ROUTLEDGE HANDBOOK OF CORRUPTION IN ASIA

Corruption in Asia ranges from the venal rent-seeking of local officials to the million-dollar bribes received by corrupt politicians; from excessive position-related consumption to future job offers in the private sector for compliant public servants; from money-laundering to 'white elephant' projects that do little more than line the pockets of developers and their political partners.

The *Routledge Handbook of Corruption in Asia* addresses the theories, issues and trends in corruption and anticorruption reform that have emerged from this diverse experience. The book is divided into four major parts: corruption and the state; corruption and economic development; corruption and society; and controlling corruption: strategies, successes and failures. Chapters compare and contrast corruption in different social and institutional contexts, examine both successful and unsuccessful attempts to control it, and consider what lessons can be drawn from these Asian experiences.

This academically rigorous and insightful book will be of interest to a wide range of students and scholars, particularly those of Asian studies, politics and sociology.

Ting Gong is Professor in the Department of Public Policy, City University of Hong Kong.

Ian Scott is Visiting Professor in the Department of Public Policy at the City University of Hong Kong and Emeritus Professor at Murdoch University in Perth, Australia.

ROUTLEDGE HANDBOOK OF CORRUPTION IN ASIA

Edited by Ting Gong and Ian Scott

LONDON AND NEW YORK

First published 2017
by Routledge
2 Park Square, Milton Park, Abingdon, Oxon OX14 4RN

and by Routledge
711 Third Avenue, New York, NY 10017

Routledge is an imprint of the Taylor & Francis Group, an informa business

British Library Cataloguing-in-Publication Data
A catalogue record for this book is available from the British Library

Library of Congress Cataloging-in-Publication Data
Names: Gong, Ting, 1955- editor. | Scott, Ian, 1943- editor. | Container
of (work): Scott, Ian, 1943- Institutional corruption and the state in Asia.
Title: Routledge handbook of corruption in Asia / edited by Ting Gong and Ian Scott.
Description: New York: Routledge, 2017. | Includes bibliographical references and index.
Identifiers: LCCN 2016027657| ISBN 9781138860162 (hardback) | ISBN 9781315716732 (ebook)
Subjects: LCSH: Corruption—Asia. | Political corruption—Asia.
Classification: LCC HV6771.A758 R68 2017 | DDC 364.1/323095—dc23
LC record available at https://lccn.loc.gov/2016027657

ISBN: 978-1-138-86016-2 (hbk)
ISBN: 978-1-315-71673-2 (ebk)

Typeset in Bembo
by codeMantra
Printed and bound by CPI Group (UK) Ltd, Croydon, CR0 4YY

Visit the [companion website/eResources]:
[insert comp website/eResources URL]

CONTENTS

Contents

LIST OF FIGURES

LIST OF TABLES

LIST OF ACRONYMS

1MDB	1Malaysia Development Berhad
AAC	Agency Against Corruption (Taiwan)
AAP	Aam Admi Party (India)
ABS	Asian Barometer Survey
ACA	Anti-Corruption Agency
ACN	Anti-Corruption Network for Eastern Europe and Central Asia
ACT-NET	Network of Anti-Corruption Authorities and Law Enforcement Agencies
ADB	Asian Development Bank
APEC	Asia Pacific Economic Cooperation
APG	Asia/Pacific Group on Money Laundering
BN	Barisan Nasional or National Front (Malaysia)
CBI	Central Bureau of Investigation (India)
CCP	Chinese Communist Party (China)
CPI	Corruption Perceptions Index
CPIB	Corrupt Practices Investigation Bureau (Singapore)
DIC	Discipline Inspection Commission (China)
DPP	Democratic Progressive Party (Taiwan)
FATF	Financial Action Task Force
GCB	Global Corruption Barometer
GI	Global Integrity
GOPAC	Global Organization of Parliamentarians Against Corruption
IAC	India Against Corruption movement
ICAC	Independent Commission Against Corruption (Hong Kong)
ICW	Indonesia Corruption Watch
KMT	Kuomintang (Taiwan)
KPK	Komisi Pemberantasan Korupsi (Indonesia)
LDP	Liberal Democratic Party (Japan)
MACC	Malaysian Anti-Corruption Commission (Malaysia)
MKSS	Mazdoor Kisan Shakti Sangathan (India)
NACC	National Anti-Corruption Commission (Thailand)
NCPRI	The National Campaign for People's Right to Information (India)

OECD	Organization for Economic Development and Co-operation
OMB	Office of the Ombudsman (The Philippines)
PAP	People's Action Party (Singapore)
PRC	People's Republic of China (China)
PRD	Pearl River Delta region
RTI	Right to Information
SEAPAC	Southeast Asian Parliamentarians Against Corruption
SMEs	Small- and Medium-Sized Enterprises
SPP	Supreme People's Procuratorate (China)
SWS	Social Weather Stations
TI	Transparency International
UMNO	United Malays National Organization (Malaysia)
UNCAC	United Nations Convention Against Corruption
UNDP	United Nations Development Programme
WVS	World Values Survey

NOTES ON CONTRIBUTORS

James Babb is Senior Lecturer in the Department of Politics, University of Newcastle-upon-Tyne, UK.

Jin-Wook Choi is Professor in the Department of Public Administration, Korea University, Seoul, South Korea.

Jamie Davidson is Associate Professor in the Department of Political Science, National University of Singapore, Singapore.

Bart W. Édes is Director of the Poverty Reduction, Social Development and Governance Division at the Asian Development Bank in Manila, The Philippines.

Ting Gong is Professor in the Department of Public Policy at the City University of Hong Kong, Hong Kong.

Robert Gregory is Emeritus Professor of Politics in the School of Government, Victoria University of Wellington, New Zealand.

Thomas Johnson is Lecturer in Politics/International Politics and Asia in the Department of Politics at the University of Sheffield, UK.

Michael Johnston is Charles A. Dana Professor of Political Science, Emeritus, Colgate University, New York, USA.

David S. Jones was formerly with the Universiti Brunei Darussalam and the National University of Singapore, Singapore.

Natalia Matukhno is Research Associate in the Centre of Public Policy, University of Strathclyde, Glasgow, UK.

Erik Mobrand is Associate Professor in the Graduate School of International Studies, Seoul National University, Seoul, South Korea.

Jon S.T. Quah is a retired Professor of Political Science at the National University of Singapore and an anti-corruption consultant in Singapore.

John Rand is Professor in the Department of Economics, University of Copenhagen, Denmark.

Susan Rose-Ackerman is Henry R. Luce Professor of Jurisprudence (Law and Political Science), Yale University, Connecticut, USA.

Sofie Arjon Schütte is Senior Advisor with the U4 Anti-Corruption Resource Centre at the Chr. Michelsen Institute, Bergen, Norway.

Ian Scott is Emeritus Professor of Politics and Fellow of the Asia Research Centre at Murdoch University in Perth, Australia.

Mitu Sengupta is Associate Professor in the Department of Politics and Public Administration, Ryerson University, Toronto, Canada.

Finn Tarp is Director of UNU-WIDER, based in Helsinki, Finland, and Professor at the University of Copenhagen, Denmark.

Wen Wang is Associate Professor in the School of Public Affairs and Administration, Rutgers University-Newark, USA.

Andrew Wedeman is Professor in the Department of Political Science, Georgia State University, Atlanta, USA.

Jong-sung You is Senior Lecturer in the Department of Political and Social Change, The Australian National University, Canberra, Australia.

Chilik Yu is Professor of Public Policy and Management at Shih Hsin University, Taipei, Taiwan.

Jiangnan Zhu is Assistant Professor in the Department of Politics and Public Administration, University of Hong Kong, Hong Kong.

ACKNOWLEDGEMENTS

We have relied heavily on the good will and expertise of many people and organizations in preparing this book. A grant from the Chiang Ching-kuo Foundation and support from the Global China Studies project of the College of Liberal Arts and Social Sciences at City University of Hong Kong enabled us to run a workshop at the City University in October 2015. Many of the chapters in this book are based on papers which were originally presented at that time. The contributors have benefited considerably from the comments of their fellow presenters and also from the insights of Stella Quah, Suh-on (Claire) Shin (who also supplied useful information on a Korean anti-corruption NGO), Mark Thompson, Baishun Yuan and others who attended the workshop. Kim Hoi Ki Wong and Hanyu Xiao, supported by general staff from the Dean's office and the Department of Public Policy, ably arranged for the transportation and accommodation of the participants.

We owe particular debts of gratitude to Michael Johnston, Jon Quah and Susan Rose-Ackerman, the authors of the reflective essays which lead each section of the book. Their reviews of the chapters in their sections were very helpful to the authors and to ourselves as editors. We thank also Ross McLeod and IP Publishing Limited for permission to reproduce the chart in Chapter 4 which originally appeared in *South East Asia Research* (July 2008) and Richard Sandbrook who provided useful advice on corruption in patrimonial systems and some key references. We are also grateful to Leanne Hinves at Routledge who invited us to work on this book and Lucy McClune and Francesca Monaco who responded very promptly and helpfully to our copyediting queries and enabled us to stay within schedule.

Finally, we would like to thank our research assistants Queenie Lijun Deng, Chiling Kong, Stephanie Xinlei Sha and, especially, Hanyu Xiao, who saved us a great deal of time by diligently checking references and statistics. The authors, of course, bear responsibility for any errors contained herein.

Ting Gong
Ian Scott
May 2016

1

INTRODUCTION

Ting Gong and Ian Scott

This handbook aims to provide a critical review of the principal issues, trends and challenges of corruption and anti-corruption reform in Asia. The approach to a task of this magnitude required some consideration. If we were simply to evaluate the state of corruption and anti-corruption reform in each Asian country, we might produce some interesting empirical material, but probably we would be analytically deficient in terms of comparisons within Asia and contributions to the broader issues raised by corruption studies elsewhere. Instead, we have chosen to focus on some central questions relating to corruption which have received some attention from scholars and practitioners around the world but are critically important in the Asian context. Within Asia, there is rich material that can be brought to bear on these questions which can serve to deepen our understanding of the issues and perhaps even help to provide some answers.

Virtually every form of corruption imaginable has been experienced in Asia in the most diverse political, economic and social circumstances. Politically, the spectrum stretches from democracies, such as Japan, Taiwan and South Korea, through many hybrid liberal authoritarian regimes, to the corrupt dictatorships of some Central Asian countries, to countries where the issue of whether there is a state is itself in question. Although the relationship between types of corruption and types of regime remains contentious, it is clear that no leader can afford to ignore the effects of corruption. Several leaders have been overthrown because of their corrupt activities, and corruption, in fact or as a pretext, has frequently been used to justify coups. More broadly, political leaders need to be concerned about corruption because there is ample evidence to suggest that, over time, corruption undermines legitimacy and trust in government (Seligson 2002; Ch. 2; but see also Chang and Chu 2006).

Economically, parts of Asia have undergone very rapid economic growth in a process which has often been associated with increased levels of corruption (Khan 1998; Choi and Woo 2012; Wedeman 2012; Ch. 2). However, this does not seem to be an invariable rule. China and South Korea have made striking economic progress with relatively high levels of corruption while Singapore and Hong Kong have progressed equally rapidly without it. Asia also has some of the poorest nations on earth, where grinding poverty and corruption seemingly go hand-in-hand. Corruption does impact disproportionately on the poor, but it may also contribute to the continuance of a "poverty trap" from which the poor find it virtually impossible to escape (Ch. 8). It is sometimes argued that it is not so much corruption but the neo-liberal policies of government that contribute to poverty. In some Asia countries, however, corruption and neo-liberal policies go hand-in-hand, which is of little comfort to those contained in the trap.

Asia's corruption is also often said to have a cultural flavour. The emphasis given to the group rather than the individual and the existence of a protective spirit in Asian culture opens the door to nepotism, cronyism and patronage (Sculli 2003), where government and business elites become mutual hostages in an informal system of corrupt practices (Kang 2002). Asian societies are also, of course, diverse in their composition, beliefs, prosperity, educational levels and degree of urbanisation. Although these settings may result in different mixes, corruption has often become embedded in the social structure and forms an integral part of the way people interact with the economic and political systems. "Street-level" corruption becomes an institutionalised facet of life, the way through which things are usually done.

Rampant corruption is manifest in Asia in the common forms of bribery, embezzlement, kickbacks, extortion, misappropriation, crony capitalism, financial fraud, illegal campaign financing and election rigging. Although sometimes these may all be found within the same country, diverse political and social settings often mean that the focus of major corrupt activities may range considerably across the region: for example, from the venal rent-seeking of local officials in India to the million-dollar bribes received by corrupt politicians in Macao; from excessive position-related consumption in China to future job offers in the private sector for compliant public servants in Hong Kong; from cross-border money-laundering to "white elephant" projects that do little more than line the pockets of developers and their political partners in Southeast Asia. For the researcher, this diversity presents the considerable challenge of finding the underlying political, economic and social causes of corruption, of discerning similar patterns of behaviour within the continent and elsewhere, and of examining possible remedies.

Before analysing further the interplay of these political, economic and social variables on patterns and forms of corruption, we need, first, to define what corruption is and then to attempt to assess the extent of the problem. Corruption is conventionally defined as the "abuse of public office for private gain" (World Bank 1997:8). We use this definition but it should be noted that it may or may not coincide with perceptions of what constitutes corruption in any particular country. In China, for example, corruption is very widely defined to include many different forms of unethical behaviour beyond the abuse of public office, while in other places its meaning may be largely restricted to bribery (Gong et al. 2015). "Abuse of public office" might be taken to focus largely on political and bureaucratic corruption although we extend the definition to include abuse of positions of trust in the private sector.

Although corruption has long been believed to be an endemic problem in Asia, measuring the level of corruption in any country is a notoriously difficult, probably impossible, task (see Chs. 7, 12, 16). The best that can be done, it seems, is to report what surveys reveal about perceptions of the extent of corruption. These are then taken as proxies for the level of corruption although they should not be regarded as much more than, at best, an order of magnitude. On this basis, according to the Corruption Perceptions Index published annually by Transparency International, Asian countries displayed stable, yet high, levels of corruption between 2006 and 2015 (see Ch. 17, Table 17.1). The average score of the 25 countries in East, Southeast and South Asia has been consistently below the global average, even including three of the world's cleanest places: Hong Kong, Japan and Singapore.

2

In 2015, 68 per cent or 17 of the 25 of Asian countries scored less than 50, which, according to Transparency International criteria, would then be considered to suffer from serious corruption (TI 2015).

While these figures suggest, and other evidence confirms, that many Asian countries have serious corruption problems, there is a need for deeper analysis to explain how these problems arise and what patterns and forms of corruption are represented. To do so, we have divided the book into four sections dealing with corruption and the state; corruption and economic development; corruption and society; and controlling corruption. Each section is introduced by a reflective essay on the concepts, literature and academic concerns related to that section. The chapters themselves focus on some central questions which have critical relevance in Asia but which may also resonate with corruption studies elsewhere.

Corruption and the state

First, we consider issues that relate primarily to political and bureaucratic corruption. How corrupt are government officials? What form does corruption take? What impact does corruption have on the level of trust in government? Are there "normal" levels of corruption that can be tolerated? Does the institutional framework impede or promote corruption? Does democracy prevent corrupt practices? How does corruption affect the conduct of elections?

The relationship between political institutions and corruption merits special attention. In Asia, virtually all forms that the state can take are present; within these various political settings, governments are organized and relate to their economies and peoples in many different ways. Yet, despite the political and institutional variations, corruption has nonetheless reached every single corner of Asia. Does the nature of state institutions matter in explaining the occurrence of corruption? It is sometimes argued that democracy may reduce corruption by increasing the possibility of throwing corrupt officials out of public office or preventing them from being elected in the first place, by enhancing effective checks and balances within government, and by allowing greater freedom for the public and the media to expose corruption (Goel and Nelson 2005; Ades and Di Tella 1999; Myerson 1993). But does this actually happen in Asia? Babb's analysis of corruption in Japan (Ch. 5) indicates that while institutional reforms have led to a decline in the number of prominent scandals, corruption continues to haunt Japanese society at a normal "background" level. Davidson and Mobrand (Ch. 6) show that, even within Asia's democracies, there is substantial sophisticated electoral manipulation which favours incumbent elites.

If corruption survives and often thrives under virtually any type of political system, then a related question is whether and to what extent political institutions influence its forms, patterns and persistence. Again, Asia's experience in the process of democratisation has seen an increase in money politics and more corrosive corruption developing alongside political decentralisation, as shown in the cases of Indonesia (Robison and Hadiz 2004) and Thailand (Hicken 2001). In this volume, Zhu (Ch. 3) provides evidence of how three institutional features of post-reform China, fragmented authoritarianism, business-government collusion, and the prevalence of informal politics, account for the surge in corruption networks. In Indonesia, as Schütte (Ch. 4) shows, some governmental organizations, particularly the police and the Attorney General's Office, have sought to dilute the impact of anti-corruption reform efforts. Despite public scandals in many Asian countries, entrenched corrupt syndicates embedded within the bureaucracy or in crony capitalist relationships or in prevalent practices within the society itself have proved very difficult to overturn.

Corruption and economic development

Second, we ask questions about the impact of corruption on the economy. Does corruption impede economic growth? Does corruption promote inequality? Or does inequality promote corruption? At the critical interface between government and business, can measures be implemented to prevent dubious or corrupt practices? Are small firms more likely to engage in bribery than large ones? Or are small firms more likely to be victimised by corrupt officials than large ones?

The relationship between corruption and economic development in Asia is puzzling. Some Asian economies are beset by widespread corruption, which lowers their growth rates, decreases capital inflows, distorts budget allocations, and results in flawed or non-existent environmental regulations. Many, as Jones shows in Ch. 9, are further afflicted by poor management of procurement which is perceived to be an easy means of obtaining a supplementary income. Yet, despite the resulting inefficiencies in government, there is a positive correlation between high levels of corruption and dramatic economic growth rates in some Asian countries. In China, for example, rapid economic development and worsening corruption have coexisted for decades, giving rise to what Wedeman (2012) refers to as a "double paradox". While it remains a moot point among scholars how and why some Asian countries are able to achieve spectacular economic growth while suffering rampant corruption, the economic consequences of corruption are subject to debate as well.

Corruption exacerbates social inequality, but it may also be likely that it is caused by inequality. You examines this convoluted relationship in Ch. 8 and points out that reciprocal causality may create a vicious cycle of high corruption and high inequality and that breaking this vicious cycle is a great challenge for many Asian countries. A similar situation of reciprocal causality may be seen in the relationship between firm behaviour and corruption. Asia is the home of numerous small and medium-sized enterprises (SMEs) and they are particularly vulnerable to corruption. Rand and Tarp (Ch. 10) investigate the evolution and nature of bribe-paying behaviour among SMEs in Vietnam to show how bribe incidence, tax avoidance and firm informality are interwoven. In their investigation of the behaviour of Hong Kong SMEs operating in the neighbouring Chinese mainland province of Guangdong, Johnson et al. (Ch. 11) argue that regulatory capture is a two-way process of corrupt exchanges through which both the regulated and the regulators seek to exert influence over state regulations to their own advantage.

Corruption and society

Third, we ask questions about the impact of corruption on society. If broad-brush references to culture offer insufficient explanations for corruption, how can we make our research more focused in this respect? How do popular protests against corruption arise and with what results? How do anti-corruption social movements emerge? What role can civil society play in mitigating corruption? Are women less corrupt than men and, if so, under what circumstances? Can we measure the impact of corruption on a society?

Asia has a long tradition of civil society movements but their impact through "bottom-up" attempts to control corruption has not yet been sufficiently explored. A critical question is how to assess the contribution of civil society organizations to the introduction of effective anti-corruption reform measures. This is further related to some more specific questions, such as how the public perceives and responds to corruption and under what conditions, how and to what extent non-government actors and organizations (NGOs) are able to play watchdog functions in high-corruption societies and what motivates the public to participate actively in the fight against corruption. Some give a pessimistic answer to these questions, "[i]f there was one common challenge to unite the Asia Pacific region, it would be corruption. From campaign pledges to media coverage to civil society forums, corruption dominates discussion. Yet despite all this talk, there's little sign of action.... Has Asia Pacific stalled in its efforts to fight corruption?" (TI 2015).

It may be true that the fight against corruption has stalled in a few Asian societies but not in all of them. The role of civil society as a deterrent to corruption varies from organization to organization, from place to place, and from time to time. Using India as a case, Sengupta (Ch. 14) identifies two important factors in mobilising society against corruption. First, she notes that "bottom-up" mobilisation against corruption depends on linking corruption with livelihood issues; where there is no such link, popular protests may dissipate quickly. Second, she observes that the relationship between the social movement or NGO and the government is a critical variable in achieving change; purely confrontational tactics are unlikely to succeed in the longer term. In his study of popular protests against corruption in China (Ch. 13), Wedeman also raises the issue of the dynamic between the protest and the political authority and finds that protests are usually local, specific and unconnected and consequently are unlikely to turn into wider social movements. "Bottom-up" corruption efforts in the form of social movements or NGOs are prevalent in Asia but their effectiveness seems to depend on positive supportive circumstances, which are only occasionally found, or on goals which need to be achieved, such as the right-to-information in India, before corruption can be mitigated.

In examining gender differences in reaction to corruption and the means to prevent it, Matukhno (Ch. 15) also stresses the importance of a supportive environment and of equality in enabling women to resist corruption. She finds that, in many Asian countries, women are less likely to resist corruption if they find themselves in a position where they feel they have no option but to succumb to it. Findings such as these bring us back to the perennial question of how to measure corruption and identify different perceptions of corruption in Asian countries. Yu (Ch. 16) discusses some of these issues, obtaining a more balanced picture than previous studies by using data from both the Corruption Perceptions Index and the Asian Barometer Survey. Importantly, he is able to show that there are enormous gaps between elite and citizens' perceptions of corruption in Vietnam, Taiwan, South Korea and Japan. Such findings take us into territory where we can begin to make constructive corruption comparisons among countries although, as Yu points out, measurement remains a continuing problem.

Controlling corruption: strategies, successes and failures

The fourth section of the book considers the successes and failures of anti-corruption strategies and of local and international organizations in corruption prevention. What are the criteria for successful corruption prevention? How can such measures be introduced? Why do some anti-corruption agencies (ACAs) fail to have any impact? Does corruption prevention need to be seen in the wider context of integrity management and increased attention to strengthening the commitment to values of those who work in public organizations? What role can regional and international agencies play in corruption prevention?

As far as anti-corruption enforcement is concerned, Hong Kong and Singapore are often cited as two of the most successful cases in the world. By contrast, many other Asian countries such as Afghanistan, Myanmar, Bangladesh, Cambodia, Laos, Indonesia and Pakistan, have been rated among the worst, or nearly the worst, on the entire CPI (Corruption Perceptions Index). Why are there only a few success stories even after decades-long anti-corruption endeavours? In Ch. 17, Quah examines the reasons behind the success and failure of the ACAs in Asia. What is clear from his account is that simple transfers of institutional and legal form from one successful case, such as Hong Kong or Singapore, to an Asian country with corruption problems do not usually work in the expected way. A critical variable, as Choi points out in Ch. 18, is whether the political will exists, as it did in both the Hong Kong and Singapore cases, to bring about real change. Beyond this, a range of different cultural factors, such as embedded social attitudes supportive of corruption, and organizational difficulties, such as over-centralisation, have shown over time that establishing effective ACAs is no easy matter.

If top-down approaches are often ineffective in combatting corruption, would a "bottom-up" approach, focusing on changing social attitudes and engaging with the public, work any better? Would value-based approaches serve to curb corruption better than rule-based ones? As Gregory shows in Ch. 19, there has been interest in some Asian countries in supplementing the traditional rule-based approach to corruption prevention with integrity measures which would attempt to raise the moral standards of public servants in particular so that potential conflicts of interest can be identified as soon as possible. A number of new anti-corruption initiatives in the international and regional fields have also sought to bring a fresh dimension to corruption prevention. In Ch. 20, Edes describes how these initiatives have been introduced in such areas as collaboration on the prevention of money-laundering, the ethics of parliamentarians and the exchange of information on successful anti-corruption practices. Nevertheless, each of these new approaches to corruption prevention has its limitations. "Bottom-up" approaches in which attempts are made to change social attitudes towards corruption are potentially expensive and may meet with cultural resistance (Scott and Gong 2015). A value-based approach can never fully replace a rule-based approach and may well become absorbed within it. And international and regional initiatives are always subject to the willingness of governments to implement agreed collaborative action.

The anti-corruption agenda

In the first three sections of the book, the contributors uncover a variety of different types of corruption in Asian countries. They reflect the concerns and experiences of the informed public, which may be defined as international and regional agencies, scholars, NGOs, journalists, professionals and, of course, the people who suffer the adverse consequences of corrupt activities. In the final section of the book, the authors address the question of what action officialdom, usually in the form of an ACA, is taking to prevent corruption and with what success.

Anti-corruption is at least formally a goal which is shared by most, if not all, governments and their informed publics. In reviewing the chapters in this book, however, what strikes us is that the ACA and the public seem to have different anti-corruption agendas which have relatively little to say to each other. What concerns the informed public is often only of marginal interest to the ACA. To some extent, this is not entirely surprising. If positive action were directed to the perceived principal corruption issues of the informed public, then it might be expected that their complaints would be less vocal and the gap between their expectations and reality less noticeable. In India, in the face of official inaction over corruption, the gap became so sizeable that anti-corruption pressure groups and parties sought, with some success, to pursue their own political agendas and to bring about change.

In other parts of Asia, such as Japan, Singapore and Hong Kong, institutions have gained public trust and respect and do appear to represent widely held values. Yet, even in those places, there may still be an alternative, if muted, corruption agenda which the informed public feels should receive more attention. In Hong Kong, for example, control over money-laundering, which is not always corrupt money but may still represent tax evasion or illegal activity, is in the hands of the police force. In 2015, the police had only 50 investigators to deal with, potentially, more than 37,000 cases (Lam 2015). In 2016, the Mossack Fonseca papers showed that the Hong Kong office was their busiest office in the world (Mai 2016). Hong Kong still retains a reputation as a clean place to do business, but money-laundering would seem to be one area where it clearly needs to tighten its regulations and increase the number of its investigators and where the agendas of the government (rather than the ACA in this case) and the informed public diverge considerably.

In most of Asia, the work of ACAs does not usually speak to the concerns of the informed public; often, it is only when a scandal attracts the attention of the agency that there is some congruence between public demands for action and what the agency is actually doing. Based on the chapters in this book and on the sources listed here, we outline the perceived principal concerns of the informed public and those of the ACAs in some Asian countries in Table 1.1.

Table 1.1 Anti-corruption agendas in selected Asian countries/regions

	Agenda of the informed public	*Agenda of the anti-corruption agency*
Cambodia	Land grabs, money politics	Not clear; ineffective
China	Land grabs, official privileges, official-business collusion, rent seeking	Campaigns against high-level corrupt officials and action against some corruption networks
Hong Kong	Cross-border corruption, money-laundering, crony capitalism	Strict enforcement of laws defining corruption as bribery
India	Venal local-level bureaucratic corruption	Official action overtaken by the efforts and agenda of anti-corruption pressure groups and parties
Indonesia	Post-Soeharto corruption legacies, especially bureaucratic corruption	Jurisdictional disputes hampering action and limiting effectiveness
Japan	Bid-rigging and parachuting former senior officials into lucrative private sector positions	Strict enforcement of the electoral laws
Malaysia	Money politics	Some work on bureaucratic corruption and involvement in the 1MDB scandal
Myanmar	Judicial corruption, land grabs; illegal drugs and trade transactions	Ineffective
Singapore	Electoral manipulation	Strict enforcement of the anti-corruption laws
South Korea	Crony capitalism	Bureaucratic corruption; jurisdictional issues limiting effectiveness
Taiwan	Political corruption	Political differences and jurisdictional disputes limiting effectiveness
Vietnam	Land grabs	Not clear; ineffective

Source: The table is derived from the chapters in this book and from Black (2004); Carter and Harding (2015); Cheesman (2012); Gomez (2012); Global Witness (2013); Global Witness (2015) Gomez (2002); Kang (2002); Ko et al. (2015); Mietzner (2015); Quah (2013); Tan (2013); Teh (2002). *Note*: Japan does not have an anti-corruption agency, but there is a Special Prosecutor who strictly enforces the electoral laws (see Ch. 5).

Two questions arise. First, why is the agenda of the informed public so often disregarded in terms of official anti-corruption priorities? Second, by what means could greater voice be given to the ACAs' wider remit and how might it better reflect the voice of the informed public? Aside from resource issues which afflict many Asian ACAs, a common answer to the first question is that, when a political system is run by corrupt leaders, the ACA will not be permitted to investigate their affairs. The activities of the agency, if it exists, are restricted to matters of little concern to the elite. In other cases, ACAs take on some duties because of factionalism within the elite itself. Their work may actually enhance the incumbent's retention of power against political opponents. If an agency shows signs of independence or exercising its powers to the fullest extent, it will, in the words of a critic of the Nepalese system, be "de-fanged" (Manandar 2015). The experience of the Indonesian ACA, the *Komisi Pemberantasan Korupsi*, at the hands of the police represents a similar attempt to undermine the work of an agency (Ch. 4).

However, there are also occasions when corruption issues, which had previously been non-decisions and off the agenda as far as the agency was concerned, take on a different character because a scandal puts sufficient political pressure on the agency to require it to take action. For example, in Malaysia, money politics has been the leading item on the agenda of the informed public for some decades (Teh 2002; Gomez 2002). The issue is that the ruling party, the United Malays National Organization (UMNO), owns a large number of businesses which, it is alleged, receive favourable treatment in the awards of government contracts, loans and concessions (Gomez 2012). For most of its history, this has been a non-issue as far as ACAs are concerned. In the 1 Malaysia Development Berhad scandal, however, a government company's funds were allegedly used to finance an UMNO election campaign and US$700 million found its way into the personal accounts of the Prime Minister. UMNO was not united in its view of the appropriate treatment of the issue. ACAs, under public pressure, responded by conducting an investigation and submitted two reports to the Attorney General who had the power to prosecute. The Attorney General, who had been appointed after the Prime Minister dismissed his predecessor, found no wrong-doing. The agency, at the time of writing, has vowed to appeal the decision.

The Malaysian example, the Indian Right-to-Information campaign and public support for the *Komisi Pemberantasan Korupsi* all show that public pressure matters in efforts to close the gap between the agendas of ACAs and the informed public. Anti-corruption efforts require some congruence between political will and public demands; if there is no such congruence, the agency may lose support and complaints about corruption, often the agency's major source of information, may well dry up. To make the voice of the informed public more influential in setting anti-corruption agendas, it may be necessary initially to focus on the means of achieving a more transparent society in which the media is prepared to report corruption and perhaps even engage in investigative journalism. Without societal and institutional support for the anti-corruption agenda of the informed public and without pressure on the ACA to do something about it, many ACAs will continue to justify a limited remit which fails to address the major corruption issues.

Research tools

The selected bibliography on corruption in Asia in Appendix 1 and the list of significant Asian anti-corruption NGOs in Appendix 2 are intended to provide tools for further research. The bibliography attempts to capture scholarly analysis of different kinds of corruption and anti-corruption activities either comparatively or within the confines of individual Asian countries and localities. There is broad coverage of many such activities in China, India and Indonesia from which a reasonably comprehensive picture of corruption can be derived. In medium-sized Asian countries, coverage tends to be less comprehensive, sometimes focusing on a particular research area. On Vietnam, for example, there is an excellent literature on firm-level corruption but much less on the issue of land grabs. In the smaller places, with the exception of Hong Kong and Singapore, there are generally only a few sources. Scholars have, however, used comparative statistical material to good effect to examine such relationships as democracy and corruption, trust and corruption, inequality and corruption, and economic growth and corruption, providing oversights on the effects of corruption on the continent. We hope that the bibliography will prove useful as a basis for future research which is certainly necessary to supplement and to expand upon the rather uneven coverage of published research at the moment.

The second research tool provided by this book is a very preliminary list of some of the most important NGOs in Asia. Anti-corruption NGOs have not themselves been the subject of a great deal of research in Asia. Yet they are particularly important in countries which suffer rampant corruption, where awareness of the effects of corruption is limited, and where governments are seeking advice on how to combat it. The list in Appendix 2 is limited by the fact that many web-sites are not in English and by a lack of information on the activities of some NGOs.

This book is a call for scholars to question the applicability of existing assumptions, explanations and theories about corruption. We hope that the book can help academics to identify new research areas and enable practitioners to become familiar with best practices and solutions for corruption problems, which have emerged in the Asian region. The findings and analyses in this volume are based on Asia but we expect that they will have relevance beyond Asian borders and that they will help enrich the literature on corruption studies.

References

Ades, A. and R. Di Tella (1999) "Rents, competition and corruption", *The American Economic Review*, 89(4): 982–993.

Black, W. K. (2004) "The dango tango: why corruption blocks real reform in Japan", *Business Ethics Quarterly*, 14(4): 603–623.

Carter, C. and A. Harding (eds.) (2015) *Land grabs in Asia: what role for the law?* London: Routledge.

Chang, E.C.C. and Y.-H. Chu (2006) "Corruption and trust: exceptionalism in Asian democracies", *The Journal of Politics*, 68(2): 259–271.

Cheesman, N. (2012) "Myanmar's courts and the sound money makes", in N. Cheesman, M. Skidmore and T. Wilson (eds.) *Myanmar's transition: openings, obstacles and opportunities*, Singapore: Institute of Southeast Asian Studies, 231–248.

Choi, E. and J. Woo (2012) "Political corruption, economy and citizens' evaluation of democracy in South Korea", *Contemporary Politics*, 18(4): 451–466.

Global Witness (2013) "Rubber barons: how Vietnamese companies and international financiers are driving a land grabbing crisis in Cambodia and Laos", https://www.globalwitness.org/en/campaigns/land-deals/rubberbarons/ (accessed 13 May 2016).

Global Witness (2015) *Jade: a Global Witness investigation into Myanmar's "big state secret"*, London: Global Witness.

Goel, R. K. and M.A. Nelson (2005) "Economic freedom versus political freedom: cross-country influences on corruption", *Australian Economic Papers*, 44 (2): 121–133.

Gomez, E.T. (2002) "Political business in Malaysia: party factionalism, corporate development, and economic crisis", in E.T. Gomez (ed.) *Political business in East Asia,* London: Routledge, 82–114.

Gomez, E.T. (2012) "Monetizing politics: financing parties and elections in Malaysia", *Modern Asian Studies*, 46(5): 1370–1397.

Gong, T., S. Wang and J. Ren (2015) "Corruption in the eye of the beholder: survey evidence from mainland China and Hong Kong", *International Public Management Journal*, 18(3): 458–482.

Hicken, A. (2001) "Governance and growth in Thailand", in J.E. Campos (ed.) *Corruption: the boom and bust of East Asia,* Manila: Ateneo de Manila University Press, 163–182.

Kang, D.C. (2002) *Crony capitalism: corruption and development in South Korea and the Philippines,* Cambridge: Cambridge University Press.

Khan, M.H. (1998) "Patron-client networks and the economic effects of corruption in Asia", *The European Journal of Development Research*, 10(1): 15–39.

Ko, E., Y-C Su and C. Yu (2015) "Sibling rivalry among anti-corruption agencies in Taiwan: is redundancy doomed to fail?" *Asian Education and Development Studies*, 4(1): 101–124.

Lam, L. (2015) "Just one investigator for every 740 potential money laundering cases", *South China Morning Post*, 8 February.

Mai, J. (2016) "Hong Kong was the busiest office of Panama papers law firm", *South China Morning Post,* 7 April.

Manandar, N. (2015) "How to corrupt an anticorruption commission: the case of Nepal", *The Global Anticorruption Blog*, http://globalanticorruptionblog.com/2015/08/26/how-to-corrupt-an-anticorruption-commission-the-case-of-nepal/ (accessed 13 May 2016).

Mietzner, M. (2015) "Dysfunction by design: political finance and corruption in Indonesia", *Critical Asian Studies*, 47(4): 587–610.

Myerson, R. B. (1993) "Effectiveness of electoral systems for reducing government corruption - a game-theoretic analysis", *Games and Economic Behavior*, 5(1): 118–132.

Quah, J.S.T. (2013) *Curbing corruption in Asian countries: an impossible dream?* Singapore: Institute of Southeast Asian Studies.

Robison, R. and V.R. Hadiz (2004) *Reorganizing power in Indonesia: the power of oligarchy in an age of markets*, London: RoutledgeCurzon.

Scott, I. and T. Gong (2015) "Evidence-based policy-making for corruption prevention in Hong Kong: a bottom-up approach", *Asia Pacific Journal of Public Administration*, 37(2): 87–101.

Sculli, D. (2003) "Culture and level of industrialization as determinants of corruption in Asia", in J. Kidd and F-J Richter (eds.) *Fighting corruption in Asia: causes, effects and remedies*, Singapore: World Scientific, 203–220.

Seligson, M.A. (2002) "The impact of corruption on regime legitimacy: a comparative study of four Latin American countries", *The Journal of Politics*, 64(2): 408–433.

Tan, N. (2013) "Manipulating electoral laws in Singapore", *Electoral Studies*, 32(4): 632–643.

Teh, Y.K. (2002) "Money politics in Malaysia", *Journal of Contemporary Asia*, 32(3): 338–345.

TI (Transparency International) (2015) *Corruption Perceptions Index Reports,* http://www.transparency.org/research/cpi/overview (accessed 18 May 2016).

Wedeman, A. (2012) *Double paradox: rapid growth and rising corruption in China,* Ithaca: Cornell University Press.

World Bank (1997) *Helping countries combat corruption: the role of the World Bank,* Washington, DC: The World Bank.

PART I

Corruption and the state

2

INSTITUTIONAL CORRUPTION AND THE STATE IN ASIA

Ian Scott

Public corruption may be divided into individual acts that violate laws, regulations or norms for personal gain and organizational situations in which officials and others collectively adapt state institutions, procedures and rules for their own ends. This distinction has been employed for some time. Sherman (1980), for example, working on an earlier idea of "deviant organizations", devised models of organizational corruption in agencies of social control. Thompson (1995: 27–28) further developed the notion into the concept of institutional corruption, subsequently defining it as a situation in which benefits were received in exchange for a service that tended to undermine procedures that supported the primary purposes of the institution (Thompson 2013: 3).

Two important features characterise this type of corruption. First, it is necessarily collusive, involving at its inception the creation of new subversive organizational arrangements, sometimes within and between legitimately constituted departments or agencies (Gong 2002; Jancsics and Jávor 2012). A collective action approach may consequently be rather more useful in analysing this kind of corruption than the more traditional principal-agent perspective (Persson et al. 2013). A second critical feature of institutional corruption is "the perversion of the mechanisms of control and the conversion of an institution from a means of preventing illicit behaviour to a means of organizing illicit acts" (Wedeman 1997: 807). The purpose of the institution is subverted to provide collective benefits for at least some of its members.

In this chapter, collusion resulting in new and deviant organizational forms and the process of attempting, successfully or otherwise, to subvert the rules are taken to be central to the concept of institutional corruption. They are explored with a view to disaggregating the concept to provide an aid for the comparison of different forms of institutional corruption in Asia and a tentative answer to the question of whether the type of state makes any difference to the form which this kind of corruption takes.

The state and institutional corruption

Most states take the maintenance of a legal/rational order as their formal *raison d'etre* and the means by which some vision of the public good may be realised. When that vision is consistently and deliberately violated by officials for self-serving organizational or collective ends, a situation of institutional corruption may be said to exist. In Western systems, such situations are often depicted as political decay, a fall from grace in which formerly high standards of integrity are replaced with dubious ethical practices, overt conflicts of interest and more tolerant public attitudes towards corruption (Dobel 1978; O'Toole 1993). In Asian countries, it might be asked whether such a state of grace ever existed outside the realm of political myths and whether situations involving institutional corruption may instead simply mirror entrenched social attitudes reflected in accepted procedures within public organizations. However, as Johnston (Ch. 12) warns, we should be wary of attributing particular cultural practices to "Asian corruption"; there are very significant variations in types of institutional corruption within the region which may have more common with what is happening elsewhere than with what is happening in other parts of Asia.

The distinction between individual and institutional corruption leads to rather different assumptions about the nature of the political order. In combatting individual corruption, if a case comes to public attention and is being dealt with according to the law, the underlying premise is that public office is not normally abused, that controls are in place and that the system is working reasonably well. Corruption then simply becomes an aberrant act committed by individual officials which conflicts with prevailing legal and moral norms relating to the integrity of the office. If the public believe the system is working well, there may be confidence that the rotten apples in the barrel can be rooted out, that rules can be tightened and enforced, and that standards of integrity can be improved. Practical measures and academic studies alike reflect a bias towards preventing corruption within an existing system that is regarded as largely acceptable. Institutional corruption, by contrast, could potentially encompass almost the entire system; practices may be tolerated that cannot be seen to be compatible with the public good and political and administrative systems may be consistently perverted to achieve self-serving official ends.

Analytically, the distinction between individual and institutional corruption is clear. However, there are moral and practical issues which create problems in applying the concept to empirical cases. Moral attitudes towards institutional corruption sometimes become entangled with the analysis. Denunciation of regimes may be couched in terms ranging from blanket moral condemnation ("all politicians are corrupt") to cynicism ("what do you expect?") to resignation ("that's the way it is"). None of this helps us understand how institutional corruption occurs and what its relationship with the system actually is. A further practical difficulty is that critical information is often absent in determining whether a particular instance represents individual or institutional corruption. In the case of a corrupt president, for example, an evaluation of whether the offence is a one-off case of individual corruption or whether the decision-making processes of the presidency as an institution have been systematically perverted would require a detailed analysis of the facts. Further, because opacity is frequently the key to successful efforts to achieve institutional corruption, it is often not clear how processes actually result in corrupt end products.

Types of state provide only general indications of the kinds of institutional corruption that may occur. It may be that in kleptocracies, such as the Philippines under Marcos or Indonesia under Soeharto, the entire state was captured and then re-designed to serve the personal ends of the leader and his immediate families and cronies (Hellman et al. 203; Ch. 4). Yet whether there can ever be a "totally corrupt" state is doubtful. First, within any governmental system, there are likely to be "dry" areas from which not much wealth can be extracted and which may not attract the interest of a corrupt elite (Quah 2013: 371–72, 464). Second, it may be in the interests of the regime to allow legal/rational procedures to continue in some parts of government in the interests of political and social stability. If a system was so perverted that it failed to deliver any formally prescribed services except at a price, then that would seem to be a recipe for social unrest. Regimes with high levels of corruption may still create "pockets of efficiency" in which some departments are insulated from the corrupt practices prevalent in most parts of the administration (Whitfield and Therkildsen 2011: 13). Third, even in the most corrupt governments, it would be surprising if there were no honest bureaucrats and if legal/rational norms were not observed in some processes. Finally, the reach of the state and what has actually been "captured" needs to be taken into account. In weak states, even if a corrupt elite seizes power, it may be that the extent of illicit activities is constrained by institutional failures and local social structures. In Afghanistan and the Central Asian states, for example, the strength of local patronage networks and clans prevents central penetration and state-building (Collins 2006: 40–41, 338–342; Murtazashvili 2015).

The kleptocracies of the Philippines and Indonesia clearly had the capacity to engage in different forms of widespread institutional corruption. However, there is no necessary correlation between this type of regime and the specific means used to attain its ends; its rulers may simply have made pragmatic choices about the best way to maximise wealth extraction which could well result in potentially different forms of institutional corruption. Control over the central state apparatus may also preclude the need to engage in some forms of institutional corruption. A president who has emergency powers does not have to turn to electoral manipulation to bring a recalcitrant legislature to heel. The negotiating strengths of corrupt companies may also be reduced in the face of centralised authoritarian state power. Alternatively, of course, this type of regime could simply use forms of institutionalised corruption to disguise its activities.

Some states tolerate certain types of institutional corruption while strongly prohibiting others. In Japan, for example, there are clearly efforts to prevent institutional corruption in many domains but there are also some grey areas in which accepted practice could be construed as perverting natural justice to favour the few (Ch. 5). Institutional corruption is often thought to weaken the state system, damaging political legitimacy and the efficiency with which public functions are performed (Seligson 2002; Lessig 2013). Yet, in line with traditional "lubrication" theories of corruption, there may be circumstances in which a degree of institutional corruption, in Japan and elsewhere, might actually strengthen the way in which the state functions (Cox 2008: 3; Thompson 2013). Institutional corruption could theoretically provide incentives for better government performance of its formal legal/rational purposes. A system which tolerates the acceptance of bribes by public servants but is able to retain control over the amount collected might have a positive effect on performance although this does assume that the government is sufficiently strong to control the behaviour of its officials (Rose-Ackerman 2002). Non-monetary benefits might also provide some incentives for at least partial performance of public functions; some shirking, for example, might be tolerated if the major purpose of the department or agency was still fulfilled.

Such possibilities, however, are often given short shrift in an academic literature which has repeatedly shown that corruption, both individual and institutional, erodes trust and legitimacy in institutions, especially in democratic countries where corruption is often seen as the antithesis of the moral purpose of the state (Seligson 2002; Clausen et al. 2011; Rothstein 2011). Warren (2015: 42), for example, argues that corruption and democracy are intrinsically linked concepts: "to identify 'corrupt' actions, practices or institutions is also to identify ways in which the actions, practices or institutions that comprise 'democracy' are failing". We should be careful, however, in drawing the conclusion that more democracy might result in less corruption. In Asia, there is no monotonic or linear relationship between democracy and corruption (Campbell and Saha 2013; You 2015: 7, 45). Numerous studies have shown that new democracies in the region generally experience more rather than less corruption (Sung 2004; Chang and Chu 2006). Sun and Johnston (2009) conclude that prospects for corruption reform in a poor democracy are not encouraging even in comparison with authoritarian regimes. The best that can be hoped for from democratisation, according to Sung (2004), is that, despite upsurges in corruption in the early stages of political liberalization, it will eventually help to create cleaner government.

Political change of whatever kind generates opportunities for corruption because it almost invariably involves either the creation of new institutional rules or an absence of rules in areas that may be exploited by the corrupt. In new democracies, elections provide fertile ground for manipulation and fraud; legislators and ministers are more visible and accessible targets for subornation; support for the government from business may come at a price (Moran 2011: 33–59). Even the perception that the rules might change or not be enforced seems enough to spark increased corruption both of an individual and an institutional kind. In Hong Kong, for example, there was a sharp increase in corruption reports, prosecutions and convictions in the period shortly before and after the retrocession to China in 1997. Only when it became clear that the anti-corruption agency would continue to pursue the corrupt did the reports and prosecutions drop (Lai 2001). The lesson is that rules do matter and that the institutionalisation of those rules within a bureaucratic system is much more important for preventing all kinds of corruption than the type of regime.

While regime change may present the most striking examples of the emergence of new forms of corruption, what the state does in organizing its own administrative system and introducing policies may also create opportunities for corruption. For example, while decentralisation may not always create opportunities for greater institutional corruption, there are certainly some circumstances in which it may reduce monitoring arrangements and provide an environment where bureaucratic capture and the perversion of rules for collective benefit becomes possible (Gainsborough 2003; Bünte 2011; Ko 2013). As with democracy, there is no necessary progression from decentralisation to the institutionalisation of transparency and the encouragement of local political participation, both of which might have positive advantages for corruption prevention. Similarly, new public management practices, which are designed to reduce rules and regulations, could result in attempts to subvert the system to ensure that there is no level playing field when it comes to contracts and the privatisation of state assets (Frederickson 1999). New policies often present opportunities for rent-seeking if they are not accompanied by sufficient checks on the ways in which they will be implemented; in areas where a government has little experience of implementing policy, the prospects for reinventing the rules to suit particular groups seems to be even greater.

Rapid economic growth is, or has been, a major objective of almost every Asian state. Modernisation of this kind, according to one school of thought, sees corruption as an "inseparable byproduct" of this process (Werner 1983). However, it does not seem to be associated with any particular state form or regime type. In South Korea and Taiwan, where developmental efforts were based on close ties between the bureaucracy and business, levels of institutional corruption increased in the process of economic growth (You 2015). Yet, similarly, in the post-communist systems of China and Vietnam, in the aftermath of economic liberalization measures, there was a rise in institutional corruption (Gong 2002; Gillespie 2002; Zhu: Ch. 3). In the free market capitalist systems of Singapore and Hong Kong, however, the governments took measures to ensure that their bureaucracies were clean both before and during economic take-off (Quah 2013: 218–224, 253–257). The state form does not seem to be the significant variable; rather, the opportunities presented for rent-seeking or the creation of patron-client networks in the process of seeking rapid economic growth appear to be more important (Khan 1998). As Johnston (2005: 38) suggests, we need to look first at underlying social and economic forces rather than to assume that particular types of state will display particular types of institutional corruption.

Types of institutional corruption

Institutional corruption can be seen as a form of goal displacement in which a legitimately sanctioned state objective is subverted for an illicit objective which enhances the personal gain of the organization's employees (Sherman 1980). How does organizing to achieve an illicit purpose occur? Who are the key actors? What shape does the illicit organization take? What is the scale of their operations? What means do they use to achieve their objectives? What is their ultimate objective? We should be able to analyse the development of deviant organizations from inception to fruition and compare across states the means and the processes the key actors use to attain their aims.

The classification and disaggregation of institutional corruption may be more fruit-fully approached by considering the way in which organizing to achieve an illicit purpose occurs. It is assumed that the collaborators are rational actors who (a) need to collude to achieve their goal and (b) will choose the most appropriate organizational form consis-tent with the achievement of that goal. The framework aims to identify four types of institutional corruption on this basis but it recognises that whatever organizational form is adopted, modifications may occur which may sometimes, but not always, be related to specific types of state characteristics or to other political, social or economic factors. In states which have decentralised systems, for example, institutional corruption might be concentrated on the opportunities available at the local level. Alternatively, where power is concentrated in the centre attempts to subvert the institutions may occur at that level. In other systems, the capacity of the state itself may be an important variable influencing the type of institutional corruption which occurs. Nonetheless, the central assumption is that the process of organizing collectively to subvert institutional rules and practices will be directly related to corrupt objectives and that this will be manifest in the organizational form which is adopted.

With this in mind, we examine four ways in which institutional corruption might be organized: patrimonialism; crony capitalism; bureaucratic capture; and electoral manipu-lation and fraud. Each of the categories could (and should) be further disaggregated into sub-categories to identify distinct organizational types which may relate to specific political, economic or social factors. For example, Kang (2002) breaks down crony capitalism into various categories; Jancsics and Jávor (2012) classify corrupt networks; and Jones (Ch. 9) suggests distinct types of organized corruption in procurement. Similarly, different corrup-tion strategies, and consequently organizational forms, arise from Davidson and Mobrand's (Ch. 6) useful distinction between the rule-making and rule-breaking means of electoral manipulation where one could envisage sub-categories based on the differing capacities of states to engage in such manipulation.

Bearing in mind the utility of further disaggregation, Table 2.1 outlines the key features of each of the four broad types of institutional corruption comprising the framework.

Table 2.1 Organizational forms of institutional corruption

Types of institutional corruption	Key actors	Organizational form	Scale	Means to achieve objectives	Objectives
Patrimonial	Usually a single leader supported by family members and henchmen	Networks; nepotism; patron-client relationships	Potentially system-wide but may also be restricted to national or local levels or to linkages between them	Attempts to pervert the rules in any area to which the network has access and where there are opportunities for wealth extraction	Wealth extraction for members of the network across the political, bureaucratic and economic system or parts of it
Crony capitalism	Senior politicians/ officials and heads of private companies	Collaborative arrangements between senior personnel in government and private companies; private sector cartels	Limited to specific events although the process may become institutionalised and may occur at central or local level	Fixing tenders, contracts, land sales, procurement	To maximise the mutual personal benefits from kickbacks derived from government contracts and other commercial activities
Bureaucratic capture	Officials and politicians at all levels and pressure groups seeking control of departmental decision-making	"Extractive institutions" comprising networks of senior officials within government departments; politicians in charge of departments; external pressure groups	May occur throughout a department or agency or may be limited to a part of a department or agency	Perversion of the department's rules and procedures	Utilisation of the organizational machine of the department or agency to extract illegal payments for the benefit of members of the corrupt network
Electoral manipulation and fraud	Central politicians and/or political parties	Political networks seeking to maintain power or local efforts to influence the vote	May be central rule making or local rule breaking	Rule making or rule breaking. Vote buying, intimidation, ballot-stuffing	To maintain political control or to win elections

Sources: For a list of relevant sources, please see the references. For definitions of the terms, please see the following:

1. **Patrimonial:** Clapham (1985: 48) defines patrimonialism as "a form of organization in which relationships of a broadly patrimonial type pervade a political and administrative system which is formally constructed on legal-rational lines".

2. **Crony capitalism:** Kang (2002: 3) defines collusion (or crony capitalism) as a situation where there is "a balance of power among a small and stable set of government and business elites… [which] make long term agreements and investments more efficient… while enriching those fortunate few who collude together".

3. **Bureaucratic capture:** Common definitions of bureaucratic capture imply that a bureaucracy becomes beholden to interest groups and cannot act autonomously. Here we also employ it to describe situations in which a department or agency is captured by its own members, either politicians or bureaucrats, who then use its organizational structure illicitly to extract benefits for themselves (see Acemoglu and Robinson 2012: 79–83; White 2015: 185–187).

4. **Electoral manipulation:** There are two elements in electoral manipulation encapsulated in Davidson and Mobrand's (Ch.6) distinction between rule making, which are attempts to change the rules to favour particular outcomes, and rule breaking measures taken to affect the result of a specific election (see also Simpser 2013: 32–38).

Patrimonialism

Patrimonialism, as the term is used here, is an organizational form rather than a state system (Clapham 1985: 48). State systems in Asia have often been described as patrimonial or neopatrimonial but there has also been criticism of the generality, "catch-all" nature, of the concept (Erdmann and Engel 2006; Isaacs 2014). Here we are concerned principally with the organizational characteristics of patrimonial networks. The network is organizationally distinctive. It is usually headed by a single figure supported by family members and henchmen who are recruited through bureaucratic or political links with the leader. In this sense, it is based on "modern" organizational relationships rather than on the Weberian concept of traditional authority. Many authors note the tension between the patrimonial networks and the formal legal-rational norms of bureaucracies which they are seeking to undermine (Theobald 1982; Collins 2011). The patrimonial network is potentially highly adaptable to opportunities for institutional corruption. It may link national and local levels and could include elements of both public and private sectors or it could be concentrated in local government. Any or all of the means described in the other categories of institutional corruption, collusion, bureaucratic capture or electoral manipulation, could be employed but the patrimonial organization remains distinctively different from those forms, serving as the parent network overseeing various types of corrupt activities. What particularly distinguishes the patrimonial network from other organizational forms is the element of personalism: individual control over the network and dependence on contacts built up through the family and through political and administrative connections.

Although the organizational form of the patrimonial network may be similar whatever the arenas in which it chooses to operate, its scale may vary enormously. Zhu (Ch. 3) describes a network in China which comprised a significant part of the state petroleum industry, a provincial bureaucracy and the National Security Bureau all under the suzerainty of a single figure aided by trusted family members and cronies. When a network operates on that scale, it must surely fear competition from similar networks and from the state which might well wish to shut it down. Perhaps this creates a lust to expand: an attempt "to seize the state" itself, in the words of Hellman et al. (2003), a potentially self-destructive, but possibly necessary, political dynamic to ensure survival. We do not know enough about such networks to understand the motivation of their leaders but we do know that they can expand very rapidly and that they can, as in case of the network described by Zhu (Ch. 3), incorporate very strange bedfellows within their systems of wealth extraction. By comparison, smaller patrimonial networks often seem quite content with maintaining their market share. In Indian villages, for example, stable networks may form around a "big man" who benefits from his position but may be constrained by external factors from expansion or may find the task of maintaining the existing network all time-consuming (Mines and Gourishankar 1990).

Whatever the causes of the differences between networks in terms of their scale and stability, they do appear to take a similar organizational form. In common with other forms of institutional corruption, there is a disregard of, or attempt to subvert, the rules, especially successful where bureaucracies have not been institutionalised and where nepotism is a feature of recruitment. Beyond this, however, the picture in many places is unclear; we need more information on the dynamics of these networks, how they interact with the state, the conditions under which they expand rapidly and the constraints on their activities.

Crony capitalism

Crony capitalism is a specific type of collusive relationship between senior officials, either politicians or bureaucrats or both, and heads or important figures in private companies seeking contracts or advantageous administrative decisions by bending or breaking rules which favour them over their competitors. The relationship is seen to have mutual benefits in the form of kickbacks for the senior officials and profits for the businesspeople. This form of institutional corruption has been widely evident in Asia (Kang 2002; Ip 2008; Gupta 2015; You 2015: 19–20) but there is some debate about whether it is simply a way of describing capitalism itself and whether its utility is more limited than the broad-brush explanations which it is sometimes employed to serve (Johnson 1998). For our purposes, crony capitalism represents a particular informal organizational form which meets our primary definitional criteria of collaboration and intent to pervert the rules.

In disaggregating the concept into specific types of relationships, however, both distinguishing the concept from other types of institutional corruption and the issue of the relative power of the key actors are important. The case of Ao Man, the Minister of Transport and Public Works in Macao from 1999 until 2006 when he was arrested and subsequently sentenced to 29 years in prison, may serve as an illustration. During his period in office, Ao received kickbacks of about US$100 million from some Hong Kong businessmen for contracts relating to the building of stadia for the 2005 Asian Games and for the construction of an apartment complex. At first sight, the Ao case might be regarded as a simple matter of individual bribery. However, it does meet both Kang's criterion (2002: 3) for crony capitalism that the relationship should be stable over time and the criterion for institutional corruption that attempts are made to change the rules and specific decisions. Evidence was presented at the trial, for example, that Ao had ordered that the decisions of the tendering committee (whom he appointed) should be changed (Yu 2013). While members of Ao's family were also convicted on charges of money-laundering, they do not, as far as we know, seem to have involved in direct corrupt relationships. There was also suspicion that the relationship might be wider than reported, stretching into networks within the Macao government. The judge's report on the case was not released, however, so there is no concrete evidence to support that claim. The Ao case does nonetheless serve to illustrate the difficulties in identifying crony capitalism, useful as the concept might be in disaggregating types of institutional corruption.

Kang's second criterion in identifying crony capitalism is that there should be "a balance of power" between government and business. Davis (2004), in her research on India and Pakistan, provides an example where there was no balance of power in the relationship and where it might be more appropriate, based on the actual facts, to classify the case as one of bureaucratic capture. She describes a situation in which a cartel of water and sanitation contractors colluded to fix the price of contracts. When the official in charge aborted the tender process because of collusion and ordered a new tendering exercise, the cartel came back with an even higher price. At least three hypothetical outcomes are possible. First, the official might simply agree the price in which case we would have an example of bureaucratic capture. Second, the official could seek to redress the balance of power, say, by allowing outside contractors to tender but still possibly seeking kickbacks from present contractors in exchange for favourable tendering decisions; in this case, we would have crony capitalism. Finally, the official could declare the existing contractors ineligible to bid which would mean that the attempt at institutional corruption through subversion of the rules would have failed. This case shows the importance of meeting the "balance of power" criterion before classifying situations as crony capitalism.

Bureaucratic capture

Bureaucratic capture is normally associated in Western countries with a situation in which an interest group is able to dictate policy outcomes and administrative decisions to a department or an agency. While bureaucratic capture of this kind certainly does occur in Asia, particularly in relationships between business and government, there may also be more effective organizational means, such as crony capitalism or bribes, of attaining the same end. What does seem to be quite common in Asia is the capture of bureaucracies by their own members with the aim of engaging in illicit activities contrary to the legitimate aim of the department or agency (Gong 2002; White 2015: 185–187; Ch. 4). The distinguishing feature of this type of bureaucratic capture is not that bureaucrats individually take bribes but that they use the organizational structure of the department and act as a syndicate to obtain and distribute corruptly obtained money. An example from Hong Kong shows how an organization can be adapted for illicit purposes and the consequences for the way in which the department functions.

In the 1960s, the Hong Kong Police Force was riddled with institutional corruption. The Force had a long history of illicit activities which gradually became established as an organizational network superimposed on the wider department. New recruits were tempted by money seemingly left inadvertently among official documents (a recruitment technique that is apparently common in other police forces). If the recruit accepted the "sweetener", they were inducted into the network; if they reported it, they were excluded. Individual corruption or "freelancing" was "frowned upon" and could result in an officer who was working outside the system, and even honest police officers, being ostracised or passed over for promotion (Blair-Kerr 1973: 24). Bribes were collected systematically from, among others, small businesses, taxi and mini-bus drivers, and hawkers and prostitutes with the proceeds distributed upwards to senior officers through a pyramidal organizational system which mirrored the formal police structure. Some areas of policing, such as on-the-beat patrols in the urban areas, were regarded as lucrative pickings while others, such as the Special Branch, were thought to be "dry". Viewed from within the corruption "bus", as it was called (Blair-Kerr 1973: 24), institutional corruption of this kind could perhaps have promoted camaraderie and a sense of collective enterprise but the costs were enormous. Not only were public resources diverted for the purpose of illegal rent-collecting, but misery was inflicted on those least able to bear the cost. Public trust was undermined and police corruption was thought to be an underlying cause of the 1966 riots.

There is also a type of bureaucratic capture in which members at the lower levels of the organization take advantage of circumstances in which supervision and the rules are not properly enforced and subsequently collectively benefit from the ensuing laxity. In some cases, paradoxically, this may occur because too much attention is being paid to the enforcement of anti-corruption rules in other parts of the organization (Scott 2015: 193, 199–201).

Bureaucratic capture of these kinds are worthy of much more research than they have received. We need to know how the syndicate is created in the first place, how members are recruited and what means are used to collect and distribute corrupt funds. The relationship between this kind of institutional corruption and the implementation of bureaucratic rules and regulations is an important element in corruption prevention. Provided that sufficient capacity and political will are present, it is an area of institutional corruption that can be successfully addressed.

Electoral manipulation and fraud

In contrast to other kinds of institutional corruption, electoral manipulation and fraud have received considerable attention (from a voluminous literature, see, for example, Ockey 2004: 44–45; Croissant and Martin 2006; Acharya et al. 2015; Christensen 2015; Weiss 2015). This is partly because there has been an abiding interest in whether Asian elections are democratic or whether they are corrupt and, as such, antithetical to democracy. In a comparative study of elections in Cambodia, Indonesia, the Philippines, Malaysia and Thailand, Croissant and Martin (2006: 18) remarks that the long history of elections in these countries is one of "electoral ritualism, limited competition, or 'manipulated' elections". The same is probably true of many other parts of Asia. Elections are very often simply intended to be a symbolic re-affirmation of the right of elites to continue to rule. They are not fair and do not provide choice.

In this classification, I employ Davidson and Mobrand's (Ch. 6) useful distinction between rule-making and rule-breaking in electoral manipulation and fraud. Two points are relevant in this context. First, rule-making is a much more sophisticated way to influence the system and cannot easily be countered by simple attention to the rules; it is the rules themselves that are being manipulated. As the citizens of Hong Kong have discovered after more than thirty years of painful constitutional debate, elites will obfuscate, lie and change the rules in order to maintain power through elections. Second, rule-breaking is a far less sophisticated means and can be countered, as Babb (Ch. 5) shows, by assiduous implementation of the rules even if these are sometimes used for expressly political purposes. The distinction between these two forms of institutional corruption is important and provides the kind of disaggregation which is necessary to develop the concept further.

Conclusions

This essay began with a definition of institutional corruption which rested on the notion of collaborative action aimed at perverting rules and regulations with the purpose of obtaining illicit collective gains. There is no apparent direct connection between this kind of corruption and regime type. Any regime may be exposed to institutional corruption. Under conditions of rapid political and/or economic change and weak institutionalisation of the rules, democracies, such as India, are as prone to institutional corruption as the dictatorships of central Asia. Even within democratic systems, such as Japan, regime attitudes towards different types of institutional corruption may range from zero tolerance to relatively relaxed attitudes towards dubious practices. While in the longer term there may be a relationship between democracy and reduced levels of institutional corruption, in the short run traditional democratic values seem to offer little protection. What is clear is that institutional corruption thrives under conditions in which there is rapid political, social and economic change and where rules and regulations are only weakly institutionalised. Opportunities for institutional corruption arise when rules are poorly formulated or are being made up as the government goes along or in new policy areas which are insufficiently regulated.

In consequence, there has been some academic interest in identifying variables in bureaucratic systems which may aid in the prevention of attempts to pervert the rules. Dahlström

(2015: 118), for example, has argued that there are "good reasons to expect a Weberian bureaucracy to have a deterrent effect on corruption" and notes that patrimonial administrative systems come with much higher risk (see also Rauch and Evans 2000; Dahlström et al. 2012; Rothstein and Teorell 2015). As far as individual corruption is concerned, there is support for this position in the Weberian bureaucracies of Hong Kong and Singapore which are usually cited as the cleanest governments in Asia and which both pay very considerable attention to the ways in which their rules and regulations might be subverted by those with corrupt intentions. With institutional corruption, however, the challenge is that those in power may themselves seek to manipulate the rules to their own advantage. In principle, it should still be beneficial to provide bureaucratic and legal checks on such action; it is common sense that, if the aim is to pervert the rules, efforts should be made to ensure that those rules are watertight and institutionalised. But it may also be important to ensure that values are well understood and endorsed and that social empowerment is encouraged as additional protection against those who seek to manipulate the rules to their advantage (Johnston 1998; Lewis and Gilman 2012: 14).

In examining the relationship between regime type and corruption, while the nature of the bureaucratic system and the degree to which rules are institutionalised appears to be of primary importance, it does not in itself provide much guidance on the nature of the threats that the system may experience. For this, as I have argued, it is more useful to disaggregate the various types of institutional corruption. I suggest, tentatively, that it may be helpful to begin by analysing the organizational form which this might take. Since, by definition, institutional corruption requires collaboration, there must be some formal or informal organizational means of seeking to achieve the corrupt objective. The categories I have chosen (patrimonialism; collusion; bureaucratic capture; and electoral manipulation) are organizationally distinct. In each case, the organizational form, the key actors, the scale of the operation and the means of achieving the objective differ. However, they may still not be sufficiently distinct to make meaningful comparisons about the methods that might be usefully employed to prevent corrupt objectives from being achieved. For that, it may be necessary to break the categories down further by scale and objective. While this task is beyond the scope of this chapter, there is evidence in the work of Kang (2002), Jancsics and Jávor (2012) and in other chapters in this book (see, particularly, Chs. 3–6, 10) that meaningful comparisons relating to methods and procedure can be made by further disaggregating what is meant by institutional corruption. To do so would enhance our understanding of the processes involved and enable us to examine successful strategies for prevention and to move beyond the blanket terms we presently use to describe such phenomena.

References

Acemoglu, D. and J.A. Robinson (2012) *Why nations fail: the origins of power, prosperity and poverty*, New York: Crown Publishers.

Acharya, A., J.E. Roemer and R. Somanathan (2015) "Caste, corruption and political competition in India", *Research in Economics*, 69(3): 336–352.

Blair-Kerr, A. (1973) *Second report of the Commission of Inquiry under Sir Alastair Blair-Kerr*, Hong Kong: Government Printer.

Bünte, M. (2011) "Decentralization and democratic governance in Southeast Asia: theoretical views, conceptual pitfalls and empirical ambiguities", in A. Croissant and M. Bünte (eds.) *The crisis of democratic governance in Southeast Asia*, London: Palgrave Macmillan, 131–150.

Campbell, N. and S. Saha (2013) "Corruption, democracy and Asia Pacific countries", *Journal of Asia Pacific Economy*, 18(2): 290–303.

Chang, E.C.C. and Y.-H. Chu (2006) "Corruption and trust: exceptionalism in Asian democracies", *The Journal of Politics*, 68(2): 259–271.

Christensen, R. (2015) "The rules of the election game in Japan", in R.J. Hrebener and A. Nakamura (eds.) *Party politics in Japan: political chaos and stalemate in the twenty-first century,* London: Routledge, 22–55.

Clapham, C. (1985) *Third world politics: an introduction,* London: Helm.

Clausen, B., A. Kraay and Z. Nyiri (2011) "Corruption and confidence in public institutions: evidence from a global survey", *World Bank Economic Review*, 25(2): 212–249.

Collins, K. (2006) *Clan politics and regime transition,* New York: Cambridge University Press.

Collins, R. (2011) "Patrimonial alliances and failure of state penetration: a historical dynamic of crime, corruption, gangs and mafias", *The Annals of the American Academy of Political and Social Sciences*, 636(1): 16–31.

Cox, M. (ed.) (2008) *State of corruption, state of chaos,* Lanham, MD: Lexington Books.

Croissant, A. and B. Martin (eds.) (2006) *Between consolidation and crisis: elections and democracy in Southeast Asia,* Munster: Lit Verlag.

Dahlström, C. (2015) "Bureaucracy and corruption", in P. Heywood (ed.) *Routledge handbook of political corruption,* Abingdon: Routledge, 110–120.

Dahlström, C., V. Lapuente and J. Teorell (2012) "The merit of meritocratization: politics, bureaucracy and the institutional deterrents of corruption", *Political Research Quarterly*, 65(3): 658–670.

Davis, J. (2004) "Corruption in public service delivery: experience from South Asia's water and sanitation sector", *World Development*, 32(1): 53–71.

Dobel, J. P. (1978) "The corruption of a state", *American Political Science Review*, 72(3): 958–973. Reprinted in M. Johnston (ed.) *Public sector corruption,* Vol. 1, London: Sage, 27–51.

Erdmann, G. and U. Engel (2006) *Neopatrimonialism revisited – beyond a catch-all concept,* GIGA Working Paper No.17.

Frederickson, H.G. (1999) "Ethics and the new managerialism", *Public Administration and Management*, 4(2): 299–324.

Gainsborough, M. (2003) "Corruption and the politics of economic decentralisation in Vietnam", *Journal of Contemporary Asia*, 33(1): 69–84.

Gillespie, J. (2002) "The political-legal culture of anti-corruption reforms in Vietnam", in T. Lindsey and H. Dick (eds.) *Corruption in Asia: rethinking the governance paradigm,* Annandale, NSW: Federation Press, 167–200.

Gong, T. (2002) "Dangerous collusion: corruption as a collective venture in contemporary China", *Communist and Post-Communist Studies*, 35(1): 85–103.

Gupta, V. (2015) *Indian administrative service (IAS) and crony capitalism: a review paper,* Ahmedabad: Indian Institute of Management.

Hellman, J. S., G. Jones and D. Kaufmann (2003) "Seize the state, seize the day: state capture and influence in transition economies", *Journal of Comparative Economics*, 31(4): 751–773.

Ip, P.K. (2008) "Corporate social responsibility and crony capitalism in Taiwan", *Journal of Business Ethics*, 79: 167–177.

Isaacs, R. (2014) "Neopatrimonialism and beyond: reassessing the formal and the informal in the study of Central Asian politics", *Comparative Politics,* 20 (2): 229–245.

Jancsics, D. and I. Jávor (2012) "Corrupt governmental networks", *International Public Management Journal*, 15(1): 62–93.

Johnson, C. (1998) "Economic crisis in East Asia: clash of capitalisms", *Cambridge Journal of Economics*, 22(6): 653–661.

Johnston, M. (1998) "Fighting systemic corruption: social foundations of institutional reform", *European Journal of Development Research*, 10(1): 85–104.

Johnston, M. (2005) *Syndromes of corruption: wealth, power and democracy,* Cambridge: Cambridge University Press.

Kang, D.C. (2002) *Crony capitalism: corruption and development in South Korea and the Philippines,* Cambridge: Cambridge University Press.

Khan, M.H. (1998) "Patron-client networks and the economic effects of corruption in Asia", *European Journal of Development Research*, 10(1): 15–39.

Ko, K. and H. Zhi (2013) "Fiscal decentralization: guilty of aggravating corruption in China?" *Journal of Contemporary China*, 22(79): 35–55.

Lai, A. N. (2001) "Keeping Hong Kong clean: experiences of fighting corruption post 1997", *Harvard Asia Pacific Review*, 5(2): 51–54.

Lessig, L. (2013) *Institutional corruptions*, Edmond J. Safra Working Papers No. 16 Cambridge, MA: Harvard University, March.

Lewis, C. W. and S.C. Gilman (2012) *The ethics challenge in public service: a problem-solving guide,* 3rd ed., San Francisco: Jossey-Bass.

Mines, M. and V. Gourishankar (1990) "Leadership and individuality in South Asia: the case of the South Indian big-man", *The Journal of Asian Studies*, 49(4): 761–786.

Moran, J. (2011) *Crime and corruption in new democracies: the politics of (in)security*, London: Palgrave Macmillan.

Murtazashvili, J. (2015) "Gaming the state: consequences of contracting out state building in Afghanistan", *Central Asian Survey*, 34(1): 78–92.

Ockey, J. (2004) *Making democracy: leadership, class, gender and political participation in Thailand*, Honolulu: University of Hawaii Press.

O'Toole, B. J. (1993) "Editorial: the loss of purity: the corruption of public service in Britain", *Public Policy and Administration*, 8(2): 1–6.

Persson, A., B. Rothstein and J. Teorell (2013) "Why anticorruption reforms fail - systemic corruption as a collective action problem", *Governance*, 26(3): 449–471.

Quah, J.S.T. (2013) *Curbing corruption in Asia: an impossible dream?* Singapore: Institute of Southeast Asian Studies.

Rauch, J.E. and P.B. Evans (2000) "Bureaucratic structure and bureaucratic performance in less developed countries", *Journal of Public Economics*, 75(1): 49–71.

Rose-Ackerman, S. (2002) "When is corruption harmful?" in A. Heidenheimer and M. Johnston (eds.) *Political corruption: concepts and context,* 3rd edition, New Brunswick, NJ: Transaction Publishers, 353–371.

Rothstein, B. (2011) *The quality of government: corruption, social trust and inequality*, Chicago; University of Chicago Press.

Rothstein, B. and J. Teorell (2015) "Causes of corruption", in P. Heywood (ed.) *Routledge handbook of political corruption*, Abingdon: Routledge, 79–94.

Scott, I. (2015) "Governance and corruption prevention in Hong Kong", in L. Van den Dool, F. Hendriks, A. Gianoli and L. Schaap (eds.) *The quest for good urban governance: theoretical reflections and international practices*, Berlin: Springer, 185–204.

Seligson, M. (2002) "The impact of corruption on regime legitimacy: a comparative study of four Latin American countries", *Journal of Politics*, 64: 408–433.

Sherman, L.W. (1980) "Three models of organizational corruption in agencies of social control", *Social Problems*, 27(4): 478–491.

Simpser, A. (2013) *Why governments and parties manipulate elections*, New York: Cambridge University Press.

Sun, Y. and M. Johnston (2009) "Does democracy check corruption? Insights from China and India", *Comparative Politics*, 42(1): 1–19.

Sung, H-E (2004) "Democracy and political corruption: a cross-national comparison", *Crime, Law and Social Change*, 41: 179–194.

Theobald, R. (1982) "Patrimonialism", *World Politics*, 34(4): 548–559.

Thompson, D. F. (1995) *Ethics in congress: from individual to institutional corruption*, Washington, DC: Brookings Institution.

Thompson, D. F. (2013) *Two concepts of corruption,* Edmond J. Safra Working Papers No. 16, Cambridge, MA: Harvard University, August.

Warren, M.E. (2015) "The meaning of corruption in democracies", in P. Heywood (ed.) *Routledge handbook of political corruption*, Abingdon: Routledge, 42–55.

Wedeman, A. (1997) "Stealing from the farmers: institutional corruption and the 1992 IOU crisis", *The China Quarterly*, 152: 805–831.

Weiss, M.L. (2015) "The antidemocratic potential of party system institutionalization in Malaysia", in A. Hicken and E.M. Kuhonta (eds.) *Party system institutionalization in Asia: democracies, autocracies and the shadows of the past*, New York: Cambridge University Press, 25–48.

Werner, S.B. (1983) "New directions in the study of administrative corruption", *Public Administration Review*, 43(2): 146–154.

White, L. T. III (2015) *Philippine politics: possibilities and problems in a localist democracy,* Abingdon: Routledge.

Whitfield, L. and O. Therkildsen (2011) *What drives states to support the development of productive sectors? Strategies ruling elites pursue for political survival and their policy implications,* DIIS Working Paper 15, Copenhagen.

You, J-S (2015) *Democracy, inequality and corruption: Korea, Taiwan and the Philippines compared,* Cambridge: Cambridge University Press.

Yu, E.W-Y (2013) "Anti-corruption approaches in Macau: lawmaking and legal enforcement", *Journal of Contemporary China,* 22(79): 93–108.

3

CORRUPTION NETWORKS IN CHINA

An institutional Analysis

Jiangnan Zhu

Introduction

Rapid economic growth provides opportunities for institutionalising new forms of corruption and for re-enforcing existing networks of wealth extraction and illicit activities (Rose-Ackerman 1999). In China, since the late 1990s, there is evidence that economic growth has been accompanied by corruption of increasing severity, complexity, and scope (Gong 1997; Wedeman 2004; Guo 2008). One indication of this intensification of corruption is the high incidence of collective corruption in which a complex network of participants from different government departments, localities, and private sectors operate like a syndicate. These corrupt networks have in some cases developed into corruption on a grand scale involving very high-level officials and the establishment of corrupt empires. The chapter identifies three major politico-economic features leading to this form of corruption in China:

- power concentration in a geographically and functionally fragmented authoritarian regime;
- business-government collusion in a transitional economy; and
- the prevalence of informal politics, especially the factional networks within the ruling party and the privatisation of public power by family members of government officials.

These features are illustrated using the case of a former member of the Politburo Standing Committee (PSC) of the Chinese Communist Party (CCP), Zhou Yongkang, who is to date the highest official ever convicted of corruption.

Corruption in China: definitions and trends

Corruption in China is broadly defined. In addition to monetary activities such as bribery or embezzlement, a corrupt official is almost always vilified for personal failings such as having mistresses, committing adultery (a term appearing in the official media since 2014), neglecting duty, or even leaking state secrets. Corruption in China seems to be, on the one hand, similar to the generic definition of "abuse of public power for private gain" but, on the other, rather more than that in the context of the public interest and the role of the party. First, although the major actors in Chinese corruption are government officials, the staff of public organizations and even ordinary people engaged in public services may also be considered to commit corruption if their misbehaviour compromises public interests (Ko and Weng 2011). Second, corruption in China is subject to both criminal law and party discipline. The criminal law regulates not only economic corruption, such as bribery, graft, embezzlement, misappropriation, holding a huge amount of property with unidentified sources, and unauthorised disposal of state properties but also the dereliction of duties and malpractices. Party discipline holds to high formal moral standards and castigates misconduct caused by violation of administrative responsibility and official malfeasance such as shirking, torture, having mistresses, squandering and many other forms of immorality. This broad definition of corruption reflects the CCP's attempts to control both typical types of corruption and the socially unacceptable behaviour of state functionaries. However, broad definitions do not necessarily correlate with low tolerance of corruption or help in efforts to constrain it (Gong and Wang 2013).

Several scholars argue that corruption in China increased in the late 1990s and can be gauged by the rising percentage of major cases filed, the number of senior officials charged, and the growing amounts of corrupt funds uncovered. For instance, major cases filed by the disciplinary inspection system, which involved officials at or above county/department level (*xian/ke*) and illicit monies exceeding 10,000 yuan, jumped from approximately 6 per cent in 1987–1988 to more than 30 per cent in 2000 (Wedeman 2004). The average amount of money involved in those cases rose dramatically from 17,000 yuan between 1978 and 1991 to 2,968,000 yuan between 1991 and 2000 and increased further to 3,208,000 by 2004. After 2001, 78.6 per cent of major cases exceeded one million yuan (Guo 2008). Significantly, high-level officials, especially those at or above bureau-level (*chu, ting, ju*), accounted for 64 per cent of the major actors among publicly reported cases (Gong and Wu 2012).

Concentrating particularly on trends in high-profile corruption, I compiled a dataset from available public sources, including government publications, websites, and media reports of senior officials at or above vice-provincial/ministerial level who were charged or punished for corruption between 1986 and June 2015. Because cases involving those very high-level officials have political importance, the mass media always report them. Thus, this dataset of some 275 officials should be an almost complete list of senior officials accused of corruption since 1986. Figure 3.1 illustrates the distribution of these officials over time. It shows a steadily increasing number of senior officials charged with corruption. Between 1986 and 1994, corrupt senior officials only appeared sporadically and in very small numbers. From 1995 onwards, corrupt senior officials began to show up in consecutive years and in several years the number reached double digits. After 2013, 126 officials were investigated for corruption, accounting for 46 per cent of the whole dataset. The large number after 2013 is apparently the result of the large scale anti-corruption campaign launched by President Xi Jinping after he came to power at the end of 2012. However, many newly investigated officials were involved in corruption long before that. For example, although the former mayor of Nanjing, Ji Jianye, was only arrested in early 2015, he had been engaged in corrupt activities since 1992 when he was only a county party secretary. The dataset also shows that, after 2005, the average amount of illicit money purloined was constantly more than 50 million yuan with the highest amount reaching 200 million yuan.

Underlying these numbers are constantly changing forms of corruption with increasingly sophisticated causes and characteristics, reflecting the changing social environment (Gong 1997, 2002). In the 1980s, the most popular form of corruption was official speculation, taking advantage of the dual-price system between the low state-set prices and the much higher

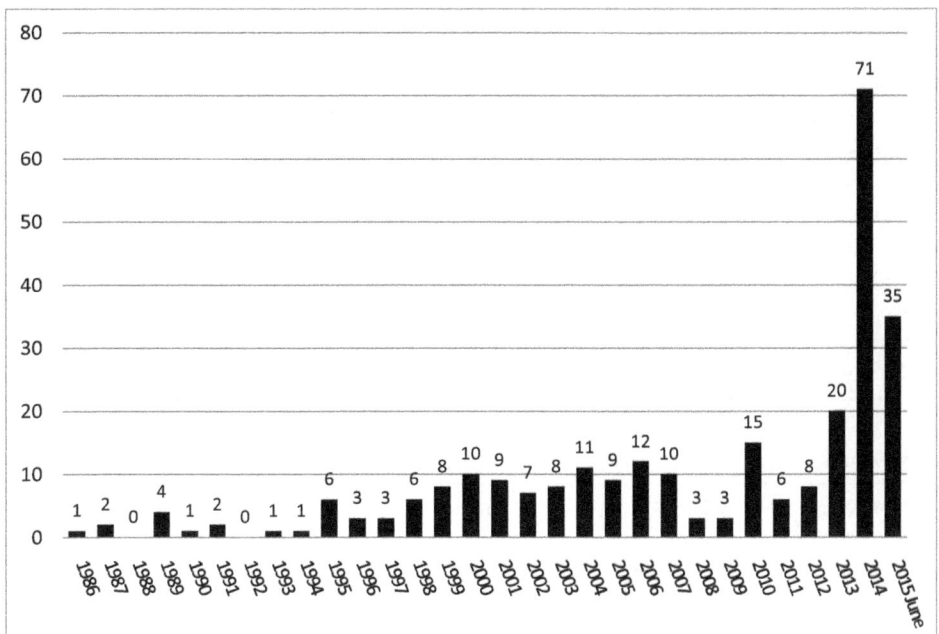

Figure 3.1   Number of disciplined vice-provincial/ministerial-level officials, 1986–June 2015

Source: Based on the author's dataset of 275 senior officials drawn from cases reported in the Chinese press.

market prices for raw materials. In the 1990s, when the state further liberalised the prices and carried out taxation, banking, and housing reforms, many new corrupt activities appeared (Gong 1997). While stock market violations, speculation in the burgeoning real estate markets, and smuggling tended to be more frequent in the economically active coastal regions, tax evasion, financial fraud, and buying and selling official positions were more common types of corruption in less-developed areas (Sun 2004; Zhu 2008, 2012). Government procurement and outsourcing of services were also plagued with high incidences of corruption (Gong and Wu 2012).

Since the late 1990s, collective corruption, in which groups of officials working collaboratively like a mafia, has been particularly noticeable (Gong 2002). Although some cases, such as collective embezzlement, only involve government officials, most collective corruption includes complex corrupt networks, which transfer interests among officials in different local bureaucratic systems and to actors outside the government (Gong 2002). For instance, in the notorious Yuanhua smuggling case investigated in the late 1990s, Lai Changxing, the boss of a smuggling empire in Xiamen suborned the entire custom house in Xiamen and cultivated the support of public security officials, local leaders, banks and even the military in Xiamen and in other parts of the country (Shieh 2005). Similar cases were also discovered in Zhanjiang and Shenyang. More recently, the former head of the Chongqing public security bureau, Wen Qiang, together with his local policemen, acted as the unlawful protectors of the criminal underworld in Chongqing (Wang 2013). In these cases, the major players in the criminal networks included private entrepreneurs, state-owned enterprise (SOE) managers, gangsters, local governors, party leaders, bureaucrats, and law enforcers. Collective corruption is politically destructive, as the experience of post-communist countries shows, because corrupt networks can infiltrate and take over state institutions (Shieh 2005).

In my dataset of the 275 senior officials, 58 were involved in 17 different collective corruption cases. Several senior officials were caught because of their linkage to the same case. As Table 3.1 shows, while some cases concentrated in a single locality or functional system, such as Chen Liangyu's case in Shanghai, the downfall of the Shanxi gang, Liu Tienan's energy system, and Xu Caihou's military corruption, other cases had wider repercussions beyond a single locality or bureaucracy. Some even implicated central government leaders, such as the case of Zhou Yongkang, which is discussed later in the chapter.

I also categorise the senior officials in my dataset by their positions when they first became involved in corruption to see which government sectors were most vulnerable to

Table 3.1 Senior officials involved in collective corruption

Case No./name	Major participants (title, year of investigation)	Other participants (year of investigation)
1. Chen Xitong's case	Chen Xitong (Party Secretary of Beijing, 1995)	Wang Baosen (suicide in 1995)
2. Yuanhua smuggling case	Shi Zhaobin (Party Secretary of Xiamen and Fujian, 2001), Cong Fukui (Vice-Governor of Hebei, 2001)	Ji Shengde (1999), Li Jizhou (1999)
3. Tao Siju's case	Tao Siju (Minister of Public Security, 2002)	
4. Han Guizhi's case	Han Guizhi (Deputy Secretary of Heilongjiang, Head of Provincial Organizational Department, Chairman of the Provincial PPCC, 2004)	Fan Guangju (2003), Xu Fa (2004), Xu Yandong (2004)
5. Guo Wengui's case	Liu Zhihua (Vice-Mayor of Beijing, 2006), Ma Jian (Deputy Minister of State Security, 2015)	Wang Youjie (2005)
6. Chen Tonghai – China Petrochemical Corporation	Chen Tonghai (General Manager of China Petroleum & Chemical Corporation, Director of China Petroleum & Chemical Co., Ltd., 2007), Du Shicheng (Deputy Party Secretary of Shandong, Member of Qingdao Municipal Committee, 2007)	
7. Bo Xilai's case	Bo Xilai (Politburo Member, Party Secretary of Chongqing, 2012)	Wang Lijun (2012)
8. Xu Caihou's military corruption case	Xu Caihou (Vice-Chairman of the Central Military Commission, 2014), Gu Junshan (Lieutenant General, Deputy Minister of PLA Logistics Department, 2012)	Liu Zheng (2013) Gao Xiaoyan (2014)
9. The Petroleum Gang	Zhou Yongkang (Former PSC Member, 2014), Jiang Jiemin (Chairman of CNPC, Director of State-owned Assets Supervision and Administration Commission, 2014), Su Rong (Vice-Chairman of the Twelfth CPPCC, 2014)	Li Chuncheng (2012), Guo Yongxiang (2013), Wang Yongchun (2013), Li Dongsheng (2013), Yang Weize (2015), Ji Wenlin (2014), Li Chongxi (2013), Bai Enpei (2014), Mao Xiaobing (2014)

10. Ling Jihua's case	Ling Jihua (Vice-Chair of CPPCC, 2014), Ling Zhengce (Vice-Chairman of Shanxi Provincial PPCC, 2014)	
11. Shanxi Gang	Du Shanxue (Deputy Governor of Shanxi, 2014), Ren Runhou (Deputy Governor of Shanxi, 2014)	Jin Daoming (2014), Shen Weichen (2014), Nie Chunyu (2014), Chen Chuanping (2014), Bai Yun (2014)
12. Shanghai pension scandal	Chen Liangyu (Party Secretary of Shanghai, 2006)	
13. Liu Zhijun's railway case	Liu Zhijun (Minister of Railways, 2013)	
14. Jiangxi Jiujiang water systems	Chen Anzhong (Vice-Chair of Jiangxi Provincial PPCC, 2015)	Zhao Zhiyong (2014)
15. Kunming case	Bai Enpei (Party Secretary of Yunnan, 2014)	Gao Jinsong (2015), Zhang Tianxin (2014), Qiu He (2015)
16. Wang Jin's case	Zhao Shaolin (Member of Jiangsu Provincial PSC, Deputy Party Secretary of Jiangsu, 2014), Yang Weize (Party Secretary of Nanjing, 2015)	Wang Min (2014), He Jiacheng (2014), Wu Changshun (2014)
17. Energy system	Liu Tienan (Deputy Director of the National Development and Reform Commission, 2013)	

Source: Based on the author's dataset of 275 senior officials drawn from cases reported in the Chinese press.

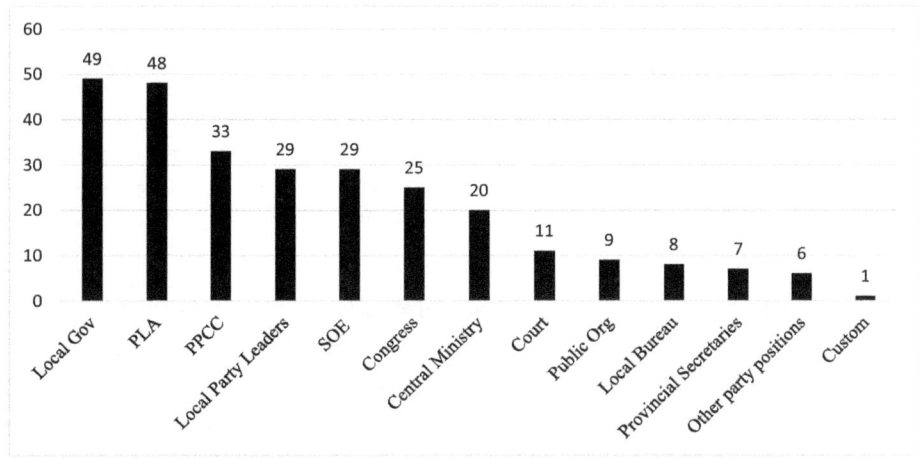

Figure 3.2 Number of disciplined vice-provincial/ministerial-level officials, by affiliations

Source: Based on the author's dataset of 275 senior officials drawn from cases reported in the Chinese press. PLA, People's Liberation Army.

corrupt intrusion. Figure 3.2 shows that 49 officials were local government leaders. This is not surprising given the large executive power and various resources controlled by local governments. This group is followed by the People's Liberation Army with 48 corrupt officers. In comparison to civilian government, power is more concentrated in the military with less public supervision and transparency given the confidentiality of national security.

Corruption in the military has become a serious problem (Chase et al. 2015). Figure 3.2 illustrates how corruption has spread across different government arenas and has often included the top leaders of a locality or a system. As Sun (2004: 121) observes, some corrupt officials are at "the very top in a local administration"; their involvement in corruption has increased the incidence of collective corruption, in which "almost an entire local government, or a large number of its officials, engage in violations".

High-profile cases, including senior officials, large sums of money, and collective corruption with complex networks, have accounted for a higher percentage of corruption in China since the late 1990s. Complex corrupt networks have also infiltrated several sectors crucial for national economic and political development, such as the real estate industry and the cadre recruitment and promotion process. The next section explores the institutional causes leading to the current form of corruption in China.

Institutional causes: major factors shaping corruption in contemporary China

The most widely attributed reason for the growth of this kind of corruption in China is probably market reform. For instance, Kwong (1997) points out that the early market transition led to an income gap between the private sector employees and the public employees. Public employees felt a sense of relative deprivation, which may have led many to engage in corruption, and justify it as an income supplement. The marketisation reforms also created many profiteering opportunities for cadres and SOE managers (Sun 2004). Officials' moral decay, a non-professional civil service system, beset by nepotism and subject to arbitrary subordination to political power, and ineffective supervision and law enforcement have also provided fertile ground for corruption (Lu 2000; Manion 2004; Johnston and Hao 1995). Although many of these problems continue to persist, these factors are especially important in explaining corruption up until the late 1990s. This section focuses on explaining the institutional roots of the corrupt networks apparent in many major collective corruption cases since the late 1990s. I argue that three related causes have been important: 1) power concentration in a geographically and functionally fragmented authoritarian regime; 2) business–government collusion in a transitional economy; and 3) the prevalence of informal politics.

Power concentration in a geographically and functionally fragmented authoritarian regime

The primary factor leading to the syndicated corruption networks is power concentration in a fragmented authoritarian regime. What "appears to be a unified, hierarchical chain of command turns out in reality to be divided, segmented, and stratified" (Lieberthal and Oksenberg 1988: 137). One significant fault line in the system is the division between the centre and the locale while the other organizing concept is that of vertical functional bureaucracies (Lieberthal and Oksenberg 1988).

From the reform era onward, China has been run in a decentralised manner with greater authority granted to local level governments, functional departments, and SOEs in economic and political decision-making (Mertha 2005). However, each decentralised provincial or functional bureaucracy is run in a clearly hierarchical way in which power is centralised in party leaders in each geographical jurisdiction or functional unit. The delegation of greater responsibility to lower level governments to optimise economic growth has inadvertently led to the development of many closed "local or vertical kingdoms" independent of central oversight and public supervision.

This pattern is especially strong at provincial level. The central government does not have direct control of policy implementation, but instead relies on local government to maintain the authority of the CCP and to implement policies. The level of autonomy granted to provinces allows them to implement policies that may differ from those of the central government if they feel that the new initiative will better promote economic growth but as a *quid pro quo* the central government requires that political stability be maintained (Lieberthal 2004). Although the centre can assert power through the armed forces and allocation of resources, once the money reaches the province, government projects and contracts are handled through the provincial government, making provincial leaders, especially the party secretaries, extremely powerful.

The central government has made some effort to recentralise by readjusting functional hierarchies and adopting a "soft centralisation" model where key bureaucracies no longer report to local officials but to leaders higher up in the chain (Mertha 2005). While this has reduced local power in village and town level units, power has not been re-delegated to the central government but to provincial governments. Provincial-level government has also been given greater control over cadres at prefecture level, who now report to provincial level units instead of to Beijing (Lam 2010). Thus soft centralisation has only served to strengthen each kingdom with power becoming more centralised in the provincial party secretary and with the prefecture/city level officials becoming more reliant on the province for support.

Given the size and increasing economic power of China, provincial leaders, especially in the more affluent coastal provinces, control economic resources similar to that of nation-states. With such wide-ranging responsibility, little oversight and lack of accountability in an authoritarian state deeply influenced by cultural ideas such as *guanxi,* provincial leaders and those close to them can more easily use their positions to develop large corruption networks. Firms seeking government contracts also look to provincial leaders and profitable SOEs to establish collusive relationships.

Business-government collusion in a transitional economy

Economic transition in China has featured step-by-step reform initiated by a centrally planned system. The economic success has resulted from the massive entry of non-state firms, a dramatic increase in competition both among state firms and between state firms and non-state firms, and improved performance of SOEs energised by state-imposed market-like incentives (McMillan and Naughton 1992). This process has driven a realignment of prices which eroded governmental resources and shifted economic power towards households. Corruption reasserted official superiority and neutralised bureaucratic resistance to reform (Manion 2004).

Several other characteristics of the transitional economy have promoted the collusive business and government relationship which forms the basis of many corrupt networks. First, to guide the economic transition, bureaucratic power has played an indispensable role. The state has maintained secure control of the commanding heights of the economy. In 2003, the state controlled 56 per cent of the national fixed industrial assets, worth $1.2 trillion yuan (Pei 2006). The state is also a dominant player in key sectors, such as energy, steel, tele-communications, and automobiles. In these sectors, despite limited competition among the state firms, private domestic firms, and foreign companies are largely blocked from entering the market to maintain the state's monopoly profits (Pei 2006). The government also keeps tight control over most investment projects using its power to issue long-term credit and to grant land-use rights. Many business actors approach government officials with the aim of stripping state assets, leading to rampant corruption, such as kickbacks to bureaucrats. Successful capitalists are often those with political connections, such as members of the CCP, or delegates to people's congresses or political consultative conferences (Li et al. 2008). Sometimes private entrepreneurs bribe local officials to secure the nomination of delegates (Sun et al. 2014).

A continuing crony relationship with businessmen also benefits government officials more than bribes for individual projects. Local officials, who are constrained by fiscal resources and pressured to promote the local economy, often require private entrepreneurs to help carry out administrative and policy orders assigned from above, such as reimbursing government purchases, aiding poorly performing SOEs, and reducing local unemployment. Private enterprises may even become the local officials' wallet to deliver bribes for political promotion (Sun et al. 2014).

The party has followed a corporatist approach to embrace economic elites. Within the state system, the relationship between Chinese political and economic elites has even been described as "nomenklatura capitalism" (Crawford 2000). Eighty-one per cent of SOE chief executives and 56 per cent of all senior corporate executives are appointed by the party (Pei 2006). The party has also tried to integrate private entrepreneurs within its ranks so as to win their ideological support and to ensure continued economic growth (Dickson 2008).

The mutual needs of businessmen and government officials have consequently generated entrenched collusive business-government relationships from top to bottom. In my database of the 275 senior officials, at least 158 cases involved bribery or collusive relations with businessmen. These symbiotic relationships are sometimes built on benefits received in exchange for bypassing rules and regulations which have led to very serious outcomes, such as accidents in coal mines (Nie et al. 2013).

The prevalence of informal politics

Another institutional factor in the growth of corrupt networks has been the prevalence of informal politics. In China today as in the past, neither a legal system nor a moral order can fully regulate the behaviour of officials (Pye 1995). As a result, informal politics becomes a convenient tool for political elites to secure power and gain protection. Unlike formal politics, which adheres to bureaucratic procedure and policies based on institutional interests and policy preferences, informal politics essentially entails loyalty towards individuals, while fixed procedures and policies are usually absent (Shih 2004). Thus, informal politics is naturally conducive to corruption. Three aspects of informal politics particularly stimulate corrupt networks in China.

First, the primary reflection of informal politics in China is factionalism. Factionalism is not limited to China or culture-given but a consequence of a structure (Nathan and Tsai 1995) which permits groups to emerge, bound by shared background, intertwined careers and bureaucratic responsibilities, and loyalty toward their leaders, seeking benefits for their members (Lieberthal and Oksenberg 1988). They include a series of patron-client pairs where patrons are higher-level officials and clients are their subordinates. Faction members rise and fall together. Without democratic elections as a way to measure which political elites are more popular, a patron may need to signal power to others through his large group of followers and clients who can obtain preferential treatment or promotions from their powerful patron. Thus, both the patron and client will strive to provide each other with protection during political struggles. Such patron–client bonds can easily degenerate into corrupt link-ages. Some clients constantly deliver benefits, including bribes, to the patron and his family members in order to show their loyalty. In other cases, the patron–client relationship is born in the mutual advantage provided by corrupt means, such as office buying and selling. When clients are investigated for corruption, the patron is incentivised to protect them because a clients' fall is considered a sign of the weakness of the patron and may even implicate the patron. Corruption buttressed by factional ties tends to operate in a relatively "safe" setting and is consequently difficult to combat.

Second, because of the enduring influence of informal power, corruption networks can be extended as the faction itself expands. Shih (2004) observes that factions have developed com-munication networks, which enable the faction to increase in size. A patron has the power to mobilise the primary, secondary, and tertiary ties of his network to engage in politics (Nathan 1973). Corruption networks could also develop into tiers through the multiple patron–client relations. For example, when Chen Xitong, the former party secretary of Beijing, was inves-tigated for corruption, the authorities discovered a large corruption network in the Beijing Municipal Party Committee resulting from Chen's broad and deep links in Beijing (Miller 2015). Moreover, because clients' personal loyalty forms the patrons' powerbase, influences from informal networks extend beyond the term in office. Informal power may have a long-lasting effect even after a leader leaves a position (Huang 2000). In many corruption cases, a leader apparently can still seek rents from the system or localities in which he previ-ously worked. If the leader has been promoted to a higher position, his former subordinates would anticipate a pecuniary advantage in meeting his demands. Thus, a corrupt network not only develops along a single patron–client hierarchical line, it also expands across systems and/or localities following an official's career track. Zhou Yongkang's case well exemplifies this point. Even after Zhou left the China National Petroleum Corporation (CNPC) and Sichuan province, he was still able to use his corrupt kingdom to extract profits from both places.

Finally, with the prevalence of informal politics, family members of government officials often become involved in a leader's political network, leading to the privatisation of public power. Family members' involvement in politics is an inherent tendency within informal politics. As Nathan and Tsai (1995) argue, amongst the political networks formed by leaders in China, memberships are mostly based primarily on kinship or marriage. The offspring of top leaders, or princelings, have more opportunities for promotion (Shih et al. 2012) and informal politics consequently blurs the boundary between the public and private. Many lower level officials try to obtain patronage from their superiors through establishing per-sonal connections with family members and relatives of their leaders. Personal connections also benefit leaders' family members and relatives. The princelings, for example, use their family status to smooth the road to success by means of *guanxi* or personal connections (Pye 1995). In many cases, family members, including mistresses of officials, become the means for officials to collect profits. For instance, instead of owning or running businesses directly, officials often retain control by proxy, establishing new firms run by their relatives or trans-ferring ownership of publicly owned assets to private enterprises owned by "cadre kin" (Power et al. 2012). Thus, many corruption networks deeply involve officials' families, who in turn further extend the corruption networks.

These institutional causes have led to the creation and sustainability of complex corrup-tion networks. The collusive business-government relationship has encouraged crony inter-actions between businessmen, and sometimes even gangsters, and government officials. The power concentration in the fragmented authoritarian regime has provided a way of building corrupt independent kingdoms. Informal politics further supplements the growth of corrupt networks. Zhou Yongkang's case exemplifies how a top leader developed his corrupt empire within a state characterised by these three features.

The case of Zhou Yongkang

A former member of the PSC, Zhou Yongkang is so far the highest-ranking official indicted on corruption charges. At the time of his arrest in December 2014, Zhou's family assets, estimated at 90 billion yuan (14 billion US dollars), were also seized (Lim and Blanchard 2014a). More than 300 of his close family members and political allies were arrested or investigated (Lim and Blanchard 2014b). Corresponding to the three features of the state, Zhou expanded his corrupt empire by building networks within different geographical or departmental systems where he was once the head, tightening his control over the lucrative petroleum business and assigning important posts to his family members or loyal henchmen. Zhou's trajectory in establishing this formidable kingdom can be traced roughly according to his career path: his early years in the oil sector, his stint in Sichuan and his peak years overseeing the security apparatus. His family members became increasingly involved in all parts of this corrupt empire (see Figure 3.3).

Zhou Yongkang (originally Zhou Yuangen) was born in the coastal Jiangsu province in 1942 to a poor rural family of five. His two younger brothers, Zhou Yuanxing and Zhou Yuanqing, also amassed enormous wealth through Zhou Yongkang's network. In 1961, Zhou

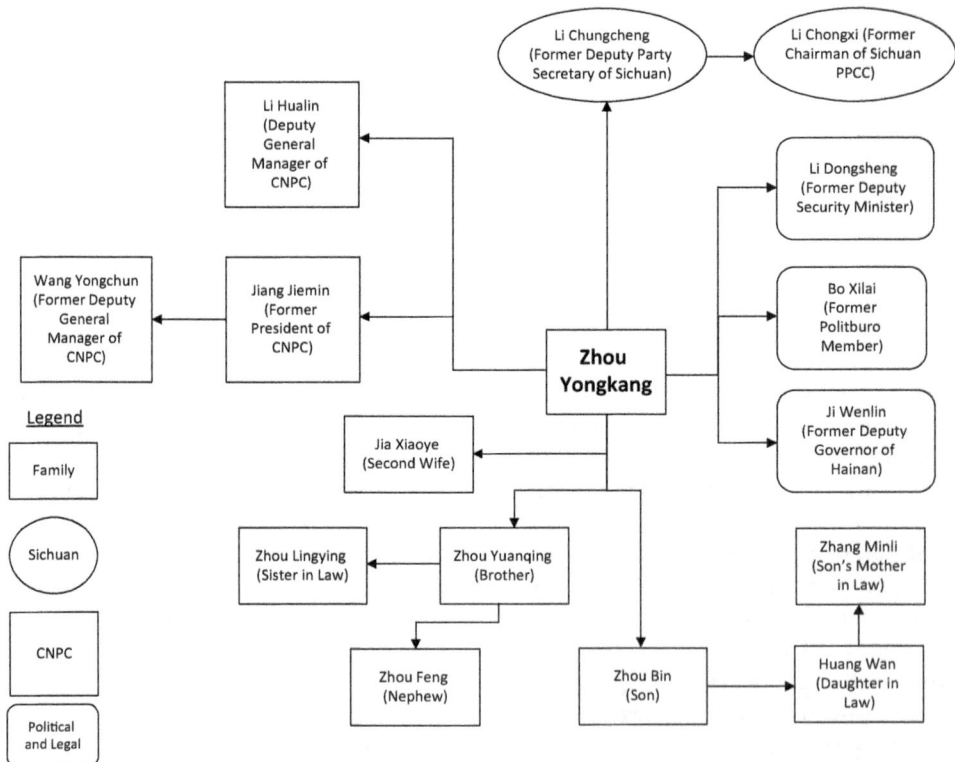

Figure 3.3 A simplified illustration of Zhou's corrupt network

Source: Based on news reports cited in the section of Zhou Yongkang's case.

Yongkang was admitted to the Beijing Institute of Petroleum to study oil exploration, a rare occurrence in those days for someone from his backward home town. In 1964, he became a member of the CCP. After graduation in 1966, he worked as a geological surveyor in the northeastern Liaoning province and lived a thrifty life. He was promoted several times during the Cultural Revolution and in 1976 became the deputy director of the Liao River Petroleum Exploration Agency's political department, shifting his work from technical labour to political management. At that time, there was some suspicion that Zhou was accumulating wealth illegally (Xie and Wang 2014). Nonetheless, in 1984, he was appointed mayor and deputy party secretary of Panjin, a city in Liaoning province. In 1996, Zhou became general manager and party secretary of the CNPC, reaching his next political milestone.

In the CNPC, Zhou took advantage of his power over the natural resources sector to accumulate enormous personal influence. The oil sector offered Zhou a great opportunity to develop a corrupt empire rapidly, partly due to its state-owned nature, partly because it was a relatively mature and independent department. Zhou also drew on the inter-personal relationships he had cultivated over several decades in the oil sector to ensure that he had the support of important individuals in the system. For example, Jiang Jiemin, the first official who was publicly linked with Zhou and investigated for corruption, was Zhou's successor as the deputy party secretary of the CNPC (Chen and Areddy 2015). Jiang had been Zhou's aide since they had worked together in Shandong province in the late 1980s (Gan 2015). Under Zhou's patronage and Jiang's direct operation, the assets of the CNPC rose six-fold during Zhou's tenure on the PSC from 2007 to 2012. PetroChina, the listed arm of the CNPC, also with Jiang as its head, became China's largest oil producer, the largest company in China by market capitalisation, and the most profitable company in Asia enjoying an expanding global presence. Including Jiang, more than 40 members of the "Petroleum Gang" have been investigated, including high-ranking officials such as the CNPC's Li Hualin and Wang Yongchun and former vice-president of PetroChina, Ran Xinquan. Several implicated officials had also worked in the oilfields, enabling Zhou to prolong his personal influence not only in the giant oil companies but also in the backstage oilfields such as the Daqing and Liao River oilfields which he frequently revisited even after he left his positions in the oil sector (Xie and Wang 2014). By filling the important posts in the state-owned oil sector with his own people, Zhou Yongkang consolidated his power over the business which in turn bolstered his long-lasting political network.

Zhou's oil empire involved many of his family members, who found various ways to make money from the CNPC and PetroChina, further entangling Zhou's political and economic interests with the oil sector. His elder son Zhou Bin's father-in-law, Huang Yusheng, who had settled in the United States in the 1980s, registered a company in 1992 called Hysco Corporation selling wellhead equipment exclusively to the CNPC (*Want China Times* 2013). Family members' involvement in his petroleum kingdom further increased when Zhou's career reached its zenith in the PSC from 2002 to 2012.

From 1999 to 2002, Zhou served as party secretary of Sichuan province in mid-west China which developed into a second major venue for corrupt activities. Once again, he reserved the most important positions for his allies, including his several personal secretaries. For instance, Li Chuncheng, the first official on the provincial level to be investigated after the Eighteenth Party Congress, was rapidly promoted to the position of the mayor of Chengdu, Sichuan's capital city, as well as elected an alternate member of the Sixteenth and Eighteenth Central Committees of the CCP. Li finally reached the position of deputy party secretary of Sichuan before he was targeted during the anticorruption campaign in 2012. Ji Wenlin, Li Chongxi, and Guo Yongxiang were all Zhou's personal secretaries during his time in Sichuan and were among the core figures of his Sichuan system. Subsequently, they all attained higher office and had control over various kinds of local businesses, such as tourism, electronics, and the wine industries. Even after Zhou Yongkang left Sichuan, his indirect and extensive influence in the state-owned business sectors remained, making it difficult for the central government to control.

In 2002, Zhou was promoted into the politburo as the minister of public security, followed by his appointment as secretary of the central political and legal affairs commission in the PSC, the highest state organ of China, in 2007. During his 10 years in the public security system, he became the "security tsar" and built up extraordinary power over the Chinese legal system because of such politically sensitive events as the Beijing Olympics, unrest in Tibet and Xinjiang, and the Arab Spring. He took strong action to maintain social stability and his dealings with the court system and other levels of the Chinese society enabled him to develop an even larger patronage network. A greater degree of overlapping of Zhou's three mini-kingdoms gradually occurred during his 10 years in the security sector. For example, Ji Wenlin, Zhou's long-time personal secretary, followed him to the Central Government, linking the Sichuan system with the security sector.

During this time, Zhou used his influence in the CNPC to give preferential treatment to family members, such as his sister-in-law Zhou Lingying, who had enormous stakes in firms closely tied to the CNPC. The firms included, for instance, Jiangyin Benyue Automobile set up in 2010 for an Audi dealership, Beijing Honghan Investment Company for potash mining, and Kunlun Energy, a CNPC subsidiary which specialises in the liquefied gas business (Xie 2014). Another sister-in-law Jia Xiaoxia, was the general manager of CNPC International (Canada) (Huang 2014). Zhou Yongkang's son, Zhou Bin, took an 80 per cent stake in a firm called Beijing Zhongxu Yangguang Petroleum and Natural Gas Technology that deals extensively with the CNPC, in addition to selling computer software to CNPC gas stations. Zhou Bin's parent-in-laws were shareholders of the America-based Hysco Corporation closely tied to CNPC, which was eventually replaced by two newly registered companies in California, Hysco Corporation and Newrun International, running businesses similar to the old Hysco. The new companies reportedly embezzled the CNPC, selling dry oil wells in the United States to the company to reap exorbitant profits (*Xinhua Net* 2013).

Zhou Yongkang received great benefits not only via his close family members but also by means of "white glove" methods using agents who performed illegal transactions that appeared to be legal and so protected their leader from direct involvement. Wu Bing, portrayed in the Chinese media as a "mysterious wealthy businessman", acted as a Zhou family puppet in various businesses in Sichuan (*Xinhua Net* 2013). In 2001, Wu featured in several lucrative deals such as the construction of two hydroelectric stations in the region worth billions of yuan (Zhai and Chiu 2013). Liu Han, who was executed in early 2015, was also Zhou's white glove agent though much more high profile and notorious. Liu worked together with Zhou Bin in power generation and tourism (Lim et al. 2014). He later built his company, Sichuan Hanlong, into a prominent energy conglomerate worth an estimated 855 million yuan (*South China Morning Post* 2015). Meanwhile, Liu rose to be the gang leader of Sichuan and was ultimately accused with his brother Liu Wei (Lim et al. 2014) of responsibility for nine murders, multiple assaults, harbouring criminals, obstruction of justice, loan fraud, kidnapping, and contract rigging. In short, Zhou's family members and white glove agents amassed wealth by all kinds of means in the natural resources and public security sectors. The decentralised nature of China's political system following the reform era afforded high-ranking officials like Zhou great freedom and responsibility in handling their respective departments and in establishing separate kingdoms. By linking his three spheres of influence with key figures like his son and personal secretaries,

Zhou was able to build a colossal political-economic corruption empire. His massive corruption network only seemed to encourage Zhou to be more ambitious and reckless for power. Rumors circulated that he and Bo Xilai, the former party secretary of Chongqing, plotted a coup against Xi Jinping, which, of course, only sped up the downfall of Zhou's empire. Zhou retired from the PSC in 2012 and the investigation into his corruption started in August 2013. Fourteen months later, he was expelled from the party and indicted for corruption, abuse of power, and leaking state secrets. In June 2015, Zhou was found guilty and sentenced to life imprisonment. Yet long before his official fall his enormous empire had begun to collapse.

Zhou's empire was but one of many corrupt networks, large or small, in contemporary China. Several other national-level officials, including Ling Jihua, the former director of the Party's Central Committee General Office and vice-chairman of the Chinese People's Political Consultative Conference, Su Rong, the former vice-chairman of Chinese People's Political Consultative Conference, and Xu Caihou, former vice-chairman of the Central Military Commission, were also indicted in Xi Jinping's anticorruption campaign. Their corrupt empires all shared similarities with Zhou Yongkang's. For example, Ling Jihua, the factional head of northern Shanxi province, also developed his personal clout with the support of a group of fallen officials, such as Du Shanxue and Chen Chuanping, both former vice-governors of Shanxi, and Liu Tienan, former vice-chairman of the National Development and Reform Commission. Moreover, these corrupt empires all reflect the three decisive features of the Chinese state: power concentration in a geographically and functionally fragmented system, business–government collusion, and informal politics.

Conclusion

This chapter offers a broad overview of corruption in China based on a literature review, original data analysis, and case studies. Evidence suggests an intensification of corruption in China: a tendency toward developing oligarchic systems which institutionally nurture collective corruption involving complex networks. We identify three institutional factors that shape the form of corruption, namely: 1) power concentration in a geographically and functionally fragmented authoritarian regime; 2) business–government collusion in a transitional economy; and 3) the prevalence of informal politics, particularly factionalism and family members' involvement in public affairs. The example of the high-profile Zhou Yongkang case illustrates the influence of these features on corruption in China.

Zheng (2006) characterises the current Chinese political system as "de facto federalist", which is a consequence of two combining forces: decentralisation and globalisation. The former points to the first state feature examined in this chapter, geographical and functional fragmentation, while the latter relates to the second institutional factor, business–government collusion in a transitional economy. Taking into account the third element of pervasive factionalism and cronyism, corruption in China could well turn into an aggregation of powerful oligarchies that amass economic and political power in a certain region or government branch and perch atop enormous personal networks. Furthermore, blatant exposure of corruption cases discrediting high-ranking state officials has not only shown the government's determination to root out corruption but also revealed the alarming depth of corrupt acts within the Chinese political and economic systems, even as far-reaching as taking place in the highest decision-making body, the PSC, and consequently undermining the overall legitimacy of the government. This complicated situation poses a great challenge for the ruling party, the CCP: how to deal with the penetration of corruption into public bodies and systems while at the same time maintaining a stable regime and sustained economic growth.

References

Chase, M.S., J. Engstrom, T.M. Cheung, K.A. Gunness, S.W. Harold, S. Puska and S.K. Berkowitz (2015) *China's incomplete military transformation: assessing the weaknesses of the People's Liberation Army (PLA)*, Santa Monica, CA: RAND Corporation.

Chen, T.-P. and J.T. Areddy (2015) "Jiang Jiemin trial links key officials in China's corruption crackdown", *The Wall Street Journal*, http://www.wsj.com/articles/chinas-jiang-jiemin-goes-on-trial-over-corruption-charges-1428895277 (accessed 29 November 2015).

Crawford, D. (2000) "Chinese capitalism: cultures, the Southeast Asian region and economic globalization", *Third World Quarterly*, 21(1): 69–86.

Dickson, B.J. (2008) *Wealth into power: the Communist Party's embrace of China's private sector*. New York: Cambridge University Press.

Gan, N. (2015) "Chinese prosecutors charge Zhou Yongkang's close allies", *South China Morning Post*, http://www.scmp.com/news/china/article/1742291/chinese-prosecutors-charge-zhou-yongkangs-close-allies (accessed 29 November 2015).

Gong, T. (1997) "Forms and characteristics of China's corruption in the 1990s: change with continuity", *Communist and Post-Communist Studies*, 30(3): 277–288.

Gong, T. (2002) "Dangerous collusion: corruption as a collective venture in contemporary China", *Communist and Post-Communist Studies*, 35(1): 85–103.

Gong, T. and S. Wang (2013) "Indicators and implications of zero tolerance of corruption: the case of Hong Kong", *Social Indicators Research*, 112(3): 569–586.

Gong, T. and A.M. Wu (2012) "A research report on China's corruption cases during 2000–2009: empirical analysis of some 2800 corruption cases", *Social Science Studies*, 4: 204–220.

Guo, Y. (2008) "Corruption in transitional China: an empirical analysis", *The China Quarterly*, 194: 349–364.

Huang, J. (2000) *Factionalism in Chinese Communist politics*. Cambridge: Cambridge University Press.

Huang, K.L. (2014) "Energy executives 'held over oil deals in Canada'", *South China Morning Post*, http://www.scmp.com/news/china/article/1555914/energy-executives-held-over-oil-deals-canada (accessed 29 November 2015).

Johnston, M. and Y. Hao (1995) "China's surge of corruption", *Journal of Democracy*, 6(4): 80–94.

Ko, K. and C. Weng (2011) "Critical review of conceptual definitions of Chinese corruption: a formal-legal perspective", *Journal of Contemporary China*, 20(70): 359–378.

Ko, K. and C. Weng (2012) "Structural changes in Chinese corruption", *The China Quarterly*, 211: 718–740.

Kwong, J. (1997) *The political economy of corruption in China*. Armonk, NY: M.E. Sharpe, Inc.

Lam, T.-C. (2010) "Central-provincial relations amid greater centralization in China", *China Information*, 24(3): 339–363.

Li, H., L. Meng, Q. Wang and L-A. Zhou (2008) "Political connections, financing and firm performance: evidence from Chinese private firms", *Journal of Development Economics*, 87(2): 283–299.

Lieberthal, K. (2004) *Governing China: from revolution through reform*, 2nd ed., New York: W.W. Norton.

Lieberthal, K. and M. Oksenberg (1988) *Policy making in China: leaders, structures, and processes*. Princeton, NJ: Princeton University Press.

Lim, B.K. and B. Blanchard (2014a) "China says investigating powerful former security chief for graft", *Reuters*, http://www.reuters.com/article/2014/07/29/us-china-corruption-idUSKBN0FY0VY20140729 (accessed 29 November 2015).

Lim, B.K. and B. Blanchard (2014b) "Exclusive: China seizes $14.5 billion assets from family, associates of ex-security chief: sources", *Reuters*. [Online] 30th March. http://www.reuters.com/article/2014/03/30/us-china-corruption-zhou-idUSBREA2T02S20140330 (accessed 29 November 2015).

Lim, B.K., D. Lague and C. Zhu (2014) "Special report: the power struggle behind China's corruption crackdown", *Reuters*, http://www.reuters.com/article/2014/05/23/us-china-corruption-special-report-idUSBREA4M00120140523 (accessed 29 November 2015).

Lu, X. (2000) *Cadres and corruption: the organizational involution of the Chinese Communist Party*. Stanford, CA: Stanford University Press.

Manion, M. (2004) *Corruption by design: building clean government in Mainland China and Hong Kong*. Cambridge, MA: Harvard University Press.

McMillan, J. and B. Naughton (1992) "How to reform a planned economy: lessons from China", *Oxford Review of Economic Policy*, 8: 130–143.

Mertha, A.C. (2005) "China's 'soft' centralization: shifting tiao/kuai authority relations", *The China Quarterly*, 184: 791–810.

Miller, A.L. (2015) "The trouble with factions", *China Leadership Monitor*, 44. http://www.hoover.org/sites/default/files/research/docs/clm46am.pdf (accessed 29 November 2015).

Nathan, A.J. (1973) "A factionalism model for CCP politics", *The China Quarterly*, 53: 34–66.

Nathan, A.J. and K. S. Tsai (1995) "Factionalism: a new institutionalist restatement", *The China Journal*, 34: 157–192.

Nie, H., M. Jiang and X. Wang (2013) "The impact of political cycle: evidence from coalmine accidents in China", *Journal of Comparative Economics*, 41(4): 995–1011.

Pei, M. (2006) "The dark side of China's rise", *Foreign Policy*, 153: 32–40.

Power, M., G. Mohan and M. Tan-Mullins (2012) *China's resource diplomacy in Africa: powering development?* New York: Palgrave Macmillan.

Pye, L.W. (1995) "Factions and the politics of guanxi: paradoxes in Chinese administrative and political behaviour", *The China Journal*, 34: 35–53.

Rose-Ackerman, S. (1999) *Corruption and government: causes, consequences, and reform*, Cambridge: Cambridge University Press.

Shieh, S. (2005) "The rise of collective corruption in China: the Xiamen smuggling case", *Journal of Contemporary China*, 14(42): 67–91.

Shih, V.C. (2004) "Factions matter: personal networks and the distribution of bank loans in China", *Journal of Contemporary China*, 13(38): 3–19.

Shih, V.C., C. Adolph and M. Liu (2012) "Getting ahead in the Communist Party: explaining the advancement of Central Committee members in China", *The American Political Science Review*, 106(01): 166–187.

South China Morning Post (2015) "China executes mining tycoon Liu Han, who had links to ex-security tsar Zhou Yongkang", http://www.scmp.com/news/china/article/1708082/chinese-mining-tycoon-liu-han-linked-zhou-yongkang-executed?page=all (accessed 29 November 2015).

Sun, X., J. Zhu and Y. Wu (2014) "Organizational clientelism: an analysis of private entrepreneurs in Chinese local legislatures", *Journal of East Asian Studies*, 14(1): 1–29.

Sun, Y. (2004) *Corruption and market in contemporary China*. Ithaca, NY: Cornell University Press.

Wang, P. (2013) "The rise of the red mafia in China: a case study of organised crime and corruption in Chongqing", *Trends in Organized Crime*, 16: 49–73.

Want China Times (2013) "More details of China's oil corruption scandal seep to the surface", http://www.wantchinatimes.com/news-subclass-cnt.aspx?id=20131003000064&cid=1101 (accessed 29 November 2015).

Wedeman, A. (2004) "The intensification of corruption in China", *The China Quarterly*, 180: 895–921.

Xie, H and H. Wang (2014) "Zhou Yongkang's early years", *Caixin Online*, http://english.caixin.com/2014-08-21/100719625.html (accessed 29 November 2015).

Xie, H. (2014) "Zhou family was influential in Jiangsu City before corruption inquiry", *Caixin Online*, http://english.caixin.com/2014-03-04/100646588.html (accessed 29 November 2015).

Xinhua Net (2013) "A mysterious rich businessman Wu Bin involved in the Petro China case, employees stated that he was like a puppet", http://news.xinhuanet.com/fortune/2013-09/07/c_125339599.htm (accessed 29 November 2015). In Chinese.

Zhai, K. and J. Chiu (2013) "Wu Bing, tycoon with Hong Kong ties, believed to be in detention", *South China Morning Post*, http://www.scmp.com/news/china/article/1306528/wu-bing-tycoon-hong-kong-ties-believed-be-detention (accessed 29 November 2015).

Zheng, Y. (2006) "Explaining the sources of de facto federalism in reform China: intergovernmental decentralization, globalization, and central local relations", *Japanese Journal of Political Science*, 7(2): 101–126.

Zhu, J. (2008) "Why are offices for sale in China? A case study of the office-selling chain in Heilongjiang Province", *Asian Survey*, 48(4): 558–579.

Zhu, J. (2012) "The shadow of the skyscrapers: real estate corruption in China", *Journal of Contemporary China*, 21(74): 243–260.

4

TWO STEPS FORWARD, ONE STEP BACKWARDS

Indonesia's winding (anti-)corruption journey

Sofie Arjon Schütte[1]

Corruption in Indonesia

Hardly anyone in Indonesia today would deny that corruption is widespread and that trying to bring it under control has been an uphill journey. Indonesia has long lingered in the lower percentiles of the "control of corruption" indicator of the World Governance Index (1996–2013). Transparency International's Corruption Perceptions Index, which first covered Indonesia in 1998, scored it best towards the end of President Yudhoyono's first term but even then the country was rated in the lowest third of the countries covered worldwide. Yet, while corruption remains pervasive, big steps have been made to prevent and punish it both by government and civil society since the end of the authoritarian Soeharto regime in 1998. This chapter traces the spread and institutionalisation of corruption in post-colonial Indonesia and the efforts undertaken by the state and civil society to bring corruption under control. As in other countries where corruption has become part of, if not a sustaining element in, the political system, anti-corruption reforms have been regularly undermined by vested interests, namely those who would lose out in a more transparent and accountable environment and who fear prosecution. This chapter describes important steps forward and backwards in Indonesia's winding (anti-) corruption journey.

As in other Asian countries, the abuse of power for personal benefit in Indonesia is shaped by patrimonialism and traditional principles of hierarchy, respect, and taking care of one's extended family. According to Palmier (1985), the cause of the long-lasting resilience of traditional structures in the modern Indonesian state is the way in which Dutch colonial rule used these same structures for the exercise of power in the Dutch East Indies. The colonial administration was layered on top of local patrimonial power structures. The princes became civil servants with fixed salaries, but kept their traditional and political rank and the legal status and the legitimacy of traditional rule was preserved until the end of the colonial era (Trocki 1999).

A dual structure persisted even after independence in 1945. A formal, modern bureaucracy grew quickly to meet the challenges and the increasing administrative needs of the young nation. Evers (1987) estimates the growth of the bureaucracy from around 100,000 civil servants before independence to 420,000 in 1950. In the 1970s, the number of civil servants in Indonesia grew fourfold from 515,000 to 2,047,000, leading Evers (1987) to speak of "runaway bureaucratization". The rapid growth of the civil service after independence was founded not only on the need for more civil servants but also on the need "[...] to reward loyal followers of revolutionary movements and to redistribute income through civil-service salaries, even where this meant only the 'sharing of poverty'" (Evers 1987: 678). At the same time, old patrimonial relationships continued to exist. The first appointments in the administration were influenced by patronage and shaped a long-lasting marriage between politics and corruption: "The spoils system had been established. By 1951, corruption was well entrenched in the government service" (Palmier 1985: 198). The parties in the fledgling democracy lacked resources independent of government: "Neither the indigenous business classes nor the land interests were substantial enough. In consequence, only by being in government could the parties lay their hands on the resources necessary for effective political activity" (Palmier 1985: 201). The military, which had earlier been a counterweight to corrupt parties, through the nationalisation and takeover of previously Dutch businesses and an increasing role in the state administration, became part of an elaborate patronage system (Palmier 1985). Inflation rendered public salaries insufficient for subsistence and corruption became a strategy for survival.

Following Soeharto's takeover in 1965–1966, the economy eventually recovered and inflation was brought under control. The excuse that corruption was a temporary survival strategy in a young nation was no longer valid but vested interests remained. Indonesia under Soeharto (1966–1998) was a complex case of institutions and their enforcement serving the benefit of a few: some institutions were rendered deliberately ineffective or dysfunctional, and law enforcement overlapped with criminal structures and operations (Lindsey 2001; McLeod 2011) and the judiciary became subservient to government interests (Pompe 2005).

In several seminal pieces, Ross McLeod (2000, 2005 and 2011) has likened the Soeharto regime to the business model of a "franchise system" and has emphasised the deliberate and extortive, or rent-harvesting, character of this system. The franchise functioned by using the "coercive power of government privately to tax the general public and redistribute the revenue to a small elite" (McLeod 2011: 49–50). The legislature, political parties, judiciary, military and law enforcement, the general bureaucracy and state-owned enterprises were all part of a large franchise system in which franchisees could invest and receive a share of

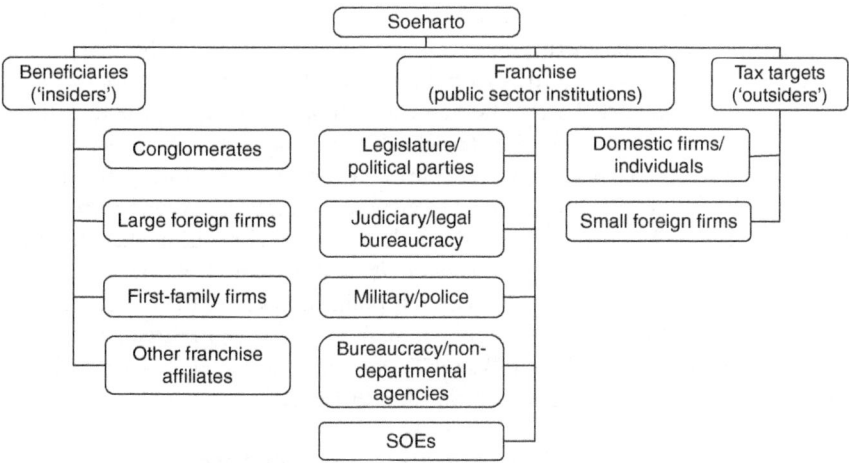

Figure 4.1 The Soeharto franchise system

Source: McLeod, R. H. (2008) "Inadequate budgets and salaries as instruments for institutionalizing public sector corruption in Indonesia", *South East Asia Research*, 16(2): 201. Reproduced with permission of IP Publishing Ltd.

the revenues extracted from the general public and firms outside the system. McLeod (2011) claims that the bureaucracy was compelled to comply with these practices because of low salaries, compared to the private sector, especially at higher management levels. Corruption had been institutionalised despite having been made a criminal offence in law (see Figure 4.1).

Soeharto's franchise system incorporated all the forms of institutional corruption discussed in Chapter 2: patrimonialism, crony capitalism, bureaucratic capture and electoral manipulation and fraud. Electoral manipulation came in the form of rule-making with the starkest example being Soeharto's political vehicle, Golkar. Golkar, standing for *golongan karya* (functional groups) and technically not a party, was by 1970 the only political vehicle for government employees who were not allowed to join political parties or to vote for them. By 1973, the remaining political parties were forced to merge into two parties.

Focusing on the question of how a state can recover from such endemic, institutionalised corruption, the rest of this chapter is devoted to a discussion of the anti-corruption efforts since the regime change in 1998 and Indonesia's return to democracy.

Anti-corruption reforms in Indonesia

The Asian Financial Crisis exposed institutional weaknesses and opened up space in Indonesia for public protests that had hitherto been repressed. The mismanagement of the financial crisis in 1997 triggered an economic and political crisis that eventually forced Soeharto to resign in May 1998 after 32 years of rule (Forrester and May 1998; Jomo 1998; McLeod and Garnaut 1998; Aspinall 2005). There ensued a period of remarkable openness and reform that became known in Indonesia as the *Era Reformasi* (Reform Era). Rampant corruption was now widely recognized to be a problem that required strong action. Many members of the elite remained in powerful positions but felt under pressure from students, other domestic activists and international creditors to commit to institutional changes. An array of reforms was therefore adopted by organizations "that were largely dominated by self-interested and often corrupt forces that in many cases had been closely tied to the Soeharto regime" (Crouch 2010: 7). Political parties mushroomed and 48 parties qualified for the first free elections in 1999. The number of seats automatically allocated to the Armed Forces was reduced to 38 in 1999 and then to zero in 2009 and government took over most of the military businesses (Mietzner 2014). The most important pieces of anti-corruption legislation were enacted in the first five years of *Reformasi* (1998 to 2002). They culminated in Law 30 of 2002 on the Corruption Eradication Commission (henceforth, KPK Law). The political monopoly on which the franchise system relied broke down with the demise of its franchisor but most of the personnel remained and patronage networks in the bureaucracy were carried over into the reform era, albeit in a less coordinated fashion (McLeod 2011). From an analysis of corporate ownership in 1996 and 2008, Carney and Hamilton-Hart (2015) draw the tentative conclusion that the proportion of large listed firms with political links was similar in 1996 and 2008, but that new players emerged and many existing players realigned their political ties after the crisis. Links between big business and politics "have become more plural, fluid, and decentralised", with some business owners such as Aburizal Bakrie (Golkar chairman) and Jusuf Kalla (vice-president) taking up key roles in politics (Carney and Hamilton-Hart 2015: 142).

Anti-KKN: public pressure for change

By the 1990s, authoritarian politics had become less acceptable to a growing middle class. Favouritism towards Soeharto's family and cronies and the inability of the government to restore market confidence and stabilise prices during the Asian Financial Crisis was widely resented and gave rise to public dissent and riots in several cities (Crouch 2010). The acronym KKN (*korupsi, kolusi, nepotisme*; corruption, collusion and nepotism) became a symbol for popular resentment towards the regime (Hamilton-Hart 2001; Eklöf 2002; Crouch 2010). As such, it was part of the much broader positive ideology of *demokrasi* (democracy) and *reformasi* (reformation). The latter was initially based on the common goal of bringing down the Soeharto regime, but would later be used for a whole array of institutional changes, such as democratic elections and amendments to the constitution. With the downfall of Soeharto and the apparent lack of capacity and/or willingness of the police, public prosecutors and courts to address corruption both by the Soeharto family and its cronies and more widely, calls for an independent anti-corruption agency grew stronger.

Another expression of the widespread demand for anti-corruption measures was the "mushrooming" of non-governmental organizations (NGOs) with a declared anti-corruption agenda (Lindsey 2002). Probably the first of these anti-corruption NGOs, and certainly by 2016 the most prominent, is Indonesia Corruption Watch (ICW), founded in June 1998. It conducts its own informal investigations into corruption cases based on reports from public. The ICW was quickly followed by a number of other organizations such as the Indonesian branch of Transparency International in 2000 and the Indonesian Society for Transparency in 1999 (Masyarakat Transparansi Indonesia, MTI). These NGOs were closely affiliated with some of the later commissioners of the anti-corruption commission such as Erry Riyana Hardjapamekas (Transparency International and MTI), Amien Sunaryadi and Chandra Hamzah (both MTI) and Bambang Widjojanto (ICW). Together with more general legal advocacy organizations, such as the Institute for Research and Advocacy for Judicial Independence (Lembaga Kajian dan Advokasi untuk Independensi Peradilan) and the Indonesian Centre for Law and Policy Studies (Pusat Studi Hukum dan Kebijakan Indonesia) established in 1999 and 1998, respectively, they have followed a cooperative approach to try to persuade government and the legislature of the need for reform. These NGOs supported the idea of a new body to combat corruption and participated in the drafting process, some as members of the official drafting team, others as participants and speakers at seminars discussing the future anti-corruption commission KPK (Komisi Pemberantasan Tindak Pidana Korupsi). Within a year of the end of Soeharto's regime, the idea of an anti-corruption agency with enforcement powers was firmly on the national political agenda.

A new legislative framework to fight corruption

During *Reformasi,* the relationship between the institutions comprising the state, the executive, legislature and judiciary, was re-negotiated and defined by several amendments to the 1945 Constitution (Lindsey 2008). After 1998, the legislature, namely the People's Consultative Assembly (Majelis Permusyawaratan Rakyat, MPR) and the House of Representatives (Dewan Perwakilan Rakyat) which had been marginalised under the Soekarno and Soeharto governments, became the main promulgator of formal institutional change in the form of constitutional amendments and new legislation (Indrayana 2008). The concepts of separation of powers (*trias politika* in Indonesian) which divides the responsibilities of the executive, legislature and judiciary, and of checks and balances, are reflected in the main changes achieved during *Reformasi*: the separation of the judiciary from the Ministry of Justice (Butt 2008) and the establishment of a Constitutional Court (Stockmann 2007); the strengthening of the House of Representatives and establishment of a Regional Representative Assembly (Dewan Perwakilan Daerah; Indrayana 2008); the direct election of the president but with reduced presidential powers (Indrayana 2008; Lindsey 2008); and the creation of additional oversight bodies such as a Financial Intelligence Unit, Judicial, Prosecutorial and Police Commissions, an Ombudsman, and the KPK.

Anti-corruption efforts in the first five years after the end of the Soeharto regime were in-itiated by the legislature. In other words, it was the "old guard", those legislators still elected in 1997 under the Soeharto regime, who passed the cornerstones of the anti-corruption legislation before the first free general elections in June 1999. MacIntyre (2003) attributes the speed of institutional changes introduced by the old elite to the enormous public pressure it faced. It was an attempt to avoid recrimination for the past, to regain credibility in the eyes of the public, and to salvage their political futures. The urgency of reform was heightened by the conditionality imposed by Indonesia's creditors, especially the International Monetary Fund. In return for a US$43 billion bailout, the International Monetary Fund "seemed to hold almost complete control of Indonesia's economic and legal reform policy" (Lindsey and Santosa 2008: 12). The motive was to rebuild political legitimacy but there was also a "shift in elite culture, based on a genuine acceptance of urgent need for institutional and regulatory reform" (Lindsey and Santosa 2008: 12–13).

Nevertheless, it is still remarkable that the elite endorsed the new anti-corruption legis-lation, considering that corruption was so widespread that this legislation could be expected to affect members of the legislature, as indeed it did. Two senior government officials com-mented to the author on the paradox: "It was the reform era. Nobody wanted to be accused of not being reformist"; and "They were afraid of being labelled "New Order". In the case of the KPK Law, discontent with the performance of the existing law enforcement agencies was a further motive which is discussed later in more detail.

From 1999 onwards, legislatures were much more wary of the repercussions of the new laws. In the following analysis of the legislation, a distinction is made between the legislative efforts of the "old guard" and the efforts (or lack thereof) of the "new guard", the democrat-ically elected legislators.

1998–1999: the "old guard"

In November 1998, during an extraordinary session, the People's Consultative Assembly issued Decree XI/MPR/1998 on a Corruption-free State Administration. The Decree spec-ifies that state officials representing the executive, legislature and judiciary are accountable to the Indonesian people and to the state. To prevent corrupt practices, all state officials must declare their assets (wealth) before assuming an office and when leaving it. They may be subject to audits by an agency (then yet to be established) staffed by members of the public as well as the civil service. Efforts to combat corruption were to be implemented consist-ently and applied to all state officials, including Soeharto and his associates but taking into account the presumption of innocence and human rights. This was not the first time that high-ranking public officials had been asked to disclose their assets in Indonesia. In the 1970s, there was an unsuccessful attempt to introduce the reporting of officials' wealth when a reason for its failure had been the lack of an authority to audit the reports.

Consequent to the People's Consultative Assembly's Decree, Law 28 of 1999 on a Corruption-free State Administration, wealth-reporting by public officials and representatives was made mandatory. Although penalties for non-compliance are merely administrative, the institutional pressure on individuals to report has increased considerably since the enactment of the law. It also provided for the establishment of a special commission, the Public Officials Wealth Audit Commission (Komisi Pemeriksa Kekayaan Penyelenggara Negara), to audit these reports. The Commission was later integrated into the KPK's prevention department.

Law 31 of 1999 on Criminal Acts of Corruption (henceforth, the Anti-corruption Law) also made reference to the MPR decree in its introduction. It replaced the New Order's

Anti-corruption Law 3 of 1971 and thus all criminal law provisions on corruption. Corporations were thereby made accountable for corruption. Minimum and maximum penalties were established. The death penalty was possible for corruption offences in state emergency situations. Article 27 allowed for the establishment of a Joint Investigation Team (Tim Gabungan Pemeriksa Tindak Pidana Korupsi) comprising police officers and public prosecutors under the Attorney General for particularly difficult corruption cases. Article 43 (2) stipulated that within two years an Anti-corruption Commission was to be established and given the tasks of coordinating and supervising corruption cases, including conducting its own pre-investigations, investigations and indictments. The Commission was to consist of members from the government (civil servants) and outside the government (Art. 43 (3)). Its organizational design, tasks and powers and operating procedures were to be regulated by law.

The provisions of Article 43 were not in the original bill which the government had submitted to the legislature. It was brought into the legislative deliberation process by the United Development Party (Partai Persatuan Pembangunan, PPP).[2]

The initiative for Article 43 of the Anti-corruption Law came from Zain Badjeber, the head of the PPP faction in the commission of the House of Representatives responsible for law enforcement and justice and head of the Legislation Council (Badan Legislasi, Baleg)[3] from 1999 to 2004 (Hamzah 2005). A former judge and advisor to the Attorney General, he believed that, if the police and the Attorney General's Office (AGO) were to bring an end to corrupt and collusive practices, a new agency was required, at least temporarily, to improve the system within the existing law enforcement agencies (Schütte 2012). In fact, the PPP proposed a complete blueprint for a commission with exclusive jurisdiction for corruption cases from investigation to prosecution[4] and a special court for corruption cases with *ad hoc* judges. These were contained in an additional chapter with 18 articles which were included in the bill's List of Issues (Hosen 2003). Ultimately, the initiative resulted in Article 43, compromising the exclusive jurisdiction proposed by the PPP in favour of a jurisdiction shared with the other law enforcement agencies. The design of the new agency was left to a separate bill which eventually became Law 30 of 2002 on the Komisi Pemeriksa Kekayaan Penyelengara Neagara, KPKPN, and later the anti-corruption commission KPK. The Anti-corruption Law was enacted in August 1999 and was the last law on corruption control produced by the "old guard". In 1999, Golkar was defeated in the first free elections in 44 years and 21 parties, 18 of which were new, won seats in the legislature.

The guidelines for a new institutional framework had been set: public officials had to report their wealth to a new commission (Komisi Pemeriksa Kekayaan Penyelengara Neagara, KPKPN, and later the anti-corruption commission KPK). The Criminal Code had been updated by the Anti-corruption Law. The Attorney General was to set up a Joint Investigation Team together with the police for difficult corruption cases and an anti-corruption commission was to be established by statutory deadline in August 2001.

1999 onwards: a "new guard"?

From 1999, the pace of reform slowed under the now democratically elected legislature and government. The 1999 elections resulted in a coalition government of the former opposition elite with minority leader Abdurrahman Wahid elected president by the MPR. Two years later, in July 2001, he was impeached and dismissed after increasing controversy about his leadership style, corruption scandals, and a failed attempt to dissolve the legislature (Lindsey and Santosa 2008). Wahid was replaced by his Vice-President and leader of the strongest party in the House of Representatives, the Indonesian Democratic Party, Struggle (Partai

Demokrasi Indonesia-Perjuangan, PDI-P). Megawati Sukarnoputri served as President until October 2004. Only 32 of a total of 120 laws planned in the national legislation programme were enacted during these five years. This poor legislative performance was partly a consequence of the instability in government but it also reflected the fact that a less reformist new legislature had just won the democratic vote and thus had less need to defend or enhance its legitimacy.

One of the 32 bills passed into law was Law 20 of 2001 amending the Anti-corruption Law. This amendment shifts the burden of proof slightly in favour of the defendant, changes some sanctions and widens the scope of admissible evidence to include electronic documents and data interchange, "namely any recorded data that can be seen, read, and/ or heard and issued with or without the help of equipment, either those printed on paper and physical material other than paper, or those recorded electronically in the form of writing, voice, picture, map, draft, photograph, letters, signs, figures or perforations that have meaning" (Art. 26 A (b), Law 20 of 2001 amending the Anti-corruption Law). This wider scope of admissible evidence was crucial for corruption investigations because commission of a crime is often supported by electronic devices, such as mobile phones to negotiate deals and computers to transfer money or information. If such evidence was not admissible, prosecutors would have to rely mostly on testimonies that are difficult to come by in corruption cases, as witnesses are often accomplices and fear prosecution themselves.

While the legislative process slowed down, the government nevertheless began to implement the legislation enacted by the "old guard": it established a Joint Investigation Team (provided for in the Anti-corruption Law) and the Wealth Audit Commission (provided for by the Law on a Corruption-free State Administration). An Ombudsman Commission was also set up by decree by President Wahid. These new entities have had little impact for various reasons (see Chalid 2001; Assegaf 2002; Sherlock 2002; Hosen 2003; Crouch 2007) and there appears to have been little concern about overlapping jurisdictions and poor integration. Nonetheless, they were part of an important learning path and fed more or less directly into the Law on the KPK enacted in December 2002 (Schütte 2012).

The drafting and deliberation of the KPK Law took more than three years, but this delay mitigated some resistance to it, particularly from the military faction, because it did not constitute an immediate threat to Soeharto and corruption committed under the New Order regime (Schütte 2012). There was still considerable resistance from those who felt their current and future interests were threatened, such as the AGO, which, supported by Golkar, opposed the transfer of its jurisdiction over corruption cases to a new entity. In the end, the KPK was provided with a potent combination of both investigative and prosecutorial powers but it had to share jurisdiction over corruption cases with the existing law enforcement agencies.

The KPK

Law 30 of 2002 equipped the KPK with a broad mandate in both prevention and repression of corruption that go beyond the authorities of other anti-corruption agencies in the region. The KPK's tasks are to coordinate and supervise other agencies that (are supposed to) control corruption. The KPK is also tasked to conduct its own pre-investigations, investigations and prosecutions in cases that involve law enforcement personnel or public officials, give rise to particular public concern, and/or involve losses to the state budget of at least one billion rupiah (approximately US$100,000). In its supervision role, the KPK is authorised to take over cases from the police and AGO if there are irregularities. It has done so only in a handful of cases to date.

Dilemmas of reform

As soon as the KPK was established, it faced public expectations to "catch and fry big fish", as the prosecution of elite perpetrators is colloquially referred to. The quantity of cases brought to court, the number of guilty verdicts, and the social status of the defendants, whether they are small or big fish, have been the main criteria applied by the media and NGOs to assess the KPK's performance.

By the end of 2015 (since inception), the KPK had conducted a total of 752 pre-investigations, 468 investigations, 389 prosecutions and obtained 320 verdicts. In 2014, it conducted 87 pre-investigations, 57 investigations, 62 prosecutions and obtained 37 final and binding verdicts (KPK 2016). These numbers are dwarfed by those of the AGO in the same period of time. By comparison, in 2014, the public prosecution service had conducted 1815 pre-investigations, 1537 investigations and 2225 prosecutions (Kejaksaan Republik Indonesia 2015; no data on verdicts are available in this annual report). This comparison is not particularly meaningful, however, because the public prosecution service has 22,000 staff in offices all over Indonesia, whereas the KPK in 2014 had a total staff, including staff working on prevention, of about 1000. In any case, it is certainly not the number of cases that has brought the KPK fame beyond the borders of Indonesia. Rather it is the "quality" of the cases: that is, the profile of the defendants and the near 100 per cent conviction rate. The KPK has drawn national and international attention for the high profile of some of its defendants, most prominently, members of the House of Representatives and the heads and members of several national agencies as well as provincial governors. The KPK has indicted individuals in a wide range of cases, in terms of both regional distribution and the office of the defendants, party affiliation, both the givers and the takers of bribes, and government officials from all branches of the state. Table 4.1 categorises the defendants by their office and shows the high status of those convicted. The majority were mayors, heads and deputy heads of districts and senior civil servants although it is the prosecution of sitting ministers and members of the legislature from parties of all colours that has brought the KPK national and international recognition.

This would have been impossible if the KPK had succumbed to corrupt practices itself. To protect its staff from the flawed incentive system of the Indonesian civil service, the KPK management sought autonomy over its human resource management. Autonomy in internal budget allocation, recruitment practices, performance-based promotion, remuneration, and attendance control has fostered KPK staff's integrity and has made it a sought-after employer and, to a certain degree, role model for civil service reform (Kuris 2012; Schütte 2015a).

As mentioned earlier, the KPK Law established a special chamber in the district court of central Jakarta with a jurisdiction over all corruption cases investigated by the KPK. The special setup of this court and its procedures have been considered an important contributing factor to the KPK's 100 per cent conviction record in its first six years of operation (Schütte and Butt 2013). This has led to a backlash and a petition for institutional review by those convicted by the Anti-corruption Court (Butt and Schütte 2014).

In December 2006, the Constitutional Court decided that a new legislative basis was required for the Anti-corruption Court. The Constitutional Court found that the existence of two different court systems for the same kind of crime conflicted with constitutional guarantees of equality before the law. Law 46 of 2009 on the Special Court for

Table 4.1 Public and private offices held by defendants in KPK cases

Office of defendants	04	05	06	07	08	09	10	11	12	13	14	Total
Member of legislature (regional and national)				2	7	8	27	5	16	8	4	**77**
Head of agency/minister		1	1		1	1	2		1	4	9	**20**
Ambassador				2	1		1					**4**
Commissioner		3	2	1	1							**7**
Governor	1		2		2	2	1			2	2	**12**
Mayor/district head and deputies		4	5	5	12	11	31	5	17	14	15	**119**
Civil Servant Echelon I–III	2	9	15	10	22	14	12	15	8	7	2	**126**
Judge							1	2	2	4	2	**11**
Corporate sector (chief executive officer)	1	4	5	3	12	11	8	10	16	24	15	**109**
Others		6	1	2	4	4	9	3	3	7	8	**47**
Total	**4**	**27**	**31**	**25**	**62**	**51**	**92**	**40**	**63**	**70**	**57**	**522**

Source: Compiled by author based on annual reporting by KPK from 2004 to 2014.

Corruption Crimes (henceforth, Anti-corruption Court Law) which followed the Constitutional Court's decision stipulates that all cases, both from the KPK and the AGO, are to be heard by specialist anti-corruption chambers in the districts where the case is being investigated. Exceptions can be made and cases can be heard in Jakarta, for example, for security reasons.

By late 2011, the Supreme Court had established special anti-corruption courts in all 34 provincial capitals. With the new anti-corruption courts came the first acquittals. At first, these acquittals were cases submitted by the regional public prosecutors' offices but on 11 October 2011 the KPK lost its first case at the district level anti-corruption court in Bandung (Butt 2011). The KPK appealed and the Supreme Court overturned the Bandung's court ruling with its conviction rate remaining nearly intact.[5]

Even if it is impossible to measure and isolate the impact the KPK has had on corruption in Indonesia, one telling indication is the resistance it has faced, on the one hand, and, on the other, the public support it has drawn to its cause.

Vested interests vs. public support

Resistance to the KPK has mostly taken a legal form, which allows for public scrutiny and pressure and has led to a general consolidation of anti-corruption institutions. The KPK has experienced resistance ever since its inception. The first petition for constitutional review of the Law that established the KPK was launched even before it started operations. Further constitutional reviews followed although most of them were dismissed. In 2009, the already tense relationship between the KPK and the police and the AGO culminated in criminal charges against three of the KPK's five commissioners. Some claim that these charges were a form of retaliation by Susno Duadji, Chief Police Investigator, when he found out that a phone call he made had been intercepted by the KPK when it was investigating a suspect related to the Bank Century case.[6] In their own defence, KPK commissioners later released other intercepts that revealed a conspiracy against them between the Chief Police Investigator, the Deputy Attorney General for Special Crimes and the brother of a corruption suspect under investigation by the KPK.

There may be some truth in the "turf war" theory: that is, that the "invasion" of a powerful new agency, the KPK, into the territory of existing agencies deprived corrupt law enforcers of a lucrative source of income, provoking a backlash (Butt 2010). The image of a war between a new (small) agency against two long-established and much bigger agencies, was fuelled by comments of the Chief Police Investigator Susno Duadji, who likened the KPK to a gecko (*cicak*) fighting a crocodile (*buaya*), the police (*Tempo* 2009). It turned out to be a public relations blunder for the police because, unlike the crocodile, most Indonesians are fond of the gecko. NGOs promptly named their campaign for the KPK after the cicak: "Cinta(i) Indonesia, Cinta(i) KPK" (Love Indonesia, love the KPK) or "Cinta(i) Indonesia, Cinta(i) Anti-Korupsi" (Love Indonesia, love anti-corruption). A day after the detention of Commissioners Bibit Samad Rianto and Chandra Hamzah on 29 October 2009, 40 mass media editors petitioned the AGO and Head of Police to release the two commissioners. Seventeen Facebook groups were opened, the most prominent being aptly called "Movement of One Million Facebookers in Support of Chandra and Bibit". Indeed, more than a million Facebookers joined solidarity declarations within the next few weeks. A similar "One billion in support of the Police" garnered the support of only 29,000 Facebookers (Haryadi 2009). Demonstrations in support of the KPK took place in several cities, engaging organizations well beyond the regular network of anti-corruption watchdogs.

The Constitutional Court also supported the KPK by allowing recordings of a conspiracy against the commissioners to be publicly aired. It decided that KPK commissioners could not be permanently discharged when becoming criminal suspects but must first be found guilty by a court. This closed the door for potential further "criminalisation" (*kriminalisasi*)[7] of commissioners which would have hindered KPK operations. The timing of the Constitutional Court's hearing of Rianto's and Hamzah's petition, just a few days after their arrest, and the Court's decision to listen publicly to four and a half hours of interception recordings that incriminated members of the Police and AGO, strongly indicate the Court's support for the KPK. This hearing tipped the scales in the case brought against the two commissioners, who were reinstalled within a month by President Yudhoyono.

Formal support from the Constitutional Court for the KPK gained considerable political leverage from the public support that organized and manifested itself through informal networks, such as the social media. Rather than suppressing public expression, as would have been the case under Soeharto, Yudhoyono consulted public opinion polls.

The public provided unprecedented support for the KPK again in 2012. In July and August 2012, street hawkers and students collected money for an unlikely cause: a new office building for a state institution, the KPK. Initially spread over two old buildings near the Presidential Palace, the KPK moved into its current office building in Kuningan, a renovated bank building, in 2007. The office in Kuningan was meant to host about 350 staff but by 2012 the KPK had more than 700 staff who could no longer fit into the building. The administration was moved to rental premises, a 15-minute drive away during normal traffic conditions. By 2008, the KPK had already applied to construct its own building on vacant land next to its current premises at a cost of Rp70 billion for up to 1300 staff. In 2012, the new building was part of a total of a proposed Rp225 billion annual budget for the KPK. The proposal was approved by the Department of Finance but was stalled by the legislature. The legislature believed that the KPK should rent existing, vacant government office space. Anti-corruption activists saw this as another attempt by legislators to weaken the KPK by withholding resources and support. Although renting vacant government office space has some plausibility, the building became a symbol of the support or, lack thereof, for the KPK (Schütte 2013).

The collection of money for the new building, led by Indonesia Corruption Watch, began in July 2012. Per person donations of up to Rp1 million were accepted. By mid-August, a total of US$35,000 had been gathered (*New York Times* 2012). In-kind contributions, such as bags of cement, bricks, wood and iron bars for future prison cells of the KPK, were also deposited in front of the current KPK office (Schütte 2013). In October 2012, the House of Representatives gave in to public pressure and finally approved the budget for the new building. In December 2015, the new KPK office in Kuningan was officially opened.

Two steps forward, one step backwards

The presidential candidature of Joko Widodo ran on the popular hope that he could do for the country what he had previously done as mayor of Surakarta (in Central Java) and Jakarta: clean up the administration and increase government responsiveness towards citizens (Aspinall and Mietzner 2014; Majeed 2015). He was voted into office through direct elections in mid-2014, with his party, the PDI-P, forming a minority government with three other parties and facing stiff opposition in the House of Representatives. What was at first welcomed by anti-corruption campaigners, including staff of the KPK, has since turned to disappointment. With the real power in PDI-P residing with its chairwoman, former President Megawati Soekarnoputri, Jokowi appeared indecisive, if not powerless, in addressing yet another power struggle between the KPK and the police. When General Budi Gunawan, a former aide of Megawati, was nominated to become head of the police, the KPK somewhat abruptly brought charges against him. A second round of "gecko vs. crocodile" unfolded that has yet to be concluded at the time of writing. Gunawan managed to avoid charges and was eventually appointed deputy head of the police (Majeed 2015). The Police have once more brought charges against three of the five KPK commissioners and their cases are pending. Meanwhile, the regular appointment process of new commissioners has been completed (*Jakarta Post* 2015; for an analysis of the KPK appointment process, see Schütte 2011).

Conclusion

While there are less of the "isms" (patrimonialism and crony capitalism) in Indonesia today, bureaucratic capture and electoral manipulation and fraud in the form of rule-making and breaking are still highly problematic. The case of the KPK is indicative of the state of anti-corruption and governance efforts in Indonesia in two respects. On the one hand, it is itself a result of reforms. The sequential leadership appointment process shared between the executive and legislature,[8] a process that has been replicated for other commissions, is an example of increased awareness and application of checks and balances in Indonesia. On the other hand, its mandate brings the KPK to the forefront of public frustration with corruption by senior state officials. Its indictments of members of the legislature show that democratic processes are still hampered by corruption. Mietzner (2015: 589) refers this to a flawed party financing framework, deliberately designed by the political elite to protect its "traditions of self-financing and rent seeking".

The next hills to climb on the road to less corruption are comprehensive civil service reform and an overhaul of the party financing system.

Notes

1 This chapter draws on parts of the author's PhD dissertation completed at the University of Melbourne in 2012.
2 The United Development Party was established in 1973 when the Soeharto government forced the Islamic parties to merge. After 1973, only two parties were allowed to contest against the

government's Golongan Karya (Golkar) in elections: the PPP and the Indonesian Democratic Party (Partai Demokrasi Indonesia, PDI). A fourth, unelected, faction represented in the legislature was the Armed Forces. The process of deliberating a bill in Indonesia depends on whether the bill is initiated by the government or the House of Representatives. All of the anti-corruption bills were submitted by the government and then deliberated in the legislature including hearings and critical discussions with the government. Part of these critical discussions is a so-called "List of Issues" (Daftar Inventarisasi Masalah) in which the factions formally comment on the individual articles of a bill and which constitutes the basis for negotiations with the government (Sherlock 2003).

3 The House of Representatives' Legislation Council is a permanent body established in 1999. Its membership consists of House of Representatives' members who are appointed at the beginning of each legislative period. The most important function of the Legislation Council is the compilation of the national legislative programme and to determine the order of the bills to be deliberated. It is responsible for the coordination of the legislative programme between the government and the House of Representatives. It is also tasked to facilitate the development of bills originating from within the House of Representatives based on the priority list (Sherlock 2003).

4 There is contradictory evidence on whether this proposed commission was to be independent or under the Attorney General's Office.

5 For a discussion on why a 100 per cent conviction rate is not necessarily a good thing and an insufficient measure of performance on its own, see Butt and Schütte 2014.

6 Bank Century was bailed out by the Indonesian Government during the Global Financial Crisis of 2008–2009. The bailout, approved by a committee headed by then Finance Minister Sri Mulyani and Governor of the Bank Indonesia, Boediono, was much more costly than initially anticipated and amounted to Rp6.76 trillion in July 2009. After the re-election of Yudhoyono, the Bank Century case was used by the political opposition in an attempt to oust Sri Mulyani and Boediono. For comprehensive accounts see Von Luebke (2010) and Patunru and Von Luebke (2010). Susno Duadji claimed to have been intercepted by the KPK, allegedly when talking to a client of Bank Century. The weekly *Tempo* (6 July 2009) reported that Susno had asked for a Rp10 billion payment for his services to expedite the release of PT Lancar Sampoerna Bestari funds from Bank Century after it had made investments without the consent of PT Lancar Sampoerna Bestari.

7 The term *kriminalisasi* has been frequently used in the context of the legal attacks against KPK commissioners by employees of the KPK, NGOs and the media. Literally it translates as "criminalisation" and implies that unfounded criminal allegations are made to damage a person and give him/her a criminal reputation.

8 Candidates are selected sequentially, with one institution (here: the president) suggesting a shortlist from which another institution (here: the House of Representatives) picks the appointees (Schütte 2011, 2015b).

References

Aspinall, E. and M. Mietzner (2014) "Indonesian politics in 2014: democracy's close call", *Bulletin of Indonesian Economic Studies,* 50 (3): 347–369.

Aspinall, E. (2005) *Opposing Soeharto: compromise, resistance, and regime change in Indonesia,* Stanford: Stanford University Press.

Assegaf, I. (2002) "Legends of the fall: an institutional analysis of Indonesia law enforcement agencies combating corruption", in T. Lindsey and H. Dick (eds.), *Corruption in Asia: rethinking the governance paradigm,* Annandale, NSW: Federation Press, 127–146.

Butt, S. (2008) "Surat Sakti: the decline of the authority of judicial decisions in Indonesia", in T. Lindsey (ed.), *Indonesia: law and society* (2nd ed.), Annandale, NSW: Federation Press, 346–362.

Butt, S. (2010) "Asian law in transition: translator's note on the Indonesian corruption court law - the unravelling of Indonesia's anti-corruption framework through law and legal process", *Australian Journal of Asian Law,* 11(2): 302–307.

Butt, S. (2011) "Anti-corruption reform in Indonesia: an obituary?" *Bulletin of Indonesian Economic Studies,* 47(3), 381–394.

Butt, S. and S. A. Schütte (2014) "Assessing judicial performance in Indonesia: the court for corruption crimes", *Crime, Law and Social Change,* 62(5): 603–619.

Carney, R. W. and N. Hamilton-Hart (2015) "What do changes in corporate ownership in Indonesia tell us?" *Bulletin of Indonesian Economic Studies,* 51 (1): 123–145.

Chalid, H. (2001) "A personal experience in combating corruption in Indonesia: the wrongful dissolution of the joint investigating team against corruption", paper presented at the Australia-Indonesia Legal Fellowship Seminar, Asian Law Centre, Faculty of Law, University of Melbourne, 18 October 2001.

Crouch, M. A. (2007) "The Yogyakarta local ombudsman: promoting good governance through local support", *Asian Journal of Comparative Law,* 2(1): 1–30.

Crouch, H. (2010) *Political reform in Indonesia after Soeharto.* Singapore: ISEAS.

Eklöf, S. (2002) "Politics, business, and democratization in Indonesia", in E.T. Gomez (ed.), *Political business in East Asia,* London: Routledge, 216–249.

Evers, H. D. (1987) "The bureaucratization of Southeast Asia", *Comparative Studies in Society and History,* 29(4): 666–685.

Forrester, G. and R. J. May (eds.) (1998) *The fall of Soeharto.* Bathurst: Crawford House Publishing.

Hamilton-Hart, N. (2001) "Anti-corruption strategies in Indonesia", *Bulletin of Indonesian Economic Studies,* 37(1): 65–82.

Hamzah, A. (2005) *Pemberantasan korupsi melalui hukum pidana nasional dan internasional,* Jakarta: RajaGrafindo Persada.

Haryadi, R. (2009) *Chandra-Bibit. Membongkar perseteruan KPK, Polri, dan Kejaksaan,* Jakarta: Hikmah.

Hosen, N. (2003) "The Habibie Government and the law on eradication of corruption in Indonesia", *European Journal of Law Reform,* 5(1/2): 293–321.

Indrayana, D. (2008) *Indonesian constitutional reform 1999–2002: an evaluation of constitution-making in transition,* Jakarta: Kompas.

Jakarta Post (2015) "KPK at risk from 'Trojan horse,' activists warn", 19 December, http://www.thejakartapost.com/search?q=KPK+at+risk+from+%E2%80%98Trojan+horse%2C%E2%80%99+activists+warn (accessed 20 December 2015).

Jomo, K. S. (1998) *Tigers in trouble: financial governance and the crises in East Asia.* London: Zed Books.

KPK (Komisi Pemberantasan Korupsi) (2016) "Rekapitulasi penindakan pidana korupsi", http://acch.kpk.go.id/en_US/home (accessed 20 January 2016).

Kejaksaan Republik Indonesia (2015) *Laporan tahunan 2014.* Jakarta: Kejaksaan Republik Indonesia.

Kuris, G. (2012) *Holding the high ground with public support: Indonesia's Anti-Corruption Commission digs in, 2002–2007,* Princeton: Innovations for Successful Societies, Princeton University.

Lindsey, T. (2001) "The criminal state: premanisme and the new Indonesia", in G. J. Lloyd and S. L. Smith (eds.), *Indonesia today: challenges of history,* Lanham: Rowman and Littlefield, 283–297.

Lindsey, T. (2002) "Anti-corruption and NGOs in Indonesia", in R. Holloway (ed.), *Stealing from the people: 16 studies on corruption in Indonesia,* Vol. 4, Jakarta: Aksara, 29–70.

Lindsey, T. (2008) *Indonesia: law and society* (2nd ed.), Annandale, NSW: The Federation Press.

Lindsey, T., and M.A. Santosa (2008) "The trajectory of law reform in Indonesia: a short overview of legal systems and change in Indonesia", in T. Lindsey (ed.), *Indonesia: law and society,* 2nd ed., Annandale, NSW: The Federation Press, 2–22.

MacIntyre, A. J. (2003) *The power of institutions: political architecture and governance,* Ithaca: Cornell University Press.

Majeed, R. (2015) "The gecko's bite", *Foreign Policy,* 24 July, http://foreignpolicy.com/?s=The+gecko%E2%80%99s+bite (accessed 23 December 2015).

McLeod, R. H. (2000) "Soeharto's Indonesia: a better class of corruption", *Agenda,* 7(2): 99–112.

McLeod, R.H. (2005) "The struggle to regain effective government under democracy in Indonesia", *Bulletin of Indonesian Economic Studies,* 41(3): 367–386.

McLeod, R. H. (2008) "Inadequate budgets and salaries as instruments for institutionalizing public sector corruption in Indonesia", *South East Asia Research,* 16(2): 199–223.

McLeod, R. H. (2011) "Institutionalized public sector corruption: a legacy of the Soeharto franchise", in E. Aspinall and G. v. Klinken (eds.), *The state and illegality in Indonesia,* Leiden: KITLV Press, 45–63.

McLeod, R. H. and R. Garnaut (1998) *East Asia in crisis: from being a miracle to needing one?* London: Routledge.

Mietzner, M. (2014) "Successful and failed democratic transitions from military rule in majority Muslim societies: the cases of Indonesia and Egypt", *Contemporary Politics,* 20(4): 435–452.

Mietzner, M. (2015) "Dysfunction by design: political finance and corruption in Indonesia", *Critical Asian Studies,* 47 (4): 587–610.

New York Times (2012) "Indonesia antigraft agency seeks donors", 3 August, http://www.nytimes.com/2012/08/04/world/asia/anti-graft-agency-corruption-eradication-commission-asks-ordinary-indonesians-for-funds.html?_r=0 (accessed 4 August 2012).

Palmier, L. H. (1985) *The control of bureaucratic corruption: case studies in Asia,* New Delhi: Allied Publishers.

Patunru, A. A. and C. Von Luebke (2010) "Survey of recent developments", *Bulletin of Indonesian Economic Studies,* 46(1): 7–31.

Pompe, S. (2005) *The Indonesian Supreme Court: a study of institutional collapse,* Ithaca, NY: Southeast Asia Program, Cornell University.

Schütte, S. A. (2011) "Appointing top officials in a democratic Indonesia: the corruption eradication commission", *Bulletin of Indonesian Economic Studies,* 47(3): 355–379.

Schütte, S. A. (2012) "Against the odds: anti-corruption reform in Indonesia", *Public Administration and Development,* 32(1): 38–48.

Schütte, S. A. (2013) "Coins for the KPK", *Inside Indonesia,* January–March, http://www.insideindonesia.org/coins-for-the-kpk (accessed 1 February 2016).

Schütte, S. A. and S. Butt (2013) The Indonesian Court for Corruption Crimes: circumventing judicial impropriety? *U4 Brief:* 5.

Schütte, S. A. (2015a) "Keeping the new broom clean: lessons in human resource management from the KPK", *Journal of the Humanities and Social Sciences of Southeast Asia,* 171(4): 423–454.

Schütte, S. A. (2015b) "The fish's head: appointment and removal procedures for anti-corruption agency leadership", *U4 Issue,* 12: 1–50.

Sherlock, S. (2002) "Combating corruption in Indonesia? The Ombudsman and the Assets Auditing Commission", *Bulletin of Indonesian Economic Studies,* 38(3): 367–383.

Sherlock, S. (2003) *Struggling to change: The Indonesian Parliament in an era of Reformasi. A report on the structure and operation of the Dewan Perwakilan Rakyat (DPR),* January, Canberra: Centre for Democratic Institutions.

Stockmann, P. (2007) *The new Indonesian Constitutional Court. A study into its beginnings and first years of work.* Jakarta: Hans Seidel Foundation and Watch Indonesia.

Tempo (2009) "Susno Duadji: Cicak kok mau melawan buaya [The gecko dares to fight the crocodile]", 6 July, 94.

Trocki, C. A. (1999) "Political structures in the nineteenth and early twentieth centuries", in N. Tarling (ed.) *The Cambridge History of Southeast Asia,* volume 2, Cambridge: Cambridge University Press, 5–123.

Von Luebke, C. (2010) "The politics of reform: political scandals, elite resistance, and presidential leadership in Indonesia", *Journal of Current Southeast Asian Affairs,* 29(1): 79–94.

5

"NORMAL" CORRUPTION IN JAPAN

James Babb

It is not helpful to assume that political corruption is endemic in a society. If we assume that such corruption will always exist, we must ask if there is some way to differentiate between random and individual cases or minor violations of strict laws and those that reveal a pattern of systematic and pervasive corruption. This chapter focuses on Japan to examine the extent to which one can define a "normal" level of political corruption.

Attempts to fight corruption in Japan, particularly since the 1990s, might be judged a success. However, the historical record of past cases of political corruption in Japan can obscure the decline in corruption in recent years. In fact, most recent studies appear to be focused on the past (for example, Cox and Thies 2000; Nyblade and Reed 2008). This begs the question: is Japan still corrupt?

First, as a baseline, we must consider the nature of corruption in Japan when it was considered highly corrupt during the heyday of the political machine operated by the former Prime Minister Tanaka Kakuei. His political faction systematised fundraising, including the use of questionable means, and was imitated by other major faction leaders in the Liberal Democratic Party (LDP), which led the national government in Japan from 1955 until 1993. The major scandals leading to political reform in the early 1990s were primarily associated with his faction, and subsequent scandals, including the *Zencon* construction scandal in 1996, are typical of the Tanaka political machine and its imitators. The persistence of "bid-rigging" (*dango*) scandals, discussed later in this chapter, may be evidence that Japan has a deeply rooted corruption problem.

Even so, attempts at political reform since the early 1990s have been dramatic and far-reaching. One of the main changes was to reform the electoral system with the abolition of multi-member constituencies, in which candidates from one party often had to compete with others from the same party, and the introduction of a mixed single-member constituency and proportional representation system. The argument supporting the change was that intra-party competition in the same district led to disproportionate spending by candidates to attract the same voters. However, there was little evidence to back this assumption and, although the change in the electoral system had an impact, its effect on corruption practices was small and perhaps not relevant at all (Lin 2006: 120). The claim that the new electoral system would create a competitive two-party system seemed to be correct when the Democratic Party of Japan (DPJ) came to power with a large majority in 2009 but the continuing weakness of the party in subsequent elections and the revival of the LDP raises doubts about this effect.

The main force against corruption in Japan in the early part of the twenty-first century has been the weakening of links between the LDP and major interest groups, such as the temporary end of funding from Keidanren, the main Japanese business federation, when the LDP was out of power between 1993 and 1994. After 2001, the destruction of LDP political links, for example, with interest groups such as postmasters or doctors, was brought about by Prime Minister Koizumi, who was the President of the LDP. In his 2001 bid for the party leadership, Koizumi vowed to reform the LDP to such an extent that he would destroy it. When the party fell from power in 2009, his prophecy was seemingly fulfilled. It was not political reform legislation but the self-inflicted destruction of the LDP through the agent of Prime Minister Koizumi that changed the political landscape (Pempel 2010).

Despite all the reforms and other changes, the taint of corruption continues to characterise Japanese politics.

Normal corruption: different shades of grey

The current record of political scandals needs to be assessed to determine if political corruption is chronic and self-perpetuating or natural and self-correcting. Even if there are more publicly known cases of corruption, it may be due to higher awareness and the greater likelihood of getting caught. There has always been monitoring of "minor" violations of laws relevant to assessing corruption (election, political finance, and bribery laws, for example). Are we at the point where we can say Japan has a "normal" amount of corruption?

The notion of "normal" corruption requires explanation. All societies have some degree of corruption. This is not the same as saying all politics is corrupt everywhere. A definition is needed of what the level of corruption is within the parameters of "normal" and how we know that corruption is a serious problem in a given society. Japan is a good test case of a society in which corruption appeared to be culturally ingrained and endemic but can now be reasonably argued to have reached a normal "background" level of corruption. Even if Japan is still corrupt, then we need to know how we would know it is still corrupt despite a decline in the number of prominent cases of political corruption.

In the context of "normal", regulation can create an image of corruption through minor or technical violations of rules rather than deep-seated corruption. Similarly, if rules are too tight, then the possibility of minor or technical violations not only creates a false impression of impropriety but also undermines respect for the law. In Japan, the laws covering the behaviour of politicians are very strict and arguably the most stringent in the world. Many violations of the law, which might be viewed as evidence of political corruption in Japan, would not be illegal elsewhere and so do not provide clear evidence of a serious problem in Japan as opposed to other countries. The Public Offices Election Act, for example, which controls campaigning, has features that are surprisingly limiting (Government of Japan 2015).

First, individual politicians cannot purchase advertising space on television, radio or in newspapers. Free time is provided on television and radio (*seiken hōsō*), but it only permits the politician to explain their political views on his or her own with few props in a studio in the blandest setting imaginable. There is no opportunity for the slick advertisements produced by top marketing firms in many other countries. Aspects of the law covering public broadcasts have been relaxed slightly in recent years due to ambiguity over the use of the internet (particularly YouTube) in political campaigns. Posting YouTube videos is now allowed, but emails to individual voters are not. With the proliferation of social media, there are many questions about the regulation of this aspect of campaigns.

During campaigns, the size and placement of posters is also restricted to officially designated billboards where candidates' posters are placed in a row. There are strict limits on the distribution of campaign literature with leaflets limited to two distinct types. For Lower House elections in a single member constituency, a candidate can only distribute 35,000 postcards and 70,000 leaflets. For an Upper House Proportional Representation list, each candidate on the list can distribute 150,000 postcards and 250,000 leaflets. A candidate for the Upper House multimember prefectural election districts is permitted 350,000 postcards and 100,000 leaflets. The postcards and leaflets are restricted in size and must not be attached to objects or scattered indiscriminately. The postcards and leaflets must also be registered with the local Election Commission. Similar restrictions exist for local elections.

One other widely used mode of campaigning, the use of cars with loudspeakers, is also regulated (see, for example, Nobeoka Police Department 2013). This is probably the most common form of canvassing and one which politicians find useful to raise name recognition. Candidates and their supporters travel along public roads in sound trucks reminding people of their name and requesting that they go to vote. Small rallies with the candidates standing on a sound truck (which often has built-in platforms) in front of train stations are also common, particularly when famous politicians come to speak in support of a candidate, but other venues, such as Shinto shrines, are also used.

Most other activities are prohibited and there are strict laws covering campaign violations. Obstruction of the freedom to campaign is prohibited and includes damage to campaign posters as well as more serious actions such as assault on candidates. It is also an offence to campaign prior to the official start of the campaign period, which is only a short period before an election. This does not stop potential candidates putting up posters or arranging meetings as an individual or as an existing member of the Japanese parliament but they must not mention that they are a potential candidate for a particular office. Door-to-door canvassing is prohibited. This is a legacy of the potential intimidation of tenant farmers by landlords in pre-war Japan and, despite the disappearance of tenant farmers and urbanisation of Japanese society, this rule is still strictly followed.

The ban on canvassing was extended to prohibit phone calls to voters by supporters of a candidate after an incident in 2003 when a DPJ candidate in Miyagi prefecture allowed a labour union to telephone supporters to encourage them to vote. Printed material must not be sent by post but handwritten letters are permitted. It is also a crime to publicise which candidates are most popular. Voter surveys published by newspapers are excluded but are limited in the details that can be revealed. There are also restrictions on who can participate. Public employees cannot participate in campaigns. Positions of authority cannot be misused and public servants, including judges, police, prosecutors and teachers, are not allowed to use their position to campaign though they may join campaigns as individuals if their title and position is not mentioned.

The most serious crime is vote buying. This is defined as providing gifts of money or goods to voters. It is illegal at all times and not just during election campaigns. Examples of vote buying activities include distributing money, providing alcoholic beverages or food, giving out gift cards, and invitations to hot springs, concerts and plays. Overpayment for services provided by voters is also prohibited including compensating those working on the campaign with money, food and gifts. Regular salaried employees of the politician must only receive their normal pay. Nonetheless, gift-giving is a major expense for Japanese politicians. They complain that they are expected to make generous contributions to festivals (*matsuri*), local events of community groups, school activities and even to constituents for weddings, funerals, and when people are hospitalised. In addition, there are major annual gift-giving seasons in Japan. There have been campaigns to encourage voters and candidates to refuse to "give, ask for, or receive" such gifts and money. Politicians and candidates for office are prohibited from doing so by law but gift-giving in a personal capacity without mention of the political office being sought or outside the official election campaign period seems to be a major loophole because the practice is still widespread (see Kokusei Jōhō Sentaa 2012: 13).

It has been argued that Japanese politicians do not take advantage of all their tools to campaign effectively (Klein 2011) but the election regulations in Japan are relatively strict by international standards. It is often the violation of these strict rules, especially in minor or ambiguous cases, which gives rise to many cases of alleged corruption in Japan.

The *renza* system and its application

Japanese election campaign law has particularly severe provisions relating to the candidate's responsibility for the behaviour of staff and family members. If a campaign staff member or a family member of a candidate is found to have violated election campaign law, then the candidate will be punished as a result (the *renza* system). This provision was added to the Public Offices Election Act as part of the changes introduced in 1994.

The law designates particular types of individuals which the campaign must identify and who are collectively responsible for campaign law violations. The designated individuals are a general or regional agent (responsible for the campaign overall or in one area), an accountant (in charge of campaign funds), a family member (father, mother, spouse, child, brothers and sisters of a candidate or potential candidate), a secretary (anyone who acts on behalf of the candidate) and a manager (responsible for overall planning of the campaign or specific activities such as the distribution of posters and leaflets). Both the violator and the candidate can face fines and probation in addition to the possibility of the election being declared void and the candidate banned from seeking the same office for five years (Government of Japan 2015).

Table 5.1 shows that the number of offences at the national level has been small, and falling, but a problem still remains at the local level. Secretaries are important for members of the House of Representatives because of the demands of constituency service. This is reflected in the higher number of prosecutions for secretaries at the national level compared to the local level. Campaign staff constitute the greatest number of prosecutions. They are the most numerous and in direct contact with voters during the election so they are perhaps more prone to the temptation to secure results by unscrupulous means. Even if these activities are not condoned by the politicians involved, they are legally responsible for the behaviour of their subordinates to a degree that is unimaginable in most other advanced democracies. This can involve relatively minor infractions such as damage to the campaign posters of another candidate or offering a small amount of food or drink to a potential voter. Prosecutions are rare and tend to be centred on more serious violations of the law.

Table 5.2 provides details of national level *renzasei* violations by type, perpetrator and party with the long-term consequences. Initially, LDP politicians were most numerous violators but later politicians from other parties, notably the DPJ, were also involved. The party in each case was gaining support in opinion polls so that there were more candidates winning from that party during the period in question. When parties expand rapidly, they often have trouble finding adequate numbers of good candidates and the quality of those running in the margins of a large field of new candidates consequently declines. There is

Table 5.1 Prosecutions for *renza*-related election rule violations, 2001–2005

	2001			2002			2003			2004			2005		
	HR	HC	L	HR	HC	L	HR	HC	L	HR	HC	L	HR	HC	L
Family	5	0	30	5	0	33	5	0	34	6	0	49	6	0	49
Secretary	7	0	1	7	1	1	7	1	1	10	1	1	12	1	1
Staff	11	0	59	11	1	61	13	1	64	16	1	79	21	4	79
Total	23	0	90	23	2	95	25	2	98	29	2	129	36	5	129

Source: Japanese Police Agency, *Keisatsu Hakusho* (Police White Paper), 2002–2006.
Keys: HR = House of Representatives; HC = House of Councillors; L = Local Elections.
Note: The data are only available until 2006 after which it was judged that the number of cases at the national level was too few to warrant inclusion in the Police White Paper. (Response of Taki Makoto, Justice Vice-Minister, to a question by Matsushita Shinpei in the House of Councillors Legal Affairs Committee 28 March 2012 in Matsushita 2012.)

Table 5.2 National politicians prosecuted for *renza* violations and their consequences

Election	Party	Outcome	Relationship	Violation	Consequences
LH 1996	Indp.	Lost	Koenkai officer	Vote buying	Mayor
LH 1996	LDP	Won	Secretary's son	Vote buying	Resigned/end
LH 1996	LDP	Won	Secretary's assistant	Vote buying	Removed
UH 2001	LDP	Won	Koenkai officer	Public official	Resigned/end
UH 2001	Indp.	Lost	Secretary	Vote buying	Lost in 2007
LH 2002★	Indp.	Lost	Accountant	Obstruction	End
LH 2003	LDP	Won	MP and accountant	Vote buying	Resigned
LH 2003	LDP	Won	Koenkai officer	Obstruction	Resigned
LH 2003	DJP	Won	Koenkai officer	Obstruction	Resigned
LH 2003	LDP	Lost	Secretary	Vote buying	Banned/lost 2012
LH 2003	DPJ	PR	Campaign staff	Vote buying	Resigned/mayor
UH 2004	DPJ	Lost	Campaign staff	Vote buying	End
LH 2005	DPJ	PR	Secretary	Vote buying	Resigned/end
LH 2005	LDP	Won	Accountant	Vote buying	Resigned/lost 2009
UH 2007	LDP	Won	Accountant and campaign staff	Vote buying	Resigned
LH 2009	DPJ	Won	Accountant	Vote buying	Resigned
LH 2009	DPJ	Won	Campaign staff	Vote buying	Resigned
LH 2009	LDP	Won	Support group	Paid volunteer	Resigned
LH 2014	JRP	Won	Campaign staff	Vote buying	Pending

Sources: Various newspaper reports.
Keys:
- *Election*: LH = Lower House/House of Representatives; UH = Upper House/House of Councillors; ★By-election.
- *Party*: LDP = Liberal Democratic Party; DPJ = Democratic Party of Japan; JRP = Japan Renovation Party; Indp. = No Party.
- *Outcome*: PR = Did not win in district but won in proportional representation block.
- *Violation*: Public official = use of a public official in a campaign; Paid volunteer = paying volunteers for campaign work; Obstruction = Obstruction of the campaign of an opponent.
- *Consequences*: Resigned/end = Resigned and end of political career; Removed/end = Removed from office and end of political career; Lost (year) = Ran for office again but lost in later election in the year indicated; Mayor = Won post as mayor in later election; Banned = Banned from running for office for 5 years.

also the corollary that independents who have little chance of winning will use all possible means to try to win.

For most of the politicians implicated in these charges, the consequences were resignation and the end of a political career. Two who did maintain a political career were only able to win again at the local level. The violations were primarily attempts at vote buying with three cases of obstruction of opponents' campaigns and one of the use of a public official in support of the campaign. Relationship of the offender to the politician is the most varied but most common in the *koenkai* support organization for the politician, the personal secretary, the accountant for the campaign and senior campaign staff. This covers a range of possible relationships although there is only one case of a family member who was a family member of a secretary of a politician and not related to the politician.

Finally, the number of cases has diminished significantly. There were no prosecutions for the 2010 House of Representative election nor for the 2013 House of Councillors' election, and only one for the 2014 House of Representative election. It might seem that the system is working and politicians and their campaign organizations are more careful. At the same time, there is evidence that in the 2014 House of Representatives election there were minor violations that have not been prosecuted (discussed later). Again, it is likely that minor violations are ignored at all levels but that raises the issue of the threshold over which a violation is deemed a prosecutable offence.

Political finance law in Japan

Laws governing financial contribution for political purposes are also very demanding. There has been an obligation to report political contributions since 1948 (Government of Japan 2014c). But it was only after the scandals associated with former Prime Minster Tanaka in the 1970s that stronger financial regulations began to be introduced. After the Recruit scandal in 1988, popular pressure for political reform grew. The government of Kaifu Toshiki (August 1989-November 1991) foundered in the face of opposition to his political reform plans. The subsequent government of Miyazawa Kiichi (November 1991-August 1993) made some changes, including restrictions on the sale of tickets for political fundraising "parties", requiring political groups to publish their financial records and introducing limitations on the use of political funds. This desperate attempt to appease public opinion failed and the LDP lost power for the first time since 1955.

In early 1994, political reform legislation saw a significant change from a multi-member constituency system to a combination of single-member constituency with regional proportional representation. The changes to political finance were just as important. Political financial contributions could only be made to designated political funding organizations (*Shikin Kanri Dantai*) such as political parties and not to individual politicians. This provision was somewhat weakened by the fact that contributions to the local branch of a political party were often effectively contributions to the local member of Parliament (MP) or party candidate in that constituency and that individual politicians created political funding organizations to collect and manage funds on their behalf.

In 1999, contributions by business firms and other organizations such as business federations and trade unions were prohibited; only contributions by individuals to designated funding organizations (donors) are now legally permitted. The amount that can be contributed to a political organization in any one year is also limited by law. In 2005, after the Japan Dental Association Political Funds scandal, the Act was revised to add a requirement for all political contributions by political funding organizations to be transferred through financial institutions, prohibiting cash contributions which were difficult to monitor. The transfer of funds between political funding organizations was limited to 50 million yen per year. In 2007, due to issues raised by office accounting irregularities, political funding organizations were prohibited from real estate transactions and procedures for reporting requirements were strengthened. Finally, in 2008, the designated political funds organizations (the recipients) of individual MPs were required to present receipts for all expenditures and to have their accounts audited by an independent third-party.

The person responsible for the accounts of the political funds organization must report all income, expenditure and assets held by the organization to the 31st December every year with a report to be submitted by the end of March in the following year. Reports can be made slightly later if an election is held in the first five months of the year. The reports made by the organization are in principle open to the public on the 30th November and can be viewed for a period of three years. However, the data are held by the General Affairs Ministry or the local electoral commission. Reports must be viewed in person and photocopying the reports is prohibited, severely limiting the ability of the public to monitor the process.

Political contributions from foreign citizens are prohibited. The violation of this provision led to the resignation of former Foreign Minister Maebara Seiji, a senior DPJ politician, in 2011 when it was revealed that he had accepted a political contribution from a South Korean citizen. However, the "South Korean" was a member of the Korean minority of permanent residents in Japan so it was more of a grey area than might at first appear. Originally, this provision also meant that foreign firms and firms or organizations in which foreigners played a major role were banned from political activity including financial contributions. However, in 2006, Japanese corporation law (Government of Japan 2014a) was revised to define as "foreign" only those firms in which the majority of the shares were held by foreign investors or corporations, thus permitting firms with foreign executive staff to make political contributions.

Is Japan too strict or not strict enough?

There is a recent trend to question these restrictions on political activity, including political finance regulations, especially in the United States (Oritz 1998; Evertsson 2013; Casal Bértoa et al. 2014). Some see the present regulations as a restriction of freedom of expression (Esenberg 2010; Kang 2012; Redish and Dawson 2012; see also Beer 1991 on Japan). Strict laws are also often counter-productive in that reducing the legal amount of political campaign contributions can actually create more corruption (Nichols 2011). Regulation can also undermine grassroots politics (Smith 2000). In Japan, the constitutionality of *renzasei* is also questionable (Agata 1990, 1992). It is true that politicians have historically hidden behind their staff to avoid prosecution but there may be genuine cases where a member of staff acted independently and it might be argued that it is unfair to punish the politician as a result. The incessant search for scandal contains the danger of the demonisation of politics and politicians as inherently corrupt and this too can undermine faith in democracy (Flinders 2012).

Recent cases are often individual instances and do not suggest a clear pattern of corrupt behaviour. Even ones that have the classic features of widespread implication of several politicians are no longer straight forward. The scandal involving the veteran politician Ichiro Ozawa, for example, is complex. He had long been associated with the most corrupt politicians in Japan so it was no surprise that he was implicated in another scandal in 2009, the Nishimatsu Construction scandal. Ozawa was not the only one to be involved and yet he seemed to be specially targeted by prosecutors. His party, the DPJ, had just come to power and he was taking on the Japanese bureaucracy to an extent never attempted before. Eventually he was cleared of corruption (McCurry 2012). The charges may have been politically motivated but it is unclear. Indeed, those who investigate corruption may have their own political agendas (Adut 2004).

In this context, there have recently been concerns about how unreasonable and bullying the Special Prosecutor can be during investigation of politicians and others for corruption (Shionoya 2010; Murayama 2012). This is a widespread perception from different ends of the political spectrum. The argument is that the Special Prosecutor has felt compelled to over-compensate for appearing to turn a blind eye to corruption in the past. The Office is seen to be too suspicious and engaged in tactics that border on harassment to the extent that they have lost their legitimacy in the eyes of some (Gōhara 2012). It was recently revealed, for example, that most ruling party MPs rely on the party to check their expenses because they are terrified of making a mistake due to the complicated nature of the reporting rules (Yomiuri online 2015). This demonstrates that, even under normal conditions, a strict reporting regime creates the potential for inadvertent violations.

Even the most recent scandals in Japanese politics are not clear proof of endemic corruption. One set of scandals has focused on the misuse of expenses, an issue which highlights the high formal ethical standards demanded of politicians. In 2014, Trade and Industry Minister Miyazawa Yōichi was accused of mis-spending political funds after allegations surfaced that he allowed one of his secretaries to claim expenses to take members of his *koenkai* local constituency political support group in Hiroshima to a sadomasochist sex club. In December 2011, the then-deputy minister of the Ministry of Agriculture, Forestry and Fisheries Iwamoto Tsukasa of the DPJ was also alleged to have spent political funds in nightclubs, including those where money was slipped into the clothing of the hostesses. Neither Iwamoto nor Miyazawa was forced to resign nor were they prosecuted.

There have also been two alleged vote buying cases. In 2014, Obuchi Yūko, then Minister of Economy, Trade and Industry, was forced to resign after irregularities in her political funding organization reports suggested an attempt to cover up the use of political funds to provide gifts and food and drink during an election campaign. Even though her secretaries were implicated, the prosecutor felt that there were grounds for suspecting she was aware of the problem and invoked the possibility of pursuing her via the *renza* system. Obuchi believed it was a simple accounting error. Justice Minister Matsushima Midori was accused in 2014 of allowing her campaign organization to distribute handheld fans (*uchiwa*) with slogans on them to people attending a summer festival in her Tokyo constituency. She was also forced to resign even though the charge was relatively trivial.

These examples of political accountability for direct spending on constituents all have grey areas. Rather than these relatively minor or ambiguous infractions, there are areas that, it could be argued, should be given more attention. The first problem is conflict of interest. Japan has relatively weak rules and practices when it comes to possible conflicts of interest. This became clear in 2014 when it was revealed that Miyazawa Yoichi, the minister responsible for regulating the nuclear power industry in Japan, held shares in Tokyo Electric Power. This was particularly problematic given the expressed desire of the government to consider restarting nuclear power plants, which was an unpopular policy. In many countries, a blind trust would be created to manage the politician's assets while in office but such trusts do not seem to be a feature of Japanese political life (Saitō 2008: 37).

The increasing tendency of politicians to be directly approached and influenced by lobbyists is also a problem. Lobbying in Japan has always been a feature of the political system but there is evidence that changes to the electoral system, among other factors, have led to an increase in lobbying politicians rather than the bureaucracy, which was more common in the past (Naoi and Krauss 2009). Lobbying is usually carried out by groups that already share similar views to those that they lobby and at best these groups have greater access to politicians but not necessarily greater influence. Since lobbying of politicians is relative new in Japan, there are less stringent rules in place than for other aspects of interactions with politicians.

Another, and perhaps the most serious area of concern, is bid-rigging (*dango*) and the role that politicians play as go-betweens (*assen*) for which they receive payment. Historically, bid-rigging has been a major problem in Japan especially at the local level (Black 2004). Firms, particularly construction firms, collude to put forward bids to supply government services, especially for public works and projects (Woodall 1996). Suspicions of collusion are usually raised because the amount bid is often close to 99 per cent of the estimated maximum cost the public agency is willing to pay. This is a problem when the estimated cost is meant to be secret to encourage competition or is artificially inflated to benefit the firms bidding.

Some observers do not see a problem with bid-rigging in Japan (Miyazaki 2014). Rather than increasing public expenditure, this might allow firms to plan work to fit local budgets. Bid-rigging can also be a distributional mechanism by sharing out the work to as many firms as possible and spreading the benefits of public works spending to the local community. Miyazaki argues that it is part of Japanese culture and need not be abandoned if it works. The problem is that bid-rigging is illegal and encourages firms and politicians to collude in a way that is not compatible with democratic oversight. It has also been used as an illegal fundraising activity by politicians who could act as brokers for the process.

With a few exceptions (George Mulgan 2010), the major cases of bid-rigging implicating politicians are now primarily, if not exclusively, at the local level. In 2007, three prefectural governors were arrested and subsequently resigned over bid-rigging. Ando Tadahiro, the governor of Miyazaki Prefecture, was involved in securing a contract for a disaster reconstruction project for an engineering firm; Kimura Yoshiki, the governor of Wakayama Prefecture, was alleged to have arranged rigged bids for sewers and other public works construction projects; and Sato Eisaku, the governor of Fukushima Prefecture, was associated with bid-rigging for a dam construction project. These were the first cases since the enactment of a law in 2006 aimed at politicians or other local government officials who co-ordinate or even leak information on a bid. The punishment for violations is up to five years in prison and fines of up to 2.5 million yen. Nonetheless, there is considerable evidence that the problem continues to exist.

The bureaucracy and political corruption in Japan

The definition of political corruption involves both politicians and bureaucrats but bureaucratic corruption is sometimes overlooked in the analysis of corruption in Japan. This is because the bureaucracy has been viewed as relatively free from corruption (Johnson 1986; Reed 1999). The tendency has been to emphasise how the relationship between bureaucrats and business leaders facilitated government-industry coordination and fostered strategies for growth with minimal, if any, damage to the economy and political institutions, especially when compared to other countries. However, historically, bureaucrats have also been involved or at least complicit in corruption practices (Babb 1995).

There have been many corruption scandals involving bureaucrats, especially in early post-war Japan. Fukuda Takeo was still a Finance Ministry official when he was implicated in the Showa Denko scandal of 1948. The Silk scandal (1949), the Electric Power Distribution scandal (1952) and the Sugar scandal (1953) only involved bureaucrats. It is true that politicians were the main focus of corruption scandals between 1960 and 1990, but individual senior civil servants were often implicated in these cases as well. Prosecution of civil servants for bribery, including higher civil servants, has not been uncommon throughout the post-war period although not widely publicized.

It was only in the late 1990s that the problem appeared to be systemic. In 1998, both the Ministry of Finance (MoF) and the Ministry of Defence were embroiled in scandals. The MoF scandal initially centred on the lavish entertainment of officials by the firms that they were meant to oversee but soon expanded to arrests of officials in the MoF and Bank of Japan on bribery charges. However, despite some high-profile arrests, most officials were given written or oral warnings and one or two were temporarily suspended or had their pay reduced. The only major long-term impact was on entertainment which is now so strictly curbed that officials doubt whether they can even accept a cup of coffee. The Ministry of Defence scandal was more serious because it was based on kickbacks received on the inflated price paid for the procurement of defence supplies and parts. It also revealed a systematic pattern of bid-rigging and provision of jobs in industry for retired officials (*amakudari*) even though bid-rigging and *amakudari* were common throughout the post-war period. In this case, two bureaucrats were given prison sentences and one of those was also heavily fined.

The scandal involving the Ministry of Foreign Affairs and the LDP politician Suzuki Muneo in 2001–2002 was revealing as a case study in bureaucratic corruption, which might be called "networking" corruption or policy tribe (*zoku*) corruption. Policy tribes or *zoku* are politicians who specialise in particular aspects of policymaking to advance their careers. This expertise is helpful in securing posts in government and enables the politician to gain knowledge of government programmes and to access the senior civil servants who manage the programmes. Most specialise in areas such as agriculture and industry which are most advantageous to constituents. However, Suzuki appeared to have carved out a relationship with the Foreign Ministry in a particularly lucrative way. Suzuki's case was not unusual but it stood out because it was not a normal area for exploiting the bureaucracy. He maintained that he did nothing wrong but he and his bureaucratic allies were punished for their activities.

One area that most would agree is criminal and not acceptable is bribery of public officials. There are very few data on the scale of bribery in Japan involving civil servants and it has been declining over the years. Prior to the late 1990s, however, it was not uncommon (see Figure 5.1).

Even more instructive is a comparison between bureaucrats and politicians at both the national and local levels in the most serious cases considered for prosecution. As is clear from Table 5.3, the number of cases of national politicians involved in bribery is negligible. Those implicating local politicians are higher but also falling. However, senior civil servants are just as likely to be involved as politicians. Local civil servants are much more likely to be involved in bribery although a large number of cases at this level appear to involve police officers.

Blatant bribery is an obvious problem but there are also more subtle forms of bureaucratic corruption in Japan (Jones 2013). One is the practice of *amakudari* where retired officials obtain employment in the industries and firms that they were previously responsible for regulating. The *Kokkakomuin Hō* makes it illegal for civil servants to lobby the agency for which they previously worked for a period of two years (Government of Japan 2014b). However,

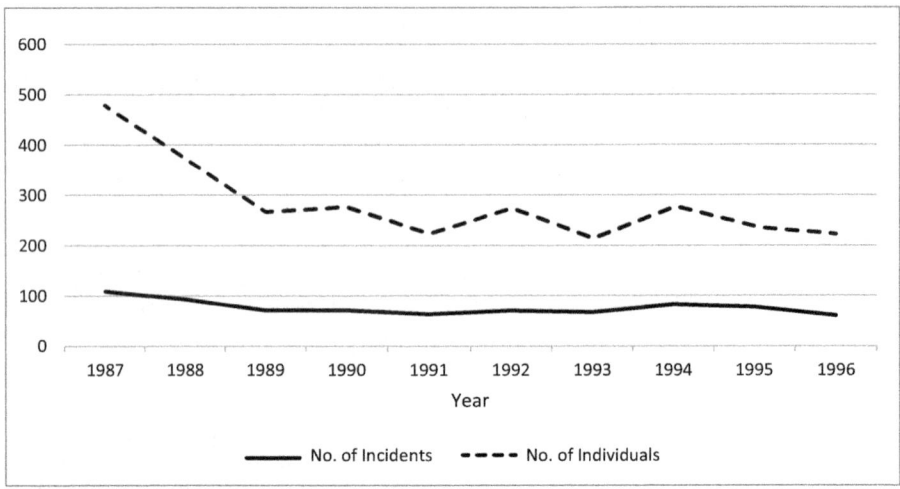

Figure 5.1 Bribery incidents involving central agency personnel, 1987–1996
Source: Japanese Police Agency, *Keisatsu Hakusho* (Police White Paper), 1997.

Table 5.3 Cases of bribery investigated (number of prosecutions), 2001–2013

	2001	2002	2003	2004	2005	2006	2007	2008	2009	2010	2011	2012	2013
National	1	2	2	0	0	1	0	0	1	0	0	0	0
Politicians	(0)	(2)	(0)	(0)	(0)	(0)	(0)	(0)	(0)	(0)	(0)	(0)	(0)
Local	35	34	16	11	28	24	9	7	7	8	18	2	1
Politicians	(27)	(19)	(15)	(9)	(21)	(24)	(8)	(5)	(5)	(8)	(5)	(1)	(0)
Senior Civil	24	15	30	59	11	8	21	22	11	8	4	10	8
Servants	(23)	(13)	(8)	(18)	(9)	(5)	(10)	(24)	(3)	(7)	(3)	(5)	(2)
Local Civil	95	104	68	72	75	111	52	41	36	28	34	22	37
Servants[1]	(78)	(92)	(53)	(55)	(55)	(73)	(41)	(33)	(34)	(23)	(30)	(14)	(21)
Other State	5	17	26	27	9	14	10	1	2	12	5	10	9
Employees	(5)	(14)	(25)	(18)	(10)	(12)	(10)	(1)	(2)	(8)	(3)	(10)	(7)

Source: Japanese Police Agency, *Keisatsu Hakusho* (Police White Paper), 2013.
Note: The data on local civil servants includes local police, which were listed separately until 2007. Up to that point, cases involving police constituted approximately 20 per cent of the combined cases at the local level for most years. Senior civil servants include ministerial employees seconded to regional offices. Other state employees include government funded organizations. The number of cases has decreased to a level where the table is no longer recorded in the Police White Paper but the pattern probably still holds in terms of more local than national cases and more bureaucrats than politicians involved.

two years is a relatively short period of time and there is a suspicion that this does not stop bureaucrats who aim at receiving deferred benefits by establishing a relationship which favours potential future employers.

There was some progress in this area under the government of Prime Minister Koizumi when many of the semi-governmental organizations were privatised or abolished. These organizations had often been set up with public money and subsidised by the government but were often used as opportunities for former civil servants to assume a post for a short period of time and obtain an additional generous second (or third or fourth) pension from the organization indirectly at public expense. These opportunities are now fewer but it is still possible to gain additional salary and pensions in private organizations and business.

Conclusion

For Japan or any country to be considered corrupt, several key features would have to be present. It would have to be intentional, systematic, widespread and explicitly or tacitly condoned by persons in positions of authority who should be monitoring and curbing "bad practice". Grey areas exist everywhere but it is the extent to which they are exploited that creates a problem. A "normal" degree of corruption is perhaps inevitable and those in authority must be sufficiently responsible not to allow it to get out of control.

As in the case of political finance, over-regulation or over-zealous implementation can be a problem as well. It can make others contemptuous of the rules and limit political activity and free speech. The difficulty is finding a balance and using discretion in dealing with minor infractions.

Nothing in this chapter should be construed as justifying corruption or arguing that it does not matter. There is a need, however, to separate political point-scoring and normative distaste for corruption from the analysis of why it exists, who benefits and the harm it causes. Scholars should distinguish between "normal" corruption and endemic systemic corruption. By doing so, we may highlight not only the damage caused by deeply embedded corruption but also enable the analyst to understand who benefits and why it is difficult to tackle corruption. Perhaps we also need to acknowledge when it is bad but not as bad as it has been or could be. Portraying politics in democracy as inherently corrupt when it is not so bad might undermine democracy as much as corruption itself.

References

Adut, A. (2004) "Scandal as norm entrepreneurship: strategy, corruption and the French investigating magistrates", *Theory and Society*, 33: 529–578.

Agata, Y. (1990) "Kōshiki senkyo hō ni okeru renzasei no gokensei nit suite (jō)" [On the constitutionality of the involvement system in the Public Office Election Law, part 1], *Annual Report*, Faculty of Literature, Otsuma Women's University, 22: 1–21.

Agata, Y. (1992) "Kōshiki senkyo hō ni okeru renzasei no gokensei nit suite (ge)" [On the constitutionality of the involvement system under the Public Office Election Law, part 2], *Annual Report*, Humanities and Social Sciences, Otsuma Women's University, 24: 5–25.

Babb, J.D. (1995) "Japan's Ministry of Finance and the politics of complicity", *Review of International Political Economy*, 2(3): 536–560.

Beer, L.W. (1991) "Freedom of expression: the continuing revolution in Japan's legal culture", Occasional Papers in Contemporary Asian Studies, School of Law, University of Maryland, 3(104).

Black, W.K. (2004) "The dango tango: why corruption blocks real reform in Japan", *Business Ethics Quarterly*, 14(4): 603–623.

Casal Bértoa, F., F. Molenaar, D.R. Piccio and E.R. Rashkova (2014) "The world upside down: delegitimising political finance regulation", *International Political Science Review*, 35(3): 355–375.

Cox, G. W. and M.F. Thies (2000) "How much does money matter: buying votes in Japan 1967–1990", *Comparative Political Studies*, 33(1): 37–57.

Esenberg, R. M. (2010) "The lonely death of public campaign financing", *Harvard Journal of Public Policy*, 33: 283–330.

Evertsson, N. (2013) "Political corruption and electoral funding: a cross-national analysis", *International Criminal Justice Review*, 23(1): 75–94.

Flinders, M. (2012) "Debating demonization in defence of politics, politicians and political science", *Contemporary Politics*, 18(3): 355–366.

James Babb

George Mulgan, A. (2010) "The perils of Japanese politics", *Japan Forum*, 21(2): 183–207.

Gōhara, N. (2012) *Kensatsu hōkai—ushinawareta seigi*, Tokyo: Mainichi Shinbun Sha.

Government of Japan (2014a) *Kaisha Hō*, http://law.e-gov.go.jp/htmldata/H17/H17HO086.html (accessed 23 August 2015). In Japanese.

Government of Japan (2014b) *Kokkakōmuin, Hō*, http://law.e-gov.go.jp/htmldata/S22/S22HO120.html (accessed 28 August 2015). In Japanese.

Government of Japan (2014c) *Seiji Shikin Kisei Hō*, http://law.e-gov.go.jp/htmldata/S23/S23HO194.html (accessed 23 August 2015). In Japanese.

Government of Japan (2015) *Kōshoki, Senkyō Hō*, http://law.e-gov.go.jp/htmldata/S25/S25HO100.html (accessed 23 August 2015). In Japanese.

Johnson, C. (1986) "Tanaka Kakuei, structural corruption, and the advent of machine politics in Japan", *Journal of Japanese Studies*, 12(1): 1–28.

Jones, C. P. A. (2013) "Amakudari and Japanese law", *Michigan State International Law Review*, 22: 879–959.

Kang, M. S. (2012) "The end of Campaign Finance Law", *Virginia Law Review*, 98(1): 1–65.

Klein, A. (2011) "The puzzle of ineffective election campaigning in Japan", *Japanese Journal of Political Science*, 12(1): 57–74.

Kokusei Jōhō Sentaa (2012) *Seiji shikin kisei hō ihan jitsurei shu*, Tokyo: Kokusei Jōhō Sentaa.

Lin, J-W. (2006) "The politics of reform in Japan and Taiwan", *Journal of Democracy*, 17(2): 118–131.

Matsushita, S. (2012) "Questions before the House of Councillors Legal Affairs Committee, 28 March", www.shinnpei.com/diet/houmu_24_03_28.htm (accessed 12 August 2015). In Japanese.

Murayama, O. (2012) *Ozawa Ichirō vs Tokusō Kensatsu 20-nen sensō*, Tokyo: Asahi Shinbun Shuppan.

McCurry, J. (2012) "Japan court clears Ichiro Ozawa, prompting talk of challenge to PM", *The Guardian*, http://www.theguardian.com/international (accessed 16 August 2015).

Miyazaki, M. (2014) *Dango bunka: Nihon o shietekita mono*, Tokyo: Shodensha.

Naoi, M. and E. Krauss (2009) "Who lobbies whom? Special interest politics under alternative electoral systems", *American Journal of Political Science*, 53(4): 874–892.

Nichols, P. M. (2011) "The perverse effect of campaign contribution limits reducing the allowable amounts", *American Business Law Journal*, 48(1): 77–118.

Nobeoka Police Department, Traffic Division (2013) "Senkyo undōyō jidōsha no setsumei shiryō 1", http://www.mi-n.net/koukai/%E5%BB%B6%E5%B2%A1%E5%B8%82/%E5%B8%82%E9%95%B7%E9%81%B8%E6%8C%99%E7%AB%8B%E5%80%99%E8%A3%9C/%E9%81%B8%E6%8C%99%E9%81%8B%E5%8B%95%E8%A6%81%E8%87%AA%E5%8B%95%E8%BB%8A%E3%81%AB%E3%81%A4%E3%81%84%E3%81%A6.pdf (accessed 15 August 2015).

Nyblade, B. and S.R. Reed (2008) "Who cheats? Who loots? Political competition and corruption in Japan 1947–1993", *American Journal of Political Science*, 52(4): 926–41.

Oritz, D. R. (1998) "The democratic paradox of campaign finance reform", *Stanford Law Review*, 50(3): 893–914.

Pempel, T. J. (2010) "Between pork and productivity: the collapse of the liberal democratic party", *The Journal of Japanese Studies*, 36(2): 227–254.

Redish, M. H. and E. N. Dawson (2012) "'Worse than the disease': the anti-corruption principle, free expression, and the democratic process", *William and Mary Bill of Rights Journal*, 20: 1053–1084.

Reed, S. R. (1999) "Review of Richard H. Mitchell's *Political Bribery in Japan* (Honolulu: University of Hawai'i Press, 1996)", *Social Science Japan Journal*, (1): 126–127.

Saitō, K. (2008) "Seiji rinri o meguru kyaku koku no dōkō—Amerika, Eikoku oyobi Kanada", *Refurensu*, 692: 27–40.

Shionoya, A. (2010) *Jitsuroku: seiji vs Tokusō Kensatsu —Aru josei hishō no kokuhaku*, Tokyo: Bungei Shunjū.

Smith, B. A. (2000) "Regulation and the decline of grassroots politics", *Catholic University Law Review*, 50: 1–12.

Woodall, B. (1996) *Japan under construction: corruption, politics, and public works*, Berkeley, CA: University of California Press.

Yomiuri online (2015) "'Seiji to kane' tenken, Jimintō 9 wari ga irainoriyū", 2 May 2015. https://premium.yomiuri.co.jp/pc/#!/news_20150502-118-OYT1T50014 (Accessed 15 August 2015). In Japanese.

6

RULE MAKING AND RULE BREAKING

Electoral Corruption in East Asia

Jamie S. Davidson and Erik Mobrand

Benjamin Reilly (2006, 2007), based on a comprehensive comparison of electoral regimes in Northeast and Southeast Asia, suggests that a loose but discernible model of Asian democracy has emerged. For Reilly, its prime characteristic has been the movement of parties toward the centre of a political spectrum where consensus or majoritarian forms of electoral democracy prevail. Notably, as the number of parties has declined, party systems have stabilised around a handful of established, sizeable parties that are vaguely programmatic in orientation. Reilly speculates that reasons behind this phenomenon could include: 1) a deep-seated culture of "Asian values" that prioritises consensus; 2) incumbent advantage as political elites "rejig" the electoral process in their favour; and/or 3) efforts to staunch regional or separatist tendencies. In this chapter, we take Reilly's second hypothesis seriously and deploy it as a launching point for an exploration into the role corruption plays in electoral management in East Asia.

If political elites really do seek incumbent advantage through the manipulation of electoral governance, as Reilly suggests, one must consider how they then justify these politically motivated changes in the electoral process to the public. Clearly, they cannot admit that the electoral rules and regulations were altered in the name of incumbent advantage. No self-respecting public that sees fit to call itself a democracy would readily accept such shamelessness. Instead, we argue that political elites in East Asia tend to use the guise of fighting corruption as cover for their electoral machinations. Elites often propose, for example, that the bribery and coercion characteristic of local politics must be subdued through reforms that place greater weight on the orderly discipline of the national level. Or that new parties, overly eager to make their mark, are more susceptible to extra-legal methods of campaigning and financing than established parties, leaving mainstream elites little choice but to constrain newcomers.

Predicated on this supposition, we contend that electoral management in East Asia is best described by political elites battling corruption on two fronts. On the one hand, they are concerned with diminishing what they believe to be the illegitimate or illegal practices of upstart opponents and the perceived adolescent behaviour and limited cognitive abilities of the average voter. On the other hand, they are equally concerned with the masking of their own malfeasance through incessant tinkering with the electoral architecture. In other words, it is our view that contestation over rule making is as much part of the spirited debate over the corruption of electoral politics in East Asia as rule breaking.

What we see emerging in East Asia is not convergence on a single model of Asian democracy but the formation of three discernible categories whose primary determining variable is the extent to which contestation is dominated by rule making or rule breaking. Our first cluster of countries contains strong states with restrictive electoral regimes because the governing political elites have a tight rein over the contestation behind rule making. In this box, we place Singapore, Korea, and Malaysia. As a second grouping, we suggest that the ubiquitous clientelism of the Philippines in part resembles the political bossism of pre-1990s Japan where rule breaking took prominence over the struggle behind rule making. Lastly, electoral governance in Indonesia, Thailand, and Taiwan displays a mix of politicking over rule making and efforts to dampen the pervasive clientelism that fosters rule breaking.

Below we place our taxonomy in the context of the corruption and institutional electoral literatures, teasing out some conceptual implications of our argument. This is followed by abbreviated case studies that provide the empirical evidence behind our tripartite classificatory schemata. We conclude by positing some of the policy implications of our argument, with particular respect to methods of combatting political corruption.

Conceptual concerns

Kunicová and Rose-Ackerman (2005) remark perceptively on the recent emergence of a literature that has made great strides in merging two voluminous bodies of work: that on corruption and that on the interplay among elections, institutions, and voter behaviour. For example, only slightly more than a decade ago in their seminal study on the characteristics of electoral systems that give rise to personal votes, Carey and Shugart (1994) hardly mention the problem of electoral corruption. Today, there is strong belief that electoral systems that produce personal votes tend to be more corrupt than those that generate party votes. Beyond this dichotomy, however, on finer grain evaluations, such as open vs. closed lists in parliamentary representative systems and the differential effect of district magnitudes (Kunicová and Rose-Ackerman 2005; Chang and Golden 2007), we take stock of Lambsdorff's view that the findings of this cutting-edge research remains contradictory and inconclusive (2007: 45, Box 13).

Instead, in this chapter, we adopt a less strictly institutional approach to examine the link between corruption and elections in East Asia. In so doing, our tripartite taxonomy engages directly with the corruption literature in two ways. First, we take issue with the distinguished life-cycle theory of corruption. This theory proposes that there is an inverted U-shaped relationship between wealth and corruption, that is, as countries become wealthier, corruption worsens. At a certain elevated level of economic development, however, the theory contends that there is a tipping point where corruption recedes considerably to tolerable levels. (It is too costly and unrealistic to expect zero corruption (Bardhan 1997; Gundlach and Paldam 2009).) This is the theoretical framework that informs the work of economists, for example, who measure levels of corruption in China and the United States at different stages of their historical economic development (Ramirez 2014). The assertion, however, that corruption declines with wealth in the context of elections is problematic on two fronts. First, it is widely recognised that where campaign costs are high, which happens in those wealthier countries that lack public political financing and/or strict regulations on campaign spending, politicians are forced to raise funds in ways that inexorably contravene domestic campaign electoral laws (Walecki 2004). Second, this theory is predicated on an apolitical understanding of rule making, which is fundamental to the electoral process. As Schaffer (2008) has observed, efforts to make elections "cleaner" often have the effect of skewing the playing field. Where electoral rules are followed, which might happen with more regularity in higher income countries, the rules themselves are a site of struggle. In other words, the adjustment of electoral rules is an intensely political activity. To say that electoral corruption will decline in parts of East Asia is imprecise. It is more accurate to state that politics has, in places, shifted from breaking rules to making them.

Our second concern has to do with the preoccupation in the corruption literature with quantification, as evidenced by the way in which international rankings of perceived corruption function as analytical pivots. Instead, we maintain that privileging the forms that corruption assume rather than their quantity or abundance improves our analytical leverage in the study of electoral politics in East Asia. With the introduction of our taxonomy, we endeavour to shift the focus from "how much?" to "what kind?" In the context of electoral politics, forms of rule breaking may encompass such conspicuously coercive means as clientelism and vote buying or even acts of public violence and intimidation. These forms might be contrasted with those that obtain in environments where the struggle over rule making prevails. These qualitative modes may be characterised by more covert, private or modernised efforts with the aim of tilting the playing field disproportionately in favour of incumbents.

Finally, by classifying electoral politics in East Asia along the axis of rule making and rule breaking, we seek to dispel the dichotomous stereotype of the violent, coercive-filled elections of Southeast Asia and the cold, calculated discipline of those in Northeast Asia. After all, Singapore's tight grip on rule making and its disproportionate vote-to-seat conversion mechanism recalls the electoral management style of Northeast Asia while the rough-and-tumble of Taiwan's local elections invokes the supposed Southeast Asian variety. That said, we are not the first to attempt to integrate cases from Northeast and Southeast Asia analytically. Of late, such comparative efforts have focused on state-building and development outcomes (Thompson 1996; Booth 1999; Kang 2002; Doner et al. 2005; You 2015). But an implicit judgement running through these studies puts Northeast Asia above Southeast Asia; scholars ask why the latter, with the partial exception of Singapore (Haggard 1990), has not been as successful as the former. Our classificatory schema does not rest on this premise. Alongside the state-building and development literature, a comparative party system literature has also emerged (Choi 2012; Croissant and Völkel 2012; Hicken and Kuhonta 2015). Its primary focus has been the causes and consequences of party system institutionalisation, not electoral malpractice. But because of the latter's pervasiveness, which has been defined as "*the manipulation of electoral processes and outcomes so as to substitute personal or partisan benefit for the public interest*" (Birch 2011: 11, emphasis in original), we believe the integrity of the region's electoral exercises can be called into question (Norris 2013). To show how, we now turn to examples of electoral management in East Asia.

Cases

In the first category, which we call "electoral tweakers", we place Singapore, Malaysia, and South Korea. In each of these places, the leaders of the most powerful parties draw on legal instruments to weaken opponents and secure their rule. In Singapore, the Election Department reports directly to the Prime Minister's office. Election campaigns are highly regulated with short campaign periods and rules to limit opportunities for campaigning. South Korea, despite being widely acknowledged as a democracy, has surprisingly similar features. Authoritarian-era elections laws and the election commission were strikingly little reformed as the regime allowed elections to become more competitive. In Malaysia, the ruling coalition has also relied on its election commission and redistricting so that the influence of the popular vote is minimised. The techniques used in each of these countries involve not directly inducing voters to vote one way or another but restricting how much impact voting can have in the first place. Many of these techniques are introduced in the name of fighting corruption.

The second category brings together the Philippines and pre-1990s Japan. These are places where dominant forces have relied more heavily on illicit voter mobilisation than on electoral tweaking. In many instances, local bosses rely on networks of vote canvassers to distribute individual inducements to voters. In Japan, electoral support was mobilised through support networks that were specific to individual politicians.[1]

The third category is illustrated by Indonesia, Thailand, and Taiwan. These countries have histories of targeted mobilisation that are also overlaid with manipulation of the electoral environment. In Indonesia, political elites have adjusted laws related to elections many times since the beginning of the post-Soeharto transition. These efforts have systematically hurt certain actors such as reform-minded independent candidates. In Taiwan, there is a long history of regime-led clientelism. Over time, the state has turned more to legal instruments, such as laws on parties, to shape the electoral sphere. Elections continue to involve high degrees of personalistic mobilisation, especially in rural places. For Thailand, features of rule breaking is more appropriate for an earlier period prior to the enactment of the reform-oriented 1997 constitution and the rise of Thaksin Shinawatra's Thai Rak Thai Party in 2001 when local business bosses were pulled into competitive electoral politics.

These categories point to the limits of thinking about individual electoral inducements and group (or programmatic) inducements as opposites. It may well be the case that the opposite of individual inducements is electoral tweaking. This point pulls together the arc of transformation in political mobilisation theorised by Scott (1969) with the more recent suggestion by Reilly that there is a common Asian pattern of electoral design. We suggest that Reilly's observation sits better at the "modern" end of the trajectory than does programmatic mobilisation.

Category 1: rule making

Malaysia

Analysing the role elections have played in Malaysia's politics has provided a conundrum for the country's scholars. On the one hand, few deem them as free and fair expressions of political choice. The ruling National Front (or BN) coalition, headed by the United Malay National Organization (UMNO), has won each national election since they were instituted under British rule in the 1950s. UMNO, the BN, and the federal government have used this dominant position to its fullest advantage. It is well known that the country's electoral rules skew the playing field by exploiting such strategies as mal-proportioned voting districts and gerrymandering that disproportionately favour the BN. This is especially so in terms of inflating the magnitude of rural Malay votes, which violates the foundational principle of one person-one vote upon which democratic elections rest. For instance, in the general elections of 2013, the BN garnered about 60 per cent of parliamentary seats, having won less than 48 per cent of the total vote. Historically, the government has not been shy about spending rural development funds in particularistic ways either as vote enticements or as rewards for voter loyalty.

"Money politics" is a noticeable blot on Malaysia's electoral record, especially since the then-Prime Minister Mahathir Mohamad embarked on a thorough yet selective program of liberalisation and privatisation of the country's economy in the 1980s (Gomez 2012). The few legal restrictions on campaign funding that exist are not enforceable. UMNO itself owns a host of large businesses, many of them via proxies including media outlets (television and print). This situation has led to a purposeful blurring of the public and private sectors. In addition, legions of well-connected tycoons who have been granted government concessions, licenses, and contracts are expected to donate generously to UMNO's coffers. Money politics was considered to be even more rampant in UMNO's internal party elections since these contests are the ones that determine the country's future political leadership. But this may no longer be accurate on account of a sensational scandal that erupted in 2015. It is alleged that Najib Tun Razak, the prime minister, used as much as US$700 million from a government investment fund named 1 Malaysia Development Berhad to ensure BN's victory in the 2013 elections (*BBC News* 2016).

As in Singapore, the Electoral Office comes under the auspices of the office of the Prime Minister. Because of the BN's dominance in parliament, which typically has seen it possess at least the two-thirds majority needed to amend the constitution (although currently its majority is below the threshold due to some recent opposition gains), debates over reforming the electoral system lose traction quickly; reforms are still unlikely even with the 1 Malaysia Development Berhad fiasco. The firm grip the powers-that-be have over the electoral process is further strengthened by restrictions on the freedom of press, speech, and assembly. Opponents (or critics) who authorities deem to have stepped out of line will be jailed under the provisions of draconian laws rather than being sued as happens in Singapore. Manipulation of vote tabulation is rare but manipulation of voter rolls that allow for "ghost voters" is extensive (Wong et al. 2010).

On the other hand, electoral-related intimidation and violence is rare, and has not occurred since the gruesome riots that followed the May 1969 elections, as is direct vote buying. Even the main opposition parties, the People's Justice Party, the Pan-Islamic Party, and the Chinese-oriented Democratic Action Party, are well-rooted in society. Significantly, Malaysians exhibit fair levels of party identification and accord the country's less-than-democratic elections with a sizeable degree of legitimacy (Weiss 2015).

South Korea

Following democratisation in the late 1980s, South Korea has seen periodic high-profile scandals involving money and elections but a remarkably low level of persistent minor electoral corruption. A series of corruption episodes shook South Korean politics in the mid-1990s. Two former presidents were put on trial for abuses of office and there were investigations into illicit financial support from big business. Yet, the local-level forms of electioneering seen elsewhere in the region are difficult to find in democratic South Korea. There are almost no reports of violence surrounding election campaigning or voting. While it is understood that candidates offer small sums to voters in some rural districts, vote buying scarcely features in Korean politics.

Several institutions govern the operation of elections and participation. These include an election law with a long list of campaign restrictions, a law on parties, constitutional rules on establishing and cancelling parties, and an election commission. Each of these institutions was founded well before the country's democratisation. Rigidities in the laws on parties and campaigning can favour politicians associated with the major parties. Indeed, the laws were written in a Cold War context with precisely this goal in mind. By forcing parties to divulge information at registration and by limiting opportunities for candidates to contact voters, these laws were intended to weaken any organization representing socialist or labour forces. After democratisation, lawmakers have chosen to leave the bulk of these laws intact and even in some cases to further restrict political activities in ways that harm independent candidates and minor parties (Sŏ 2013). An example is the 2004 abolition of local-level party offices.

These restrictions have recently raised concerns that elections are not only skewed to the major parties but that elections are not as free as they once seemed to be. In 2013, the president ordered a minor party's registration to be cancelled, invoking a clause in the constitution for the first time, and in 2014 the constitutional court upheld the law. Restrictions on political speech in the months before an election have also drawn criticism. Defamation suits are increasingly used, especially by office-holders, to weaken rivals (Haggard and You 2015). Blatant government intervention is now known to have occurred in the 2012 presidential election. The intelligence agency took the lead in organizing an attempt to tarnish the reputation of the rival of the eventual winner, Park Geun-hye.

Tight electoral regulations have been maintained or made more rigid in the name of fighting electoral corruption. Lawmakers and court decisions have repeatedly cited the dangers of over-spending in campaigns and of allowing candidates to have excessive contact with voters. While these concerns may have some justification, the effort to separate politicians and voters also conveniently works to benefit the most influential sets of politicians. Independent candidates, local politicians, and members of minor parties find themselves disadvantaged by rules that make it difficult for them to build support bases.

Singapore

Elections in Singapore have never deposed the ruling People's Action Party (PAP). The party today relies mostly on institutionalised means to maintain its dominance. In other words, the party need not break electoral rules because it can use legal methods for gaining an advantage. These methods include a variety of techniques that limit the political sphere. Some relate to restrictions on political speech. Threats of defamation suits can stifle critical views. The media environment makes it difficult for alternative voices to be heard. This end is accomplished not so much through outright censorship but through the licensing regime and the recruitment of ambitious people into the official news agencies (George 2012).

Electoral rules advantage the PAP as well (K.P. Tan 2011; N. Tan 2013). Single-member districts mean that there is very little proportionality in representation. Group Representation Constituencies in which teams of candidates win or lose together favour a big party. In the 2011 general election, the ruling party won sixty per cent of the popular vote and eighty-one of eighty-seven seats. In 2015, a 69 per cent vote share translated into eighty-three of eighty-nine seats. As in other parliamentary systems, the government announces elections. In a context where opportunities are limited for non-incumbent politicians to gain public exposure, this procedure allows the ruling party to gain a massive advantage in preparing well in advance of an election.

Electoral regulation in Singapore is not separated from political power. The Election Department reports to the Prime Minister's office. The government also redraws districts in preparation for an election. Observers note that much of the redistricting focuses on areas where opposition figures have made inroads.

A similarity can be found between Singapore and South Korea in the ways elites describe how elections should run. Singapore's rulers stress the importance of clean, orderly elections.

If campaigning is allowed to produce too much mobilisation, the logic runs, politics could become chaotic and electoral results might be dubious. This argument justifies short campaign periods of nine days and detailed regulation of campaign events. The PAP, of course, does not need campaigns in order to win. Its reputation as the governing party gives voters what they need to know. For other candidates, who have no such way of making themselves known, restrictions on campaigning are damaging. Although Singapore's political system hardly meets the expectations of a liberal democracy, the techniques of regulating elections share something in common with what is found in South Korea.

These countries do, however, have many differences. South Korea is understood to be far more liberal than Malaysia or Singapore. Electoral outcomes are not known in advance and there has been turnover in office. Ruling elites have clung to power in the Southeast Asian countries but techniques of control differ. There is greater open contestation in Malaysia and general elections can be intense affairs. In Singapore, by contrast, there are few open debates. Yet in each of these places leaders have turned away from illicit inducements to voters in order to remain in power. Instead, they rely more on institutional frameworks.

Category 2: rule breaking

Japan

The operation of elections in Japan might be thought to be similar to Category 1 countries, such as South Korea. After all, the architects of South Korea's restrictions on campaigning also drew on the Japanese example. Japan's election law features myriad restrictions on political speech. At the same time, however, there are elements of voter mobilisation that stand in sharp contrast to a reliance on electoral laws that separate citizens and candidates. The Liberal Democratic Party (LDP), which has dominated politics since the mid-1950s, was long run as an alliance of factions. These factions were formally separate and their leaders competed within the party for influence. Patronage norms informed factional operation. Patron–client networks stretched from the pinnacle of power down to grassroots supporters. The electoral system encouraged such networks. Japan's lower house until 1994 had multi-member districts, which meant that candidates needed to develop their own networks for mobilising support. The success of clientelist strategies, especially in rural places, created a situation where "[v]oters are manipulated by local social elites and machines so they will vote for conservative party nominees" (Richardson 1997: 3).

The most notorious institution of patronage has been the *koenkai* or support association. Each individual candidate has such an association. These associations raise funds and connect candidates to large numbers of voters. While candidates may be affiliated with a party, *koenkai* operate independently of party organization. *Koenkai* make election campaigning more personal. Candidates, even those with the LDP, cannot rely on party funding or the party name to win seats. Instead, they must use their own organizational resources to bring out votes. This effect was compounded, at least until the 1994 electoral reforms, by the single, non-transferable vote system in which a party would nominate multiple candidates who might compete against each other. For this and other reasons, "the LDP was one of the most decentralized major parties in the world" (Krauss and Pekkanen 2011: 279).

The development of personal electoral machines can be tied to practices that might from a legal perspective be deemed corrupt (see Ch. 5). An example is that of Tanaka, a former prime minister and long-time heavyweight in the LDP. He built his career on funneling resources to his backwater district. Lucrative deals with developers helped facilitate his pork-barrel politics. Grateful for his assistance, voters in his district repeatedly returned Tanaka to office, even when he gained a national reputation for his shady manoeuvres and after his conviction for taking funds in the Lockheed scandal (Schlessinger 1999). A national poll later found that Japan's most scandalous prime minister was also deemed its most effective (Bowen 2003: 5–6).

The personalisation of electoral mobilisation in Japan sets it apart from what can be found in either South Korea or Taiwan. In South Korea, leading politicians have depended more on the legal status of their parties and on party names to dominate. In Taiwan, the relationship between party organization and local agents has been more complicated with candidates depending more on one or the other at different times. In Japan, however, local systems of support had enduring significance for the perpetuation of a political elite. To maintain this support, politicians focused their energy on activities that can spill into concrete, specific inducements to voters. These patterns were clearest before the shift away from multi-member districts in 1994.

The Philippines

The Americans introduced limited-suffrage elections in the early twentieth century. With the granting of commonwealth status and then independence, elections obtained even more significance, particularly as a means to distribute spoils to supporters and clan or family members. A two-party presidential system was devised although party switching between the Liberals and Nacionalistas was commonplace. Party elites originated from similar backgrounds and little separated the two parties ideologically. Prior to Ferdinand Marcos's 1972 suspension of electoral democracy under Martial Law, fiercely contested elections were marred by violence, intimidation, vote buying, and vote padding.

The evolution of electoral politics following its reintroduction after Marcos was overthrown by a People Power Revolution in 1986 has puzzled observers. Most notably, a two-party system failed to reemerge. In its stead, a weak, highly personalistic, multi-party system emerged with frontrunners often forming new parties as their own electoral vehicles. Changes to electoral rules upon the return to democracy were instrumental. For instance, a single presidential term limit of six years has discouraged party building because the urgency to do so is lessened as the incumbent is unable to run for a second term. Another post-Marcos reform was the introduction of a party-list system, which was designed to provide marginalised social groups with parliamentary representation. But it took more than a decade for the party-list system to be instituted. Since then, it has been captured in part by regular politicians who were not returned to Congress. Equally important, since the immediate post-Marcos period some thirty years ago, there has been little debate on major reforms to the electoral process because party elites have essentially stifled such discussions (Hicken 2015).

Continuities with the pre-Marcos era are evident. One is the lack of ideological differentiation among parties (with the Communists boycotting elections and the Catholic Church abstaining from electoral politics). Another characteristic, similar to Thailand, is pervasive pork-barreling. Not only do politicians display their pictures on the projects they fund (although that practice is now prohibited by law), but the eruption in 2014 of one of the largest political scandals to hit the country displayed its true detriment when it was learned that scores of Congress members had established bogus non-governmental organizations through which to channel pork-barrel benefits for their constituencies. Similar to Thailand, local bossism is rampant in the poor countryside, characterised by accusations of direct vote buying, vote canvassing, intimidation, coercion, and vote tampering (Teehankee 2013).

But more egregiously than Thailand has been the use of overt violence, such as the killings of journalists who openly criticise local power holders or the murder of opposition candidates (Aguilar et al. 2014). The most graphic illustration was the massacre in broad daylight of some nearly sixty opposition supporters, women, children, and journalists in 2009 in Maguindanao on the island of Mindanao. The slaughter was perpetrated by a local clan who were political supporters of then-President Gloria Macapagal Arroyo. Arroyo herself had been embroiled in a poll-fixing scandal which helped to swing the 2004 elections, although she out-manoeuvred her parliamentary opposition by nipping impeachment proceedings in the bud. Some scholars call for the deeper institutionalisation of the country's party system as a means of combatting the corruption and pork emblematic of electoral politics in the Philippines.

In Japan, we do not see the blatant elections-related violence that flares up periodically in the Philippines. Still, in both places, one finds a personalisation of electoral mobilisation. In neither place has party building taken the expected form. Japan's LDP is a powerful electoral force but it is more of an umbrella organization that holds together separate factions.

Category 3: mixed forms

Indonesia

Contestation over electoral outcomes and electoral management has figured prominently in Indonesia's democratisation following the forced resignation of its long-time authoritarian ruler, Soeharto, in May 1998. A revamp of the electoral laws was hotly negotiated among technocrats and parliamentarians. The 1999 foundational elections were contested by nearly fifty parties, which was seen as an advance in political freedom. In these elections, the president and heads of local government (provinces, cities, and districts) were still indirectly elected via parliament. Since then, Indonesia's electoral system has undergone constant reform. Electoral thresholds, for example, were introduced to help produce more stable governments, according to some, or to favour large, established parties, according to others. Extensive corruption surrounding the local parliamentary elections of regional executives demanded attention. So, in 2004, direct elections of executives were introduced, designed to lessen corruption because expanded electorates would be too expensive to bribe (Horowitz 2013: 129, 171). In large part, corruption has remained prevalent; it has just changed forms. The distribution of cash to voters is common in local and national elections although voter intimidation and coercion do not appear to be widespread. Indonesia lacks a hegemonic party like that of Singapore and Malaysia, but the established parties have at times collaborated to advance their collective interests. In the nomination process, as an illustration, mainstream parties have ensured the prohibition of independent candidates. In this way, parties are not excluded from the widespread distribution of spoils and patronage as a result of electoral success. This explains why the winner of the 2014 presidential election, Joko "Jokowi" Widowo, was forced to join an established party, a procedural necessity but one that has nevertheless tarnished his reformist credentials. But parties have suffered setbacks, too. Notably, in 2008, the Constitutional Court declared closed party lists unconstitutional. The open lists have loosened party elite control over their candidates. As a result, this has interjected more individual-oriented candidacies into parliamentary campaigns.

Indonesia's Electoral Commission is an independent body but not free of scandals. Some corruption has pertained to the procurement of electoral-related supplies but this has had limited impact on outcomes of national elections. Technical miscues persist as does the lack of public funding. At the local level, however, corruption appears to be more damaging. In 2013, news broke that a number of judges of the post-Soeharto Constitutional Court had accepted bribes in cases concerning disputes over local electoral outcomes. The revelation was a blow to Indonesia's electoral democracy. That said, Indonesia has held more than a thousand local elections since Soeharto's 1998 forced ouster, the majority of which have been reasonably free and fair and violence free, notwithstanding vote buying and the evident distribution of post-electoral patronage to campaign donors. While there have been a few dozen incidents where local electoral commission offices were stoned or set alight by partisans, there has been a tendency to overstate the impact of these events. Some conservative national elites have sought to exploit the supposed deficiencies of local elections to re-introduce indirect executive elections. Indonesia's rather active civil society thus far has successfully prevented such a rollback of the country's democracy (Aspinall et al. 2015).

Thailand

Vote buying, the prominence of vote canvassers, and the pork-barreling of post-electoral projects are as much a part of Thailand's elections as the mal-proportionment and gerrymandering of Malaysia's elections. For most of the twentieth century, Thailand's political parties have been self-serving and weakly rooted in society, which in part explains the ease with which the army has been able to interfere in the country's politics extra-constitutionally, most notoriously via coups. Targeted incidents of electoral-related violence in rural Thailand among rivals of so-called godfathers in the 1970s and 1980s signified the increased significance with which local elites accorded elections (Anderson 1990). The practice of rural dwellers selling their votes has been pervasive and has sparked a spirited debate over the degree to which this practice constitutes a form of electoral corruption. Despite the vote buying, which is often mediated by canvassers who are paid to deliver blocks of votes, there is also a tangible norm of local performance legitimacy to which citizens hold local representatives accountable. If their representative does not deliver on the selected or particularistic good, even if it is in the form of a paved road or school, locals have no compunction to sell their votes to another candidate in the subsequent election (Callahan 2005).

A majority of Thais still live outside cities, and as these so-called rural ruffians began to hold sway in parliament, the Bangkok-based elite and influential segments of the middle class sought to revamp the system. Such reforms were enacted through constitutional amendments passed in 1997; the rarity of sweeping electoral reforms in the country lent them their notoriety. Under the guise of improving the country's democracy, reforms included increased access to information and the establishment of an anti-corruption court and an independent electoral commission. Reformists measures also sought to improve the quality of parliament's representatives, moves that many interpreted as an attempt to undercut the rural-based parties. Holding a bachelor's degree was now required to become a member of parliament and an upper chamber or senate was established, designed to be non-partisan or "above politics". Bachelor's degrees were subsequently purchased and the senate became known as a den of politician's wives and families. With Thaksin Shinawatra's dramatic rise to power following the 1997–1998 Asian Financial Crisis and his strategic promotion of such populist policies as free healthcare, monarchial and other conservative elites, including the army, grew worried. One coup was not enough; Thaksin-related parties in different guises continued their electoral dominance (Chachavalpongpun 2014). Against the backdrop of days of street violence between Thaksin's supporters (red shirts) and conservative supporters (yellow shirts) and the 2011 electoral victory of Thaksin's sister, Yingluck, the army stepped in once again and toppled her administration in 2014. It remains to be seen how temporary this setback will be to Thailand's electoral democracy but the army seems intent on rewriting the rules of the game to an extent that when elections are eventually reintroduced, the resulting restrictions on freedoms, rights, and the electoral system will, at least on paper, invoke more of the Singaporean variety than that of pre-2014 coup Thailand.

Taiwan

In Taiwan, there are aspirations to attain the regulated political atmosphere of South Korea or Singapore. As in South Korea, there is a law governing political parties. Regulations on campaigning are, at least formally, also detailed. However, the institutions governing elections in Taiwan have passed through an evolutionary path distinct from South Korea's despite both regimes apparently following parallel processes of democratisation. The Kuomintang (KMT) did not permit elections for national office but it did institute island-wide local elections in 1950. Taiwan's rulers also imposed rigid campaign laws. During the 1980s, the regime began to liberalise the laws with an eye to combatting vote buying specifically rather than limiting speech. This course of reform followed other gradual liberalisations in the same period, including a relaxing of limits on party organizing and the holding of elections for offices at higher levels.

Legacies of local-level electoral mobilisation have been important in post-transition Taiwan. The republic maintained local elections at the township and county levels from the early 1950s. These elections had been highly mobilising affairs. Local posts could be lucrative and candidates invested financial and social resources in contesting them. The ruling KMT became dependent on alliances with sets of local business bosses, called "local factions", to win these local elections (Rigger 1999). In the 1990s, this situation put the party in a bind. The opposition Democratic Progressive Party and the open media atmosphere of the 1990s forced the party to condemn vote buying and underworld influence in politics (Gobel 2004). However, to win elections, the party needed to work with these allies to make the electoral machinery operate. The problem of "black-gold politics", or cooperation between underworld elements and politics, was a major theme of the 1990s.

Lucien Pye (1997) has argued that corruption paradoxically advanced democratisation in Taiwan since it forced corrupt officials to confront an angry public. The KMT gradually overcame its dilemma. Depoliticisation of the judiciary made the KMT less able to control agents (Wu and Huang 2004). Electoral competition forced the party to mobilise voters more through mass appeals to social interests rather than through local, clientelist organization. The opposition had earlier wooed some local factions away from the KMT, but the Democratic Progressive Party never truly gained its own local clients (Wang 2006: 36). By the 2000s, elections had become much more civil affairs than they once were.

Election campaigns still involve local mobilisation on a significant scale. There is debate over whether the tactics of mobilisation are the side effects of giving representation to communities or simply corrupt practices. The distribution of small sums to voters is illegal and might be called vote buying (although it is unclear whether such inducements encourage voting in a particular way or just increase turnout). Others point out that mobilisation of voters through meaningful networks, such as clan or temple groups, comes with the cultural requirement of giving a token gift when campaigning. These local bosses inhabit a contested space, viewed by their supporters as legitimate representatives but by the legal regime as agents of corruption.

In each of these places, we see politicians both continuing to break electoral rules while also setting in place new rules that benefit the rule makers. Indonesia's regulations on parties and Thailand's constitutional criteria for standing for office resonate with the forms of electioneering that Reilly's work brings into the spotlight. Taiwan has a state that is more effective at enforcing rules, but it also has a history of intense local electoral mobilisation. Laws made in the name of fighting corruption directly serve political purposes.

Conclusion

This discussion challenges suggestions that electoral corruption simply declines with increases in income. We have pointed to similarities among countries at different income levels. Moreover, we have noted that in several places politics centres more on rule making than on rule breaking. In contrast to a modernisation theory-inspired view that personal mobilisation eventually gives way to its programmatic counterpart (Scott 1969), we observe that the use of rules can often supplant the breaking of rules as an elite strategy for perpetuating power. We caution against associating electoral corruption with low-income contexts and "clean" politics with high-income places. To say that corruption is less in a particular place can be to overlook the ways that elites deliberately design electoral frameworks so that they need not engage in corrupt behaviour. Whether such designs are good for democratic competition is a separate matter.

Note

1 We acknowledge Hutchcroft's (2014) imaginative grouping of these two countries (along with Thailand) in the context of how patronage and clientelism shapes governance patterns over the extent of each of these state's territories.

References

Aguilar, F.V. Jr., M. P. Meynardo and A.L.K. Candelaria (2014) "Keeping the state at bay: the killing of journalists in the Philippines, 1998–2012", *Critical Asian Studies*, 46(4): 649–77.
Anderson, B. (1990) "Murder and progress in modern Siam", *New Left Review*, 181: 33–48.
Aspinall, E., M. Mietzner and D. Tomsa (2015) "The moderating president: Yudhoyono's decade in power", in E. Aspinall, M. Mietzner and D. Tomsa (eds.) *The Yudhoyono presidency: Indonesia's decade of stability and stagnation*, Singapore: Institute of Southeast Asian Studies, 1–22.
Bardhan, P. (1997) "Corruption and development: a review of issues", Journal *of Economic Literature*, 35(3): 1320–46.
BBC News (2016) "1MDB: the case that has riveted Malaysia", 26 January, http://www.bbc.com/news/world-asia-33447456 (accessed 27 January 2016).
Birch, S. (2011) *Electoral malpractice*, Oxford: Oxford University Press.
Booth, A. (1999) "Initial conditions and miraculous growth: why is South East Asia different from Taiwan and South Korea?" *World Development*, 27(2): 301–21.
Bowen, R.W. (2003) *Japan's dysfunctional democracy: the Liberal Democratic Party and structural corruption*, Armonk, NY: M.E. Sharpe.
Callahan, W. A. (2005) "Social capital and corruption: vote buying and the politics of reform in Thailand", *Perspectives on Politics*, 3(3): 495–508.
Carey, J. M. and M. S. Shugart (1994) "Incentives to cultivate a personal vote: a rank ordering of electoral formulas", *Electoral Studies*, 14(4): 417–39.
Chachavalpongpun, P. (2014) "'Good coup' gone bad: Thailand's development since Thaksin's downfall", in P. Chachavalpongpun (ed.) *"Good coup" gone bad: Thailand's development since Thaksin's downfall*, Singapore: Institute of Southeast Asian Studies, 3–16.

Chang, E.C.C. and M.A. Golden (2007) "Electoral systems, district magnitude and corruption", *British Journal of Political Science*, 37(1): 115–137.

Choi, J. (2012) *Votes, party systems and democracy in Asia*, London: Routledge.

Croissant, A. and P. Völkel (2012) "Party system types and party system institutionalization: comparing new democracies in East and Southeast Asia", *Party Politics*, 18(2): 235–65.

Doner, R. F., B.K. Ritchie and D. Slater (2005) "Systemic vulnerability and the origins of developmental states: Northeast and Southeast Asia in comparative perspective", *International Organization*, 59(2): 327–61.

George, C. (2012) *Freedom from the press: journalism and state power in Singapore*, Singapore: National University of Singapore Press.

Gobel, C. (2004) "Beheading the hydra: combating political corruption and organised crime", *China Perspectives*, 56: 14–25.

Gomez, E. T. (2012) "Monetizing politics: financing parties and elections in Malaysia", *Modern Asian Studies*, 46(5): 1370–97.

Gundlach, E. and M. Paldam (2009) "The transition of corruption: from poverty to honesty", *Economics Letters*, 103(3): 146–48.

Haggard, S. (1990), *Pathways from the periphery: the politics of growth in newly industrialised countries*, Ithaca: Cornell University Press.

Haggard, S. and J. You (2015) "Freedom of expression in South Korea", *Journal of Contemporary Asia*, 45(1): 167–79.

Hicken, A. (2015) "Party and party system institutionalization in the Philippines", in A. Hicken and E. M. Kuhonta (eds.), *Party system institutionalization in Asia: democracies, autocracies, and the shadows of the past*, Cambridge: Cambridge University Press, 307–327.

Hicken, A. and E. M. Kuhonta (2015) "Introduction: rethinking party system institutionalization in Asia", in A. Hicken and E. M. Kuhonta (eds.) *Party system institutionalization in Asia: democracies, autocracies, and the shadows of the past*, Cambridge: Cambridge University Press, 1–24.

Horowitz, D. L. (2013) *Constitutional change and democracy in Indonesia*, Cambridge: Cambridge University Press.

Hutchcroft, P. (2014) "Linking capital and countryside: patronage and clientelism in Japan, Thailand, and the Philippines", in D.A. Brun and L. Diamond (eds.) *Clientelism, social policy and the quality of democracy*, Baltimore: Johns Hopkins University Press, 174–203.

Kang, D. C. (2002) *Crony capitalism: corruption and development in South Korea and the Philippines*, Cambridge: Cambridge University Press.

Krauss, E.S. and R.J. Pekkanen (2011) *The rise and fall of Japan's LDP: political party organizations as historical institutions*, Ithaca, NY: Cornell University Press.

Kunicová, J. and S. Rose-Ackerman (2005) "Electoral rules and constitutional structures as constraints on corruption", *British Journal of Political Science*, 35(4): 573–606.

Lambsdorff, J. G. (2007) *The institutional economics of corruption and reform: theory, evidence and policy*, Cambridge: Cambridge University Press.

Norris, P. (2013) "The new research agenda studying electoral integrity", *Electoral Studies*, 32(4): 563–75.

Pye, L. W. (1997) "Money politics and transitions to democracy in East Asia", *Asian Survey*, 37(3): 213–28.

Ramirez, C.D. (2014) "Is corruption in China 'out of control'? A comparison with the U.S. in historical perspective", *Journal of Comparative Economics*, 42(1): 76–91.

Reilly, B. (2006) *Democracy and diversity: political engineering in the Asia-Pacific*, Oxford: Oxford University Press.

Reilly B. (2007) "Democratization and electoral reform in the Asia-Pacific Region. Is there an 'Asian model' of democracy?" *Comparative Political Studies*, 40(11): 1350–71.

Richardson, B. (1997) *Japanese democracy: power, coordination, and performance*, New Haven: Yale University Press.

Rigger, S. (1999) *Politics in Taiwan: voting for democracy*, New York: Routledge.

Schlessinger, J.M. (1999) *Shadow shoguns: the rise and fall of Japan's postwar political machine*, New York: Simon and Schuster.

Schaffer, F.C. (2008) *The hidden costs of clean election reform*, Ithaca: Cornell University Press.

Scott, J. C. (1969) "Corruption, machine politics and political change", *American Political Science Review*, 63(4): 1142–58.

Sŏ P. (2013) "Chehanjŏk kyŏngjaeng ŭi chedohwa: 1958-yŏn sŏn'gŏpŏp ch'eje" (The institutionalization of limited competition: the system of the 1958 election law), *Sŏn'gŏ yŏn'gu* (Electoral studies), 3: 109–38.

Tan, K.P. (2011) "The People's Action Party and political liberalization in Singapore", in L.F. Lye and W. Hofmeister (eds.), *Political parties, party systems, and democratization in East Asia*, Singapore: World Scientific, 107–132.

Tan, N. (2013) "Manipulating electoral laws in Singapore", *Electoral Studies*, 32(4): 632–43.

Teehankee, J.C. (2013) "Clientelism and party politics in the Philippines", in D. Tomsa and A. Ufen (eds.) *Party politics in Southeast Asia: clientelism and electoral competition in Indonesia, Thailand and the Philippines*, London: Routledge, 186–214.

Thompson, M. R. (1996) "Late industrialisers and late democratisers: developmental states in the Asia-Pacific", *Third World Quarterly*, 17(4): 625–47.

Walecki, M. (2004) *Political money and corruption*, IFES Political Finance White Paper Series, http://www.legislationline.org/topics/topic/16 (accessed 16 November 2015).

Wang, J. (2006) "Taiwan shicongzhuyi shidai de jieshu" (The end of the clientelist period in Taiwan), *Dangdai* (Contemporary), 227: 26–37.

Weiss, M. L. (2015) "The antidemocratic potential of party institutionalization: Malaysia as a morality tale?" in A. Hicken and E. M. Kuhonta (eds.) *Party system institutionalization in Asia: democracies, autocracies, and the shadows of the past*, Cambridge: Cambridge University Press, 25–48.

Wong, C.H., J. Chin and N. Othman (2010) "Malaysia - towards a topology of an electoral one-party state", *Democratization*, 17(5): 920–949.

Wu, C.-L. and C. Huang (2004) "Politics and judiciary verdicts on vote-buying litigation in Taiwan", *Asian Survey*, 44(5): 755–70.

You, J.S. (2015) *Democracy, inequality and corruption: Korea, Taiwan and the Philippines compared*, Cambridge: Cambridge University Press.

PART II

Corruption and economic development

7

CORRUPTION IN ASIA

Trust and Economic development[1]

Susan Rose-Ackerman

Corruption frequently surfaces in Asia, as it does throughout the world. Sometimes the existence of bribes, kickbacks, and official self-dealing is clear cut. In other cases the information is circumstantial. A scandal arises that could have been the result of official negligence or incompetence but the scale of the violation often suggests that illicit *quid pro quo*s were present. Behaviour that arises from the long-term buildup of patronage, connections, and cronyism can form the background conditions within which the search for private gain substitutes for the public interest. In the extreme, state agencies or even whole governments may be "taken over" by self-seeking networks that milk the institutions for private gain.

If innocent people are injured and killed or are unfairly excluded from public benefits, corruption has serious social costs. Even if kickbacks allocate public contracts to firms that actually perform, the result is increased budgetary costs and an inappropriate choice of the quantity and quality of infrastructure and of public goods and services. Payoffs are not just a way for individuals and businesses to pay for services that they deserve or to induce officials to work hard. Even if payoffs benefit businesses by reducing taxes and tariffs and limiting regulatory burdens, the state loses needed revenue and the costs fall on workers, customers and ordinary citizens, and on honest businesses that cannot compete.

To illustrate, consider a few recent scandals in Asia. In some cases, overt evidence of payoffs has not (yet) surfaced, but a description of the situation strongly suggests illicit private gains fueled by payoffs. In August 2015, hazardous chemicals exploded at a storage site in Tianjin, China. The explosion reportedly killed an estimated 150 people and injured more than 750. *The New York Times*, using a term that often signals corruption, wrote that the "company exploited weak governance in one of the party's showcase economic districts and used political connections to shield its operations from scrutiny" (Jacobs et al. 2015). Observers noted the collaboration of business and corrupt officials that was fueled by the Communist Party's emphasis on economic growth, which tied career advancement to economic success. In other words, neither the government in Tianjin nor the Party had an incentive to provide strong oversight of the regulatory lapses in Tianjin. In addition, the firm's owners had close personal ties to high officials in the police and fire departments. A safety management report was issued by a firm described by some as a "red hat intermediary", that is, a firm set up by officials to extract payments from businesses (Jacobs et al. 2015). Thus, we see a complex and institutionalised system of interpersonal ties where health and safety regulations existed but were effectively neutralised.

Overall, Chinese firms whose top executives are politically connected had worker death rates that were up to five times the rates in firms without such connections (Fisman and Wang 2015: 89). In response, China has imposed worker "death ceilings" that affect officials' career prospects, and some localities followed up with their own programmes (Fisman 2015). Apparently, Tianjin was not one of those localities. The web of connections needed to maintain the system of mutual favour-giving depended on trust to support self-interested dealings. The ties of friendship and family linkages may well be genuine, but they are used in ways that undermine the public interest.

Corruption often subverts the legal rules of the game. One's view of such payoffs depends upon the social value of the public programmes. Those who condemn the proliferation of rules by calling them "red tape" are often tolerant of bribes paid to smooth bureaucratic approvals. In contrast, if the rules serve beneficial functions, as do many health and safety and environmental rules, bribery distorts government goals. Of course, even in the former case of red tape, the first and best option is to remove some rules and streamline others, and for the latter, programmatic reforms can lead to more effective regulation. If corruption determines benefits and costs, the public programme will favour the well-off and the unscrupulous. A similar problem arises in public benefit programmes that aim to help the poor, an increasingly common form of assistance (Ravallion 2013). Bribes may speed up the approval process but open the way for the well-off and the unqualified to obtain public benefits, undermining programme goals, lowering quality, and increasing the cost per qualified beneficiary. Thus, in India, one study found that ration cards designed for the poor were routinely obtained by unqualified households of higher income, suggesting corruption (*The Economist* 2015). In response, biometric data are being used in some Indian programmes to combat fraud and corruption. Similarly, Indonesia has proposed mobile payment systems using SIM cards (Gelb and Decker 2012). In Lahore, Pakistan, a mosquito eradication programme was plagued by corruption; workers resold the insecticide rather than applying it as required or demanded bribes from residents. The response was to give city workers smart phones so that they could take before and after shots of their work to be posted on-line. The increased monitoring not only reduced corruption, it also increased productivity. Another effort involved random calls to users of public services to report on their interactions with public servants (*The Economist* 2013a). These innovative programmes suggest that corruption in the routine provisions of government services and the application of regulations can be controlled so long as malfeasance does not extend up the hierarchy. Such reforms, however, assume that there are honest supervisory officials seeking solutions. Unfortunately, that is not always the case.

In particular, corruption is a serious risk when the state contracts for infrastructure and awards concessions for natural resources. Natural resource concessions are an area of high risk. In Southeast Asia, timber concessions have been a particular locus of corruption. There are many examples of problematic deals. Logging firms and their bankers may claim to comply with sustainable logging principles but allegations of corruption repeatedly surface. Recently, for example, Global Witness documented the award of massive land concessions to Vietnamese firms in Cambodia and Laos in "opaque circumstances" for both rubber plantations and timber (Global Witness 2013; *The Economist* 2013b). In the aftermath of war, the legal situation was murky. The report suggests that payoffs were likely, but unclear property rights make proving malfeasance difficult. Property development rights can be similarly at risk of corruption, especially because there, too, property rights may be unclear. Thus, in India, a report linked "rent-seeking" in the property market in Mumbai to the existence of unclear and excessive rules. For example, a programme to allow taller buildings in return for constructing housing for the poor reportedly was "opaque and vulnerable to corruption" (Crabtree 2014).

Corruption is one way to reduce taxes and tariffs. The problem is not only vague laws but, in the extreme, state capture or takeover. Complex tax and customs laws can induce individuals and businesses to pay to get reduced rates on a one-off basis, but sometimes corruption can undermine the entire system of revenue collection. For example, in China, a powerful individual essentially took over the collection of tariffs in Xiamen in the 1990s. Wank (2009) describes what happened as the mastermind of the scheme, Lai Changxing, gradually built up a network of connections that eventually stretched to the top of the hierarchy. At its high point, Lai essentially created a parallel business that organised smuggling activities, including "hiring" officials as members of his firm. Wank describes the lavish gifts used to cement Lai's patronage empire. Often, they were not tied to an explicit *quid pro quo* but were part of a long-term business plan to control the port and gain illicit influence. The state's loss in revenue was huge.

These are simply a few examples, but they illustrate several common corrupt patterns. I want especially to highlight the role of trust as a necessary condition for long-term corrupt deals. Trust, which can support many positive aspects of state/society relations, here operates to keep a corrupt system in place based on patronage and clientelism, often facilitated by family and professional ties. Thus, I next consider the link between corruption and trust in Asia followed by a discussion of the chapters in this section.

Corruption, trust, and culture

Asian countries contain a wide diversity of cultures, ethnicities, income levels, and state structures. Market principles govern their economies to varying degrees, and state involvement in the economy and society varies. Some countries are competitive democracies, others are authoritarian, and still others are in the middle with periods of military rule. One key to understanding inter-state differences in the type and incidence of corruption is the level of trust in government officials and institutions. But we need to unpack the notion of trust (Rose-Ackerman 2001a, 2001b). Lack of trust in state institutions fuels corruption, and corruption, in turn, generates lack of trust in government in a vicious cycle. People, instead, rely on interpersonal trust between friends and family, but interpersonal trust can also fuel corruption as corrupt public officials provide services, sign contracts, and enforce the law. Corrupt dealings outside of the law may only be possible if the perpetrators trust each other not to turn each other in. Such trust may depend upon having a friend or relative inside the state bureaucracy or in a political position. Thus, trust is a two-edged sword.

Survey evidence indicates a wide range of levels of trust in government officials in Asia (Table 7.1). But what do these responses mean? When trust is high, do people trust government to be fair and impartial or do they trust it to favour their own interests? Does trust in government simply reflect the fact that most people's household income has grown in recent years? Does lack of trust reflect cynicism about government or does it signal a healthy scepticism about government and a willingness to hold officials to account? Finally, in some states, those surveyed may be reluctant to express their true opinions for fear that the survey is not actually anonymous.

Some believe that a high level of generalised trust in others translates into trust in public institutions. I am sceptical about this claim, and the Asian cases demonstrate that it is oversimplified. In Asia, there are three different relationships between generalised trust and trust

Table 7.1 Corruption and trust in national government in selected Asian countries

Country	1. Trust most people -%, ABS, Wave 2	2. Trust relatives "a great deal" or "a lot" -%, ABS, Wave 2	3. Trust neighbours "a great deal" or "a lot" -%, ABS, Wave 2	4. "Almost everyone" or "most national officials" are corrupt-%, ABS, Wave 2	5. "Almost everyone" or "most local government officials" are corrupt-%, ABS, Wave 2	6. Trust national gov. "a great deal" or "a lot", ABS, Wave 2	7. Trust in gov. officials -%, ABS, Wave 2	8. Trust national gov. "a great deal" or "a lot" -%, ABS, Wave 3	9. Trust in gov. officials -%, ABS, Wave 3	10. Confidence in national gov. a "great deal" or "a lot"-%, WVS, Wave 5	11. Reporting bribe payments for one of 8 services-%, TI, GCB, 2012–2013,	12. TI-CPI-2015[1]
East Asia												
China	61	77	36	14	48	95	61	97	44	94	N/A	37
Indonesia	8	92	78	49	39	68	78	61	72	56	36	36
Japan	31	88	74	44	42	23	41	12	41	31	1	75
Korea (S.)	33	88	74	48	43	15	22	23	27	46	3	56
Malaysia	5	78	67	45	43	74	74	78	75	75	3	50
Mongolia	11	50	54	75	47	58	89	36	87	N/A	45	39
Philippines	8	89	75	66	60	41	47	44	51	N/A	12	35
Singapore	30	91	78	2	N/A	91	85	88	78	N/A	N/A	85
Taiwan	34	86	74	67	66	39	23	36	20	32	36	62
Thailand	46	94	74	29	20	66	74	59	73	39	18	38
Vietnam	59	3	12	17	6	98	95	98	95	98	30	31
South Asia												
Bangladesh	N/A	N/A	N/A	N/A				N/A	N/A	N/A	39	25
India	N/A	N/A	N/A	N/A				N/A	N/A	N/A	54	38
Nepal	N/A	N/A	N/A	N/A				N/A	N/A	N/A	31	27
Pakistan	N/A	N/A	N/A	N/A				N/A	N/A	N/A	34	30
Sri Lanka	N/A	N/A	N/A	N/A				N/A	N/A	N/A	19	37

Sources: Columns 1 to 7: ABS, Wave 2 (2005 to 2008). Columns 8 and 9: ABS, Wave 3 (2010 to 2012). From more information about ABS, see: http://www.asianbarometer.org/data/data-release (accessed 12 April 2016). Column 10: WVS, Wave 5 (2005 to 2009), http://www.worldvaluessurvey.org/WVSOnline.jsp (accessed 11 April 2016). Column 11: Percentage of people who used a service and reported that they paid a bribe for at least one of eight benefits from public officials. Transparency International, Global corruption barometer, 2013, http://www.transparency.org/gcb2013/report (accessed 12 April 2016). Column 12: Data from the TI-CPI 2015, https://www.transparency.org/cpi2015/#results-table (accessed 12 April 2016).
Keys: n.a. = not available. WVS: World Values Survey, ABS: Asian Barometer Surveys, GCB: Global Corruption Barometer, TI-CPI: Transparency International Corruption Perceptions Index.
Notes: 1. The range is 1–100, with 100 being the best.

in institutions. At one extreme are one-party states with a socialist history and high levels of reported trust in the national government (China and Vietnam). In China and Vietnam, those surveyed by the Asian Barometer Survey (ABS) express both high levels of trust in public officials and relatively high levels of generalised trust (more than 50 per cent). However, the Vietnamese are especially distrustful of both family and neighbours compared to their Asian counterparts, at least in the 2005–2008 ABS findings. The rest of the countries surveyed expressed lower levels of generalised trust (from 5 per cent to 43 per cent). This group can be subdivided into two groups: countries listed by the ABS as liberal democracies and others that they categorise as electoral democracies. In the 2005–2008 survey, many citizens in the liberal democracies (Taiwan, Korea, Japan) distrusted the national government, with less than 40 per cent saying that they have "quite a lot" or a "great deal of trust" in the national government, reaching a low of 15 per cent for Korea. It is not clear what causal story one can tell based on this cross-country variability. At the very least, a simple claim that high interpersonal trust and democratic structures lead to more trusted states is not proven. Similarly, some countries express low levels of general trust in other people combined with high levels of trust in family and neighbours. Consider, in particular, the Philippines whose pattern is the reverse of Vietnam.

Adding corruption further complicates the picture. Global cross-country work suggests that income equality, low corruption, and generalised trust tend to go together (Rothstein and Uslaner 2005). However, in Asia the pattern is mixed. In some countries relatively strong performance on the Corruption Perceptions Index of Transparency International (CPI) goes along with citizens' quite low levels of trust in government officials and a belief that corruption is widespread (Japan, Taiwan, Korea). (Note that high scores on the CPI indicate low levels of corruption.) Singapore is the best performer in the region. Perhaps citizens' scepticism about public institutions in the Asian democracies helps keep corruption in check (Hardin 2002). However, if the state apparatus is, in fact, quite honest, this should promote trust, but that does not seem to be the result overall. Conversely, in China, household surveys reveal that the per cent who trust the government "a great deal" has fallen from 93 per cent to 51 per cent between 2001–2002 and 2010–2011 (Wang 2013). The surveyed individuals also reported that corruption was quite low, but the CPI, in contrast, gives poor scores to both countries (37 and 31 to China and Vietnam, respectively, of a possible 100). Furthermore, a survey in Vietnam found that 30 per cent reported paying at least one type of bribe, and in the ABS, 14.4 per cent of respondents identified corruption as the most important problem, much higher than in any other country. (Mongolia was a distant second at 7.8 per cent.) General trust in officials in the rest of the countries surveyed is quite high, but individuals also think that corruption is widespread. Omitting Singapore where corruption is minimal, about one third of those surveyed think that "almost everyone" or "most officials" at the national level are corrupt, ranging from 29 per cent in Thailand to 75 per cent in Mongolia.

In many countries, there are interesting differences in perceptions of corruption between local and national government officials. In China, the difference is particularly stark with perceptions of corruption much higher at the local level while trust is lower. In other countries, however, national officials are both distrusted and thought to be more corrupt. Here, Thailand and Mongolia stand out on both measures, and in Japan trust in the national government is very low.

These data are difficult to interpret. Perhaps they just indicate the difficulty of doing survey research. A cluster of highly corrupt countries, mostly in South and Southeast Asia, are a mixed bag in terms of the trust variables. One wonders if the relatively high levels of trust in some institutions are the result either of ignorance or of a belief that officials can be "trusted" to show favouritism, not impartial rule-bound behaviour.[2] Favouritism seems to be behind Sapio's (2009: 33) claim that Chinese officials gave untied gifts of cash to a newly transferred official to build up trust and "as paving the ground on which corruption or rent seeking may subsequently develop". The secrecy required for corruption can be better maintained if bonds of trust exist (Sapio 2009: 36). These complexities are a challenge to research that associates generalised inter-personal trust with trust in government and trust in government with a lack of corruption. That association does not hold as a general matter in Asia, and there are many anomalous cases outside Asia as well.

One explanation for the survey results is that citizens in some states have low expectations for government so that the survey responses indicate that they are pleasantly surprised by how well the state performs. This positive attitude may be strengthened by a country's good economic performance. If a country is growing rapidly, that fact may dominate concerns about official corruption. In stagnant economies, confidence in government is likely to suffer especially if the state is blamed for slow growth. Further, in a robust democracy citizens trust government only if it is reliable and conforms to the rules, and they are alert for evidence of waste and malfeasance. Broad cross-country studies cannot sort out these conflicting explanations, but we do have survey and experimental evidence that sheds light on some of the mechanisms at work.

Corruption combined with collectivist values could lead to satisfied insiders operating through reciprocal trust. The mass of outsiders and excluded businesses, however, could view the government as corrupt or unresponsive and, as a consequence, they would not trust the system to operate fairly (Chang and Chu 2006). In such cultures, surveys, such as those reported in Table 7.1, would show that generalised trust is relatively low at the same time as internal or in-group trust is high. For example, one study showed that societies based on close family ties (reciprocal affect-based trust) are particularly likely to experience lower levels of generalised inter-personal trust (Realo et al. 2008). There is a negative relationship between familism and interpersonal trust as measured by the World Values Survey (WVS) for the period of 1999 through 2002.

But does everyone understand the concept of "trust" in the same way in answering surveys? Delhey et al. (2011) compare types of trust across 51 countries based on the WVS from 2005 through 2009. They hypothesise that the overall trust question is interpreted differently in different countries and that in Asia many respondents include only friends, kin, and neighbours. The WVS responses unpacked the notion of trust into in-groups and out-groups. The authors calculate a "radius of trust" as the difference between the two trust values. Most Asian countries in the sample had relatively high overall levels of trust in "most people", and higher levels of in-group trust compared to out-group or general trust. An exception was Taiwan with both relatively low generalised trust and even lower levels of in-group trust. The authors argue that measures of generalised trust in the WVS may, in fact, weight in-group trust more highly than trust in the mass of others in society. The data on generalised trust in "most people" hence do not seem to measure the same phenomenon across the globe. Furthermore, in comparing the WVS data with that from the ABS and even across studies apparently drawing from the same data, further anomalies appear.

These data problems exacerbate the difficulty of tracing the link from in-group reciprocal trust, to generalised trust in other people, to trust in government reliability, to reductions in corruption. The worry is that if people depend on reciprocal trust within their in-group, they will seek to help their members achieve political power and economic advantage, as indicated in the cases from China outlined previously in this chapter. In return, they will expect to receive individual or group benefits. Outsiders, both inside and outside the country, will see a corrupt, patronage-based system based on the mutual exchange of favours that often look indistinguishable from bribes. Favoured insiders see in-group reciprocal trust and mutual support. However, in an ethnically homogeneous society almost everyone may feel like an insider so that perceptions of corruption are concentrated in the international business and investment community. Investors may be accused of cultural insensitivity, but in reality, in-group control limits overall investment and entrepreneurship opportunities. Consistent with this observation, one study of China found that ethnically heterogeneous provinces have higher levels of corruption than less diverse provinces (Dong and Torgler 2013). Although the difference was not large, it may result from the lower need to make arms-length payoffs when everyone is part of the same in-group.

Unfortunately, it is not clear exactly what mechanisms are at work. Are people simply prejudiced so that strong in-group affiliation reflects a belief in their group's inherent superiority? Does it matter if the out-group is poor and disadvantaged, such as lower caste individuals in India, or wealthy and economically dominant, such as the Chinese in parts of Southeast Asia (Chua 2003)? In strong collectivist cultures, does the in-group supply its members with needed services, resolve disputes and provide security that in other societies are provided by the state? If so, does that mean those in such groups do not need to trust either outsiders or state officials? Then the surveys measure not just attitudes but also state capacity. We do not know, but such analyses ought to be done to help sort out the underlying factors at work. Building on my distinction between generalised trust in others, reciprocal trust, and trust in the impartiality and fairness of institutions, research should study how citizens could maintain close trusting relations and also create a modern state that is trustworthy because it uses impartial, fair criteria, and not in-group connections, to allocate benefits.

A laboratory experiment using subjects from two Southeast Asian countries tried to get at some of these issues (Carpenter et al. 2004). The subjects all perceived themselves to be part of the same in-group. Using a game in which the individually rational response was not to cooperate, the researchers found high levels of cooperation, indicating high inter-personal trust. The authors argue that high levels of behavioural and associational social capital are the reason for high trust. However, although in one country both generalised trust in other people and trust in impartial institutions is high, in the other general trust is quite high but institutional trust is quite low. Corruption is reportedly high in both countries. Once again, we see the weak link between the individual interactions of those who trust or empathise with each other and trust in the reliability and impartiality of state institutions.

Perhaps education is one route to more competent, impartial and less corrupt government. A study using European data found a link between an individual's level of education and his or her trust in government mediated by the level of corruption (Hakhverdian and Mayne 2012). The more highly educated a person was, the less trust he or she placed in a corrupt government and, conversely, the more that person trusted an honest government. The result is consistent with the finding that in highly corrupt countries those with the least education trust government the most and vice versa in countries with little corruption. The basic idea is that, as overall levels of education improve, so will public demands for cleaner and more effective government. This seems a plausible hypothesis that is consistent with a view that citizens trust government only if it behaves in an impartial, transparent way. It would be contradicted, however, by a case where the state managed educational opportunities to prevent independent, critical thought and to make the elite dependent upon favours and patronage as a route to advanced training (Rose-Ackerman 2001b).

To understand corruption and its impact, one needs to understand citizens' relationships to each other and to the state. In Asia, strong in-group trust translates both to weak out-group trust and to a distrust of government officials who are thought to be corrupt. The exceptions are China, Vietnam and Singapore, at least judging by survey responses. Similarly, corruption can be high in states that otherwise have gained the trust of their citizens. This does not mean, however, that corruption is benign. Perhaps payoffs and cronyism favour some over others and the disadvantaged are not willing to speak up. Perhaps trust is genuine but ill-informed or built on a history of deference to authority. We need a deeper understanding of what it means to trust other individuals and to trust institutions and to connect expressions of trust with the actual performance of public and private institutions in furthering public values and operating without corrupt self-dealing.

Given the uneasy relationship between trust, corruption, and government performance, the implications for anti-corruption policy are complex. Any explanation that relies on culture, such as observations of in-group solidarity and generalised trust, is a challenge to policymakers. If culture is deep and immutable, policy can only operate at the margins. Furthermore, if what others call corruption is acceptable to most citizens and is understood as a valid cultural practice, reform is not plausible. The rest of the world needs to accept as given these cultural practices and decide whether or not to engage with societies where they are prevalent. For those convinced of the long-run negative impact of corruption in undermining economic growth, human flourishing, and government legitimacy, that is a discouraging result.

In practice, however, so-called cultural attitudes need not be immutable and changed circumstances can lead to changed practices. If traditionally powerful in-groups are challenged by democratic and popular pressures, entrenched systems can change. If old practices are dysfunctional under more modern conditions, demonstrating that fact can plausibly change both attitudes and behaviour. Changes in the fundamental conditions of political and social life can change behaviour in ways that increase or decrease corruption and trust in the state. For example, in Indonesia, trust in government grew in the first decade of the twenty-first century in spite of declines elsewhere. The explanation, according to one study, is government reform after the fall of Soeharto in 1998 aimed at reducing corruption and strengthening state institutions (Tjiptoherijanto and Rowen 2010). Similarly, in South Korea, successful reform in the tax system depended on institutional reform, not a major transformation in public values (Kim 2010). In other words, past distrust of state institutions turned into trust, not because of a change in culture but because of a change in state behaviour. One can argue, in fact, that the original high level of (justified) distrust was one of the motivations for the policy change. It will be important to study the present crackdown on corruption in China to see whether it translates into higher public perceptions of corruption or improved service provision and greater fairness in the allocation of public goods and services. After the crackdown on smuggling in Xiamen, the government collected much more revenue, but the prices of imports rose, many businesses shutdown, and those consuming the cheap imports suffered (Wank 2009: 83).

Corruption and economic development

Given the links between corruption, trust, and culture, what can one say about the connection between corruption and economic development? It is clear that if a high percentage of the benefits of public programmes are siphoned into the pockets of the few, be they top government officials or private business owners (domestic or foreign), then these programmes will provide few benefits to ordinary people. As many have claimed, such corruption is like an opaque tax that eats away at the value of public programmes. It can then result in the spread of corrupt payoffs throughout society as a reaction to the dysfunctional state. This has been the thrust of Jong-sung You's scholarship that focuses on corruption in Asia. His chapter for this volume builds on his book (You 2015) and on You and Khagram (2005), both of which begin with the high correlation between corruption and measures of inequality. You argues that a corrupt elite can capture a polity through payoffs that induce public officials to favour them and ignore the interests of the general public, maintaining and reinforcing inequality. The influence of private wealth may extend to the selection of bureaucrats who owe their jobs to patronage and engage in corruption to benefit their patrons as well as themselves. For You, the emphasis of anti-corruption policy should be less on the average growth rate of income and wealth and more on the way in which the gains are distributed. If one considers the position of those in the bottom tiers of the income distribution, an honest but slowly growing state may be superior to one that grows quickly but where the public and private elites benefit from corrupt gains. As he writes, "corruption is likely to increase inequality, and inequality may increase corruption" (see Ch. 8). He focuses on South Korea, Taiwan, and the Philippines and he claims that land reform in South Korea and Taiwan helped to undermine the power of the landed elite opening the way for economic growth that was widely shared. In contrast, no such reform occurred in the Philippines. This restrained growth and permitted the elite to retain power, in part, through corruption and patronage. In other words, inequality of wealth and income is the key factor with corruption arising as a result of this concentration of resources (see Blunt et al. 2012). Thus, he recommends interfering with existing vicious cycles. Using only law enforcement to crack down on corruption attacks a symptom rather than the underlying reasons for slow growth. However, as the survey data indicate, perceptions of government corruption remain high in Taiwan and South Korea although in Korea few report actually paying bribes. These data suggest that perceptions of corruption are a moving target. If You is correct that South Korea and Taiwan are much less corrupt than the Philippines, then survey results should not be taken at face value in making cross-country comparisons. The results for Taiwan and South Korea may simply represent a rise in citizens' awareness of the issue and expectations of honesty in public officials and the businesses that deal with them.

Nevertheless, even accepting You's claims about the structural determinants of corruption, polities that have not experienced fundamental reform can make marginal gains through policies that are less drastic than a massive redistribution of wealth. The other chapters in this section concentrate on that intermediate level, dealing with procurement, with tax avoidance by small and medium-sized firms in Vietnam, and with regulatory capture in China. Of course, none of the reforms suggested in these chapters would be feasible in a state that has been captured by elite actors.

Procurement is a key feature of government service provision and competition for contracts can easily become a site for corrupt dealings. David S. Jones outlines the loci of corruption, and I would add to his list collusive arrangements that determine the projects supported with public money. If a government has been captured in You's sense, the elite in the public and private sectors can collude to select projects especially suited to the capacities of corrupt private firms and that can be designed to make it easy to hide payoffs. Officials may favour complex, one-of-a-kind projects that outsiders cannot check for cost padding. Similarly, if payoff amounts rise with scale, officials may favour projects that are too large and too expensive relative to society's needs as a way of increasing the volume of potential payoffs. Such projects are unlikely to be the best way for the state to further economic growth. The search for private gain distorts public choices and, if widespread, can limit the state's role in promoting growth and development. Interestingly, the data presented by Jones are not always consistent with You's claims. For example, the World Economic Forum data from 2014 on the frequency of bribe payments from firms to officials places South Korea and the Philippines close together at 2.9 and 3.1 on a scale of 1 to 7, with 7 standing for "never occurs". Taiwan is at 4.1. (The Asian countries range from 2.2 for Bangladesh to 5.4 for Singapore.) You's claims are supported, however, when respondents are asked about favouritism by officials to well-connected firms. The Philippines, however, is by no means the worst. Consistent with You's emphasis on the fundamental distribution of property rights and wealth, Jones finds that the reforms, even though extensive on paper, have had a limited effect. Implementation has been seriously lacking. Deals linked to nepotism and cronyism are rampant. Powerful political figures exercise behind the scenes influence from the top. The problem occurs in both democracies and in authoritarian states.

John Rand and Finn Tarp's chapter is an object lesson on the difficulty of making reforms stick. They show how initial successes in curbing corruption in small- and medium-sized businesses in Vietnam in 2005 appear to have evaporated. Formally organised firms are more likely to pay bribes as are larger and more profitable firms; those in the informal sector, especially small firms, simply hide from the state and are less likely to bribe. However, bribes do not seem to be a tax avoidance device, although one is then left to ask what they did accomplish. Perhaps officials could threaten to take other costly actions so that the bribes were pure extortion payments. The authors report that bribes were paid "to get connected to public services", "to deal with tax and tax collectors", and "to gain government contracts". The authors do not try to estimate the social cost of corruption. In the Vietnamese case, however, the cost is not a reduction in tax revenue but, instead, the reluctance of small firms to expand and to organise in the formal sector in order to access the banking system. The indirect impact on tax collections is the loss in economic output from firms that fail to expand to take advantage of economic opportunities. If this phenomenon is widespread enough, the result will be slower growth.

The final chapter in this section by Thomas Johnson, Ting Gong, and Wen Wang considers the corruption risks faced by Hong Kong small- and medium-sized enterprises operating in China's Pearl River Delta. Their focus is on the region's dysfunctional regulation. Officials seek rents under a complex and unclear regulatory structure where both firms and officials seek to maximise their gains. Corruption affects regulation, and regulation creates opportunities for corruption in a mutually reinforcing cycle. The Pearl River Delta case is just one of many examples of vicious and virtuous cycles in corruption. Business registration and daily operations, such as customs and inspections, are the primary loci of corrupt dealings. The corruption risks are completely conventional worldwide and arise from the complexity and ambiguity of rules and the business need for speed and certainty in order to run profitable businesses. Some officials reportedly create extra red tape and delay to extort higher payoffs. There is nothing distinctly "Asian" about the corruption reported here, but it does indicate the general risk of business regulation rules that are cumbersome and unclear, whatever their core social value. As the example of the explosion in Tianjin illustrates, the answer is not the wholesale elimination of corrupt incentives but rather the reform of bureaucratic processes to clarify and streamline the rules and to provide a complaint mechanism for those who wish to report extortion.

In general, the connection between corruption and growth is multi-faceted. Cultural factors and the underlying structure of property rights can encourage corruption and distrust in government. In some cases, quite major changes in those conditions have helped a society move in the direction of a system that is more fair and equitable. Even when culture and past practice favour corruption, marginal reforms in particular sectors can help spur reform and help restore trust. Corruption can also be controlled indirectly by limits on political power and by changes in public attitudes toward the exercise of that power. Such strategies give people and groups a way to complain about poor government service provision. To facilitate these activities, the government supplies information about its actions, the media and the public voice complaints, and private organizations and individuals push for public account-ability. The goal is to increase governmental openness, leaving it more vulnerable to popular discontent. Many regimes, even nominally democratic ones, may view such policies with suspicion. They are, nevertheless, an essential check on corruption and on other forms of dishonest self-dealing that can arise if officials are insulated from popular oversight. Institu-tions need to hold officials to account over and above criminal investigations for malfeasance. Reforms that concentrate on particular sectors or loci of corruption are less dramatic than a massive criminal law crackdown or a transformative shift in property rights, but they can contribute to changed behaviour over time so long as they retain the active support of public officials, citizens, and the business community.

Notes

1 Portions of this essay are drawn from a paper prepared for the International Corruption Confer-ence, Bangkok, Thailand, November 2010, but all of the material has been rewritten and updated. I wish to thank Rory Truex for excellent research help on the original essay and Leo O'Toole for locating some recent scholarship linking trust and corruption. I thank Shitong Qiao for comments on an earlier draft.

2 I leave to one side Hong Kong and Singapore, which score 75 and 85, respectively, out of 100 on Transparency International's Corruption Perceptions Index. Although they are often held up as models, it appears difficult to generalise their situation to other Asian countries.

References

Blunt, P., M. Turner and H. Lindroth (2012) "Patronage's progress in post-Soeharto Indonesia", *Public Administration and Development*, 32(1): 64–81.

Carpenter, J. P., A.G. Daniere and L.M. Takahasji (2004) "Cooperation, trust and social capital in Southeast Asian urban slums", *Journal of Economic Behavior & Organization*, 55 (4): 533–551.

Center for East Asian Democratic Studies (2015) *Asian Barometer Surveys* (Taipei, Taiwan) http://www.asianbarometer.org/intro (accessed 27 January 2016).

Chang, E.C.C. and Chu, Y. (2006) "Corruption and trust: exceptionalism in Asian democracies?" *The Journal of Politics*, 68(2): 259–271.

Chua, A. (2003) *World on fire: how exporting free market democracy breeds ethnic hatred and global instability*, New York: Doubleday.

Crabtree, J. (2014) "Mumbai's towering ambitions brought low by legal disputes", *Financial Times*, October 10, http://www.ft.com/cms/s/2/98751ce6-4a41-11e4-bc07-00144feab7de.html# (accessed 27 January 2016).

Delhey, J., K. Newton and C. Welzel (2011) "How general is trust in 'most people'? Solving the radius of trust problem", *American Sociological Review*, 76(5): 786–807.

Dong, B. and B. Torgler (2013) "Causes of corruption: evidence from China", *China Economic Review*, 26: 152–169.

The Economist (2013a) "Zapping mosquitos, and corruption", June 1, http://www.economist.com/news/technology-quarterly/21578520-technology-and-government-how-clever-use-mobile-phones-helping-improve (accessed 27 January 2016).

The Economist (2013b) "Logging in South-East Asia: rubber barons", May 18.

The Economist (2015) "Targeting social spending: casting a wide net", January 10, http://www.economist.com/news/international/21638127-developing-countries-are-cutting-fraud-and-waste-anti-poverty-schemes-deciding-who (accessed 27 January 2016).

Fisman, R. (2015) "Political connection and corruption—a global perspective", in S. Rose-Ackerman and P. Lagunes (eds.) *Greed, corruption, and the modern state: essays in political economy*, Cheltenham: Edward Elgar, 71–91.

Fisman, R., and Y. Wang (2015) "The mortality cost of political connections", *The Review of Economic Studies*, 82(4): 1346–1382.

Gelb, A., and C. Decker (2012) "Cash at your fingertips: biometric technology for transfers in developing countries", *Review of Policy Research*, 29(1): 91–117.

Global Witness, *Rubber barons* (2013) available at https://www.globalwitness.org/en/campaigns/land-deals/rubberbarons/ (accessed January 28, 2016).

Hakhverdian, A. and Q. Mayne (2012) "Institutional trust, education, and corruption: a micro-macro interactive approach", *The Journal of Politics*, 74(3): 739–750.

Hardin, R. (2002) *Trust and trustworthiness,* New York: Russell Sage Foundation.

Jacobs, A., J. C. Hernández and C. Buckley (2015) "Behind deadly Tianjan blast, shortcuts and lax rules: Chinese firm at center of tragedy becomes symbol of corrupt system", *The New York Times*, August 31, http://www.nytimes.com/2015/08/31/world/asia/behind-tianjin-tragedy-a-company-that-flouted-regulations-and-reaped-profits.html (accessed 27 January 2016).

Kim, B. S. (2010) "Building trust in government in the Republic of Korea: the case of the national tax service reforms", in G. S. Cheema and V. Popovoski (eds.) *Building trust in government: innovations in governance reform in Asia*, New York: United Nations University Press, 190–203.

Ravallion, M. (2013) *The idea of anti-poverty policy*, NBER Working Paper 19210, Cambridge Mass.: NBER.

Realo, A., J. Allik and B. Greenfield (2008) "Radius of trust: social capital in relation to familism and institutional collectivism", *Journal of Cross-Cultural Psychology,* 39(4): 447–462.

Rose-Ackerman, S. (2001a) "Trust and honesty in post-socialist societies", *Kyklos,* 54(2–3): 415–443.

Rose-Ackerman, S. (2001b) "Trust, honesty, and corruption: reflection on the state-building process", *Archives of European Sociology*, 42 (3): 526–570.

Rothstein, B. and E.M. Uslaner (2005) "All for all: equality, corruption, and social trust", *World Politics,* 58 (1): 41–72.

Sapio, F. (2009) "Rent seeking, corruption, and clientelism", in T.-W. Ngo and Y. Wu (eds.) *Rent seeking in China*, New York: Routledge, 22–42.

Tjiptoherijanto, P., and M. Rowen (2010) "Promoting trust in government: the case of Indonesia", in G. S. Cheema and V. Popovoski (eds.) *Building trust in government: innovations in governance reform in Asia*, New York: United Nations University Press, 204–220.

TI (Transparency International) (2013) *Global corruption barometer,* Berlin: Transparency International, http://www.corruptionwatch.org.za (accessed 27 January 2016).

TI (Transparency International) (2016) *Corruption perceptions index 2015*, https://www.transparency.org/cpi2015/#results-table (accessed 22 February 2016).

Wang, Z.-X. (2013) *Institutional trust in East Asia*, working paper No. 92, Asian Barometer and Global-barometer, http://www.asianbarometer.org/publications (accessed 27 January 2016).

Wank, D. (2009) "Local state takeover as multiple rent seeking in private business", in T.-W. Ngo and Y. Wu (eds.) *Rent seeking in China*, London: Routledge, 79–97.

You, J.-S. (2015) *Democracy, inequality, and corruption: Korea, Taiwan, and the Philippines compared*, Cambridge: Cambridge University Press.

You, J.-S. and S. Khagram (2005) "A comparative study of inequality and corruption", *American Sociological Review*, 70(1): 136–157.

8

CORRUPTION AND INEQUALITY IN ASIA

Jong-sung You

Corruption has been often discussed as a problem of efficiency and economic development (Mauro 1995; Rose-Ackerman 1999). However, many people perceive it to be more a problem of injustice than a problem of inefficiency. Corruption creates unequal influence, leading to unequal benefits and costs (Johnston 2005), and undermines the principle of impartial administration and equal treatment before the law (Mungiu-Pippidi 2006; Rothstein and Teorell 2008). Thus, corruption is likely to reinforce and widen existing inequalities of power, wealth and influence. Corruption poses a particular challenge to democracy which is supposed to give everyone equal voice and equal rights. A well-functioning democracy may reduce existing inequalities but corruption prevents democracy from properly functioning.

Higher inequalities in power, wealth and influence may lead to higher levels of corruption by undermining democratic accountability mechanisms. The powerful and the wealthy may seek favourable administrative decisions and preferential treatment before the law using corrupt means but the powerless and the poor may be more immediately vulnerable to often-visible extortion and petty corruption. In well-functioning democracies, voters should be able to punish corrupt politicians and various checks and balances mechanisms should contribute to curbing corruption. However, the wealthy elite, less visibly, may capture policy-making and implementation processes and corrupt elections (Johnston 2005; You 2015). Thus, corruption is likely to increase inequality and inequality may increase corruption. The reciprocal causality may create a vicious cycle of high corruption and high inequality (Rothstein 2011; Uslaner 2008; You 2015). Breaking this vicious cycle is a great challenge for many countries in Asia.

The purpose of this chapter is to explore the relationships between corruption and inequality theoretically and empirically, focusing on Asian countries. It will examine the correlation between corruption and inequality; causal effects from corruption to inequality and from inequality to corruption; and the joint effects of corruption and inequality on development. It will also examine successful cases of breaking out of the vicious cycle of corruption and inequality.

Data and methodological issues in the study of corruption and inequality

For quantitative studies of corruption and inequality, there are two difficult issues: data quality and endogeneity (You and Khagram 2005; Treisman 2007).

First, both corruption and inequality are difficult to measure. Measuring corruption is inherently difficult because most corrupt acts are conducted secretively. Due to the difficulty in objectively measuring corruption, measures of "perceived corruption" such as the Corruption Perceptions Index (CPI) of Transparency International (TI) and Control of Corruption Indicator (CCI) (Kaufmann et al. 2010) have been widely used in cross-national studies. Another widely used index of corruption is the International Country Risk Guide (ICRG) published by the Political Risk Services Group. However, these perceived measures are likely to contain large measurement errors. They may also suffer from systemic biases because country analysts and survey respondents may assume, for example, that richer countries are less corrupt. As an alternative measure of corruption, surveys of "experienced corruption" have been developed, notably TI's Global Corruption Barometer (GCB) surveys. However, the GCB data on "experience of bribery" shows large yearly fluctuations within countries, which indicate substantial measurement errors rather than actual changes in the frequency of bribery. Also, such surveys are likely to reflect only petty bribery and the definition of bribery or corruption may vary from country to country.

Since no single measure of corruption is reliable, this chapter will employ multiple indicators of corruption. It will use Kaufmann et al.'s CCI, the GCB data on "experience of bribery", and the Quality of Government (QoG) Institute's survey data on "impartial public administration", which is also considered a good indicator of the control of corruption (Mungiu-Pippidi 2006; Rothstein and Teorell 2008). The Institute at Gothenburg University has constructed a dataset on bureaucratic structure for 105 countries around the world through a survey of experts (Dahlström et al. 2015).

Inequality can be objectively measured. However, high-quality data on income inequality is available for only a small number of rich countries, notably the data from the Luxembourg Income Study. There is a problem of data quality in many of the sources. While most data are based on household surveys, many surveys are not representative of the whole population. Moreover, survey data are derived from different methodologies such as income versus expenditure, individual versus household, and market income versus net income. This chapter uses the Gini index of household net income from Frederick Solt's (2014) Standardized World Income Inequality Database (version 5). Although not perfect, this is the most extensive dataset comparable across countries and across time (for 174 countries from 1960 to the present).

Second, corruption and inequality are likely to affect each other. Hence it is difficult to sort out causal effects. There are two ways of dealing with the endogeneity problem in econometric studies: longitudinal data analysis and the use of instrumental variables. Some researchers have employed longitudinal data analysis. However, the lack of reliable quantitative data on corruption for a sufficiently long time is still a problem. The ICRG index of corruption is available from 1984 but doubts on the data quality have been raised (Knack 2006; Lambsdorff 2006). The CPI and CCI, available from 1995 and 1996 respectively, are generally considered slightly more reliable. Although there are large variations in these measures across countries for any given year, there are only small variations across time within countries. A large part of yearly fluctuations is likely to come from measurement errors rather than actual changes in the level of corruption. Hence, reliability of cross-national longitudinal analysis is still a concern.

Many scholars have used the instrumental variables method to address the endogeneity issue. However, none of the instruments for corruption used by these studies looks convincing. While Mauro (1995) and some researchers have used ethnolinguistic fractionalisation and legal origin as instruments for corruption in growth regressions, neither is a good instrument for corruption because they are only weakly correlated with corruption (Shaw et al. 2011). Predicted trade share that Shaw et al. (2011) have used as an instrument for corruption is likely to be correlated with economic development other than through corruption because trade openness, with which predicted trade share is highly correlated, must be correlated with economic development. Gupta et al. (2002) used "democracy" as an instrument for corruption. However, democracy is likely to be correlated with inequality and development other than with corruption. All of these instruments seem to violate the exclusion restrictions.

As for instruments for inequality, existing studies have used "*mature cohort size*" and "*wheat to sugar ratio*". You and Khagram (2005) used "mature cohort size" (the ratio of population aged 40–59 to the whole adult population) as an instrumental variable for inequality. Higgins and Williamson (1999) found that mature cohort size is a powerful predictor of inequality. Easterly (2007) used "wheat to sugar ratio", or the log of [(1 + share of arable land suitable for wheat)/ (1 + share of arable land suitable for sugar)], as an instrument for inequality. This is based on Engerman and Sokoloff's (1997) finding that factor endowments such as the exogenous suitability of land for wheat vs. sugarcane were a central determinant of inequality across the Americas. Both instruments seem to reasonably satisfy the exclusion restriction. When I used both instruments together, they passed the over-identification test (You 2015: 233–235).

Although most studies of the causes and consequences of corruption have relied on quantitative methods, qualitative methods can also be used for such studies. In particular, comparative historical analysis can be used to explore the causes and consequences of corruption (Mahoney and Rueschemeyer 2003). Systematic and contextualised comparisons of similar and contrasting cases paired with careful analysis of historical sequences can be a powerful tool for causal analysis. It helps to reveal not only the causal direction between the variables of interest, but also the causal mechanisms. This chapter will provide a summary of major findings from my comparative historical investigation of the causal relationship between inequality and corruption in South Korea, Taiwan and the Philippines (You 2015).

Correlation between corruption and inequality

Table 8.1 presents correlations between income inequality (Gini index of net income inequality) and various indicators of corruption. It shows that income inequality is highly correlated negatively with perceived levels of control of corruption (r = −0.4142, N = 103) and "impartial public administration" (r = −0.6445, N = 67). Income inequality is strongly correlated positively with the natural logarithm of the average percentage of respondents whose family members have bribed public officials during the last year (r = 0.5403, N = 65). Also, the table shows high correlations among various indicators of corruption.

The high correlation between corruption and inequality is reflected in the stylised regional patterns. Advanced democracies, particularly Scandinavian countries, tend to have both low levels of corruption and low levels of inequality. Many countries in sub-Saharan Africa and Latin America tend to have both high corruption and high inequality.

Table 8.1 Pairwise correlations

	Gini	CCI	Impartial	Bribery
Net income Gini (2010–12)	1			
Control of corruption (2010–12)	−0.4142	1		
Impartial administration (2011)	−0.6445	0.8971	1	
ln bribery (2004–10)	0.5403	−0.8497	−0.8044	1

Sources: *Standardized World Income Inequality Database*, version 5 (Solt 2014); *Worldwide Governance Indicators* (Kaufmann et al. 2010); *QoG expert survey dataset* (Dahlström et al. 2015); natural logarithm of the average percentage of respondents whose family members have bribed public officials during the last year, from Transparency International's *Global Corruption Barometer Surveys* (2004–10).

The high correlations between income inequality and various indicators of corruption are also confirmed among Asian countries. Figures 8.1–8.3 clearly show that countries with higher income inequality tend to have higher levels of corruption (or lower levels of control of corruption). In particular, three East Asian countries, Japan, South Korea and Taiwan, enjoy the lowest levels of income inequality as well as the lowest levels of bribery experience and highest levels of impartial administration.

Although we have confirmed the strong correlation between income inequality and various indicators of corruption, both globally and within Asia, correlation does not necessarily mean causation. Causality could run from corruption to inequality, from inequality to corruption, or from a third factor affecting both corruption and inequality.

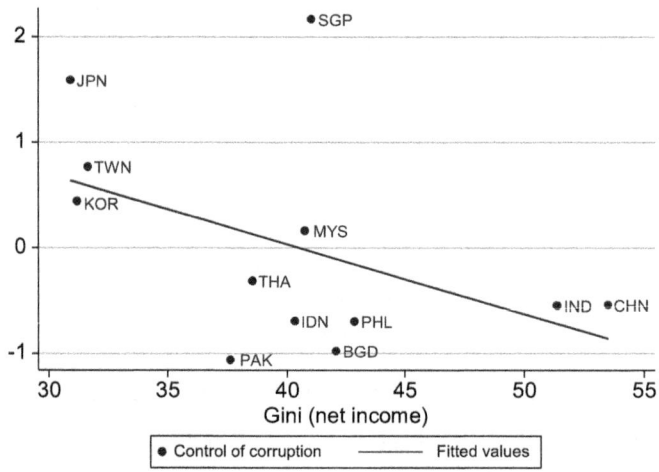

Figure 8.1   Gini (net income) and control of corruption for Asian countries
Sources: Solt (2014) and Kaufmann et al. (2010).

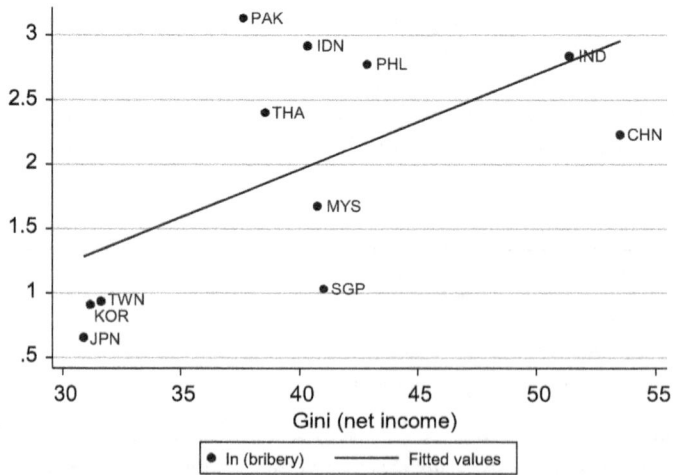

Figure 8.2   Gini (net income) and ln (bribery) for Asian countries
Sources: Solt (2014) and TI (2011).

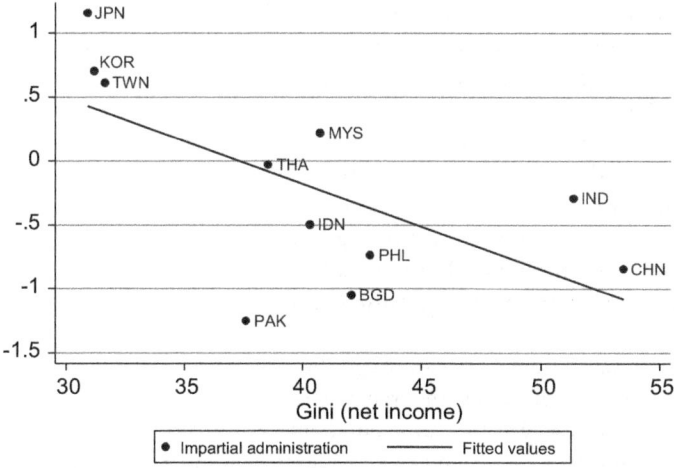

Figure 8.3 Gini (net income) and impartial administration for Asian countries
Sources: Solt (2014) and Dahlström et al. (2015).

Causality from corruption to inequality

As Johnston (2005: 29) notes, corruption typically benefits the "haves" at the expense of the "have-nots". Grand corruption is likely to favour large corporations and the wealthy elite as well as high-level public officials. Petty corruption is likely to impose higher costs on the poor, at least relative to income, if not in absolute terms. There are many empirical studies to support these claims.

Empirical studies of state capture by large corporations and conglomerates show that state policies are often bought and directed by special business interests (Hutchcroft 1998; Hellman et al. 2000; Kang 2002). State capture by industrial-financial conglomerates, or crony capitalism, was an important cause of the Asian financial crisis of 1997 (Haggard 2000). State capture is pervasive in the extraction of natural resources. In the Pacific Islands, international logging companies have been accused of bribing government officials to in-fluence policy decisions. In Mongolia, political elites entered into numerous deals and joint ventures with mining companies (UNDP 2008: 92).

Transparency International's Global Corruption Barometer Survey (2010/11) reveals that the poor suffer from petty corruption much more than the rich. The survey asked people around the world if they had paid bribes in the previous year when they contacted any of nine public service agencies.[1] The survey shows that the police force is the institution most often reported for taking bribes around the world. Almost three in ten of those who had contact with the police report paying a bribe. The survey further finds that the poor are more frequently penalised by bribery. In eight of nine services, users who belong to the lowest income quintile pay bribes more frequently than those with higher income levels. In parti-cular, the poor are three times more likely to pay bribes than the rich when they contact customs, utilities, medical services and the education system. To receive basic social services, poor people are effectively paying higher prices (TI 2011).

The United Nations Development Programme's Asia-Pacific human development re-port on corruption documents in detail the impact of corruption on the poor. It notes that the poor are "vulnerable to police corruption because they lack the influence needed to defend themselves when they get into difficulties". Street vendors are especially vulnerable to police extortion. The sums extorted by the police are not very large but they constitute a significant proportion of the income of poor people. On the other hand, poor people tend to get less attention when they want to register a complaint with the police (UNDP 2008: 44).

The poor also suffer from judicial corruption. According to a household survey conducted by TI Bangladesh in 2005, two-thirds of the respondents who went through the lower tiers of courts in the previous year paid bribes of around $108 per case on average. This amounted to about one-quarter of their average annual income. Often, the poor cannot rely on the legal system for protection. Being unable to defend their rights and properties, they are subject to arbitrary judgments that cause them to lose their land, homes, or livelihoods (UNDP 2008: 50).

Some cross-national studies have examined the effect of corruption on inequality. Li et al. (2000) found that corruption affects income distribution in a slightly inverted U-shaped way (the least corrupt countries are the most equal and countries with medium-high levels of corruption are the most unequal) and that corruption alone explains a large proportion of the Gini differential across developing and developed countries. Gupta et al. (2002), using a cross-country analysis, suggested that corruption increases inequality and poverty by perpetuating an unequal distribution of asset ownership and unequal access to education, minimising the progressiveness of the tax system, lowering the level and effectiveness of social spending and lowering economic growth.

Causality from inequality to corruption

Although it is quite obvious that corruption increases inequality and poverty, the reverse causal direction is less clear. Earlier cross-national studies found no significant effect of income inequality on corruption (Husted 1999; Paldam 2002). However, my own cross-country studies indicate that economic inequality increases corruption significantly across countries, using the instrumental variable method (You and Khagram 2005; You 2015). My studies show that the impact of inequality on corruption is particularly pronounced in democracies. Easterly (2007) and Uslaner (2008) also presented empirical evidence of the effect of inequality on corruption. Dutta and Mishra (2013) presented a formal model in which inequality increases corruption in the presence of an imperfect credit market.

Why does economic inequality affect corruption? Why is this effect stronger in democracies than in autocracies? First, high levels of inequality will increase the risks of state capture by a wealthy elite, especially in countries with formal institutions of democracy (You 2015: 33–34). Democracy is supposed to allow equal voice to every citizen. In democratic countries with high inequality, redistributive pressures will be high. Thus, the rich will have higher stakes and greater expected returns in influencing policy-making and policy-implementing processes at higher levels of inequality. Hence, the wealthy elite will try to defend and further advance their interests through lobbying, legal and illicit political contributions and bribery. Acemoglu and Robinson's (2008) model of "captured democracy", in which the *de jure* political power of citizens is offset by the *de facto* political power of the elite, is more likely at higher levels of inequality.

Although state capture by the elite can theoretically occur without corruption (i.e. through legal lobbying and campaign contributions), capture by special interests often involves corruption. In addition, capture by the elite will spread corruption to the entire private sector (You 2015: 176–7). As large firms and business groups exert great abilities for state capture through both legal and illegal means, smaller firms will be also drawn to corruption. Since the latter have weaker influence and connections to the state power, they will be compelled to rely more on extra-legal means, such as bribery and illegal political contributions.

Hellman et al. (2000) created a dataset on "capture economy index" for 22 transition economies based on the 1999 Business Environment and Enterprise Performance Survey data. The index incorporates responses to questions such as how much a firm's business is influenced by the sale of parliamentary votes on laws and presidential decrees to private interests, the sale of court decisions, and illicit political contributions by private interests. When the capture economy index was regressed on per capita income and inequality of income, per capita income was not significant but income inequality was significantly positive (You 2015: 242).

Second, countries with higher economic inequality are likely to experience more prevalent and persistent clientelism in electoral mobilisation (You 2015: 11–2, 32–3). Clientelism involves exchanges of particularistic benefits for political support between politicians and voters. Clientelism is not necessarily illegal or corrupt but it often involves illegal and corrupt acts of vote buying in cash, gifts and entertainment. In addition, electoral clientelism is likely to encourage high-level political corruption, because clientelistic politicians often collect clientelistic resources through corrupt means (Stokes 2007; Hicken 2011). Clientelistic politicians lack the genuine will to fight against corruption and many anti-corruption reforms are merely rhetorical. Also, clientelistic voters lose the ability to punish corrupt politicians at the poll.

The literature on clientelism supports the proposition that the poor are more prone to clientelism than middle-class voters (Stokes 2007; Hicken 2011). Since countries with higher levels of inequality tend to have higher proportions of the poor at a given level of economic development, inequality will be associated with clientelism, controlling for the level of economic development. At the same time, higher inequality will encourage the wealthy elite to promote clientelism rather than programmatic politics. Since programmatic competition under high levels of inequality is likely to empower the relatively poor population and to strengthen leftist parties that pursue significant redistributive policies, the rich will have an incentive to sponsor clientelistic politicians and to help them buy votes from the poor. In return, clientelistic politicians are likely to be captured by the wealthy. Thus, both the demand side (the poor) and the supply side (the rich) of clientelism suggest that high economic inequality is likely to deter the development of programmatic competition and encourage the prevalence and persistence of clientelistic competition.

Robinson and Verdier (2013) demonstrated through formal modelling that clientelism becomes an attractive political strategy for the elite in situations of high inequality. Acemoglu et al. (2011) presented a theory that emergence and persistence of inefficient states based on patronage politics is more likely when there is higher income inequality. Debs and Helmket (2010) found that the probability of the left candidate to be elected was lower at high levels of inequality based on the data on 110 elections in 18 Latin American countries from 1978 to 2008. They suggested that this is because the rich bribed the poor voters to avoid redistribution. Markussen (2011) showed a strong association between economic inequality and political clientelism across local governments in South India.

Kitschelt's (2013) dataset on democratic accountability and linkages provides cross-national data on clientelism. The data are based on expert surveys of 88 countries about various features of clientelistic and programmatic politics. Employing both ordinary least squares and instrumental variable regressions, I find that income inequality is significantly associated with clientelism across countries, controlling for age of democracy and per capita income (You 2015: 236–9). Inequality retains significance even when poverty is controlled for. I also find that clientelism is significantly associated with political corruption. Figure 8.4 shows that the levels of income inequality and clientelism are closely correlated across Asian countries.

Third, countries with high inequality are more likely to suffer from bureaucratic patronage and corruption (You 2015: 33). Clientelistic politics typically involves provision of public sector jobs in exchange for political support (Calvo and Murillo 2004). Where clientelism is prevalent, meritocratic recruitment of civil servants is hindered by political interference for patronage jobs. Also, the rich may directly participate in politics and penetrate the bureaucracy through political appointments. Bureaucratic penetration by the rich will further increase patronage appointments and promotions. Ziblatt (2009) found that land inequality led to penetration of local institutions by landed elites in late nineteenth-century Germany.

Bureaucratic patronage will increase bureaucratic corruption. Public officials who have obtained their jobs through patronage are also likely to seek promotion via patronage and thus have incentives for engaging in corruption to reward their patrons (Hodder 2009). Weberian bureaucracy, and in particular meritocratic recruitment, is found to be closely associated with lower corruption (Rauch and Evans 2000; Dahlström et al. 2012). Rauch and Evans (2000) constructed a dataset on bureaucratic structure for 35 developing countries, based on expert surveys. They found that their measure of meritocratic recruitment is a statistically significant determinant of the ICRG index of corruption across countries. Using the QoG survey data on "professional bureaucracy" (absence of patronage appointments in bureaucracy) and the CCI, Dahlström et al. (2012) reached the same conclusion.

I have tested the effect of inequality on bureaucratic structure, using the QoG survey data. I find that income inequality is significantly negatively associated with "professional bureaucracy" (You 2015: 240–1). Also, I find that professional bureaucracy is strongly associated with lower levels of perceived corruption (higher CPI) and experience of bureaucratic corruption (percentage of respondents whose family members have bribed public officials

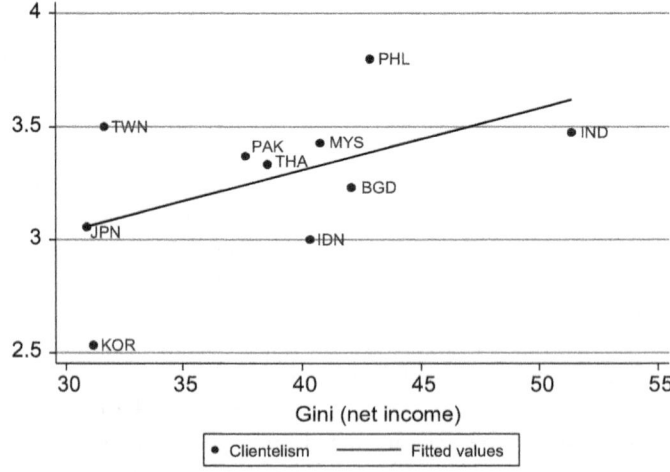

Figure 8.4 Inequality (net income Gini) and clientelism in Asia
Sources: Solt (2014) and Kitschelt (2013).

during the last year, from TI's Global Corruption Barometer Survey data). Figure 8.5 shows the strong negative correlation between income inequality and the professional civil service across Asian countries.

Fourth, inequality may negatively affect education and thereby corruption. A number of studies show that high inequality of income and land lowers educational levels by constraining the poor population's investment in education (Easterly 2007; Galor et al. 2009; Cinnirella and Hornung 2011; Cingano 2014). Also, studies show that education has been linked to lower levels of corruption (Goldin and Katz 1999; Botero et al. 2012; Uslaner and Rothstein 2016). Uslaner and Rothstein (2016) found that countries with a more egalitarian distribution of land were more likely to introduce universal education in the late nineteenth century, which in turn was strongly linked to corruption levels in 2010 across 78 countries.

Last, inequality is likely to erode social trust (generalised interpersonal trust), which in turn may increase corruption. Under high levels of inequality, many relatively poor people are likely to perceive that the rules of the game are unfair or that the rich have made their fortunes unfairly (You 2012). Hence, the overall level of social trust will decline as economic inequality increases. Low social trust is likely to breed corruption (Uslaner 2004, 2008). People are more likely to follow the rules of the game honestly when they trust that others will do the same. When they do not trust others to act honestly, their own incentives for cheating and corruption will increase as well. Corruption can be understood as a problem of collective action (Rothstein 2011: 99–110; Persson et al. 2013). It is harder to overcome the collective action problem at lower levels of generalised trust.

Uslaner (2008) presented cross-national evidence to support this causal chain from inequality to social trust and then to corruption. Other cross-national studies also found the significantly negative effect of income inequality on social trust (Zak and Knack 2001; Leigh 2006; You 2012). Regarding the causal relationship between social trust and corruption, causal direction may run both ways. Uslaner (2004, 2008) found that social trust is associated with lower corruption, while Rothstein (2011) and You (2012) found that corruption is associated with lower social trust.

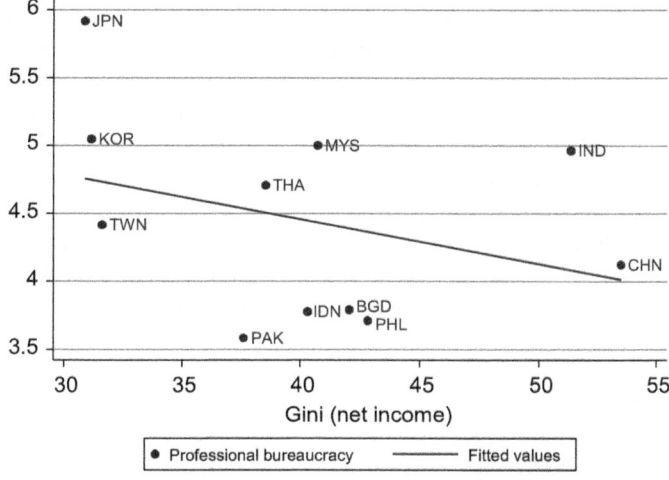

Figure 8.5 Inequality and professional bureaucracy across Asian countries
Sources: Solt (2014) and Dahlström et al. (2015).

Vicious cycle of high inequality and high corruption

There may be a vicious cycle of high inequality and high corruption, considering the two-way causality between inequality and corruption. Chong and Gradstein (2007) found cross-national evidence and Apergis et al. (2010) presented evidence from the US states supporting the two-way causal relationship between inequality and corruption (or institutional quality, more broadly).

Rothstein (2005, 2011) and Uslaner (2008) added social trust to this vicious cycle. Rothstein proposed the concept of "social trap", or a vicious cycle of "high corruption ⇒ low social trust ⇒ low redistribution ⇒ high inequality ⇒ high corruption". Uslaner proposed an "inequality trap", or a vicious cycle of "high inequality ⇒ low social trust ⇒ high corruption ⇒ high inequality". In the end, they both reach the same conclusion, irrespective of precise causal directions and mechanisms. Countries trapped in a vicious cycle of "high corruption, high inequality and low trust" will find it difficult to break out of this trap.

Corruption, inequality and development in Asia

The vicious cycle of inequality and corruption is likely to have negative impact on economic development. Several empirical studies show that inequality is harmful for growth (Alesina and Rodrik 1994; Deininger and Olinto 2000; Esterly 2007; Cingano 2014; Ostry et al. 2014). Also, many studies suggest corruption deters economic development (Mauro 1995; Keefer and Knack 1997; Mo 2001; Kaufmann and Kraay 2002; Pellegrini and Gerlagh 2004; Johnson et al. 2011).

There is no consensus among researchers about the negative effects of inequality and corruption on growth. However, an increasing number of studies are confirming the negative impact of inequality on growth, including studies published by researchers at the World Bank (2006), International Monetary Fund (Ostry et al. 2014), and OECD (Cingano 2014). Also, there has been strong consensus about the negative impact of corruption on economic and human development in the international development community.

Table 8.2 compares the long-run economic growth performances (average annual growth of gross domestic product per capita between 1960 and 2010 and between 1980 and 2010) of 12 Asian countries. It divides the countries into four groups by levels of corruption in 1980–85 (CPI 1980–85) and land inequality around 1960. Most countries belong to either the "high corruption or high land Gini group" or the "low corruption and low land Gini" group. For the "high corruption and high land Gini group", which consists of five countries (Indonesia, the Philippines, Pakistan, Thailand and India), the average CPI (1980–85) is 1.77 and the average land Gini (circa 1960) is 51.5. For the "low corruption and low land Gini" group comprising five countries or regions (Singapore, Japan, Taiwan, China, and South Korea), the average CPI (1980–85) is 6.23 and the average land Gini (circa 1960) is 33.5. Land inequality around 1960 is a strong predictor of income inequality in the 1980s: the former group's average income Gini (1980s) is 39.9, and the latter group's 30.5.

There are significant differences in the long-run growth performances between these two groups. The high corruption and high inequality group's average annual growth rate for the 50-year period from 1960 to 2010 is 3.08 per cent, while that for the low corruption and low inequality group is 5.50. The high corruption and high inequality group's average annual growth rate for the 30-year period from 1980 to 2010 is 3.06 per cent while that for the low corruption and low inequality group is 5.17.

Table 8.2 Growth performances by corruption (CPI 1980–85) and inequality (Land Gini 1960)

Country	CPI 1980–85	Land Gini c.1960	Income Gini 1980s	Average Annual Growth 1960–2010	Average Annual Growth 1980–2010
High corruption, high land Gini					
Indonesia	0.2	52.7	33.3	3.42	3.64
Philippines	1.04	52.3	42.6	1.41	0.77
Pakistan	1.52	50.1	33.5	2.54	2.23
Thailand	2.42	43.5	44.4	4.91	4.32
India	3.67	59	45.5	3.12	4.32
(Average)	1.77	51.5	39.9	3.08	3.06
High corruption, low land Gini					
Bangladesh	0.78	41.8	34	–	2.68
Low corruption, high land Gini					
Malaysia	6.29	66	43.8	–	3.34
Low corruption, low land Gini					
S. Korea	3.93	32.3	33	5.93	5.89
China	5.13	–	29.2	6.34	8.92
Taiwan	5.95	39	27	5.69	4.95
Japan	7.75	41.5	24.5	4.03	1.86
Singapore	8.41	29.1	38.6	–	4.21
(Average)	6.23	35.5	30.5	5.5	5.17

Sources: Annual growth rates have been calculated based on data from Penn World Table (version 8.1) (Feenstra et al. 2015). Land Gini (circa 1960) is the average value of the land Ginis from the two datasets provided by Deininger and Olinto (2000) and Frankema (2010). Income Gini (average for 1980–89) is the net household income Gini, from Solt's (2014) data.

It has been long recognised that East Asia's miracle economies such as Japan, South Korea and Taiwan have had low levels of inequality in income and wealth. Table 8.2 shows that these countries also had low levels of land inequality around 1960 and low levels of income inequality in the 1980s. It is notable that these countries all experienced land reform (Kuznets 1988; Rodrik 1995; Kay 2002; Kim 2009).

Rodrik (1995) emphasised the role of favourable initial conditions such as low inequality of wealth and income and a large educated labour force in the sustained economic growth of South Korea and Taiwan. He shows that almost 90 per cent of the growth experience of both South Korea and Taiwan since 1960 "can be *explained* by these initial conditions". Kim (2009) showed, via macro-historical comparison, significant land reforms in Northeast Asian countries explain their superior long-term economic performance to Southeast Asian countries. However, these studies do not consider the association between inequality and corruption or the role of corruption in economic development.

My comparative historical study of South Korea, Taiwan and the Philippines focuses on the causal relationship between inequality and corruption and their impact on economic development (You 2014, 2015). The three regions were all similarly poor, very corrupt and highly unequal at the time of independence after World War II. In fact, the Philippines had a somewhat higher per capita income and substantially higher educational attainment than South Korea and Taiwan. Also, inequality of land was greatest in South Korea. However, South Korea and Taiwan implemented far-reaching land reforms in the early years of post-independence while the Philippines failed to do so.

Successful land reform in South Korea and Taiwan and failed reform in the Philippines produced starkly different levels of inequality of land and income which in turn led to different levels of corruption and development. In the Philippines, failed land reform has maintained the domination of the landed elite and led to persistent electoral clientelism, bureaucratic patronage and capture of the policy-making and implementation processes by the elite. These problems were evident throughout the early period of democracy (1946–72) as well as the post-Marcos democratic era (1986-present). Meritocratic recruitment of civil servants via civil service examinations has been increasingly replaced by patronage appointments. Clientelistic politicians have often promised to implement anti-corruption reforms but the reform measures have been largely rhetorical. Corrupt public officials are rarely prosecuted, and voters have been unable to punish corrupt politicians at the polls because of endemic practices of clientelism. The Philippine state, captured by the powerful landed-industrial-financial family conglomerates, has never been able to formulate and implement coherent industrial policy. The persistent clientelism and capture have not only constrained the anti-corruption efforts but hindered economic development.

In contrast, sweeping land reform in South Korea and Taiwan dissolved the landed elite and created relatively egalitarian societies. Land reform contributed to the rapid expansion of education by enabling the tenant-turned-owner-cultivators to educate their children. Expansion of education led to increased pressures for meritocracy. Clientelism was somewhat limited due to the separation of the political and economic elites and the relatively low levels of absolute poverty, as well as the growing size of the educated middle class. The gradual development of meritocratic bureaucracy was accompanied by declining bureaucratic corruption. Although clientelistic practices, such as vote buying, were endemic during the early years of democracy, both South Korea and Taiwan have been able to curb clientelism with strict prosecution of vote buying practices and voters' punishment of corrupt politicians at the polls. The decline of clientelism has been accompanied and reinforced by the gradual development of programmatic party politics in both countries. There was some progress in corruption control both during the authoritarian period and during the democratic period in South Korea and Taiwan. Both regions enjoyed high state autonomy in the absence of an influential economic elite and were able to formulate and implement coherent industrial policies.

Although both South Korea and Taiwan achieved rapid economic growth, South Korea's *chaebol*-centered industrialisation led to increasing economic concentration and policy capture by powerful business interests compared to the small-and-medium-sized-enterprises-centered industrialisation in Taiwan. This explains South Korea's historically higher level of corruption than that of Taiwan (Table 8.2 shows that CPI 1980–85 for South Korea was 3.93 and that for Taiwan 5.95).

The divergent developmental trajectories of these countries that initially shared similar conditions provide compelling evidence for the vicious and virtuous cycles hypothesis. The Philippines represents a case trapped in a vicious cycle of high inequality, high corruption and underdevelopment while South Korea and Taiwan represent a virtuous cycle of low inequality, low corruption and high economic development. It is notable, however, that Korea and Taiwan started in no better condition than the Philippines did. These countries or regions demonstrated that a vicious cycle is not pre-destined. South Korea and Taiwan were able to break the vicious cycle by implementing sweeping land reforms and by a series of anti-corruption reforms, including the establishment of meritocratic bureaucracies. Their stories demonstrate that a vicious cycle is not inevitable. Countries that are seemingly trapped in a vicious cycle may well be able to break it and move toward a virtuous cycle by implementing major reforms to reduce inequality and curb corruption. Also, countries that have enjoyed a virtuous cycle may find themselves in danger of falling back into a vicious cycle. If inequality and/or corruption rise over time, the virtuous cycle may be broken. In this regard, increasing inequality in many countries in Asia over the last decades should be of a great concern.[2]

Notes

1 The average percentage of respondents who paid bribes to any of the nine institutions in the previous year in the Asia-Pacific region was 11 per cent, but there were large differences across countries in the Global Corruption Barometer survey of 2010: Cambodia (84 per cent), Afghanistan (61 per cent), India (54 per cent), Pakistan (49 per cent), Vietnam (44 per cent), Papua New Guinea (26 per cent), Thailand (23 per cent), Solomon Islands (20 per cent), Indonesia (18 per cent), Philippines (16 per cent), Vanuatu (16 per cent), Fiji (12 per cent), Singapore (9 per cent), Japan (9 per cent), China (9 per cent), Malaysia (9 per cent), Taiwan (7 per cent), Hong Kong (5 per cent), New Zealand (4 per cent), Australia (2 per cent), South Korea (2 per cent).
2 In this regard, South Korea is facing a dangerous trend of rapidly rising inequality, according to a study of top income shares by Kim and Kim (2015). The top 1 per cent's share of income dropped dramatically from around 20 per cent during the 1930s to around 7 per cent during the 1980s and 1990s, which must be due to the sweeping land reform between these periods. However, it began to rise again starting from the late 1990s. It surpassed 12 per cent in 2012 and has been rising continuously.

References

Acemoglu, D. and J. A. Robinson (2008) "Persistence of power, elites, and institutions", *American Economic Review,* 98(1): 267–93.

Acemoglu, D., D. Ticchi and A. Vindigni (2011) "Emergence and persistence of inefficient states", *Journal of the European Economic Association,* 9(2): 177–208.

Alesina, A. and D. Rodrik (1994) "Distributive politics and economic growth", *Quarterly Journal of Economics,* 109(2): 465–490.

Apergis, N., O. C. Dincer and J. E. Payne (2010) "The relationship between corruption and income inequality in U.S. States: evidence from a panel cointegration and error correction model", *Public Choice,* 145(1/2): 125–35.

Botero, J., A. Ponce and A. Shleifer (2012) *Education and the quality of government,* NBER Working Paper No. 18119, http://www.nber.org/ (accessed 11 February 2016).

Calvo, E. and M. V. Murillo (2004) "Who delivers? Partisan clients in the Argentine electoral market", *American Journal of Political Science,* 48(4): 742–57.

Chong, A. and M. Gradstein (2007) "Inequality and institutions", *Review of Economics and Statistics,* 89(3): 454–65.

Cingano, F. (2014) *Trends in income inequality and its impact on economic growth,* OECD Social, Employment and Migration Working Papers, No. 163, OECD Publishing, http://dx.doi.org/10.1787/5jxrjncwxv6j-en (accessed 11 February 2016).

Cinnirella, F. and E. Hornung (2011) *Landownership concentration and the expansion of education,* EHES Working Paper, No 10, ehes.org/ (accessed 11 February 2016).

Dahlström, C., V. Lapuente and J. Teorell (2012) "The merit of meritocratization: politics, bureaucracy, and the institutional deterrents of corruption", *Political Research Quarterly,* 65(3): 656–68.

Dahlström, C., J. Teorell, S. Dahlberg, F. Hartmann, A. Lindberg and M. Nistotskaya (2015) *The QoG expert survey dataset II,* University of Gothenburg: The Quality of Government Institute, http://qog.pol.gu.se/data/datadownloads/qogexpertsurveydata (accessed 17 March 2016).

Debs, A. and G. Helmket (2010) "Inequality under democracy: explaining the left decade in Latin America", *Quarterly Journal of Political Science,* 5(3): 209–41.

Deininger, K. and P. Olinto (2000) *Asset distribution, inequality, and growth*, World Bank Research Working Paper, No 2375, June.

Dutta, I. and A. Mishra (2013) "Does inequality foster corruption?" *Journal of Public Economic Theory,* 15(4): 602–619.

Easterly, W. (2007) "Inequality does cause underdevelopment: insights from a new instrument", *Journal of Development Economics,* 84(2): 755–776.

Engerman, S. L. and K. L. Sokoloff (1997) "Factor endowments, institutions, and differential paths of growth among new world economies: a view from economic historians of the United States", in S. Haber (ed.) *How Latin America fell behind: essays on the economic histories of Brazil and Mexico, 1800–1914*, Stanford, CA: Stanford University Press, 260–306.

Feenstra, R. C., R. Inklaar and M. P. Timmer (2015) "The next generation of the Penn World Table (version 8.1)", www.ggdc.net/pwt (accessed 17 March 2016).

Frankema, E. (2010) "The colonial roots of land inequality: geography, factor endowments, or institutions?" *Economic History Review,* 63(2): 418–451.

Galor, O., O. Moav and D. Vollrath (2009) "Inequality in landownership, the emergence of human-capital promoting institutions, and the great divergence", *Review of Economic Studies,* 76(1): 143–179.

Goldin, C. and L. F. Katz (1999) "Human capital and social capital: the rise of secondary schooling in America, 1910–1940", *Journal of Interdisciplinary History,* 29(4): 683–723.

Gupta, S., H. Davoodi and R. Alonso-Terme (2002) "Does corruption affect income inequality and poverty?" *Economics of Governance,* 3: 23–45.

Haggard, S. (2000) *The political economy of the Asian financial crisis*, Washington, DC: Institute for International Economics.

Hellman, J. S., G. Jones and D. Kaufmann (2000) *Seize the state, seize the day: state capture, corruption and influence in transition*, World Bank Policy Research Working Paper, No. 2444. Washington, DC: World Bank.

Hicken, A. (2011) "Clientelism", *Annual Review of Political Science,* 14(1): 289–310.

Higgins, M. and J. G. Williamson (1999) *Explaining inequality the world round: cohort size, Kuznets Curves, and openness*, NBER Working Paper 7224.

Hodder, R. (2009) "Political interference in the Philippine civil service", *Environment and Planning C: Government & Policy,* 27(5): 766–782.

Husted, B. W. (1999) "Wealth, culture, and corruption", *Journal of International Business Studies,* 30(2): 339–359.

Hutchcroft, P. D. (1998) *Booty capitalism: the politics of banking in the Philippines*, Ithaca, NY: Cornell University Press.

Johnston, M. (2005) *Syndromes of corruption: wealth, power, and democracy*, Cambridge: Cambridge University Press.

Johnson, N. D., C. L. LaFountain and S. Yamarik (2011) "Corruption is bad for growth (even in the United States)", *Public Choice,* 147(3/4): 377–393.

Kang, D. C. (2002). *Crony capitalism: corruption and development in South Korea and the Philippines*, Cambridge: Cambridge University Press.

Kaufmann, D. and A. Kraay (2002) *Growth without governance*, World Bank Policy Research Working Paper, No. 2928.

Kaufmann, D., A. Kraay and M. Mastruzzi (2010) "The worldwide governance indicators: methodology and analytical issues", *World Bank Policy Research Working Paper No. 5430*, www.govindicators.org (accessed 17 March 2016).

Kay, C. (2002) "Why East Asia overtook Latin America: agrarian reform, industrialisation, and development", *Third World Quarterly,* 23(6): 1073–1102.

Keefer, P. and S. Knack (1997) "Why don't poor countries catch up? A cross-national test of an institutional explanation", *Economic Inquiry,* 35(3): 590–602.

Kim, N. N. and J. Kim (2015) "Top incomes in Korea, 1933–2010: evidence from income tax statistics", *Hitotsubashi Journal of Economics,* 56(1): 1–19.

Kim, W. (2009) "Rethinking colonialism and the origins of the developmental state in East Asia", *Journal of Contemporary Asia,* 39(3): 382–399.

Kitschelt, H. (2013) *Democratic accountability and linkages project, 2008–9 dataset* (version: April 1, 2014), Duke University, http://sites.duke.edu/democracylinkage/data/ (accessed 11 February 2016).

Knack, S. (2006) *Measuring corruption in Eastern Europe and Central Asia: a critique of the cross-country indicators*, Washington, DC: World Bank.

Kuznets, P. W. (1988) "An East Asian model of economic development: Japan, Taiwan, and South Korea", *Economic Development and Cultural Change*, 36(3): S11-S43.

Lambsdorff, J. G. (2006) "Measuring corruption - the validity and precision of subjective indicators (CPI)", in C. Sampford, A. Shacklock, C. Connors and F. Galtung (eds.) *Measuring corruption*, Aldershot: Ashgate, 81–100.

Leigh, A. (2006) "Does equality lead to fraternity?" *Economics Letter*, 93(1): 121–125.

Li, H., L. C. Xu and H. Zou (2000) "Corruption, income distribution, and growth", *Economics and Politics*, 12(2): 155–82.

Mahoney, J. and D. Rueschemeyer (eds.) (2003) *Comparative historical analysis in the social sciences*, Cambridge: Cambridge University Press.

Markussen, T. (2011) "Inequality and political clientelism: evidence from South India", *Journal of Development Studies*, 47(11): 1721–38.

Mauro, P. (1995) "Corruption and growth", *Quarterly Journal of Economics*, 110(3): 681–712.

Mo, P. H. (2001) "Corruption and economic growth", *Journal of Comparative Economics*, 29(1): 66–79.

Mungiu-Pippidi, A. (2006) "Corruption: diagnosis and treatment", *Journal of Democracy*, 17(3): 86–99.

Ostry, J. D., A. Berg and C. G. Tsangarides (2014) *Redistribution, inequality, and growth*, IMF Staff Discussion Note SDN/14/02 (February).

Paldam, M. (2002) "The cross-country pattern of corruption: economics, culture, and the seesaw dynamics", *European Journal of Political Economy*, 18(2): 215–240.

Pellegrini, L. and R. Gerlagh (2004) "Corruption's effect on growth and its transmission channels", *Kyklos*, 57(3): 429–456.

Persson, A., B. Rothstein and J. Teorell (2013) "Why anticorruption reforms fail—systemic corruption as a collective action problem", *Governance*, 26(3): 449–471.

Rauch, J. E. and P. B. Evans (2000) "Bureaucratic structure and bureaucratic performance in less developed countries", *Journal of Public Economics*, 75(1): 49–71.

Robinson, J. A. and T. Verdier (2013) "The political economy of clientelism", *Scandinavian Journal of Economics*, 115(2): 260–291.

Rodrik, D. (1995) "Getting interventions right: how South Korea and Taiwan grew rich", *Economic Policy*, 10(1): 55–107.

Rose-Ackerman, S. (1999) *Corruption and government: causes, consequences, and reform*, New York: Cambridge University Press.

Rothstein, B. (2005) *Social traps and the problem of trust*, Cambridge: Cambridge University Press.

Rothstein, B. (2011) *The quality of government: corruption, social trust, and inequality in international perspective*, Chicago: University of Chicago Press.

Rothstein, B. and J. Teorell (2008) "What is quality of government? A theory of impartial political institutions", *Governance*, 21(2): 165–190.

Shaw, P., M. S. Katsaiti and M. Jurgilas (2011) "Corruption and growth under weak identification", *Economic Inquiry*, 49(1): 264–275.

Solt, F. (2014) *The standardized world income inequality database*, Working paper, http://myweb.uiowa.edu/fsolt/swiid/swiid.html (accessed 11 February 2016).

Stokes, S. C. (2007) "Political clientelism", in C. Boix and S. C. Stokes (eds.) *The Oxford handbook of comparative politics*, Oxford: Oxford University Press, 604–627.

TI (Transparency International) (2011) Global Corruption Barometer Survey 2010/11, http://www.transparency.org/gcb201011 (accessed 17 March 2016).

Treisman, D. (2007) "What have we learned about the causes of corruption from ten years of cross-national empirical research?" *Annual Review of Political Science*, 10(1): 211–244.

UNDP (United Nations Development Programme) (2008) *Tackling corruption, transforming lives: accelerating human development in Asia and the Pacific*, New Delhi: Macmillan India.

Uslaner, E. M. (2004) "Trust and corruption", in J. G. Lambsdorff, M. Taube and M. Schramm (eds.) *The new institutional economics of corruption*, London: Routledge, 76–92.

Uslaner, E. M. (2008) *Corruption, inequality, and the rule of law: the bulging pocket makes the easy life*, Cambridge: Cambridge University Press.

Uslaner, E. M. and B. Rothstein (2016) "The historical roots of corruption: state building, economic inequality, and mass education", *Comparative Politics*, 48(2): 227–248.

World Bank (2006) *World development report 2006: equity and development*, Washington, DC: World Bank and Oxford University Press.

You, J.-S. (2012) "Social trust: fairness matters more than homogeneity", *Political Psychology,* 33(5): 701–721.

You, J.-S. (2014) "Land reform, inequality and corruption: a comparative historical study of Korea, Taiwan and the Philippines", *The Korean Journal of International Studies,* 12(1): 191–224.

You, J.-S. (2015) *Democracy, inequality and corruption: Korea, Taiwan and the Philippines compared*, Cambridge: Cambridge University Press.

You, J.-S. and S. Khagram (2005) "A comparative study of inequality and corruption", *American Sociological Review,* 70(1): 136–57.

Zak, P. J. and S. Knack (2001) "Trust and growth", *The Economic Journal,* 111: 295–321.

Ziblatt, D. (2009) "Shaping democratic practice and the causes of electoral fraud: the case of nineteenth-century Germany", *American Political Science Review,* 103(1): 1–21.

9

CORRUPTION AND PROCUREMENT IN ASIAN STATES

David S. Jones

Introduction

In most Asian states, corruption has been prevalent in the public procurement of goods, services and public works. This has in turn prevented the development of well-resourced public services and a high quality infrastructure and has resulted in poor value for money and financial waste. A further consequence is the lack of equal and fair access to government contracts for business. Corruption has been evident in these states during the various stages of the procurement process from initial registration to contract implementation.

In recent years, reforms have been introduced in many countries in Asia to combat corruption in government procurement. They have been introduced to both deter and prevent corruption, sometimes as part of a package of reforms to improve the overall standards of procurement or to combat corruption in general. However, the impact of these reforms has varied and implementation has often been weak (ADB/OECD 2006).

The chapter will be divided into two parts. The first part will consider the extent and types of corruption found in procurement in Asian states, viz. bribery, collusion, nepotism and cronyism, embezzlement and fraud. These different types of corruption procurement are inter-linked and one type of corrupt practice is often accompanied by another. The second part will then consider the reforms that have been introduced to combat corruption in procurement. It will highlight the limited effectiveness of the reforms through various shortcomings in their implementation. The conclusion will note how these may be attributed to the control of the procurement process by powerful elites in politics, business and administration working through a culture of informal practices in the government bureaucracy in many of the less-developed Asian states.

Bribery

Purposes of bribery in procurement

The most common form of corruption in procurement in Asia is bribery in which companies offer bribes to officials and politicians to secure an advantage in the procurement process or officials and politicians solicit bribes from companies for the same purpose.

The bribe given or solicited may be intended to achieve any of the following outcomes in the procurement process:

- to enable a company to secure registration as a government trading partner or contractor even though the company may not meet all the criteria for registration;
- to allow it to pass a pre-qualification test even if it fails to meet key standards laid down in the test;
- to influence the specifications of the products, services or works so that only one company can meet them;
- to waive competition so that only one company can tender for the project (commonly known as direct contracting);
- to obtain a favorable assessment of a company's bid in the tender evaluation and to secure the award of the contract even though other bids were more advantageous in terms of price and quality;
- to allow an increase in price subsequent to the award of the contract;
- to ensure that false documents and declarations submitted by a company in execution of a contract (such as the amount of work done, goods supplied and costs incurred) are accepted by procurement officials;
- to ensure that procurement officials turn a blind eye to collusion or that the bids of other companies not party to the collusion are rejected.

In the last two outcomes, the bribe is a reward for forbearance by procurement officials in respect of fraudulent submissions and collusion.

The extent of bribery in procurement

Tables 9.1, 9.2 and 9.3 provide a measure of the extent and distribution of bribery in procurement in different Asian states. Table 9.1, which covers seventeen countries, provides an estimate based on ratings 1 through 7 given by business executives of the frequency of bribe payments for public contracts and licences in a survey conducted by the World Economic Forum in 2015. A rating below 4 indicates that bribery is a serious and frequent problem while ratings at 4 and above indicate that bribery is less common. In about two-thirds of the countries in the list, it appears that bribery occurs on a frequent basis including bribery in procurement. All of these countries, with the exception of Korea, are developing countries. Most of the countries where bribery was less frequent are developed countries or regions (Singapore, Japan, Taiwan and Hong Kong).

Table 9.2 refers to expectancy of bribery to secure government contracts and is based on the Enterprise Surveys of the World Bank between 2009 and 2014 (the year of the survey varied from country to country). In South Asian countries in 2014, an average of 46 per cent of firms expected to pay bribes and, in East Asia and the Pacific, the average in 2013 was 29.7 per cent. In four countries (Nepal, Indonesia, the Philippines and Vietnam), businesses in the sample expected to pay bribes in more than 50 per cent of contracts to stand a chance of winning. In India in 2014, the figure was almost 40 per cent. The surprising outlier is Cambodia, where the figure was only 7.1 per cent, which is in direct contrast to its very low rating in Table 9.1. The frequency of bribe payments did not vary much by size of the firm. Firms employing 100 or more staff expected to pay bribes for 32 per cent of contracts; the figure for smaller firms was 36 per cent.

Table 9.1 Rating of frequency of bribe payments by firms for public contracts and licences, 2015

Country	Rating	Country	Rating
Bangladesh	1.8	India	3.5
Nepal	2.4	Indonesia	3.7
Sri Lanka	2.6	China	3.9
Cambodia	2.7	Korea	4.1
Pakistan	2.8	Malaysia	4.6
Vietnam	2.9	Taiwan	5.1
Philippines	3.1	Hong Kong	6.0
Lao PDR	3.1	Japan	6.1
Thailand	3.2	Singapore	6.4

Source: World Economic Forum (WEF) 2015.
Note: 1 = very common; 7 = never occurs.

Table 9.2 Percentage of firms indicating the need to pay bribes to secure a procurement contract in selected Asian countries, 2009–2014

Country	Year of survey	% of all firms	% of small firms <20 employees	% of medium firms 20–99 employees	% of large firms >100 employees
Vietnam	2009	53.7	50.8	67.4	44.2
Philippines	2009	53.3	94.0	17.6	55.8
Indonesia	2009	53.0	50.9	59.2	59.4
Nepal	2013	51.3	27.1	79.7	0.0
India	2014	39.8	43.2	37.3	35.4
Bangladesh	2013	35.5	37.0	21.7	54.3
Sri Lanka	2011	18.2	26.3	1.8	4.9
China	2012	8.8	1.3	10.0	12.0
Cambodia	2013	7.1	1.2	29.7	33.1

Source: World Bank 2015.

The survey in Table 9.3, which was conducted by Ernst and Young on bribery by companies in six Asian countries, is informative. It shows that companies engaging in bribery were widespread in Indonesia, frequent in Malaysia and Vietnam and infrequent in Korea and Singapore. A similar pattern exists for bribery to secure contracts in both the government and private sectors. The very low incidence of bribery to secure contracts in Korea is, however, inconsistent with its rating in Table 9.1, in which the World Economic Forum survey shows frequent company bribery of government agencies.

The polling organization Social Weather Stations (SWS) provides an in-depth assessment of corruption in the Philippines including corruption in procurement. In its most recent survey conducted in 2013, a sample of 913 private sector managers and owners were interviewed. On a 4-point scale measuring the extent of corruption from "a lot" to "none", 56 per cent of the sample indicated that there was "a lot". In addition, 42 per cent of respondents stated that 'almost all/most companies' in their line of business paid bribes to secure a public contract while the

Table 9.3 Responses to statements on bribery and corruption in certain Asian states (sample N = 681)

Country	Bribery/corruption is frequent: per cent who agree	Bribery to win contracts is common: per cent who agree	Government policies to fight bribery have an impact: per cent who agree
Indonesia	79	36	50
Malaysia	39	15	56
Vietnam	36	26	13
China	21	9	35
South Korea	2	0	9
Singapore	1	0	15

Source: Asia Pacific Fraud Survey, EY Fraud Investigation and Dispute Services 2013: 7.
Note: Sample includes business executives, senior managers and employees.

corresponding figure for private sector contracts was lower at 23 per cent (SWS 2014: 4–6). According to a previous SWS survey, the median amount paid as a bribe was 15 per cent of the contract value (SWS 2009: 4–6).

The SWS 2013 survey data corroborate the figures for the Philippines in Tables 9.1 and 9.2 which also show that bribery in procurement in Indonesia is equally prevalent. Data on bribery in procurement and also collusion in Indonesia are supplied by its Competition Commission (Komisi Pengawas Persaingan Usaha [KPPU]). Between 2000 and 2013, it received 2,078 reports/complaints of competition violations of which nearly 80 per cent related to "tender conspiracy" in the procurement of goods and services. In 2013, 150 reports of "tender conspiracy" were received. This term refers both to bribery to influence the procurement process and bid awards and to collusion or price-fixing. Of eight cases under investigation in 2014, five concerned contractors in building and infrastructure projects and two were suppliers of heavy equipment and vehicles (OECD 2014a: 5).

Collusion

Another form of corruption affecting government procurement in Asia is collusion. This involves companies cooperating in a collusion ring to limit competition in a tender and so fix a high price. This practice was declared a form of corruption by the World Bank in 2004. Four main types of collusion may be identified:

- bid suppression or single bidding in which only one company ultimately submits a bid and the other companies in the collusion ring refrain from bidding or withdraw their bids;
- cover bidding in which, through a prior agreement, one company submits a high bid and complies with the specifications and others deliberately submit even higher bids and/or do not comply (in some cases, they are invited to join the collusion ring to give the impression of genuine competition);
- rotational bidding in which companies in the collusion ring supplying similar products or projects take turns to submit a bid from one procurement to another;
- market allocation which is an arrangement to give each company in the collusion ring a monopoly in a particular segment of the market on the basis of geography or product.

The first three forms of collusion are usually accompanied by a reward given by the company awarded the contract to the companies who did not submit a bid or whose bid failed. The reward often involves the company awarded the contract passing on part of the payments received to the other companies or giving them profitable sub-contracts. Procurement officials and politicians frequently aid and abet the collusion by turning a blind eye or by disqualifying or rejecting the bids of other companies not party to the collusion (OECD 2009: 1–3; 2012: 5).

Country procurement assessment reports by the World Bank, project reviews by the Asian Development Bank, Organization for Economic Co-operation and Development, the United Nations Development Programme and the World Bank, reports of the Competition Commission and of the State Auditor, as well as media reports, have consistently referred to the frequency of collusion in Asian states. It arises particularly when companies are closely linked through business associations, through overlapping ownership, and through family and crony ties. Procurement of highly specialized products or services in which there is a limited range of suppliers or contractors, such as pharmaceutical products, medical equipment, certain types of military hardware and large infrastructure projects, are most vulnerable to collusion (OECD 1998: 10, 19, 50, 73–75; 2009: 1–3; 2010: 10).

Indonesia has long been identified as a country in which collusion is widespread. In 2014, the KPPU court proved five cases of collusion entailing nineteen companies. The procurement concerned high-value contracts: two were infrastructure projects, one the purchase of heavy equipment and two the procurement of medical equipment. The collusion involved cover bidding with firms participating so as to "create false competition". The evidence for collusion was the almost exact similarity in the details of the bid submissions, close associations between the companies through ownership and family ties, high price offers above the market rate and information provided by a whistleblower. In these cases, it was also found that the procurement committees chose to overlook this evidence and there was suspicion that they had connived in the collusion (KPPU 2013: 7; 2014: 12–13).

Collusion continues to be an issue in public procurement in India. The Competition Commission of India (CCI) regularly refers to collusive bidding. In 2012, it referred to the "wide-scale prevalence of cartelisation and bid rigging in public procurement". It further noted:

> Bid rigging is a highly pernicious form of collusive price-fixing behaviour and ... can cause serious economic harm. It increases prices artificially and lowers quality, leading to loss of taxpayers' money.... Inefficient procurements have a detrimental impact on the quality of key public infrastructure and services and hurt the interests of the poor largely relying on public provision (CCI 2012: 5).

In 2014, the CCI found "that often suppliers take advantage of inadequate specifications and lack of vigil by procuring authorities and through collusive conduct raise the cost of procurement, causing a drain on the exchequer" (CCI 2014: 6). Particular areas subject to collusion were purchases of equipment for the railways and the military and the procurement of pharmaceuticals.

Collusion is also frequent in Korea. The Korean Fair Trade Commission (KFTC) found 172 cases of collusion from 2009 to 2014 including 51 in 2014 (2015a: 62). Up until April 2015, eight high-profile cases of collusion had been identified in infrastructure projects covering water embankment construction, dam construction, sewerage disposal, waste water processing and an environmental energy center. The companies involved all agreed on virtually the same price offers, which were noticeably high, and it may be surmised that the winning company shared some of the profits or apportioned sub-contracts to the other companies (KFTC 2015b).

Even in Japan, collusion in public bidding occasionally occurs. In 2013, companies in 10 collusion cases were convicted on the grounds that "the enterprises jointly designated a successful bidder for each work and managed to have the designated bidders receive the order". Three were high value contracts for developing the electrical power transmission grid, procurement of snow-melting equipment for the railways and road and pavement works (OECD 2014b: 5–6).

Small economies are also vulnerable to collusive bidding because there are usually few local suppliers. An example is Nepal where, according to one observer, collusion "has become an institutionalized practice … leading to unscrupulous competition and rise of corruption". There are identifiable common collusive practices which "can include, for example, assigning 'turns' among the cartel members for winning public bids, or agreeing to internal compensation payments for submitting high or other 'failed bids'" (Adhikari 2015: 7, 8–11; Ministry of Finance, Nepal 2011: 14). The author was informed by civil servants in another small state, Brunei, that the government often pays much higher than the market rate for goods and services due to collusion and price fixing by local suppliers who are small in number and known to each other through personal and family ties.

Nepotism and favoritism

A good deal of corruption in procurement in Asia involves favoritism; contracts are awarded to companies owned by senior figures in the governing class, their family members (nepotism) and personal and political associates (cronyism). Such companies often belong to a favored network of businesses dominated by the governing and business elites.

Favoritism may often be exercised by leading politicians, top bureaucrats and leaders in local government, who either arrange for the award of the contract directly to the favored company, bypassing the procurement committee or instruct the procurement committee to award the contract to that company. In such cases, competitive bidding, though required by the procurement legislation, is avoided and the company is appointed without competition.

According to the ratings given by the World Economic Forum on favoritism in Table 9.4 (rating below 5 indicating "a lot" of favoritism), it would appear that in about two-thirds of

Table 9.4 Rating of the extent of favouritism of government officials to well-connected firms and individuals in policies and contracts in selected Asian countries

Country	Rating	Country	Rating
Bangladesh	2.2	Lao DPR	3.7
Sri Lanka	2.7	Indonesia	3.8
Cambodia	2.8	India	3.9
Nepal	2.8	China	4.0
Korea	2.9	Taiwan	4.1
Thailand	3.0	Hong Kong	4.6
Pakistan	3.0	Malaysia	4.6
Philippines	3.0	Japan	5.1
Vietnam	3.2	Singapore	5.6

Source: World Economic Forum 2015.
Note: 1 = always show favoritism; 7 = never shows favoritism.

the countries listed, being a favored company is important in winning contracts. It may be surmised that such favoritism in many cases is exercised for personal gain or family advantage or for the advantage of cronies.

Favoring certain companies in procurement contracts on self-serving family and friend-ship grounds has been entrenched in the Philippines with companies earmarked for con-tracts belonging to a network of well-connected business leaders and landowning families (Johnston 2010: 16, 40–41; Jones 2013: 378, 395–396). In the indictment of two senior officials in the Department of Transportation and Communications, the Ombudsman found that they "exhibited manifest partiality" in awarding a contract of switching gear worth US$560,000. There was no competitive tender and the Bids and Awards Committee, which rightfully should have handled the procurement, was bypassed. There was suspicion that the guilty parties or their families had a stake in the company (Office of the Ombudsman, Philippines 2015). Another case, which is subject to an ongoing investigation, involves Vice-President Jejomar Binay and his wife, Elenita. It is alleged that when they served as the mayors of Makati City (1998–2001 and 2004–2010), they regularly instructed the procure-ment committee of the Council to award contracts directly to favored companies without competitive bidding as required by law. The procurement officials were themselves paid off for permitting the irregularities. The allegations, which are presently subject to a Senate inquiry and an investigation by the Ombudsman, are being contested by the Binay family (Cupin 2014a, 2014b; OOP 2015).

Fraud and embezzlement

Fraud is another form of corruption affecting procurement in government agencies and in-volves submitting false or misleading information or acting dishonestly in other ways which affect the procurement process, the award of a contract, and the execution of the contract.

Fraud may entail submitting false information to secure or expedite registration as a government trading partner or contractor, to pass the pre-qualification test in a selec-tive tender, or to obtain favorable consideration in a tender evaluation. The false disclo-sures may cover: a) the company's track record determined by the size and value of recent projects; b) present or impending projects; c) financial health (including cash flow, credit lines, and existing assets, reserves and liabilities); d) levels of expertise and professional qualifications amongst staff; and e) technical resources such as equipment, facilities and technology. Such disclosures are normally required in registration and pre-qualification. Procurement in Pakistan has been blighted by the submission of false or fake documents. For example, of 11 firms blacklisted by procuring entities in 2014, eight had submitted false or fake documents in the pre-qualification (Public Procurement Regulatory Authority, Pakistan 2015).

Fraud may also occur in the implementation of the project if a company supplies a lower quality and quantity of product and work than agreed and submits invoices and receipts overstating the price of goods provided and the amount of work done. Third, fraud may occur in collusive arrangements when a fake bid proposal is submitted by a company in the name of another company so as to give the impression of competition. Fraudulent practices may also involve officials who award contracts knowing full well that the eligibility of the company to tender had not been met and who in their disbursement of funds deliberately avoid keeping proper accounts and entries.

Closely linked to fraudulent submissions is embezzlement. This entails the misappropri-ation of funds and resources by officials and politicians for personal enrichment, which are

Table 9.5 Rating of frequency of diversion of public funds in selected Asian countries

Country	Rating	Country	Rating
Bangladesh	2.7	Lao DPR	3.5
Thailand	2.9	Indonesia	3.6
Cambodia	3.0	China	3.8
Nepal	3.1	India	4.1
Pakistan	3.1	Taiwan	4.5
Philippines	3.1	Malaysia	4.8
Sri Lanka	3.2	Japan	5.6
Vietnam	3.4	Hong Kong	5.9
Korea	3.4	Singapore	6.1

Source: World Economic Forum 2015.
Note: 1 = very common; 7 = never occurs.

earmarked for procurement projects. Table 9.5 shows the frequency of diversion of public funds for personal enrichment in Asian countries as indicated in the World Economic Forum's Business Executive survey of 2014. The figures given are ratings on a scale of 1 through to 7 with a rating below 4 indicating that diversion is frequent. A pattern similar to that in the previous tables is evident with frequent embezzlement of public funds in developing countries and much less embezzlement in the developed countries, with Singapore the least corrupt in this regard. The public funds listed are for all programmes and services but a good proportion would have been earmarked for procurement. An example of how funds for procurement may be embezzled occurred in the Corrupt Practices Investigation Bureau of Singapore. In 2013, an Assistant Director was convicted of embezzling S$1.7 million of funds to be used in procuring goods and services (Quah 2015: 77, 81–85).

Reforms to combat corruption in procurement

Most developing Asian states have now introduced reforms based on international best practices to combat corruption in procurement, which provide a comprehensive legal and institutional framework for this.

Procurement laws

Legal reforms, introduced over the past 10 to 15 years, are an important means to combat corruption. The reforms usually take the form of an umbrella sovereign law passed by the legislature rather than a presidential or government decree. The reforms may directly prohibit explicitly stated corrupt practices in the procurement process with express penalties for committing such offences and, in addition, may also stipulate requirements to be followed to prevent conflicts of interest.

Indirectly, the procurement reforms may combat corruption by stipulating open competitive tendering for most types of procurement, laying down strict guidelines when competition should be waived in favor of alternatives such as limited tenders and direct contracting. The reforms may also discourage corruption by mandating transparency in the procurement process and by splitting the function of bid evaluation and bid selection, each to be undertaken by separate personnel. For example, the major reform of procurement in Vietnam is the Law on Tendering, No. 61 of 2005, subsequently extended in 2013. The 2005 reform prohibits "giving, accepting or requesting any object of value by an individual or organization involved in the process of selection of a contractor or of contractual performance, resulting in dishonest or partial behavior when deciding on selection of contractor or when signing and implementing the contract". It further prohibits "using personal influence to affect or to intervene in, or intentionally making a false or dishonest report about information thus distorting the result of selection of a contractor or the signing and implementation of the contract" (National Assembly, Vietnam [NAV] 2005a: s. 12).

A key law governing procurement in Thailand is the Act Concerning Offences Relating to the Submission of Bids to Government Agencies, 1999, which details various types of collusive practice and bribery (including bribery to alter product specifications to suit a company) as major offences. The Act also specifies the powers of investigation of the National Counter Corruption Commission in these cases and the penalties attaching to such offences (ThaiLaws.com 2015: ss. 4–15).

In contrast, the main procurement reform in Indonesia, the Presidential Decree No. 60 of 2003, refers to corrupt practices in much less detail. Such practices are referred to simply as "corruption, collusion and nepotism" and are accompanied by a broad prohibition on the involvement of procurement officials, procurement committees and tender participants in such practices. If this occurs, the tender is cancelled and a new tender undertaken. The official procurement committee or company committing the corrupt offence is replaced or debarred for the repeat tender. The penalties for corrupt offences against individuals are only broadly referred to as "sanctions in accordance with the provisions of laws in force" although a company may face the additional penalty of being debarred for two years from public sector contracts (OECD 2007: ii, iii, 5, 7–9, 12–13; President of the Republic of Indonesia [PRI] 2003: ss. 1, 3, 27, 35, attachment II).

Laws relating to monopolies, cartels and unfair competition

Another legal instrument to combat corruption in procurement is the laws restricting monopolies and cartels and prohibiting unfair competition. These normally include provisions prohibiting actions to undermine competition in public procurement through collusion and bribery.

For example, the anti-monopoly law in Korea, the Monopoly Regulation and Fair Trade Act, under the heading "Prohibition on improper concerted practices", proscribes a wide range of collusive practices to limit competition and fix prices in bids for both public and private sector contracts or to decide the outcome of a tender beforehand (KFTC 2016: Ch. 4, s. 19). In Indonesia, the anti-monopoly law No. 5 of 1999 specifies that "Entrepreneurs are prohibited from conspiring with other parties to arrange and/or determine the winner of the tender thus causing unfair business competition". This covers principally collusion amongst companies to fix the price but also includes the bribery of officials to influence the outcome of a tender (PRI 1999: s. 22; Hadiputranto et al. 2013).

Anti-corruption laws

Anti-corruption laws (both specific anti-corruption laws and the penal code) may be used to deal with corruption in public procurement although in the majority of cases procurement is not specifically mentioned. For example, in India, the Prevention of Corruption Act,

1988, and other anti-corruption measures such as Lokpal and Lokayuktas Act, 2013, do not mention procurement but the offences listed and powers of enforcement could be applicable to procurement.

In addition, certain anti-corruption laws, such as the Malaysian Anti-Corruption Commission (MAC) Act, 2009, mandate prevention and education to combat corruption as part of the role of the anti-corruption agency. These include identifying weaknesses in procedures and systems in government agencies which increase the opportunity for corruption, and also raising awareness of corruption in the public service, business, schools and colleges, and the community and of the need to avoid and report it. In such efforts, attention is partly focused on the issue of corruption in procurement (MAC 2009: s. 7).

Some anti-corruption laws do specify corrupt practices in procurement. For example, in the Philippines, Law No. 3019, 1960 (Section 3) specifically prohibits offering, soliciting, and accepting bribes in the procurement process. Sections 4–5 proscribes acts involving nepotism, cronyism, favoritism, and influence pedaling, and any arrangement giving rise to conflicts of interest in the procurement process. Another law, No. 7080, 1991, subsequently amended in 1993, covers high-value corruption known as plunder in which personal gain is more than PHP50 million (US$1,050,000). The law specifies receipt of gifts and bribes in connection with any government contract or project and also embezzlement of public monies (Congress of the Philippines [COP] 1960; COP, 1991: s. 1; 1993: s.12). In Vietnam, the Anti-Corruption Law of 2005 mandates transparency in bidding for public procurement including infrastructure projects and lays down a list of requirements which procuring entities must follow (NAV 2005b: ss. 13–14).

Agencies to fight corruption in procurement

The reforms to combat corruption in procurement are implemented by a variety of watchdog and enforcement bodies, most of which deal with corruption in all areas of public administration and not just in procurement. Some agencies, such as the state auditor, committees in the legislature, and the central procurement authority, are responsible for unearthing initial evidence of possible corruption in procurement. Others go further and conduct criminal investigations that could lead to prosecution based on evidence provided by them, most notably the anti-corruption agency, the anti-monopoly body and the ombudsman. Prosecution is handled by the state attorney's office and conducted before a normal criminal court.

In some Asian countries, however, trials for corruption offences are conducted before a special anti-corruption court: for example, the Sandiganbayan in the Philippines, the Special Court for Corruption Crimes in Indonesia and the Corruption Session Courts in Malaysia (MAC 2012: 38; Schütte and Butt 2013: 2–3; Sandiganbayan 2015). In Korea and Indonesia, the KFTC and the KPPU, may not only investigate anti-competitive practices, many of which involve collusion and bribery in public procurement, but also perform a quasi-judicial role of prosecution and conviction, imposing fines and other penalties on errant companies (KFTC 2014: 8, 23; OECD 2014a: 7–8).

Limited impact of the reforms: weak implementation

Despite the legal and institutional reforms, progress in reducing corruption in government procurement has been limited in the developing states of Asia and also in Korea. The reforms have been quite far-reaching with the notable exception of India, where the Lok Saba has yet to pass a statute to govern procurement. However, there have been serious shortcomings in implementation both by officials in procuring entities and by watchdog and enforcement bodies. This is the main reason why corruption in procurement remains widespread.

Weaknesses in implementation by procurement officials

A key problem in implementation has been the tendency of officials in procuring entities, and procurement committees in developing Asian states not to adhere to their responsibilities laid down in the law. Bribes to alter procurement specifications, bid evaluations and contract awards in favor of certain companies, continue to be solicited or accepted. Nepotistic and crony deals in favor of well-connected businesses remain prevalent, money continues to be embezzled for earmarked projects, and goods and services received and payments made are still fraudulently recorded. Failure to enforce conflict of interest rules benefits procurement officials and their family members (Jones 2009: 166–167). Typical is the Philippines, where some procurement officials continue to by-pass their legal obligations by not holding open competitive tenders, taking bribes and favoring certain companies (ADB 2013: 41; Jones 2013: 389–392).

Furthermore, corrupt practices followed by companies in offering bribes, making false submissions, by-passing contractual obligations and engaging in collusive practices may be encouraged or ignored by the procuring entity. Global Integrity (GI) in its survey of corruption in India in 2011 gave the government a score of 25 out of 100 with respect to the frequency of debarment of corrupt companies from future tenders, although the procurement manuals expressly mandate debarment (GI 2011). In 2012, the Cambodian government received a score of 0 out of 100 in its enforcement of the debarment provision in the Anti-Corruption Law and the Penal Code (GI 2012). Likewise, in 2011, the Vietnamese government received a zero score for non-enforcement of debarment provisions although debarment is permitted by various laws (GI 2011; NAV 2005b: s. 75; 2013: s. 2).

Procuring entities and committees have also been limited by capacity constraints. GI's reports covering Asian countries since 2011 (India, Vietnam, Indonesia and Cambodia) indicate the absence of comprehensive training of officials in procurement in all these states, which denies them the opportunity to develop skills to detect bribery, collusive practices and fraudulent submissions, and in managing competitive tenders (GI 2011; GI 2012; GI 2013). A report by Transparency International highlighted the lack of training of officials at subnational level, with particular reference to Indonesia, as an obstacle to controlling corruption in procurement (2014: 20).

Failings of watchdog and enforcement bodies

Another factor that has contributed to failings in implementing the reforms to combat procurement corruption is the weakness of watchdog and enforcement bodies. These agencies include the central procurement authority, the state audit office, the anti-corruption agency, the anti-monopoly commission, the ombudsman, the public prosecutor's office and the courts. They are responsible for monitoring and exposing the conduct of officials, politicians and businesses, enforcing legal provisions which prohibit corrupt practices and mandating transparency and open and fair competition in tenders.

One weakness is the absence of the necessary cooperation between the different watchdog and enforcement agencies. Watchdog agencies, whose remit is to identify evidence of possible corruption in procurement, may not be able to count on further investigation and prosecution by other bodies such as the anti-corruption agency, and the public prosecutor's office. This has been the experience, for example, of the State Audit Office in Indonesia and Bangladesh, the Government Inspectorate in Vietnam, and the Central Vigilance Commission in India (GI 2011; GI 2013; GAN Integrity Solutions [GIS] 2015). One report of procurement in Indonesia in 2007 referred to staff in enforcement bodies as "not wanting to take responsibility" for prosecution in corruption cases (OECD 2007: 11).

Implementation has also been affected by the inability of investigative and enforcement bodies to secure convictions in the courts in corruption cases, including procurement corruption cases. An example is the Competition Commission of Indonesia. Of 204 decisions made by the Commission to penalize anti-competitive practices between 2006 and 2012 (74 per cent relating to bid rigging), 49 were overturned by either the District Courts or the Supreme Court (OECD 2014a: 7–8).

Capacity constraints also hinder the watchdog and enforcement agencies. This is particularly evident in Cambodia where the Anti-Corruption Unit set up in 2010 has suffered from low budgets, resulting in poor salaries and an inability to attract well-qualified staff. This has been exacerbated by limited training especially in detecting corruption. GI remarked that the Anti-Corruption Unit's "low budget ... will continue to paralyse its potential to tackle corruption, both petty and grand corruption" (GI 2012). In Indonesia, the staffing of the Ombudsman's Office, according to one of its senior officials, was "woefully inadequate". In 2013, it had only 56 staff to process 4,000 complaints. A similar predicament confronted the Corruption Eradication Commission, which in 2013 had only 75 investigators with a case load on average of five concurrent investigations (GI 2013).

A third failing is the vulnerability of watchdog and enforcement bodies themselves to bribery and favoritism when dealing with corruption offences. For example, in 2011, Merceditas Gutierrez, head of the Ombudsman's Office in the Philippines, resigned in the face of charges of irregular conduct. One charge concerned a failure to act when money earmarked for the purchase of fertilizers by the Department of Agriculture was embezzled to fund President Gloria Aroyo's 2004 presidential campaign (Torres et al. 2011).

Even the judicial system may be implicated in corruption. A recent report for the Konrad Adenaur Foundation referred to such corruption in Indonesia.

> In 2012, independent corruption watchdog groups implicated 84 anticorruption court judges in corruption cases. Bribes and extortion influenced prosecution, conviction, and sentencing in civil and criminal cases. Key individuals in the justice system were accused of accepting bribes and of turning a blind eye to other government officers and agencies suspected of corruption. Legal aid organizations reported cases often moved very slowly unless a bribe was paid.
>
> *(Abjorensen 2014: 99)*

This observation was consistent with the evidence of bribery and favoritism in the judiciary of Indonesia in TI's Global Report of 2007 on judicial corruption (judicial corruption was also reported in Bangladesh, Cambodia, Nepal, Pakistan, the Philippines, Sri Lanka, and Thailand) (2007: 161). It is likely that judicial corruption in these two reports included cases of alleged corruption in public procurement.

Where such weaknesses in watchdog and enforcement bodies exist, the chances of those engaged in procurement corruption being investigated, prosecuted, convicted and adequately punished are small. In the event of high-value procurement and infrastructure contracts, that risk is worth taking given the potential for lucrative gains. This makes procurement corruption a "low risk, high rewards activity" (Quah 2003: 13–15, 74, 99–100).

Interference by politicians and senior officials

To a certain extent, the failings of implementation stem from indirect controls exercised by powerful figures in the political establishment and the bureaucracy. Such figures can wield behind-the-scenes influence to determine procurement specifications, methods of tendering, evaluation of tender submissions, contract awards, disbursement of funds, and the implementation of contract obligations. Anti-corruption organizations and web sites have consistently referred to the top-down interference of politicians and senior officials in the procurement process for corrupt purposes. GAN Integrity Solutions in its country profile of Bangladesh, for example, states that, since 2012, "governments have been using political patronage to award jobs or lucrative government contracts in transportation, utilities, construction projects and government supplies" (GIS 2015).

Equally, political interference has undermined watchdog and enforcement bodies, resulting in delay or termination of investigations and prosecutions or in acquittals by the courts in corruption cases, as shown in surveys of the ombudsman, state audit authorities, and anti-corruption agencies in Bangladesh, Cambodia, China, India, the Philippines and Vietnam. An exception has been Indonesia where the Corruption Eradication Commission, the Audit Board and Ombudsman's Office remained free from such interference (GI 2010; 2011; 2012; 2013). Political interference may equally occur in both autocratic one-party states (Vietnam and China) and in two-party or multi-party democratic states (the Philippines and India).

Conclusion

Public procurement in Asian states has been particularly susceptible to various types of corruption. These include bribery, collusion, nepotism and cronyism, embezzlement and fraud. All stages of the procurement process have been affected from registration of suppliers and contractors and drafting of specifications to contract awards, execution of contracts and disbursement of funds.

Reforms introduced to combat corruption in procurement have had a limited impact mainly due to shortcomings in their implementation. Among the shortcomings is corruption by officials themselves in procuring entities in violation of relevant laws and regulations. This is compounded by capacity constraints, such as the lack of training of procurement officials in detecting bribery, fraud and collusion and in managing competitive tenders. Shortcomings in implementation have also been evident in watchdog and enforcement bodies. These include lack of support from the government and legislature and the failure of enforcement bodies to undertake follow up investigative and judicial action in response to corruption allegations. They have been further handicapped by capacity constraints such as limited financial resources and insufficient well-trained staff. Equally detrimental has been the susceptibility of officials in watchdog and enforcement bodies to bribery and favoritism.

To a significant extent, corruption in procurement stems from interference by politicians and senior bureaucrats in both the procurement process and the investigative and judicial processes. Such interference is designed to ensure that lucrative contracts are awarded to certain companies to which politicians and senior bureaucrats or their families and cronies are connected. To safeguard themselves, their cronies and political associates, politicians and senior bureaucrats may be equally prepared to interfere in investigative and judicial processes undertaken by watchdog and enforcement bodies to ensure that they do not proceed with an investigation or that they acquit the accused.

Two key factors explain the persistence of corruption in the implementation of procurement. One is the strength of political, bureaucratic and business elites in the less developed Asian states, which are often inter-connected through political party associations, business links and family and crony ties. The other factor is the informal culture of bureaucracies in these states. The elites have been able to control or capture the procurement process by working through the informal culture to influence procurement outcomes and spending in their favor.

References

Abjorensen, N. (2014) *Combating corruption: implications of the G20 Action Plan for the Asia-Pacific Region*, Tokyo: Konrad-Adenauer-Stiftung.

ADB (2013) *Philippines country procurement assessment report (CPAR) 2012*, Washington, DC: World Bank Group.

ADB/OECD (2006) *Curbing corruption in public procurement in Asia and the Pacific: progress and challenges in 25 countries*, Geneva, http://www.oecd.org/site/adboecdanti-corruptioninitiative/37575976.pdf (accessed 15 November 2015).

Adhikari, R.P. (2015) "Public procurement issues and challenges in Nepal", *Journal of Engineering Economics and Management*, 2(3): 3–27.

CCI (Competition Commission of India) (2012) *The Quarterly Newsletter of the Competition Commission of India (CCI): Fair Play,* 3 (Oct-Dec), New Delhi, http://www.cci.gov.in/sites/default/files/Newsletter_document/Newsletter_Dec.pdf (accessed 6 August 2015).

CCI (Competition Commission of India) (2014) *The Quarterly Newsletter of the Competition Commission of India (CCI): Fair Play*, 8 (Jan-March), New Delhi, http://www.cci.gov.in/sites/default/files/Newsletter_document/nwl8.pdf (accessed 6 August 2015).

COP (Congress of the Philippines) (1960) *Anti-Graft and Corrupt Practices Act*, Republic Act No. 3019, Manila, http://www.lawphil.net/statutes/repacts/ra1960/ra_3019_1960.html (accessed 7 August 2015).

COP (Congress of the Philippines) (1991) *Act Defining and Penalizing the Crime of Plunder, Amendment 1993*, Republic Act No. 7059, Manila, http://www.dole.gov.ph/files/RA%207080.pdf (accessed 7 August 2015).

COP (Congress of the Philippines) (1993) *An Act to Impose the Death Penalty on Certain Heinous Crimes, Amending for that Purpose the Revised Penal Laws, as Amended, Other Special Penal Laws, and for Other Purposes*, Republic Act No. 7659, Manila, http://www.lawphil.net/statutes/repacts/ra1993/ra_7659_1993.html#s12 (accessed 29 February 2016).

Cupin, B. (2014a) "Former official: rigged bids in Makati under VP Binay, wife", *Rappler.com*, 25 September, http://www.rappler.com/nation/70140-rigged-bids-makati-binay (accessed 23 July 2015).

Cupin, B. (2014b) "Binay skips Senate blue ribbon hearing", *Rappler.com*, 7 November, http://www.rappler.com/nation/70140-rigged-bids-makati-binay (accessed 23 July 2015).

EY Fraud Investigation and Dispute Services (2013) *Building a more ethical business environment: Asia-Pacific Fraud Survey 2013*, London, http://www.ey.com/Publication/vwLUAssets/2013_Asia-Pacific_Fraud_Survey/$FILE/EY-Asia-Pacific-Fraud-Survey.pdf (accessed 5 May 2015).

GI (Global Integrity) (2010) *Country reports, 2010: Bangladesh; China; Philippines - scorecards*, Washington, DC, https://www.globalintegrity.org (accessed 7 August 2015).

GI (Global Integrity) (2011) *Country reports, 2011: India; Vietnam - scorecards*, Washington, DC, https://www.globalintegrity.org (accessed 7 August 2015).

GI (Global Integrity) (2012) *Country reports, 2012: Cambodia - scorecard*, Washington, DC, https://www.globalintegrity.org (accessed 7 August 2015).

GI (Global Integrity) (2013) *Country reports, 2013: Indonesia- scorecard*, Washington, DC, https://www.globalintegrity.org (accessed 7 August 2015).

GIS (GAN Integrity Solutions) (2015) *Business-Anti-Corruption Portal: country profiles, South Asia – Bangladesh; India,* Copenhagen, http://www.business-anti-corruption.com/country-profiles/south-asia/bangladesh/snapshot.aspx (accessed 6 August 2015).

Hadiputranto, Hadinoto and Partners (2013) *Guide to competition law in Indonesia*, Jakarta, http://www. hhp.co.id/files/Uploads/Documents/Type%202/HHP/bk_hhp_competitionlawindonesia_2013. pdf (accessed 30 July 2015).

Johnston, M. (2010) *Political and social foundations for reform: Anti-corruption strategies for the Philippines*, Asian Institute of Management, Manila.

Jones, D.S. (2009) "Curbing corruption in government procurement in Southeast Asia: challenges and constraints", *Asian Journal of Political Science,* 17(2): 145–172.

Jones, D.S. (2013) "Procurement reform in the Philippines: the impact of elite capture and informal bureaucracy", *International Journal of Public Sector Management*, 26(5): 375–400.

KPPU (Komisi Pengawas Persaingan Usaha) (2013) *Newsletter on Indonesian competition law and policy: Kompetisia*, Jakarta, vol. 1, http://eng.kppu.go.id/wp-content/uploads/2013/07/kompetisia_vol1_ 2013_26062013_LAST.pdf. (accessed 16 July 2015).

KPPU (Komisi Pengawas Persaingan Usaha) (2014) *Newsletter on Indonesian competition law and policy: Kompetisia*, Jakarta, vol. 2, http://www.apeccp.org.tw/doc/Indonesia/Publication/nl2014/ KOMPETISIA_Vol2_2014.pdf (accessed 16 July 2015).

KFTC (Korean Fair Trade Commission) (2014) *Fair Trade Commission Republic of Korea Annual Report*, Sejong City, http://eng.ftc.go.kr/bbs.do?command=getList& type_cd=53&pageId=0301 (accessed 16 July 2015).

KFTC (Korean Fair Trade Commission) (2015a) *Statistical Yearbook of 2014*, Sejong City, http://eng.ftc. go.kr/bbs.do?command=getList&type_cd=51&pageId=0303 (accessed 16 July 2015).

KFTC (Korean Fair Trade Commission) (2015b) *Press Releas*, Sejong City, http://eng.ftc.go.kr/bbs. do?command=getList&type_cd=52&pageId=0305 (accessed 16 July 2015).

KFTC (Korean Fair Trade Commission) (2016) *Monopoly Regulation and Fair Trade Act* (amended 2016), Sejong City, http://eng.ftc.go.kr/bbs.do?command=getList& type_cd=62&pageId=0401 (accessed 28 February 2016).

MAC (Malaysian Anti-Corruption Commission) (2009) *Malaysian Anti-Corruption Commission Act 2009*, Putrajaya.

MAC (Malaysian Anti-Corruption Commission) (2012) *On the road to a corruption free nation: anti-corruption initiatives in Malaysia*, Putrajaya.

Ministry of Finance, Nepal (2011) *Nepal portfolio performance review (NPPR) 2011: portfolio performance and aid effectiveness*, Kathmandu, http://mof.gov.np/uploads/document/file/NPPR2011_ 20130715123906.pdf (accessed 12 August 2015).

NAV (National Assembly, Vietnam) (2005a) *Law on Tendering*, No. 61/2005/QH11, Hanoi, http:// www.slideshare.net/IFADVietnam/vietnam-law-on-tendering-number-61-2005qh11 (accessed 20 August 2015).

NAV (National Assembly, Vietnam) (2005b) *The Anti-Corruption Law*, No.55/2005/QH11, Hanoi, http://www.oecd.org/site/adboecdanti-corruptioninitiative/46817414.pdf (accessed 20 August 2015).

NAV (National Assembly, Vietnam) (2013) *Amended Law on Tendering*, No. 43/2013/QH13. Hanoi, http:// www.slideshare.net/iZibook/new-points-in-law-on-bidding-of-vietnam (accessed 20 August 2015).

OECD (1998) *Competition policy and procurement markets,* Geneva, www.oecd.org/regreform/ sectors/1920223.pdf (accessed 16 November 2015).

OECD (2007) *Snapshot assessment of Indonesia's public procurement system as at June, 2007*, Geneva, http:// www.oecd.org/dac/effectiveness/39254688.pdf (accessed 16 November 2015).

OECD (2009) *OECD principles for integrity in public procurement*, Geneva, http://www.oecd.org/gov/ ethics/48994520.pdf (accessed 15 November 2015).

OECD (2010) *Collusion and corruption in public procurement*, Geneva, http://www.oecd.org/competition/ cartels/46235884.pdf (accessed 16 November 2015).

OECD (2012) *Guidelines for fighting bid rigging in public procurement: Helping governments to obtain best value for money*, Geneva, http://www.oecd.org/competition/cartels/42851044.pdf (accessed 17 November 2015).

OECD (2014a) *Annual report on competition policy developments in Indonesia, 2013*, Geneva, http://www. oecd.org/officialdocuments/publicdisplaydocumentpdf/?cote=DAF/COMP/AR(2014)48&doc Language=En (accessed 17 November 2015).

OECD (2014b) *Annual report on competition policy developments in Japan*, Geneva, http://www.oecd.org/ officialdocuments/publicdisplaydocumentpdf/?cote=DAF/COMP/AR(2014)32&docLanguage= En (accessed 30 July 2015).

OOP (Office of the Ombudsman, Philippines) (2015) *Ombudsman Morales preventively suspends Mayor Binay Jr., et al. pending investigation*, Manila, http://www.ombudsman.gov.ph/index.php?home=1&pressId= NjEw (accessed 28 July 2015).

PRI (President of the Republic of Indonesia) (1999) *Law of the Republic of Indonesia Concerning the Ban on Monopolistic Practices and Unfair Business Competition*, Sovereign Law 5/1999, Jakarta, http://www. wipo.int/edocs/lexdocs/laws/en/id/id050en.pdf (accessed 16 July 2015).

PRI (President of the Republic of Indonesia) (2003) *Technical Guidelines on Procurement of Government Goods/Services*, Presidential Decree No. 80/2003, Jakarta, http://www.4shared.com/get/W3rcaYCA/ Keppres_No_80_Th_2003_-_Englis.html (accessed 16 July 2015).

Public Procurement Regulatory Authority, Pakistan (2015) *Blacklisted firms - Pakistan*, Islamabad, http://www.ppra.org.pk/pakblack.asp (accessed 4 August 2015).

Quah, J.S.T. (2003) *Curbing corruption in Asia: a comparative study of six countries*, Singapore: Eastern Universities Press.

Quah, J.S.T. (2015) "Singapore's corrupt practices investigation bureau: four suggestions for enhancing its effectiveness", *Asian Education and Development Studies*, 4(1): 76–100.

Sandiganbayan (2015) *About us*, Manila, http://sb.judiciary.gov.ph/ (accessed 2 August 2015).

Schütte, S.A. and S. Butt (2013) *The Indonesian court for corruption crimes: circumventing judicial impropriety?* Bergen: U4 Anti-Corruption Resource Centre, http://www.u4.no/publications/the-indonesian-court-for-corruption-crimes-circumventing-judicial-impropriety/ (accessed 17 June 2015).

SWS (Social Weather Stations) (2009) *Transparent accountable governance: the 2008 SWS surveys of enterprises on corruption*, Quezon City, Asia Foundation, http://www.sws.org.ph/TAG%208_NCR%20 Handout%20Nov21.pdf (accessed 29 July 2015).

SWS (Social Weather Stations) (2014) *The 2013 SWS survey of enterprises on corruption: The fight against public sector corruption has mixed findings*, Quezon City, Asia Foundation, https://www.sws.org.ph/ pr20140115b.htm *(accessed 29 July 2015)*.

ThaiLaws.com (2015) *Act Concerning Offences Relating to the Submission of Bids to Government Agencies B.E. 2542 (1999)*, Bangkok, http://thailaws.com/law/t_laws/tlaw0002_3.pdf (accessed 2 August 2015).

Torres, T., M. Ramos and J. Quinto (2011) "Ombudsman resigns", *Philippine Daily Inquirer*, 29 April.

TI (Transparency International) (2007) *Corruption report 2007: corruption in judicial systems*, Cambridge: Cambridge University Press.

TI (Transparency International) (2014) *Curbing corruption in public procurement: a practical guide*, http:// www.transparency.org/whatwedo/publication/curbing_corruption_in_public_procurement_a_ practical_guide (accessed 20 February 2016).

World Bank (2015) *Enterprise surveys: country profiles*, Washington, http://www.enterprisesurveys.org/ reports (accessed 17 June 2015).

WEF (World Economic Forum) (2015) *Competitiveness rankings,* Geneva, http://reports.weforum.org/ global-competitiveness-report-2015-2016/competitiveness-rankings/ (accessed 15 October 2015).

10

BRIBES AND TAXES: SPATIALLY CONCENTRATED OR RANDOMLY DISTRIBUTED?

Evidence from three sources
of firm level data in Vietnam[1]

John Rand and Finn Tarp

Introduction

With the enactment of the 2005 law on corruption, the establishment of the National Anti-Corruption Committee in 2006, and the ratification of the United Nations convention against corruption in 2009, the Vietnamese government signaled that the fight against corruption was at the top of the policy agenda. From 2005, media coverage on combating bribes also intensified. This increased public awareness, combined with a series of punitive actions against corrupt public officials and bribe paying firms, made clear to civil society that government legislative action against corrupt behavior would be progressively enforced.

Nevertheless, corrupt behavior remains widespread in the Vietnamese business environment. While bribe incidence decreased shortly after the enactment of the Law on Corruption (Rand and Tarp 2012), updated data show that bribe levels are back to their pre-2005 level. Biannual small- and medium sized enterprise (SME) tracer-survey data demonstrate that bribe incidence went from 41 per cent in 2005 to 26 per cent in 2007 and subsequently increased to 33 per cent, 37 per cent and 45 per cent in 2009, 2011 and 2013, respectively (CIEM 2010, 2012 and 2014).

Over the same period, the burden of corruption for bribe paying firms remained relatively constant at an average 1.6 per cent of reported profits of these firms. It is generally agreed that corruption is costly because of the associated efficiency losses in the allocation of resources related to the distorting and uncertain nature of the corruption "tax" (Fisman and Svensson 2007). With this background, it is important to analyze in more detail the nature, evolution and dynamics of the spatial distribution of firm level bribe payments over time to help formulate effective policy measures.

Several scholars have discussed the potentially close relationship between tax avoidance and informal payments. It is suggested that bribes are paid in order to avoid taxes (Johnson et al. 1998 and Tenev et al. 2003 in the case of Vietnam). On this basis, we would *ceteris paribus* expect to find a negative relationship between firm level bribe payments and tax burden (at least for firms with formal status). This relationship has however been questioned by Svensson (2003) among others, who emphasize firm visibility and relative bargaining power as the main drivers of observed bribe patterns. From this perspective, the observed positive correlation between tax and bribe incidence is seen as a function of firm level visibility (firm size and formality status) and unobserved heterogeneity in relative bargaining power between firms and civil servants/tax collectors.

Within the framework of the bargaining model (see Shleifer and Vishny 1993, for an exploration), a firm is with some probability faced with a tax collector, who can choose to extract a bribe which the firm needs to pay in order to get taxes reduced and perhaps even to stay in business. The discretionary power of the tax collector in implementing, executing, and enforcing rules relevant to the firm will affect the threat point in the negotiation between the tax collector and the firm. Moreover, the bargaining power of the tax collector will depend on tax reduction benefits that he/she can offer relative to the firm's outside option of not paying the bribe. In other words, a reduction in corporate income tax (CIT) should *ceteris paribus* reduce the bargaining power of tax collectors.

Over the period 2009 and 2013, the statutory corporate tax rate was 25 per cent and the CIT remained an important source of government revenue (approximately 16 per cent of total tax income). However, after the international crisis in 2008, a temporary CIT reduction/ exemption programme (30 per cent reduction) for SMEs was introduced. One might have expected this would have contributed to a continuation of the observed decline in SME bribe incidence. Instead bribe incidence has, as noted, been on the rise.

In this chapter, we aim to come to grips with the countervailing forces at play regarding SME bribe incidence in Vietnam, and provide an in-depth analysis of bribe-paying behavior based on different data sources that rely on different bribe incidence identification approaches. Contrary to previous studies of Vietnam, we focus especially on the relationship between tax avoidance and bribe incidence. The basic question we ask is whether tax avoidance and bribe incidence are spatially, identically or randomly distributed. First, we draw on a 2009–2013 panel dataset (CIEM 2010, 2012 and 2014). This includes both direct and indirect bribe incidence information on 1,169 manufacturing SMEs. Second, we combine the Provincial Competitiveness Index and the annual, nationwide Vietnamese Enterprise Survey (VES) data (GSO 2014) on manufacturing firms in all provinces to study whether corporate tax evasion is found in high bribe incidence locations. We conclude by highlighting a set of policy implications.

Data

For our main analysis, we rely on three SME surveys conducted in 2009, 2011 and 2013 in a Danida-supported project. All surveys cover around 2,600 enterprises in 10 provinces, including Ho Chi Minh City (HCMC), Ha Noi and Hai Phong, Long An, Ha Tay, Quang Nam, Phu Tho, Nghe An, Khanh Hoa and Lam Dong. In the years and areas covered, samples were stratified by type of ownership to ensure that all types of non-state enterprises (officially registered [with a business registration license], formal household, private, cooperative, limited liability and joint stock enterprises and non-official [informal] household firms) were represented. For reasons of implementation, the surveys were confined to specific areas in each province/city. Subsequently, stratified random samples were drawn from a consolidated list of formal enterprises and an on-site random selection of informal firms. While the sampling was adjusted over time to accommodate the rapidly changing business environment in Vietnam, other aspects, including the questionnaires, were maintained in a virtually identical form. After data cleaning and checking consistency of time-invariant variables between the three survey rounds, a balanced panel of 1,169 firm observations in each year was left. It is especially the lack of financial accounts that reduced the number of observations and no systematic attrition effects along observable dimensions were found.[2]

Given our focus on bribe incidence, we start by describing how we measure our main variable of interest. Firms were asked both an indirect and a direct question, in specifically designed survey instruments, about whether they were faced with informal payment requests. In the pilot phase of the project, more specifically, firms were asked the following initial question: "Do firms in your line of business (with the same location, size and sector) normally have to pay informal fees to public servants in order to "get things done?" Subsequently, the following more direct question was posed: "Do you have to pay informal fees to public servants in order to "get things done?" Surprisingly, answers to the indirect and direct questions were close to identical. In what follows, therefore, we report results based on the answers to the direct question only. Based on the answers to these questions, an indicator variable taking the value of one was generated if the firm paid bribes/informal fees and zero otherwise.

Table 10.1 shows the number of enterprises (in a transition matrix) which paid bribes in 2009 and 2013, respectively. Some 38 per cent of firms provided an informal payment in 2009 (the same level as in 2005; see Rand and Tarp 2012) and this share increased substantially to 50 per cent in 2013.[3] As in previous tracer studies, we observe significant variation in bribe payments across firms over time; only 22 per cent of firms paid bribes in both periods. However, during the period under consideration 2009–2013, most firms at some point found it necessary to pay bribes.

In the survey instrument, enterprises were also asked about the main purpose for paying bribes. Responses do not differ much from the patterns described in Rand and Tarp (2012). Thus, most bribes are said to be paid "to get connected to public services", "to deal with tax and tax collectors" and "to gain government contracts". Moreover, the size of the informal payments also remained fairly constant from 2005 onwards at approximately 1.6 per cent of recorded profits for bribe paying firms. However, although many firms see informal payments as a "normal feature of doing business", two-thirds of the firms in our data said that they never know in advance why they have to pay, when they have to pay, and how much they have to pay in informal fees. The uncertain and random nature of bribes therefore seems to have continued in Vietnam, with potentially detrimental effects on firm level growth and investment behavior (Fisman and Svensson 2007).

Turning to potential bribe determinants (see summary statistics in Table 10.2 and Appendix Table A by year), we basically follow the model structure outlined in Rand and Tarp (2012). Firm exposure and visibility and the degree of interaction with public officials has been shown to influence bribe incidence. Firm size (number of employees) captures one aspect of visibility and exposure, as larger firms are more visible and less likely able to avoid

Table 10.1 Bribe incidence dynamics

		2013					
		No		Yes		Total	
2009	No	408	(56)	320	(44)	728	
		(69)		(55)		(62)	
	Yes	181	(41)	260	(59)	441	
		(31)		(45)		(38)	
	Total	589	(50)	580	(50)	1169	

Note: Number of enterprises (percentage in parentheses).

Table 10.2 Firm characteristics by bribe incidence category

	Total		Bribe-payers		Non-bribers	
	Mean	Std	Mean	Std	Mean	Std
Bribe (Yes = 1)	0.423	0.494	1.000	0.000	0.000	0.000
Firm size (Number of employees, log)	12.9	23.9	18.1	30.5	9.0	16.6
Capital-Labor ratio (million VND, log)	6.6	1.2	6.7	1.1	6.5	1.3
Profit per employee (million VND)	145.9	115.6	155.4	126.4	138.8	106.5
State customer (Yes = 1)	0.201	0.401	0.257	0.437	0.160	0.367
Trade (Yes = 1)	0.048	0.214	0.069	0.253	0.033	0.178
Government assistance (Yes = 1)	0.199	0.400	0.223	0.416	0.182	0.386
Informal/Not registered (Yes = 1)	0.271	0.445	0.142	0.349	0.366	0.482
Pay taxes	0.908	0.289	0.968	0.177	0.865	0.342
Bribe incidence redefined (Yes =1)	0.520	0.500	1.000	0.000	0.167	0.374
Number of observations	3,507		1,483		2,024	

Note: Summary statistics based on 1,169 firms over three years (2009, 2011 and 2013).

potentially corrupt public officials/tax collectors. Table 10.2 also shows that bribe-payers are on average larger than non-bribe-payers. Firm informality (indicator variable taking the value one if the firm does not have a business registration license and zero otherwise) captures another aspect of the visibility/exposure dimension. SMEs without a formal business registration licence can, on the one hand, hide more easily and avoid bribes. On the other hand, informality may be part of a firm's strategy to avoid paying taxes; in order to access these tax benefits of informality, they are willing to pay an informal fee associated with the tax benefit service. Consequently, informality may have opposing effects on bribe incidence so the net effect on the probability of paying bribes of being informal is an empirical issue. Table 10.2 shows an (unconditional) larger share of informal firms among non-bribers.

We also include proxies for firm ability or willingness to pay (profits per employee) and firm refusal power (capital-labor [K/L] ratio), where a high profit level and K/L ratio will *ceteris paribus* weaken the firm's bargaining position, and will result in public officials/ tax collectors demanding higher informal fees. In addition, following Svensson (2003) and Hansen et al. (2009) a series of variables (having the state as a customer, receiving direct government assistance and engaging in international trade/with customs) that captures the degree to which firms interact directly with public officials is also included. Unconditional means in Table 10.2 indicates that bribe payers tend to be more profitable, capital intensive and engage more frequently with public officials than their non-bribing counterparts.

Given the focus in this chapter on the relationship between tax avoidance and bribe incidence and consistent with Svensson (2003) (who interprets the "pay tax" dummy as a control rights measure), we include an indicator variable taking the value one if the firm pay taxes and zero otherwise. Table 10.2 shows that almost 97 per cent of bribe payers also pay taxes, whereas this number is 87 per cent among the non-bribe paying segment. However, several of the informal firms record tax payments. We therefore also constructed a second bribe incidence measure taking the value one if firms pay a bribe or if an informal firm records official corporate income tax (CIT) payments and zero otherwise. We see from Table 10.2 that this moves 16.7 per cent of the non-bribers into bribe payer category. This is an issue to which we return in the analysis that follows as it may influence the inter-relationship between bribe incidence, tax avoidance and informality.

Finally, in accordance with Rand and Tarp (2012), we include location and sector indicators. Vietnamese provinces are relatively autonomous and have to follow different implementation strategies of centrally planned initiatives and sector (based on 2-digit level International Standard Industrial Classification (ISIC) codes) may capture additional aspects of the sunk cost component of physical capital.

Econometric results

We focus on three issues in our econometric analysis. First, we investigate the association between bribe determinants identified in traditional theory and the probability of providing informal payments. Second, we seek to disentangle whether there exists a systematic relationship between informal payments, effective corporate tax rates (ECTR) and formality status. We do so by taking a close look at the bribe gap for the average ECTR and try to disentangle the gap into explained and unexplained components applying a generalized Blinder-Oaxaca (BO) decomposition. Furthermore, we illustrate that firm size is an important determinant of the average adjusted ECTR and, importantly, firm size has differential impacts among bribe-paying and non-bribe-paying firms. Third, we try to uncover whether the bribe incidence increase in post-2007 Vietnam can be explained by underlying firm specific observables changes, including changes in effective corporate tax rates.

Bribe incidence, tax avoidance and informality

In column 1 of Table 10.3, we report results from pooled probit models using contemporaneous measures of potential bribe determinants. Province, sector and time indicators are included in all regressions and they are significant as groups.

Results are consistent with those reported in Rand and Tarp (2012). First, we note that the time indicator for 2013 is positive and significant throughout Table 10.3 (not reported). This highlights the unfortunate trend reversal observed in the bribe incidence pattern among Vietnamese SMEs. According to our data, more SMEs now face bribes than during the period around 2005 when there was intensified political commitment to combat corruption. Second, our "exposure/visibility" variable represented by firm size (log employment) is positive and well-determined in all specifications. Larger firms are more likely to pay bribes. Third, firm outside options (captured by the K/L ratio) also have the expected statistically well-determined positive sign throughout. Fourth, profit per employee estimates is also positive and well-determined in all specifications. This confirms that visible/exposed and high-profit firms are more likely to pay bribes. Fifth, among our "interaction with government" controls we find no systematic relationship between dealing with customers and observed bribe incidence. However, contrary to previous results studying the same SMEs, firms that receive government assistance are not more likely to be bribe payers, which may partly be explained by the sharp decline between 2009 and 2013 in the number of firms receiving such assistance. Finally, we note that having the state as customer and formality status remain important for understanding bribe paying status. Firms linked via the supply chain to state-owned enterprises (SOEs) are more likely to pay bribes and this is consistent with the view that hiding (and avoiding interaction with potentially corrupt public officials) is easier when the firm has informal status. In fact, being informal reduces the probability of making informal payments by 13.5 per cent in the base specification (column 1).

Table 10.3 Bribe incidence determinants

	1	2	3	4	5
Firm size	0.136★★★	0.132★★★	0.131★★★	0.132★★★	0.129★★★
	(0.012)	(0.012)	(0.012)	(0.012)	(0.012)
Capital-Labor ratio	0.024★★	0.023★★	0.021★★	0.023★★	0.021★★
	(0.009)	(0.009)	(0.009)	(0.009)	(0.009)
Profit per employee (★100)	0.018★	0.017★	0.019★	0.017★	0.019★
	(0.008)	(0.008)	(0.008)	(0.008)	(0.008)
State customer (Yes = 1)	0.047★★	0.047★★	0.044★	0.047★★	0.044★
	(0.023)	(0.023)	(0.023)	(0.023)	(0.023)
Trade (Yes = 1)	−0.044	−0.042	−0.046	−0.043	−0.054
	(0.041)	(0.041)	(0.042)	(0.041)	(0.042)
Government assistance	0.025	0.027	0.025	0.026	0.027
(Yes = 1)	(0.023)	(0.023)	(0.023)	(0.023)	(0.023)
Informal/Not registered	−0.135★★★	−0.104★★★	−0.136★★★	−0.208★★	−0.158★★★
(Yes = 1)	(0.024)	(0.026)	(0.024)	(0.116)	(0.026)
Pay taxes		0.130★★★		0.033	
		(0.035)		(0.124)	
ECTR adjusted			−0.031		−0.046
			(0.056)		(0.056)
Informal★Pay taxes				0.118	
				(0.135)	
Informal★ECTR					0.967★
					(0.420)
Sector dummies included	Yes	Yes	Yes	Yes	Yes
Province dummies included	Yes	Yes	Yes	Yes	Yes
Year dummies included	Yes	Yes	Yes	Yes	Yes
Firm observations	3,507	3,507	3,507	3,507	3,507
Pseudo R-squared	0.13	0.14	0.13	0.14	0.14

Note: Dependent variable: indicator variable taking the value one if the firm pay bribes, zero otherwise. Probit estimates, marginal effects. Standard errors (reported in parenthesis) are cluster robust. ★, ★★, ★★★ indicate significance at a 10 per cent, 5 per cent and 1 per cent level, respectively.

Digging deeper into the triangular relationship between informality, taxes and bribes, we include, in column 2 in Table 10.3, the indicator variable for paying taxes, and find a positive association between paying taxes and paying bribes (even when conditioning on informality status). This is consistent with the positive relationship found in Svensson (2003) in the case of Uganda.

To obtain a deeper insight into whether bribe payments and firm level tax avoidance are related independently of formality status, we look more closely at the combined burden of taxes and bribes for corporate balance sheets. Following the recommendations in Hanlon and Heitzman (2010), we define tax avoidance broadly, such that our tax avoidance measure represents a variety of tax planning strategies. More specifically, we use two measures of tax avoidance. First, we calculate the annual effective corporate tax rates (ECTR) as the ratio of profit taxes paid over calculated pre-tax gross profit. In what follows, we refer to this as the *unadjusted ECTR* measure. The second measure is the *adjusted ECTR* calculated as ECTR plus the ratio of bribe paid over calculated pre-tax gross profit. None of the ECTR measures control for nondiscretionary items (depreciable and amortizable assets) and they also contain measurement errors related to previous year's tax refunds and tax dispute settlements. As a robustness check, we therefore use the five-year effective corporate tax rate (5ECTR) for both measures. This is the ratio of the sum of corporate tax payments and bribe payments over the past five years divided by the sum of pre-tax profits over the same five-year period (Dyreng et al. 2008). Since statutory corporate tax rates differ along firm size during the period under consideration, we use all measures relative to their respective compliance rates as a robustness check (rel5ECTR). We only report results for the unadjusted and adjusted ECTR which are qualitatively the same as conclusions obtained using 5ECTR or rel5ECTR.

Appendix Table B provides summary statistics for bribe amounts and effective corporate tax rates, split by bribe status, tax payer status and formality status. First, we see that the average ECTR is somewhat below the statutory corporate tax rate (ranging between 17 per cent and 25 per cent depending on firm size). Second, the ECTR is almost 16 times higher than bribes paid on average for the full sample. The financial "burden" of taxes therefore clearly dominates bribe payments even among bribe paying firms. Third, formal enterprises on average pay larger bribes and face higher tax payments than informal firms. Finally, bribe paying firms pay 47 per cent more in taxes (as a percentage of profits) than non-bribers, an amount that increases to 65 per cent if bribes are included in tax measure (adjusted ECTR).

Returning to Table 10.3, we do not find in column 3 a clear systematic pattern between bribe incidence and average ECTR, both adjusted and unadjusted for bribe amounts. However, this effect may be non-linearly related to informality status. In columns 4 and 5, we therefore look into the relationship between bribe incidence, taxes and informality status. We find only limited evidence that informal firms which pay taxes are more likely to pay bribes. Overall, our results from Table 10.3 seem to suggest that firm formality is strongly associated with bribe incidence whereas the relationship between taxes and bribes is less clear, even when distinguishing firms along the informality dimension. We therefore proceed to explore the latter relationship further.

One problem with the analysis in Table 10.3 is the way in which it distinguishes between taxes and bribe payments in a context of firms without a registered tax code (informal firms). The two plots in Figure 10.1 illustrate the point. The figure shows the association between firm size and the share of bribe paying firms, split by formality status. The black curve is the share of informal bribe paying firms while the grey curve is the share of formal bribe paying firms. The shaded area indicates the point-wise 90 per cent confidence interval. In the "bribes only" plot we clearly see that the probability of paying bribes is increasing with firm size and that formal firms are significantly more likely (at least for smaller firms) to pay bribes than informal firms. This confirms the results in Table 10.4. However, when considering self-reported taxes as bribes for informal firms (panel B: Bribes + Taxes) this changes the picture, as one would expect. The share of informal firms paying bribes increases dramatically and stochastically dominates formal firms throughout the firm size distribution. Consequently, it may be of more relevance to look at the relationship between the financial burden of bribes and taxes, respectively, and their inter-relationship.

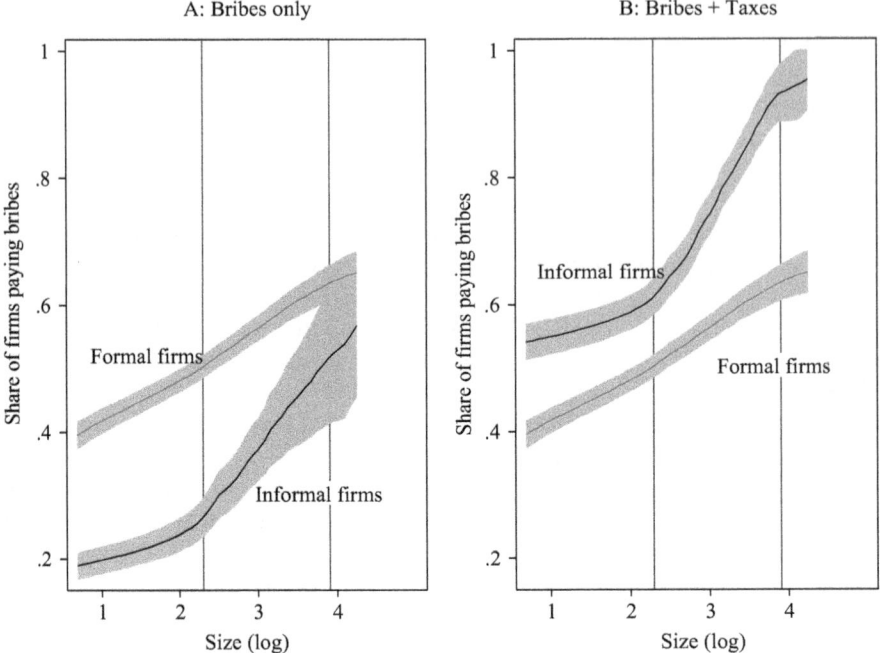

Figure 10.1 Bribe incidence, taxes and informality by firm size

Note: Kernel weighed local mean smoothing using the Epanechnikov kernel and a bandwidth of 0.8. Black curves are for informal firms; grey curves are for formal firms. Shaded areas are point-wise 90 per cent confidence intervals. The two vertical lines are at 2.30 and 3.91 and indicate the upper limits on the size of micro (up to 10 employees) and small (up to 50 employees) enterprises using the standard World Bank definition.

Accordingly, we turn to the Blinder-Oaxaca (BO) decomposition, which essentially identifies two components of the unconditional gap in ECTR (both unadjusted and adjusted), that is, the difference between ECTR for bribe payers and the ECTR for non-bribers. The first component is a measure of the importance of differences in observable characteristics between bribers and non-bribers. Following the literature, we refer to this component as the "characteristics effect". The second component is a measure of the importance of differences in parameters for the two groups. It is often described as capturing variation in the returns to the characteristics between bribe-paying and non-bribe-paying firms. In the following, it is denoted as the "coefficient effect" or the unexplained component. Algebraically, the tax gap between bribers and non-bribers can be described by the following decomposition into two components where Δ is the ECTR gap given both bribe specific characteristics and coefficients (the "average difference", or gap):

$$\Delta = \left[E_{\beta_B}(C_{iB} \mid X_{iB}) - E_{\beta_B}(C_{iN} \mid X_{iN}) \right] + \left[E_{\beta_B}(C_{iN} \mid X_{iN}) - E_{\beta_N}(C_{iN} \mid X_{iN}) \right] \quad (1)$$

The first term in brackets on the RHS is difference in expected ECTR for bribers (B) and non-bribers (N) where the expectation is evaluated under bribers' parameters (β_B). This is the explained component because it extracts the importance of differences in endowments and weighing these using the same weights (the bribers' parameters). The second term in brackets is the difference in expected ECTR for non-bribers when the expectation is evaluated under the bribers' parameters and the non-bribers parameters, respectively. This is the unexplained component of the tax gap. The decomposition in (1) is formulated from the viewpoint of bribing firms, which means that group differences in the characteristics are weighted by the coefficients of bribers to determine the endowments effect. For the unexplained component, the difference in expectations for the two different coefficient sets are weighted by non-briber firm characteristics, that is, the coefficient effect measures the change in expectations of non-bribers' outcome, if they had bribers' coefficients. The formulation in (1) can be changed such that the non-bribers' and bribers' characteristics and coefficients are interchanged. This weighting difference may lead to different component estimates for a given average tax gap. Next, we therefore report results using both briber and non-briber coefficients as reference parameters.

Table 10.4 shows the results of our BO decompositions by bribe category and formality status. For the full sample, we see a statistically significant unconditional combined tax and bribe gap of 5.9 percentage points between bribers and non-bribers confirming the summary statistics in Table 10.2. Splitting the sample into formal and informal firms, respectively, reduces the combined tax and bribe gap to around 3 percentage points within each formality group. Generally the characteristics effect is positive and significant. This indicates that if the combined burden of taxes and bribes were allocated based on differences in observable characteristics, bribers would be more heavily taxed than non-bribers. The result is robust to the exclusion of bribes from the ECTR measure. More than 73 per cent of the variation in the tax gap can be attributed to explained differences in characteristics between bribers and non-bribers. Moreover, differences in firm size and formality status are the main contributors for explaining the observed differences in the tax gap between bribers and non-bribers. Hence, the result in Table 10.4 leads to the conclusion that the observed tax gap is

Table 10.4 Blinder-Oaxaca decomposition: effective corporate tax rates and bribes

	All		Formal		Informal	
	(1)	*(2)*	*(3)*	*(4)*	*(5)*	*(6)*
Difference	0.059***		0.031***		0.032***	
	(0.007)		(0.008)		(0.006)	
Characteristics	0.046***	0.043***	0.025***	0.015***	0.001	0.010*
(explained) effect	(0.005)	(0.005)	(0.005)	(0.004)	(0.002)	(0.006)
Coefficients	0.013	0.016***	0.006	0.016**	0.031***	0.022***
(unexplained) effect	(0.008)	(0.005)	(0.010)	(0.008)	(0.006)	(0.005)
Reference Group	Bribers coefficients	Non-bribers coefficients	Bribers coefficients	Non-bribers coefficients	Bribers coefficients	Non-bribers coefficients
Detail (explained – % of total difference)						
Firm size	55.1	50.1				
Informality	22.8	22.9				

Note: Dependent variable: Effective Corporate Tax Rate (ECTR). Blinder-Oaxaca decomposition. Standard errors reported in parenthesis. *, **, *** indicate significance at a 10 per cent, 5 per cent and 1 per cent level, respectively.

not strongly linked to the unexplained component. If anything the positive coefficient effect suggests a discrimination against bribe payers in terms of effective corporate taxation. As such, the level of taxation (unadjusted and adjusted for bribe payments) does not seem to be affected (on average) by bribe payer status, when one controls for other observable firm level attributes.

Figure 10.2 illustrates this lack of close correspondence between observed ECTR (obtained at the district and province level from the VES average 2009–2013) and levels of informal charges (obtained at the provincial level from the provincial competitiveness index average 2009–2013) at a more aggregate level. A high score in Figure 10.2 indicates relatively big discrepancies between the individual rankings of firm level taxes and bribes whereas a low score indicates close ECTR and informal charges rankings. The overall unconditional correlation is −0.11 (conditioning on province level gross domestic product (GDP) reduces the correlation to −0.04). Moreover, sorting provinces according to ECTR and informal charges, respectively, the rank correlation is clearly relatively low according to Figure 10.2. So, also at the more aggregate level, we cannot find a clear relationship between effective rates of taxation and informal charges facing firms, even when controlling for province income levels.

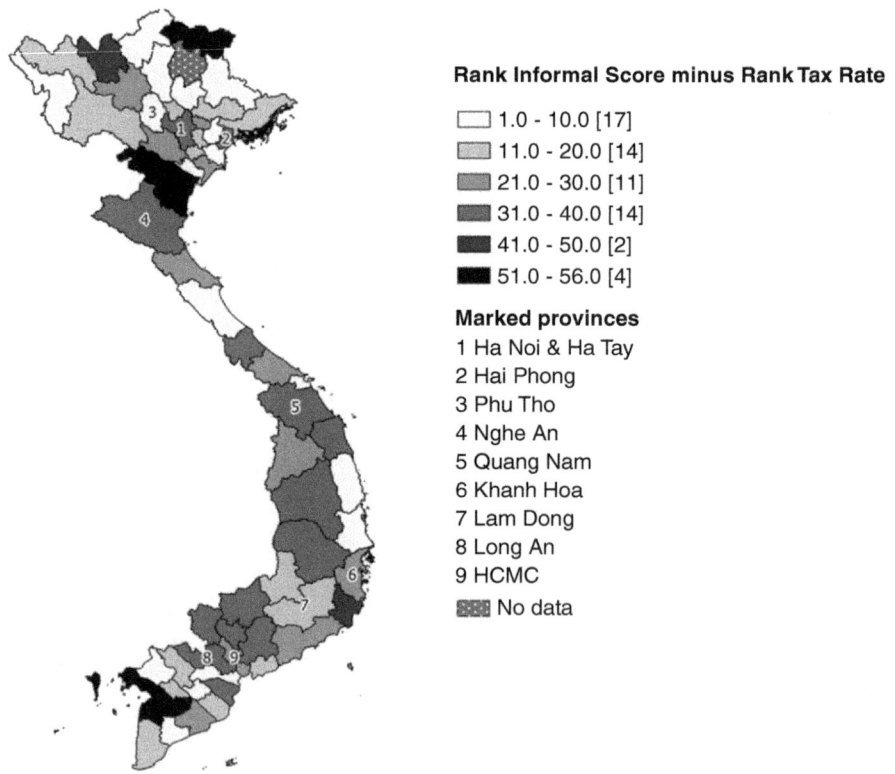

Rank Informal Score minus Rank Tax Rate

☐ 1.0 - 10.0 [17]
▨ 11.0 - 20.0 [14]
▨ 21.0 - 30.0 [11]
▨ 31.0 - 40.0 [14]
▨ 41.0 - 50.0 [2]
■ 51.0 - 56.0 [4]

Marked provinces
1 Ha Noi & Ha Tay
2 Hai Phong
3 Phu Tho
4 Nghe An
5 Quang Nam
6 Khanh Hoa
7 Lam Dong
8 Long An
9 HCMC
▨ No data

Figure 10.2 Rank correlations between ECTR and informal payments

Note: ECTR is calculated from the Vietnam Enterprise Survey (VES) (GSO 2014). Informal payments have been calculated from the provincial competitiveness index (PCI) (VNCI 2014).

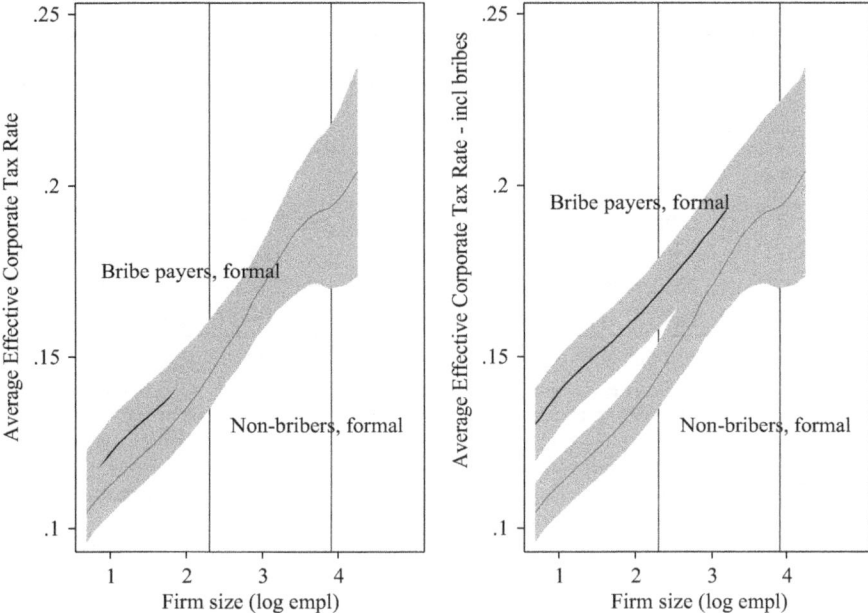

Figure 10.3 Average effective corporate taxes and bribes by firm size

Note: Kernel weighed local mean smoothing using the Epanechnikov kernel and a bandwidth of 0.8. Black curves are for bribers; grey curves are for non-bribers. Shaded areas are point-wise 90 per cent confidence intervals. The two vertical lines are at 2.30 and 3.91 and indicate the upper limits on the size of micro (up to 10 employees) and small (up to 50 employees) enterprises using the standard World Bank definition.

Given the importance of firm size for bribe incidence, we return in Figure 10.3 to the SME data and illustrate the estimated ECTR for formal firms conditional on firm size. Panel A illustrates the situation without adjusting the ECTR for bribe payments; Panel B shows the situation for the adjusted ECTR measure. The upper black curves are for bribers; the grey curves are for non-bribers. Panel A illustrates that bribers and non-bribers face more or less the same ECTR along the firm size distribution. However, Panel B shows that the ECTR gap between bribers and non-bribers is more pronounced for smaller firms, signaling that the burden of bribes for micro formal firms is just added to compliance-related tax payments. Even though the adjusted ECTR increases with firm size the tax gap narrows and we estimate that the combined burden of taxes and bribes is not statistically different between bribers and non-bribe payers for firms with 20 employees and above.

Change in bribe incidence

Turning to the significant increase in bribe incidence between 2009 and 2013, which followed a decrease from 2005, we aim to uncover the underlying reasons using a generalized BO decomposition. The change in bribe incidence between 2009 and 2013 (*B13 – B09*) can be described by the following decomposition into two components:

$$B_{13} - B_{09} = \left[\Phi\left(\sum X_{13}\beta_{13}\right) - \Phi\left(\sum X_{09}\beta_{13}\right) \right] + \left[\Phi\left(\sum X_{09}\beta_{13}\right) - \Phi\left(\sum X_{09}\beta_{09}\right) \right] \quad (2)$$

Table 10.5 Blinder-Oaxaca decomposition: bribe incidence changes

	All		Formal		Informal	
	(1)	*(2)*	*(3)*	*(4)*	*(5)*	*(6)*
Difference	−0.119★★★		−0.078★★★		−0.149★★★	
	(0.019)		(0.024)		(0.032)	
Characteristics	−0.003	−0.013	−0.028★★	−0.054★★★	0.001	0.018
(explained) effect	(0.014)	(0.012)	(0.011)	(0.010)	(0.021)	(0.017)
Coefficients	0.122★★★	0.132★★★	0.106★★★	0.131★★★	0.148★★★	0.131★★★
(unexplained) effect	(0.019)	(0.022)	(0.026)	(0.025)	(0.036)	(0.033)
Reference Group/	2009	2013	2009	2013	2009	2013
Year	coefficients	coefficients	coefficients	coefficients	coefficients	coefficients

Note: Blinder-Oaxaca decomposition. Dependent variable: Bribe incidence changes. Mean estimates in 2013 and 2009 for the full sample are 0.496 (0.015) and 0.377 (0.014), respectively (see Appendix Table A). Robust standard errors reported in parenthesis. ★, ★★, ★★★ indicate significance at a 10 per cent, 5 per cent and 1 per cent level, respectively.

where Φ is the cumulative normal density function; X_{13} and X_{09} include the mean values of the explanatory variables used in the probit estimation described in Table 10.3; and β_{13} β_{09} contains the estimated coefficients for each year. The first and second part of the right-hand side reflects respectively the characteristics and the coefficients effect (as described above). Since decomposition of non-linear models share the problem of the linear BO decomposition with regard to the choice of reference group, we report findings using both 2009 and 2013 coefficients as the reference group.

In our sample, the mean bribe incidence is 0.377 in 2009 and 0.496 in 2013. This yields a significant difference or gap of 0.119. This bribe incidence gap has been divided into: (1) a characteristics (explained) and (2) a coefficients (unexplained) part. In Table 10.5, BO decompositions have been done for all firms (column 1), for formal firms only (column 2) and for informal firms only (column 3). The BO decomposition in Table 10.5 suggests that most of the bribe incidence increase of 11.9 percentage points is explained by differences in coefficients rather than by changes in observed characteristics, which is in accordance with Rand and Tarp (2012). This suggests that changes in "preferences" in the Vietnamese SME business environment played as important a role for the increase in bribe incidence from 2009–2013 as for the decrease observed between 2005 and 2009.

Turning to the formality split (columns 2 and 3 in Table 10.5), we observe a higher bribe incidence increase among informal firms (14.9 percentage points) than for formal firms (7.8 percentage points). Moreover, we see that it is differences in characteristics within formal firms that bring the bribe incidence increase to a lower level. Detailed BO decompositions (not reported) reveal that firm size changes (reductions in number of employees) and changes (reductions) in government assistance to formal firms are the main drivers of this characteristics effect. Although decreases in average firm size and the significant decline in direct government support may contribute to reduced bribe incidence, this finding may be of less relevance from a policy perspective if job creation is at the center of Vietnamese policy priorities for the future.

Summary and conclusions

At the outset of this chapter, we wanted to come better to grips with the evolution and nature of bribe-paying behavior among SMEs in Vietnam from 2009 to 2013. Using three different up-to-date data sources with information on bribe incidence, tax avoidance and firm informality, we broadly followed the approach of Rand and Tarp (2012), who focused on the 2005–2007 years. This earlier period saw a decrease in bribe incidence while the opposite is the case for the years studied in this chapter. As such, the present chapter was meant to establish any changes between the two periods and provide further illuminating insights into the underlying driver(s) of bribe incidence.

Our analysis in the section on bribe incidence, tax avoidance and informality showed, first, that relatively larger, more profitable, more visible, and formally registered firms are more likely to provide informal payments. This is in line with Rand and Tarp (2012) and confirms that the *visibility* effect continues to dominate the *bribes-to-hide* effect when analyzing Vietnamese SMEs in 2009 to 2013. Second, at a first glance we do not find a clear systematic relationship between tax avoidance and bribe incidence, when controlling for relevant firm level attributes. This conclusion is, however, firm size-dependent, as the financial (balance sheet) burden of bribes is especially detrimental for formal micro-SMEs. Smaller registered SMEs (fewer than 20 employees) do not seem to get the observable preferential tax benefits from paying bribes that SMEs with more than 20 employees seem to enjoy. But even for larger SMEs the preferential tax benefit received from paying bribes does not bring any significant tax balance sheet effects as compared to larger SMEs not paying bribes. Although the tax "benefit" of paying bribes is not easily observed among Vietnamese SMEs, we do not discount the possibility that bribes may be facilitating other growth enhancing opportunities such as easier access to certain government contracts (as shown in Rand and Tarp 2012).

Our decomposition approach in the section on change in bribe incidence suggests that the recent increase in bribe incidence observed among Vietnamese SMEs does not reflect changes in firm characteristics. If anything changes in characteristics (especially for enterprises with a business registration license) are leading to decreasing bribe incidence, which is, however, dominated by a coefficients effect pulling in the other direction. This means that the increase in bribe incidence would have occurred even without changes in observable firm characteristics. Moreover, without the significant reductions in firm size and reductions in direct government support to SMEs the observed bribe incidence would have been even higher. In fact, most of the bribe incidence increase in the full sample is explained by the coefficient effects, meaning that the increase in bribe incidence between 2009 and 2013 is strictly related to behavioral changes among firms in relation to bribe provision. This is in line with Rand and Tarp (2012) and unfortunately confirms that the greater political commitment and improved law enforcement around 2005 (and the immediate observed effects hereof) were short lived.

Turning to policy implications, we reiterate that behavioral changes are at the centra of the non-sustainability of previous progress. Arguably, these behavioral changes are associated with the weakening attention and declined political commitment to improved law enforcement during the 2009– 2013 period, including also less media focus on punitive actions against corruption. This reinforces the line of argument that in settings where bribe behavior has become intrinsic, the role of political leaders and the publicity given to punitive action have a key role to play in counteracting and overcoming corrupt behavior.

Appendix Table A Firm characteristics by year

	2009		2011		2013	
	Mean	*Std*	*Mean*	*Std*	*Mean*	*Std*
Bribe (Yes = 1)	0.377	0.485	0.395	0.489	0.496	0.500
Firm size (Number of employees, log)	14.3	28.7	12.9	23.1	11.4	18.9
Capital-Labor ratio (million VND, log)	6.5	1.2	6.8	1.2	6.6	1.1
Profit per employee (million VND)	145.9	115.6	145.9	115.6	145.9	115.6
State customer (Yes = 1)	0.180	0.384	0.234	0.424	0.189	0.392
Trade (Yes = 1)	0.054	0.226	0.049	0.215	0.041	0.199
Government assistance (Yes = 1)	0.318	0.466	0.150	0.357	0.130	0.336
Informal/Not registered (Yes = 1)	0.320	0.467	0.256	0.436	0.239	0.426
Pay taxes	0.874	0.332	0.924	0.265	0.926	0.261
Bribe incidence redefined (Yes =1)	0.502	0.500	0.492	0.500	0.565	0.496
Number of observations	1,169		1,169		1,169	

Note: Summary statistics based on 1,169 firms over three years (2009, 2011 and 2013).

Appendix Table B Bribe amounts and effective corporate tax rates

	Bribe amount (Share of profits, %)	Effective Corporate Tax Rate (ECTR, %)	Combined Tax + bribe (%)	No of firms
All Firms	0.7	10.9	11.6	(3,507)
Non-bribers	0.0	9.1	9.1	(2,024)
Bribers	1.6	13.4	15.0	(1,483)
Non-tax payers	0.3	0	0.3	(322)
Tax payers	0.7	12.0	12.7	(3,185)
Informal	0.3	1.6	1.9	(952)
Formal	0.8	14.4	15.2	(2,555)

Note: Numbers in percentages (of gross profits). Number of firms in each category in parenthesis.

Notes

1 We thank Kasper Brandt (Development Economics Research Group [DERG], Department of Economics, University of Copenhagen) for excellent research assistance. We furthermore acknowledge our productive and stimulating collaboration with the survey teams from the Vietnamese Institute of Labor Science and Social Affairs (ILSSA) and the staff at the Central Institute for Economic Management (CIEM) and General Statistics Office (GSO) in Vietnam. The usual caveats apply.

2 For full details on the surveys and sampling procedures, see CIEM (2010, 2012, and 2014).
3 In the Provincial Competitiveness Index (PCI) survey (VNCI 2014) formal (registered) enterprises were also asked whether it is common for firms to pay informal charges. Some 52 per cent of firms answered yes to this question in 2013.

References

CIEM (Central Institute for Economic Management) (2010) *Characteristics of the Vietnamese business environment: evidence from a SME Survey in 2009*, Hanoi: CIEM.

CIEM (Central Institute for Economic Management) (2012) *Characteristics of the Vietnamese business environment: evidence from a SME Survey in 2011*, Hanoi: CIEM.

CIEM (Central Institute for Economic Management) (2014) *Characteristics of the Vietnamese business environment: evidence from a SME Survey in 2013*, Hanoi: CIEM.

Dyreng, S.D., M.H. Hanlon and E.L. Maydew (2008) "Long-run corporate tax avoidance", *The Accounting Review*, 83(1): 61–82.

Fisman, R. and J. Svensson (2007) "Are corruption and taxation really harmful to growth? Firm level evidence", *Journal of Development Economics*, 83(1): 63–75.

GSO (General Statistics Office) (2014) *The real situation of enterprises: through the results of surveys conducted in 2010, 2011, 2012*, Hanoi: Statistical Publishing House.

Hanlon, M. and S. Heitzman (2010) "A review of tax research", *Journal of Accounting and Economics*, 50(2–3): 127–178.

Hansen, H., J. Rand and F. Tarp (2009) "Enterprise growth and survival in Vietnam: did government support matter?" *Journal of Development Studies*, 45(7): 1048–1069.

Johnson, S., D. Kaufmann and P. Zoido-Lobatón (1998) "Regulatory discretion and the unofficial economy", *American Economic Review*, 88(2), 387–392.

Rand, J. and F. Tarp (2012) "Firm level corruption in Vietnam", *Economic Development and Cultural Change*, 60(3): 571–595.

Shleifer, A. and R.W. Vishny (1993) "Corruption", *Quarterly Journal of Economics*, 108(3): 599–617.

Svensson, J. (2003) "Who must pay bribes and how much? Evidence from a cross section of firms", *Quarterly Journal of Economics* 118(1): 207–230.

Tenev, S., A. Carlier, O. Chaudry and Q.-T. Ngyuen (2003) "Informality and the playing field in Vietnam's business sector", photocopy, Washington DC: IFC, World Bank and MPDF.

VNCI (Vietnam Competitiveness Initiative) (2014) *The Vietnam Provincial Competitiveness Index 2014*, Hanoi: Vietnam Chamber of Commerce and Industry (VCCI) and United States Agency for International Development's Vietnam Competitiveness Initiative (VNCI).

11

REGULATORY CAPTURE AS A TWO-WAY STREET

Hong Kong small and medium enterprises in the Pearl River Delta Region

Thomas Johnson, Ting Gong and Wen Wang

Introduction

Since the onset of China's reform and the introduction of the "opening up" policy in 1978, the Pearl River Delta region (PRD) has been a key driver of the country's remarkable economic transformation. This economic zone, which includes the cities of Guangzhou, Shenzhen, Dongguan, Foshan, Zhongshan, Zhuhai and Jiangmen, as well as parts of Huizhou and Zhaoqing, has experienced rapid economic growth in the past decades. In 2013, the gross domestic product (GDP) of the PRD grew at an average of 9.4 per cent and accounted for 9.3 per cent of the country's total GDP and 27.5 per cent of national exports. The region is also a global manufacturing base, playing a leading role in the production of toys, footwear, lighting fixtures, furniture and other products (HKTDC 2015).

Small- and medium-sized enterprises (SMEs) have made a significant contribution to the PRD's economic success. Healthy SME development has long been considered critically important for economic growth, innovation, job creation and market competition in developed and developing countries alike (Aidis 2005). Approximately 80,000 Hong Kong companies operate in the region (GPPP and ICAC 2008). Most are SMEs, which are defined as manufacturing enterprises with fewer than 100 employees and non-manufacturing enterprises with fewer than 50 employees (Hong Kong General Chamber of Small and Medium Business 2015). These firms have contributed significantly to the region's rapid economic growth and derive their own substantial benefits from the Chinese market.

Despite the importance of Hong Kong SMEs to the PRD's economy, they operate in an environment that presents great corruption risks. The academic literature recognises that corruption is a serious problem in many transitional economies, jeopardising long-term economic growth and social development. Corruption has been shown to have adverse effects on the rate at which firms grow (Beck et al. 2005), to distort their investment and distribution decisions (Johnson et al. 2011), and to harden their disbelief in the possibility of constructive dialogue with governments (Olmpieva 2009), and even to drive companies out of business (Bliss and Di Tella 1997). SMEs are particularly vulnerable to corruption, with studies showing a negative correlation between firm size and corruption impact

(Beck et al. 2005). Whereas large firms are more likely to view bribing officials as a way of gaining advantages, smaller firms experience bribery as akin to an extra form of regressive taxation inimical to innovation and growth (Safavian et al. 2001). Corruption also represents a significant barrier to entry for new firms (Broadman 2000), and a strong correlation has been found between bribing government officials and the concealment of output, resulting in problems such as reduced tax revenue (Johnson et al. 2000).

This chapter analyses the corruption risks faced by Hong Kong SMEs operating in the PRD through the lens of regulatory capture, whereby regulated entities exert influence over regulators. Drawing on interviews and survey data, we find that corruption is endemic and is closely correlated with the failure of state regulation in the PRD. SMEs take advantage of an unpredictable regulatory structure that alternates between highly flexible and rigid enforcement styles (McAllister 2010). However, instead of simply blaming the regulated entity for state capture, we argue that Hong Kong SMEs operating in the PRD face a complex regulatory environment that provides great discretion for local officials, who are strongly motivated and well-placed to seek rents. Thus our study reveals how far corruption affects regulation and, vice versa, how gravely ill-performing regulation exacerbates corruption. Rather than representing a regulatory capture model, where regulated entities capture regulators, or a simple inversion of this model with local officials deriving bribes from SMEs, we find that regulatory capture is a two-way process through which both the regulator and SMEs seek to maximize private gains. The outcome is that corruption has become a normal part of doing business and an embedded institutional feature of state regulation in the PRD.

Regulatory capture

Regulatory capture is associated with an economic theory of regulation, which assumes that actors aim to maximise their own material interests instead of being driven by the public good (Baldwin et al. 2012). It refers to "the process through which special interests affect state intervention in any of its forms" (Dal Bó 2006: 203). Scholars distinguish between direct capture, whereby regulated entities directly influence the regulator's behaviour, and indirect capture, where regulated entities affect decisions made by political principals through a variety of methods (Agrell and Gautier 2012). Capture may take place in both legal ways, such as lobbying, and in illegal acts by such means as bribery and coercion (Dal Bó and Di Tella 2003). Scholars have also distinguished between the capture of decisions and the capture of information (Agrell and Gautier 2012). The objective of the former is to influence the making of regulations while the latter seeks to distort information and obstruct the effective implementation of regulations (Dal Bó 2006; Estache and Wren-Lewis 2011). Tirole (1986), for example, focuses on the informational asymmetry that exists between political principal and the regulated firm. This is conceptualised as a three-tier principal-agent model comprising the political principal at the top, the regulator in the middle, and the regulated entity at the bottom (Agrell and Gautier 2012). It assumes that firms have private information that political principals cannot access, leading the latter to establish a regulatory agency to monitor the firm (Dal Bó 2006: 220). In this configuration, information is a critical resource, and gathering it is one of regulator's main tasks (Agrell and Gautier 2012). When the regulator has good information that, if acted upon could lead to a decrease in firm profits, the firm has an incentive to bribe the regulator to hide information from the political principal (Dal Bó 2006).

Early models of regulatory capture were based on the assumption that incentives (including bribes, other payments such as campaign contributions, and industry jobs) would flow from firms to regulators (Dal Bó 2006). The "revolving doors" phenomenon is the practice whereby regulators are recruited from industry whilst industry employs regulators after they leave the government (Estache and Wren-Lewis 2011). Although such practice is relatively common, there is little empirical evidence that revolving doors between regulatory agencies and the industries they monitor result in regulatory capture (Dal Bó 2006). Similarly, evidence of capture through bribery is scant (Agrell and Gautier 2012). Agrell and Gautier refer to this as the "paradox of capture" (Agrell and Gautier 2012). Despite this, regulatory capture can be a useful concept for analysing relations between firms and regulators. It is necessary to reveal "the many faces of corruption in regulation" (Boehm 2011) before effective measures can be taken to prevent regulatory capture.

Data

The empirical data for this study were collected in 2010 from multiple sources, including semi-structured interviews, a questionnaire survey, and documentary evidence. We conducted 98 in-depth, semi-structured interviews with Hong Kong SME operators, local government officials, and intermediaries in the PRD. Among them were 58 SME operators from 56 enterprises working in the manufacturing sector (74 per cent) and service sector (26 per cent), who shared with us their experience of conducting business in the PRD and their encounters with local government officials and intermediaries. Our interviewees also included 30 local officials from eight government units at the township, district, and municipal level, including customs, foreign trade and economic cooperation, taxation, industry and commerce, environmental protection, quality inspection, labour and social security, hygiene, and production safety supervision. We also interviewed ten people from six intermediary organizations, including individuals from a law firm, an accounting firm, an inspection firm, an auditing agency, and a labour rights non-governmental organization, as well as five customs brokers. We supplemented interviews with a questionnaire survey, which was distributed to approximately 2,000 Hong Kong SME operators in the PRD. The survey was designed to collect general information about respondents, their understanding of corruption, perception of corruption risks, and suggestions on how to reduce corruption. The questionnaires were mailed to the SMEs, followed by the second round of mailing to those who had not responded after one month, and 350 follow-up phone calls. We obtained 227 valid responses, equating to a response rate of 12.67 per cent, which we consider adequate given the fact that it was one of the few early attempts to conduct empirical research on such a sensitive issue of corruption risks faced by Hong Kong SMEs in China. A total of 194 of these respondents were from firms based in the PRD. Finally, we collected documentary evidence to obtain a fuller picture of the regulatory environment facing SME operators in the PRD.

A corruption-prone regulatory environment

SMEs in the PRD must navigate a complex regulatory environment, both during the registration process and in the course of their daily operations. A multitude of applications must be filed to set up a new enterprise and various administrative licenses must be obtained before the enterprise begins to operate in the PRD. In addition, enterprises deal directly with local government units including village committees or enterprise management offices of sub-district committees, and foreign commerce investment service centres at different administrative levels. Enterprises whose products are sold on domestic and overseas markets must also deal with the Bureau of Quality and Technology Supervision and Entry-Exit Inspection and Quarantine Bureaus.

The complexity of the regulatory environment is exacerbated by the fact that officials have considerable discretion in enforcing rules. This provides local officials with multiple opportunities to solicit favours from SME operators and SMEs have few channels for recourse when maltreated. According to our survey, SME operators perceive corruption to be endemic in the PRD. Data presented in Table 11.1 show that only 12 per cent and 13 per cent of respondents claimed never to have experienced bribe extortion by government officials and intermediary agencies, respectively. In contrast, more than half our respondents had "often" or "sometimes" experienced bribe extortion from officials and intermediaries. Corruption in the PRD is endemic to the extent that 56 per cent of our survey respondents believed that conducting business would be impossible without resorting to it.

The prevalence of corruption in the PRD was also reflected in respondents' perceptions of government officials. As Figure 11.1 shows, only 2 per cent of respondents viewed PRD government officials as "extremely clean" whereas 16 per cent of them regarded these officials as being "extremely corrupt". Slightly more respondents (40 per cent) viewed officials as "relatively clean" rather than "relatively corrupt" (37 per cent), but this nevertheless represents a high degree of perceived official corruption. When asked whether it would be impossible for Hong Kong SMEs to operate in the PRD without bribes and other forms of corruption, 16 per cent of respondents "completely agreed" with the statement and a further 40 per cent "quite agreed" with it. By comparison, 28 per cent and 12 per cent of respondents respectively either "quite" or "completely disagreed" with the statement.

Although corruption appears widespread, we found that corruption risks varied considerably between government departments. As Table 11.2 shows, customs, environmental protection, and taxation were seen as closely associated with high corruption risks by our survey respondents, while labour and social security, industry and commerce, and foreign trade and economic cooperation were less likely to involve corruption risks.

Similarly, Table 11.3 presents the corruption risks faced by the SMEs when liaising with intermediary agencies in the PRD. Customs declaration agents are most likely to engage in corruption with 49 per cent of the respondents equating them with extremely or relatively high corruption risks. Respondents indicated that, in general, all other intermediary agencies are unlikely to bring about corruption risks.

Table 11.1 Perception of external and internal corruption: (Total number of respondents: 194)

Occurrence	Often	Sometimes	Rarely	Never	Missing Values
Perceived corruption phenomena of government officials	28%	50%	14%	2%	5%
Perceived internal corruption	21%	50%	16%	3%	10%
Incidents of corruption involving government officials in vicinity	18%	57%	16%	5%	4%
Incidents of corruption involving intermediary agencies in vicinity	14%	53%	20%	9%	4%
Experience of bribe extortion by government officials	13%	42%	22%	12%	11%
Experience of bribe extortion by intermediary agencies	9%	42%	24%	13%	12%

Sources: Authors' survey.
Note: The total percentage of each item may not add up to 100% due to rounding errors.

The results from our questionnaire reveal a certain amount of disagreement among SME operators concerning what types of behaviour constitute corruption. Although the majority of respondents agreed that the giving of gifts or cash to government officials was a form of corruption, less than half equated inviting officials to dinners or arranging jobs for officials'

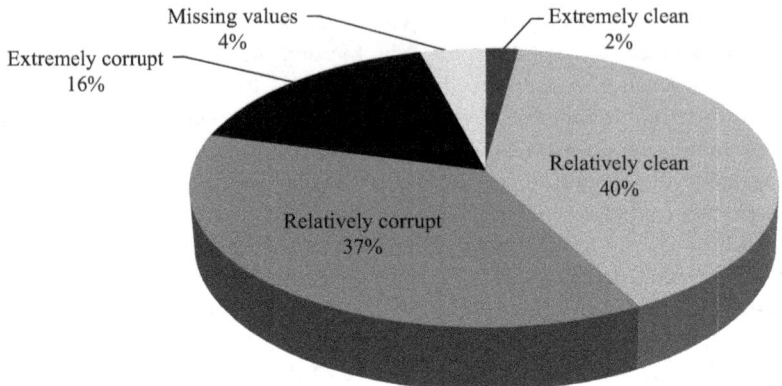

Figure 11.1 Survey respondents' impression of government officials in the PRD region: (Total number of respondents: 194)

Sources: Authors' survey.

Table 11.2 Corruption risks while liaising with local government agencies: (Total number of respondents: 194)

Local government agencies	Extremely high	Relatively high	Relatively low	Extremely low	No contact	Missing values
1) Customs	25%	39%	13%	9%	9%	5%
2) Foreign Trade and Economic Cooperation	4%	25%	31%	20%	9%	10%
3) Taxation	13%	40%	23%	17%	2%	6%
4) Industry and Commerce	5%	29%	35%	20%	3%	9%
5) Environmental Protection	18%	41%	15%	11%	10%	5%
6) Quality Inspection	13%	30%	30%	10%	9%	7%
7) Labour and Social Security	7%	27%	35%	21%	4%	7%
8) Hygiene	5%	27%	32%	16%	12%	8%
9) Bureau of Production Safety Supervision	8%	30%	32%	14%	9%	7%
10) Town/District/ Municipal Government	10%	21%	29%	19%	7%	14%
11) Others	1%	3%	3%	3%	5%	86%

Sources: Authors' survey.
Note: The total percentage of each item may not add up to 100% due to rounding errors.

Table 11.3 Corruption risks while liaising with intermediary agencies: (Total number of respondents: 194)

Intermediary agencies	Extremely high	Relatively high	Relatively low	Extremely low	No contact	Missing values
1) Banks	2%	13%	41%	34%	4%	7%
2) Accounting firms	2%	22%	33%	30%	8%	5%
3) Law firms	3%	19%	32%	28%	11%	7%
4) Guarantee companies	6%	19%	28%	19%	20%	9%
5) Customs declaration agents	14%	35%	20%	14%	12%	5%
6) Quality inspection centres	7%	27%	30%	15%	12%	9%
7) Insurance companies	2%	18%	31%	31%	11%	8%
8) Others	1%	3%	3%	2%	5%	87%

Sources: Authors' survey.
Note: The total percentage of each item may not add up to 100% due to rounding errors.

friends and relatives with corruption. This finding suggests that many enterprises regard maintaining a close relationship with officials as a normal and necessary aspect of conducting business in the PRD. To some extent, this may also suggest that the legal system still suffers from sufficiently serious weaknesses that SMEs either do not trust or cannot rely upon it in the course of doing business.

While the survey findings indicated the existence of corruption risks, our interview data enabled us to better understand the nature and scale of these risks. We found that corruption risks are manifested in two major areas: the business registration process and during SMEs' daily operations.

Corruption risks in the business registration process

The business registration process in the PRD is complex and cumbersome, providing ample rent seeking opportunities. Our interviewees complained bitterly about the business registration procedure because of its excessive length and the involvement of too many government agencies. Some government officials concurred with this view. As one official from a quality inspection bureau stated:

> Take the application for permits as an example. Companies have to submit an application for permission and wait for approval by different layers of the government before they are allowed to start business. The application process is full of redundant or pointless procedures, and costs SMEs too much energy and time. The normal approval time is three months. For companies, three months is too long and constitutes a big opportunity cost. After the approval is granted, they still cannot start production, because they need to find manpower. Companies have to pay rent

and loan interests as usual while waiting for approval, so they are actually burning money, instead of making money, every day (O#11).[1]

According to another interviewee, business registration normally takes between three and a half to six months (E#52). Although local governments have reportedly promised to speed up or simplify the registration process, lengthy and cumbersome procedures persist, and some SMEs resort to bribery to expedite the process. At the same time, local officials also solicited favours from SMEs. Interviewees reported that it was particularly difficult to obtain an Environmental Impact Assessment (EIA) approval from the Environmental Protection Bureau (EPB), a Fire Prevention Certificate from the Fire Department, and a Production Safety Permit from Production Safety Supervision departments. Hence, the solicitation of favours between SMEs and some government officials is a two-way street.

Environmental impact assessment

According to China's Environmental Protection Law, enterprises that may cause pollution during production, construction or other activities must pass an EIA and obtain an official permit issued by the local EPB (Guangzhou Environmental Protection Bureau 2015). Interviewees complained that the complicated and time-consuming nature of the approval process yields opportunities for corruption (E#17). To obtain approval, an enterprise must first hire an intermediary agency to conduct a preliminary assessment of the environmental impact of its construction project. After the assessment, relevant documents should be submitted to the EPB for initial approval, and the enterprise may hire a certified company to begin construction. However, upon the completion of the construction, an official on-site inspection must be conducted by the EPB before issuing final approval for the project. The whole process takes at least two to three months (O#7). To expedite the approval process "some companies may provide 'wining and dining' or other types of bribes for officials to grant approval quickly.... Such informal practices have become widespread and indicate that doing so is feasible" (E#17). An interviewee, who had EPDS certification, indicated that the requirements were very strict and that even local governments found difficulty in coping with them. He said, "the Environmental Protection Bureau is the toughest among all the government units I have dealt with" (E#57).

Fire prevention certification

Government regulations state that manufacturing plants and warehouses exceeding a certain size must be officially certified by the Fire Prevention Unit of the local Public Security Bureau (PSB) before they are used. The application process for a Fire Prevention Certificate consists of two steps. First, the company should file a fire prevention assessment application for its proposed construction site containing the following documents in addition to the application form: an urban land use certificate issued by the local land planning department; architectural drawings provided by the design company; and certificates for fire prevention devices to be used. After preliminary approval is obtained, a certified company may be hired to install the fire prevention system. According to the Fire Prevention Law, if an enterprise fails to obtain approval, all of its construction projects must be suspended. Second, after the first stage has been completed, a quality assurance inspection of the fire prevention system is conducted. Similar to the EIA, official approval (this time from the PSB) is required for business registration. Some interviewees complained of a protracted approval process and an unreasonably high standard for fire prevention, with one interviewee claiming that, "if you abide by the Fire Prevention Law, you won't be able to start your business for two years" (E#25).

Although the difficulties associated with obtaining fire safety approval through normal channels are not necessarily linked with corruption, we found that some enterprises have resorted to informal and backdoor connections or "wining and dining" to expedite the process (E#17, E#52, E#54, E#25). An employee from the Enterprise Management Office of a village committee in Dongguan City admitted that when an enterprise in his jurisdiction failed to pass the fire safety inspection, it would very likely try to bribe the inspector to let it pass. Some interviewees also mentioned that local PSB Fire Prevention Units might collude with suppliers of fire prevention products to make money. Under this type of scenario, enterprises could do nothing but comply. As stated by an interviewee,

> It is easy for the fire prevention products provided by certain suppliers to pass inspections because these suppliers have special relationships with the inspectors. The prices of these products may be 10–15 per cent higher than those provided by other companies. However, you would have to use these products since those from other companies often fail the inspection even though the products are actually the same. Thus, despite paying higher prices, enterprises are inclined to purchase fire prevention products from those providers who have a close relationship with public officials in charge of fire prevention certification (E#30).

Production safety permits

According to state regulations, certain industries such as those involving chemicals, paints, and hazardous materials, need special permission from the Bureau of Production Safety Supervision. For SMEs, this represents yet another complicated procedure. Even if it is granted, a production safety permit is only valid for three years; the enterprise must repeat the same cumbersome process to apply for a renewal before its expiry (E#51).

Corruption risks in the daily operation of SMEs

After registering and starting their businesses, Hong Kong SME operators continue to face considerable corruption risks in their daily operations in the PRD. These risks were mainly manifested through inspections, annual assessments, and in dealings with customs departments and entry–exit inspection and quarantine bureaus.

Customs

Almost all our interviewees reported that customs procedures are associated with high corruption risks. Corruption takes place in one or some combination of the following situations. First, whereas an enterprise can only predict the volume of production for the next year, actual production volume almost invariably deviates from the estimate. Customs officers may question the discrepancy between the predicted and actual production volumes and hence deny approval. To complete the customs process smoothly, enterprises may choose to bribe customs officers (E#25). An interviewee told us, "once bribed, the customs officers will surely let you go" (E#24).

Second, problems concerning product codes may also lead to corruption. Customs provides a product code for each exported product. Exported goods can only pass customs when their codes are verified. Because of contractor changes, enterprises sometimes need to apply to customs for new codes, which is often highly cumbersome (E#49, E#37). The difference between the international code system and the Chinese one further complicates the problem. Enterprises may try to explain their situation to customs officers but very often they do not listen. As a result, some resort to bribing frontline officials to enable them to pass customs checks (E#48).

Third, some customs officials solicit bribes by purposely slowing down the customs process or making it more difficult. Because time is crucial for exports, companies may be willing to pay bribes. An interviewee reported that a customs officer who came to his factory to check company accounts found a minor problem caused by normal wear and tear of production materials. When this officer threatened to fine the factory, the factory management bribed him to minimize possible losses (E#17). Some interviewees indicated a willingness to pay bribes as long as the "payment" they demanded was within an affordable range (E#19, E#18). An interviewee provided an example:

> We export clothes to Malaysia and Singapore. Sometimes, customs officers create troubles for us by not allowing our goods to leave or asking us to reload them to delay the departure time. Nevertheless, we need to export the clothes to Hong Kong tonight and then ship them to Malaysia and Singapore the next day. If they delay the customs clearance, we would have to pay penalties to our customers. Thus, we are forced to pay bribes to those officers (E#23).

Fourth, corruption occurs when enterprises violate regulations and are asked to pay fines. In this situation companies may bribe customs officers in exchange for a reduced penalty. This might include taking the officers to dinner or contacting them through backdoor connections (E#25).

Fifth, customs officers often enjoy great discretion in customs clearances. They may ignore illicit practices or they may strictly enforce laws and regulations (O#13). This discretion creates corruption risks for SMEs. As some interviewees noted, "if the customs officers want to find problems with your company, they can easily do it, even if you run your business properly. They can always come up with something that puts you in trouble. If they consider your behaviour to be illegal, it is illegal" (E#7-E#11).

Regular and occasional inspections

SMEs operating in the PRD face two types of official inspections: regular and *ad hoc*. Regular inspections include those concerning production safety supervision, environmental protection, and fire prevention. These inspections usually number five or six per year (O#6, O#7). Once again, interviewees bemoaned the great discretion enjoyed by inspectors. Enterprises may buy off inspectors to avoid trouble (E#54, E#55). However, some interviewees revealed that "during the course of an inspection, the types of problems that could be settled by bribing inspectors were usually relatively minor ones. In the case of a serious problem, the problem must be rectified [through means other than bribery]" (E#7-E#11). One interviewee noted that bribing inspectors was problematic, "because each time you have different inspectors, you may have to bribe them separately. The best way is to deal with the problem by yourself by meeting the standards so you will not leave any excuse for inspectors to seek bribes" (E#46).

Ad hoc inspections are mainly conducted by Customs and Entry-Exit Inspection and Quarantine Bureaus. State regulations classify finished goods and commodities for export into two categories: those subject to compulsory inspection and those subject to general inspection. For goods under general inspection, officials usually give quick and easy approval. However, the compulsory inspection process may be difficult and time consuming and often involve on-the-spot checks in factories inspection. Our interviewees linked commodity inspection with corruption risks, because, similar to customs officers, commodity inspection officers enjoy considerable enforcement discretion. They sometimes used this power to create difficulties for SMEs in order to solicit bribes (E#17, E#23, E#3, E#7-E#11). An interviewee complained, "inspection officials say that, for example, there is a problem with the knitting, or a problem with the thread, in relation to your commodities. Actually, there is no such problem, but they purposefully do not let our commodities pass the inspection or impose repeated tests" (E#23).

Annual assessments

All enterprises must pass a cumbersome annual assessment conducted by the Bureau of Industry and Commerce or risk losing their business license. Enterprises are required to submit various documents for annual check-up, which include their balance sheets, income statements, audit reports issued by accounting firms, and reports from other government agencies such as state and local tax bureaus, customs, foreign trade and economic cooperation departments, and labour and social protection institutes. For some special industries, additional documents are needed, such as those concerning fire safety, environmental protection, security and supervision, and hygiene. SMEs have to contact these departments one by one. Some interviewees had to arrange for three or four staff members to prepare for the assessment. Each staff member had to make five or six trips lasting up to a day to complete the required documentation (E#7-E#11). The situation has improved somewhat with cities such as Guangzhou providing a one-stop service. However, in places where this was not possible, some interviewees resorted to hiring intermediaries to handle the process in order to save time (E#7-E#11, E#53). In cases where enterprises had missed procedures or lost documents, they hired intermediary agencies to prepare the reports (E#7-E#11, E#24). Some interviewees complained that the annual assessment process was unnecessarily complex and difficult, creating opportunities for officials to engage in rent seeking (E#53).

Intermediaries

Intermediary organizations have proliferated in the PRD. An Internet key word search for the phrases "agent services for business registration" and "Guangzhou City" using China's Baidu search engine and conducted in 2010 generated over 772,000 results. Three types of intermediary organizations are frequently involved in SME business. The first type, agent service intermediaries, helps enterprises complete business registration, annual assessments, and pre-approvals of various licenses. These agencies are familiar with administrative procedures and requirements and can provide much needed information and timely assistance for SMEs. The second type, professional service intermediaries, mainly consists of professional institutions specialised in areas such as law, finance, accounting and auditing, insurance, and recruitment. They are market-oriented and compete with each other to provide services so that enterprises can choose which one to hire. Finally, inspection service intermediaries provide assessments and accreditations on various matters, and include agencies working on commodity inspection, quality control, environmental protection, and production safety evaluation. These intermediaries comprise accreditation centres directly subordinated to, or authorised by, governmental departments, as well as professional assessment institutions holding domestic or international qualifications.

We observed a modified version of the "revolving doors" phenomenon. In the PRD, many intermediary organizations are staffed by former government officials (E#7–E#11). These former officials are well placed to help SMEs navigate a complex regulatory landscape and the revolving doors phenomenon is not seen to be problematic (Dal Bó, 2006). However, intermediaries are also well placed to exploit their close ties with local officials to take advantage of SMEs. Since officials cannot charge money for their services and view taking bribes as risky, intermediaries sometimes help collect money on officials' behalf (E7#–E11#, E#24, E#25).

Our data reveal some differences in the corruption risks associated with each of the three intermediary organization types.

Agent services intermediaries

SME operators hire this type of intermediary in order to overcome difficulties associated with applying for various approvals. Interviewees indicated that intermediary organizations of this type actually had a close relationship with governmental departments (E#7–E#11, E#24, E#25). According to some interviewees, most staff in these intermediary organizations had previously worked in the government (E7#–E11#) and were consequently capable of dealing with difficulties that SMEs had failed to resolve (E#24, E#25). Conversely, however, intermediary organizations sometimes acted as surrogates for officials who could not directly accept bribes themselves but who could do so indirectly via the intermediaries (E#7–E#11, E#25, E#24). Several SME interviewees had been cheated by intermediary organizations although they declined to provide details due to the sensitivity of the topic (E#7–E#11). As expected, the government officials we interviewed denied the existence of connections between their departments and intermediary organizations (O#9, O#18).

Professional service intermediaries

Professional service intermediaries were associated with relatively low corruption risks. One explanation was that these organizations feared jeopardizing their business or good reputation. For example, banks might be less corruption prone because they had to consider commercial profits and would therefore avoid providing loans for unqualified firms (E#47). As one interviewee stated, "the overall situation of the PRD, particularly the bank system in this area, is market driven. The banks are expected to perform well, so they will only provide loans for you if your company meets the required standards" (E#52). Some claimed that banks tended to have a low level of corruption because they were well regulated. For example, "since the Banking Regulatory Bureau issued strict regulations for this industry, banks seldom behaved irregularly" (E#19).

Low corruption risk may also hold true for accounting and law firms. Some interviewees said that accounting firms worked relatively well in accordance with regulations, resulting in a low level of corruption risk for SMEs (E#19, E#30, E#31, E#47). Others believe that because accounting firms and law firms were hired by enterprises, the latter would have no need to bribe them: "law firms will be delighted if they are asked to work for you on a law suit; accounting firms will also be happy to serve you. Many accounting firms are competing in mainland China. So when you offer them a business opportunity, they will do what you ask them to do" (E#31). Because accounting firms and law firms do not monopolise the market, enterprises can choose which one to hire (E#19). Another reason for the lack of kickbacks was that the level of compensation for their staff was relatively high. As one intermediary staff member said, "for example, in a trade with a payment of HK$20,000, how much kickback can I give him? The small amount of money means nothing" (I#2).

Inspection service intermediaries

Inspection service intermediaries are powerful and are associated with high levels of corruption risk. In some cases, SMEs colluded with intermediaries to circumvent government regulations. An interviewee from the Guangdong Provincial Bureau of Production Safety Supervision mentioned that, in order for his department to approve and issue a safety production license, "it is necessary for the enterprise to acquire a certificate issued by an intermediary organization based on its assessment. So it is possible that the intermediary may collaborate with the applicant to cheat us" (O#1). One SME operator expressed a similar view:

> Corruption might emerge when third party notaries and assessment agencies conduct an inspection over an enterprise. The enterprise, which does not actually meet the standards, may bribe the inspectors in order to get the certificates from, for example, ICTI [International Council of Toy Industries], ISO [International Standardization Organization], and C-TPAT [Customs-Trade Partnership Against Terrorism] (E#17).

We interviewed the director of a certification agency engaging in corporate social responsibility assessments in the PRD. His institution was the very first non-governmental organization in mainland China to provide advisory services on social responsibility and has close contact with Hong Kong SMEs in the PRD. For that reason, this interviewee was able to provide us with detailed information (I#1). He told us that the inspectors sent by his institutions could check an enterprise's financial accounts and even its bank statements. He also noted that the overall profit making ability of Hong Kong SMEs declined dramatically after 2004 due to the worsening economic environment and exchange rates and that, partly for that reason, "Hong Kong SMEs have not done very well in abiding by law and following regulations, especially in the areas of protecting workers' rights and interests. They are familiar with Chinese culture. They bribe the government first and then exploit workers. And they have serious corruption problems". He mentioned that when inspecting some factories, his institution found their documents to be totally faked. The interviewee said",

> Because there are too many audits, they have used some computer software designed by Hong Kong companies to prepare fake documents. There are also Hong Kong consulting firms to teach them how to cope with inspections conducted by institutions like us. They have many different ways to deal with us. This is the bad element of Chinese culture. We may say that they take to their business in China just like a duck to water. They play tricks, give false information, engage in corruption, and exploit their workers (I#1).

This interviewee estimated that about half the factories they inspected each year attempted to bribe them. When their inspectors went to Hong Kong SMEs for the first time, they were almost completely sure that they would be offered bribes, just like the situation with regard to mainland factories. The most common form of bribery was to give a "'red envelope', then they will ask you 'do you need anything else?'" For example, they would offer to take males to "entertainment" places. Another reason, according to him, is that Hong Kong enterprises often hire mainland people to serve as managers, unlike Taiwanese companies where the management teams are usually from Taiwan. "This way those mainland managers will deal with or bribe government officials on behalf of their Hong Kong boss. The Hong Kong boss provides money, but if there is anything wrong, it is the responsibility of those mainland managers, not them".

He also revealed that there were many cases in which inspectors themselves became corrupt. "They often take bribes from their clients and therefore cannot make fair and honest assessments". His institution has taken many measures to prevent corruption among its own staff. In addition to providing education and a high salary, for example, his institution often sends two inspectors to a factory together so they can keep an eye on each other; it will try to avoid sending the same inspector to a factory more than once unless it is absolutely necessary; a review of completed assessments is sometimes performed to verify the results; and clients are welcome to lodge complaints against its employees. The institution also has very detailed regulations about how to deal with gifts or invitations for dinner. It is stipulated that inspectors can only eat a working lunch at the factory being inspected and may accept a small souvenir worth RMB 10 or less.

Conclusion

Corruption is a normal part of doing business for many Hong Kong SMEs operating in the PRD. Its root cause lies in the failure of state regulation. SMEs encounter a complex and unpredictable regulatory environment that gives considerable discretion to local officials whilst providing insufficient oversight of their actions. This in turn provides numerous opportunities for corruption, ranging from "wining and dining" and arranging jobs for officials' friends and relatives, to gift giving and cash payments to officials. These corruption risks manifest themselves in the various stages of the business registration process and in the daily operations of SMEs. Even government officials do not deny the ubiquity of corruption in the PRD. In some cases, intermediary organizations, many of which are staffed by former officials, serve as surrogates and share the proceeds of corruption with government officials.

Although SMEs are vulnerable to predation by local officials and intermediaries, many of them also seek to benefit illicitly from regulatory uncertainty by offering bribes to officials and their agents. In addition, they sometimes attempt to solicit favours from intermediaries. Our findings reveal that, in some cases, inspectors were offered bribes by half of the factories they inspected.

Whilst regulatory capture is traditionally associated with the unidirectional influence of regulated entities over regulators, our study of SMEs in the PRD highlights the complex relationship between corruption and regulation. Corrupt exchanges take place between the regulator and the regulated not only as a result of enforcement loopholes but also because regulators enjoy ample discretion and actively engage in rent seeking. Bribe giving by business operators and bribe seeking by government officials are two sides of the same coin and both contribute to the spread of corruption in the PRD.

In order to control official corruption, the regulation process should be rule-based, transparent, and closely monitored. The government should simplify procedures, improve efficiency, and empower the public to report the wrongdoings of government officials and hold them accountable. The government should also enhance anti-corruption efforts, tighten punishment measures against the corrupt activities of officials and business people, and crack down on collusion between the two groups. Mechanisms for handling complaints against corruption should also be strengthened.

Corruption risks facing Hong Kong SMEs operating in the PRD testify to the importance of inter-government collaboration. The Hong Kong government must work closely with local PRD governments to create a clean business environment and to minimise opportunities for corruption. Improving communication channels and enhancing collaborative governance between the two regions are imperative. At the same time, Hong Kong SMEs should improve their own corporate governance and integrity management to ensure that their staff abide by laws, ethical standards, and international norms. Whilst one should caution against adopting a linear view of any anticorruption measures, controlling corruption is not mission impossible. Future studies may wish to explore the tactics of tackling corruption and their prospects.

Note

1 The interview code indicates the category of interview (E = enterprise operators, O = officials, I = intermediaries) and the sequence (e.g. #1=the first interview conducted in that category).

References

Agrell, P. J. and A. Gautier (2012) "Rethinking regulatory capture", in J. E. Harrington Jr. and Y. Katsoulacos (eds.) *Recent advances in the analysis of competition policy and regulation*, Cheltenham: Edward Elgar, 286–302.

Aidis, R. (2005) "Institutional barriers to small and medium sized enterprise operations in transition countries", *Small Business Economics*, 25(4): 305–318.

Baldwin, R., M. Cave and M. Lodge, (2012) *Understanding regulation: theory, strategy, and practice (second edition)*. Oxford: Oxford University Press.

Beck, T., A. Gemirgüç-Kunt and V. Maksimovic (2005) "Financial and legal constraints to growth: does firm size matter?", *The Journal of Finance*, 60(1): 137–177.

Bliss, C. and R. Di Tella (1997) "Does competition kill corruption?", *Journal of Political Economy* 105(5): 1001–1023.

Boehm, F. (2011) "Is there an anti-corruption agenda in regulation? Insights from Colombia and Zambia water regulation", in S. Rose-Ackerman and T. Søride (eds.) *International handbook of the economics of corruption*, Vol. 2, Cheltenham: Edward Elgar, 299–329.

Broadman, H. (2000) "Reducing structural dominance and entry barriers in Russian industry", *Review of Industrial Organization*, 17: 155–76.

Dal Bó, E. (2006) "Regulatory capture: a review", *Oxford Review of Economic Policy*, 22(2): 203–225.

Dal Bó, E. and R. Di Tella (2003) "Capture by threat", *Journal of Political Economy*, 111(5): 1123–1154.

Estache, A. and L. Wren-Lewis (2011) "Anti-corruption policy in theories of sector regulation", in S. Rose-Ackerman and T. Søride (eds.) *International handbook of the economics of corruption*, Vol. 2, Cheltenham: Edward Elgar, 269–298.

Guangzhou Environmental Protection Bureau (2015) "Approval form of environmental impact assessment of construction projects", http://www.gzaic.gov.cn/download/blsptable/ (accessed on 9 January 2010).

GPPP (Guangdong Provincial People's Procuratorate) and ICAC (Independent Commission Against Corruption) (2008) "Integrity and compliance with the law: a guide to the prevention of corruption for SME entrepreneurs investing in Guangdong and Hong Kong", www.icac.org.hk/filemanager/en/content_1231/sme.pdf (accessed 9 January 2016).

Hong Kong General Chamber of Small and Medium Business (2015) Homepage. http://www.hkgcsmb.org.hk/ (accessed 1 January 2016).

HKTDC (Hong Kong Trade Development Council) (2015) "PRD economic profile", http://china-trade-research.hktdc.com/business-news/article/Fast-Facts/PRD-Economic-Profile/ff/en/1/1X000000/1X06BW84.htm (accessed 9 January 2016).

Johnson, N. D., C. L. LaFountain and S. Yamarik (2011) "Corruption is bad for growth (even in the United States)", *Public Choice*, *147*(3–4): 377–393.

Johnson, S., D. Kaufmann, J. McMillan and C. Woodruff (2000) "Why do firms hide? Bribes and unofficial activity after communism", *Journal of Public Economics,* 76: 495–520.

McAllister, L. K. (2010) "Dimensions of enforcement style: factoring in regulatory autonomy and capacity", *Law & Policy*, 32(1): 61–78.

Olmpieva, I. (2009) "Background corruption in small and medium-size business: a 'weapon of the weak'?", *Russian Politics and Law*, 47(4): 28–42.

Safavian, M., D. Graham, and C. Gonzalez-Vega (2001) "Corruption and microenterprises in Russia", *World Development,* 29(7): 1215–1224.

Tirole, J. (1986) "Hierarchies and bureaucracies: on the role of collusion in organizations", *Journal of Law, Economics, & Organization*, 181–214.

APPENDIX I

List of Interviewees

1. Interviews with SME operators

E#1	Board president, home appliance factory/Shenzhen
E#2	Managers in the department of external affairs, watch-manufacturing factory/Shenzhen
E#3	Administrative manager, plastic and rubber products factory/Shenzhen
E#4	Chief inspectors of operations, plastic and rubber products factory/Shenzhen
E#5	Director, luggage and bag factory/Dongguan
E#6	Director, educational consultancy company/Guangzhou
E#7	Financial affairs staff, clothing factory/Guangzhou
E#8	Financial affairs staff, vehicle inspection company/Guangzhou
E#9	Financial affairs staff, vehicle inspection company/Guangzhou
E#10	Financial affairs staff, cargo company/Guangzhou
E#11	Administrative staff, leather goods factory/Guangzhou
E#12	Administrative staff, clothing factory/Guangzhou
E#13	Financial affairs staff, clothing factory/Guangzhou
E#14	Administrative staff, real estate agency/Guangzhou
E#15	Financial affairs staff, product testing company/Guangzhou
E#16	Board president, sewing products company/Guangzhou
E#17	General manager, sports goods factory/Shenzhen
E#18	Board president, decorating materials factory/Dongguan
E#19	Director, clothing factory/Dongguan
E#20	Board president, plastic and rubber hardware factory/Dongguan
E#21	Administrative staff, electric goods factory/Dongguan
E#22	Factory director, toy factory/Dongguan
E#23	General manager, clothing factory/Shenzhen
E#24	Manager, trading company/Shenzhen
E#25	Board president, clothing factory/Dongguan
E#26	Manager, building materials factory/Shenzhen
E#27	Factory director, knitting mill/Dongguan
E#28	Factory director, handbag factory/Dongguan
E#29	Director, electronic hardware trade company/PRD
E#30	Director, clothing factory/Panyu
E#31	Board president, battery factory/Panyu
E#32	Manager, hardware factory/Dongguan
E#33	Factory director, door and window accessories factory/Dongguan
E#34	Assistant to the factory director, domestic electrical appliance factory/Taiwan
E#35	Accounting staff, hardware factory/Dongguan
E#36	General manager, clothing factory/Panyu
E#37	Manager, clothing accessories factory/Dongguan
E#38	Factory director, hardware factory/Dongguan
E#39	Factory director, knitting mill/Dongguan
E#40	Factory director, clothing factory/Dongguan
E#41	Manager, building materials factory/Dongguan

E#42	Assistant to the manager, furniture factory/Shenzhen
E#43	Director, financial service company/Guangzhou and Shenzhen
E#44	Manager, digital goods trading company/Shenzhen
E#45	Manager, electronic devices trading company/Shenzhen
E#46	General manager, restaurants/Zhongshan
E#47	General manager, clothing factory/Dongguan
E#48	Deputy general manager, electric wire factory/Dongguan
E#49	Administrative staff, electric wire factory/Dongguan
E#50	Factory customs broker, textile factory/Dongguan
E#51	Factory director, paint factory/Dongguan
E#52	Board president, technology service company/Shenzhen
E#53	Manager, technology service company/Shenzhen
E#54	General manager, plastics and rubber factory/Shenzhen
E#55	Director, electronic devices trading company/PRD
E#56	General manager, automobile electronic accessories trading company/Shenzhen
E#57	Director, financial investment company/Guangdong and nationwide
E#58	Product manager, toy company/Guangzhou

2. Interviews with local government officials

The officials we interviewed are affiliated with the following government institutions:

O#1	Bureau of Production Safety Supervision
O#2	Bureau of Industry and Commerce
O#3	Foreign Trade and Economic Cooperation Bureau
O#4	Foreign Business Section of Local Taxation Bureau
O#5	Foreign Trade and Economic Cooperation Bureau
O#6	Bureau of Production Safety Supervision
O#7	Environmental Protection Bureau
O#8	Local Taxation Bureau
O#9	Town Government
O#10	Enterprise Management Office of Village Committee
O#11	Bureau of Quality and Technology Supervision
O#12	Enterprise Management Office of Village Committee
O#13	Customs
O#14	Enterprise Management Office of Village Committee
O#15	Entry-Exit Inspection and Quarantine Bureau
O#16	Entry-Exit Inspection and Quarantine Bureau
O#17	Customs
O#18	Customs
O#19	Anti-smuggling Bureau, Customs
O#20	Bureau of Trade and Industry
O#21	Local Branch of Industry and Commerce Bureau
O#22	Payment Centre of National Treasury
O#23	Sanitation Management Bureau
O#24	Sanitation Supervisory Office
O#25	Neighbourhood committee
O#26	Labour and Social Security Bureau
O#27	Local Local branch of the Disciplinary Inspection Commission of the Chinese Communist Party

O#28   Bureau of Quality and Technology Supervision
O#29   District government
O#30   Bureau of Quality and Technology Supervision

3. Interviews with local intermediaries

The interviewees are from the following intermediary organizations:

I#1   An NGO working on labour rights protection (Shenzhen)
I#2   Accounting firm (Shenzhen)
I#3   Law firm (Dongguan)
I#4   Audit section of an accounting firm (Dongguan)
I#5   Customs broker (Dongguan)
I#6   Customs broker (Dongguan)
I#7   Customs broker (Dongguan)
I#8   Customs broker (Dongguan)
I#9   Customs broker (Shenzhen)
I#10   Certification Centre, Guangdong Food and Drug Supervision and Management
        Bureau (Guangzhou)

PART III

Corruption and society

12

THINKING ABOUT CORRUPTION AS THOUGH PEOPLE MATTERED

Michael Johnston

An analytical mismatch

By now, it is widely recognized that corruption is not just an external event that "happens to" a society nor is it merely an anomaly that can be eradicated by punishing bad people. The types and amounts of corruption found in organizations, communities and whole societies have systemic roots and implications and the patterns and variations that we see around the world exhibit a certain amount of regularity or predictability, as a generation's statistical work has shown.

Still, it is easy to overplay that hand and to assume that aggregate data and system-level attributes tell the whole story. Too often corruption is depicted as a kind of national attribute, like gross domestic product per capita or population density[1], whose significance more or less speaks for itself and which can be compared across cases just by looking at the numbers. That perspective is only reinforced by our frequent reliance upon single-dimension indices, ranking whole countries with a single score for each, in quantitative analysis. The short-comings of such indices have been widely noted: they obscure intra-country variations, tell us nothing about contrasting types of corruption and suggest in effect that corruption is the same thing everywhere, varying only in amounts or extent. When plugged into an equation they imply that the causes and effects of corruption are the same everywhere. The indices, and the research they have spawned, have definite value but they miss a great deal: arguably, the most important parts of the story.

Corruption is a systemic problem, to be sure. *But it is also a lived experience for real people*, affecting their wellbeing, their values and choices, their political voice (or lack of it), their relationships with other citizens as well as with officials and their future chances in life. All of those individual-, household- and enterprise-level experiences, expectations and reactions help shape a society's options and realistic chances for reform. It is not as though such connections and implications have been completely ignored in the research literature: important work on trust (Uslaner 2004; Rothstein and Uslaner 2005; Uslaner 2009), collective action problems (Persson et al. 2013), cultural influences and responses to incentives (Cameron et al. 2005; Banuri and Eckel 2012), and patronage and clientelism (Manzetti and Wilson 2007) are all valuable parts of the analytical repertoire.

But too often the social aspects of corruption have been treated in much too general ways. One such error is to make, and then be satisfied with, broad-brush references to culture. Frequently such references are practically content-free: "cultural and historical factors" certainly must shape, and be shaped by, corruption; after all, it raises questions of right and wrong, fairness and justice, the sources and legitimacy of authority and tests important social boundaries. But what are those effects specifically? Some cultural claims are speculative: might there be "cultures somewhere" in which corruption and bribery are acceptable? Yes, there might, but exhaustive research (for example, Noonan 1984) has not found them. In other settings, cultural factors are invoked as reasons why we cannot compare different sorts of societies or reach conclusions about places other than our own. Certainly, cultural influences can tell us much about the *significance* of corrupt dealings within a society but as any sort of general explanation of corruption they encounter logical problems (Bufacchi and Burgess 1998: 90). Such arguments assume that very general, historically distant and relatively constant influences can explain detailed and variable processes and outcomes in the here and now. Moreover, those influences have a hard time accounting for change. Worst of all is the risk of circular arguments: culture shapes what people do, we are told, but to learn what the culture is like we must…observe what people do.

Another approach to understanding the social dimensions of corruption, which is, again, far from worthless but in need of sceptical examination, is the resort to economic or behavioural determinism. "Determinism" is a strong word, and many analysts doing this sort of work are careful to qualify their findings and to specify the assumptions and circumstances under which they apply. But in the broader discussion such arguments are sometimes assumed to constitute near-laws of behaviour. Make the costs of corruption exceed the benefits and sharp reductions in the problem must surely follow. Raise the pay of civil servants and the same good results will occur. Enact new laws with harsher penalties and intensify monitoring and surveillance and again the quality of government will rise. Usually, costs and benefits are calculated primarily in material terms; likelihood of benefiting or being penalised is assumed to be knowable, known to participants, and reckoned in the same ways by all. (Here, perhaps, might be a fertile domain for some subtle cultural analysis: can we incorporate differing conceptions of, and attitudes toward, risk among different groups of people?)

If we take those ideas as hypotheses, rather than as laws of human nature, they can spur insightful work. But qualifications are in order: people are not necessarily as rational we might wish; self-images and erroneous understandings of costs, benefits and probabilities all shape the ways we respond to incentives, opportunities and risks. For frequently repeated kinds of corruption and for conspiracies to cover them up, past experience can affect both the actual and (not necessarily in the same ways) perceived risks and benefits of a series of deals. Costs and benefits can take intangible forms and those intangibles can mean different things to different people or in contrasting situations. Klitgaard's frequently cited account (1988: Ch. 1) of the effects of publishing corrupt officials' names in the newspapers in the Philippines, a society where family name and honour are valued above almost all else, is a good example. Rational behavioural models of corruption also need to take into account whether people have, or believe they have, alternatives to paying off an abusive official or selling their votes; levels and manifestations of mutual trust; the presence or absence of guarantors for a given deal; and so forth.

All of these quibbles and *caveats* should themselves be judged in a larger context. One reason we have so much research to criticise, and one reason why we can point out the problems with existing data, is that we have so much more of both than was once the case. But there is still a need to get beneath the surface and to understand corruption as a day-to-day individual and social experience. That need is more pressing than ever, for the efforts of a generation have built up a broad consensus on the causes and most promising cures for corruption – one marked by anti-corruption strategies that are strikingly similar even though they are intended to deal with the situation in quite different settings. That consensus has solidified (though to be fair, it is hardly monolithic) despite the indifferent-at-best track record of the anti-corruption movement overall.

Back to basics?

The four chapters included in this section are welcome departures from those trends because they get beneath the surface in a variety of ways. To be sure, they are not the only such efforts: anthropologists and ethnographers have looked at the social settings of corruption in a number of ways, making important contributions even though some have indulged in a kind of cultural exceptionalism that regards comparisons and analytical judgments by outsiders as inherently illegitimate. Case studies of corruption and reforms, along with process-tracing methodologies, can also illuminate social dimensions of corruption. Numerous surveys of households, businesses, citizens and officials highlight such experiences, too. The four contributions in this section take up specific aspects of corruption as a social experience in highly productive detail.

Whose perceptions?

Chilik Yu begins with familiar corruption indices, but raises the fascinating question of how and why the perceptions of elites and citizens might diverge. At stake here is not only a broader assessment of how corruption is viewed in actual societies; equally important questions have to do with the validity and reliability of the national perception-based indices we so often employ, which in many countries draw upon the views of few actual citizens. Abramo (2008) has shown substantial divergence between country level scores on the Transparency International Corruption Perceptions Index (TI-CPI) and on data from TI's Global Corruption Barometer. While the data from each source showed strong internal consistency, the two bodies of evidence were much less strongly correlated with each other, suggesting that differing target populations, sampling, and survey methods substantially influenced the resulting scores. In somewhat similar ways, Yu employs CPI and Asia Barometer data for thirteen Asian societies to compare elite and citizen appraisals of domestic corruption situations. In some instances, such as Vietnam, elites and citizens seem to be reacting to quite different things. For elites, their concern is the perceived overall corruption situation; for citizens, the changed expectations in the aftermath of government anti-corruption moves. Are the two data streams even measuring the same things? Should either or both even be believed, given the authoritarian nature of the system? Yu is appropriately sceptical of the data. Thai citizens' views, as he shows, may reflect an understanding of corruption that is considerably more subtle, differentiated, and multi-layered than the relatively straightforward definitions underlying omnibus indices.

For perception-based indices to hold any validity and reliability, those being surveyed must perceive essentially the same things and judge them against widely shared standards; but in Vietnam and Thailand at least such may not be the case. Overall, people do see corruption as bad news and react to it as such. But in the case of Taiwan, as Yu suggests, the real bad news has been gaps and deficits in the democratisation process, notably, the influences of scandals involving a couple of Presidents, the first family at one point, and the business class. To add, perhaps, another modifier to Collier and Levitsky's (1997) "democracy with adjectives", "democracy with deficits" is likely to be replayed in most democratising and reforming societies in any number of differing ways. We would expect such reactions to affect expectations, actual corruption and responses to it at the grassroots level in complex and context-dependent ways that cannot be divined from one-number national indices. By contrast, even meaningful reforms often fail to move the needle in terms of the expert and (largely) elite perceptions factoring into TI-CPI scores; numerous governments that have devoted political capital and other resources to checking corruption have observed that their index scores seem to change very little.

Yu also raises the fascinating possibility that ratings of corruption might break down, in practice, into qualitatively different scenarios (for a similar argument, see Johnston 2014, 2005). His categories are open to debate but they come as another welcome counterweight to generalisations about "Asian corruption". Exploring qualitatively different kinds of corruption problems is a significant research challenge and will not be welcomed by all as it will tend to produce nominal- rather than interval-level corruption comparisons and undermine many generalisations across large numbers of cases. But it may also yield a more nuanced and context-rich view of both corruption and reform and assessments of both that will still say a great deal about complex cases. A full set of qualitative distinctions will also make it possible to include categories that apply to affluent market democracies. Do the corruption indices we have now give those countries a "pass" in terms of corruption? Taking Yu's logic to heart, the divergence between generally good index scores in the United States, for example, and the three-quarters of survey respondents who regularly say that money in politics is corrupting democracy, makes a compelling case for such a re-examination.

Yu concludes by noting the large gaps between our current corruption measuring sticks and the standards we would hope to attain and his call for further research must be taken seriously. Recent years have witnessed the long-overdue spread of useful scepticism regarding some of the most commonly used indices. Any effort to improve upon current methods must begin with a careful reassessment of just what we seek to learn from any approach to measurement and of how our methods relate to corruption as citizens experience it.

The gender dimension

Natalia Matukhno offers a broad-gauged look at the intersections between gender and corruption, beginning with notion of women as "the fairer sex" in terms of corruption control. Might women tend to be less corrupt, or corruptible, than men (Dollar et al. 2001)? The evidence is ambiguous. Some efforts to test that idea in action, notably the well-known Mexico City experiment with women as traffic wardens, based on the assumption that male drivers would not want to plead for, or buy, leniency from a female official, have yielded results that were mixed at best.

From a research standpoint, it is difficult to disentangle any independent effects of gender upon corruption from the systemic context, as Matukhno notes. In general (with some clear exceptions), women are more likely to win elective office and exercise other public powers in liberal democracies than in other systems. The setting will shape the powers they hold, the institutions within which they hold them, popular expectations of government and officials and the sorts of influence tactics that are or are not seen as acceptable. Any independent effects of gender upon corruption will be mediated through the values and institutions of the societies in question; that does not mean that there are no such effects but rather that they will be difficult to tease out. Meanwhile, we risk drawing upon stereotypes in the formation of policy.

A similar problem stems from treating "corruption" as a single undifferentiated problem. Consider the implications of women's subordinate positions in many societies and situations. While some corruption (say, a firm's bribery of a bureaucrat to obtain tax breaks) involves the aggressive and illegitimate use of power and influence, other cases, such as, for example, inspectors who extort payments from stallholders in a market, revolve around vulnerability. In the latter situations, any inherent gender differences in corruptibility may well be beside the point. A great many, of course, involve both: consider official extortion of women applying for much-needed family benefits, for example, or law enforcement officers who extract payments from women using threats of sexual violence. Other variations on this theme include the question of whether reports by women or men are more likely to be believed by authorities, and whether cases involving women, particularly those of low status, will be given priority by supervisors, the courts, and the press.

Status and vulnerability considerations are linked, in turn, to the range of alternatives to corruption that women and men might have. Matukhno rightly observes that in Southeast Asia, the former Soviet region, Latin America and sub-Saharan Africa where women's rights are weak, women suffer more from corruption and are less able to take a stand against it than elsewhere. At the same time, however, she notes that subordinate status, vulnerability and repression might give women an extra incentive, and occasionally opportunities, to resist corruption and to organize others around such causes.

Matukhno also makes it clear that we would do well to move beyond general propositions about corruptibility to look at more subtle contrasts in attitudes and dispositions. On the whole, she notes, women are more risk-averse. That tendency might inhibit a certain amount of corruption but could also make women reluctant to report abuses by powerful figures. Risk aversion could also invite, or require, more carefully contrived incentives and penalties as parts of our overall corruption-control repertoire. Are women more strongly influenced by social sanctions such as "naming and shaming", shunning and the like? Would such a contrast suggest means of deterrence other than criminal punishment? On the other hand, would it invite gratuitous shaming and defamation of women under the guise of corruption control?

Matukhno tests a number of hypotheses and points to some surprising country-by-country contrasts. She is careful to set up those comparisons of gender in the context of both internal (individual influences linked to gender) and external structures (a range of contextual factors). Women's resistance to corruption tends to be strong in some unexpected places, such as Afghanistan, India, Japan and Pakistan, once education, age and urbanisation have been taken into account. There are also significant contrasts among countries in terms of whether women are likely to be asked for bribes. Those differences are linked not only to whether women are in powerful or subordinate positions as individuals but also to the persistence of "old-boy networks" in society. Thus, she cites Afghanistan, Bangladesh, India, Nepal, Pakistan and Sri Lanka as cases where those networks remain strong and entrenched. Related to this is the question of whether, under what circumstances and how frequently, women have the opportunity to manifest opposition to corruption in meaningful ways. Japan, Korea, and Taiwan, not surprisingly, are countries in which women are more likely to have refused to pay a bribe but so is Afghanistan, a case that reminds us that values and systems of authority can persist in the absence of a strong and credible state. Willingness of women to report corruption varies considerably, too, with Japan, Vietnam and Pakistan ranking surprisingly low in those terms. Might unwillingness to file reports shift the anti-corruption burden back in the direction of personal refusals to pay? In some highly corrupt settings (Fiji, for example), women report paying more bribes but are also more willing to file reports.

In the end, the question of whether women are "the fairer sex" when it comes to corruption control has no single answer. We are discussing, after all, a little more than half of humanity living in situations that run the full global gamut; indeed, women seem to vary more among themselves than do men in terms of their responses to corrupt pressures and opportunities. A critical finding of her chapter is that women may play a special anti-corruption role where they are supported in legal, institutional, economic and social ways; where such support is absent, being risk-averse and often vulnerable make them more compliant with corrupt pressures. Thus, anti-corruption hopes or actual policies based on gender alone are likely to prove unwise. Fundamentally, it is up to society to support women, or anyone vulnerable to corruption and official abuse, if we expect lasting popular support for reform. Simply shoving women out to the front line and expecting them to check corruption based on presumed aspects of gender alone is likely, in many settings, to place women upon a more vulnerable pedestal than before and is an abdication of society's broader obligations to pursue and guarantee justice for all.

Behind the façade, resistance

If liberal democratic systems shape or reward characteristic responses to corruption, what is to be said about undemocratic societies? It is easy to assume that in authoritarian or dictatorial political systems corruption is carried out with impunity and that the domestic politics of corruption will be unimportant or non-existent – or that corruption and resentment will culminate in systemic crisis. Similarly, when undemocratic regimes accede to international anti-corruption agreements such as the United Nations Convention Against Corruption, or take specific steps toward reform, it is tempting to argue that they do so primarily to reduce interference from outside interests, to solidify the regime's hold over its own domain, or to engage in reprisals against domestic critics via "reform" purges.

But undemocratic regimes and responses to corruption come in many flavours (Yadav and Mukherjee 2016), varying among themselves more than do democracies. Moreover, corruption is a widely shared grievance in such societies, and protests against it do make headlines. But generally we know few details; American mass media accounts of protests abroad, when they appear at all, are often filed by correspondents from a great distance and jammed into a ritualised formula. If we were to get beyond such simplistic news frames and understand the reality of anti-corruption activities in an undemocratic regime, what might we learn?

A great deal, according to Andrew Wedeman. For starters, there is a strong, if not perfect, relationship between political stability and success at controlling corruption, at least as measured by the World Governance Indicators. While both axes of that comparison are subject to the usual *caveats* about whole-country, single-dimension indices, it also fits with experience. At one end of the continuum, we might speculate that both control of corruption and overall stability are aspects of control in general, via generalised political and institutional effectiveness and, quite likely, workable levels of political trust. But the real interest lies at the other end: many regimes ineffective at controlling corruption, and probably less stable as well, are also authoritarian. At times that instability is overt. At other times, it may take the form of more subtle systemic fragility: systems that cannot bend become more likely to break. At the very least, undemocratic systems deserve more, not less, analytical attention in terms of reactions to corruption.

Wedeman presents and analyses a sizeable database of news reports on protests within China. The data resist any simple interpretation: not all discontent culminates in protest. Connections between the two are complex. Not all protests are necessarily anti-regime and not all grievances relate to corruption. Even when corruption is the nominal focus of a protest, the events at issue might not fit an analyst's definition of the term. In authoritarian regimes, corruption can be a way to raise a range of issues and to attack the conduct of specific officials without directly challenging the regime's legitimacy or claims to rule: individual officials or agencies can be criticised for running afoul of the regime's own proclaimed values. Some protests are one-off local events; others spread geographically and persist over time and in that latter instance, according to Wedeman, violence, be it attacks on protestors or on the police, becomes more common. Overall, violence occurs in around a third of the protests.

Wedeman estimates that corruption enters into about one-quarter of the more than 4,000 protests in his database, usually in combination with other grievances. Many issues revolve around land, always a pivotal issue in China and now all the more strategic as the economy has been transformed. In rural areas, land is formally held in communal fashion and farmers are supposed to be compensated when those lands move into private hands. Tension between farmers and villagers, on the one hand, and alliances of developers and local officials can be intense, with the latter at times resorting to violence and intimidation in order to convert land into development projects. Some protests are over the injustice of such deals and alliances but in other cases, Wedeman reports, the emphasis is mostly on getting a better price. By contrast, protests directly aimed at official corruption comprise only about 2 per cent of the cases.

Resentment of corruption, broadly defined, is real in China. That there is a domestic politics of corruption, albeit largely informal and extra-systemic, in an authoritarian society is of great interest. At the same time, anyone hoping to harness such resentments for reform purposes or in hopes of more sweeping systemic change should find Wedeman's evidence sobering. After all, hundreds of millions in China are now living better and, in some respects, freer lives than they once did. Efforts at improving services and facilities in rural areas have been impressive over the past decades. Triggering linkages that turn diffuse discontents into focused, anti-corruption mass action are complex and usually involve issues and grievances that stretch our analytical definitions. Much more needs to be known about how values (and varieties of value confusion), expectations, conceptions of authority, and non-governmental/non-party social linkages, such as *guanxi,* might shape responses to corruption. Land deals can be a compelling grievance for villagers or farmers whose communal holdings have been sold out from under them or have brought insufficient compensation but may not strongly affect those in other areas. Such issues might operate in a kind of patchwork fashion across the country, not as a factor mobilising hundreds of millions.

Those are all reasons why, once again, an exclusive national-level focus may miss a great deal. Wedeman's data show us both that a great deal is happening in widely varying ways at local levels and yet that local protests rarely aggregate into coherent regional or national unrest. An emerging wild-card factor is the spread of social media. After the 2011 high-speed rail crash in Wenzhou, Zhejiang Province, that killed 40 people, the government literally attempted to bury much of the evidence. But passengers and spectators had quickly begun to circulate photographs of the event and the cover-up was unsuccessful. Subsequent investigations and safety reviews confirmed corruption as a contributing cause to the signal failures that allowed two trains to collide (Osnos 2012). Partially as a result of social media and citizen action, the result was neither the suppression of the event nor a mass political outcry but rather a more measured and possibly constructive response on all sides to corruption.

The future implications of Wedeman's analysis are tantalising but complex. We might hope discontent over corruption might help open up the system somewhat. By that, I do not mean anything like a systemic political transition but perhaps more positive responsiveness to local issues and grievances. Against that, we must consider the overall power of the regime: despite its internal stresses and the challenges of responding to the current economic slowdown, its basic dominance remains intact. Citizens, confronted with a choice between confrontation even at a local or regional level and continuing adaptation to the realities of the new China, could be forgiven for choosing the latter, particularly if economic trends turn upward again. A third option, cooperative action involving both citizens and officials, would require massive changes on both sides; as Mitu Sengupta's chapter makes clear, civil society action against corruption requires critical resources, opportunities, and skilled leadership that cannot be taken for granted. Meanwhile, corruption continues to evolve, and Wedeman is correct in observing that as it becomes a more high-level and collusive phenomenon, citizens might be less likely to know much about it or to challenge it openly.

That in turn invites speculation about even longer term trends: if there are multiple distinct syndromes of corruption (Johnston 2005, 2014), much depends upon whether China's current style of "Official Moguls" corruption changes into the somewhat more open and politically resilient "Elite Cartels" syndrome, or into the chaos of "Oligarchs and Clans". Yan Sun's observations (1999) about the ways China's party-state resisted a Soviet-style implosion by retaining political hegemony while pursuing economic change remain valid today, and despite the system's manifest tensions, a change toward "Elite Cartel" corruption seems more likely. Wedeman's idea of elite-focused corruption surfacing in the form of extensive collusion and tactical accommodations to other groups and interests in society fits that scenario well. Perhaps we might even imagine an eventual shift toward "Influence Markets" in China, albeit with a more limited range of issues open to contention than we would see in a democracy. In both cases, corrupt processes would likely become even more remote from citizens' immediate experience, and in the "Influence Market" case, it could become difficult to say where routine market processes end and corruption begins. All this is speculative and, as with our other three contributions in this section, a clear implication is that any credible prognosis will entail knowing much more about corruption as a lived experience. For those seeking that sort of understanding, Wedeman's data and interpretations give us critical guidance in terms of some important places to look.

Civil society: hopes versus realities

If any concept has been a staple of anti-corruption thought over the past generation, it is the potential strength of *civil society*. Strong civil societies are often found in relatively well-governed countries. If, however, Lessig (2013) and others are correct that much of what we might call corruption in those countries is legal and enjoys the protection of strong institutions, we might wonder just how much civil society is actually doing to check corruption. Similarly, we might ask whether a strong civil society is a cause of moderate corruption, or whether limited corruption and a strong civil society are both outcomes of deeper democratising changes (Johnston 2014). Many high hopes and no small amount of romance revolve around mass movements in other societies; the "people power" movements that helped topple Ferdinand Marcos and, 15 years later, Joseph Estrada, in the Philippines are well-known and help fuel arguments that similar movements can curtail corruption in other settings (Beyerle 2014). Such movements, however, are not the same thing as a strong civil society nor is overturning a corrupt ruler the same thing as lasting reform (for a more hopeful assessment, see Chenoweth and Stephan 2011). An even bigger problem, in specific cases, is whether civil society is real or more of a wish. We observe a certain level of democracy, or the existence of a middle class, or the appearance of individuals and groups critical of the government of the day, and assume or hope that the sort of civil society we envision is present or emerging. But autonomous, sustained civil society action is all too rare in high-corruption settings and even more difficult to jump-start from without.

For those reasons, Mitu Sengupta's contribution is of particular importance. India poses the most difficult and momentous test of reform thinking about civil society. It is a democracy of nearly 70 years' standing and one that has survived despite episodes of severe stress. At the same time, democracy has not been able to contain corruption; in some ways, in fact, mass electoral democracy has intensified corrupt connections and the power of money (Sun and Johnston 2009). Has civil society failed India in some sense, or are such expectations misplaced and ill-informed?

Sengupta reminds us that the emergence of a strong civil society is a tall order. Some challenges are practical: poverty, the sheer scale of Indian society, poor performance by official institutions, parties with top-down patterns of influence, the power of local and regional political potentates and the collective action problems confronting civil society everywhere are enduring difficulties. Another problem is conceptual: when we expect or hope that "civil society" as an abstract entity will move against corruption, we are in effect assigning it a life of its own, where instead we must remember that civil society is at best an aggregation of the actions, interests, expectations and values of millions of individuals and small groups, none of which is necessarily acting in "civic" or altruistic ways. For example, the anti-corruption movement led by Anna Hazare that began to make headlines in 2010 appeared to have great potential for reform and for introducing civil society as a more autonomous force in politics. But for reasons, Sengupta makes clear, the movement gradually lost strength: issues of nationalism, among others, cut across Hazare's appeal, a fact that is disappointing in terms of national reform but much less puzzling from a bottom-up point of view.

Our challenge is to revise our expectations of civil society: of what it can do, why it would do it and what its likely effects might be. While a top-down view might lead us to hope civil society would lead a nationwide crusade for better government as a good in itself, a grassroots view reminds us of what an immense undertaking that would be and leads us to ask why citizens might ever take on the risks and uncertainties it would entail. "Livelihood struggles", Sengupta reminds us, are far more likely than civic values for their own sake to motivate citizen action against corruption. That means there must be far more specific goals and convincing incentives and appeals, if anti-corruption action is to be sustained. Similarly, what would success really look like in practice? Certainly not an India cleansed of all corruption: no precedent for that exists anywhere. More of a voice in local decision-making and service provision? That might seem a less inspiring goal but one that falls far closer to the realm of possibility.

On that level, in fact, there have been successes. *Mazdoor Kisan Shakti Sangathan* (MKSS), a social movement founded in Rajasthan State in India's northwest, has parlayed its own people power, along with some international aid, into a continuing presence monitoring government performance in the region. Data are gathered and discussed in people's assemblies where they are discussed and analysed. Citizen representatives then work with state and local officials to implement positive changes. An early initiative involved going through government employment rolls name by name with citizens helping spot the many "ghost employees" officials had enrolled in order to siphon off salary funds. MKSS was able to reduce payroll abuses and demonstrate its potential effectiveness in ways that all could easily understand. While the group encountered considerable official resistance at first, it became a respected presence in state and local politics and an active partner both in reforming existing practices and developing new ones.

The National Campaign for People's Right to Information (NCPRI), launched in 1996, achieved major successes as well by harnessing grassroots energy in lasting ways. Its early push for a Right to Information (RTI) law was bottled up in parliamentary committees and stonewalled by powerful elected and appointed officials, but citizens kept up the pressure partly because the goal was specific and linked directly to their own interests and wellbeing. A breakthrough came when a top agency unilaterally allowed access to its information, showing citizens that success was possible, and may have persuaded some bureaucrats that citizen access to information would not cause the sky to fall. Reversals in the courts only intensified demands for a national RTI law, while the visible scope of NCPRI and its following created political opportunities for elites willing to back the proposal. A new government, elected in 2004, came out in favour of sweeping transparency improvements, and created a commission including NCPRI representatives that framed an RTI bill which was enacted in 2005. Despite implementation problems and weaker support from subsequent governments, India's RTI law and NCPRI have both attracted worldwide praise.

Civil society advocates can learn at least as much from failures, however. Where MKSS and NCPRI both provided believable incentives to citizens and officials alike to support specific anti-corruption proposals, Anna Hazare's forays into the reform arena were marked by more diffuse appeals and antagonistic relationships with government. India Against Corruption (IAC) in particular attracted worldwide attention in 2010 and 2011, its appeals dramatised by Hazare's hunger strikes and massive public demonstrations of support. But in the end IAC's effects were minimal. Hazare's adversarial stance succeeded in winning some official concessions but was an unlikely foundation for sustained cooperation. In making himself the issue Hazare enjoyed Gandhian appeal but that and the presence of what Sengupta calls other "celebrity" leaders led to rivalries in the movement and weaker ties to IAC's citizen base. Worse yet, the celebrities antagonised the leadership of other progressive groups such as NCRI. That citizen base had been thinner than the sheer numbers of demonstrators alone might have suggested. Early on, many people showed up as spectators or marchers at IAC events, but for most, that was the extent of their involvement, a major contrast, Sengupta notes, with the ability of MKSS and NCRTI to involve citizens and volunteers in their work and successes. Hazare was in the untenable position of mobilising the weak against the strong rather than building modes of cooperation and of doing so without a solid system of sustaining incentives and appeals (see Johnston and Kpundeh 2002). By the end of 2012, Hazare's movement and influence had largely dissipated.

Lessons from India, and from Sengupta's discussion, are many and valuable. Citizens must be given "livelihood" reasons to join or support an anti-corruption movement. Reform appeals often seem to assume that fighting corruption means putting one's own interests aside but many more people will get involved when it is clear that their wellbeing is at stake and when believable goals are kept clearly in view by leaders. Visible and understandable results, the MKSS case shows, are essential. Further, NCRTI's success puts civil society forces into a more favourable position, going forward, as they will be defending the RTI legislation and its continuing implementation, rather than seeking sweeping change. Civil-society movements will also be more effective when they offer positive incentives to officials, such as political support, cooperation in pursuit of specific goals, or sharing the credit for accomplishments, than when they take a wholly adversarial stance.

Civil society strategies can also become more effective if we rethink our criteria for success. A national corruption-index score will be a far less useful way of understanding citizen experiences with corruption, and their likely responses to reform appeals, than (say) a series of skillfully designed household surveys on dealings with officials and bribes paid. In somewhat different fashion, the "Shudify" movement in Bangalore (Global Changemakers 2012) for example, was able to produce useful and provocative data through "exit interviews" of citizens leaving district Transport Offices. Student interviewers asked a handful of quick questions: Were you well-treated? Was the office clean? Were you asked for bribes? Did you get what you needed from the office? On that basis, they were able to map out the city's best and worst Transport Offices and to give citizens a clear sense that somebody wanted to help them avoid future mistreatment. Success on limited objectives, such as MKSS efforts to root out "ghost employees", has much more appeal than calls for political transformation or "zero tolerance" of corruption. Civil society groups that can show that they are more reliable and effective allies than the touts and "fixers" who ply their trade outside government offices can make considerable headway in winning citizen support. Halfway outcomes involving partial cooperation from officials on a few goals may not be fully satisfying but may also signal valuable progress.

Civil society groups do, however, face delicate choices in their relationships with government. Too much cooperation runs the risk of losing public credibility and of being used by venal officials. Too much of an adversarial stance risks repression or the stony indifference of entrenched interests and officialdom. A mix of carrots and sticks, combining demonstrated popular support for change with positive incentives for cooperation and a specific rather than an omnibus agenda would seem to be a promising mix, but such decisions must be based on extensive knowledge of citizen experiences and expectations and of the likely reactions of officials and corrupt figures. No single set of "best practices" can define such choices in advance.

Conclusion

We often refer to corruption as an "embedded" problem in the sense of endogeneity: that corruption can be both cause and effect of more general problems such as poverty, weak institutions, low levels of social and political trust, and so forth. But it is also embedded in a second sense: it is embedded in daily life. That refers not just to how common an experience corruption can be for people but also to the ways it is mediated through personal experience and networks, opportunities and choices, and the problems and reciprocities of everyday life. Analysts and reformers, on the one hand, and citizens, on the other, may be talking about quite different things when they mention "corruption", and can have very different reactions to it. I have been struck, in the course of working with people in some reputedly quite corrupt places, how experiences with the problem vary from one person to the next and also by the levels of optimism that sometimes jump out in surprising ways. Even in the least promising settings, people might see corruption as a fact of life, but they do not like it, accept it, or believe nothing can be done. The challenge is to learn about and connect with their experiences and outlooks.

At the same time, reformers must remember that in the short term at least, many people may benefit from corruption if only by receiving a few crumbs from the feast, or at least believe they stand to benefit in the future. That such hopes may strike us as futile and as drastically underestimating the long-term, intangible, and shared costs of corruption may be both true and beside the point. For some people, trading the known, even if it is difficult, for the risks and uncertainties of change may seem a dubious proposition, particularly if past reform efforts have changed nothing or even made matters worse. That is one more reason why citizen backing for reform must be built patiently, step-by-step and focused upon real and understandable goals and successes. If what we offer is a national morality campaign or a popular crusade against the bankers, bureaucrats, generals and politicians entrenched at the top of the system, chances are citizens have heard all of that before.

One positive aspect of that grassroots perspective for reformers view is that it keeps *justice* squarely at center stage. It is easy, in fighting corruption, to lose sight of that overriding goal in the midst of wrangling with administrative processes and developing targeted but short-lived projects. Working for justice is a long-term enterprise and like corruption control, the job never ends. But it is, or should be, the reason why we care about corruption in the first place and it is the most enduring foundation on which sustained popular backing for and participation in reform can be built.

A different social dimension, and one on which we arguably know even less, has to do with the corrupt themselves. How do such officials, politicians, and their private clients understand their roles? Do they want to follow a more honest path but doubt its outcomes? Do they see themselves as having any choice in the matter at all? Many private parties regularly pay bribes, for example, but do not like it; at least some officials want to do the jobs they are nominally expected to do but believe they are alone in that wish. Will corrupt figures dig in and defend their existing advantages, resort to repression and revenge, or perhaps see well-crafted reforms as a way to reduce risks and conflict, and to live a quiet life? Much depends upon whom we have in mind, of course: a dictator with ill-gotten real estate holdings in his portfolio, a political following to keep paying off, and a loyal army at his disposal will differ greatly from a long-suffering police officer or inspector who must collect bribes in order to pay off the superiors who gave him his job. Sometimes, however, reformers may find allies in surprising places, and functionaries involved in corrupt processes (as opposed to those who orchestrate them from above) may act out of motivations other than greed. Often, our reform models focus on corrupt offenders as free agents, responding to a climate of costs, risks, and benefits; but those influences (and how they are perceived by corrupt figures themselves) may be poorly understood, and those figures' alternatives and choices may be much more complex than we have suspected.

A final idea is that perhaps we should be more sceptical of whole-country efforts to measure corruption and the effects of reforms. Even if we had demonstrably valid and reliable ways to arrive at such measures, how much would they really tell us? Middle-level methods such as surveys of households and businesses can produce valuable and highly detailed insights. Anthropological and ethnographic methods hold great potential if we do not insist on obtaining quantitative indicators. Indicators and benchmarks of government performance likewise can shed detailed light on the specific connections, gaps, and procedural problems that give rise to or harbour corruption (Johnston 2010), and can do so at much less cost than surveys. The difficulty with that idea, of course, is getting agency managers and officials on board, and involving citizens in evaluating the results and implementing changes. Still, knowing that issuing licenses in City A involves many more steps and takes much more time than it does in City B, or that Agency Y in a local region is paying 50 per cent more for petrol than does Agency Z, could be extremely valuable knowledge for reformers. Extending such measures over time could track the effects of reform, and where indicators are improving over time, send clear messages to citizens and potential malefactors alike that reform is for real. Conversely, where trends are negative the message for reformers is that quite specific new ideas, and/or better implementation, are needed. Integrity Action's "fix rate" scheme, evaluating units of government in terms of their responses to problems, is a similar idea that has proven effective in the course of trial runs in a number of settings (Integrity Action 2016).

When we do look at government processes at those sub-national levels, we often see striking variations. A 2009 Tsinghua University survey, for example, found significant variations across five major Chinese cities in terms of the time, cost and steps involved in registering a business and obtaining permits (Hills Program on Governance 2009). Similarly, in Europe, there are striking differences in the quality of governance across the sub-national regions of the EU (Charron et al. 2013; 2014).

The four contributions in this section can only address some of these issues but they show the critical importance of understanding corruption as a lived experience. Together with work being done elsewhere, we have both the need and the opportunity to put our understanding of corruption and the prospects for reform on a much more complete and realistic footing.

Note

1 I am indebted to the late Clifford Geertz for that analogy, offered in the course of a seminar at the Institute for Advanced Study.

References

Abramo, C. W. (2008) "How much do perceptions of corruption really tell us?" *Economics,* 2:3, http://www.economics-ejournal.org/economics/journalarticles (accessed 22 January 2016).

Banuri, S. and C. C. Eckel (2012) *Experiments in culture and corruption: a review,* World Bank Policy Research Working Paper No. 6064 (May 1), http://ssrn.com/abstract=2055105 (accessed 22 January 2016).

Beyerle, S. M. (2014) *Curtailing corruption: people power for accountability and justice,* Boulder, CO: Lynne Rienner.

Bufacchi, V. and S. Burgess (1998) *Italy since 1989: events and interpretations,* New York: St. Martin's Press.

Cameron, L. A., A. Chaudhuri, N. Erkal and L. Gangadharan (2005) "Do attitudes towards corruption differ across cultures? Experimental evidence from Australia, India, Indonesia and Singapore", http://ssrn.com/abstract=778464 (accessed 25 January 2016).

Charron, N., L. Dijkstra and V. Lapuente (2014) "Regional governance matters: quality of government within European Union member states", *Regional Studies,* 48(1): 68–90.

Charron, N., V. Lapuente and B. Rothstein (2013) *Quality of government and corruption from a European perspective: a comparative study of good government in EU regions,* Cheltenham: Edward Elgar Publishing.

Chenoweth, E. and M. J. Stephan (2011) *Why civil resistance works: the strategic logic of nonviolent conflict,* New York: Columbia University Press.

Collier, D. and S. Levitsky (1997) "Democracy with adjectives: conceptual innovation in comparative research", *World Politics,* 49(3): 430–451.

Dollar, D., R. Fisman and R. Gatti (2001) "Are women really the 'fairer' sex? Corruption and women in government", *Journal of Economic Behavior and Organization,* 46(4): 423–429.

Global Changemakers (2012) "*Shudify*", http://www.global-changemakers.net/#home (accessed 21 January 2016).

Hills Program on Governance (2009) "Report of the China city governance and integrity education curriculum projects", Tsinghua University (Beijing), summary tables of municipal process indicators available from Michael Johnston.

Integrity Action (2016) "Statistics – measuring a fix", http://integrityaction.org/index.php/ (accessed 13 January 2016).

Johnston, M. (2005) *Syndromes of corruption,* Cambridge: Cambridge University Press.

Johnston, M. (2010) "Assessing vulnerabilities to corruption: indicators and benchmarks of government performance", *Public Integrity,* 12(2): 125–142.

Johnston, M. (2014) *Contention, conflict, and reform: the power of deep democratization,* Cambridge: Cambridge University Press.

Johnston, M. and S. J. Kpundeh (2002) "*Building a clean machine: anti-corruption coalitions and sustainable reforms*", Washington, DC: World Bank Institute Working Paper number 37208.

Klitgaard, R. (1988) *Controlling corruption,* Berkeley, CA: University of California Press.

Lessig, L. (2013) "'Institutional corruption' defined", *Journal of Law, Medicine, and Ethics,* 41(3): 553–555.

Manzetti, L. and C. J. Wilson (2007) "Why do corrupt governments maintain public support?" *Comparative Political Studies,* 40(8): 949–970.

Noonan, J. T. (1984) *Bribes: the intellectual history of a moral idea,* Berkeley: University of California Press.

Osnos, E. (2012) "Boss rail: the disaster that exposed the underside of the boom", *The New Yorker,* October 22: 44–53.

Persson, A., B. Rothstein and J. Teorell (2013) "Why anticorruption reforms fail – systemic corruption as a collective action problem", *Governance,* 26(3): 449–471.

Rothstein, B. and E. M. Uslaner (2005) "All for all: equality, corruption, and social trust", *World Politics,* 58(1): 41–72.

Sun, Y. (1999) "Reform, state, and corruption: is corruption less destructive in China than in Russia?" *Comparative Politics,* 32(1): 1–20.

Sun, Y. and M. Johnston (2009) "Does democracy check corruption? Insights from China and India", *Comparative Politics,* 42(1): 1–19.

Uslaner, E. M. (2004) "Trust and corruption", in J. G. Lambsdorf, M. Taube and M. Schramm (eds.) *The new institutional economics of corruption,* London: Routledge, 76–92.

Uslaner, E. M. (2009) "Corruption", in G.T. Svendsen and G. L. H. Svendsen (eds.) *Handbook of social capital: the troika of sociology, political science and economics,* Cheltenham: Edward Elgar, 127–142.

Yadav, V. and B. Mukherjee (2016) *The politics of corruption in dictatorships,* Cambridge: Cambridge University Press.

13

CORRUPTION AND COLLECTIVE PROTEST IN CHINA

Andrew Wedeman

Introduction

Over the past two decades, China has experienced worsening corruption and a surge in mass unrest. Whereas there were a reported 8,700 reported mass incidents in 1993, an average of 25 per day, in 2012 there were an estimated 187,000, an average of about 500 a day (Tanner 2004; Yu 2012).[1] Since then, it is said that the number has exceeded 200,000 a year. Corruption, which had been a widespread but low-level problem during the pre-reform era, first increased in raw numbers in the 1980s and then intensified in the 1990s (Wedeman 2004). As measured by the total number of indictments for corruption, it then seemed to level off for the better part of a decade. However, the advent of a new major anti-corruption campaign following the selection of Xi Jinping as General Secretary of the Chinese Communist Party in November 2012 has yielded evidence that, while the quantitative incidence of corruption may not have changed significantly since the 1990s, there has been a qualitative worsening of its severity, particularly among senior party and state officials, as well as within the ranks of senior officers in the People's Liberation Army. Corruption has also emerged as a major source of discontent. In polls conducted annually by Pew Research between 2012 and 2015, half of those surveyed said that corrupt officials were a "very big problem" and an additional third said corrupt officials were a "moderately big problem". Only 8 to 12 per cent said corrupt officials were a minor problem or not a problem (Pew Research 2015a and 2015b). Since a 2008 poll, those saying corruption was a moderate problem has decreased and those saying it was big problem has increased.[2]

Are the concurrent increases in reported mass incidents and the apparent qualitative worsening of corruption connected? More specifically, has the worsening of corruption led to increased unrest? Are China's workers, farmers, and members of the new middle class reacting to an increasingly venal and predatory regime whose officials and functionaries have usurped their official authority and converted their public offices into private money-making machines? More critically, is corruption linked to violent protests and, if so, what kinds of violent protests?

Corruption is frequently associated with unrest. In China during the eighteenth century, for instance, Park (1997: 996) argues that even though corruption was "extremely widespread" and the source of deep feelings of injustice, it did not generate unrest, in part because the Qing state was strong enough to convince commoners that resistance was "futile". Over time, however, "the simmering hostility of the populous... and the Qing regime's failure to deal ..." with corruption "affected the long-term health and stability of the empire, ultimately contributing to the social upheavals of the nineteenth century". In his "Report on an Investigation of the Peasant Movement in Hunan", Mao Zedong (1927: 27) argued that it was "corrupt officials" who were behind the cruelty of "the local tyrants, the evil gentry, and the lawless landlords" whose abuses drove peasants to rise up "like a hurricane" to smash and sweep away China's autocrats, warlords, and imperialists. Michael (1948: 162) argued that, during the civil war, China's "leading businessmen and bankers... intellectual leaders... labor leadership ..." and "urban middle class... bitterly resented misgovernment" by the Kuomintang and that the officer corps had become "discontent[ed] with the corruption and inefficiency of the military command". Corruption thus sapped popular support for the Kuomintang, contributing to its enfeeblement. According to Wright (2015: 123), corruption has become the single most serious "shortcoming" of China's post-Mao regime and has "been the general cause for most of the collective popular contention" in contemporary China. She specifically points to "arbitrary taxes and fees", "unfair land acquisitions", and environmental issues as causes of protests. Similarly, Fewsmith (2013: 23) argues that corruption is "widespread" in poor rural areas and that the friction created by a combination of corruption, a heavy handed, repressive approach to "stability maintenance" and ties between local cadres, police, and organized crime creates conditions in which tensions are kept at a constant simmer and are only prevented from boiling over by "some combination of resignation, intimidation, and the simple desire to pursue one's own livelihood". Under such conditions, he asserts, a single seemingly petty confrontation between citizens and the authorities can quickly explode into violent mass incidents.

More broadly, Rotberg (2004: 9) argues that corruption contributes to political instability because it leads citizens to believe that their rulers are "working for themselves and their kin, not the state" and that "the state increasingly comes to be perceived as being owned by an exclusive group, with all others pushed aside", which causes citizens to transfer their loyalties to rival organizations. The State Failure Task Force (2000) asserted that corruption was highly correlated with government performance and lists it as a factor in regime failure in Ghana (1972), cult violence in Nigeria (1980), the suspension of constitutional rule in Uganda (1966), and the overthrow of the Obote government (1972).

Individual case studies of state failure also point to corruption as a major contributing factor in the incapacitation of specific states. Khan (2007), for instance, argues that decades of systemic corruption have crippled the Pakistani state and rendered it incapable of providing basic public goods, thereby de-legitimating successive governments, and opening the way for the proliferation of grassroots challengers. Research in Africa and Peru links corruption to popular protests and the rise of revolutionary groups (Taylor 1987; Harsch 1993). In Bolivia, Gingerich (2009) found evidence that individuals who said that they had experienced corruption first hand were much more likely to join protests than those who were not exposed to corruption, especially if they thought it was directly linked to the regime. Measures generated by the World Bank's Governance Indicators, finally, appear to validate the impression that corruption is associated with political stability (see Figure 13.1).

The literature on rebellion and the connection between grievance and open challenges to authority makes clear, however, that while there may be a visual relationship between corruption and instability, the mechanisms that cause latent discontent to boil over in collective resistance and violent confrontation are complex. First, not all discontent leads to collective protest (Gurr 1971; Lichbach 1995; Tilly 2003). As Olson (1971) observes, what is most noteworthy about discontent is how rarely it erupts into collective protest. Mounting corruption

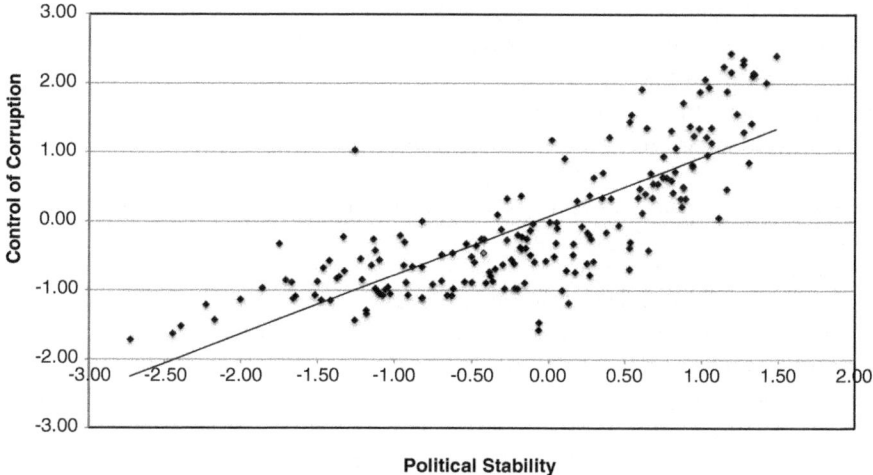

Figure 13.1 Political stability and control of corruption

Source: World Bank Governance Indicators, average 1996 to 2012, http://info.worldbank.org/governance/wgi/index. aspx#home (accessed 6 October 2015).

may, therefore, generate discontent without triggering a transition from latent grumbling to collective protest. Second, collective protests may confront local state institutions without challenging the regime as a whole. As O'Brien and Li (2006) found, protestors involved in "rightful resistance" often seek to bring higher-level bureaucratic pressure to bear on the "street-level bureaucrats", believing that the upper levels of government will bring them relief from injustices inflicted on them by local officials. A rising tide of protests may not, therefore, lead to a deterioration in regime legitimacy. In fact, public opinion polls suggest that, although between 2012 and 2015 an average of about 85 per cent of those surveyed said corruption was a problem, overall support for the regime has remained high in China (Dickson 2008; Chen and Dickson 2010; Whyte 2010; Chen 2013).

Third, not all mass incidents are political or plausibly linked to official corruption. Workplace protests triggered by low wages, poor working conditions, and wage arrears might be viewed as "political" in the sense that they are battles over the authoritative allocation of value and, in some instances, may involve state-owned enterprises. But even in such instances, the core conflict is between employers and employees, not between the regime and its citizenry. Fourth, some types of protests simply do not combine with others in ways that would make them "additive" in the sense that protests in one issue area combines with protests in another issue area to generate a greater combined threat. Protests by ethnic Uighurs in China's far west, for instance, do not combine and complement labour protest in the rustbelts of Northeast China or the export-led industrial enclaves of Southern China. Mass incidents should not, therefore, be treated as a unitary political phenomenon.

Data, sources, and definitions

If mass incidents are not a unitary phenomenon, then to determine if changes in the level of corruption and number of protests are correlated, it is first necessary to identify specifically how and where corruption and protest connect. Thus, I first decompose mass incidents writ large into more specific categories, identify which categories are logically linked to and driven by corruption, and then assess the trends in these types of protests. To this end, I have compiled a database of approximately 6,000 cases involving collective protests. Data were drawn from major international newspapers such as the *New York Times*; major regional newspapers such as *The South China Morning Post*; the official *Xinhua News Agency*; international newswires such as *United Press International*; the *Associated Press, Reuters*, and *Agence France-Presse*; the US government-backed *Radio Free Asia*; the Hong Kong-based China Labour Bulletin and its *CLB Strike Map*; and a number of Chinese language sources, including *Boxun*. Because the latter uses social-media reports to generate stories about protests and its reporting is not tightly checked for facts and is not subject to strict editorial scrutiny, it is often seen as providing some uncertain combination of fact and rumour, as well as being subject to anti-regime bias. There are obvious questions about the veracity and reliability of social media-based news sources. Perceptions of the extent of collective protests and unrest are, arguably, shaped not by cold hard facts, but rather by what people see on the social media. Moreover, stories that originate on sites such as *Boxun* are often picked up by more mainstream sources such as *Radio Free Asia*. For purposes of the current analysis, I have used 4,282 mass incidents reported between 1990 and 2012.

News and media stories were coded according to: a) where protests took place; b) when they took place; c) who were the principal participants; d) what were the participants protesting; e) whether the protest turned violent; and f) the size of the protest. Violence was defined as any sort of physical confrontation beyond minor pushing and shoving and included cases in which protesters were beaten by police, security guards, or others acting on behalf of the authorities. At present, additional data on whether protests that turned violent resulted in arrests, police shootings, or deaths have been collected but is not yet complete. The database does not contain protests by individual petitioners, except in instances where groups of petitioners coalesced into collective protests. Petitioning the state for redress of grievances is a common form of protest but it is most often an individualised form of protest that involves asking authority for redress of injustice. As such, petitioners often put themselves in the position of supplicants to power rather than challengers (Chen 2012). As a result, I prefer to treat petitioning as a separate form of protest from mass incidents.

In this analysis, I treat protest and unrest as analytically distinct. Protests, as Tilly (1978, 2003) suggests, may be defined as short-term, issue-focused, and time-specific events that coalesce grievances along a boundary that divides a polity into temporarily antagonistic groups (see also McAdams et al. 2001). Protests are thus, according to Tarrow (1998), "modular", focus on immediate conflicts and engage proximate protagonists. When boundaries harden and begin to spread beyond those immediately involved in a particular protest, then the grievances that fueled the protest can begin to morph into political unrest, which I define as a diffuse and sustained set of conflicts between authorities and groups of citizens. Unrest may not become generalised and it is in fact likely that a majority of citizens will remain uninvolved or only participate as bystanders. Unrest in this construct involves a sporadic but sustained pattern of contention between authorities and citizens in which the citizenry remains largely unorganized, except perhaps on a local basis (Tambiah 1996). Unrest is thus the visible manifestation of relatively widespread discontent with the political status quo and the presence of grievances that citizens associate with the regime as a whole rather than its local agents. Nevertheless, unrest remains disjointed and intermittent. If sporadic unrest morphs into a sustained confrontation between discontented citizens and the authorities, unrest can produce political instability and may begin to undermine the regime's grip on society. Instability can ultimately turn into rebellion if disaffected groups organize for a direct challenge to a regime's monopoly on political power.

Although violence can erupt in even the smallest and most idiosyncratic protests, the frequency with which protests culminate in attacks on either the police or the protestors logically increases as scattered protests over localised grievances morph into more widespread unrest and mounting political instability. High incidences of violence would thus provide a secondary indicator that deepening corruption has been a factor in the observed increase in mass incidents and a possible qualitative shift from protest to unrest.

Thus conceptualised, the core research question can be restated as: is the corruption-protest nexus evolving in ways that give us reason to believe that the role of corruption as a source of popular protest is not simply a trigger for localised protest but rather a driver of widespread, sustained and violent political unrest and thus perhaps a precursor of political instability?

Corruption, protests, and mass incidents

Based on the 4,300 odd protests between 1990 and 2012 I documented, corruption was likely to be a factor in approximately one-quarter of the reported protests. Overall, workers accounted for approximately one-quarter of all documented protests (see Table 13.1). If, however, other occupational groups such as bus and cab drivers, teachers, migrants, miners, sanitation workers, and doctors and nurses are combined with workers, these groups accounted for 40 per cent of documented protests. The second largest group was farmers-villagers who accounted for 18 per cent of protests, followed by Tibetans 13 per cent and urban residents 11 per cent. Other significant groups included nationalists (4 per cent), students (2 per cent), petitioners (2 per cent), veterans (2 per cent), and retirees (2 per cent).

As a result, workplace issues account for over one-third of the documented protests (see Table 13.2) and the majority of workplace-based protests were over wages, jobs, and working conditions (see Table 13.3; Lee 2007). In many cases, protesting workers frame their grievances in terms of "corruption", decrying the evil actions of their "black hearted" bosses and the theft of their "blood and sweat" money. In theory, management misconduct could be

Table 13.1 Groups involved in mass incidents

Group	Number of incidents	Per cent incidents	Cumulative per cent
Workers, cab drivers, teachers, migrant workers, miners, sanitation workers	1,629	38.04	38.04
Farmers/Villagers	750	17.52	55.56
Tibetans	554	12.94	68.50
Residents	486	11.35	79.85
Nationalists	190	4.44	84.28
Students	99	2.31	86.60
Petitioners	86	2.01	88.60
Veterans	80	1.87	90.47
Retirees	78	1.82	92.29
Vendors	76	1.77	94.07
Uighurs	51	1.19	95.26
Other	203	4.74	100.00
Total	4,282		

Source: Author's database.

construed as a form of corruption if the company is state-owned and hence the managers are de facto state officials. If corruption is defined as the misuse of delegated authority, then even the managers of private companies could be included because they are "agents" of the company and hence theft of company funds would be a violation of their fiduciary responsibility.

Protests against management corruption do not, however, necessarily target the regime. In most instances, the core issue is money (wages, benefits, wage arrears, layoffs, and restructuring) and the critical line of conflict is between employers and employees, not between citizens and the state. Workplace protests may thus contribute to the overall rise in the number of mass incidents and perhaps a sense of social instability. It is not clear, however, that

Table 13.2 Protest issue

Issue	Number of incidents	Per cent incidents	Cumulative per cent
Wages and working conditions	1,525	35.61	35.61
Ethnic conflict	632	14.76	50.37
Land	460	10.74	61.12
Police/Official corruption or misconduct	392	9.15	70.27
Quality of life	260	6.07	76.34
Demolitions	175	4.09	80.43
Nationalism: anti-Japanese	172	4.02	84.45
Pensions	163	3.81	88.25
Redress/Injustice	96	2.24	90.50
Scam	69	1.61	92.11
Campus conditions	63	1.47	93.58
Taxes	46	1.07	94.65
Other	229	5.35	100.00
Total	4,282		

Source: Author's database.

Table 13.3 Workplace incidents

Issue	Number of incidents	Per cent incidents	Cumulative per cent
Wage arrears	340	22.30	22.30
Wages and benefits	336	22.03	44.33
Layoffs	286	18.75	63.08
Gas and operating costs	227	14.89	77.97
Restructuring	94	6.16	84.13
Pay cuts	58	3.80	87.93
Working conditions	41	2.69	90.62
Management misconduct	40	2.62	93.25
Relocation	31	2.03	95.28
Other	72	4.72	100.00
Total	1,525		

Source: Author's database.

they represent a significant source of political unrest or instability so long as worker protests are not merged into a larger labour movement, which has not occurred in China to date.

The second most common source of protests was ethnic conflict (15 per cent), most of which occurred in Qinghai, Gansu, Sichuan, and the Tibetan Autonomous Region. In total, the database documents 631 protests related to ethnic conflict, of which 554 (88 per cent) involved protests by Tibetans. Protests by ethnic Uighurs totaled 51, which may appear anomalously small. Because the ongoing conflict between the Chinese state and what it brands "separatists" often straddles the line between contentious politics in the form of protest and armed conflict, I have opted to treat political unrest in Xinjiang in a separate analysis.

The trigger for ethnic protests should be considered independently of corruption. Corruption may, of course, play a role in fueling tensions between Han officials, who are often condemned as arrogant, insensitive, and corrupt by minority groups. The driving force behind ethnic conflicts is, however, conflicting identities and the belief by these groups that they do not belong to the Chinese "nation" and do not wish to be forced to conform to norms laid down by the Han-dominated state. To the extent that corruption plays a role in ethnic conflict, therefore, it is likely to act as a visible irritant, adding to underlying sources of tension and providing a trigger for protest. Ethnic unrest is, finally, not additive to protests involving the Han majority. On the contrary, there is anecdotal evidence that attacks on Han civilians by Uighurs and Tibetans have actually hardened Han opposition to their demands and increased Han support for repressive measures.

Arguably, the single most direct and explosive link between corruption and protest is land. Overall, protests involving land accounted for 11 per cent of protests between 1990 and 2012, with the number of documented land protests rising sharply, beginning in about 2002 (see Figure 13.2). As the Chinese economy boomed and cities were redeveloped and expanded, new industrial parks and logistics bases were built and infrastructure expanded, the demand for land soared, pushing market prices upward dramatically (Guo 2001; Walker 2006; Ding 2007; Ho 2014). Because land in rural areas remains collectively owned by the community, local officials, and cadres are positioned to negotiate deals with would-be developers whereby use rights are sold and the land transferred. Because the land is owned communally, the farmers are supposed to be fairly compensated for the loss of "their" land. In reality, local officials and cadres are positioned to cut deals whereby buyers overtly pay one price but covertly transfer part of the gap between the nominal price and the actual market value of the land to their interlocutors in the form of bribes or kickbacks. As a result, disputes over the value of the land and how much compensation farmers are due are common (He and Xue 2014). So, too, are charges of corruption. Many of these same patterns are found in the protests against the demolition of urban residences by developers, which accounted for 4 per cent of documented protests. In some cases, developers have hired gangs of "security guards", thugs, or triad members to evict those who refused to sell out, leading to charges that the police failed to intervene or that they acted in league with developers to force residents out. In general, according to Lagerkvist (2015), protests against land expropriation and demolitions do not seek regime change but are oriented toward "policy change". In some cases, in fact, it appears that what land and housing protesters are really seeking is a better deal.

Press reports document numerous land protests. Longstanding tensions over land boiled over in the village of Wukan in Lufeng City, Guangdong, in September 2011 after village officials sold 800 acres of village land to developers. Protesters blocked roads, attacked businesses, and besieged a police station where several villagers were being held (Jacobs 2011a). Soon after the protests in Wukan, villagers in Longguang, Guangdong, moved to seize

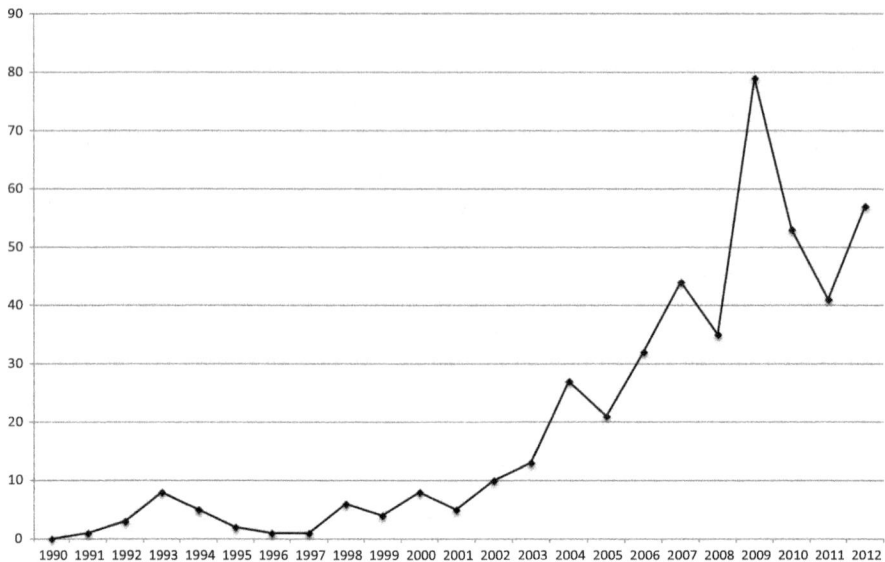

Figure 13.2 Protests involving land

land sold to developers (Choi 2011). In November, police clashed with upwards of 3,000 villagers outside Zhongshan in a protest against a land grab by local officials (Clem 2011). In December, the trouble reignited in Wukan after one of the villagers' informal leaders died in police custody (Chan 2012). After driving local officials out of the villages, the protesters armed themselves with homemade weapons, stones, bricks, and petrol bombs, threw up barricades to prevent riot police from entering the village, and prepared for a siege (Jacobs 2011b). Ultimately, provincial authorities intervened with promises of new village elections and an inquiry (Wong and Wines 2011).

Protests specifically against official corruption represent a very small percentage of the total number of documented protests. In all, of nearly 4,300 documented protests, official corruption was identified as the cause of just 84, only 2 per cent of the total. Twenty-five other protests were attributed to disputes over village elections and electoral malfeasance.

Protests triggered by confrontations between the police, city management officers, security guards, and thugs accounted for more than 7 per cent of documented protests. Out of 304 such protests, police misconduct accounted for 52 per cent, misconduct by city management offices (*chengguan*) 20 per cent and misconduct by officials 4 per cent (see Table 13.4). Murders and rapes in which the police or officials were said to have had a hidden hand triggered 23 protests. Sixteen protests were sparked by demands for government compensation for deaths attributed to government dereliction.

Protests triggered by confrontations between police and citizens in China are similar to many urban riots in the United States, the United Kingdom, and elsewhere. Urban rioting or disorder often erupts after a combination of factors lead residents to feel politically disenfranchised, thus heightening tensions in the streets. In such a situation, a seemingly minor incident such as a beating by police or the death of an individual under suspicious circumstances can produce a "flash" that transforms simmering grievances into outbursts. Not only those angry at the authorities take to the street to vent their anger and frustration, but so, too, do opportunists pursuing objectives ranging from making mayhem to seeking loot, as well as onlookers who simply get caught up in the excitement and join the crowd (Kritzer

Table 13.4 Official corruption and abuse of power

Type of interaction	Number of incidents	Per cent of incidents	Cumulative per cent
Police misconduct	154	39.69	39.69
Official corruption	84	21.65	61.34
Chengguan misconduct	61	15.72	77.06
Death, murder, or rape	23	5.93	82.99
Attacks by hired thugs	20	5.15	88.14
Compensation	16	4.12	92.27
Official misconduct	13	3.35	95.62
Other	17	4.38	100.00
Total	388		

Source: Author's database.

1977; Body-Gendrot 2013; King 2013). Thus, as Fewsmith (2008) argues in the case of the 2008 Weng'an disturbance in Guizhou, although the discovery of the body of a 16-year-old woman who had apparently been murdered may have triggered the initial confrontation, the root cause of the riot was a long history of bad blood between local residents, mining interests, local criminal gangs, and the police. Thus when police attempted to disperse a crowd of 10,000 who had gathered to demand the return of her body, angry residents fought back and ended up storming government offices and overturning a dozen police cars in what was described as an "anger venting social incident".

Overall, about one in three protests (1,535 of 4,282) resulted in some violence (see Table 13.5). Protests triggered by police misconduct and land, however, witnessed violence in nearly two-thirds of the cases. By contrast, strikes and other workplace-related protests, the largest single type of protests, turned violent in less than 20 per cent of cases. In fact, the three issues most closely associated with corruption (land, police misconduct and demolitions) accounted for 24.6 per cent of all documented incidents but 42 per cent of violent incidents.

There are numerous examples of anger venting protest. In 2012, a thousand villagers in Haifeng County, Guangdong, fought with police after the villagers protested the local government's refusal to pay the funeral expense of a woman who died at the age of 106. The protest left a number of villagers injured, eleven police cars smashed and overturned, and a number of protesters under arrest. The protesters said that it was a tradition for the local government to pay the funeral expenses of centenarians. In reality, the clash was the outgrowth of a bitter land dispute (*Radio Free Asia* 2012a). In another case in the same year, a thousand villagers surrounded local government offices to protest police handling of a murder case they said involved the children of local officials (*Want China Times* 2012). In 2010, 20 villagers were injured in a clash in Huaiji County, Guangdong, over what local authorities said was an illegal graveyard (*Radio Free Asia* 2010). Two years later in that same county, hundreds of residents attacked police after a patrol car pursuing another car hit two bystanders. When the officers attacked an old man, the crowd smashed their patrol car and then blocked roads for several hours and damaged other police cars (*Radio Free Asia* 2012b). Also in 2012, more than 100 villagers in Shanwei City, Guangdong, smashed police cars after the local government ordered a family to exhume the body of a woman they had "illegally" buried so that she could be cremated (Deng 2012).

In June 2012, in Shaxi Township, Zhongshan City, Guangdong, a fight between two boys triggered a two-day riot by several thousand migrant workers. The rioters broke into

Table 13.5 Violence

Issue	Number of incidents	Violent incidents	Per cent of violent incidents	Per cent of incidents that turned violent
Wages and working conditions	1,525	263	17.13	17.25
Ethnic conflict	632	235	15.31	37.18
Land	460	292	19.02	63.48
Police/Official misconduct	392	255	16.61	65.05
Quality of life	260	124	8.08	47.69
Demolitions	175	91	5.93	52.00
Nationalism: anti-Japanese	172	36	2.35	20.93
Pensions	163	21	1.37	12.88
Redress/Injustice	96	16	1.04	16.67
Scam	69	23	1.50	33.33
Campus conditions	63	33	2.15	52.38
Taxes	46	25	1.63	54.35
Local dispute	45	41	2.67	91.11
Other and less than five	35	17	1.11	48.57
Religion	31	8	0.52	25.81
Elections	25	9	0.59	36.00
Nationalism: anti-American	19	6	0.39	31.58
Medical malpractice	16	9	0.59	56.25
Political	13	2	0.13	15.38
Evictions	12	7	0.46	58.33
Sports	11	11	0.72	100.00
Airport delays	8	4	0.26	50.00
Prices	7	5	0.33	71.43
Rents	7	2	0.13	28.57
Total	4,282	1,535		35.85

Source: Author's database.

businesses, set fires, looted shops, and overturned cars (*Radio Free Asia* 2012c). A year earlier in Chaozhou City, Guangdong, thousands of migrant workers clashed with police during a protest over claims that police had covered up an assault by thugs hired by a local businessman on a crippled worker who had been seeking back wages. Scores of protesters were beaten and several dozen cars burned in two days of rioting (*Radio Free Asia* 2011). A thousand migrant workers in Xintang, Guangdong, rioted that same month after city management officers allegedly beat a pregnant street hawker. During three days of disturbances, protesters attacked local government offices and police stations with bricks and stones (Lau 2011d). In April 2011, several thousand residents of the Songjiang district in Shanghai battled with police after a vehicle driven by city management officers tried to force its way through a group of pedestrians while running a red light. When a man refused to get out of their way, the officers beat him, which drew a huge crowd that blocked streets who set vehicles on fire. Police arrested dozens before they were able to quell the disturbance (*Want China Times* 2011).

Corruption, mass incidents, and political unrest

Based on the preceding data, it is clear that corruption, or at least perceptions of corruption in the sale of land use rights and in the way the police and other authorities treat the public, play a role in fomenting protests in China. But does an increase in the number of protests signal a shift from localised discontent and protest to a more generalised situation of political unrest? In 1998, as the reported total number of mass incidents rose from around 10,000 in 1993–1995 to 25,000 in 1998 (Tanner 2004), a group of scholars attempted to answer the question "is China unstable?" (Shambaugh 2000). In the concluding chapter, Whyte (2000: 160) argued that based on the sector-by-sector analyses presented:

> We can expect a high level of contentiousness and conflict to persist in China in the future… Despite this turbulence, there is no particular group or grievance that appears very likely to pose a fundamental challenge to the leadership in the next few years… Stability seems an odd and quite inappropriate term to use for the scenario envisioned here. Terms such as "rocky stability" or "stable unrest" seem closer to the mark.

Dichotomizing the analysis into a question of "chaos" versus "stability", Miller (2000) argues, is a fundamental error because societies are never at a stable equilibrium but are always unstable to some degree. And while Whyte argues that many ordinary Chinese welcomed the "return to normalcy" after the disorder and incipient "chaos" of the Cultural Revolution, many had become "suspicious, cynical and angry" because economic reforms had led to the reemergence of "the 'social evils' that socialism was supposed to eliminate" and hence they "increasing(ly)…see their society as characterized by an amoral, man-eat-man struggle and in this context leaders at all levels are seen as venal and self-serving". At the time, Whyte (2000: 145–7) concluded that latent discontent had not reached levels suggesting that the regime was sitting atop a "social volcano" that could "erupt at any moment".

If Chinese society was perhaps in a "normal" state of "turbulence" in 1998, does the increase in mass incidents from the 25,000 reported in 1998 to the estimated 187,000 in 2010 signal a shift to a level of turbulence that suggests the emergence of widespread and increasingly coherent political unrest? And can the increase in mass incidents be ascribed to some significant degree to worsening corruption? Superficially, an increase from a daily average of 68 mass incidents nationwide in 1998 to 512 in 2010, a 7.5-fold jump, would seem to suggest that China has become considerably more turbulent. The key issue is not, however, simply whether the level of turbulence has increased in aggregate quantitative terms but rather whether the observed turbulence has begun to take a more coherent form, one which suggests that protests in one locality and about a specific issue have become linked with protests in other localities and over other issues?

On one level, there seems little question that increasing use of the social media has given many Chinese more access to reports of protests outside of their immediate surroundings and that news about protests in one area may have fueled protests in other areas. Social media reports on Wickedonna, the social media website, show there is a striking similarity in the modalities of protest, including the use of what might be called "selfie" protests in which a small group of protestors pose for photos with a banner listing their grievances and post the pictures on social media. Social media has also likely led to a considerable increase in the number of protests reported on sites such as *Boxun*, *Duowei*, and other social media-based sources.

Evidence that the quantitative increase in the number of mass incidents signals a qual-itative shift from scattered protests to more cohesive political unrest is not strong. Most protesters' demands continue to focus on immediate grievances, with farmers demanding better compensation for the loss of their land; workers demanding payment of wages and wage increases; urban residents opposing the construction of nuisance facilities such as incin-erators and chemical plants; retirees demanding better pensions and social security benefits; and students demanding better campus conditions. The bulk of protests thus remain oriented toward localised and particularistic issues. Moreover, survey data from the Asian Barometer suggests that while ordinary Chinese regard the national level as relatively corruption free, they see local officials as much more likely to be corrupt. By extension, therefore, they con-tinued to view the regime as legitimate even if its agents are corrupt and dishonest.[3]

Some protests do, however, transcend localised issues. Nationalism, for example, has turned out large crowds across China. In 1999, for example, my database documents anti-American protests in 15 provinces after the 1999 Belgrade Embassy bombing. Three years later, it records anti-Japanese demonstrations in 27 provinces, many of which involved tens of thousands of protestors who in some instances overturned Japanese brand cars and attacked Japanese-owned stores and restaurants. Nationalist protests are, however, oriented toward an external "enemy" and not the regime itself. Similarly, ethnic nationalism may unite some disaffected Tibetans in both the Tibetan Autonomous Region and the "Inner Tibet" belts of traditional Tibetan areas of Qinghai, Gansu, and Sichuan and some alienated Uighurs across Xinjiang. But the common opposition to the regime and the political status quo that unites Uighurs, Tibetans, and, to a lesser extent, Mongols does not necessarily create a united anti-government front. Moreover, such ethnic nationalism estranges them from the Han majority and pits them against a regime that is adamantly opposed to making any significant concessions to what it considers "separatism" and "terrorism".[4]

Within the Han-dominated regions of the country, protests do not seem to have coalesced into a coherent pattern of sustained political unrest. If the three categories of protest most directly associated with corruption: land, police misconduct and demolitions, are combined and juxtaposed with workplace protests that pit employees against employers it becomes clear that the major surge in unrest in recent years is most likely driven by increases in workplace related protests, not protests directed against the state and, more specifically, its local agents (see Figure 13.3).

Evidence derived from my analysis of 4,300 odd protests between 1990 and 2012 largely reaffirms the conclusions of the 1998 analysis (Shambaugh 2000). The data suggest that Chinese society is more tumultuous than it was in 1993. But the primary source of turbu-lence continues to come from scattered and localised protests rather than widespread and sustained political unrest. The primary axes of conflict remain the employee-employee axis and community-local authority axis, not the society-regime axis.

Conclusion

Given that corruption and collective protest link primarily through the nexus of police misconduct and expropriation of land, it is perhaps not surprising that the observable trends in corruption and mass incidents are not tightly connected. Using the number of crimi-nal indictments handed down by the Procuratorate for economic crimes as one proxy for changes in the level of corruption in China and the number of disciplinary investigations initiated by the party's Discipline Inspection Commission (DIC) as a second, it appears that the major increases in mass incidents occurred at a time when the number of criminal

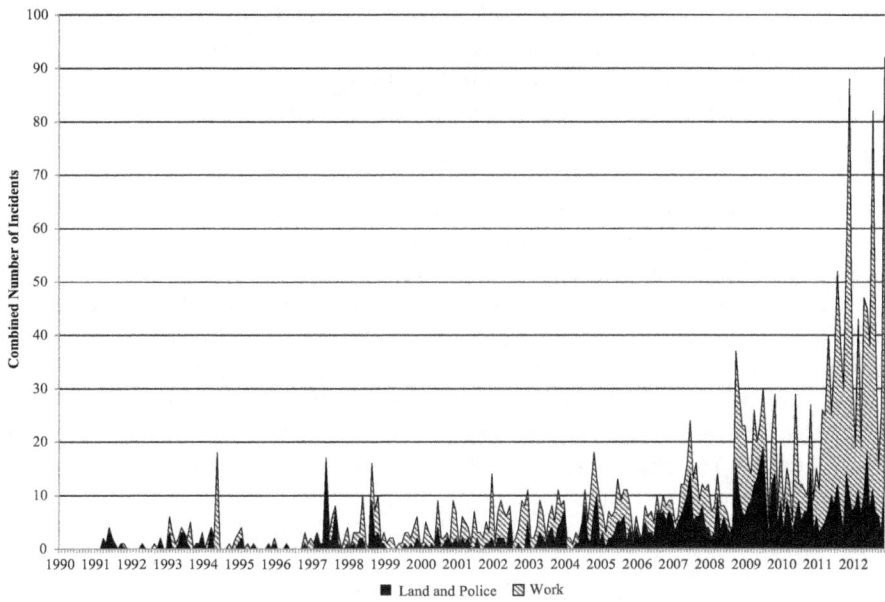

Figure 13.3 Anti-government vs. workplace protests (by month)

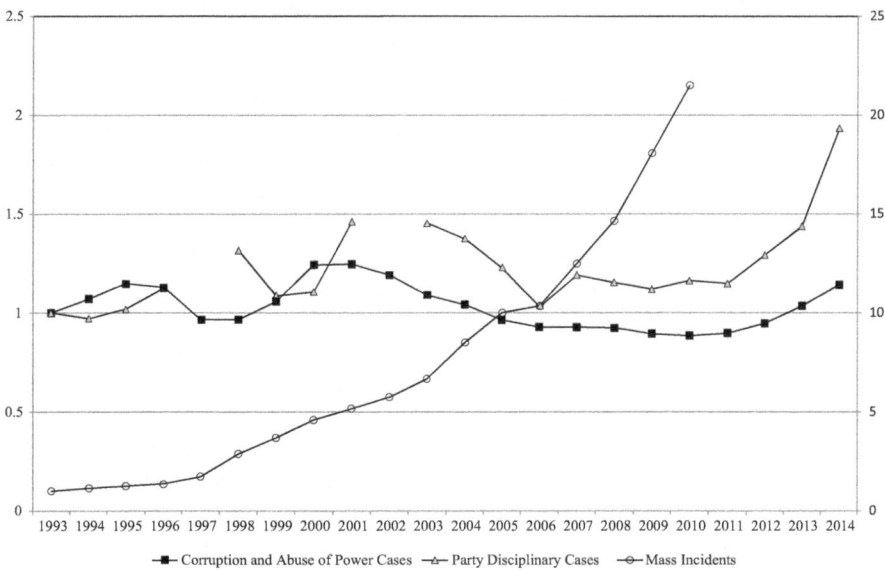

Figure 13.4 Trends in "street-level" corruption and mass incidents

Sources: *Number of indictments for corruption and abuse of power from Procuratorial Office (various years) and Supreme People's Procuratorate of the People's Republic of China (2016). Data on mass incidents from Tanner (2004, 2005); Pei (2005); McGregor (2006); Wong (2009); Johnson (2009); Cheng Ming (2009); and Bloomberg (2011). Data on investigations by the DIC are from People's Republic of China Yearbook (1997–2007 and 2012) and Fu (2015).*

Note: *In 1998, the implementation of a new criminal code led to a 50 per cent drop in the number of indictments for corruption. Because the drop was caused by the reclassification of a wide range of what had been deemed criminal offences in the 1979 Criminal Code as non-criminal administrative offences, I have normalised the trend by assuming that given a constant definition of criminal corruption, the number of indictments in 1997 and 1998 would have been roughly equal.*

indictments was actually gradually decreasing (see Figure 14.4). The number of disciplinary investigations by the party, on the other hand, seems to rise in parallel with the rise in mass incidents in the late 1990s but the two trends then diverged with the number of party investigations remained relatively constant in the early 2000s while the number of mass incidents continues to rise.[5]

Data on the number of indictments handed down or investigations are, of course, imperfect proxies for changes in the level of corruption since changes in the "revealed rate of corruption" may be driven by changes in the intensity of enforcement rather than changes in the "actual rate of corruption" and also by qualitative changes in the severity of corruption as reflected in the seniority and amounts of dirty money of those involved. There is reason, in fact, to posit that the flat or declining trends in indictments and investigations masked a significant qualitative worsening of corruption during the last decade and a half. The anti-corruption campaign launched by Chinese Communist Party General Secretary Xi Jinping in late 2012 has brought to light impressionistic evidence of extensive high-level corruption. Thus far, more than 130 officials, including four former members of the Politburo, and state-owned enterprise managers holding ranks equivalent to vice minister/vice governor, known in the Chinese press as "tigers", and close to 90 generals have been taken down since 2012 (Wedeman forthcoming). Indictments of officials at the county and department levels by the DIC have risen 44 per cent since 2012. Indictments of prefectural and bureau level officials have increased 222 per cent. Because many of those detained during the current campaign became involved in corruption well prior to the advent of the crackdown,[6] it stands to reason that the worsening of corruption occurred earlier. If so, then the observed increase in mass incidents would have coincided with a worsening of corruption.

There is, however, reason to discount a connection between the rise in the mass incidents and worsening corruption. Whereas citizens may see and encounter "street-level" corruption, they are not likely to experience high-level corruption directly. High-level corruption takes place behind closed doors and in discrete places. To the extent that ordinary citizens "know" about high-level corruption, it is most likely through rumours or reports in the media. High-level corruption thus exists at "arms' length" rather than directly affecting ordinary citizens. Moreover, whereas the leadership may be somewhat willing to tolerate protests against grassroots corruption, it is highly unlikely to tolerate protests against high-level corruption. The potential costs for protesting high-level corruption are thus presumably much higher than protesting low-level corruption. As a result, although they may feel, and tell pollsters, that corruption is a "big problem", it seems unlikely that they would take to streets in mass protests against what is essentially an abstract issue. Consequently, we can explain the apparent contradiction between citizens reacting strongly to street-level corruption in the form of protests and the near absence of protests against high-level corruption as a joint function of the potentially greater political risks of taking to the street to protest against high-level corruption and the lack of a tangible connection between high-level corruption and the everyday lives of ordinary citizens.

Notes

1 In police parlance, a mass incident is an illegal assembly of 10 or more people.
2 Three years into Xi's Jinping's anti-corruption drive, the number of those polled saying that corruption was a "very big problem" actually dropped from 53 per cent in 2013 and 54 per cent in 2014 to 44 per cent in 2015. When respondents were asked if they thought corruption would get better or worse in the next five years, 63 per cent said it would get better versus 18 per cent who said it would get worse and 15 per cent who said it would stay the same.

3 Whereas 75.5 per cent of those surveyed by the Asia Barometer between 2001 and 2012 said that no or only a few national officials were corrupt and 24.6 per cent said that most or all national officials were corrupt, 24.6 per cent said no or only a few local officials were corrupt and 48.6 per cent said that most or all local officials were corrupt (see Ch. 16).

4 Half of the 38 protests documented in the database involving Mongols were classified as being about ethnic conflicts. Twelve were classified as land issues. The line between ethnic conflict and land is, however, blurred because protests were often triggered by disputes between Mongol herders and Han developers. In these cases, it becomes unclear if the dispute was over the loss of the land *per se* or the loss of the land to Han Chinese.

5 In addition to prosecuting ordinary criminal offences, the Procuratorate is responsible for investigating and prosecuting economic crimes, which include graft, bribery, and embezzlement; and dereliction of duty crimes, which include abuse of authority, dereliction of duty, and nepotism. Although what Chinese law defines as economic crime corresponds closely to what is generally defined as corruption, dereliction of duty does not. In the past, the annual Procuratorial Work Report provided separate figures for economic crime and dereliction of duty. In more recent years, it has provided only a combined figure. I have thus used the sum of economic crime and dereliction of duty indictments.

6 Among 950 individuals charged with corruption between 2011 and 2015, almost half were reported to have first engaged in corruption prior to 2006 while only 25 per cent became corrupt after 2009. (Source: authors database.)

References

Bloomberg (2011) "China cracks down in wake of riots bombings", 13 June, http://www.bloomberg.com/news/articles/2011-06-13/china-cracks-down-in-wake-of-riots-bombings (accessed 15 March 2016).

Body-Gendrot, S. (2013) "Urban violence in France and England: comparing Paris (2005) and London (2011)", *Policing and Society*, 23(1): 6–25.

Chan, M. (2011) "Villagers rage anew over leader's death", *South China Morning Post*, 16 December, http://www.scmp.com/article/987884/villagers-rage-anew-over-leaders-death (accessed 1 March 2016).

Chen, J. (2013) *A middle class without democracy: economic growth and the prospects for democratization in China*, New York: Oxford University Press.

Chen, J. and B.J. Dickson (2010) *Allies of the state: China's private entrepreneurs and democratic change*, Cambridge: Harvard University Press.

Chen, X. (2012) *Social protest and contentious authoritarianism in China*, New York: Cambridge University Press.

Cheng Ming (2009) "Over 120,000 group protests take place in China in 2008", No.1: 10–13.

Choi, C.Y. (2011) "Rural land grab protests spread", *South China Morning Post*, 25 September, http://www.scmp.com/article/980022/rural-land-grab-protests-spread (accessed 1 March 2016).

Clem, W. (2011) "Land grabs blamed again for rioting in Guangdong", *South China Morning Post*, 14 November, http://www.scmp.com/article/984756/land-grabs-blamed-again-rioting-guangdong (accessed 1 March 2016).

Deng, J. (2012) "Forced cremation upsets village", *Global Times*, 8 May, http://www.globaltimes.cn/content/708314.shtml (accessed 1 March 2016).

Dickson, B. J. (2008) *Wealth into power: The Communist Party's embrace of China's private sector*, New York: Cambridge University Press.

Ding, C. (2007) "Policy and praxis of land acquisition in China", *Land Use Policy*, 24(1): 1–13.

Fewsmith, J. (2008) "An 'anger-venting' mass incident catches the attention of China's leadership", *China Leadership Monitor*, 26: 2–10.

Fewsmith, J. (2013) *The logic and limits of political reform in China*, New York: Cambridge University Press.

Fu, K. (2015) "An iron hand on corruption and a win-win cooperative approach", May 13, http://www.icac.org.hk/symposium/2015/pdf/FU%20Kui.pdf (accessed 26 December 2015).

Gingerich, D. W. (2009) "Corruption and political decay: evidence from Bolivia", *Quarterly Journal of Political Science*, 4(1): 1–34.

Guo, X. (2001) "Land expropriation and rural conflicts in China", *The China Quarterly*, 166: 422–439.

Gurr, T.R. (1971) *Why men rebel*, Princeton, NJ: Princeton University Press.

Harsch, E. (1993) "Accumulators and democrats: challenging state corruption in Africa", *The Journal of Modern African Studies*, 31(1): 31–48.

He, S. and D. Xue (2014) "Identity building and communal resistance against land grabs in Wukan village, China", *Current Anthropologist*, 55(S9): S126–S137.

Ho, P. (2014) "The 'credibility thesis' and its application to property rights: (in)secure land tenure, conflict, and social welfare in China", *Land Use Policy*, 40: 13–27.

Jacobs, A. (2011a) "Farmers in China's south riot over seizure of land", *New York Times*, 23 September, http://www.nytimes.com/2011/09/24/world/asia/land-dispute-stirs-riots-in-southern-china.html?_r=0 (accessed 1 March 2016).

Jacobs, A. (2011b) "Village revolts over inequities of Chinese life", *The New York Times*, 14 December, http://www.nytimes.com/2011/12/15/world/asia/chinese-village-locked-in-rebellion-against-authorities.html (accessed 1 March 2016).

Johnson, I. (2009) "China sees protest surge by workers", *Wall Street Journal*, 10 July, http://www.wsj.com/articles/SB124713050245617293 (accessed 15 March 2016).

Khan, F. (2007) "Corruption and the decline of the state in Pakistan", *Asian Journal of Political Science*, 15(2): 219–247.

King, M. (2013) "Birmingham revisited – causal differences between the riots of 2011 and 2005?" *Policing and Society*, 23(1): 26–45.

Kritzer, H. M. (1977) "Political protest and political violence: a nonrecursive causal model", *Social Forces*, 55(3): 630–640.

Lagerkvist, J. (2015) "The unknown terrain of social protests in China: 'exit', 'voice', 'loyalty', and 'shadow'", *Journal of Civil Society*, 11(2): 137–153.

Lau, M. (2011) "Curfew order for riot-hit Xintang", *South China Morning Post*, 14 June, http://www.scmp.com/article/970568/curfew-order-riot-hit-xintang (accessed 1 March 2016).

Lee, C. K. (2007) *Against the law: labor protests in China's rustbelt and sunbelt*, Berkeley: University of California Press.

Lichbach, M. I. (1995). *The rebel's dilemma*, Ann Arbor: The University of Michigan Press.

Mao, Z. (1927) "Report on an investigation of the peasant movement in Hunan", in *Selected works of Mao Tse-tung*, https://www.marxists.org/reference/archive/mao/selected-works/volume-1/mswv1_2.htm (accessed 6 October 2015).

McAdams, D. S. Tarrow and C. Tilly (2001) *Dynamics of contention*, New York: Cambridge University Press.

McGregor, R. (2006) "Data show social unrest on the rise in China", *Financial Times*, 19 January, http://www.ft.com/intl/cms/s/0/171fb682-88d6-11da-94a6-0000779e2340.html#axzz42xKXXfuq (accessed 15 March 2016).

Michael, F. (1948) "A revolutionized Kuomintang?" *Far Eastern Survey*, 17(14): 161–164.

Miller, H. L. (2000) "How do we know if China is unstable?" in D.L. Shambaugh (ed.) *Is China unstable?* Armonk: M.E. Sharpe, 18–25.

O'Brien, K. J. and L. Li (2006) *Rightful resistance in rural China*, New York: Cambridge University Press.

Olson, M. (1971). *The logic of collective action: public goods and the theory of groups*, Cambridge, MA: Harvard University Press.

Park, N. E. (1997) "Corruption in eighteenth-century China", *The Journal of Asian Studies*, 56(4): 967–1005.

Pei, M. (2005) "China is paying the price of rising social unrest", *Financial Times*, 11 July, http://carnegieendowment.org/2005/11/07/china-is-paying-price-of-rising-social-unrest (accessed 15 March 2016).

People's Republic of China Yearbook (1997–2007 and 2012) Beijing: People's Republic of China Yearbook Publisher.

Pew Research Global Attitudes Project (2015a) "Environmental concerns on the rise in China: many also worried about inflation, inequality, corruption", *Pew Research Center*, http://www.pewglobal.org/2013/09/19/environmental-concerns-on-the-rise-in-china/ (accessed 28 September 2015).

Pew Research Global Attitudes Project (2015b) "Corruption pollution, inequality, are top concerns in China: many worry about threats to traditions and culture", *Pew Research Center*, http://www.pewglobal.org/files/2015/09/Pew-Research-Center-China-Report-FINAL-September-24-2015.pdf (Accessed 28 September 2015).

Procuratorial Office (various years) *Chinese procuratorial yearbook*, Beijing: China Procuratorial Press.

Radio Free Asia (2010) "Six detained in graves clash", 7 January, http://www.rfa.org/english/news/china/graves-clash-01072010095222.html (accessed 1 March 2016).

Radio Free Asia (2011) "Migrant worker disabled over pay", 7 June, http://www.rfa.org/english/news/china/migrant-06072011190157.html (accessed 1 March 2016).

Radio Free Asia (2012a) "Villagers fume over centenarian's burial costs", 7 May, http://www.rfa.org/english/news/china/burial-05072012180427.html (accessed 1 March 2016).

Radio Free Asia (2012b) "Mob attack police for 'abusive' behavior", 26 March, http://www.rfa.org/english/news/china/mobs-03262012180650.html (accessed 1 March 2016).

Radio Free Asia (2012c) "Township wakes to chaos", 27 June, http://www.rfa.org/english/news/china/wakes-06272012161642.html (accessed 1 March 2016).

Rotberg, R. I. (2004) "The failure and collapse of nation-states: breakdown, prevention, and repair", in R.I. Rotberg (ed.) *When states fail: causes and consequences*, Princeton, NJ: Princeton University Press, 1–50.

Shambaugh, D.L., (ed.) (2000) *Is China unstable?* East Armonk, NY: M.E. Sharpe.

State Failure Task Force (2000) *State failure task force report: phase III findings,* http://www.raulzelik.net/images/rztextarchiv/uniseminare/statefailure%20task%20force.pdf (accessed 2 September 2015).

Supreme People's Procuratorate of the People's Republic of China (Various years) "Procuratorial work report", http://www.spp.gov.cn/gzbg/ (accessed 14 March 2016).

Tambiah, S. J. (1996) *Leveling crowds: ethnonationalist conflicts and collective violence in South Asia*, Berkeley, CA: University of California Press.

Tanner, M. S. (2004) "China rethinks unrest", *The Washington Quarterly*, 27(3): 137–156.

Tanner, M. S. (2005) "Chinese government responses to rising social unrest", testimony presented to the US-China Economic and Security Review Commission, 14 April, http://www.rand.org/pubs/testimonies/CT240.html (accessed 15 March 2016).

Tarrow, S. (1998) *Power in movement: social movements and contentious politics*, New York: Cambridge University Press.

Taylor, L. (1987) "Agrarian unrest and political conflict in Puno, 1985–1987", *Bulletin of Latin American Research*, 6(2): 135–162.

Tilly, C. (1978) *From mobilization to revolution*, New York: McGraw-Hill.

Tilly, C. (2003) *The politics of collective violence*, New York: Cambridge University Press.

Walker, K.L.M. (2006) "'Gangster capitalism' and peasant protest in China: the last twenty years", *The Journal of Peasant Studies*, 33(1): 1–33.

Want China Times (2011) "Shanghai protests triggered by traffic incident", 14 April.

Want China Times (2012) "Wukan revolt encourages similar protests across China", 2 April.

Wedeman, A. (2004) "The intensification of corruption in China", *The China Quarterly*, 180: 895–921.

Wedeman, A. (forthcoming) "Xi Jinping's tiger hunt: anti-corruption campaign or political purge?" *Modern China*.

Whyte, M.K. (2000) "Chinese social trends: stability or chaos?" in D.L. Shambaugh (ed.) *Is China stable?* Armonk: M.E. Sharpe, 143–163.

Whyte, M. K. (2010) *Myth of the social volcano: perceptions of inequality and distributive injustice in contemporary China*, Stanford, CA: Stanford University Press.

Wong, E. (2009) "Chinese question police absence in ethnic riots", *New York Times*, 18 July, http://www.nytimes.com/2009/07/18/world/asia/18xinjiang.html?_r=0 (accessed 15 March 2016).

Wong, E. and M. Wines (2011) "Provincial officials meet leaders of protesters who took over Chinese village", *New York Times*, 20 December, http://www.nytimes.com/2011/12/21/world/asia/top-provincial-leaders-to-meet-with-protesting-chinese-villagers-in-wukan.html (accessed 1 March 2016).

Wright, T. (2015) *Party and state in post-Mao China*, Malden, MA: Polity Press.

Yu, G. (2012) "China: one fire may be out, but tensions over rural land rights are still smoldering", *The Christian Science Monitor*, 6 February, http://www.csmonitor.com/Commentary/Opinion/2012/0206/China-One-fire-may-be-out-but-tensions-over-rural-land-rights-are-still-smoldering (accessed 2 March 2016).

14

CIVIL SOCIETY AND ANTI-CORRUPTION INITIATIVES IN INDIA

Towards a citizen's perspective

Mitu Sengupta[1]

Introduction

India has provided some of the most dramatic examples of tensions between civil society and the state on the perceived failure of government action to control corruption. This chapter will examine a number of significant episodes in the development of anti-corruption civil society action in India, including the campaign for public audits in Rajasthan by the Mazdoor Kisan Shakti Sangathan (MKSS), the quest for strong access to information laws by the National Campaign for People's Right to Information (NCPRI), and the demand for a powerful public ombudsman by the India Against Corruption movement (IAC). Drawing upon these examples, this chapter will strive to provide a bottom-up, citizens' perspective on the nature of corruption in India and on the remedies that are required. The chapter will also aim to shed light on whether anti-corruption civil society action has actually achieved success, be this defined in terms of reducing the magnitude of corruption, or in emboldening anti-corruption reformers within government to push through specific laws and policies, or in shifting public discourses on corruption in enduring ways. Finally, by exploring tensions as well as moments of compromise in the relationship between the state and civil society, and between different civil society groups, the chapter will reflect upon the politics of anti-corruption reform and why some civil society mobilisations have endured better and had more impact than others.

Civil society and corruption: making the connection

Citizen demands for anti-corruption reform in India have become particularly strident in recent years. In 2011, tens of thousands gathered in Delhi, India's national capital, to support social activist Anna Hazare's hunger strike against corruption. In 2014, a major election study found that anti-corruption sentiment was the primary issue in that year's national election, and the main reason why the Bharatiya Janata Party (BJP) won an outright majority in parliament after being out of power for more than nine years (CSDS 2014). In early 2015, a new party, the Aam Admi Party (AAP), won an overwhelming majority of seats (67 of 70) in the Delhi State Legislative Assembly election on an almost exclusively anti-corruption platform. Another notable development in recent years is that an increasing number of people have raised their voice against corruption through innovative social media outlets such as www.ipaidabribe.com, a website that allows citizens to report bribes they were forced to pay. At the time of writing, the site claimed millions of visits and more than 65,000 reports from more than 1,000 cities across India.

Heightened citizen interest in corruption has followed on the heels of a series of high-profile corruption scandals involving billions of dollars, including the multiple cases of fraud connected with the 2010 Commonwealth Games, the bribery-driven allocation of telecommunications licenses in the "2G spectrum scam" of 2011, and the graft-infused purchase of a fleet of helicopters in the "choppergate scam" of 2013. According to Sukhtankar and Vaishnav (2015: 3), who have compiled an inventory of the biggest corruption scandals since the year 2000, the mean scam value in the past 15 years was Rs. 36,000 crore (approximately US$54 billion), and the median was Rs. 12,000 crore (about US$18 billion), numbers that the authors justifiably consider "eye-popping". Nonetheless, while citizen demands for anti-corruption reform have become more vociferous in recent years, they are hardly new. Either individually or organized into civil society groups and social movements, ordinary citizens have been speaking out against corruption for decades and have offered many creative solutions to the problem. A notable example is former World Bank economist Samuel Paul's ground-breaking work in the creation of citizens' report cards, a civil society initiative that aims to gather citizen feedback on the performance of public agencies. Another example, discussed later, is the NCPRI, a broadly based social movement that is recognised as the force behind the passage of India's powerful Right to Information Act (RTIA) in 2005. Yet another example, also discussed later, is the MKSS, a grassroots group, whose trailblazing work in organizing social audits against corruption has won praise both in India and internationally (Roberts 2006).

This brief review should leave little doubt that civil society in India, broadly construed as the individuals and organizations in the society that are formally independent of the government, has been an important actor in the quest for anti-corruption reform. Yet discussions of civil society are rarely robust in the academic and policy literature on corruption in India. An assumption that runs through both the India-specific and general literature on corruption is that, although ordinary people, especially poor people, suffer greatly from the problem, they lack the organizational power necessary to hold powerful government officials to account. This is seen as especially true in India, a country marked by sharp divisions along lines of class, caste, and ethnicity (Jayaram 2005); the very term "civil society" is often greeted with scepticism and with the question, "whose civil society?" (for a critical view on corruption and conceptualisations of "civil society", see Chatterjee 2004; Harriss 2007; Webb 2012). It is also assumed that ordinary people are unable to develop coherent positions on what they seek from anti-corruption reform. The wisdom of the *aam admi* (a popular Hindi term for "common man") may be doubted, for example, by asking why people continue to vote for politicians tainted by allegations of corruption.

This chapter takes heed of such objections but presses beyond them to suggest important reasons why civil society struggles should be taken seriously in the study of corruption, not only in India. Specifically, it analyses the objectives, strategies, and achievements of three major civil society mobilisations against corruption in India, namely, the MKSS, the NCPRI, and the IAC. This exercise is valuable on normative grounds alone, since turning the spotlight on civil society means giving due recognition to the agency of ordinary citizens. It also assists in building a view of corruption from the ground up, providing insights into how ordinary people, especially poor people, experience corruption, thus pushing past the high-profile "scams" that the media tend to highlight. A citizen's perspective on corruption also promises to broaden horizons beyond what have become mainstays of the anti-corruption policy literature: top-down public administration mechanisms, such as ombudsmen and vigilance commissions, and civil service reforms focused on remunerating public officials more effectively. One lesson, for example, is that while much of the literature on the relationship between corruption and development is focused on corruption's impact on economic efficiency and growth, poor people's struggles against corruption usually begin as broader livelihood struggles, over such matters as the timely payment of wages and the availability of subsidised food. In seeking remedies, moreover, their focus is on improving access to state programmes and services, and strengthening their provision, which provides a counterpoint to the anti-corruption literature's emphasis on deregulation and other modes of market reform. Improving citizens' access to government records also seems to matter greatly to ordinary people, presumably because it empowers them to challenge corrupt officials directly. Indeed, the demand for direct forms of accountability, and the technique of shaming corrupt officials into publicly taking responsibility for their misdeeds, appears to cut across class lines. A final reason why anti-corruption civil society action should be taken seriously in the study of corruption is that it opens a window into the elusive *politics* of anti-corruption reform and the compromises and alliance-building that are needed, both *among* civil society actors and *between* civil society and the state, for anti-corruption initiatives to succeed.

MKSS

The MKSS was formed in 1990 in rural Rajasthan and is one of India's leading social movements (it calls itself a "non-party people's movement"). Described as "a combination of local residents and a handful of committed activists from other parts of India" (Jenkins and Goetz 1999: 603), the MKSS is known not only for its pioneering work in organizing village-level social audits but also for its key role in India's right to information movement. The organization's interest in access to information emerged out of its concern with local livelihood issues, such as the Rajasthan state government's failure to enforce minimum wage regulations or to ensure the availability of subsidised food through the national Public Distribution System (PDS) (www.mkssindia.org). The MKSS came to understand corruption as the root cause of such problems and strong access to information laws as the primary solution.

In the years leading up to its formation, activists working on local livelihood issues came to learn that authorities were diverting food from the PDS system and its "ration shops" to the open market in order to reap a profit and were also billing the central government for wages that were not being paid out to workers enrolled in government employment generation programmes. The underpayment of wages was a particularly serious concern in the famine relief work sites set up by the government to provide a basic income for poor people in drought-prone areas of Rajasthan. Since men from these areas tended to migrate to towns and cities in search of jobs, large numbers of women worked at the sites which included projects to build roads and dig wells. When workers confronted local officials over failure to pay wages, they were told that there was no proof of their having worked. It was then that the MKSS campaigned on their behalf and demanded access to the government's employment registers. Jenkins (2004: 223) points out that a key document sought was the muster roll, an employment register listing the names of people employed at each site, the days they worked, and the amount paid to each worker. The MKSS organized public hearings (*jan sunwais*) where the muster roll was read aloud to assembled villagers and systematically cross-checked by MKSS volunteers for evidence of fraud. Although *jan sunwais* were organized independently of official, statutorily recognized village assemblies, local officials and elected representatives were invited to attend, including the village *sarpanch* (the elected head of the village government). Each event was presided over by a panel of respected individuals, such as lawyers, academics, and journalists, from both within and outside the area.

The MKSS's innovative strategy of connecting livelihood concerns to corruption and holding *jan sunwais* has received high praise from academics and activists alike. This has been described as a "ground-breaking" approach (Jenkins 2004: 224–225) that operationalised transparency and drove home the importance of the otherwise abstract concept of information to ordinary people's lives. Furthermore, even though the *jan sunwais* organized by the MKSS relied solely on the power of shaming people, there were instances of tangible success. Baviskar (2007: 8) highlights some of these triumphs:

> The *jan sunwais* brought to light the huge discrepancies between the official record and actual practice. Scams relating to fictitious works, forged muster rolls, over-billing, and under-payment of wages were uncovered, and the culprits identified. The effect was often dramatic. In 1998, for instance, the *sarpanches* of Kukarkheda (Rajsamand district), Rawatmal and Saurajpura (Ajmer district) apologized for committing fraud and publicly returned money after being confronted with incontrovertible documentary evidence at a *jan sunwai*.

Baviskar also notes that *sarpanches'* fear of public humiliation led to swift payment of outstanding wage claims and to action against officials found guilty of embezzlement. Given such accounts, one can understand why the MKSS's example inspired other civil society groups rallying against corruption, such as the Delhi-based *Parivartan*, to organise *jan sunwais* as well (Pande 2007). It must be said, however, that the MKSS's strategy did not always yield results. Jenkins and Goetz (1999: 606) point to numerous occasions where it was fiercely (and successfully) resisted by local officials. In 1996, for example, there was a statewide strike of village-level development officers in response to a district chief administrative officer's directive to cooperate with the MKSS. In another case, an elected village chairperson who had admitted to committing fraud during a *jan sunwai* was persuaded by her counterparts in neighbouring villages to recant her statement of guilt. No further action was taken against her. Overall, extracting information from government officials proved to be very difficult and subsequent action on misdeeds brought to light through *jan sunwais* was rare. The Officials Secret Act of 1923, which has been held over from the colonial period, was regularly cited to block demands for access to government accounts records and the MKSS found that its public hearings were almost entirely reliant on the cooperation of sympathetic government officials.

In order to break its dependence on the goodwill of individual government officials, the MKSS, in alliance with other civil society groups in the state, sought legislative and regulatory reform that would provide a legal basis for citizens to obtain government documents. After many mass rallies and *dharnas* (sit ins), this effort was rewarded with the passage of a state-level RTIA in the year 2000. It was a hard-won victory, however, that took a full decade to achieve (Jenkins and Goetz 1999; Mander and Joshi 1999). For example, the government first issued an order that allowed inspection but not photocopying. Then it issued an order that allowed the photocopying of records related only to development works under the authority of local governments, a rule that did not apply to the PDS, which is jointly controlled by the state and central governments. The government also tried, albeit unsuccessfully, to exclude the MKSS from the process of drafting the new right to information law.

It is important to note, however, that there were two sides to the MKSS's relationship with government officials. On the one hand, there was predictable hostility and foot-dragging, especially on the part of local officials during the early years of *jan sunwais*. On the other hand, the MKSS was treated with respect and had allies within government, especially within the upper levels of the Rajasthan state administration. Jenkins notes that, even in the stormy years leading up to the passage of the state RTI act, the MKSS and state government officials communicated directly with one another and while such "face-to-face communication was not lacking in the normal hardball negotiating tactics and duplicitous public-relations diplomacy that one expects of seasoned politicians and bureaucrats", there was "a level of civility" beneath which proceedings did not sink (Jenkins 2004: 248). The MKSS also enjoyed good relations with other state and national-level civil society groups working on development and civil liberties with whom it participated intensively in state and national-level campaigns for employment guarantee schemes, the right to food, and the right to information.

Jenkins contrasts the MKSS's experience, in these respects, with that of the Maharashtra-based anti-corruption movement, the Brashtachar Virodhi Jan Andoloan (BVJA). The BVJA was founded by Anna Hazare in the early 1990s, two decades before he exploded onto the national stage as a leader of the IAC, in order to combat corruption in government-sponsored irrigation schemes in his native village of Ralegaon Sidhi. Like the MKSS, the BVJA arrived at its analysis of corruption through broader development work, specifically, on irrigation and watershed management projects (Jenkins 2004: 222). Like the MKSS, the BVJA viewed access to official documents as essential to its struggle against corruption, and like the MKSS, it launched a campaign for a state-level right to information law. A key difference between the two organizations, however, was the Maharashtra state government's hostile relationship with the BVJA. "On more than one occasion", writes Jenkins, "Anna called off a hunger strike – the ultimate form of sacrificial politics – when the state government refused to even take official notice of his actions" (Jenkins 2004: 247). Jenkins suggests that the BVJA's antagonistic relationship with the government reduced its impact as a movement, as did Hazare's willingness to work alongside Hindu nationalist in-dividuals and groups (see also Sharma 2006). This alienated most groups working on issues related to development and civil liberties, which tended to be intensely committed to pro-moting secularism as a philosophy as well as a form of politics. Thus, while Maharashtra did finally adopt an right to information law in 2003, the BVJA's footprint in precipitating the shift is regarded as smaller than the MKSS's effect in Rajasthan.

Several reasons may be advanced for explaining the MKSS's talent for forging alliances. Its key leader, Aruna Roy, is a former civil servant from the elite Indian Administrative Services (IAS) cadre. From the beginning, therefore, Roy was well-networked in govern-ment circles and, along with other leaders of the MKSS, consciously followed an inclusive approach towards state officials. The MKSS has consistently maintained that it is not against government and does not seek to undermine the state's authority. Roy is quoted by Baviskar (2007: 16–17) as saying, "we want a powerful state, but one that is also open and account-able", and "we had to make the *patvari* (revenue official), *thanedar* (policeman) and retired *javan* (soldier) realise that it was in their interest too". Baviskar indicates, furthermore, that the MKSS also made conscious appeals across *class* lines, and "encouraged alliances, incor-porating a range of social groups under a common broad umbrella" (2007: 17). It maintained a distance, however, from Hindu nationalist individuals and groups. Other factors that may have worked in the MKSS's favour, in building its movement, were Rajasthan's political cul-ture where there still remained "norms of civil behaviour between bureaucrats and elected leaders, and between these officials and ordinary citizens or their associations" (Jenkins 2004: 248) and the relatively homogenous *caste* profile of the MKSS's home region (Jenkins 2004: 235–236). A relatively homogenous caste profile reduced the potential of the confrontational *jan sunwai* to disintegrate into outright conflict. Indeed, Jenkins indicates that such situational factors were an important reason why the MKSS's *jan sunwais* could not be replicated on a large scale across different regions and states.

NCPRI

On June 15, 2005, the Parliament of India passed a historic RTIA that applies to every state and union territory in the country with the exception of Jammu and Kashmir. The RTIA entitles any citizen to request information from a public authority and requires the authority to respond to the request within 30 days.

India's RTIA is a powerful legal text that has drawn worldwide acclaim. In 2012, the Centre for Law and Democracy, a global human rights watchdog, ranked the RTIA as the second best right to information law in the entire world based on its overall score in the categories of right of access, scope, requesting procedures, exceptions and refusals, appeals, sanctions and protections, and promotional measures (Sukhtankar and Vaishnav 2015: 23). Moreover, even though Indian civil liberties advocates and anti-corruption activists tend to express deep concern over the many problems in the RTIA's implementation (Shreyaskar 2014; Venkat 2015), they are also quick to point to its strengths. Many reports and articles appearing in 2015, the RTIA's tenth anniversary, highlighted the ways in which the law has advanced anti-corruption struggles in India, such as by equipping the public with credible information about the notoriously opaque selection processes of the University Grants Commission, expensive foreign trips taken by cabinet ministers, and the abuse of allowances by members of parliament (Worthy and McClean 2015; Yadav 2015). Sukhtankar and Vaishnav (2015: 26) suggest that, even in the absence of follow-up sanctions, information, or in most cases, the *threat* of exposing unsavoury information, is a valuable tool, as it puts more bargaining power in the hands of citizens when they interact with the government as applicants or beneficiaries. This, in turn, can help reduce everyday corruption.

There is little doubt that the RTIA has had a significant impact on the functioning of government in India. Perhaps the most remarkable aspect of this historic law, however, is that, unlike most other acts of parliament, the RTIA was initiated by sustained civil society action from below. This action was ably coordinated and led by the NCPRI, an organization founded in mid-1996, when a number of locally based groups, including the MKSS, joined together with larger interest groups, such as the Press Council of India, along with senior faculty members of the National Academy of Administration (an organization that trains IAS officers), to demand the enactment of a national right to information law. It is because of its central role in staging a vibrant and ultimately fruitful nationwide campaign, with the support of a multitude of other movements and groups, that the NCPRI has come to be regarded as one of India's foremost civil society organizations. Yet, despite its many friends within civil society, the NCPRI's journey was still difficult and arguably would not have culminated in success were it not for the support of allies at the highest levels of government.

Shekhar Singh's summary of "milestones in the RTI journey" (2010: 51) provides a helpful snapshot of the NCPRI's tortuous route to triumph. It began in 1996, when the NCPRI and the Press Council of India sent a draft right to information bill to the government, which promptly appointed a committee to study the proposal. The committee submitted its report in 1997 but the government took no action. Two years later, however, there was a major breakthrough, when Ram Jethmalani, a prominent lawyer and then Union Minister for Urban Development, unexpectedly issued an administrative order permitting citizens to inspect and receive photocopies of files in his ministry. This "unilateral" step, according to Singh (2010: 58), exposed "internal contradictions within and among different levels of government" about the merits of RTI. The Prime Minister reversed Jethmalani's order and activists seized upon this decision to file a petition with the Supreme Court in protest. The Supreme Court found for the petitioners and issued an ultimatum to the government, which precipitated the passage of the Freedom of Information Act (FIA) in 2002. However, the FIA was not given presidential assent and thus did not officially come into effect, giving the government "the last laugh", according to Singh (2010: 59).

The national elections of 2004 provided a fresh opportunity for the right to information movement to mobilize its extensive networks within elite political circles. Following its victory over the centre-right National Democratic Alliance, the Congress-led United Progressive Alliance (UPA) government adopted a National Common Minimum Programme pledging to provide a government which was "corruption free, transparent, and accountable at all times" (cited in Webb 2012: 212). The UPA established a high-level National Advisory Committee that included NCPRI members Aruna Roy and Jean Dreze (an economist who is known for his work in India's right to food campaign). The National Advisory Committee formulated amendments to strengthen the FIA of 2002 and the amended bill was passed by the new government as the RTIA in June 2005. The law received presidential assent and came into effect in October, 2005.

The NCPRI remains active today, with an emphasis on raising awareness about the RTIA, monitoring its implementation and safeguarding the law from being watered down through amendments of its provisions. The NCPRI has also pushed for electoral reforms, judicial accountability, the institution of a public ombudsman, and most crucially, for the protection of whistleblowers. It was arguably because of the NCPRI's aggressive campaigning alongside families of murdered right to information activists that the landmark Whistleblowers Protection Act, passed by the lower house of parliament in 2011, was finally given presidential assent and brought into effect in 2014. Yet such significant victories notwithstanding, there is reason to believe that the right to information movement has been faced with more rather than less resistance with the passage of time (Rukmini 2015). In 2009, the UPA coalition once again won the national election, but the government, in its second incarnation (UPA-II), was viewed as considerably less progressive than the first by civil liberties and human rights groups, and as a consequence, their relations with the new government became strained. Tensions have only escalated with UPA-II's dramatic electoral defeat in 2014 by the centre-right BJP-led National Democratic Alliance coalition. The BJP is not known to be supportive of right to information and other rights-based causes, to put it mildly. The NCPRI and other rights-based civil society groups have found themselves with few reliable allies within the upper echelons of the new government. One can only hope that the RTIA is now too firmly entrenched and too internationally well-regarded to be a serious candidate for repeal by the BJP government.

IAC

The demand for a strong, autonomous, and quasi-judicial ombudsman (Lokpal) has dominated anti-corruption reform debates in India since the early 1960s. The first Lokpal bill, proposed in 1968, was passed by the lower house of parliament in 1969 but was stalled in the upper house. In 2010, the UPA-II government created a draft Lokpal bill that was circulated to various ministries for review. Many civil society groups, including the IAC and NCPRI, were critical of the government's bill and argued that the proposed ombudsman would be too weak to address corruption at the highest levels of government. The IAC stole everyone else's thunder, however, when its key leader, Anna Hazare, proposed a hunger strike in August 2011 to protest the UPA-II's draft bill. The government arrested Hazare on the eve of the planned protest, sparking candle-lit marches across the country. Although the government ordered his release within 12 hours, Hazare refused to leave. Playing upon Mahatma Gandhi's legacy of civil disobedience, Hazare started a "fast-unto-death" in Tihar Jail, South Asia's largest maximum security prison. He walked out of Tihar four days later, a free man and national hero, and took up residence in the expansive grounds of Delhi's Ramlila Maidan, surrounded by thousands of supporters, a sea of national flags, and a giant portrait of Gandhi.

At Ramlila, Hazare refused to eat for eight more days, breaking his fast only when the Indian parliament had passed an unprecedented "sense of the house" motion relenting to some of his key demands. Tens of thousands poured into the streets of Delhi, rejoicing in what they saw as a "people's victory". Hazare was hailed as a leader of Gandhian proportions, and celebrated by the media in India and beyond. In 2011, for example, *Foreign Policy* magazine placed him on its list of the world's "top 100 global thinkers".

Within a year of the Ramlila protest, however, it was evident that Hazare's movement had lost steam. A poorly attended three-day hunger strike in Mumbai, held at the end of 2011, was called off within 24 hours. Candidates endorsed by Hazare did not fare well at the Uttar Pradesh state assembly elections in early 2012. By mid-2012, the press no longer showed much interest in Hazare, and when it did, negative reports, laced with ridicule, overwhelmed the positive. It was also clear, by mid-2012, that conflict between movement's key leaders had intensified. In November 2012, the IAC suffered a major blow when Arvind Kejriwal broke away to form a political party, the AAP, which went on to achieve major victories in the Delhi state legislative assembly elections of 2013 and 2015 (Sharma 2014). When Hazare announced, in January 2013, that the IAC would now organize under the banner of *Jantantra Morcha* (Democratic Front), it was clear that the movement was in shambles. This point was driven home when the parliament finally passed the Lokpal and Lokayuktas Act (commonly known as the Lokpal Act) at the end of 2013. It was evident that most of the IAC's demands had not been met and that, albeit with a few exceptions, the government had followed the parameters of its original bill, which had sparked its conflict with the IAC in the first place.

Several reasons may be advanced to explain why the IAC lost momentum and eventually crumbled and why its experience was at striking variance with that of the NCPRI. First, the IAC leadership possibly had too many celebrity leaders, including star policewoman Kiran Bedi and spiritual guru-to-the-influential Swami Agnivesh, who had come together to form the movement having already achieved recognition elsewhere. Arguably, they were not fully invested in the movement's survival and their relationships were competitive rather than collaborative. This contrasted markedly with the leadership profile of the MKSS or even the NCPRI. In those organizations, the leaders had worked together on common struggles for years and had achieved recognition *through* the right to information movement rather than outside of it.

Second, while the Ramlila protests organized by the IAC had drawn tens of thousands of people, many of these were office workers and shopkeepers who had taken the day off, or young people, even children, who had been bussed in from Delhi's schools and colleges. This was a far cry from the committed, volunteer base of the MKSS and various other organizations that comprised the NCPRI.

Third, the IAC's demands had brought it into direct confrontation with the government. There were two reasons for this. One, the IAC was not only seeking evidence about corruption which is the focus of right to information struggles but was also demanding that public officials suspected of corruption be investigated and punished. Its approach, therefore, was quite different from the NCPRI's, though it was arguably closer to that of the MKSS and the BVJA. The strategy of these grassroots groups of making government officials answer for their misdeeds at public hearings had brought them into direct confrontation with the local state. Resistance was fierce, and in the BVJA's case, it was debilitating. The IAC was going a step further than the MKSS and BVJA because it was advocating a mode of accountability beyond naming and shaming. It should be no wonder, then, that it won little or no cooperation from the government.

Another related reason why the IAC came into open confrontation with the government was that it had advanced a bill (which it named the "Jana Lokpal" bill) that was directly at odds with the government's version (known simply as the "Lokpal" bill) on a number of salient provisions. For example, the Jana Lokpal bill proposed to bring the sitting prime minister and cabinet ministers under the scope of the ombudsman whereas the government's version excluded this option (PRS Legislative Research 2011). Unsurprisingly, the government was vigorously opposed to the idea. Hazare's maximalist demands and high profile hunger strikes had made him a threat to the government in a way that the NCPRI never was. Various elite politicians and bureaucrats, including eminent lawyer and union minister for Human Resource Development, Kapil Sibal, spoke out fervently against Hazare, portraying him as an anti-parliament, anti-democracy populist demagogue who was about to unleash mob rule on India (PTI 2011). Hazare had sold flowers at a railway station in Mumbai and served as an army truck driver and his humble origins most likely reinforced such imaginings. Hazare was not a genteel IAS officer, like Aruna Roy, who could be counted upon to follow accepted norms of engagement with the government (on how class prejudice coloured perceptions of Hazare, see Nigam and Menon 2011).

Roy, for her part, made it clear that she did not accept Hazare's demands, even though the two civil society giants had long fought for similar objectives, including the right to information and a public ombudsman. Roy said that Hazare's idea of a strong Lokpal to cover "the entire gamut of corrupt practices" had left her "with a great sense of disquiet", not least because it "does not address the arbitrary use of power" (Roy 2011a). With Roy at the helm, the NCPRI advanced a third "civil society" Lokpal bill that differed from the IAC's on several provisions, including the key point that the Lokpal should not be a single institution, but that "there should be multiple institutions and that a basket of collective and concurrent Lokpal anti-corruption and grievance redress measures should be evolved" (Roy 2011a).

The NCPRI's distancing itself from the IAC was reflective of the extent to which Hazare had become alienated from the progressive sections of India's intelligentsia, media, and civil society. This turned out to be very damaging indeed (Sengupta 2014). As the IAC was propelled into the spotlight, a wave of anti-Hazare sentiment swept through the country's universities, policy think-tanks, and English-language media. One criticism was that Hazare's movement did not connect sufficiently with the concerns of poor people, but was, rather, wholly a creature of India's new middle classes (Sitapati 2011). Arundhati Roy (2011b), a celebrated author and social activist, accused Hazare of silence on issues, such as illegal mining and land acquisition for special economic zones, where marginal farmers and indigenous communities were hurt by corruption, rather than issues concerning the urban middle class, which Roy saw as Hazare's primary base of support. While Hazare's experience with the BVJA in Maharashtra should have lent him authenticity as a grassroots leader, it ultimately worked against him because, it was discovered, Hazare had "led a violent campaign of fear and intimidation" in his home village of Ralegan Siddhi, flogging alcoholics, among other things (Nelson 2011). His ties with Hindu nationalist groups were also an issue. Hazare was targeted by leading progressive academics, such as Neera Chandhoke, for his "top-down decision-making process [and] expectations of uncritical obedience" (Chandhoke 2011: 19), and the IAC's Ramlila rally was described as a "classic mass fascist fantasy" (Appadurai 2011).

Concluding thoughts

It is useful to reflect upon the three questions posed at the onset of the chapter: (1) is it possible to distinguish a citizens' perspective on corruption? (2) why have some mobilisations endured better than others? and (3) have civil society mobilisations against corruption reduced the magnitude of the problem? In order to respond effectively to these questions, it is helpful to recall Samuel Paul's distinction between three different ways in which corruption surfaces (1998: 4). First, there is "collusive corruption", a form of corruption that involves the willing and planned cooperation of the giver and the taker. Paul suggests that most cases of political corruption, and "scams" involving large contracts, fall into this category. However, another dimension of collusive corruption that does not draw as much notice, and is not taken into account by Paul, is the type of corruption unearthed by groups such as the MKSS, BVJA, and *Parivartan* through the use of public hearings. Second, there is "extortionary corruption", which involves the forced extraction of bribes or other favours by people in authority. Third, there is "anticipatory corruption", which involves, say, paying a bribe or making a gift in anticipation of future favourable actions by those in authority. As Paul points out, it is difficult to detect and quantify collusive and anticipatory corruption, as those engaged in it are unlikely to complain (Paul 1998: 4).

When it comes to identifying a citizens' perspective on corruption, the key consideration is that everyday people care most about the corruption that directly affects their everyday lives. Cutting across class, ethnicity, and locality, extortionary corruption is the most obvious area of concern from a citizens' perspective. It was primarily anger over extortionary corruption that impelled tens of thousands to Delhi's Ramlila grounds to rally around Anna Hazare and the IAC movement. The struggles of groups such as the MKSS indicate, however, that collusive corruption can also have a very direct impact on people's lives when it affects the quality or delivery of welfare programmes and services. Thus, ordinary people may also be motivated to mobilise against collusive corruption.

It is unwise, nonetheless, to try to formulate a citizens' perspective on corruption without taking into consideration the multiple fractures created by differences in class, ethnicity, and locality. The experience of grassroots groups such as the MKSS suggests that while poor people stridently oppose corruption in the delivery of government subsidies, programmes, and services, they do not wish to see these welfare measures withdrawn. Mobilisations against corruption by poor people in rural areas often begin as livelihood struggles, over food, water, the payment of minimum wages, and so on. As MKSS leaders have repeatedly stressed, their objective is on improving the functioning of the state, not in reducing its size. Middle and upper classes residing in urban areas, in contrast, are less reliant on government programmes and are thus more likely to view deregulation, privatisation, and other measures that scale back the state as the best antidote to corruption. Notably, the IAC was thought to represent this middle class anti-state or neoliberal perspective, which is why it failed to garner the support of progressive opinion in the country. Whether or not the charge was fair, the perception of class bias was enough to prompt the NCPRI, which was otherwise a natural ally, to keep the IAC at arm's length. An avowedly secular group, the NCPRI was also deterred by Hazare's pro-Hindu nationalist reputation. Certainly, aside from class, factors such as ethnicity, caste and religion also seem to matter when it comes to developing a cohesive position on corruption from below. The mystery of why Indians vote in droves for politicians tainted by allegations of corruption and other forms of criminal behaviour is partially solved when one realises that Indian voters tend to cast ballots along ethnic and caste lines (see Chandra 2004; Vaishnav 2012). Among other things, this suggests that "clean government" is not the only relevant objective for voters.

Is it impossible, then, to discern a common thread that underlies citizens' demands for anti-corruption action? Given the distinctions based on class and other social categories noted above, it is best not to venture too bold a claim. Yet a common thread that may be detected is that while ordinary people have reason to value top-down anti-corruption efforts such as civil service reform, vigilance commissions, and tougher punishments for corruption-related crimes, what they ultimately want are mechanisms that will impel corrupt officials to answer directly to citizens and publicly take responsibility for their actions. The MKSS's *jan sunwais* are the clearest expression of this demand for a more restorative form of justice but the quest for direct accountability was also key to the IAC and NCPRI's struggles. A major source of conflict between the IAC and the government was that the IAC wanted sitting prime ministers to be brought under the jurisdiction of the Lokpal so that they would be directly answerable to the public. This demand was fiercely resisted by the government but it was supported by the NCPRI. Moreover, both the IAC and NCPRI, and also the MKSS and BVJA, were committed advocates of access to information laws: tools that empower citizens to seek answers directly from government.

The second question of why some civil society mobilisations fare better than others has already been partially answered. Given India's highly diverse and deeply stratified society, anti-corruption movements, like all other social movements, tend to splinter along lines of class, caste, ethnicity, language, region, and locality. In this inhospitable climate for collective action, a civil society mobilisation's growth and survival will depend on its talent for horizontal alliance-building with other, like-minded civil society groups and its ability to steer away from potential alliances that may enhance vertical divisions. The leaders of the right to information movement were skilled in this respect, finding common cause with many development, civil liberties, and human rights-focused groups while carefully avoiding association with individuals and groups presumed to be sympathetic to Hindu nationalism. Right to information leaders also tread carefully in their interactions with the government, at both state and national levels, always emphasising the point that theirs was a cause not against the state but for the rule of law and the better functioning of the state. This was a prudent move that the IAC should have learned from, given the intense concern about mob rule that has weighed upon Indian democracy since the early days of the republic.

On the question of whether civil society mobilisations against corruption have reduced the magnitude of the problem, a cynic might claim that, given the only sluggish improvement in the country's Corruption Perceptions Index score in recent years, from 36 in 2013 to 38 in 2014, civil society could not have made much of a difference and, even if it did, its contribution would be difficult to measure. While such points are well-taken, it is important to note that civil society action has been crucial in unearthing many instances of collusive corruption, first through *jan sunwais* organized at the local level, even before citizens had a legal basis to demand access to government records, and then, following the passage of state and national right to information laws, through right to information requests. Many high-profile "scams" including those connected with the Commonwealth Games, were brought to light by right to information requests. Moreover, a recent study has found (RAAG and TAG 2014) that right to information is also relevant at the local level: indeed, it is being used more extensively to seek information about the decisions and finances of local authorities than those of higher levels of government.

Civil society action has been a factor in precipitating a number of important legal and policy shifts in India. Bills to create a national ombudsman, for instance, had been floating around for decades. It was only after the dramatic protests staged by the IAC at Ramlila, however, that an actual Lokpal act came to pass even though the IAC did not succeed in influencing the contents of the new law to the extent that it wanted. Civil society action was, without doubt, also a precipitating factor in the passage of right to information laws in Rajasthan and other states and at the national level. It was due to pressure from the NCPRI, furthermore, that the Whistleblowers Protection Act finally received presidential assent in 2014, following a gap of almost three years after its passage by the lower house of parliament. Last, it is also reasonable to claim that civil society action has altered the public discourse on corruption in India in enduring ways. Citizens are actively demanding change with a greater sense of empowerment, as suggested by the BJP's stunning defeat in the Delhi state assembly elections by the AAP, which ran on an aggressively anti-corruption platform. Corruption is now a primary issue in most state and national level elections.

Note

1 The author gratefully acknowledges the valuable support of her research assistant, Prashant Rayaprolu, a student at the University of Toronto.

References

Appadurai, A. (2011) "Our corruption, our selves: Arjun Appadurai", *Kafila*, https://kafila.org/2011/08/30/our-corruption-our-selves-arjun-appadurai/ (accessed 5 December 2015).

Baviskar, A. (2007) *Is knowledge power? Winning the right to information campaign in India*, Brighton: The Institute of Development Studies, University of Sussex, https://www.ids.ac.uk/files/dmfile/IndiacaseOctober06final.doc (accessed 10 December 2015).

Chandhoke, N. (2011) "Our latest democratic predicament", *Economic and Political Weekly*, 46(19): 17–21.

Chandra, K. (2004) *Why ethnic parties succeed: patronage and ethnic head counts in India*, Cambridge: Cambridge University Press.

Chatterjee, P. (2004) *The politics of the governed: reflections on popular politics in most of the world*, New York: Columbia University Press.

CSDS (Centre for Study of Developing Societies) (2014) *All India post-poll 2014 survey findings*, New Delhi: Centre for Studies of Developing Societies, http://www.lokniti.org/pdf/All-India-Postpoll-2014-Survey-Findings.pdf (accessed 3 July 2015).

Harriss, J. (2007) "Antinomies of empowerment: observations on civil society, politics and urban governance in India", *Economic and Political Weekly*, 42(26): 2716–2724.

Jayaram, N. (2005) *On civil society: issues and perspectives*, New Delhi: Sage Publications.

Jenkins, R. (2004) "In varying states of decay? The politics of corruption and anti-corruption in Maharashtra and Rajasthan", in R. Jenkins (ed.) *Regional reflections: comparing politics across India's states*, New Delhi: Oxford University Press, 219–252.

Jenkins, R. and A.M. Goetz (1999) "Accounts and accountability: theoretical implications of the right-to-information movement in India", *Third World Quarterly*, 20(3): 603–622.

Mander, H. and A. Joshi (1999) *The movement for right to information in India: people's power for the control of corruption*, New Delhi: Commonwealth Human Rights Initiative, http://www.humanrightsinitiative.org/programs/ai/rti/india/articles/The%20Movement%20for%20RTI%20in%20India.pdf (accessed 30 September 2015).

Nelson, D. (2011) "Fear and intimidation in Anna Hazare's 'model' village", *The Telegraph*, 25 August, http://www.telegraph.co.uk/news/worldnews/asia/india/8723270/Fear-and-intimidation-in-Anna-Hazares-model-village.html (accessed 13 December 2015).

Nigam, A. and N. Menon (2011) "Anti-corruption movement and the Left", *Economic and Political Weekly*, 46(37): 16–18.

Pande, S. (2007) "The Right to Information and societal accountability: the case of the Delhi PDS campaign", *IDS Bulletin*, 38(6): 47–55.

Paul, S. (1998) "Corruption in India: who will bell the cat?" *Asian Journal of Political Science*, 6(1):1–15.

PTI (Press Trust of India) (2011) "Hazare seeks parallel government without accountability", *Economic Times*, 24 June, http://articles.economictimes.indiatimes.com/2011-06-24/news/29699097_1_kapil-sibal-bjp-leader-corruption-issues (accessed 15 January 2015).

PRS Legislative Research (2011) "Comparison of the Lokpal bill and the draft Jan Lokpal bill, 2011", http://www.prsindia.org/administrator/uploads/media/Lokpal/official%20Lokpal%20bills%20comparison.pdf (accessed 15 December 2015).

RAAG (Right-to-information Assessment and Advocacy Group) and TAG (Transparency Advisory group) (2014) *Who uses the Right to Information Act in India and for what?* New Delhi: Right-to-Information Assessment and Advocacy Group and Transparency Advisory Group, http://www.snsindia.org/raag-final-report-raag-applications-16-revised-may-2014.pdf (accessed 16 December 2015).

Roberts, A. (2006) *Blacked out : government secrecy in the information age*, New York: Cambridge University Press.

Roy, A. (2011a) "The Lokpal – NCPRI approach: the right to differ", (A letter from Aruna Roy), *Kafila*, 19 August, http://kafila.org/2011/08/19/the-lokpal-ncpri-approach-the-right-to-differ/ (accessed 12 December 2015).

Roy, A. (2011b) "I'd rather not be Anna", *The Hindu*, 10 February, http://www.thehindu.com/opinion/lead/id-rather-not-be-anna/article2379704.ece (accessed 12 November 2015).

Rukmini, S. (2015) "CIC turning down more RTI requests now", *The Hindu*, 29 October, http://www.thehindu.com/news/national/central-information-commission-turning-down-more-rti-requests-now/article7811266.ece?homepage=true (accessed 10 December 2015).

Sengupta, M. (2014) "Anna Hazare's anti-corruption movement and the limits of mass mobilization in India", *Social Movement Studies: Journal of Social, Cultural and Political Protest*, 13(3): 406–413.

Sharma, M. (2006) "The making of moral authority: Anna Hazare and watershed management programme at Ralegan Siddhi", *Economic and Political Weekly*, 41(20): 1981–1988.

Sharma, P. (2014) "From India against corruption to the Aam Admi Party: social movements, political parties and citizen engagement in India", in R. Cordenillo and S. Van Der Staak (eds.) *Political parties and citizen movements in Asia and Europe*, Stockholm, Sweden: Asia-Europe Foundation, 39–56.

Shreyaskar, P. (2014) "RTI under threat", *The Hindu Business Line,* 1 October, http://www.thehindubusinessline.com/opinion/rti-under-threat/article6466194.ece (accessed 14 December 2015).

Singh S. (2010) "The genesis and the evolution of right to information regime in India", in S. Anam, S. Bakshi, S. Candah, T. Dahal, R. Edrisinha, I, Idris, V. Nayak, T. Rahman, P. Sharma and S. Singh (eds.) *Transparent governance in South Asia*, Delhi: Indian Institute of Public Administration, 43–78.

Sitapati, V. (2011) "What Anna Hazare's movement and India's new middle classes say about each other", *Economic and Political Weekly*, 46(30): 39–44.

Sukhtankar, S. and M. Vaishnav (2015) "Corruption in India: bridging research evidence and policy options" in S. Shah, A. Panagariya and S. Gokarn (eds.) *India Policy Forum 2014–2015,* Vol.11, New Delhi, Sage Publications, 193–261.

Vaishnav, M. (2012) *The merits of money and 'muscle': essays on criminality, elections and democracy in India*, New York: Columbia University, Ph.D. http://academiccommons.columbia.edu/catalog/ac%3A146579 (accessed 17 December 2015).

Venkat, V. (2015) "10 years after RTI: transparency under cloud", *The Hindu*, 16 May, http://www.thehindu.com/news/cities/Delhi/10-years-after-rti-transparency-under-cloud/article7213480.ece, (accessed 14 December 2015).

Webb, M. (2012) "Activating citizens, remaking brokerage: transparency activism, ethical scenes, and the urban poor in Delhi", *Political and Legal Anthropology Review (PoLAR)*, 35(2): 206–222.

Worthy, B. and T. McClean (2015) "Freedom of Information and corruption", in P.M. Heywood (ed.) *Routledge Handbook of Political Corruption*, London: Routledge, 347–358.

Yadav, S. (2015) "10 ways in which RTI has changed the functioning of govt. officials", *The Indian Express*, 28 October, http://indianexpress.com/article/explained/10-ways-in-which-rti-has-changed-the-functioning-of-govt-officials/ (accessed 17 December 2015).

15

WOMEN AND CORRUPTION

When being the fairer sex becomes a myth

Natalia Matukhno[1]

Introduction

Countries where women occupy senior positions in parliaments, governments, and businesses are generally considered less corrupt. Is it, therefore, reasonable to conclude that women are the fairer sex? The foundations of research on women and corruption were laid by Swamy et al. (2001) and Dollar et al. (2001), both of whom posited that women are less likely to be corrupt than men. Since then, evidence has been presented on both sides and support for the notion that women are a more powerful anti-corruption force has been ambiguous (Sung 2003; Alatas et al. 2009; Torgler and Valev 2010). Women are less likely to pay bribes but they are also less likely to be asked for bribes and somewhat less likely to refuse to pay. They are also less likely to report corruption. Even if in terms of the payment of bribes, women appear to be the fairer sex, they are not the fairer sex when it comes to refusing to pay or to report corruption. I suggest that women have a wide range of behaviour regarding corruption. Given favourable internal and external structures, they may be less pre-disposed to corruption than men. However, if political and social structures are unsupportive and repressive of women, then they are less likely to take a stand because they tend to be risk-averse, critical of themselves and unable to stand against corruption if the safest option is to comply. Using multilevel models and Global Corruption Barometer data, I find that women are not always the fairer sex. Women have a greater range of attitudes and behaviour than men; extortion and resistance to bribes trigger different responses from men and women depending on the context. Women are affected by internal propensities to resist bribes but they are also less likely to be asked. External structures may exert a greater influence on them than men to comply with bribes or to resist bribes. I test four dependent variables: paying bribes, refusing to pay bribes, being asked for a bribe, and reporting bribery using cross-national data focusing on a subsample of Asian countries.

The reasons why women are less likely to engage in corruption may be aggregated, according to Wangnerud (2012), into theories about relationships with liberal democracy; gender differences/sex roles; and opportunity structures. As Wangnerud (2012: 234) sees it, the association with liberal democracy involves a spurious correlation between gender and corruption; the views about gender differences argue for a positive direct effect from two perspectives: women are more risk-averse, have more self-control, are less likely to engage in criminal activities, and are more caring and helping of others; and at the same time opportunity structures are thought to have an indirect effect: women have more domestic roles, are less engaged in interactions with public officials and are excluded from "'old boys' networks". Some recent studies have nonetheless suggested that the pure gender effect is not so significant and that women are not the fairer sex by definition and in all circumstances (McGabe et al. 2006; Alatas et al. 2009). Swamy et al. (2001) note, for example, that "we do not claim to have discovered some essential, permanent or biologically determined differences between men and women…gender differences … may be attributable to socialization, or to differences in networks of corruption, or in knowledge of how to engage in corrupt practices, or to other factors".

I argue that women's propensity to engage or resist corruption depends on a number of external and internal factors and should not be treated as a natural condition. Internal factors have mostly been explored using experimental studies. Some experimental evidence suggests that women are more risk-averse and are more responsive to monitoring and less likely to engage in bribery. However, other studies have found that women are more likely to bribe, as Armantier and Boly's (2008) study of Burkina Faso shows or as likely as men to bribe in Singapore, India, and Indonesia, as Alatas et al. (2009) show.

Another strand of research has focused on external factors: whether political and economic institutions shape women's proclivity to corruption. Alatas et al. (2009) touch on the contextual research even though their study is primarily experimental. They find that women in Australia are less likely to engage in corruption but women in India, Indonesia, and Singapore are not. Esarey and Chirillo (2013) posit that liberal democratic institutions shape women's proclivity to act corruptly but conclude that women are not more or less corrupt in authoritarian environments. Jha and Sarangi (2015) find that the improved social status of women and more women in local government lead to reductions in corruption.

I utilise survey evidence to show that women have a stronger potential to be less corrupt than men but at the same time have a stronger propensity to do nothing about corruption (such as not to report the offer of a bribe) if no support structures for women's participation or collective action exist. The complexities of cross-national surveys hide large differences in women's propensity to pay bribes or resist bribes and I therefore analyse results from the surveys as a whole and random coefficients for gender in each individual country.

External and internal structures influence women's decisions to pay bribes or refuse to pay bribes, whether they are more likely to be asked for bribes or to report corruption. External structures which do not empower women lead to feelings of hopelessness and compliance with corrupt systems. Non-supportive external structures involve lack of social institutions that promote egalitarianism and heavy reliance on favouritism and connections in addition to more visible forms of corruption, such as bribery. Under such circumstances, women become at least as likely as men to pay bribes and in many contexts more likely to pay bribes, less likely to refuse them, and less likely to report corruption.

Internal structures involve women's propensity to follow the rules, to be more risk-averse and to be capable of collective action. In more corrupt societies, following the rules means paying bribes and not reporting corruption. In cleaner societies, following the rules is the opposite. Hence women have a wide range of behaviour: in societies more conducive to corruption, they are more complicit and in societies less conducive to corruption they are more resistant than men. Women are often more limited in their options and have fewer connections and less influence. In societies with less institutional support, they may resort to bribery because they feel the rules tell them to bribe officials and because they do not have many other options. With no outlets for collective action, women comply with corruption at a greater rate than men. I demonstrate these tendencies using data from Asian countries. Wangnerud (2012) proposes an agency perspective arguing that women, as a subordinate group, have fewer assets and consequently may participate less in corruption and often have to rely on alternative power bases from those of men. This perspective is only partially confirmed by my data analysis and by looking at bribery only. It is not confirmed in terms of resistance to bribes or in terms of taking a stand against corruption. Paying bribes may be a reflection of the subordinate role of women. When women are less independent in societies, they tend to be more likely to pay bribes. If familial and societal support structures recognise women as equal partners in exchanges, then they may decide not to participate in corrupt transactions.

Collective action allows women to take a stand even in very corrupt societies. Having external structures that are supportive of women is another way to keep them motivated to refuse bribes and report corruption; therefore, we cannot generalise about whether women are less likely than men to engage in corruption. They can be either more or less likely depending on the circumstances. Recognising these wider dynamics puts policy makers and activists in the unambiguous situation of needing to improve gender equality.

Internal structures

Internal structures that help women avoid corruption are risk-taking, self-criticism, and collective action. If it is riskier not to engage in corruption, if standing against corruption is followed by repercussions, then women succumb to corruption. Women are more prone to self-criticism and self-justification and more likely to abide by formal rules (whether these rules are corruption-free or corruption-prone depends on the society).

If a society disapproves of "making waves", then it is easier for women to feel that corruption is justified. Some anti-corruption movements challenge women's inherent need not to become involved in risks and their greater propensity to self-criticise. Anti-corruption movements can create cognitive dissonance, making women ashamed of their behaviour but nevertheless may not be able to stop them from complying with corrupt norms. In some countries, standing against corruption can be taken as revolutionary behaviour. Moreover, women may be subjected to similar pressures as men. Joshi et al. (2015) note that women can be involved in discrimination, power dominance and competition just as much as men can. Women are less likely to be empowered individually but are more likely to respond to collective action. Therefore, collective action may enable women to gain courage to speak against unfair and corrupt systems.

Women who are subjugated under corrupt structures want validation and justification and are less likely to let others break the chain of corruption in part because that would invalidate their previous decisions. Collective associations, such as clubs, unions, and companies, are often formed by men who generally have more experience in working together for a common purpose. Women have been traditionally deprived of such opportunities in many societies. As a result, they have less experience in participating in groups where members can assist each other, work interchangeably, and aim for common goals. Their skill levels for collective action are generally less developed.

Some disillusioned women accept corruption as an unavoidable evil. There is a need, however, to differentiate between women who continue to oppose corruption and are a significant driving force behind anti-corruption groups and reforms and women who have suffered from corruption and accepted it. The second group can become fervent supporters of the existing status quo: they are more likely to pay bribes and less likely to reject corruption and report it. More women have suffered from corruption and decide to comply with it in the regions such as Southeast Asia, former Soviet republics, Latin America, and sub-Saharan Africa, because women tend to have fewer rights in many societies in these regions.

Women's internal incorruptibility is a myth. They are capable of heightened integrity and a sense of justice, but when faced with prolonged and extended exposure to corruption, they give up more readily than men, become more compliant, condone bribe-taking, and may even start participating in the system. Women are more concerned about justifying their actions than men. When faced with hard choices and unfair systems, women justify their corrupt behaviour according to their own integrity criteria. Women can be more prone to internal moral dilemmas. When faced with hardship, they are more likely to accept the justification that they cannot refuse to pay bribes or to report corruption. For women, when their behaviour comes in direct conflict with their internal values, they go the extra mile to find justifications and eventually become convinced that there is no other way.

Studies relating to findings on gender differences during negotiations (Bowles et al. 2005) or in terms of public goods (Andersen et al. 2008) have found that women are more risk-averse (Eckel and Grossman 2008). In no-risk environments, women are not different from men. They are equally corruption-prone and are not necessarily more intrinsically honest than men, although they do react more strongly to a given risk of detection (Frank et al. 2011). Other studies find that men are more corrupt than women and that men bribe significantly more often than women (Rivas 2007).

Women can be more corrupt if they believe it is the only way to survive and if they believe nothing happens to either corrupt or non-corrupt individuals. Therefore, a proper institutional framework helps women more, not because they are intrinsically fairer but because broken rules exert more pressure on them than on men. Men appear to be more immune to variations in the rules and structures while women are more susceptible both to losing hope and to acting with integrity; hence their range of behaviour is wider.

Collective action as an antidote for corruption

Given the higher dependency of women on rules and institutions, one of the means of reversing women's propensity to comply with corrupt systems is to allow and motivate women to take collective action. Chile is one of the best performers in terms of anti-corruption activities and integrity scores. How did it go from being very corrupt to not so corrupt? I argue that women's handling of their ability to organize and become an anti-corruption force played a role. In Chile, women were able to organize without abandoning their traditional roles. During the atrocities of the Pinochet regime in the 1970s, women organized as mothers, wives, and daughters to express support for men who were victims of the dictatorship. Such organizations were later able to evolve and expand into the political and economic arena (Noonan 1995).

During Pinochet's regime, women acted as "big mothers", entering public service and advocating more health care, education, and welfare. Groups formed around relatives (mothers, wives, sisters) of victims of the regime and of the thousands who disappeared. Those groups demanded justice. However, Pinochet specifically worked with women's groups "to deepen their consciousness as mothers" which pushed them to be apolitical. The "true womanhood" was also supported by the church in terms of such qualities as morality, self-abnegation, devotion to others, and domesticity. Poor women joined protests against Pinochet for survival and became increasingly politicised, turning to government to address their grievances about health, quality of life, and human rights. Women accepted their role in the family and upholding of the traditional issues but at the same time were able to pursue radical politics. "Many women publicly stood by their convictions for the first time, entered positions of leadership in the community, and learned how to manage organizations" (Noonan 1995: 103). Some of those organizations specifically did not take help from men in order to learn how to self-organize and to self-manage their organizations.

Women can thus become a powerful anti-corruption force even under circumstances of authoritarian political rule and great adversity. Noonan (1995) explains:

> How did they do it? The answer… lies in collective action frames. When the state forms changed, women mobilized the pre-existing maternal frame, thus manipulating dominant cultural themes in a safe manner, to identify the culpable parties, guide their action, and justify their "non-traditional" behaviour… Women had a mobilizational opportunity men did not have. Ostensibly Pinochet respected motherhood and family, and these women were only performing their duties as "good" women… women most likely perceived an opportunity to mobilize on this basis.
>
> *(Noonan 1995: 104)*

Similarly, in Japan, Fusae Ichikawa, a political activist and later a senator, became politically active by pushing for women's right to vote. The right to vote struggle took more than 20 years; full suffrage for women was not granted until 1945. From the 1950s until the 1970s, Ishikawa focused on clean political campaigns and corruption issues and was re-elected to the Diet on many occasions (Kiyoko 1984; Vavich 1967).

Ichikawa collaborated with other movements that took up broader feminist issues and was aware that the power of women had to be addressed in the form of unified action across a range of issues. For her, for women to have a voice and some political influence was a step in the right direction. In terms of her anti-corruption work, Ichikawa took pride in running "the ideal campaign" and she published her expenses and kept her accounting books transparent, showing that a campaign could be won without using an excessive amount of money (both legal and illegal) (Vavich 1967; Kiyoko 1984).

Mongolia has also made some progress in combatting corruption, in part because of the significant involvement of women leaders in civil society. For example, Sanjaasuren Oyun, one among many strong women in Mongolia's anti-corruption efforts, started a foundation, the Zorig Foundation, in memory of her assassinated brother. The foundation focused mainly on the media as an effective tool against corruption. In 2001, it launched a campaign, *Today or… It May Be Too Late*, which was a competition among journalists and artists to produce media products and posters on anti-corruption issues. There were 411 entries for the competition, which subsequently resulted in a broad media campaign that made corruption issues prominent on the national agenda. The Mongolian parliament responded with the National Anti-Corruption Programme and created a National Council to coordinate the programme (Landell-Mills 2013).

Introducing the programme was a breakthrough, but shortly thereafter Sanjaasuren Oyun realised that implementation was lagging. The scenario is typical of many anti-corruption initiatives in developing countries. Local elites often stall and create obstacles while local media, civil activists, and non-governmental organizations lack resources, access and capacity to monitor the initiatives. Very often, anti-corruption initiatives end without even having a chance. Due to the Zorig Foundation's efforts, this was not the case in Mongolia. The foundation made an assessment of the progress of the National Anti-Corruption Programme, found it poorly implemented, and suggested ways to move forward. For example, local authorities were found to be more innovative than the centre, giving rewards for reporting corruption, working with local non-governmental organizations, forming local anti-corruption commissions, introducing hotlines and conducting local surveys on corruption (Landell-Mills 2013). As a result, an anti-corruption commission with special powers was introduced. Another project was a movement against special interests which eventually resulted in the passage of a Conflict of Interest Act in 2012.

Sanjaasuren Oyun entered politics shortly after her brother's assassination and followed his steps as a pro-democracy leader. In 2000, she founded the Civil Will Party, which has won about 10 per cent of the seats in Parliament. She also served as the Vice-Speaker of Parliament, Minister of Foreign Affairs, and Minister of Environment and Green Development of Mongolia. She has broadened her efforts, but her first major campaign was against corruption because she realised that in a very corrupt society even perfectly planned and well-endowed initiatives could be predicted to fail.

In corrupt societies, women need to be shown the tools that can be used to stand up for their rights without alienating traditional structures. Full equality cannot be achieved overnight and corrupt societies can occasionally use traditional values as a reason not to modernise and address corruption. That is not to say that corrupt societies always display conservative values. For instance, modern Ukraine is corrupt but more liberal than its neighbours. Saudi Arabia is more conservative than most countries in the Middle East but not the most corrupt.

Women can become either fully compliant or they can become radicalised and lose patience with unfair regimes. Hirschman's (1970) concepts of exit, voice, and loyalty are relevant here. Many women in corrupt societies choose loyalty and women usually have fewer opportunities to exit. How likely are women to voice their concerns? Under which conditions are they likely to take a stand? Loyalty is considered a virtue for women who have traditionally been appreciated for their nurturing, supportive and domestic roles. Being proactive, vocal, and exiting the system were not considered good qualities in a woman. Women do not often have role models who use voice or exit as options. Loyalty is considered a preferable virtue. How do women become more political and more involved in the bigger issues of society? How do they move away from focusing mostly on social issues to focusing on broader or more specialised, non-social issues?

Women are more comfortable initially with bridging their traditional social roles and collective action. Collective action is constrained by the societal expectations that women should be passive and not assume leadership roles. In addition to these expectations, women are constrained by often excessive domestic demands and by a lack of resources. Even if they have resources, they have less control over them. Money is an obvious one, but housing and availability of space for gatherings are also resources. Since men are more likely to be in control of space (especially in developing countries), they can organize meetings, brainstorming sessions, focus groups, or host other organizational gatherings while women cannot. In politics, there are obvious links between domesticity and public roles and female candidates and activists are more inclined to work on issues in education, health care, and family (Dodson and Carroll 1991). Voters tend to expect women to perform better on issues requiring compassion (Huddy and Terkildsen 1993).

The existing paradigms create obstacles for collective action. Without an ability to organize and motivate each other, women are perceived to be more gentle, compassionate, and forgiving and are not expected to take an aggressive stand against corruption. The compassionate and caring nature of women, however, can motivate them to unite and organize to protect their loved ones and their communities. Over time, such local organizations may evolve into political and social ones.

External structures

External structures include social institutions that support gender equality, democratic institutions, and social norms which guide women's behaviour. External structures support internal structures that incline women to avoid bribery. External structures can make bribery more risky and can also encourage women to participate in public life and to become organized around shared concerns. Previous research suggests that there are indeed cross-country variations in women's propensity to engage in corruption. For instance, women were less likely to engage in corruption in Australia, but there were no gender differences in India, Indonesia, and Singapore (Alatas et al. 2009).

In societies where women are more controlled, freedom of choice would be less recognised and a woman's personality would, to a larger extent, be formed by the society she lived in. She would not in consequence be able to recognise or to follow her own choice to the same extent as a woman living in a freer society (Holmgren 2015: 7). I argue that, in countries where women are empowered and better represented, they are more likely to refuse to pay bribes. Women are also less likely to be asked for bribes in such contexts. Bribe extortion and resistance to bribes trigger different responses from men and women depending on the context. Empowering women is a path to reduce corruption, however, without support structures women are more likely to be asked for bribes and less likely to say no to bribes generally. Women are less corrupt (namely, they are able to refuse bribes and to oppose corruption) only when women-empowering structures are already in place.

Women are also more risk-averse. Therefore, installing a different set of rules, such as accountability, democratic institutions, and fair social institutions that keep corruption in check, allows for less corruptible individuals to act according to their values. Armantier and Boly (2008) conducted an experiment in Burkina Faso in which they inserted bank notes among papers to be graded, asking for a better mark. Given the ubiquity of corruption in Burkina Faso, female graders were in fact more likely to take bank notes, but this tendency decreased in a scenario where graders were monitored. In many countries, corruption is a way of life and is not monitored. Frank et al. (2011) also found that women were more likely to accept bribes if there was no real danger of whistleblowing but this did not necessarily mean that women's moral predisposition was different. It might simply be "driven by strategic considerations: if women do not expect negative reciprocity, that is, whistle-blowing by firms that were cheated and seek retaliation, they might guess that opportunism is the most profitable strategy" (Frank et al. 2011: 66).

Research on gender and political candidates indicates that women are more likely to run for public offices if they are asked to run, supported, and encouraged to run. Men usually do not need to be asked to become political candidates. In less egalitarian countries, women are less likely to be encouraged to run for political office. Women may also have a stronger need to be encouraged in order to make a public statement against corruption. Kenney (2013) studied the gendered norms of recruiting women into politics and points out that gender norms shape recruitment. Not only do gatekeepers prevent some women from entering politics, gendered norms influence which candidates are seen as viable and more appealing to voters and to the electorate. Women can thus be discriminated against directly or indirectly.

What kind of support do women need? They need structures that recognise their equal status and structures that support their ability to organize and unite. Previous research suggests that democratic institutions support the recruitment of women of integrity (Esarey and Chirillo 2013) while autocratic institutions do not. However, external structures do not fully explain why women decide to comply more with corrupt systems after they have themselves been unfairly treated. Internal motivations come into play. In part, this stems from being suppressed in more corrupt societies and in being more risk-averse. Abstaining from corruption is risky in very corrupt societies, where a woman is more likely to be scolded and branded as a rebel and women have fewer rights and hold fewer positions of power.

In societies with more gender equality and inclusion, women do indeed become a stronger anti-corruption force. Women have the capacity to be the fairer sex but they are less likely to do so if their rights are not upheld and enforced. Dollar et al. (2001) suggest that women are more trustworthy and public-spirited than men. If the structures to promote gender equality are already in place, then women who consider corruption to be wrong are less likely to engage in corruption. Gender differences in behaviour do exist, therefore, and women are more capable of integrity given the proper environment. Nevertheless, women who are suppressed in their societies are equally likely to defend their decision to bribe.

Esarey and Chirillo's (2013) argument may consequently be extended. Women are more powerful if social norms promote equality but those women who believe more strongly in such social norms may find themselves in a tenuous position because they tend to be more complaisant about existing corrupt practices. If women embrace their rights, they are stronger than ever. If women shun their rights, they may just become more complaisant with destructive systems but do not oppose them.

Women who see possible punishment from traditional structures are less courageous despite the fact that those punishments may or may not be stronger for women compared to men. But some evidence suggests that women's misdemeanours are punished more harshly than men's. The ethical expectation of many societies is that women should know better than to be caught in misdemeanours or corruption (Stolberg 2011; Esarey and Chirillo 2013). If they transgress, they are punished emotionally and made to feel ashamed of what they did. What does this mean in practical terms? Women are more susceptible to societal norms. If norms are against bribery, they are cleaner. If norms condone bribery, they participate in corruption at the same rate as men, if not to a greater degree.

Corrupt organizations may sustain old boys' networks that also serve to keep women disempowered. Sundström and Wängnerud (2016) found that shadowy corrupt arrangements maintain the power of an already privileged stratum of which men are in the majority and support structures of nepotism, favouritism, and corruption. In the countries where old boys' networks are prevalent, women feel hopeless and give in to those networks. They believe that the only way is to fit in or comply with informal structures. Sundström and Wängnerud (2016) point out that women are dependent on impartial formal and informal institutions that allow them to claim equal space in political and economic affairs. If they are allowed to claim that space, then they become the fairer sex.

My argument goes partially against the myth of women as the fairer sex, but it does not diminish the importance of support structures for collective action and individual responsibility that allow women to display their integrity openly. Quotas do seem to improve the situation because they provide women with support structures to organize and to voice opinions. In Peru and Mexico, for example, more women police traffic officers were introduced which helped reduce corruption (Rose-Ackerman and Palifka 2016).

The common assumption that women are less likely to take risks plays a role here, too. If it is less risky to report corruption and to be a law-abiding citizen as in the countries with developed democratic structures and progressive informal institutions, then women are more inclined to do so than men. The opposite is true as well. If corruption is a way of life and old boys' networks permeate the society, women have no other option but to comply. Where there is not much chance of greater equality, many women may feel that their quest for equal rights is hopeless. They do not wish to be perceived as irrational or as rebels, which would also damage their domestic reputation.

New research shows the high importance of gender equality in social institutions. Branisa et al. (2013), for example, using a Social Institution and Gender Index found positive results when they tested social institutions that were unequal to see whether this affected corruption. Their recommendation was to reduce gender inequalities in social institutions which in turn should lead to reductions in corruption. Social institutions differ from political institutions in that they affect opportunity structures so that women are less restricted to solely domestic roles and have alternative venues to engage in public life. In addition, social institutions provide opportunities for collective action and solidarity. If women do achieve greater equality with men, corruption declines.

My analysis shows how women vary in their propensity to resist or react to various corrupt activities and how their propensities are linked to the kind of internal and external structures that affect them. In part gender differences are due to the situation in developing nations, where women are less comfortable voicing their opinion and play a more passive role in the public domain (Chaudhuri 2012). Therefore, participating in corrupt transactions might itself be a sign of women's empowerment, as women may be allowed to go outside by themselves, to conduct business and official transactions, and to represent themselves and their families.

Women are more reciprocal in any transaction, which means that they are more likely to bribe if asked (Chaudhuri 2012). What reciprocity is can be interpreted differently in different societies. In some societies, reciprocity means watching out for the collective good and keeping the lawful structures functioning and, therefore, women uphold greater principles of fairness. In other societies, familial structures are entrenched and watching for local groups' interests becomes the first priority; as a result, a deviation, such as taking a stand against corruption, would not go unnoticed.

Women are more risk-averse and, in some societies, failing to participate in corrupt transactions bears a higher cost. Women are more subject to violence and coercion. Sometimes an alternative to paying a bribe is an exchange of sexual favours, which in essence is sexual violence against vulnerable women who are unable to pay. In such situations, women will choose to pay bribes and participate in corrupt transactions to avoid being abused.

Method and data

To assess whether women are less likely to be corrupt than men, I utilise a cross-national survey on bribery and corruption; namely the Transparency International Global Corruption Barometer 2013 conducted in 76 countries. I chose only Asian countries that were included in the survey. After some deliberation, I have decided to keep Taiwan in the sample, even if the sampling strategies employed by a polling firm from the People's Republic of China were not ideal. Global Corruption Barometer 2013 contains questions on experiences of corruption, perceptions of corruption, contact with authorities, willingness to be involved in fighting corruption as well as the basic demographic questions.

Chaudhuri (2012: 22) notes that "survey responses do indicate that women are less tolerant of corruption, yet, such responses seem to be both culture and context-specific and attitudes revealed by survey responses may not accurately indicate true behaviour when confronted with an actual situation involving corruption". My research focuses more on women's behaviour in corrupt situations, such as the ability to say no to corruption, to pay a bribe, or to report corruption.

Since women's behaviour is analysed both at the individual and at the country level, I chose multilevel logistic regressions as a primary method of analysis. The questions used are dichotomous, such as whether a person paid a bribe or whether a person reported corruption and, therefore, a logistic regression is best suited for the analysis. Given the multilevel data structure, I have included both random coefficients and random intercepts for the main independent variable of interest, gender. Multilevel logistic regression equations include all the countries in the sample, but for the purposes of the analysis it is less interesting to learn whether gender in general is significant or not, but to learn that statistical significance at 0.05 level hides the real story of great variation in gender variable coefficients. In the results section, I report and analyse gender effects (using random coefficients for each country) on corruption variables.

Results

In order to show that women's response to corruption varies across countries, I look at a sub-sample of Asian countries only. Following is the ranking of some Asian countries in terms of control of corruption scores to provide the context where each country stands. Control of corruption is the most widely accepted measure of general corruption that can be used and compared across time and space. It has been used by the World Bank as part of the Worldwide Governance Indicators and is defined as "perceptions of the extent to which public power is exercised for private gain, including both petty and grand forms of corruption, as well as 'capture' of the state by elites and private interests" (Worldwide Governance Indicators 2015).

Table 15.1 Ranking of some Asian countries in terms of control of corruption 2012

Country	*Control of corruption score*
Singapore	2.15
Japan	1.61
Taiwan	0.72
South Korea	0.47
Malaysia	0.30
Sri Lanka	−0.24
Thailand	−0.34
China	−0.48
Mongolia	−0.52
Vietnam	−0.56
India	−0.57
Philippines	−0.58
Indonesia	−0.66
Nepal	−0.83
Bangladesh	−0.87
Cambodia	−1.04
Pakistan	−1.06
Afghanistan	−1.41

Source: Worldwide Governance Indicators (2013).

My analysis is based on a number of multilevel logistic regressions for four dependent variables: paying bribes, refusing to pay bribes, being asked for a bribe, and reporting bribery. Furthermore, I have calculated random coefficients for gender as the primary independent variable. The figures display gender coefficients for the selected Asian countries only. I have included education, age, and level of urbanisation as control variables.

The statistical results for paying bribes as a dependent variable and gender as the independent variable are quite interesting. Women are less likely to pay bribes and this trend is universal. The gap between men and women paying bribes is somewhat smaller in Bangladesh, Indonesia, Mongolia, Pakistan, Philippines, and Taiwan. This indicates some variation, because Pakistan, for instance, is quite corrupt, while Taiwan is cleaner, but I assume that support structures for women play a greater role, which I will test later.

Who was asked for bribes? Men are more involved in nepotism and favouritism than women. They can rely on old boys' networks, while women either have to rely on more egalitarian structures or pay bribes. Women are less likely to be asked for bribes. The gap between men and women is smaller in Cambodia, India, Mongolia, Taiwan, and Vietnam. If anything, a smaller gap indicates a more egalitarian structure where women are treated more like equals even if it concerns such predatory practices as being asked for a bribe. The countries where women face somewhat equal pressure as men are not the most corrupt on the list but are in the mid-range.

In which countries are women more capable of saying "no" to bribes? Women are more likely to refuse to pay bribes in Cambodia, Japan, Pakistan, and Thailand. At the same time, they are much less likely to refuse in Afghanistan, the Philippines, Sri Lanka, and Vietnam. The ability to say "no" is one of the clearest indicators of a society where women are the fairer sex. They follow the rules, they feel more confident in themselves, they are not restricted to domesticity, and they are capable of collective action. They can act together because they know that when they say "no" somebody or some organization will back them

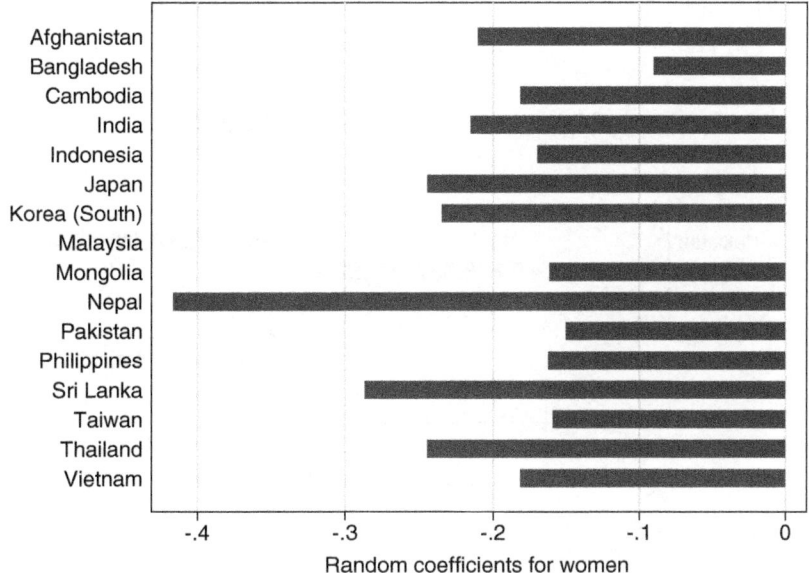

Figure 15.1 Random coefficients for women for paying a bribe as a dependent variable
Source: TI (2013).

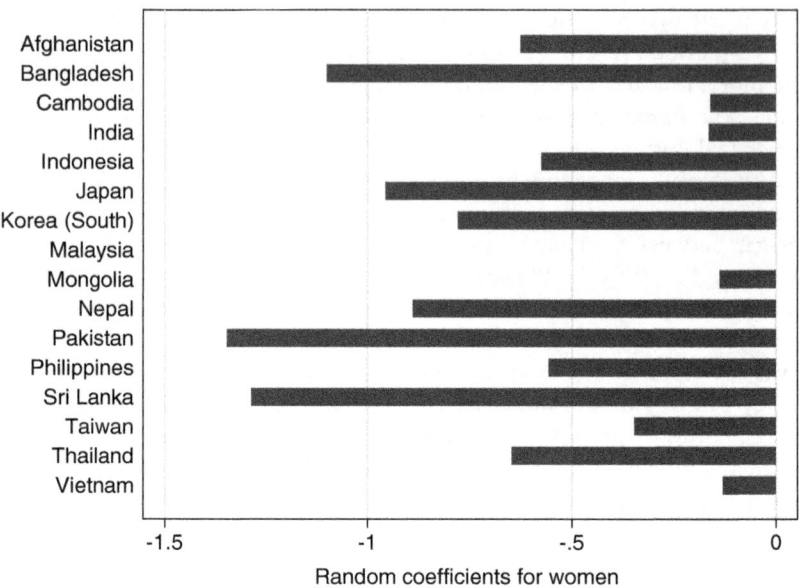

Figure 15.2 Random coefficients for women for being asked for a bribe as a dependent variable
Source: TI (2013).

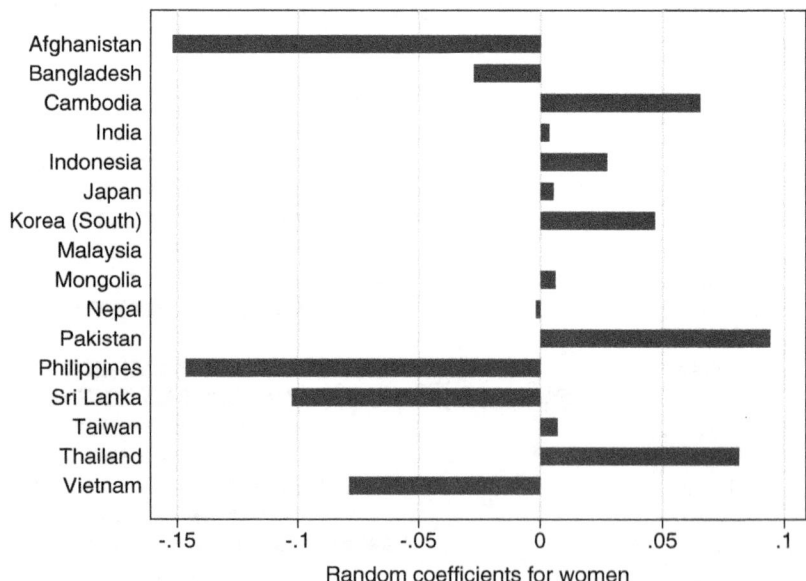

Figure 15.3 Random coefficients for women for refusing to pay a bribe as a dependent variable
Source: TI (2013).

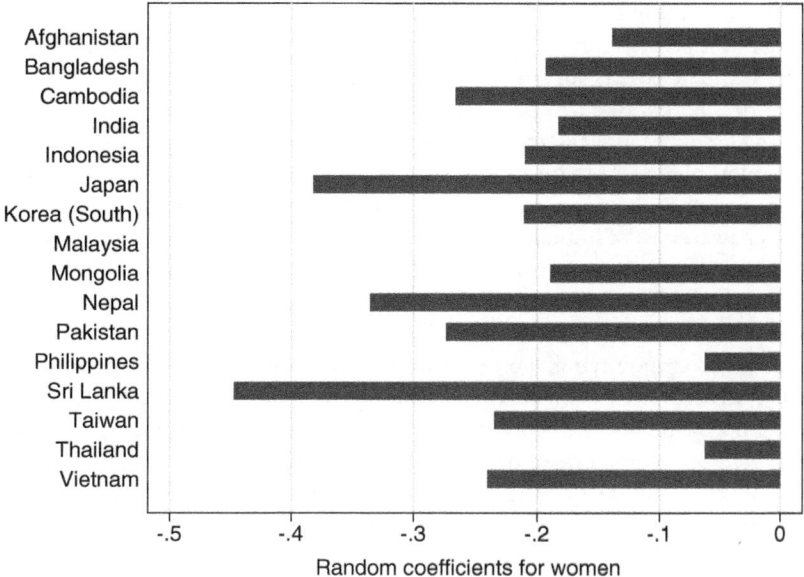

Figure 15.4 Random coefficients for reporting corruption as a dependent variable
Source: TI (2013).

up. They are risk-averse and agreeing to pay bribes becomes riskier behaviour. Empowering women in societies where social institutions become more egalitarian and women can organize themselves has an effect on making them the fairer sex.

When women are less empowered, they would not feel safe to report bribery. They know that everybody pays extra, and they know they are not as protected by connections and old boys' networks. They might have suffered in the past for refusing to pay bribes so they are used to bribery. Under such circumstances, women become a detrimental force in corruption control. In such countries, women would need more motivation than men to stop complying with the corrupt system.

Women need to be empowered both internally and externally (such as in Korea where they are more empowered compared to other neighbouring countries) to become an anti-corruption force. Otherwise, women become participants in corruption and they may do so at greater rates than men.

Women are not the fairer sex when it comes to reporting corruption. Across the Asian countries analysed here, women are less likely to report corruption. In some corrupt countries, such as the Philippines or Thailand, women become almost as likely as men to report corruption. Other than that, the results are consistent with women being more risk-averse and following the rules. If corruption is systemic, following the rules means not taking a stand against it. If women lack societal and family support and the ability for collective action to do something about corruption, they are less likely to do it.

Conclusion

Are women the fairer sex? The answer is "not always", and it depends on the type of action. Women are less likely to pay bribes, but they are also less likely to be asked to bribe, and they are less likely to do something about corruption (such as refuse to pay or report corruption).

Building anti-corruption policy on gender requires a note of caution. Social context matters. While women can be the fairer sex, in some societies they are not supported nor prepared to be the fairer sex. The results suggest that women display variation across countries in terms of paying bribes, being asked to pay, refusing to pay, or reporting bribes. Asia provides a fruitful testing base, because the region has countries that are very clean (such as Singapore) and very corrupt (such as Afghanistan). If women are not supported, their propensity to follow the rules and not take risks can be manifested in not resisting corruption. The findings call for greater awareness of importance of gender equality and women's rights. Women need to be empowered if only not to worsen the already detrimental effects of corruption.

How can all this be applicable for anti-corruption discourses? First, knowing which country people come from is paramount, because context adds great variation to corrupt behavior. Second, empowering women socially and politically by providing them with gender-equal structures and make them equal participants in groups and organizations can lead to improvements. Third, expecting women to stand up for their rights individually is unrealistic. Women need to be invited and validated to become a fairer sex, learn organizational skills, and start acting in order to promote gender equality and social justice. Individually they are not the fairer sex but if allowed to unite and attain equal status in society, they become the fairer sex.

Note

1 This research has been supported in part by the Economic and Social Research Council grant #ES/13482X/1.

References

Alatas, V., L. Cameron, A. Chaudhuri, N. Erkal, and L. Gangadharan (2009) "Gender, culture, and corruption: insights from an experimental analysis", *Southern Economic Journal*, 75(3): 663–680.

Andersen, S., E. Bulte, U. Gneezy and J.A. List (2008) "Do women supply more public goods than men? Preliminary experimental evidence from matrilineal and patriarchal societies", *The American Economic Review*, 98(2): 376–381.

Armantier, O. and A. Boly (2008) "Can corruption be studied in the lab? Comparing a field and a lab experiment", Social Science Research Network working paper, http://papers.ssrn.com/sol3/papers.cfm?abstract_id=1324120 (accessed 9 April 2015).

Bowles, H.R., L. Babcock, and K.L. McGinn (2005) "Constraints and triggers: situational mechanics of gender in negotiation", *Journal of Personality and Social Psychology*, 89(6): 951–965.

Branisa, B., S. Klasen and M. Ziegler (2013) "Gender inequality in social institutions and gendered development outcomes", *World Development*, 45: 252–268.

Chaudhuri, A. (2012) "Gender and corruption: a survey of the experimental evidence", in D., Serra and L. Wantchekon (eds.) *New advances in experimental research on corruption*, Bingley: Emerald Group Publishing, 13–50.

Dodson, D. L. and S. J. Carroll (1991) *Reshaping the agenda: women in state legislatures*, New Brunswick, NJ: Center for the American Woman and Politics (CAWP) Eagleton Institute of Politics, Rutgers, the State University of New Jersey.

Dollar, D., R. Fisman and R. Gatti (2001) "Are women really the 'fairer' sex? Corruption and women in government", *Journal of Economic Behavior & Organization*, 46(4): 423–429.

Eckel, C. C. and P. J. Grossman (2008) "Men, women and risk aversion: experimental evidence", in C.R. Plott and V.L. Smith (eds.) *Handbook of experimental economics results*, New York: Elsevier, Volume 1: 1061–1073.

Esarey, J., and G. Chirillo (2013) "'Fairer sex' or purity myth? Corruption, gender, and institutional context", *Politics & Gender*, 9(4): 361–389.

Frank, B., J. G. Lambsdorff and F. Boehm (2011) "Gender and corruption: lessons from laboratory corruption experiments", *European Journal of Development Research*, 23(1): 59–71.

Frank, B., and G. G. Schulze (2000) "Does economics make citizens corrupt?" *Journal of Economic Behavior & Organization*, 43(1): 101–113.

Hirschman, A. O. (1970) *Exit, voice, and loyalty: responses to decline in firms, organizations, and states*, Cambridge, MA: Harvard University Press.

Holmgren, V. (2015) Women and corruption, http://www.diva-portal.org/smash/record.jsf?pid=diva2:815012 (accessed 20 April 2016).

Huddy, L. and N. Terkildsen, (1993) "Gender stereotypes and the perception of male and female candidates", *American Journal of Political Science*, 37(1): 119–147.

Jha, C. and S. Sarangi (2015) "Women and corruption: what positions must they hold to make a difference?" http://papers.ssrn.com/sol3/papers.cfm?abstract_id=2434912 (accessed 10 August 2015).

Joshi, A., B. Neely, C. Emrich, D. Griffiths and G. George (2015) Gender research in AMJ: an overview of five decades of empirical research and calls to action thematic issue on gender in management research, *Academy of Management Journal*, 58(5): 1459–1475.

Kenny, M. (2013) *Gender and political recruitment: theorizing institutional change*, Basingstoke: Palgrave Macmillan.

Kiyoko, T. (1984) "Ichikawa Fusae: pioneer for women's rights in Japan", *Japan Quarterly*, 31(4): 410.

Landell-Mills, P. (2013) *Citizens against corruption: report from the front line*, Cornwall: Troubador Publishing Ltd.

McCabe, A. C., R. Ingram and M. C. Dato-on (2006) "The business of ethics and gender", *Journal of Business Ethics*, 64(2): 101–116.

Noonan, R. K. (1995) "Women against the state: political opportunities and collective action frames in Chile's transition to democracy", *Sociological Forum,* 10(1): 81–111.

Rivas, M. F. (2013) "An experiment on corruption and gender", *Bulletin of Economic Research*, 65(1): 10–42.

Rose-Ackerman, S. and B. J. Palifka (2016) *Corruption and government: causes, consequences, and reform*, 2nd edition, Cambridge: Cambridge University Press.

Stolberg, S. G. (2011) "When it comes to scandal, girls won't be boys", *New York Times,* 11 June, http://www.nytimes.com/2011/06/12/weekinreview/12women.html?_r=0 (accessed March 2016).

Sundström, A., and L. Wängnerud (2016) "Corruption as an obstacle to women's political representation: evidence from local councils in 18 European countries", *Party Politics*, 22(3): 354–369.

Sung, H.E. (2003) "Fairer sex or fairer system? Gender and corruption revisited", *Social Forces*, 82(2): 703–723.

Swamy, A., S. Knack, Y. Lee and O. Azfar (2001) "Gender and corruption", *Journal of Development Economics*, 64(1): 25–55.

TI (Transparency International) (2013) *Global Corruption Barometer 2013*, http://www.transparency.org/whatwedo/publication/global_corruption_barometer_2013 (accessed 20 April 2016).

Torgler, B. and N. T. Valev (2010) "Gender and public attitudes toward corruption and tax evasion", *Contemporary Economic Policy*, 28(4): 554–568.

Vanderbilt, T. (2009) *Traffic: why we drive the way we do (and what it says about us)*, London: Penguin UK.

Vavich, D.A. (1967) "The Japanese woman's movement: Ichikawa Fusae, a pioneer in woman's suffrage", *Monumenta Nipponica*, 22(3/4): 402–436.

Wängnerud, L. (2012) "Why women are less corrupt than men", in S. Holmberg and B. Rothstein (eds.) *Good government: the relevance of political science*, Cheltenham: Edward Elgar Publishing Limited, 230–250.

Worldwide Governance Indicators (2013) http://info.worldbank.org/governance/wgi/index.aspx#home (accessed 20 April 2016).

Worldwide Governance Indicators (2015) http://info.worldbank.org/governance/wgi/pdf/cc.pdf (accessed 20 April 2016).

16

MEASURING PUBLIC PERCEPTIONS OF CORRUPTION IN ASIA

Chilik Yu

Introduction

Since the mid-1990s, empirical studies seeking to determine the causes and consequences of corruption have multiplied. Scholars from many disciplines are interested in understanding why corrupt practices occur more frequently in some countries than in others and, consequently, in understanding the political, economic, and social consequences of these illicit acts. The majority of these empirical investigations can be said to share three common traits: first, they are comparative in nature, mostly cross-country analyses of the extent of corruption in various countries; second, they tend to focus on public rather than private corruption; and third, they tend to rely on subjective measures (or perceptions) of corruption for their data sources. To date, the availability of an unusually large number of high-quality review-and-synthesis papers on the causes and consequences of corruption obviates the need for yet another comprehensive review on the topic. One can be assured, however, that most meta-reviews point to the fact that the study of corruption has greatly benefitted from this empirical turn as the field moves beyond anecdotal descriptions, purely theoretical considerations, and compilations of individual scandals or cases that had dominated previous research (Lambsdorff 2006a).

Although more is now known about the origins, nature, patterns, and outcomes of corruption than ever before, paradoxically, the state of corruption research remains hampered by the twin fundamental problems of "definition" and "measurement". The process of either defining or measuring the true level or extent of corruption is notoriously difficult and complex and there is simply no universally accepted method to define or measure corruption satisfactorily (Heywood and Rose 2014; Lin and Yu 2014). In fact, the United Nations Convention against Corruption, the world's first legally binding instrument aimed at combating and preventing corruption at the global level, deliberately does not include an explicit definition of corruption in its text, relying instead on the various enumerated acts within the convention to characterise different types of corrupt behavior.

Even if corruption scholars have yet to (re)solve the dual problems of definition and measurement, researchers nevertheless have been able to advance the study of corruption by taking some very pragmatic and cautious steps. Many have adopted Transparency International's (TI) working definition of corruption—the abuse of entrusted power for private gain—as a starting point in their discussions. As for the measurement problem, TI's Corruption Perceptions Index (CPI) is perhaps the most important and most widely used perception-based indices of corruption for cross-national studies.

Despite its popularity, critics have become increasingly aware that the CPI may not be as valid, reliable or robust a measure of the underlying phenomenon as was first thought (Andersson and Heywood 2009; Ko and Samajdar 2010). A common criticism of these composite perception-based measures of corruption such as the CPI is that they rely solely on the surveys of international business executives and expert assessments of foreign analysts. As such, the CPI mainly reflects the perceptions of (mostly foreign) elites which may be highly disconnected with the perceptions of the general public (average citizens) for each country in question. Although TI's own study (TI 2010) and a few empirical studies (Canache and Allison 2005; Ko and Samajdar 2010) have provided evidence of a strong correlation between the average citizen and elite assessments of the extent of public sector corruption, results obtained from other studies are not quite as definitive and some even arrive at opposite conclusions (Razafindrakoto and Roubaud 2010; Hawken and Munck 2011; Lin and Yu 2014).

Accordingly, this chapter uses data from both an international elite-based approach and a domestic citizen-based approach to demonstrate the corruption conditions in various countries/territories in Asia. Specifically, this chapter will focus on 13 countries/territories in East and Southeast Asia found in the Asian Barometer Survey (ABS), which adopts a domestic citizen-based approach to corruption measurement. These 13 countries and territories are Cambodia, China, Hong Kong, Indonesia, Japan, South Korea, Malaysia, Mongolia, the Philippines, Singapore, Taiwan, Thailand, and Vietnam. The data from the ABS will be compared with that from the CPI, which represents an international elite-based approach to corruption measurement. By compiling and comparing both the ABS and the CPI data, this chapter answers four research questions: (1) What are the elite and public perceptions of corruption in these countries/territories? (2) Does a corruption perception gap exist between the elite and the public? (3) Why does such a gap exist? (4) How can corruption be measured more appropriately? Understanding and comparing both elite and public perceptions will advance the study of corruption in Asia as well as providing new insights into the problem of corruption measurement. Before discussing the findings of the data analysis, the next section reviews the literature on measuring corruption with an emphasis on Asia.

Measuring corruption: mission indispensable

Can corruption be measured? Before we ask this empirical question, we need to briefly address a normative question: Should we devote our scarce research resources to the issue of corruption measurement? The answer is obviously we should! Since corruption undermines good governance and the sound development of a country, fighting corruption has become a worldwide movement. Many governments have developed institutional designs, policy initiatives and action plans hoping to cure this illness. The solid test of these cures is whether the problem has at least been alleviated, if not completely solved. As such, the development of a valid and reliable measure of corruption provides the reform movement with an important foundation which enables corruption problems to be correctly diagnosed and solutions to be properly evaluated.

Although measuring corruption deserves attention and is a long-standing concern of scholars and practitioners, how we can effectively measure the extent of corruption is never an easy task and arouses heated discussions. The measurement of corruption is difficult because corruption is usually illicit and concealed; measuring corruption for the purpose of cross-national comparison is especially difficult because the definition of corrupt behavior varies according to cultural, legal and other factors (Svensson 2005). Although Caiden (2001) has already identified the nineteen "most commonly recognized forms of corruption", his efforts did not close the definition debate. Nor do such definitional efforts provide a solid foundation for measurement because the operational definitions of these forms of corruption may still be unclear.

Even if the definition of corruption remains unsettled, scholars and practitioners have not been deterred from attempting to measure it. Lin and Yu (2014) classify these efforts by using two types of data: objective and subjective measurements. Similarly, Heywood and Rose (2014) provide a detailed review of non-perceptual and perception-based approaches to the measurement of corruption. While the early efforts of using objective measures and the currently innovative attempts of non-perceptual measures enhance our capacity for corruption measurement, they still suffer from many inherent deficiencies. This is especially true when research is aimed at cross-national comparison. Accordingly, the perception-based measures of corruption have been used widely over the past 20 years.

Perception-based measures are subjective data about the extent of corruption in a specific area collected from the opinions of stakeholders, which could include global elites and/or local citizens. The use of subjective perception for the measurement of corruption, especially from the public, might be justifiable from a philosophical point of view. Hilgartner and Bosk (1988), for example, argue that public issues are a projection of the collective cognition of the society as a whole rather than simply a reflection of the objective reality. From a practical perspective, corruption researchers often have difficulty in collecting valid objective data so the alternative is to survey subjective perceptions of corruption from various stakeholders (Kaufmann et al. 2010). Attempts to measure corruption by using subjective data abound. Many countries have conducted surveys to understand their own corruption problems. For example, in Taiwan, a longitudinal research project, the Taiwan Integrity Survey sponsored by the Ministry of Justice since 1997, is probably one of the most systematic measures of corruption in the world (see Yu et al. 2008, 2013). Although these kinds of data enhance our understanding of corruption in a particular country, it has little value for cross-national studies due to the lack of comparative data.

For the purpose of cross-national comparison, the most widely used measure of corruption is the CPI, which is produced annually by TI, a non-governmental organization (NGO) based in Berlin dedicated to raising public awareness about global corruption (Lin and Yu 2014). The CPI is a composite index (a "survey of surveys"), which relies on global expert evaluations and business opinion surveys from think tanks, NGOs, and international organizations to determine the extent of corruption. The rationale for compiling and aggregating indicators from several sources is to limit concerns about measurement errors arising from any single source. The CPI ranks countries and territories around the world each year according to the perceived level of corruption in the public sector. The number of countries and territories included in the ranking has expanded from 42 in 1995 to about 170 in recent years.

The increase in coverage and the regular annual release of data are perhaps the major reasons for the acceptability of the CPI in cross-national research. Not only has the CPI ensured the TI's power of global anti-corruption agenda setting, but it has also served the function of making possible cross-national large-N empirical studies. The popularity of the CPI has thus stimulated much academic research on corruption over the past two decades. Yet, while the CPI enhances our knowledge about global corruption conditions, strong concerns about its adequacy, validity, reliability, and utility persist (Rose 2015).

One common criticism of the CPI is that it relies mainly on elite perceptions and does not take into account the perspective of local citizens. The distinction between elites and non-elites is an important aspect of social analysis, and has been a central topic in the study of public opinion formation for many years (Yu 2007). Following this line of inquiry, an important research question related to corruption is: should we rely on "the wisdom of crowds" (Surowiecki 2004) or put our faith on the judgment of experts and other elites (Tetlock 2005)?

In responding to this criticism, the TI has supplemented the CPI with the Global Corruption Barometer (GCB), a large worldwide survey that measures ordinary people's perceptions of corruption. Starting from 2003, the TI has collected and released the GCB data eight times. In 2010, it conducted an analysis to compare the relationship between the 2010 GCB and 2009 CPI data and found a statistically significant correlation (Pearson's correlation coefficient = 0.54, p<0.01), claiming that the corruption perceptions between local citizens and international elites are not that different (TI 2010). In addition, Ko and Samajdar (2010) compared the CPI with public opinion data taken from two other multi-region surveys: the World Values Survey and the International Crime Victimization Survey; they found that the CPI scores were highly correlated with local people's responses to the bribery questions found respectively in the World Values Survey (r = −0.86) and in the Crime Victimization Survey (r = −0.75). These findings make for an argument that the CPI is not inconsistent with public perceptions of corruption in most countries and territories.

Contrary to these conclusions, results obtained from other studies show a gap between corruption perceptions of the elite and the general public. In an innovative work that surveyed both citizens and elites in eight African countries, for example, Razafindrakoto and Roubaud (2010) find that experts' views about the extent of corruption in a given society do not correlate at all with the citizens' perceptions. The authors conclude that the so-called "experts" generally overestimated the level of corruption in these eight countries. Likewise, in a study that analyzed the measurement quality of corruption indicators and indices, Hawken and Munck (2011) discover that different classes of elite evaluators would systematically generate higher or lower estimates of the level of corruption. For example, they find that experts from the commercial risk assessment agencies generally provide stricter assessments of the extent of corruption in a country than either experts from non-governmental organizations or the general public. In East and Southeast Asia, research on domestic sources of corruption perception also finds that citizens have their own unique perspective towards corruption, which is quite different from the results of the CPI (Yu et al. 2008, 2013; Lin and Yu 2014).

From a brief review of the corruption measurement literature above, one can conclude that it is impossible to measure corruption appropriately without the use of both elite-based and citizen-based subjective data. Taking into consideration the availability of valid data for cross-national study, the following section relies on two main data sources: the CPI, which provides international elite perspectives of corruption, and the ABS, which provides public opinion data on Asian citizens.[1] Each of the data sources is briefly described next.

Corruption perceptions in East and Southeast Asia

Corruption is increasingly regarded as a major challenge for many countries in Asia and as one of the foremost obstacles to Asia's growth. Despite the anti-corruption reforms of recent years, results do not seem positive and scholars have consequently asked whether curbing corruption is an impossible dream (Quah 2011). How serious is the problem of corruption in the East and Southeast Asian region? Table 16.1 depicts the CPI performance of 17 East and Southeast Asian countries and territories between 2010 and 2015 to give a snapshot of the problem.

Table 16.1 Measuring elite perceptions of corruption in East and Southeast Asia by the CPI

Country/Territory	2010 Score (Rank)	2011 Score (Rank)	2012 Score (Rank)	2013 Score (Rank)	2014 Score (Rank)	2015 Score (Rank)
Singapore	9.3 (1)	9.2 (5)	87 (5)	86 (5)	84 (7)	85 (8)
Japan	7.8 (17)	8.0 (14)	74 (17)	74 (18)	76 (15)	75 (18)
Hong Kong	8.4 (13)	8.4 (12)	77 (14)	75 (15)	74 (17)	75 (18)
Taiwan	5.8 (33)	6.1 (32)	61 (37)	61 (36)	61 (35)	62 (30)
South Korea	5.4 (39)	5.4 (43)	56 (45)	55 (46)	55 (43)	56 (37)
Macau	5.0 (46)	5.1 (46)	N/A	N/A	N/A	N/A
Malaysia	4.4 (56)	4.3 (60)	49 (54)	50 (53)	52 (50)	50 (54)
Mongolia	2.7 (116)	2.7 (120)	36 (94)	38 (83)	39 (80)	39 (72)
Thailand	3.5 (78)	3.4 (80)	37 (88)	35 (102)	38 (85)	38 (76)
China	3.5 (78)	3.6 (75)	39 (80)	40 (80)	36 (100)	37 (83)
Indonesia	2.8 (110)	3.0 (100)	32 (118)	32 (114)	34 (107)	36 (88)
Philippines	2.4 (134)	2.6 (129)	34 (105)	36 (94)	38 (85)	35 (95)
Vietnam	2.7 (116)	2.9 (112)	31 (123)	31 (116)	31 (119)	31 (112)
Laos	2.1 (154)	2.2 (154)	21 (160)	26 (140)	25 (145)	25 (139)
Myanmar	1.4 (176)	1.5 (180)	15 (172)	21 (157)	21 (156)	22 (147)
Cambodia	2.1 (154)	2.1 (164)	22 (157)	20 (160)	21 (156)	21 (150)
North Korea	N/A	1.0 (182)	8 (174)	8 (175)	8 (174)	8 (167)
Regional Average	4.33	4.21	42.43	43.00	43.31	43.44
Number of countries and territories surveyed	178	183	176	177	175	168

Source: Transparency International's Corruption Perceptions Index, 2010–2015.

In 2010 and 2011, the CPI scores ranged from 0 to 10; since 2012, the CPI has been changed to a 100 points scale. In both scales, a lower score represents a higher corruption perception. Table 16.1 shows that East and Southeast Asia is composed of diverse countries and territories perceived to be both highly corrupt (for example, North Korea, Cambodia, and Myanmar) and very clean (for example, Singapore, Japan, and Hong Kong). In 2015, more than half (ten of seventeen) of the countries and territories failed to score above 50, which is TI's transition point differentiating countries and territories that do or do not have a serious corruption problem. Yet, as discussed in the previous section, an important but not fully answered question is whether the citizens of these countries and territories hold the same views as those reflected in the CPI scores.

In order to shed light on this question and to present a more balanced picture, this study presents corruption perceptions from citizens in thirteen countries and territories in East and Southeast Asia, using data from the 2010–2012 ABS. The ABS is a collaborative regional survey network that conducts public opinion surveys on issues related to political values, democracy and governance around the region. Headquartered in Taipei, the ABS is co-hosted by the Institute of Political Science, Academia Sinica, and the Institute for the Advanced Studies of Humanities and Social Sciences, National Taiwan University. Starting in 2001, the ABS has completed three rounds: the first wave was from 2001 to 2003, the second from 2005 to 2008, and the third from 2010 to 2012. The data are freely accessible to researchers worldwide from the ABS program's website (http://www.asianbarometer.org/) upon a simple application process after the embargo date. The ABS data have been used as a statistical base for many scholarly publications (for example, Chang and Chu 2006; Chang 2013; Lin and Yu 2014).

Each round of the ABS was collected by individual national research teams in the participating countries or territories using a common research framework. Random samples with a size of large-N were required for each country and territory. Target respondents represented a cross-section of voting-age adult citizens and all interviews were conducted face-to-face by trained fieldworkers in the language of the respondent's choice. The ABS used a standard survey instrument with identical or functionally equivalent questions, thus making it possible for the comparison of results across countries and territories. For the purpose of this chapter, the following questions in the ABS are used to measure citizen perceptions of the overall level of government corruption:

1 How widespread do you think corruption and bribe-taking are in the national government?
2 How widespread do you think corruption and bribe-taking are in your local/municipal government?

For each question, respondents were presented with four choices: (1) hardly anyone is involved (coded as 1), (2) not a lot of officials are corrupt (coded as 2), (3) most officials are corrupt (coded as 3), and (4) almost everyone is corrupt (coded as 4). Higher scores indicate higher levels of perceived corruption.

Table 16.2 presents the data on the distribution of individual responses to the question about corruption in the national government, disaggregated by country, calculated by mean. By using mean = 2.5 as the transition point to differentiate countries, the ABS shows a divided picture. About half of the countries (Five of Eleven including Singapore, China, Japan, Malaysia, and Thailand), score below 2.5, indicating the citizens do not think their central governments have a serious corruption problem. Citizens in the other countries, including South Korea, Cambodia, Taiwan, Indonesia, the Philippines, and Mongolia, on the other hand, consider corruption a serious problem. As might be expected, Singapore is the only country where about two-thirds of respondents (67.6 per cent) feel that hardly any government official is engaged in corrupt behavior. Conversely, more than two-thirds of the respondents in Mongolia and Philippines believe that most or almost all government officials are corrupt. Although respondents in neither of these countries give the "almost everyone is corrupt" as the most popular response, Mongolia comes closest with 33.8 per cent followed by the Philippines at 29.5 per cent.

The results from Table 16.2 nevertheless produce some interesting and unexpected results, especially when compared to conventional wisdom and/or the CPI scores in Table 16.1. For example, the majority of Chinese respondents believe that corruption is not pervasive in their national government, where 24.8 per cent of the respondents consider hardly anyone is involved and 50.7 per cent indicate that they think not many officials are corrupt. These results, which come from a survey conducted in 2011, when Xi had not yet initiated his major anti-corruption reform, are especially unbelievable (Wedeman 2012; Quah 2015).

In Thailand, as another example, the majority (about 60 per cent of respondents) answer that hardly any or not many officials are corrupt, a result in contrast to the elite perceptions of corruption in Thailand from the CPI. This result may not reflect the level of corruption, but the high degree of citizens' tolerance for corrupt practices. Quah (2011: 290–291) has explained the Thai population's tolerance of corruption by highlighting Sakkarin Niyomsilpa's argument that Thais have identified seven levels of corruption, ranging from the less

Table 16.2 Measuring citizen perceptions of corruption in the national government by the ABS

Country	How widespread is corruption and bribe-taking in the national government?				Valid respondents	Mean
	1. Hardly anyone is involved	2. Not a lot of officials are corrupt	3. Most officials are corrupt	4. Almost everyone is corrupt		
Singapore (Year: 2010; N=1000; missing=14.6%)	577 (67.6%)	256 (30.0%)	19 (2.2%)	2 (0.2%)	854 (100%)	1.35
China (Year: 2011; N=3473; missing=34.1%)	567 (24.8%)	1160 (50.7%)	451 (19.7%)	112 (4.9%)	2290 (100.1%)	2.05
Japan (Year: 2011; N=1880; missing=0.7%)	79 (4.2%)	1333 (71.4%)	427 (22.9%)	28 (1.5%)	1867 (100%)	2.22
Malaysia (Year: 2011; N=1214; missing=13.6%)	122 (11.6%)	604 (57.6%)	259 (24.7%)	64 (6.1%)	1049 (100%)	2.25
Thailand (Year: 2010; N=1512; missing=16.1%)	81 (6.4%)	693 (54.6%)	326 (25.7%)	169 (13.3%)	1269 (100%)	2.46
South Korea (Year: 2011; N=1207; missing=3.1%)	13 (1.1%)	497 (42.5%)	572 (48.9%)	88 (7.5%)	1170 (100%)	2.63
Cambodia (Year: 2012; N=1200; missing=8.5%)	44 (4.0%)	459 (41.8%)	411 (37.4%)	184 (16.8%)	1098 (100%)	2.67
Taiwan (Year: 2010; N=1592; missing=11.2%)	48 (3.4%)	473 (33.5%)	775 (54.8%)	117 (8.3%)	1413 (100%)	2.68
Indonesia (Year: 2011; N=1550; missing=15.5%)	44 (3.4%)	523 (39.9%)	443 (33.8%)	300 (22.9%)	1310 (100%)	2.76
Philippines (Year: 2010; N=1200; missing=1.8%)	56 (4.8%)	300 (25.5%)	475 (40.3%)	347 (29.5%)	1178 (100.1%)	2.94
Mongolia (Year: 2010; N=1210; missing=5.0%)	15 (1.3%)	188 (16.3%)	558 (48.5%)	389 (33.8%)	1150 (99.9%)	3.15

Source: Asian Barometer Survey, 2010–2012.

Note: Because of rounding, percentages may not add up to 100. For each country, the year in which the survey was conducted is presented and N represents the sample size. In Hong Kong, it was not applicable to ask the question on national government. In addition, this question was omitted from the Vietnam survey due to political sensitivity.

severe form of misconduct, *sin nam jai* (gift of goodwill), to the most severe form of misconduct, *kan khorrapchuan* (corruption); of the seven levels of corruption, the first three levels are viewed as acceptable practices by Thais, whereas the remaining four levels are considered to be unacceptable practices.

As for the local/municipal government, Table 16.3 reports the distribution of citizen perceptions about the existence of widespread corruption. Seven out of twelve countries and territories in this area, (Vietnam, Hong Kong, Japan, Malaysia, Thailand, Indonesia, and Cambodia), score below 2.5, showing relatively low perceptions of corruption in their local/municipal governments. On the other hand, residents in the remaining countries, including South Korea, Mongolia, China, Taiwan, and Philippines, express concerns about the problem of corruption in their local/municipal governments. Surprisingly, the most clean local/municipal governments are found in Vietnam, according to the ABS. Only 7.4 per cent of Vietnamese respondents consider that almost every or most officials are corrupt. The majority have an extremely positive assessment of their local/municipal governments (54.0 per cent answer that not many officials are corrupt and 38.7 per cent think hardly anyone is involved). The huge gap between these perceptions and the CPI results (score 2.9 and rank 112 in 2011; score 31 and rank 123 in 2012) deserves further discussion.

The gaps between elite and citizen perceptions of corruption

What factors explain the huge gap between elite and citizen perceptions of corruption? Current developments in Vietnam might account for the extremely positive results from the ABS (Lin and Yu 2014). In recent years, Vietnam continued its push toward greater economic growth, stronger globalization, and better governance (Luong 2006). In 2005, after extensive coverage of major corruption cases by the media, the Vietnamese government passed the country's first comprehensive anti-corruption legislation to express its commitment to fighting corruption (Fritzen 2005). These developments, arguably,[2] provide Vietnamese citizens with reasons to feel better and to have more confidence in their government. In a question asked in the 2010 ABS (In your opinion, is the government working to crack down on corruption and root out bribery?), a great majority of the respondents (87.3 per cent) believe their government is doing their best or doing something, only 12.7 per cent of the respondents felt it is not doing much or doing nothing.

Although local citizens might be more sensitive to the progressive developments they have experienced than the external elites, and, as such, have quite different perceptions of corruption of their government, the overly positive results about Vietnam from the ABS are still questionable. Can we believe this beautiful picture painted by subjective measures derived from a citizen survey in an authoritarian regime? Assuming that data collection has been conducted properly and data entry errors kept at a minimal, a high percentage of missing responses (25.5 per cent) triggers caution on the validity and reliability of the data. From a methodological perspective, the percentage missing is above the generally acceptable cutoff point, 20 per cent, and has raised problems of estimation and inference (see Schlomer et al. 2010). More seriously are the reasons why so many respondents fail or refuse to answer this question. If this is a sign of fearing to voice their views, then those who choose to respond might give a government-acceptable answer to the question. This is an intriguing and unsettled problem of using survey methods on a politically sensitive issue, such as corruption, in an authoritarian regime (Mishler and Rose 2008).[3]

Following the case of Vietnam, a more systematic analysis is presented in Table 16.4 and Figure 16.1 to understand how each country and territory compares to others in the

Table 16.3 Measuring citizen perceptions of corruption in the local/municipal government by the ABS

Country/Territory	How widespread is corruption and bribe-taking in your local/municipal government?				Valid respondents	Mean
	1. Hardly anyone is involved	2. Not a lot of officials are corrupt	3. Most officials are corrupt	4. Almost everyone is corrupt		
Vietnam (Year: 2010; N=1191; missing=25.5%)	343 (38.7%)	479 (54.0%)	59 (6.7%)	6 (0.7%)	887 (100.1%)	1.69
Hong Kong (Year: 2012; N=1207; missing=11.5%)	123 (11.5%)	822 (77.0%)	117 (11.0 %)	6 (0.6%)	1068 (100.1%)	2.01
Japan (Year: 2011; N=1880; missing=0.6%)	137 (7.3%)	1409 (75.4%)	300 (16.1%)	22 (1.2%)	1868 (100%)	2.11
Malaysia (Year: 2011; N=1214; missing=11.9%)	176 (16.4%)	646 (60.4%)	199 (18.6%)	49 (4.6%)	1070 (100%)	2.11
Thailand (Year: 2010; N=1512; missing=13.0%)	250 (19.0%)	729 (55.4%)	201 (15.3%)	135 (10.3%)	1315 (100%)	2.17
Indonesia (Year: 2011; N=1550; missing=17.9%)	181 (14.2%)	562 (44.1%)	336 (26.4%)	194 (15.2%)	1273 (99.9%)	2.43
Cambodia (Year: 2012; N=1200; missing=1.4%)	88 (7.4%)	599 (50.6%)	348 (29.4%)	148 (12.5%)	1183 (99.9%)	2.47
South Korea (Year: 2011; N=1207; missing=2.6%)	41 (3.5%)	503 (42.8%)	541 (46.0%)	91 (7.7%)	1176 (100%)	2.58
Mongolia (Year: 2010; N=1210; missing=10.6%)	78 (7.2%)	410 (37.9%)	411 (38.0%)	183 (16.9%)	1082 (100%)	2.65
China (Year: 2011; N=3473; missing=17.4%)	177 (6.2%)	1010 (35.2%)	1301 (45.3%)	381 (13.3%)	2869 (100%)	2.66
Taiwan (Year: 2010; N=1592; missing=8.7%)	57 (3.9%)	447 (30.7%)	851 (58.5%)	99 (6.8%)	1454 (99.9%)	2.68
Philippines (Year: 2010; N=1200; missing=2.0%)	56 (4.8%)	409 (34.8%)	427 (36.3%)	284 (24.1%)	1176 (100%)	2.80

Source: Asian Barometer Survey, 2010–2012.
Note: Because of rounding, percentages may not add up to 100. For each country, the year in which the survey was conducted is presented and N represents the sample size. Data on the local/municipal government of Singapore were not available due to its size and government structure.

region. In order to make comparison and a clearer presentation, this study calculates standard z-scores for the CPI and the ABS for all countries/territories and then reverses the CPI scores to make them comparable to the ABS figures.[4] The ABSZ and the CPIZ' are the respective perceptions of corruption by local citizens and international elites, and the higher scores indicate more corruption. A Perception Gap Index (PGI, in the last column in Table 16.4) has also been constructed to indicate the distance from a specific point to the 45-degree diagonal in Figure 16.1.[5]

Figure 16.1 identifies four types of combinations between citizen and elite perceptions. The distribution of East and Southeast Asian countries and territories across the four quadrants is informative and interesting. In Quadrant I, both citizens and elites perceived corruption in the country to be relatively high, including Cambodia, Indonesia, the Philippines, Mongolia, and China. In Quadrant II, elites, but not the citizens, perceived corruption to be

Table 16.4 Perception gaps in the ABS and CPI data (ranked by the PGI)

Country/Territory	ABS Mean	ABSZ	CPI t+1	CPI t+2	CPIZ'	ABSZ–CPIZ'	PGI
Indonesia (t=2011)	2.60	0.59	32	32	0.83	−0.24	0.17
Malaysia (t=2011)	2.18	−0.33	49	50	−0.04	−0.29	0.21
Singapore (t=2010)	1.35	−2.16	9.2	87	−1.84	−0.32	0.23
China (t=2011)	2.36	0.06	39	40	0.46	−0.40	0.28
Philippines (t=2010)	2.87	1.19	2.6	34	0.80	0.39	0.28
Mongolia (t=2010)	2.90	1.26	2.7	36	0.73	0.53	0.37
Hong Kong (t=2012)	2.01	−0.71	75	74	−1.29	0.58	0.41
Thailand (t=2010)	2.32	−0.03	3.4	37	0.56	−0.60	0.42
Japan (t=2011)	2.17	−0.36	74	74	−1.24	0.88	0.62
Cambodia (t=2012)	2.57	0.53	20	21	1.43	−0.90	0.64
South Korea (t=2011)	2.61	0.61	56	55	−0.33	0.94	0.66
Taiwan (t=2010)	2.68	0.77	6.1	61	−0.57	1.35	0.95
Vietnam (t=2010)	1.69	−1.41	2.9	31	0.81	−2.23	1.57

Source: Transparency International's Corruption Perception Index, 2010–2014; Asian Barometer Survey, 2010–2012.

Note: In the first column, t indicates the year when the ABS was conducted. ABSZ and CPIZ are the respective z-scores calculated from the ABS values and the comparable CPI values (CPI$_{t+1}$ and CPI$_{t+2}$). The CPIZ (not shown in this Table) was then reversed to produce CPIZ' so that higher values indicate more corruption, similar to what ABSZ represents. In the table, countries are ordered from low to high according to the Perception Gap Index (PGI). The higher the PGI, the bigger the perception gap between citizens and experts.

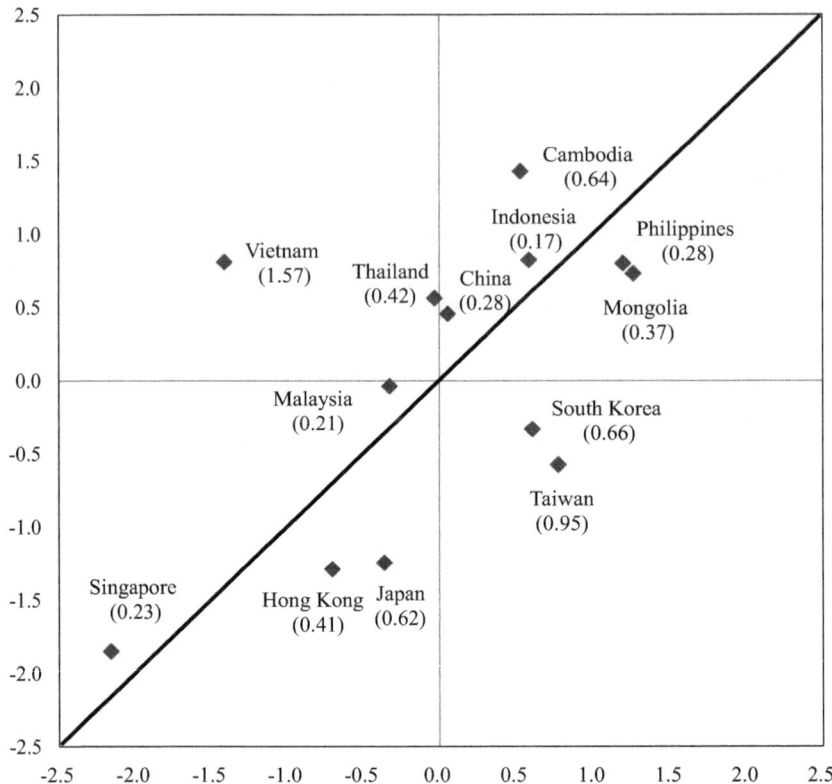

Figure 16.1 A typology of perception gaps

Source: Transparency International (2010–2014) Corruption Perceptions Index; Asian Barometer Survey, 2010–2012.

relatively high, Thailand and Vietnam are the examples. In Quadrant III, both citizens and elites perceived corruption to be relatively low, including Singapore, Hong Kong, Japan, and Malaysia. In Quadrant IV, citizens, but not the elites, perceived corruption in the country to be relatively high, with South Korea and Taiwan falling in this category.

Another way to examine the results from Figure 16.1 is the PGI, the distance from a specific point to the 45 degree diagonal, which indicates the gap between the citizen and elite perceptions of corruption for a specific country/territory. The closer the distance means the smaller difference between the values of ABSZ and CPIZ'. For example, Singapore falls close to the 45-degree diagonal (the PGI = 0.23), representing a small difference between ABSZ and CPIZ'. Although categorized in the same Quadrant as Singapore, Japan falls some distance away from the 45 degree diagonal, showing quite a large gap between citizen and elite perceptions (the PGI is 0.62). The top three countries with the biggest gaps between ABSZ and CPIZ' can be found in Quadrant II and IV, which are Vietnam (the PGI = 1.57), Taiwan (the PGI = 0.95), and South Korea (the PGI = 0.66).

The difference in perceptions of corruption between elites and citizens in three East Asian democratic countries deserves further explanation and discussion. From a measurement perspective, Hawken and Munck (2011) find corruption perceptions differ in regional comparisons and by various evaluators: East Asian countries were favored by experts from multilateral development banks but not favored by other business executives and by the citizens at large. This is especially true for Japan, which scored 74 in 2012 and 2013 by the

CPI (ranked seventeen among 176 and eighteen among 177 countries/territories, respectively) but was not perceived as such a clean country by its citizens. As Quah (2011: 58) indicates, Japan's high ranking and score on the CPI reflect the low level of petty corruption but ignore the structural corruption which is the result of the following three factors: "(1) the high cost of being elected; (2) the official income of a Diet member is inadequate to meet his or her social obligations; and (3) the collusion between politicians, bureaucrats and businessmen".

South Korea was ranked 45 (among 176 countries and territories) and 46 (among 177) with a CPI score of 56 and 55 in 2012 and 2013, which seems to be a relatively positive assessment from a global perspective. Yet corruption remains a serious problem in South Korea from the citizens' perspective because of some negative anti-corruption developments. For example, on February 29, 2008, President Lee Myung-bak weakened the Korea Independent Commission Against Corruption by merging it with the Administrative Appeals Commission and the Ombudsman to form the Anti-Corruption and Civil Rights Commission (Quah 2011: 334). During President Lee's term of office, he used his right to pardon 55 persons who had been imprisoned for bribery.

By the same token, the Taiwanese citizens' negative perception of corruption in the 2010 ABS was probably influenced by the memory of corruption scandals involving former President Chen Shui-bian and his wife. The first family was friendly with business tycoons who used their friendship to obtain political favours from the Chen administration (2000–2008). The next President Ma Ying-jeou (2008–2016) also failed to curb corruption. The July 2010 corruption scandal involving three high court judges might probably account for the extremely negative perception from the citizens in the 2010 ABS.[6] In short, the democratic transformation in Taiwan since 2000 has resulted in some deficits, one of which is that many citizens have come to view the problem of corruption as worsening, given perceptions of the low integrity of elected officials and political appointees (Yu et al. 2008, 2013).

However, these perceptions from citizens might not reflect reality. Previous literature has found a strong link between political corruption and the decline of institutional trust in Asian democracies (Chang and Chu 2006; Chang 2013). Yet this low trust could in turn trigger citizens' low assessment of the integrity of government and become one of the reasons for the extremely negative perception of corruption in Taiwan, South Korea, and Japan, which is reflected in the ABS data, but not in that of the CPI. As Wroe et al. (2013: 175) put it: "less trusting individuals are consistently more censorious of politicians' misbehaviour and more likely to perceive the presence of corruption than are their more trusting peers". This relationship should be connected with another important topic: the relationship between democracy and corruption.

From a broader viewpoint, the relationship between democracy and corruption has been an important topic for academic research. Li et al. (2016) find that people in countries with higher levels of democracy tend to perceive their governments to be more corrupt, but the relationship is not linear because in countries with more developed democratic institutions, individuals with stronger democratic values, the perception of corruption becomes lower. Campbell and Saha (2013: 290) also discover this "non-monotonic relationship" by examining data from Asia-Pacific countries: "When a country shifts from autocratic rule to highly imperfect democracy (an 'electoral democracy') it is frequently perceived that the level of corruption increases. Conversely, when the democracy level is already relatively high (approaching 'mature democracy') an increase in the level of democracy is typically expected to decrease the level of corruption". As Japan, South Korea and Taiwan have not yet reached the standards of mature democracy, the corruption perception gaps between local citizens and international elites do not seem so surprising.

Conclusions

Since TI first released its annual CPI in 1995, the CPI has quickly become the best-known measurement of corruption. Despite its enormous influence on both academic and practical communities, the CPI has been criticised because it only reflects the perceptions of international elites rather than the perceptions of the citizens from each country or territory. Accordingly, this chapter draws on two main data sources: the CPI and the ABS, to give a more balanced picture of perceptions of corruption in thirteen countries and territories in East and Southeast Asia. The results show that this region is diverse with perceptions ranging from highly corrupt to very clean by either the international elite and/or the citizens. Compiling and comparing data from the CPI and ABS, a typology of perception differences between elites and citizens is developed and presented in Figure 16.1, which clearly identifies huge gaps in corruption perceptions between elites and citizens in Vietnam, Taiwan, South Korea, and Japan. Although this chapter discusses some plausible reasons for these gaps, it remains unclear whether the existing gaps should be labeled as perceptual errors from the elites or the citizens.

Heywood and Rose (2014) have provided a detailed and excellent review of the measurement of corruption and conclude that our understanding of how best to measure corruption is "close but no cigar". The large problems encountered in compiling the present data make us wonder if we are even close to completing the indispensable mission of providing an accurate measure of corruption. Theoretically, public attitudes towards corruption, such as tolerance of corruption, vary across different groups among different societies, and consequently, affect the definition of corruption and influence the perception of the seriousness of corruption. Lambsdorff (2006a, 2006b) similarly points out that a high perception of corruption might not accurately represent the reality of corruption but rather reflect the respondents' high standard of ethics. This is an important conceptualization in the study of corruption but it has not received adequate theoretical and empirical attention, and until recently few studies have empirically examined the important concept of corruption tolerance (Truex 2011; Gong and Wang 2013; Gong et al. 2015).

In the future, academia should devote more resources on the study of attitudes toward corruption, especially corruption tolerance. As León et al. (2013: 977) note "respondents to corruption perception questions utilize different response scales in their answers, i.e. for identical levels of corruption practices, subjects from one country could answer a different level of corruption perception than subjects from another country, based on socioeconomic characteristics". The tolerance of corruption should be one of the important factors which affect the respondents' response scales. By taking into account respondents' attitudes toward corruption to correct response scale differences, we will then be able to avoid the misuse and abuse of perception-based measures in cross-country comparative studies.

Notes

1 This study does not use TI's GCB because it is not suitable for cross-country comparison.
2 Indeed, the effectiveness of the 2005 anti-corruption reform in Vietnam is questionable. In Chapter 10, Rand and Tarp indicate that the previously observed decline in corruption in Vietnam after the 2005 anti-corruption reform has not been sustained.
3 By the same token, a 34.1 per cent of missing responses for China in Table 16.2 makes the validity and reliability of the data quite questionable.
4 The CPI is a lagged index, which used data from the previous two years to calculate a country or territory's annual corruption perception score. To correct for this lag, this study calculates a

comparable CPI value which uses the average of a country or territory's CPI standardized scores for the two years immediately following its ABS implementation year. The formula for computing z-scores is $z = \dfrac{X_i - \mu}{\sigma}$, where μ is the mean and σ is the standard deviation.

5 The formula of Perception Gap Index is $d = \dfrac{|ax + by + c|}{\sqrt{a^2 + b^2}}$. In the case of the 45-degree diagonnal where $X - Y = 0$, $a = 1$, $b = -1$, and $c = 0$. Using Vietnam as an example, $x = -1.41$, $y = 0.81$, the PGI is caculated as the following: $d = \dfrac{|1 \star -1.41 + (-1) \star (0.81) + 0|}{\sqrt{1^2 + (-1)^2}} = \dfrac{-2.22}{\sqrt{2}} = \dfrac{-2.22}{1.414} = \cdot 1.57$.

6 This 2010 corruption scandal opened a window of opportunity for anti-corruption reform in Taiwan, resulting in the birth of the Agency Against Corruption in 2011. However, its institutional design has some deficiencies and has still failed to restore trust in government (Ko et al. 2015).

References

Andersson, S. and P.M. Heywood (2009) "The politics of perception: use and abuse of Transparency International's approach to measuring corruption", *Political Studies*, 57(4): 746–767.

Caiden, G.E. (2001) "Corruption and governance", in G.E. Caiden, O. P. Dwivedi, and J. Jabbra (eds.) *Where corruption lives,* Bloomfield: Kumarian Press, 15–38.

Campbell, N. and S. Saha (2013) "Corruption, democracy and Asia-Pacific countries", *Journal of the Asia Pacific Economy*, 18(2): 290–303.

Canache, D. and M.E. Allison (2005) "Perceptions of political corruption in Latin American democracies", *Latin American Politics and Society*, 47(3): 91–111.

Chang, E.C.C. (2013) "A comparative analysis of how corruption erodes institutional trust", *Taiwan Journal of Democracy*, 9(1): 73–92.

Chang, E. C.C. and Y.H. Chu (2006) "Corruption and trust: exceptionalism in Asian democracies", *The Journal of Politics*, 68(2): 259–271.

Fritzen, S. (2005) "Beyond 'political will': how institutional context shapes the implementation of anti-corruption policies", *Policy and Society*, 24(3): 79–96.

Gong, T. and S. Wang (2013) "Indicators and implications of zero tolerance of corruption: the case of Hong Kong", *Social Indicators Research*, 112(3): 569–586.

Gong, T., S. Wang and J. Ren (2015) "Corruption in the eye of the beholder: survey evidence from mainland China and Hong Kong", *International Public Management Journal*, 18(3): 458–482.

Hawken, A. and G.L. Munck (2011) "Does the evaluator make a difference? Measurement validity in corruption research", *Political Concepts*, Committee on Concepts and Methods: working papers series.

Heywood, P. M. and J. Rose (2014) "'Close but no cigar': the measurement of corruption", *Journal of Public Policy*, 34(3): 507–529.

Hilgartner, S. and C.L. Bosk (1988) "The rise and fall of social problems: a public arenas model", *American Journal of Sociology*, 94 (1): 53–78.

Kaufmann, D., A. Kraay and M. Mastruzzi (2010) "The worldwide governance indicators: methodology and analytical issues", World Bank Policy Research Working Paper No. 5430.

Ko, K. and A. Samajdar (2010) "Evaluation of international corruption indexes: should we believe them or not", *The Social Science Journal*, 47(3): 508–540.

Ko, E. C., Y. Su and C. Yu (2015) "Sibling rivalry among anti-corruption agencies in Taiwan: is redundancy doomed to fail?" *Asian Education and Development Studies*, 4(1): 101–124.

Lambsdorff, J.G. (2006a) "Causes and consequences of corruption: what do we know from a cross-section of countries", in S. Rose-Ackerman (ed.) *International handbook on the economics of corruption*, Cheltenham: Edward Elgar, 3–51.

Lambsdorff, J.G. (2006b) "Measuring corruption: validity and precision of subjective indicators (CPI)", in C. Sampford, A. Shacklock, C. Connors and F. Galtung (eds.) *Measuring corruption*, Aldershot: Ashgate, 81–100.

León, C. J., J.E. Araña and J. de León (2013) "Correcting for scale perception bias in measuring corruption: an application to Chile and Spain", *Social Indicators Research*, 114(3): 977–995.

Li, H., M. Tang and N. Huhe (2016) "How does democracy influence citizens' perceptions of government corruption? A cross-national study", *Democratization*, 23(5): 892–981.

Lin, M.W. and C. Yu (2014) "Can corruption be measured? Comparing global versus local perceptions of corruption in East and Southeast Asia", *Journal of Comparative Policy Analysis: Research and Practice*, 16(2): 140–157.

Luong, H.V. (2006) "Vietnam in 2005: economic momentum and stronger state-society dialogue", *Asian Survey*, 46(1): 148–154.

Mishler, W. and R. Rose (2008) "Seeing is not always believing: measuring corruption perceptions and experiences", Paper prepared for the Elections, Public Opinion and Parties 2008 Annual Conference, 12–14 September, 2008, University of Manchester, United Kingdom.

Quah, J.S.T. (2011) *Curbing corruption in Asian countries: an impossible dream?* Bingley: Emerald.

Quah, J.S.T. (2015) "Hunting the corrupt 'tigers' and 'flies' in China: an evaluation of Xi Jinping's anti-corruption campaign, (November 2012-March 2015)", Maryland Series in Contemporary Asian Studies (MSCAS).

Razafindrakoto, M. and F. Roubaud (2010) "Are international databases on corruption reliable? A comparison of expert opinion surveys and household surveys in Sub-Saharan Africa", *World Development*, 38(8): 1057–1069.

Rose, J. (2015) "Corruption and the problem of perception", in P. Heywood (ed.), *Routledge handbook of political corruption*, New York: Routledge, 172–182.

Schlomer, G.L., S. Bauman and N.A. Card (2010) "Best practices for missing data management in counseling psychology", *Journal of Counseling Psychology*, 57(1): 1–10.

Surowiecki, J. (2004) *The wisdom of crowds: why the many are smarter than the few and how collective wisdom shapes business, economies, societies, and nations*, New York: Doubleday.

Svensson, J. (2005) "Eight questions about corruption", *Journal of Economic Perspectives*, 19(3): 19–42.

Tetlock, P.E. (2005) *Expert political judgment: how good is it? How can we know?* Princeton: Princeton University Press.

TI (Transparency International) (2010) *Global Corruption Barometer 2010*, Available at www.transparency.org (accessed 31 March 2016).

Truex, R. (2011) "Corruption, attitudes, and education: survey evidence from Nepal", *World Development*, 39(7): 1133–1142.

Wedeman, A. (2012) *Double paradox: rapid growth and rising corruption in China,* Ithaca: Cornell University Press.

Wroe, A., N. Allen and S. Birch (2013) "The role of political trust in conditioning perceptions of corruption", *European Political Science Review*, 5(2): 175–195.

Yu, C. (2007) "Reinventing government in Taiwan: public opinion research findings", in G.E. Caiden and T.T. Su (eds.) *The repositioning of public governance: global experience and challenges*, Taipei: Best-Wise Publishing Co., Ltd., 347–368.

Yu, C., C.M. Chen, W.J. Juang and L.T. Hu (2008) "Does democracy breed integrity? Corruption in Taiwan during the democratic transformation period", *Crime, Law and Social Change*, 49(3): 167–184.

Yu, C., C.M. Chen and M.W. Lin (2013) "Corruption perception in Taiwan: reflections upon a bottom-up citizen perspective", *Journal of Contemporary China*, 22(79): 56–76.

PART IV

Controlling corruption: Strategies, successes and failures

17

CONTROLLING CORRUPTION IN ASIAN COUNTRIES

The Elusive Search for Success

Jon S.T. Quah

Introduction

In October 1952, the Corrupt Practices Investigation Bureau (CPIB) was established in Singapore (Quah 2011: 209) and on 25 February 2014, the Anti-Corruption Commission (ACC) of Myanmar was launched by President Thein Sein (Ko 2014). During this 62-year period, 29 anti-corruption agencies (ACAs) were formed in 23 Asian countries to tackle the scourge of corruption. However, an analysis of the performance of Asian countries in 2014 on Transparency International's Corruption Perceptions Index (CPI) and the World Bank's Control of Corruption governance indicator in Table 17.1 shows that corruption remains a serious problem in most of these countries with the three exceptions of Singapore, Japan and the Hong Kong SAR.

Why is success in controlling corruption in Asian countries so elusive? This chapter addresses this question by evaluating in the next section the effectiveness of these countries in curbing corruption according to their perceived extent of corruption, the political will of their governments, and the public perceptions of their ACAs' performance. The third section explains why most Asian ACAs are ineffective. The fourth section analyses the top-down approach of relying on ACAs and two bottom-up anti-corruption efforts. The fifth section compares the compliance and integrity strategies and shows that the compliance approach is gradually being supplemented by the integrity approach in some Asian countries. The chapter concludes with some suggestions for enhancing anti-corruption efforts in Asian countries.

Success and failure in corruption control

Caiden (2013: 203) defines success in combating corruption as "achieving the minimal level of how they define corruption, reducing wrongdoing and evil, pursuing the corrupt, encouraging exposure, warning possible victims, shaming offenders, and advocating and adopting anti-corruption reforms". For this chapter, three criteria are used to assess success or failure in combating corruption in Asian countries. First, their perceived extent of corruption is ascertained according to six indicators: CPI's 2014 rank and score; control of corruption indicator in 2014; and four indicators from *The Global Competitiveness Report*

2014–2015: diversion of public funds; irregular payments and bribes; organized crime; and ethical behaviour of firms (Schwab 2014: 408, 410, 420, 422). Second, the political will of their governments in curbing corruption is assessed according to the staff-population ratios and per capita expenditures of their ACAs. Third, the public perceptions of their ACAs' performance in combating corruption are used to evaluate the success of Asian countries in combating corruption.

Perceived extent of corruption

Johnston (2001: 158) observes that corruption is difficult to measure because it is "hidden" with few direct witnesses who are themselves interested in "keeping it secret". As it is impossible to measure the actual extent of corruption in a country, scholars rely on surveys on the perceptions of citizens and their attitudes toward corruption to assess their perceived extent of corruption in the country. The CPI is the most well-known and cited "poll of polls", but it has several limitations (Ko and Samajdar 2010). Accordingly, instead of relying only on the CPI, five other indicators are used to ascertain the perceived extent of 22 Asian countries in 2014 in Table 17.1. What is important is whether these countries have performed consistently on all the six indicators rather than on the CPI only. Table 17.1 confirms that Singapore is consistently ranked first on all six indicators, followed by Hong Kong and Japan. At the other extreme, Myanmar is perceived to be the most corrupt Asian country according to the six indicators, followed by Bangladesh and Cambodia.

Political will in combating corruption

Brinkerhoff (2000: 242) defines political will as "the commitment of actors to undertake actions to achieve a set of objectives – in this case, anti-corruption policies and programmes – and to sustain the costs of those actions over time". There are five indicators of political will: (1) comprehensive anti-corruption legislation; (2) the ACAs are provided with adequate personnel, budget, and operational autonomy to perform their functions effectively; (3) the anti-corruption laws are enforced impartially, regardless of the offender's position, status, or political affiliation, without political interference; (4) the government avoids using corruption as a weapon against its political opponents; and (5) anti-corruption efforts are sustained and their impact monitored by the government (Quah 2015a: 13).

Political will is needed for effective corruption control for three reasons. First, combating corruption is expensive because the ACAs need sufficient personnel and budget to enforce the anti-corruption laws impartially. Without political will, the ACAs will not be provided with these prerequisites because "the principal people who can change a culture of corruption if they wish to do so are politicians" as they "make the laws and allocate the funds that enable the laws to be enforced" (Senior 2006: 184, 187). The second reason is that corrupt individuals and organizations are powerful and have vested interests to circumvent the anti-corruption laws to avoid arrest and conviction for their offences. Third, fighting corruption is difficult and complex because it is necessary to identify the causes of corruption and to recommend appropriate measures to address these causes over a sustained period of time. Often, governments fail to conduct this analysis.

To assess whether the governments in Asian countries have provided their ACAs with adequate personnel and budgets to perform their functions effectively, data on the number of their personnel and budgets for a selected year are used to calculate their per capita expenditure (by dividing the ACA's budget in US dollars by the population for the same year) and their staff-population ratio (the ratio of the country's population to the number of ACA

Table 17.1 Perceived extent of corruption in 22 Asian countries, 2014

Country[1]	Corruption Perceptions Index 2014	Control of corruption 2014	Diversion of public funds 2014[2]	Irregular payments and bribes 2014[3]	Organized crime 2014[4]	Ethical behaviour of firms 2014[5]
Singapore	7th (84)	97.10	6th (6.1)	3rd (6.5)	4th (6.6)	3rd (6.2)
Japan	15th (76)	93.27	14th (5.6)	11th (6.2)	52nd (5.2)	7th (6.0)
Hong Kong	17th (74)	92.30	10th (5.8)	12th (6.2)	25th (5.8)	18th (5.5)
Bhutan	30th (65)	88.46	29th (4.6)	39th (4.8)	16th (6.1)	38th (4.5)
Taiwan	35th (61)	77.40	34th (4.4)	31st (5.2)	28th (5.8)	29th (4.9)
South Korea	43rd (55)	69.71	67th (3.3)	52nd (4.4)	93rd (4.3)	95th (3.7)
Malaysia	50th (52)	68.27	26th (4.8)	37th (4.9)	51st (5.2)	23rd (5.3)
Mongolia	80th (39)	38.46	103rd (2.7)	82nd (3.7)	72nd (4.7)	91st (3.7)
India	85th (38)	38.94	60th (3.4)	93rd (3.5)	114th (4.0)	88th (3.8)
Philippines	85th (38)	39.90	78th (3.1)	86th (3.6)	69th (4.7)	49th (4.3)
Sri Lanka	85th (38)	46.63	85th (3.0)	91st (3.5)	67th (4.8)	82nd (3.8)
Thailand	85th (38)	42.31	108th (2.6)	84th (3.7)	89th (4.5)	92nd (3.7)
China	100th (36)	47.12	45th (3.9)	66th (4.0)	70th (4.7)	55th (4.2)
Indonesia	107th (34)	34.13	63rd (3.4)	87th (3.6)	102nd (4.2)	47th (4.3)
Vietnam	119th (31)	37.50	76th (3.2)	109th (3.2)	78th (4.6)	109th (3.6)
Nepal	126th (29)	36.06	92nd (2.8)	119th (2.9)	129th (3.5)	128th (3.3)
Pakistan	126th (29)	21.60	94th (2.8)	123rd (2.9)	137th (3.0)	111th (3.5)
Timor-Leste	133rd (28)	29.33	75th (3.2)	111th (3.1)	98th (4.3)	114th (3.5)
Bangladesh	145th (25)	18.75	106th (2.6)	140th (2.3)	97th (4.3)	140th (2.9)
Lao PDR	145th (25)	25.00	59th (3.4)	96th (3.4)	71st (4.7)	65th (4.0)
Cambodia	156th (21)	12.50	113th (2.6)	129th (2.8)	86th (4.5)	89th (3.8)
Myanmar	156th (21)	17.30	122nd (2.4)	139th (2.3)	136th (3.1)	133rd (3.2)

Sources: Transparency International (2014); World Bank (2015); and Schwab (2014: 408, 410, 420, 422).
Notes: [1] Papua New Guinea, Afghanistan and North Korea are excluded in the *Global Competitiveness Report's* four indicators and are not included here.
[2] *The score is calculated from the respondents' answers to this question*: "In your country, how common is diversion of public funds to companies, individuals, or groups due to corruption?" The score ranges from 1 (very commonly occurs) to 7 (never occurs).
[3] *The score is calculated from the respondents' answers to this question*: "In your country, how common is it for firms to make undocumented extra payments or bribes in connection with (a) imports and exports; (b) public utilities; (c) annual tax payments; (d) awarding of public contracts and licenses; (e) obtaining favourable judicial decisions?" The score ranges from 1 (very common) to 7 (never occurs).
[4] *The score is calculated from the respondents' answers to this question*: "In your country, to what extent does organised crime (mafia-oriented racketeering, extortion) impose costs on businesses?" The score ranges from 1 (to a great extent) to 7 (not at all).
[5] *The score is calculated from the respondents' answers to this question*: "In your country, how would you rate the corporate ethics of companies (ethical behaviour in interactions with public officials, politicians, and other firms)?" The score ranges from 1 (extremely poor—among the worst in the world) to 7 (excellent—among the best in the world).

personnel for the same year) (Quah 2009: 182). To illustrate the differences in political will in combating corruption in nine Asian countries, Table 17.2 provides data on the per capita expenditures and staff-population ratios of nine ACAs[1] in 2012.

Of these selected ACAs, six are single ACAs: the Independent Commission Against Corruption (ICAC) in Hong Kong, SAR; the Corrupt Practices Investigation Bureau (CPIB) in

Singapore; the Malaysian Anti-Corruption Commission (MACC) in Malaysia; the ACC in Bhutan; the National Anti-Corruption Commission in Thailand; and the *Komisi Pemberantasan Korupsi* (KPK) or Corruption Eradication Commission in Indonesia. The other three ACAs are selected from those countries which rely on more than one ACA: the Central Bureau of Investigation (CBI) in India; the Office of the Ombudsman (OMB) in the Philippines; and the Agency Against Corruption (AAC) in Taiwan. Table 17.2 shows that the per capita expenditures and staff population ratios of the ICAC, CPIB, MACC, and ACC are better than those of the AAC, NACC, OMB, KPK, and CBI.

Public perceptions of ACAs' performance

As Singapore has a low incidence of corruption and a government committed to minimising corruption, it is not surprising that the public perceptions of the CPIB's performance are also favourable. The CPIB commissioned Forbes Research to conduct a public perceptions survey of 1,000 respondents of Singapore citizens between 16 and 60 years old in October 2002. This survey found that 13 per cent of the respondents rated corruption control in Singapore as excellent, 41 per cent as very good, 39 per cent as good, and only 7 per cent as fair. Furthermore, 71 per cent of them agreed or strongly agreed that the CPIB had done well in solving corruption offences. It was also found that 61 per cent of the respondents trusted the CPIB to keep Singapore corruption free and 56 per cent of them agreed or strongly agreed that the CPIB was world class in curbing corruption (CPIB 2003). Similarly, the 2013 public perceptions survey of 1,016 Singaporeans found that: (1) 90 per cent of the respondents

Table 17.2 Budgets and personnel of nine Asian ACAs, 2012

ACA	Budget	Personnel	Population	Per capita expenditure	Staff population ratio
ICAC Hong Kong	US$112.96 million	1,282	7.1 million	US$15.91	1: 5,538
CPIB Singapore	US$20.8 million	138	5.2 million	US$4.00	1: 37,681
MACC Malaysia	US$80.55 million	2,705	28.9 million	US$2.79	1: 10,684
ACC Bhutan	US$1.84 million	74	720,679	US$2.55	1: 9,739
AAC Taiwan	US$12.5 million	179	23.2 million	US$0.54	1: 129,609
NACC Thailand	US$35.45 million	965[1]	69.5 million	US$0.51	1: 72,021
OMB Philippines	US$35.88 million	1,222	94.9 million	US$0.38	1: 77,660
KPK Indonesia	US$35.72 million	667	242.3 million	US$0.15	1: 363,268
CBI India	US$72.41 million	5,755	1,241.5 million	US$0.06	1: 215,725

Sources: AAC (2013); ACC (2013: 20); Bureau of the Budget (2012: 82); CBI (2013); ICAC (2012, 2013); KPK (2013: 13, 54); MACC (2013); OMB (2013); Ministry of Finance, Bhutan (2012: 65); National Statistical Bureau (2012); Republic of Singapore (2014: 359); Schwab (2013: 405).
Note: [1] 2009 figure.

believed that Singapore was much better or better than most countries in the world in controlling corruption; (2) 72 per cent of them strongly agreed or agreed that the CPIB had done well in solving corruption cases; and (3) 77 per cent of the respondents indicated that the CPIB was effective in maintaining a low level of corruption in Singapore.[2]

Hong Kong's ICAC established the Community Relations Department in 1975, a year after its formation in February 1974. The ICAC found that there was widespread public awareness of its role because its 1977 survey, and every subsequent survey, found that almost everyone in Hong Kong had heard of the ICAC (Scott 2013a: 87). A recent analysis of the answers to the question: "How effective is the ICAC's work?" in the ICAC's annual surveys from 1997 through 2011 by Scott (2013a: 91) found that between 60.2 to 87.8 per cent of the respondents said that the ICAC was very effective or quite effective in its work. The ICAC's 2013 annual survey found that 95.3 per cent of the respondents said that the ICAC deserved their support, and 79.7 per cent of them believed that the ICAC's anti-corruption work was effective (ICAC 2014: 69).

Unlike the CPIB and ICAC, Mongolia's Independent Authority Against Corruption (IAAC) is less effective in curbing corruption as reflected in the public perceptions of its performance in fighting corruption in eight surveys conducted between March 2010 and April 2015. Table 17.3 indicates that the proportion of respondents with "good" or "very good" perceptions of the IAAC's performance has increased from 7.8 to 16.5 per cent during the period. On the other hand, the percentage of respondents with a negative evaluation of the IAAC's performance has declined from 62.4 to 45.5 per cent during the same period. Similarly, the Mongolian respondents' negative assessment of the IAAC as an impartial law enforcement agency is reflected in the finding that an average of 72.9 per cent of them believe that the IAAC is not an impartial law enforcement agency (Asia Foundation and Sant-Maral Foundation 2015: 25).

The final example is the public perceptions of the OMB's net sincerity in curbing corruption. The survey of the perceptions of the executives of enterprises on corruption in the Philippines conducted by the Social Weather Stations (SWS) since 2000 includes a question which asks the respondents to evaluate 30 public agencies in terms of their sincerity or insincerity in fighting corruption. The net sincerity rating is the difference between the percentage of respondents rating an agency as very or somewhat sincere and the percentage of respondents rating an agency as very or somewhat insincere (SWS 2007: 12). It can be seen from Table 17.4 that the OMB's net sincerity rating in fighting corruption has declined considerably from +22 per cent in 2005 to -8 per cent in 2009. Its net sincerity rating increased to +39 per cent, its best rating, in 2012, but dropped slightly to +36 per cent in 2014/2015.

Table 17.3 Public perceptions of IAAC's performance in fighting corruption, March 2010-April 2015

Response	March 2010	September 2010	April 2011	November 2012	March 2013	September 2013	March 2014	April 2015
Very good	1.0%	0.3%	1.2%	1.1%	0.9%	1.7%	1.7%	2.1%
Good	6.8%	7.7%	7.9%	14.5%	19.4%	27.7%	20.9%	14.4%
Not good, not bad	29.8%	38.4%	33.6%	38.7%	42.0%	38.4%	40.1%	38.0%
Bad	39.3%	32.5%	32.5%	25.8%	26.8%	24.4%	25.8%	30.3%
Very bad	23.1%	21.0%	24.4%	19.9%	10.9%	7.7%	11.5%	15.2%

Source: Asia Foundation and Sant-Maral Foundation (2015: 24).

Table 17.4 Net sincerity rating of the OMB in fighting corruption, 2005 to 2014/2015

Year	Net sincerity rating
2005	+22% (Moderate)
2006	+5% (Neutral)
2007	+9% (Neutral)
2008	+4% (Neutral)
2009	-8% (Neutral)
2012	+39% (Good)
2013	+23% (Moderate)
2014/2015	+36% (Good)

Sources: SWS (2015, 2010).
Note: The SWS did not conduct surveys in 2010 and 2011. The ratings range from Excellent (+70 and above), Very good (+50 to +69), Good (+30 to +49), Moderate (+10 to +29), Neutral (+9 to −9), Poor (−10 to −29), Bad (−30 to −49), Very bad (−50 to −69) and Execrable (−70 and below).

The performance of Singapore, Hong Kong SAR, Taiwan, Malaysia, Bhutan, Thailand, Philippines, India, and Indonesia in curbing corruption according to the eight indicators is summarised in Table 17.5. Based on their performance on these eight indicators, Singapore is ranked first, followed by Hong Kong SAR, Bhutan, Malaysia, Taiwan, Thailand, Philippines, India, and Indonesia.

Why many Asian ACAs are ineffective

The success of Singapore's CPIB and Hong Kong's ICAC has promoted the belief that ACAs are effective in combating corruption (UNDP 2011: 8) and resulted in the proliferation of many ACAs in Asia. However, in reality, the performance of many Asian ACAs has been disappointing because of the weak political will of their governments, which is reflected in their inadequate legal powers, limited budgets, lack of trained personnel, and lack of independence. The obstacles faced by Asian ACAs are illustrated by referring to the experiences of the CBI in India, the OMB in the Philippines, and the KPK in Indonesia.

India's CBI

The CBI was established as the lead ACA in India in April 1963 by incorporating the Delhi Special Police Establishment (DSPE) as the Investigation and Anti-Corruption Division (Quah 2008: 246). However, the CBI is not an effective ACA for four reasons. First, unlike the CPIB and ICAC, which are dedicated ACAs focusing only on curbing corruption, the CBI is responsible for performing both anti-corruption and non-corruption-related functions. The CBI's three core functions identified in its vision statement are: "combating corruption in public life, curb economic and violent crimes through meticulous investigation and prosecution", "help fight cyber and high-technology crime" and "play a lead role in the war against national and transnational organised crime" (CBI 2010: iv).

Among the CBI's three investigation divisions, the Anti-Corruption Division deals with corruption by civil servants, the Economic Offences Division focuses on economic crimes, and the Special Crimes Division is responsible for cases of terrorism, bomb blasts, sensational homicides, kidnapping for ransom, and organized crime. In 2014, 839 cases (71.5 per cent) were registered with the Anti-Corruption Division, followed by 169 cases (14.4 per cent)

Table 17.5 Performance of nine Asian countries on eight indicators, 2012 and 2014

Country	CPI score 2014	Control of corruption 2014	Diversion of public funds 2014	Irregular payments and bribes 2014	Organized crime 2014	Ethical behaviour of firms 2014	ACA per capita expenditure 2012	ACA staff population ratio 2012	Overall ranking
Singapore	84(1st)	97.12 (1st)	6th (1st)	3rd (1st)	4th (1st)	3rd (1st)	US$4.00 (2nd)	1:37,681(4th)	1st
Hong Kong	74 (2nd)	92.30 (2nd)	10th (2nd)	12th (2nd)	25th (3rd)	18th (2nd)	US$15.91 (1st)	1:5,538 (1st)	2nd
Bhutan	65 (3rd)	88.46 (3rd)	29th (4th)	39th (5th)	16th (2nd)	38th (5th)	US$2.55 (4th)	1:9,739 (2nd)	3rd
Taiwan	61 (4th)	77.40 (4th)	34th (5th)	31st (3rd)	28th (4th)	29th (4th)	US$0.54 (5th)	1:129,609 (7th)	5th
Malaysia	52 (5th)	68.27 (5th)	26th (3rd)	37th (4th)	51st (5th)	23rd (3rd)	US$2.79 (3rd)	1:10,684 (3rd)	4th
Thailand	38 (6th)	42.31 (6th)	108th (9th)	84th (6th)	89th (7th)	92nd (9th)	US$0.51 (6th)	1: 72,021 (5th)	6th
Philippines	38 (6th)	39.90 (7th)	78th (8th)	86th (7th)	69th (6th)	49th (7th)	US$0.38 (7th)	1:77,660 (6th)	7th
India	38 (6th)	38.94 (8th)	60th (6th)	93rd (9th)	114th (9th)	88th (8th)	US$0.06 (9th)	1:215,725 (8th)	8th
Indonesia	34 (9th)	34.13 (9th)	63rd (7th)	87th (8th)	102nd (8th)	47th (6th)	US$0.15 (8th)	1:363,268 (9th)	9th

Sources: As in Tables 17.1 and 17.2.

with the Economic Offences Division, and 166 cases (14.1 per cent) with the Special Crimes Division (CBI 2015: 8, 27).

The second reason for the CBI's ineffectiveness is the continued reliance by the Government of India (GOI) on the flawed British colonial government's method of using the police to curb corruption when police corruption is rampant. Maurice Punch (2009: 245) contends that the "golden rule" is that "the police cannot and should not be responsible for investigating their own deviance and crimes". The CBI's role is to investigate crimes handled by the DSPE and derives its investigating powers from the DSPE Act of 1946. This means that the CBI is a police agency of the central government and can only operate at the state level with the consent of the state government (Quah 2011: 97).

Police corruption is widespread in India as the *Global Corruption Barometer 2013* has confirmed that the police are the second most corrupt institution after political parties (TI 2013: 36). The success of Singapore and Hong Kong in combating corruption can be attributed to their rejection of the British colonial government's method of using the police to curb corruption and their reliance instead on the CPIB and ICAC, respectively. Singapore has taken 15 years (1937–1952) and Hong Kong has taken 26 years (1948–1974) to learn this important lesson: do not rely on the police to curb corruption because this means "giving candy to a child, expecting that it would not be eaten" (Quah 2004: 1–2). In view of this, it is surprising that the GOI has continued to rely on the CBI and DSPE for the past 75 years, even though the police are corrupt and ineffective in curbing corruption in India.

The third reason why the CBI is ineffective is that it has not been provided with an adequate budget and sufficient personnel by the GOI. Table 17.2 shows that the CBI has the lowest per capita expenditure of US$0.06 and the second least favourable staff-population ratio of 1:215,725 among nine Asian ACAs in 2012. The CBI's staff shortage is reflected in the increase in the number of vacant positions from 831 (12.6 per cent) in 2012 to 878 (13.2 per cent) in 2013 and to 1,000 (15 per cent) in 2014 (CBI 2015: 84). The decrease in the CBI's personnel from 5,755 to 5,676 from 2012–2014 and the reduction of its budget from US$72.4 million to US$65.5 million during the same period have resulted in the reduction of its per capita expenditure to US$0.05 and increase in its staff-population ratio to 1: 228,206 in 2014 (CBI 2015: 84, 94). According to B.R. Lall (2007: 230–231), the CBI is "a very small organization as compared to the quantum of crimes committed in the country".

Finally, apart from the government's inadequate allocation of budget and personnel to the CBI, the other manifestation of the GOI's lack of political will in curbing corruption is the public perception that the CBI is not independent and viewed as "a pliable tool of the ruling party, and its investigations tend to become cover-up operations for the misdeeds of ministers" (Gill 1998: 238). Similarly, a former senior civil servant, Madhav Godbole (2000: 88) criticised the CBI for being used as "an instrument of persecution" by the late Prime Minister Indira Gandhi, and for its "disgraceful" record of investigating corruption cases "involving the high, the mighty and the powerful". In the same vein, Gill (1998: 238) has accused the CBI of going "only after the small fry" as only one gazetted officer was dismissed in 1972 and two officers in 1992.

The Philippines' OMB

The Philippines relies on five ACAs[3]. The lead ACA, the OMB or *Tanodbayan*, was originally established by President Ferdinand Marcos on 18 July 1979 and reorganized by President Corazon Aquino in May 1988. Like the CBI, the OMB is also not a dedicated ACA because it performs these five functions: (1) investigation of anomalies and inefficiency;

(2) prosecution of graft cases in the *Sandiganbayan* (Special Anti-Graft Court); (3) administrative adjudication through disciplinary control over all elective and appointed officials except for members of the Congress and Judiciary and impeachable officials; (4) provision of public assistance by requiring public officials and employees to assist the public; and (5) graft prevention by analysing anti-corruption measures and increasing public awareness and cooperation (OMB 2009: 7–8).

An analysis of the OMB's 2012 budget by function shows that 24 per cent were allocated for preliminary investigations, followed by prosecution (21 per cent), investigation (18 per cent), corruption prevention (13 per cent), administrative adjudication (15 per cent), and public assistance (9 per cent) (OMB 2013: 28). This means that 76 per cent of the OMB's 2012 budget was devoted to combating corruption with the remaining 24 per cent allocated for the non-corruption-related functions of administrative adjudication and public assistance.

Apart from being saddled with both corruption and non-corruption-related functions, the OMB's second limitation is its limited budget and inadequate personnel, which is reflected in its per capita expenditure of US$0.38 and staff-population ratio of 1:77,660 in 2012 (see Table 17.2). According to Simeon V. Marcelo (2005: 1), a former Ombudsman, the OMB is "designed to fail because of its crippling lack of resources". He compared the OMB's personnel and budget with those of Hong Kong's ICAC in 2004 and found that the OMB's field investigator-bureaucracy ratio of 1:17045 compared unfavourably with the ICAC's ratio of 1:208. Furthermore, the OMB's staff-population ratio of 1:71,340 was much higher than the ICAC's ratio of 1:5,354. In terms of per capita expenditure, the ICAC's figure of 696 pesos exceeded that of the OMB's 6 pesos by 116 times (Marcelo 2005: 3). In 2013, the OMB's 1,211 personnel constituted only 55.1 per cent of its approved number of 2,195 positions. This means that the OMB was severely under-staffed with 985 vacant positions (OMB 2014: 26).

The OMB's third weakness is its weak leadership. Impeachment complaints were filed thrice in 1996, 2001, and 2002 against Ombudsman Aniano Desierto during his seven-year term (1995–2002) for betraying the public trust. Even though these complaints against Desierto were dismissed by congressmen, these impeachment cases had "sullied the already unsavoury reputation of the Ombudsman" (Coronel and Kalaw-Tirol 2002: 261–262). More recently, the OMB was described as "the Street Ombudsman" because the Ombudsman Merceditas N. Gutierrez was criticised for devoting its limited resources to investigating petty corruption instead of continuing her predecessor's exposure of grand corruption (*Newsbreak Online* 2006). As the former classmate of the First Gentleman, Michael Arroyo, Ombudsman Gutierrez was criticised for protecting the interests of President Gloria Arroyo, her husband, friends and political allies. Two hundred and twelve congressmen voted to impeach Gutierrez on 22 March 2011 for protecting former President Arroyo by not investigating allegations against her (Gomez 2011). Gutierrez resigned on 29 April and left her position as Ombudsman on 5 May 2011 (Cayabyab 2011).

Finally, instead of cooperation among the many ACAs in the Philippines, there is "duplication, layering and turf wars" (Quimson 2006: 30) and lack of coordination among them because of their competition for recognition, personnel and resources (Quah 2011: 145). These ACAs have overlapping jurisdictions, which diffuses anti-corruption efforts, and results in "poor coordination in policy and programme implementation, weak management and wastage of resources" (Oyamada 2005: 99). The Inter-Agency Anti-Graft Coordinating Council (IACC) was formed in June 1997 to enhance coordination among the several ACAs. However, Ombudsman Gutierrez "deactivated" the IACC by not convening it. The OMB also competed with the Civil Service Commission (CSC) by implementing the Oplan Red Plate programme, which was agreed by the IACC to be the CSC's responsibility (Quah 2011: 146).

Indonesia's KPK

The KPK was formed on 29 December 2003 according to Law No. 30 of 2002, which was passed in December 2002 (KPK 2009: 14). Unlike the CBI and OMB, the KPK is a dedicated ACA and performs these five functions: (1) coordinating with other state agencies to curb corruption; (2) supervising those state agencies authorised to combat corruption; (3) performing investigations, indictments and prosecutions of corruption cases; (4) preventing corruption by examining wealth and gratification reports, conducting anti-corruption education and socialisation programmes, and engaging in bilateral and multilateral cooperation to curb corruption; and (5) monitoring the administration of state agencies and making recommendations for making these agencies more corruption-resistant (Davidsen et al. 2006: 48).

In his comparison of the performance of the KPK and OMB, Emil Bolongaita (2010: 9) found that the KPK was more effective than the OMB even though the latter was an older agency with more personnel. He has attributed the KPK's effectiveness to its wider jurisdiction, investigative powers, consultation between investigators and prosecutors in preparing cases for prosecution, selective recruitment of qualified and experienced investigators and prosecutors, and the support provided by President Sushilo Bambang Yudhoyono and the public (Bolongaita 2010: 13–20).

Emily Hartwell (2009: 32–33) has also praised the KPK's strong record because of its high conviction rate since 2006. The KPK's effectiveness is also reflected in Indonesia's improvement in its percentile rank for the World Bank's Control of Corruption indicator from 17.07 in 2004 to 34.13 in 2014 (World Bank 2015). In 2008, a survey found that 82.11 per cent of the respondents identified the KPK as the most trustworthy law enforcement agency because of its "independent, courageous, and all-powerful anti-corruption activities" (Choi 2011: 49; see also Ch. 4).

However, in spite of the KPK's "strong start in addressing impunity for corruption", Hartwell (2009: 33–35) has identified four weaknesses: (1) it has not compelled civil servants to submit asset disclosures or made these disclosures widely accessible to citizens; (2) it has pursued corruptors in high levels of government in the executive and legislative branches' at the expense of investigating the rampant corruption in the police and judiciary; (3) it has been careful in prosecuting "big fish" in the business community or presidential allies to avoid backlash and endangering its own survival; and (4) it has faced tremendous resistance in its anti-corruption activities from those being investigated, especially after it had named 25 senior politicians as graft suspects in 2010 and detained nineteen of them on 28 January 2011 (Saragih 2011).

In spite of the KPK's efforts, corruption remains a serious problem in Indonesia as it was ranked 107th among 175 countries with a score of 34 on Transparency International's CPI and a percentile rank of 34.13 on the World Bank's Control of Corruption indicator in 2014. The KPK's success in exposing corruption scandals has earned tremendous public support. However, for the KPK to sustain its effectiveness, it must be provided with more resources by the government because its per capita expenditure has only increased marginally from US$0.14 in 2008 (Quah 2011: 455) to US$0.15 (see Table 17.2).

In 2010, the Ministry of Finance approved a sum of US$24 million to build a new building to cater for the KPK's increased staff strength of 850 personnel. When its request to a parliamentary commission to release the approved funds was blocked by several Members of Parliament, the KPK resorted to a public funding drive in late June 2012 to finance the construction of the new building. The lack of parliamentary support for the KPK's activities is not surprising because more than 30 Members of Parliament were convicted by the KPK for bribery in 2004. Many persons contributed generously to the KPK's campaign for funds and the sum of US$35,000 was raised by early August 2012 (Nazeer 2012: A11; Schonhardt 2012; see also Ch. 4).

For its long-term survival and sustained effectiveness, the KPK has to neutralise the serious threats posed by its three enemies: the police, Attorney General's Office (AGO), and the "court or judicial mafia" (*mafia peradilan*). The KPK's conflict and competition with the police and the AGO resulted in the arrest in November 2009 of two senior KPK officials by the police allegedly for bribery. The arrest of these officials in the wake of the arrest of the KPK Chairman Antasari Azhar for murder in May 2009 was widely viewed as "an apparent high-level conspiracy" by the police and AGO to weaken the KPK (Osman 2009: A9; Onishi 2009: A10). Azhar's arrest was "a huge blow to the KPK" because it changed public opinion and gave the impression that the KPK was "doing business as usual" like the police, prosecutors, judges and prison guards (Harsono 2009).

Contrary to expectations, the problem of corruption further deteriorated during the post-Suharto period because of the lack of political will and the difficulties encountered in implementing the Anti-Corruption Law of 1999 by Presidents Habibie, Wahid, Megawati, and Yudhoyono. In his analysis of the obstacles to the implementation of the anti-corruption laws in Indonesia, Roby Brata (2014: 304) concludes that the "chronic, complex, and serious systemic corruption in the law enforcement agencies popularly known as *mafia peradilan* or court mafia [has] systematically, institutionally, and seriously disabled the institutional capacity and integrity of the enforcement agencies to effectively implement the Anti-Corruption Laws".

President Joko Widodo, popularly known as Jokowi, assumed office in October 2014 and has been criticised after his first year in office for not keeping his election promise of eradicating corruption (*Jakarta Post* 2015). Following the wisdom of the Indonesian proverb that one "cannot clean the dirty floor with a dirty broom", President Jokowi must unequivocally demonstrate his political will by taking immediate steps to eradicate the pernicious influence of the well-organized and powerful court mafia, which has undermined his anti-corruption efforts and those of his predecessors. This is an important but necessary step for ensuring the impartial implementation of the anti-corruption laws and the amelioration of the perceived extent of corruption in Indonesia.

Combating corruption: top-down and bottom-up approaches

In view of their contextual differences and the fact that the causes of corruption are country specific, Shah (2007: 236) cautions that "adopting one-size-fits-all approaches" to Asian countries which vary widely in the incidence of corruption and quality of governance will fail because "policy makers need to understand the local circumstances that encourage or permit public and private actors to be corrupt".

In *Tackling Corruption, Transforming Lives,* the United Nations Development Programme (2008: 152–155) recommends an agenda for action which combines both "crushing corruption from the top" with bottom-up anti-corruption initiatives by citizens, civil society organizations and the media. As corruption is a serious problem in many Asian countries, it is not surprising that their governments have initiated many anti-corruption measures, including anti-corruption laws and ACAs. Table 17.6 confirms the dominance of the top-down approach as nineteen Asian countries have adopted the second pattern of relying on a single ACA to implement the anti-corruption laws. By contrast, six countries rely on

Table 17.6 Patterns of corruption control in 27 Asian countries

Pattern	Features	Countries
1	Reliance on anti-corruption laws without an ACA	Japan, Papua New Guinea
2	Reliance on a single ACA to implement the anti-corruption laws	Singapore, Hong Kong SAR, Malaysia, Brunei Darussalam, Nepal, Sri Lanka, Maldives, Thailand, Macao SAR, South Korea, Afghanistan, Indonesia, Bangladesh, Lao PDR, Bhutan, Mongolia, Timor-Leste, Cambodia, Myanmar
3	Reliance on multiple ACAs to implement the anti-corruption laws	China, India, Pakistan, Philippines, Taiwan, Vietnam

Source: Compiled by the author.

multiple ACAs to implement the anti-corruption laws, while Japan and Papua New Guinea are the two countries which do not have an ACA. Japan relies on the Special Investigation Departments of the Public Prosecutor's Offices in Tokyo, Osaka and Nagoya to investigate bribery cases exposed by the police (Quah 2011: 64–65). Since 1975, Papua New Guinea has relied on the Ombudsman Commission to investigate complaints of maladministration and to enforce the Leadership Code; an Investigation Task Force Sweep was established in 2011 to investigate corruption in government departments (Quah 2016: 254).

Two recent innovations to combat corruption at the local level in India and Pakistan are briefly discussed here. First, the ipaidabribe.com website was launched on 15 August 2010 by Ramesh and Swati Ramanathan, the founders of the *Janaagraha* Centre for Citizenship and Democracy in Bangalore, India. Its aim is to "uncover the market price of corruption" in Indian cities by inviting individuals to report when they paid a bribe (including the place and amount), when they did not, and when they were not asked to pay a bribe. Their stories are shared online by completing a form, blogging about their experiences, or even posting a video. By collating the data on the bribes reported by citizens, the website quantifies the extent of petty corruption in various government departments and provides a snapshot of bribery trends in India. The data collected are useful for identifying the corrupt government agencies and for diagnosing problem areas in public service delivery. The information and publicity generated by the portal alerts the general public about the prevalence of bribery in public service delivery and educates them on how best to avoid paying bribes in requesting services from government agencies (OneWorld Foundation India 2013: 129).

By 12 May 2011, the website had attracted 450,180 visits from 197 countries with 61.3 per cent of the visits coming from 86 cities in India (OneWorld Foundation India 2013: 136). By 14 September 2011, the portal reported that a total of Rs. 491,043,426 (US$10.3 million) in bribes was paid. The Police Department received the most bribes but the amount rarely exceeded Rs. 1,000. The Department of Stamps and Registration, where large sums of bribes were paid, was the most corrupt (Loh 2011). The website has not solved the problem of bribery in India, but it has shown that "ordinary people can be turned from [being] the victims of corruption into part of the solution" (Campion 2011). It has also attracted attention from non-governmental organizations and government agencies in seventeen countries

(Strom 2012). In 2011, Bhutan's ACC introduced an online form for the anonymous reporting of corruption, and Pakistan also launched a similar website: ipaidabribe.pk. By 8 November 2015, the ipaidabribe.com website reported that 64,038 reports were recorded in 1,067 cities across India.

The Punjab model of proactive governance was introduced in ten districts in Pakistan in June 2010 to reduce petty corruption, empower citizens to hold civil servants accountable through proactive engagement and improve service delivery by allowing citizens to report problems. It uses information communications technology to deter corruption among civil servants administering basic services by collecting feedback on their performance and bribe-taking from citizens requesting for such services (Callen and Hasanani 2011: 2, 17).

During the first stage, the government official records the mobile telephone number of the citizen requesting the service including his or her identity, the time and place of the transaction, and other details for identifying corruption during the transaction (for example, official duty or price paid for the property). The collected data are transmitted by short message service (SMS) to a data collection centre. At the second stage, a random subset of the mobile telephone numbers recorded are given to some supervisory officers for them to call the citizens and enquire whether there was corruption in their transaction. In view of the large number of transactions, most of the calls to the citizens are made by a call centre. The data collected during the second stage are systematically recorded in a database and analysed to identify the patterns.

The beneficiaries are contacted "to proactively engage the citizen, rather than waiting for complaints, and to remove the information bottlenecks that corrupt officials can exploit to extort citizens". If the patterns indicate that corruption can be traced to particular individuals or departments, remedial action will be taken during the third stage by counselling, warning, suspending, or, if necessary, dismissing the corrupt officials from the civil service. In June 2011, the Commissioner of Bahawalpur initiated disciplinary proceedings against nine government officials on the basis of complaints received in the Punjab model reports by Hafizabad's District Coordination Officer (Callen and Hasanani 2011: 11–13, 39).

By June 2011, one year after its implementation, the Punjab model recorded 30,941 transactions in health, 463 driver's licences, 583 character certificates, 1,582 education pension disbursements, and 51,258 property registrations. An analysis of 370 citizens' feedback SMS responses for evaluation found that 82 respondents (22.2 per cent) were grateful that the government had introduced the Punjab model, and 161 respondents (43.5 per cent) provided a positive evaluation of the office being investigated. Feedback from the 428 connected calls in the health sector revealed that 38 per cent reported that individuals were only getting some medicine and 28 per cent said that they did not get any medicine. A preliminary evaluation of the Punjab model in July 2011 described it as "intuitively appealing and potentially highly scalable and cost-effective" (Callen and Hasanani 2011: 3–4).

The Punjab model's important achievement is the implementation of a real-time performance monitoring mechanism, which enables the government to detect corruption but also to monitor the supply and demand of critical medicine. Another attractive feature of the Punjab model is its "built-in capacity for constant data-based evaluation" as large amounts of data are generated rapidly. While the Punjab model is "a very promising mechanism using existing technologies and easily replicable elsewhere", the evaluators recommended a more rigorous evaluation to validate the data collected and verify that the reports of low corruption correspond with actual decreases in corruption cases (Callen and Hasanani 2011: 49–50, 52).

Compliance and integrity approaches

Two complementary approaches are employed to combat corruption among public officials in Asian countries. The compliance or rule-based approach relies on external controls like laws and regulations and ACAs to control unethical behaviour. By contrast, the integrity approach relies on internal controls like training, education and the integrity of the individual to curb unethical behaviour (Lawton et al. 2013: 95, 117). A rule-based approach "involves administrative procedures, rules and regulations which are designed to check the behaviour of public servants, to limit their discretion and to apply sanctions if they act corruptly or improperly". On the other hand, a value-based approach ensures that "public servants acquire an ethical framework, either by osmosis through socialization in the organization or by specific training, which will enable them to arrive at appropriate, morally-acceptable decisions" (Scott 2013b: 77).

The compliance approach is based on deterrence theory and focuses on the prevention of unlawful conduct, primarily by increasing surveillance and control and by imposing penalties for wrongdoers. Furthermore, it "overemphasizes the threat of detection and punishment in order to channel behaviour in lawful directions". However, the weakness of the compliance approach is that it does not "address the root causes of misconduct" (Paine 1994: 109–111). Consequently, Paine (1994: 111) recommends the adoption of an integrity strategy for ethics management because it is "broader, deeper, and more demanding than a legal compliance initiative". She concludes that the integrity strategy creates "a climate that encourages exemplary conduct and is "the best way to discourage damaging misconduct" (Paine 1994: 117).

Among the Asian ACAs, Hong Kong's ICAC appears to be most concerned about supplementing its traditional reliance on the compliance approach with an integrity approach. Scott and Leung (2012: 41) have attributed this shift in the ICAC's strategy to changes in the traditional forms of corruption, the emergence of new patterns of corruption and conflicts of interest, and the increasing importance of "core values" for the civil service and the personal morality of the civil servants. Initially, after its formation in 1974, the ICAC focused on combating corruption in the civil service but its scope gradually widened to include private sector corruption cases, which now outnumber those in the public sector.

The localisation of the civil service and the introduction of private sector practices in government after Hong Kong's handover to China in July 1997 have resulted in more cases of conflict of interest, especially in regulating post-public employment. Civil servants were warned in a government circular in December 1992 not to use their positions to benefit themselves, their families, relatives or friends. They were also required to report any conflict of interest to their superior officers. To address the increased incidence of conflicts of interest in the civil service arising from increased interaction with the private sector, the government has enhanced integrity by introducing in September 2009 a Civil Service Code, which reminds civil servants that there should be "no actual, perceived or potential conflict of interest" between "their official duties and private interests" (Scott and Leung 2012: 41–49).

In highlighting the ICAC's decision to supplement its reliance on the rule-based approach with a value-based approach, Scott (2013b: 91–92) attributes the ICAC's effective rule-based approach to corruption prevention to three factors: (1) the establishment of corruption as the principal value; (2) the government's provision to the ICAC of sufficient personnel and funds in a budget which constitutes 0.3 per cent of the government's annual total expenditure; and (3) the acceptance of and support for corruption prevention as a principal value by all civil servants.

By contrast, China is a communist state which relies on the Central Commission for Discipline Inspection (CCDI), Ministry of Supervision, Supreme People's Procuratorate (SPP), and National Corruption Prevention Bureau, as well as periodic anti-corruption campaigns to enforce its compliance strategy (Quah 2015b: 24–29). After becoming the General Secretary of the Chinese Communist Party (CCP) in November 2012, Xi Jinping initiated an extensive anti-corruption campaign to eliminate the corrupt "tigers" (senior officials) and "flies" (lower ranking officials) in China. This campaign is the longest campaign launched by the CCP as it began its fourth year in November 2015. The CCDI investigated 71 senior officials for corruption from December 2012 to March 2015, and 30 military officers from 2014 to March 2015 (Quah 2015b: 49–54). Apart from curbing the Chinese officials' extravagance on the three public expenses of vehicles, banquets and overseas trips (*sangong xiaofei*) by means of the "Eight Directives" (*baxiang guiding*) and "Six Injunctions" (*liuxiang jinling*), the CCDI also dispatched 46 inspection teams (*xunshizu*) across China in 2013 and 2014 to investigate corruption in corruption-prone provinces, ministries, state corporations and public service organizations (Quah 2015b: 42–49).

The compliance approach's limitations for combating corruption in China are evident in the CCDI's lenient approach in dealing with corrupt CCP members (with the exception of opponents of the political leaders) and President Xi's ineffective anti-corruption campaign. As the lead ACA, the CCDI is responsible for investigating party officials accused of corruption offences. Sapio (2005: 8–9) has criticised the CCDI for protecting party cadres under investigation by shielding them "in a safe nest" and exempting them from criminal punishment. The CCP prefers not to impose the legal penalty for its corrupt members in order to save its "face" and prevent the erosion of official authority. As corrupt senior party officials are not punished but "disciplined" internally by the CCP, they believe that they would unlikely be caught or punished (Zhang 2001: 28, 33).

As not all Chinese officials who are investigated for corruption offences are convicted, Cai (2015: 130–133) explains why some corrupt officials are punished less severely than others. First, cooperative corrupt officials who make voluntary confessions, provide information on other corrupt officials, and return illegal income, receive reduced punishment. Second, some corrupt officials are punished less harshly depending on the definition of the amount of money embezzled or bribes received. Third, when there are many corrupt officials, only seriously corrupt officials are punished while the less corrupt ones are spared to prevent paralysing the operations of the city or local government. Indeed, the inconsistencies in investigating and punishing corrupt officials at both the central and local levels in China undermine the credibility of the disciplinary agencies and encourages officials to believe that they would unlikely be punished for corrupt offences.

Similarly, Xi Jinping's anti-corruption campaign has been ineffective for three reasons. First, the campaign has dealt only with the symptoms of corruption without addressing its root causes. Instead of addressing all the causes of corruption in China[4], Xi's campaign has focused on the cultural practices of *guanxi* and gift-giving by curbing official extravagance on cars, banquets, and trips abroad. The campaign's second limitation is the selective enforcement of the anti-corruption laws because corrupt CCP members are protected from investigation and prosecution by the SPP and are disciplined instead by the CCDI. The third weakness of Xi's anti-graft campaign is the CCP leaders' reliance on the use of corruption charges as a weapon against their political opponents, as shown in the persecution of Chen Xitong, Chen Liangyu, Bo Xilai, and Zhou Yongkang from 1995 to 2014 (Quah 2015b: 84–87).

Gong and Ren (2013: 8) contend that the ineffectiveness of "frequent campaigns and harsh penalties" in curbing corruption in China has resulted in the shift from "campaign-driven anti-corruption enforcement to rule-based integrity management", which also reflects the Chinese government's recognition of preventing corruption by more effective regulation of conflicts of interest arising from the increased interaction between officials and the private sector. Consequently, 173 regulations were introduced during 1980 to 2009, which focused on bribery and illegal gratuities, disclosure of information on potential or actual conflicts of interest, procedures for managing conflict of interest situations, and accountability mechanisms and penalties for ensuring compliance (Gong and Ren 2013: 9–14). However, the Chinese government's efforts to manage conflicts of interest face the difficulty of adopting a transparent approach in a communist system and the necessity to supplement the rule-based system's inability to deal effectively with conflicts of interest with value-based integrity management (Gong and Ren 2013: 15–16).

Conclusion: what can be done?

The lack of political will is the most important reason why success in combating corruption has eluded many Asian countries in spite of their anti-corruption efforts during the past six decades. Having anti-corruption laws is necessary but insufficient because these laws must be enforced impartially, without fear or favour, by adequately staffed and funded independent ACAs. Furthermore, political leaders relying on ACAs should resist the temptation to use corruption as a weapon against their opponents. While Holmes (2015: 125) agrees that the success of anti-corruption measures depends on political will, he argues convincingly that political leaders must "not only be committed, i.e. have the political will to combat corruption, but must also have the *capacity* to implement their will". Indeed, the political will and capacity to control corruption must not be confined to the political leaders only but also shared widely by civil servants, the private sector, civil society organizations, the media, and citizens.

Many Asian countries need substantial doses of political will and capacity to implement impartially comprehensive measures to address the causes of corruption and to sustain the implementation of these measures over a long period. However, this is a tall order given the scarcity and fragility of political will. Bertrand de Speville (2013: 19), a former ICAC Commissioner in Hong Kong, has aptly described the fragility of political will of a new political leader as "a candle flame" and stressed the importance of nurturing and protecting this fragile commodity from "being extinguished by any passing political breeze".

Apart from the lack of political will, the anti-corruption strategies of many Asian countries have focused on the symptoms of corruption instead of addressing the fundamental causes of low salaries of civil servants, red tape, low probability of detection and punishment of corrupt offenders, and those cultural values which condone and encourage corruption. Anti-corruption campaigns which fail to address these causes are likely to fail, as illustrated by Xi Jinping's anti-corruption campaign. It will be difficult, if not impossible, to minimise petty corruption among low-ranking civil servants if they are paid "starvation wages", an appropriate label coined by poorly paid Filipino low-ranking bureaucrats. Cumbersome administrative procedures and excessive red tape compel business persons to offer bribes to poorly paid officials to expedite their applications for permits or approve other requests. Corruption is viewed as a "low risk, high reward" activity by citizens in those Asian countries afflicted with rampant corruption because of the low probability of detection and punishment of persons found guilty of corrupt offences. Finally, the importance of *guanxi,* gift-giving, family ties and other cultural values encourage the population to tolerate or engage in corrupt practices (Quah 2011: 14–21). Without substantive reforms to address these causes of corruption in Asian countries, their anti-corruption efforts will continue to be ineffective.

There is no "one best approach" to combating corruption in Asian countries because "unfortunately, every method outlined has its drawbacks" (Holmes 2015: 122). As mentioned earlier, the success of Singapore's CPIB and Hong Kong's ICAC has led to the proliferation of single ACAs in many Asian countries, but similar success has eluded many ACAs because of the lack of political will and their unfavourable policy contexts. The preference for rule-based anti-corruption approaches in Asian countries has also a mixed record not only because the anti-corruption laws are not enforced impartially but also because the increase in private sector corruption cases has encouraged some countries like Hong Kong, Malaysia and China, to supplement their compliance strategies with integrity management approaches. However, the integrity management strategy is not easy to implement and not a silver bullet which can curb the problem of systemic corruption overnight. Holmes (2015: 99) has expressed his reservations regarding the integrity approach because "it takes a long time, sometimes generations" for ethical education to be effective. Furthermore, its impact is marginal if other factors are involved.

The success stories of the ipaidabribe.com website and the Punjabi model of proactive governance demonstrate the potential benefits of combating corruption at the local level in India and Pakistan. After evaluating the effectiveness of 15 community-based anti-corruption initiatives in six Asian countries, Richards (2006: 6) identified three factors responsible for their success: (1) the programme's well-defined focus, strategy, and flexibility; (2) a skilled and competent team for implementing the programme; and (3) the community's trust in the programme. However, the most important finding was that "there was no single condition, factor or catalyst that underpinned the success of a community anti-corruption program" as each initiative succeeded because of a combination of several factors (Richards 2006: 40).

The wise reminder by the Millennium Challenge Corporation (2007: 8) that "anti-corruption reform is a marathon, not a sprint" should be heeded by all the stakeholders in Asian countries in their efforts to minimise corruption. The anti-corruption struggle in Asian countries and elsewhere involves three groups of stakeholders: the heroes, villains, and innocent victims. The heroes are the "integrity warriors" namely, the journalists, lawyers, and community leaders "who expose corruption or fight abuse". The villains are the "corrupt officials or venal government leaders" who not only accept bribes, but also "systematically plunder the treasuries". The "hapless victims" are the "ordinary citizens confronting unresponsive bureaucrats, the legal clients who must bribe a lawyer or judge, the hospital patients who must pay off a nurse, the students who must bribe their teachers, [and] the women and children who are unprotected by corrupt police" (Sampson 2010: 321).

In sum, those governments in Asian countries that are sincerely committed to minimising the adverse consequences of systemic corruption should rely on both top-down and bottom-up approaches and supplement their emphasis on the compliance strategy with the integrity strategy to help them manage more effectively the conflict of interest situations arising from the rising number of private sector corruption cases. Holmes (2015: 107) has recommended a "smart anti-corruption" approach, which combines "stick, carrot, and other approaches" with the "mix" varying "from country to country, according to the culture, the type of political and economic system, and the resources available". Indeed, as advised by Shah (2007: 234), "for programs to work, they must identify the type of corruption they are targeting and tackle the underlying, country-specific causes, or 'drivers', of dysfunctional governance".

In the final analysis, anti-corruption programmes in Asian countries should strive to enhance the efforts of the heroes, undermine the activities of the villains, and protect and ameliorate the sufferings of the poor citizens, who are the innocent victims of corruption. In the words of another anti-corruption warrior, Frank Vogl (2012: 2), "the anti-corruption train has left the station and it is gathering speed toward a destination called good governance. The journey will be long, there will be interruptions and setbacks, and some carriages may not make it all the way, but many will". These anti-corruption programmes should ensure that more carriages will reach their destination of good governance in Asian countries, no matter how long or difficult the journey.

Notes

1 These nine ACAs are selected for comparison because of the availability of data on their budgets and personnel in their annual reports and other official reports.
2 These survey findings are provided by the CPIB's Deputy Director (Planning, Policy and Corporate Relations) by email to the author on 20 November 2015.
3 In addition to the OMB, the other four ACAs are: the Presidential Commission on Good Government; the *Sandiganbayan*; the Inter-Agency Anti-Graft Coordinating Council; and the Office of the Deputy Secretary for Legal Affairs (Batalla 2015: 55–56).
4 The other four causes of corruption in China are: low salaries, red tape, low probability of detection and punishment for corrupt offenders, and decentralisation. See Quah (2015b: 65–72) for a detailed analysis.

References

AAC (Agency Against Corruption) (2013) *Annual report 2012*, Taipei: AAC, Ministry of Justice.
ACC (Anti-Corruption Commission) (2013) *Annual report 2012*, Thimphu: ACC.
Asia Foundation and Sant-Maral Foundation (2015) *Survey on perceptions and knowledge of corruption: strengthening transparency in Mongolia project*, Ulaanbaatar: Asia Foundation, April.
Batalla, E.V.C. (2015) "Treading the straight and righteous path: curbing corruption in the Philippines", *Asian Education and Development Studies*, 4 (1): 51–75.
Bolongaita, E.P. (2010) "An exception to the rule? Why Indonesia's Anti-Corruption Commission succeeds where others don't – A comparison with the Philippines' Ombudsman", *U4 Issue*, (4), August, Bergen: Christian Michelsen Institute.
Brata, R.A. (2014) *Why did anticorruption policy fail? A study of anticorruption policy implementation failure in Indonesia*, Charlotte, NC: Information Age Publishing.
Brinkerhoff, D.W. (2000) "Assessing political will for anti-corruption efforts: an analytic framework", *Public Administration & Development*, 20: 239–252.
Bureau of the Budget (2012) *Thailand's budget in brief fiscal year 2012*, Bangkok: Bureau of the Budget, www.bb.go.th/bbhomeEng/budget_in_brief/budget_in_brief_2012.pdf (accessed 9 November 2015).
Cai, Y. (2015) *State and agents in China: disciplining government officials*, Stanford, CA: Stanford University Press.
Caiden, G.E. (2013) "Accounting for success in combating corruption", in J.S.T. Quah (ed.) *Different paths to curbing corruption: lessons from Denmark, Finland, Hong Kong, New Zealand and Singapore*, Bingley: Emerald Group Publishing, 189–217.
Callen, M. and A. Hasanani (2011) *The Punjab model of proactive governance: empowering citizens through information communication technology, findings from an early review of evidence*, Islamabad: Project Report, 25 July, 55 pages.
Campion, M.J. (2011) "Bribery in India: a website for whistleblowers", *BBC News South Asia*, 6 June.
Cayabyab, M. (2011) "PH Ombudsman behind other anticorruption agencies in Asia", *VERA Files*, 10 May.
CBI (Central Bureau of Investigation) (2010) *Annual report 2009*, New Delhi: CBI.
CBI (Central Bureau of Investigation) (2013) *Annual report 2012*, New Delhi: CBI.

CBI (Central Bureau of Investigation) (2015) *Annual report 2014,* New Delhi: CBI.

Choi, J.W. (2011) "Measuring the performance of an anticorruption agency: the case of the KPK in Indonesia", *International Review of Public Administration,* 16(3): 45–63.

Coronel, S.S. and L. Kalaw-Tirol (eds.) (2002) *Investigating corruption: a do-it-yourself guide,* Quezon City: Philippine Center for Investigative Journalism.

CPIB (Corrupt Practices Investigation Bureau) (2003) "CPIB's public perception survey 2002", Singapore: CPIB press release, 4 April.

Davidsen, S., V. Juwono, and D.G. Timberman (2006) *Curbing corruption in Indonesia, 2004–2006 - a survey of national policies and approaches,* Washington, DC, and Jakarta: United States-Indonesia Society and Center for Strategic and International Studies.

de Speville, B. (2013) "Interview by Gabriel Kuris", Princeton, NJ: Innovations for Successful Societies, 14 August: 1–25 https://successfulsocieties.princeton.edu/sites/successfulsocieties/files/interviews/transcripts/3552/bertrand_despeville.pdf (accessed 1 September 2015).

Gill, S.S (1998) *The pathology of corruption,* New Delhi: HarperCollins Publishers.

Godbole, M. (2000) *The changing times: a commentary on current affairs,* New Delhi: Orient Longman.

Gomez, J. (2011) "Philippine lawmakers impeach chief anti-corruption investigator", *Associated Press,* 22 March.

Gong, T and J. Ren (2013) "Hard rules and soft constraints: regulating conflict of interest in China", *Journal of Contemporary China,* 22(79): 1–17.

Harsono, A. (2009) "The gecko vs. the crocodile", in *Global integrity report: Indonesia 2009,* Washington, DC: Global Integrity.

Hartwell, E. (2009) *"Wild Money": The human rights consequences of illegal logging and corruption in Indonesia's forestry sector,* New York: Human Rights Watch.

Holmes, L. (2015) *Corruption: a very short introduction,* Oxford: Oxford University Press.

ICAC (Independent Commission Against Corruption) (2012) *2012 budget,* "Head 72: Independent Commission Against Corruption", 604–614, Hong Kong, http://www.budget.gov.hk/2012/eng/pdf/head072.pdf (accessed 1 September 2015).

ICAC (Independent Commission Against Corruption) (2013) *Annual report 2012,* Hong Kong: ICAC.

ICAC (Independent Commission Against Corruption) (2014) *Annual report 2013,* Hong Kong: ICAC.

Jakarta Post (2015) "Jokowi criticised for lack of commitment to corruption eradication", 18 October.

Johnston, M. (2001) "Measuring corruption: numbers versus knowledge versus understanding", in A.K. Jain (ed.) *The political economy of corruption,* London: Routledge, 157–179.

Ko, N.K. (2014) "Myanmar enters mortal combat against corruption", *The Nation,* 10 September, http://www.nationmultimedia.com/opinion/Myanmar-enters-mortal-combat-against-corruption-30242899.html (accessed 23 January 2015).

Ko, K. and A. Samajdar (2010) "Evaluation of international corruption indexes: should we believe them or not?" *The Social Science Journal,* 47(3): 508–540.

KPK (*Komisi Pemberantasan Korupsi*) (2009) *Annual report 2008,* Jakarta: KPK.

KPK (*Komisi Pemberantasan Korupsi*) (2013) *Annual report 2012,* Jakarta: KPK (in Indonesian).

Lall, B.R. (2007) *Who owns CBI: the naked truth,* New Delhi: Manas Publications.

Lawton, A., J. Rayner and K. Lasthuizen (2013) *Ethics and management in the public sector,* London: Routledge.

Loh, K. (2011) "Q & A with founder of 'I paid a bribe': India's anti-corruption online movement", *In Asia: Weekly Insight and Analysis,* San Francisco, CA: Asia Foundation, 21 September.

Marcelo, S.V. (2005) *Combating corruption in the Philippines: are we plundering our chances or doing it better?* Diliman: National College of Public Administration and Governance, University of the Philippines, Working Paper Series No. 2.

MACC (Malaysian Anti-Corruption Commission) (2013) *Annual report 2012,* Putrajaya: MACC.

Millennium Challenge Corporation (2007) *Building public integrity through positive incentives: MCC's role in the fight against corruption,* Washington, DC: Working Paper.

Ministry of Finance, Bhutan (2012) *National budget financial year 2012–2013,* Thimphu: Ministry of Finance.

National Statistical Bureau (2012) *Bhutan at a glance 2012,* Thimphu, http://www.nsb.gov.bt/nsbweb/publication/files/pub10pq3779fx.pdf (accessed 4 September 2015).

Nazeer, Z. (2012) "Anti-graft body galvanizes public support", *Straits Times,* 28 June, A11.

Newsbreak Online (2006) "The Street Ombudsman", 21 November.

OMB (Office of the Ombudsman) (2009) *Annual report 2008,* Quezon City: OMB.

OMB (Office of the Ombudsman) (2013) *Annual report 2012,* Quezon City: OMB.

OMB (Office of the Ombudsman) (2014) *Annual report 2013,* Quezon City: OMB.

OneWorld Foundation India (2011) "I paid a bribe: case study 7", in *ICT facilitated access to information Innovations: a compendium of case studies from South Asia,* 129–145 http://southasia.oneworld.net/Files/ict_facilitated_access_to_information_innovations.pdf (accessed 1 September 2015).

Onishi, N. (2009) "Indonesia officials resign in graft scandal", *New York Times,* 5 November, A10.

Osman, S. (2009) "KPK scandal captivates Indonesians: wide media coverage fuelling anger over alleged plot against graft busters", *Straits Times,* 6 November, A9.

Oyamada (2005) "President Gloria Macapagal-Arroyo's anti-corruption strategy in the Philippines: an evaluation", *Asian Journal of Political Science,* 13(1): 81–107.

Paine, L.S. (1994) "Managing for organizational integrity", *Harvard Business Review,* 72(2): 106–117.

Punch, M. (2009) *Police corruption: deviance, accountability and reform in policing,* London: Routledge.

Quah, J.S.T. (2004) "best practices for curbing corruption in Asia", *The Governance Brief,* 11: 1–4.

Quah, J.S.T. (2008) "Curbing corruption in India: an impossible dream?" *Asian Journal of Political Science,* 16(3): 240–259.

Quah, J.S.T. (2009) "Benchmarking for excellence: a comparative analysis of seven Asian anti-corruption agencies", *Asia Pacific Journal of Public Administration,* 31(2): 171–195.

Quah, J.S.T. (2011) *Curbing corruption in Asian countries: an impossible dream?* Bingley: Emerald Group Publishing.

Quah, J.S.T. (2015a) "The critical importance of political will in combating corruption in Asian countries", *Public Administration and Policy: An Asia-Pacific Journal,* 18(2): 12–23.

Quah, J.S.T. (2015b) *Hunting the corrupt "tigers" and "flies" in China: an evaluation of Xi Jinping's anti-corruption campaign (November 2012 to March 2015),* Baltimore, MD: Carey School of Law, University of Maryland.

Quah, J.S.T. (2016) "Combating corruption in six Asian countries: a comparative analysis", *Asian Education and Development Studies,* 5(2): 244–262.

Quimson, G. (2006) *National integrity systems Transparency International country study report Philippines 2006,* Berlin: Transparency International.

Republic of Singapore (2014) *Singapore Budget 2014: annex to the expenditure estimates,* Singapore: Budget Division, Ministry of Finance.

Richards, K. (2006) "What works and why in community-based anti-corruption programs", Blackburn, South Victoria: Transparency International Australia.

Sampson, S. (2010) "Integrity warriors: global morality and the anti-corruption movement in the Balkans", in M. Johnston (ed.) *Public sector corruption,* vol. 4, *Cures?* London: Sage Publications, 313–339.

Sapio, F. (2005) *Implementing anti-corruption in the PRC: patterns of selectivity,* Lund: Centre for East and Southeast Asian Studies, Lund University, Working Paper No. 10.

Saragih, B.B. (2011) "KPK vows to defy political pressure", *Jakarta Post,* 30 January.

Schonhardt, S. (2012) "Indonesia antigraft agency seeks donors", *New York Times,* 3 August.

Schwab, K. (ed.) (2013) *The global competitiveness report 2013–2014,* Geneva: World Economic Forum.

Schwab, K. (ed.) (2014) *The global competitiveness report 2014–2015,* Geneva: World Economic Forum.

Scott, I. (2013a) "Engaging the public: Hong Kong's Independent Commission Against Corruption's community relations strategy", in J.S.T. Quah (ed.) *Different paths to curbing corruption: lessons from Denmark, Finland, Hong Kong, New Zealand and Singapore,* Bingley: Emerald Group Publishing, 79–108.

Scott, I. (2013b) "Institutional design and corruption prevention in Hong Kong", *Journal of Contemporary China,* 22(79): 77–92.

Scott, I. and J.Y.-H. Leung (2012) "Integrity management in post-1997 Hong Kong: challenges for a rule-based system", *Crime, Law and Social Change,* 58(1): 39–52.

Senior, I. (2006) *Corruption - the world's big C: cases, causes, consequences, cures,* London: Institute of Economic Affairs.

Shah, A. (2007) "Tailoring the fight against corruption to country circumstances", in A. Shah (ed.) *Performance accountability and combating corruption,* Washington, DC: World Bank, 233–254.

SWS (Social Weather Stations) (2007) *The 2006–2007 SWS surveys of enterprises on corruption,* Quezon City: SWS.

SWS (Social Weather Stations) (2010) *The 2009 SWS surveys of enterprises on corruption,* Quezon City: SWS.

SWS (Social Weather Stations) (2015) *The 2014/15 SWS Survey of enterprises on corruption*, Quezon City: SWS.

Strom, S. (2012) "Websites shine light on petty bribery worldwide", *New York Times*, 6 March.

TI (Transparency International) (2013) *Global Corruption Barometer 2013*, Berlin: TI.

TI (Transparency International) (2014) "Corruption Perceptions Index 2014: results", Berlin, www. transparency.org/cpi2014/results (accessed 1 September 2015).

UNDP (United Nations Development Programme) (2008) *Tackling corruption, transforming lives: accelerating human development in Asia and the Pacific*, New Delhi: Macmillan India.

UNDP (United Nations Development Programme) (2011) *Practitioners' guide: capacity assessment of anti-corruption agencies*, New York: UNDP.

Vogl, F. (2012) *Waging war on corruption: inside the movement fighting the abuse of power*, Lanham, MD: Rowman and Littlefield Publishers.

World Bank (2015) "Worldwide Governance Indicators 2014", Washington D.C., http://info. worldbank.org/governance/wgi/index.aspx#reports (accessed 28 September 2015).

Zhang, L. (2001) "White-collar crime: bribery and corruption in China", in J. Liu, L. Zhang and S.F. Messner (eds.) *Crime and social control in a changing China*, Westport, CT: Greenwood Press, 23–36.

18

CORRUPTION PREVENTION

Successful cases

Jin-Wook Choi

Introduction

The severely negative impact of corruption is a sufficient justification for placing it high on the reform agenda, particularly since globalisation accelerated in the 1990s. In a globalised world, corruption in one country is easily transmitted to another country, forcing both countries to bear the costs. Coupled with a domestic thrust in democratic governance, this environment has pushed many countries to take steps to cope with corruption (UNDP 2014). Although genuine motivation might vary from one country to another, developed as well as developing countries have reacted to this global demand. A popular and typical response of developing countries is to enact an anti-corruption law and to establish an independent anti-corruption agency (ACA) (Rose-Ackerman 1999). This anti-corruption institution-building is usually in line with typical recommendations on anti-corruption reform articulated in the academic literature and policy reports (Meagher 2005). However, despite almost 20 years of anti-corruption reform, there are not many developing countries which have made notable progress in controlling corruption (Heilbrunn 2004; UNDP 2011).

The limited changes in the corruption landscape of developing countries demonstrate how anti-corruption reform is difficult and time-consuming. Challenges to anti-corruption reform arise from the fact that corruption is multifaceted and stems from diverse causes (Rose-Ackerman 1999). In consequence, one or two anti-corruption measures alone do not suffice to control corruption effectively. Corruption can, however, be brought under control effectively when a comprehensive reform, or a big bang approach, is carried out (Quah 1995; Rothstein 2011). Political leaders require a strong commitment and will to not only fight corruption, but also to fight any resistance to reform by vested political and economic interests (Quah 2007). An effective ACA supported by political will needs to be created to implement a zero tolerance policy. While an ACA's anti-corruption activities are essential, they are a punitive approach rather than a preventive one. For effective prevention of corruption, administrative reform towards more transparent and accountable government in order to minimise the corruption opportunities of public officials and to sanction any violation of ethics is a necessary condition for success (UNDP 2014). The complexity of corruption thus requires a government to deploy a comprehensive reform package.

The changes in Transparency International's (TI) Corruption Perceptions Index (CPI) support the claim that the corruption problem is complex and difficult to solve. When TI produced the CPI scores in 1995 for the first time, the average of 41 countries was 59.5 on a 100-point scale. In 2014, the CPI average score of 174 countries was 43.1. In a 20-year period, although the CPI scores of some countries improved (for example, the CPI score of Spain increased from 43.5 in 1995 to 60.0 in 2014), other CPI scores plummeted. In Argentina, for example, the CPI score decreased from 52.4 in 1995 to 34.0 in 2014 (TI 2016).

In searching for success factors, many studies have examined the cases of Singapore and Hong Kong which have successfully reached a new corruption-free equilibrium from a previous state in which the government was seriously corrupt (de Speville 1999; Choi 2009). In doing so, several analytical frameworks have been deployed ranging from institutional theory to socio-cultural perspective to geographical characteristics. However, no matter what lesson one learns from Singapore and Hong Kong, there is no one-size-fits-all solution. Indeed, with strong political will from their leaders, it would have been relatively easy to govern densely populated small island states or regions such as Singapore and Hong Kong. As far as the issue of corruption control is concerned, this geographic characteristic is advantageous for an effective law enforcement agency to be entrenched in every corner of the society. Yet there are additional factors that Singapore and Hong Kong ascribe to their successful corruption control.

Contrary to how developing countries are handling the corruption problem, the anti-corruption reform paths of Singapore and Hong Kong are exceptionally noteworthy (Rothstein 2011). When one tries to trace the history of fighting corruption in Singapore and Hong Kong, commonalities as well as discrepancies are easily observable, which have been well-analysed. Although most studies have lauded Singapore and Hong Kong, some recent commentaries adopt a more critical view. They ask whether Singapore and Hong Kong will continue to follow the same course in fighting corruption and whether forms of corruption other than bribery, over which both ACAs have firm control, will require more attention in the future (for example, Stephenson 2015).

The aim of this chapter is to examine how the history of anti-corruption reform in Singapore and Hong Kong has evolved over time. In doing so, the chapter adopts the perspective of institutional theory because addressing an inefficient equilibrium stemming from corruption is the primary goal of anti-corruption reform. In this light, Singapore and Hong Kong are relevant cases of institutional change. This chapter is structured as follows. The next section provides an overall theoretical framework within which the cases of Singapore and Hong Kong are analysed. Section 3 sketches the history of corruption in light of an inefficient equilibrium. Section 4 examines how Singapore and Hong Kong attempted to dismantle a corruption-ridden inefficient equilibrium through institution-building. Section 5 compares the paths to anti-corruption reform in Singapore and Hong Kong. The similarities and differences of the institutionalisation of anti-corruption policies and strategies are contrasted in this section. Section 6 attempts to assess the effectiveness of anti-corruption reform in Singapore and Hong Kong compared to selected developing countries. The last section concludes with identifying the challenges for sustainable anti-corruption efforts in Singapore and Hong Kong.

Anti-corruption reform and institutional change: from an old to a new equilibrium

At the micro-level, corruption can be characterised as the deviant behaviour of individuals from socially desirable norms. If corruption was committed by a small number of people, its negative impact would be limited and the majority of people would not be affected in their decision-making. However, when corruption is pervasive and systemic throughout society, it becomes a guiding norm that governs behavioural decisions. Assuming that corruption is socially unacceptable behaviour that should be controlled and prevented primarily by the government, systemic corruption indicates the failure of the state to do so. Moreover, in most cases of systemic corruption, the state itself is a key player which benefits from corruption. Corruption bred by society and upheld by the state dominates the norm in a way that drives everyone to extract the rents from corruption. Unchecked corruption becomes part of informal institutions, resulting in seriously negative inefficiencies for the society (Darden 2002; Helmke and Levitsky 2003).

The difficulty of counteracting corruption arises because of the complexity surrounding the corruption problem and the nature of corruption as an informal institution. As constraints over the choice of behaviour of individuals and organizations, institutions, whether formal or informal, usually resist changes (North 1990). In particular, informal institutions, like corrupt practices, are hard to change because they have been internalised over a long period and have become a focal point of reference for individual values and beliefs. In these circumstances, it is unrealistic to expect that corruption can be dealt with effectively by self-correction in society. As corruption breeds an inefficient equilibrium, formal authorities are faced with the problem that corruption endangers social stability and the development of a nation. The recognition of the problem often accompanies changes in exogenous parameters outside the corruption system. Regime change and economic shock are such examples.

In order to dismantle an inefficient equilibrium caused by corruption, there must be deliberate action by political entrepreneurs, especially by political leaders, to form a new corruption-free equilibrium. Institutional change through anti-corruption reform, to be successful, needs to be completed comprehensively. Incremental change is not likely to succeed because vested political and economic interests in systemic corruption tend to strongly oppose reform that results in drastically different distributional consequences (Rothstein 2011). Nonetheless, political leadership alone does not ensure the success of anti-corruption reform. Political leaders can transform a corrupt institutional culture successfully by mobilising and coordinating needed resources inside and outside of the government (Klitgaard 2004). For this, transforming formal institutions is critical. New formal institutions whose *modus operandi* differ from the old corruption-ridden formal institutions need to be put in place to enable effective political leadership for anti-corruption measures. By establishing new principles with an emphasis on the disutility of corruption, new formal institutions may be institutionalised so that behaviour is changed and decisions are based on the belief that the costs of corruption outweigh the gains. When new principles become the dominant norm, a new and efficient equilibrium emerges.

An old equilibrium: the historical contexts of corruption in Singapore and Hong Kong

In the past, Singapore and Hong Kong were very corrupt societies. There are many anecdotes that describe the pervasiveness of corruption in these places. It was so strongly embedded as to dominate the behaviour of the people (Quah 1995; Jing 2007). In Singapore, according to Tan (1999), bribing was a common practice if people wanted to receive services from the government. In Hong Kong, bribery was also a way of life and corruption syndicates were a part of the fabric of public administration (Lethbridge 1985; Yep 2013).

A single factor cannot account for endemic corruption. There are several explanations for the prevalence of corruption in Singapore and Hong Kong. In Singapore, the limited effectiveness of anti-corruption institutions allowed corruption to flourish during the colonial period. Quah (2001) identifies three key factors: the low salaries of local civil servants, ample corruption opportunities of civil servants in the absence of proper bureaucratic controlling mechanisms and the low risk of detection and punishment. These factors alone do not, however, provide a full explanation of the corruption that was rife in Singapore. Other factors such as the lack of political will of the colonial government and an environment in which anti-corruption laws were ineffectively implemented also played a role in breeding corruption (Quah 1995). Moreover, the socioeconomic conditions resulting from the Japanese occupation and high inflation worsened the problem. As Lee put it: "[t]he Japanese Occupation culture brought out the basic survival instincts in people and produced a society where all manner of evils could be justified because it was all about survival" (Lee 2005, as cited in Quah 2008: 88).

In the investigation of the Peter Godber case in 1973, a Commission of Inquiry under Sir Alastair Blair-Kerr attempted to answer the question of why corruption was widespread in the Hong Kong government. Quoting local Hong Kong Chinese, the report put forth a lengthy list of the causes of corruption: a Chinese dynasty-inherited legacy that characterised bribery as a natural payment to officials without consideration of morality, the behaviour of refugees from a corrupt and oppressive Kuomintang government attempting to survive in a new alien environment in Hong Kong, the Chinese custom of paying tea money that penetrated the civil service, socioeconomic circumstances under which legal business practices could not fulfill the needs of people's livelihood, inefficient administration, and stringent regulations which forced people to rely on illegal means to receive public service, and low paying public officials who sought petty corruption opportunities (Commission of Inquiry 1973: 20–22).

From an institutional perspective, if corruption is understood as a target to be curbed for various reasons, formal institutions need to be created to deal with the evils of corruption. Unfortunately, anti-corruption institutions in Singapore and Hong Kong failed to be institutionalised because formal institutions were badly designed and crucial preconditions to make institutions effective were not in place.

The control of corruption reached a turning point in 1959 in Singapore and in 1973 in Hong Kong for similar reasons but within different politico-economic contexts. Both Singapore and Hong Kong witnessed corruption scandals committed, respectively, by Chew Swee Kee and Peter Godber which incensed the public. Although Singapore was run by a self-ruling government under circumstances of economic underdevelopment, unlike capitalist Hong Kong which was ruled by a British-appointed governor, both governments recognised corruption as one of the most serious obstacles to national development. The ultimate *raisons d'être* of anti-corruption reform was the belief of political leaders that the economic and social future would be severely compromised unless corruption was eradicated.

A new equilibrium: the evolution of anti-corruption institution-building in Singapore and Hong Kong

To counteract corruption, the first step that Singapore and Hong Kong undertook was to (re)build the institutional framework for corruption prevention (Choi 2009). Comprehensive anti-corruption reforms were undertaken in 1960 when the Singapore government enacted the Prevention of Corruption Act and strengthened the anti-corruption activities of the Corrupt Practices Investigation Bureau (CPIB), and in 1974 when the Hong Kong government created the Independent Commission Against Corruption (ICAC) (Quah 1995).

However, these measures do not necessarily imply that anti-corruption institutions were completely absent in the two places. Rather, Singapore and Hong Kong adopted anti-corruption laws and corruption-fighting agencies well before the CPIB and the ICAC were created. Institutions to cope with corruption were built in the nineteenth century in both Singapore and Hong Kong. Singapore attempted to control corruption in 1871 when the Penal Code of the Straits Settlements of Malacca, Penang and Singapore was enacted (Jing 2007). Some years later, in 1898, the Misdemeanors Punishment Ordinance was legislated in Hong Kong. Reshaping the institutional framework through the replacement of defunct anti-corruption laws and the restructuring of anti-corruption organizations took place several times in Singapore and Hong Kong. The Hong Kong government enacted the Prevention of Corruption Ordinance in 1948, which was replaced by the Prevention of Bribery Ordinance of 1971. In 1956, it had established the Anti-Corruption Branch within the police and the Standing Committee on Corruption and, in 1971, created an Anti-Corruption Office that replaced the Anti-Corruption Branch. However, these early anti-corruption strategies did not bring substantial changes in corruption *per se*. There were several reasons why anti-corruption efforts were futile.

Until the outbreak of corruption scandals of the Minister of Education of Singapore, Chew Swee Kee, in 1959, and the Chief Superintendent of the Hong Kong Royal Police Force, Peter Godber, in 1973, the corruption agendas of the British colonial governments of Singapore and Hong Kong reflected incremental rather than comprehensive anti-corruption approaches (Quah 1995). Analysing recently released documents in the United Kingdom's National Archives, Yep (2013) argues that the colonial government in Hong Kong regarded corruption as a problem of low ranking Chinese officials despite the fact that British expatriates were among the culprits. This misperception meant that the colonial government tended to be passive in corruption prevention.

Moreover, the organizational structure for anti-corruption efforts was flawed because the units were located within the police, which in both places was the most corrupt of all government departments at that time (Advisory Committee on Corruption 1961). Before an independent CPIB was created in Singapore in 1952, the main anti-corruption unit was the Anti-Corruption Branch within the police. Likewise, the anti-corruption unit in Hong Kong before the ICAC was the Anti-Corruption Branch which was formed in 1948 later replaced by an Anti-Corruption Office. Because the units were located within the police, they were not able to act impartially against endemic police corruption (Quah 1995).

Finally, although both Singapore and Hong Kong dealt with corruption through detecting and punishing the corrupt, this punitive approach was not supplemented by preventive measures intended to minimise corruption opportunities in the civil service system (Quah 1995).

Similar yet different paths to a new equilibrium in Singapore and Hong Kong

An institutional perspective dictates that pervasive corruption tends to be sustained in an inefficient equilibrium (Rothstein 2011). Anti-corruption reform, thus, implies the disruption of this unfavourable equilibrium to form a new one. Institutions, particularly informal institutions like corruption, are not easy to change (North 1990). Institutional change takes place because of the unexpected result of historical accidents such as, for example, when Peter Godber fled to Britain to try to avoid corruption charges. His case provided the critical momentum needed to counteract corruption in Hong Kong. Yet a historical event alone does not guarantee institutional change. In the past, although several crises have arisen from corruption, only a few cases served as a turning point to reverse a situation of rampant corruption. If institutional change is not generated by a scandal or a major social movement such as a civil revolution, it can be steered by changes initiated by the political leadership. When these factors continuously interact with each other over time, the possibility of replacing the old equilibrium with a new one increases. Nonetheless, the actual path to institutional change can vary depending on endogenous and exogenous settings within which the institutions can be reshaped. This process of institutional change can provide an explanation of how Singapore and Hong Kong transformed their corruption situations.

In understanding the success of anti-corruption measures in Singapore and Hong Kong, three key factors are commonly underscored: strong political will; the creation of a credible, independent and effective ACA; and continuous administrative reform (Rose-Ackerman 1999). The first two factors, which are strongly linked, comprise the important principle of zero tolerance towards corruption through controlling the behavioural norm of public officials. While the first two factors are direct components of anti-corruption success, the last factor is an indirect approach because it aims at minimising corruption opportunities through diverse reform measures.

Concerning political leadership, both Singapore and Hong Kong displayed strong resolution when the government undertook substantial anti-corruption action in the late 1950s and the early 1970s, respectively. Unlike many cases where the political will to curb corruption ended in empty political rhetoric with no serious action, the leadership in both places showed a strong will and commitment to fight corruption. In Singapore, all the Cabinet members at the time of the launching of a new People's Action Party (PAP)-led government in June, 1959 sent a strong anti-corruption message to the society by wearing white shirts and slacks to symbolise purity and honesty. It was then that the newly appointed Prime Minister, Lee Kuan Yew, forged a new path to corruption prevention. In his memoirs, Lee Kuan Yew stated that "[w]hen the PAP government took office in 1959, we set out to have a clean administration. We were sickened by the greed, corruption, and decadence of many Asian leaders. ... We had a deep sense of mission to establish a clean and effective government" (Lee 2000 cited in Quah 2013a: 146).

Lee's will regarding anti-corruption has been internalised in the government of Singapore in such a way that integrity has become an important part of the ethos of public officials. In a speech to celebrate the CPIB's 60th anniversary in 2012, Prime Minister, Lee Hsien Loong, emphasised that setting high standards of honesty and integrity is not only a core value of political leaders but also a social value that makes Singapore special (Lee 2012). Since the time of Lee Kuan Yew, political leaders and the Singaporean government have continued to uphold anti-corruption and integrity as key pillars of governance. Political stability, characterised by PAP dominance under the leadership of Lee Kuan Yew, followed by Goh Chok Tong, and Lee Hsien Loong, contributes to the strenuous and consistent efforts to fight corruption.

While Hong Kong has shared similarities with Singapore in that political leadership played a crucial role in curbing corruption, its political circumstances were different. Unlike the self-ruling government of Lee Kuan Yew who took office in 1959, Hong Kong was still a British colony when the ICAC was established in 1974. Political leadership for the anti-corruption initiative in Hong Kong was under the expatriate leadership of the British Governor. Yet the stance of the then Governor of Hong Kong, Sir Murray MacLehose regarding corruption was not much different from that of Lee Kuan Yew. Facing a public outcry due to the mishandling of the Godber case and referring to Sir Alastair Blair-Kerr's report, Governor MacLehose in a speech at the Legislative Council on October 17, 1973, stated that "[c]learly the public would have more confidence in a unit that was entirely independent, and separate from any department of the Government, including the police. We have therefore decided … to set up a separate Anti-Corruption Commission under a civilian Commissioner" (Hong Kong Legislative Council 1973: 17). Although the establishment of the ICAC was the culmination of political efforts before Governor MacLehose (Yep 2013), regaining public credibility through the ICAC might not have been introduced if it were not for MacLehose's political leadership (Tsang 2004).

If political will provided a trigger to pave a new road for anti-corruption action, building and reshaping anti-corruption institutions were a critical component through which a new equilibrium could be attained. Both Singapore and Hong Kong, based on strong political support, have tried to make their dedicated corruption fighters, the CPIB and the ICAC, as effective as possible. At the same time, they attempted to bring corruption under control as soon as possible. It is claimed, for example, that the ICAC was successful in wiping out major corruption syndicates in the Hong Kong government in less than 10 years (Yep 2013).

The success of an ACA can be judged by the extent to which it institutionalises its anti-corruption mission as mandated in laws and by the degree to which it meets the expectations of the society. In so doing, it is essential for an ACA to carry out impartial and uncompromising law enforcement. The effectiveness of law enforcement is also reflected in public perceptions. Public sentiment, confirming the effectiveness of the CPIB and the ICAC, is evidenced in public polls which are further addressed in the next section.

As pioneering ACAs, the experiences of the CPIB and the ICAC allow scholars to identify the key success factors of ACAs through inductive reasoning. Through an assessment of several ACAs in Asian countries, for example, Quah (2007) suggests six preconditions with which effectiveness can be upheld: the absence of corruption in an ACA, an independent *de jure* as well as *de facto* independent status, comprehensive anti-corruption legislation, adequate levels of staff and budget, impartial law enforcement, and strong political will.

Although the effectiveness of the CPIB and the ICAC is well known, their political circumstances differed. A stable political environment enabled the CPIB, except for the first eight years from 1952 to 1960 before the Prevention of Corruption Act was enacted, to function effectively; given the political circumstances, it would be expected that this satisfactory level of performance would be maintained. By contrast, Hong Kong's political context has been very different. Around the time of the handover of Hong Kong to China on July 1, 1997, there was concern that the ICAC's independent status and its effectiveness might be crippled when it fell under the control of Beijing (Rose-Ackerman 1999). Yet this concern did not materialise. In the ICAC's 2014 survey, 80.6 per cent of the Hong Kong people perceived the Commission's functions to have been effective (ICAC 2014b). This perception of effectiveness was even higher than the 1997 survey in which 76.5 per cent of respondents replied positively.

While the initial anti-corruption measures adopted by Singapore in the 1960s and Hong Kong in the 1970s were skewed towards a detection-and-punishment strategy driven by ACAs, both governments also attempted to prevent corruption by reforming their civil services. Civil service reform, as a means of anti-corruption strategy, proceeded in two ways: minimising the corruption opportunities of public officials and reframing the corruption-prone structure and process. While the former is related to an incentive mechanism for public officials, the latter is represented by a more transparent and accountable mechanism in operating the government.

The most typical example of corruption control through incentive restructuring is improving the salary and working conditions of public officials. Since 1972, the Government of Singapore has increased the salaries of public officials not only to prevent the brain drain of talented public officials but also to remove the motivation for corrupt behaviour stemming from low salaries (Quah 1995, 2010). Likewise, following the British legacy of generous perks and benefits, the Hong Kong government provided its public officials with salaries that were on a par with those in the private sector (Lee 2003; Quah 2013b).

Apart from incentives, Singapore and Hong Kong have undertaken broader civil service reform not only to improve administrative efficiency and effectiveness but also to enhance transparency, responsiveness and accountability. The initial civil service reform was meritocracy-based human resources management. The Public Service Commission was introduced in 1950 in Hong Kong and in 1951 in Singapore to recruit and retain competent and capable public officials (Quah 2013b). In Singapore, the PS21 Initiatives were introduced in 1995 and embraced e-government systems which have contributed to corruption prevention (Koh 2011).

Along with the prevention activities of the CPIB and the ICAC, civil service reforms have enabled Singapore and Hong Kong to reduce corruption to minimal levels within their governments.

Effectiveness of anti-corruption reforms in Singapore and Hong Kong

The nexus of anti-corruption policies and strategies lies in key institutions. The effectiveness of anti-corruption institutions can be assessed in several ways. The most important one is the extent to which institutions are institutionalised so that they are embedded in society as a governing norm of the people (North 1990). In this light, anti-corruption institutions are effective when people in public and private sectors build and maintain a sense of ethics to resist corruption. As North (1990) stresses, institutionalisation is realised through implementation. This implies that the ACA's zero-tolerance law enforcement is a critical process as far as corruption is concerned. Therefore, the effectiveness of anti-corruption institutions can be measured through the impartial and effective law enforcement of ACAs and its impact on corruption occurrence and social values (Choi 2009).

In the absence of reliable objective data on the impartiality and effectiveness of the CPIB and the ICAC, the surveys conducted by the CPIB and the ICAC provide a public view on the effectiveness of the two ACAs. While annual data on the effectiveness of the ICAC are accessible, data on the CPIB are neither available nor disclosed to the public. Yet those who assess the effectiveness of the CPIB generally concede the effectiveness of the Bureau. Using the CPIB's 2002 survey results in which 71 per cent of respondents perceived that the CPIB had successfully controlled corruption in Singapore, Quah (2010) supports the position that the Bureau has an effective anti-corruption role. A more recent survey, the 2009 Global Corruption Barometer Report, shows similar results regarding the CPIB's effectiveness. Asked about the government's corruption fighting activities, 96 per cent of Singaporean respondents believed that they were effective (TI 2009). Concerning the ICAC, 74.6 per cent of respondents in the 1992 survey felt that the ICAC was effective. After more than 20 years, the 2014 annual survey reveals that 87.8 per cent of respondents perceived the ICAC to be quite effective (ICAC 2014b). Although these surveys do not fully capture the ACA's impartial and effective law enforcement functions, both the CPIB and the ICAC, as reliable guardians against corruption, have been able to garner public support.

Another aspect in assessing the effectiveness of anti-corruption institutions is changes in the occurrence of corruption. As the metaphor "the tip of the iceberg" indicates, it is not possible to measure the entire range of corruption accurately. In this regard, determining how effective anti-corruption efforts are in curbing corruption is not an easy task. Even if a measure shows that corruption decreases over time, it is still uncertain to what extent the anti-corruption role of an ACA contributes to this decrease because other variables may also be at play. Nonetheless, a measure, albeit incomplete, that captures corruption can be used to assess the effectiveness of an ACA's anti-corruption activities. Since the TI's CPI is one of the most widely used indicators to measure the degree of corruption in the public sector, it is examined to assess the effectiveness of the CPIB and the ICAC.

Along with the CPI data on Singapore and Hong Kong, the CPI scores of other developing countries are considered to see whether an ACA-driven anti-corruption strategy has worked over time. A comparison of the two ACAs of Singapore and Hong Kong with other ACAs tends to reaffirm the popular notion that an ACA is a necessary, but not sufficient, element of successful corruption control. For the past two decades, several developing countries established a separate ACA with somewhat different functions and organizational structure. Among several ACA models, there are some countries which adopted the so-called Singapore or Hong Kong model in which punitive and prevention functions are merged in an ACA. They include the state of New South Wales in Australia, Indonesia, Jordan, Latvia, Lithuania, Maldives, Mongolia, Timor-Leste, and Uganda (UNDP 2011). Although the CPI is a rough estimate to assess the effectiveness of ACAs in those countries, using the CPI to measure public sector corruption is in some sense acceptable because corruption control in the public sector is one of the core missions of an ACA. Table 18.1 displays the longitudinal CPI scores in those countries along with several other features.

First, while the CPI scores of Singapore and Hong Kong have remained high over time, they have dropped since 2012. Further exploration of why this has happened is necessary. One possible interpretation is that the CPIB and the ICAC have been unable to maintain their effectiveness. Second, the CPI scores of other countries that embraced the Singapore and Hong Kong ACA model do not show comparable results in curbing corruption in the public sector. If one assumes that the CPI scores are influenced by the effectiveness of an ACA, there are some countries which show remarkable progress and others which show backtracking even after an ACA was established. Whereas Latvia's CPI scores increased sharply from an average of 32.3 during the pre-ACA period to an average of 45.3 after its ACA was created, the CPI scores of the Maldives before and after the creation of an ACA decreased from an average of 33.0 to 25.3. As seen in Table 18.1, except for New South Wales, Australia which has maintained a high level of public integrity, other countries have not been able to make significant progress in dealing with corruption in their governments. This fact indicates that when other key factors including a strong anti-corruption will and the commitment of the political leader are not present, an ACA by itself does not ensure success.

A final aspect for judging the effectiveness of anti-corruption institutions is the value of societal ethics. The issue of ethics can be addressed according to the two perspectives of public officials and the general public. While examining the Hong Kong government, Scott and Leung (2012) and Scott (2013) observe the changing integrity management of the Hong Kong civil service from a traditional, rule-based corruption prevention approach to a value-based one. Because of the strong institutional inertia in the Hong Kong civil service in which a rule-based anti-corruption strategy had prevailed since 1974, it is still uncertain whether value-based corruption control is strongly rooted in the Hong Kong civil service. However, because the Hong Kong government continues to incorporate value-based integrity management into its civil service, ethics-driven behaviour and decisions may become another important pillar to sustain a high level of integrity in the Hong Kong government. Apart from public officials, it seems that citizens in Singapore and Hong Kong have attained

Table 18.1 Changes in the CPI scores of Singapore- and Hong Kong-modelled ACAs

Country	Name of ACA	Year of Est.	1995	1996	1997	1998	1999	2000	2001	2002	2003	2004	2005	2006	2007	2008	2009	2010	2011	2012	2013	2014	Pre-ACA	Post-ACA
Singapore	Corruption Practices Investigation Bureau	1952	93	88	87	91	91	91	92	93	94	93	94	94	93	92	92	93	92	87	86	84	N/A	91.0
Hong Kong	Independent Commission Against Corruption	1974	71	70	73	78	77	77	79	82	80	80	83	83	83	81	82	84	84	77	75	74	N/A	78.6
Australia	Independent Commission Against Corruption in New South Wales	1988	88	86	89	87	87	83	85	86	88	88	88	87	86	87	87	87	88	85	81	80	N/A	86.1
Indonesia	Corruption Eradication Commission	2003	19	27	27	20	17	17	19	19	19	20	22	24	23	26	28	28	30	32	32	34	20.6	26.5
Jordan	Anti-Corruption Commission	2008		49		47	44	46	49	45	46	53	57	53	47	51	50	47	45	48	45	49	48.7	47.9
Latvia	Corruption Prevention and Combating Bureau	2002				27	34	34	34	37	38	40	42	47	48	50	45	43	42	49	53	55	32.3	45.3
Lithuania	Special Investigation Service	1997				38	38	41	48	48	47	46	48	48	48	46	49	50	48	54	57	58	N/A	48.3

(Continued)

Country	Name of ACA	Year of Est.	1995	1996	1997	1998	1999	2000	2001	2002	2003	2004	2005	2006	2007	2008	2009	2010	2011	2012	2013	2014	Pre-ACA	Post-ACA
Maldives	Anti-Corruption Commission	2008													33	28	25	23	25				33.0	25.3
Mongolia	Independent Authority Against Corruption	2007					43					30	30	28	30	30	27	27	27	36	38	39	29.3	31.8
Timor-Leste	Anti-Corruption Commission	2010												26	26	22	22	25	24	33	30	28	24.0	28.0
Uganda	Inspector General of Government	1988		27		26	22	23	19	21	22	26	25	27	28	26	25	25	24	29	26	26	N/A	24.8

Source: Transparency International, https://www.transparency.org/ (accessed 1 April 2016).

Note: The CPI scores from 1997 to 2011 were converted from the original 10-point scale to a 100-point scale. A lower CPI score indicates more serious corruption in the public sector, a higher CPI score, less corruption.

a relatively high sense of ethics. According to the results of the 2009 Global Corruption Barometer survey, both Singapore and Hong Kong belonged to the "high" group, indicating that more than 64 per cent of respondents were willing to pay more to buy a corruption-free company (TI 2009).

Conclusion

From the angle of institutional theory, this chapter has examined how anti-corruption reform processes have evolved over time in Singapore and Hong Kong. Facing serious corruption problems throughout the entire society, both governments tried to change the old equilibrium which provided more benefits to the corrupt and to create a new one that incurred greater costs to be corrupt. Anti-corruption reform began to make substantial progress aided by changes in exogenous parameters such as a new PAP government in Singapore and the Peter Godber case in Hong Kong. These changes triggered deliberate anti-corruption reforms led by political leaders which were further reinforced by administrative reforms. The paucity of available data shows that anti-corruption reforms in Singapore and Hong Kong have not only been effective in curbing corruption in their civil services but also successful in propelling social values towards higher integrity. In sum, as institutional theory suggests, Singapore and Hong Kong provide good examples of how formal institutions affect informal institutions through the process of institutionalisation in the midst of solving social inefficiencies.

Yet this assessment is not without critics. The ever-changing corruption environment raises some challenges. In this light, regarding the occurrence of corruption in the present and in the future, private sector corruption warrants more attention. What is commonly observed in both Singapore and Hong Kong is that private sector corruption has increased over time. Concern over private sector corruption can be justified when both objective and subjective data are examined. For example, public sector corruption in Singapore accounted for 15 per cent of all cases registered for investigation in 2014. This number is a decrease from 23 per cent in 2012 and 16 per cent in 2013. In contrast, private sector corruption showed an increasing trend from 77 per cent in 2012 to 84 per cent in 2013 to 85 per cent in 2014 (CPIB 2015). The same is true in Hong Kong. In 2014, a total of 223 persons were prosecuted for corruption and related offences of which those in the public and private sectors were 54 and 169, respectively (ICAC 2014a). These objective data on corruption are in line with subjective perception-based surveys. In the 2009 Global Corruption Barometer Report, survey respondents in Singapore and Hong Kong perceived that business and private sectors are most affected by corruption. This perception contrasts with the results at the global level in which political parties and the legislature are considered corruption-prone sectors (TI 2009).

Another concern is about how to control the potential conflict of interests, particularly of high office-holders, which is legally allowed but ethically banned. Oehlers (2005) points out that what is noteworthy in Singapore is not the absence of corruption but the particular form of corruption. Although common forms of corruption such as public officials' bribe-taking and embezzlement are rare, there is criticism that the ruling PAP overuses public resources to maintain its power. Moreover, the ruling class in the Singaporean government is tied strongly to the business sector surrounding the so-called Government-Linked Companies. This can be viewed as the abuse of power for private gains (Stephenson 2015). Similarly, in Hong Kong, there have been concerns about potential increases in crony capitalism, money-laundering, and cross-border corruption.

The operation of law enforcement raises another concern although there is a significant difference between the CPIB and the ICAC. The ICAC operates its law enforcement activities within a framework of accountability and transparency, both of which are essential for holding an ACA accountable to people (Heilbrunn 2004). Internal as well as external mechanisms are designed to hold the ICAC not only accountable to the Chief Executive but also to the Legislative Council. In addition, Advisory Committees in the ICAC place the Commission under the citizens' oversight. In this way, the ICAC by law and by practice is held accountable to its key principals of the head of government, the legislature, and the public (Meagher 2002). Moreover, the ICAC pursues transparency as one of its operating principles. Accordingly, how and what the ICAC does is open to public scrutiny. By contrast, internal and external accountability mechanisms in the CPIB are weakly institutionalised and not comparable to those in the ICAC (Quah 2015).

The final, but not least important, concern is related to the political systems which are different but may have similar consequences for corruption. It is commonly observed that the level of democracy is not strong in either Singapore or Hong Kong. Hong Kong is ruled by its constitution, known as the Basic Law. Although formally under the principle of "one country, two systems" Hong Kong is supposedly granted a high degree of economic and political autonomy, in practice it falls under the political control of the Chinese government. Democracy is consequently not fully realised in Hong Kong. The dearth of a democratic political system has an effect on Hong Kong constituents who do not have a fully accountable Chief Executive even when the issue is wrongdoing (Scott 2014). The level of democracy is lower in Singapore than in Hong Kong. According to the World Bank's Governance measure, the "Voice and Accountability" indicators of Hong Kong and Singapore in 2013 were 69.19 and 52.13, respectively, which was lower than Taiwan at 73.46 (World Bank 2016).

To conclude this chapter, as observed in Singapore and Hong Kong, administrative systems and the values of the civil service that resist corruption are neither created nor sustained in the absence of an anti-corruption political will and an effective, independent and dedicated corruption-fighting agency. While a punitive approach centering on detection and punishment is one pillar of anti-corruption strategy, the experiences of Singapore and Hong Kong signify the importance of another pillar, a preventive approach through continuous government reform. Yet anti-corruption reform, propelled by these two pillars, is easy to verbalise but difficult to put into action. Academic and practical discourses on anti-corruption measures do not propose a panacea to cure the disease of corruption because each country is situated in unique circumstances. One may consider the successful anti-corruption paths of Singapore and Hong Kong as a paragon that corruption-ridden countries can follow. However, what the two countries have achieved is the result of many years of endeavour. Instead of embracing all the success factors into an anti-corruption reform strategy which is not feasible, it is more realistic, albeit challenging, for countries suffering from endemic corruption to find their own way to dismantle an inefficient corruption-dominant equilibrium.

References

Advisory Committee on Corruption (1961) "Sixth report", in *Reports of the Standing Committee and the Advisory Committee on Corruption*, Hong Kong: Government Printer, 29 December.
Choi, J. W. (2009) "Institutional structure and effectiveness of anticorruption agencies: a comparative analysis of South Korea and Hong Kong", *Asian Journal of Political Science*, 17(2): 195–214.

Commission of Inquiry (1973) *Second report of the Commission of Inquiry under Sir Alastair Blair-Kerr*, Hong Kong: Government Printer.

CPIB (Corruption Practices Investigation Bureau) (2015) "Corruption situation in Singapore under control", CPIB Press Release, 2 April, https://www.cpib.gov.sg/sites/default/files/publication-documents/CPIB%20Corruption%20Statistics_0.pdf (accessed 5 April 2016).

Darden, K. (2002) "Graft and governance: corruption as an informal mechanism of state control", Yale University Working Paper.

de Speville, B. E. D. (1999) "The experience of Hong Kong, China, in combating corruption", in R. Stapenhurst and S. J. Kpundeh (eds.) *Curbing corruption: toward a model for building national integrity*, Washington, DC: World Bank, 51–58.

Heilbrunn, J. R. (2004) "Anti-corruption commission: panacea or real medicine to fight corruption?" World Bank Institute, http://siteresources.worldbank.org/WBI/Resources/wbi37234Heilbrunn.pdf (accessed 5 April 2016).

Helmke, G. and S. Levitsky (2003) "Informal institutions and comparative politics: a research agenda", The Helen Kellogg Institute for International Studies, Working Paper #307, https://www3.nd.edu/~kellogg/publications/workingpapers/WPS/307.pdf (accessed 5 April 2016).

Hong Kong Legislative Council (1973) *Legislative Council debates*, October 17.

ICAC (Independent Commission Against Corruption) (2014a) *Annual report 2014*, Hong Kong: ICAC.

ICAC (Independent Commission Against Corruption) (2014b) *ICAC annual survey 2014: executive summary*, Hong Kong: ICAC.

Jing, S. (2007) "Corruption by design? A comparative study of Singapore, Hong Kong and mainland China", Australian National University: Crawford School of Economics and Government, Discussion Papers, http://apo.org.au/resource/corruption-design-comparative-study-singapore-hong-kong-and-mainland-china (accessed 5 April 2016).

Klitgaard, R. (2004) "Leadership under systemic corruption", paper presented to the six Mekong Delta countries at a summit meeting in Vientiane, Laos, December, http://www.cgu.edu/include/Leadership_Under_System_Corruption_12-04.pdf (accessed 5 April 2016).

Koh, T. H. (2011) "Corruption control in Singapore", Resource Material Series No. 83, http://www.unafei.or.jp/english/pdf/RS_No83/No83_17VE_Koh1.pdf (accessed 5 April 2016).

Lee, G. B. (2005) *The Syonan years: Singapore under Japanese rule, 1942–1945*, Singapore: National Archives of Singapore.

Lee, G. O. M. (2003) "Hong Kong: institutional inheritance from colony to special administrative region", in C. Hood, B. G. Peters, and G. O. M. Lee (eds.) *Reward for high public office: Asian and Pacific Rim states*, London: Routledge, 130–144.

Lee, H. L. (2012) "Fighting corruption and keeping Singapore corruption-free", speech by Lee Hsien Loong at CPIB's 60th Anniversary Celebrations, September 18, http://www.pmo.gov.sg/mediacentre/speech-prime-minister-lee-hsien-loong-cpibs-60th-anniversary-celebrations (accessed 22 April 2016).

Lee, K. Y. (2000) *From third world to first: the Singapore story: 1965–2000*, New York: HarperCollins Publishers.

Lethbridge, H. J. (1985) *Hard graft in Hong Kong: scandal, corruption, the ICAC*, Hong Kong: Oxford University Press.

Meagher, P. (2002) "Anti-corruption agencies: a review of experience", Center for Institutional Reform and the Informal Sector (IRIS) at the University of Maryland: the IRIS Discussion Papers on Institutions and Development, http://www.u4.no/recommended-reading/anti-corruption-agencies-a-review-of-experience/ (accessed 5 April 2016).

Meagher, P. (2005) "Anti-corruption agencies: rhetoric versus reality", *Journal of Policy Reform*, 8(1): 69–103.

North, D. C. (1990) *Institutions, institutional change, and economic performance*, New York: Cambridge University Press.

Oehlers, A. (2005) "Corruption: the peculiarities of Singapore", in N. Tarling (ed.) *Corruption and good governance in Asia*, New York: Routledge, 149–164.

Quah, J.S.T. (1995) "Controlling corruption in city-states: a comparative study of Hong Kong and Singapore", *Crime, Law & Social Change*, 22(4): 391–414.

Quah, J.S.T. (2001) "Combating corruption in Singapore: what can be learned?" *Journal of Contingencies and Crisis Management*, 9(1): 29–35.

Quah, J.S.T. (2007) "Anti-corruption agencies in four Asian countries: a comparative analysis", *International Public Management Review*, 8(2): 73–95.

Quah, J.S.T. (2008) "Anti-corruption agencies in four Asian countries: a comparative analysis", in B. Bowornwathana and C. Westcott (eds.) *Comparative governance reform in Asia: democracy, corruption, and government trust*, Bingley: JAI Press, 85–109.

Quah, J.S.T. (2010) *Public administration Singapore-style*, Bingley: Emerald.

Quah, J.S.T. (2013a) "Curbing corruption in Singapore: the importance of political will, expertise, enforcement, and context", *Research in Public Policy and Management*, 23: 137–166.

Quah, J.S.T. (2013b) "Curbing corruption and enhancing trust in government: some lessons from Singapore and Hong Kong", in J. Liu, B. Hebenton and S. Jou (eds.) *Handbook of Asian criminology*, New York: Springer, 25–48.

Quah, J.S.T. (2015) "Singapore's Corrupt Practices Investigation Bureau: four suggestions for enhancing its effectiveness", *Asian Education and Development Studies*, 4(1): 76–100.

Rose-Ackerman, S. (1999) *Corruption and government: causes, consequences, and reform*, New York: Cambridge University Press.

Rothstein, B. (2011) "Anti-corruption: the indirect 'big bang' approach", *Review of International Political Economy*, 18(2): 228–250.

Scott, I. (2013) "Institutional design and corruption prevention in Hong Kong", *Journal of Contemporary China*, 22(79): 77–92.

Scott, I. (2014) "Political scandals and the accountability of the Chief Executive in Hong Kong", *Asian Survey*, 54(5): 966–986.

Scott, I. and J.Y.H. Leung (2012) "Integrity management in post-1997 Hong Kong: challenges for a rule-based system", *Crime, Law and Social Change*, 58(1): 39–52.

Stephenson, M. (2015) "Does Singapore deserve its squeaky-clean reputation?" GAB: The Global Anticorruption Blog, 7 July, http://globalanticorruptionblog.com/ (accessed 1 April 2016).

Tan, A. L. (1999) "The experience of Singapore in combating corruption", in R. Stapenhurst and S. J. Kpundeh (eds.) *Curbing corruption: toward a model for building national integrity*, Washington, DC: World Bank, 59–66.

TI (Transparency International) (2009) *2009 Global Corruption Barometer*, Berlin: TI.

TI (Transparency International) (2016) Corruption Perception Index: overview, http://www.transparency.org/research/cpi/overview (accessed 1 April 2016).

Tsang, S. (2004) *A modern history of Hong Kong*, London: I.B. Tauris & Co.

UNDP (United Nations Development Programme) (2011) *Practitioners' guide: capacity assessment of anti-corruption agencies*, New York: UNDP.

UNDP (United Nations Development Programme) (2014) *Anti-Corruption strategies: understanding what works, what doesn't and why? Lessons learned from the Asia-Pacific region*, Bangkok: UNDP.

World Bank (2016) Worldwide Governance Indicators, http://info.worldbank.org/governance/wgi/index.aspx#reports (accessed 1 April 2016).

Yep, R. (2013) "The crusade against corruption in Hong Kong in the 1970s: Governor MacLehose as a zealous reformer or reluctant hero?" *China Information*, 27(2): 197–221.

19

RULE-BASED AND INTEGRITY-BASED ANTI-CORRUPTION APPROACHES IN ASIA

Robert Gregory

Introduction

A rules-based ("low road") approach to developing and maintaining standards of ethical probity in government assumes that those who work for government cannot always, if ever, be trusted to conduct themselves honestly and fairly, and that they must be induced or coerced to comply with the authority that is embedded in hierarchically and vertically imposed laws, rules and regulations. On the other hand, an integrity-based ("high road") method is founded on the premise that the moral character of those who work in government service is a more important determinant of honest, fair, impartial, and non-corrupt government.[1]

In discussing the two approaches, this chapter comprises four sections. The first outlines the essential elements of these approaches to securing ethical probity among bureaucratic officials and the relationship between them. The second draws attention to the behaviour of politicians. The third shows how some Asian countries have adopted various mixes of both approaches (but does not provide any assessment of how effective these combinations have been in combatting corruption). The final section offers some concluding observations.

Taking the low road and the high road

Modern bureaucracies are essentially control systems. As Weber (1947: 337, emphasis added) said, "bureaucracy is the most rational known means of carrying out imperative control over human beings…superior to any other form in precision, in stability, *in the stringency of its discipline*, and in its reliability". The monocratic form is based on the assumption that the people who comprise the organization cannot be trusted to carry out the purposes of the organization's owners faithfully, whether those owners be the sovereign people (represented by a constitutionally elected government), or the shareholders of a private business enterprise.

In contrast to Weber's "ideal-type", in reality, officials are likely to be more or less competent, and more or less morally corrupt. Their behaviour, *qua* bureaucrats, is governed by legal-rational authority: the application, without fear or favour, of impersonally mandated, knowable rules and regulations, backed by the threat of sanctions for non-compliance. There is a clear distinction between what they are allowed to do as office-holders and what they are allowed to do as private individuals outside of the offices they hold.

A rules-based approach to public service integrity operates at different levels. All government officials are subject in the first instance to the law of the country in which they live and work and in most cases criminal laws will proscribe various forms of corrupt behaviour. As public officials, their behaviour will also be constrained by bureaucratic rules and regulations, codes of conduct, and codes of ethics. Codes of conduct and codes of ethics (especially as they are intended to govern members of professional occupations) are "some of the most important statements of civic expectation", whose appeal is as much emotional as rational, motivating individuals to see themselves as proud professionals, and guiding people as to what they should do rather than what they should not do (Gilman 2005: 3–12).[2] They generally are not laws or regulations in and of themselves but are simplified statements of principle, whose intent will be reflected in both the spirit and the letter of laws and regulations. They may be designed for particular organizations and functions or more generically for a governmental system as a whole.

Laws, regulations, rules and codes of conduct are of little value unless those people whose behaviour they are intended to regulate *voluntarily* comply with them, rather than being coerced to do so, and are motivated less by the risk of punishment and more by a firm desire to conduct themselves with honesty and integrity. As Gilman (2005: 25) observes, "Printing a code of conduct and placing it on a wall, is not implementation. There must be an institutional fabric for developing the code, communicating it, interpreting it, training or education on the code, enforcing it and assessing it". In the case of laws aimed at controlling corruption, criminal penalties will be imposed whereas lesser kinds of malfeasance perpetrated by public officials will be subject to administrative sanctions, such as dismissal, suspension, demotion, and diminished career opportunities.

In countries where patrimonial rather than legal-rational authority is the predominant source of political and bureaucratic order, codes of official conduct may be more necessary while at the same time being less effective, especially if public servants are not clear about whom they actually work for and what their roles and responsibilities are. In the absence of a bureaucratic system based firmly on legal-rational authority, as is often the case in "developing" countries, it is more difficult to implement impersonally mandated rules and regulations designed to provide proper contractual arrangements for public procurement and other areas of public administration that are by nature vulnerable to improper official behaviour.

Codes of ethics are inadequate if the people whose behaviour they are intended to constrain are incapable of reasoned and reasonable ethical and moral judgment. So in contrast to the assumptions that ultimately underpin a rules-based approach to maintaining ethical probity in government, the integrity-based method more readily assumes that individuals' baser instincts can be kept at bay through elevating people's capacity and willingness for moral suasion. As Gilman (2005: 9) argues:

>...codes of ethics do not take away one's own moral autonomy or absolve the public servant from the obligation to reason. Codes of ethics provide at most a strong prima facie reason to act in a certain way. However, these can be overridden by strong, reasoned objection. The expectation is that the norm is not to violate the code and such violations can only be justified because of a higher ethical principle.

The "high road" approach is based on the belief that satisfactory levels of individual and group compliance stem not only from the authoritative imposition of formal authority but also from the internalisation within the individual of organizational norms and values which keep in check any predisposition to engage in opportunistic behaviour. It encourages and enables the official to serve as a "fiduciary professional citizen" in a democratic society (Cooper 2012). This method is aspirational, appealing to the "better angels" of human nature. Coercive control systems, as ethics-maintaining fallback positions, are heavily complemented by informal normative acculturation, which is made more effective by personnel policies designed to recruit and promote people of good character. Ethical awareness can be developed among governmental officials through mandatory training courses, seminars, and the like, without seeking to turn people into ethical philosophers.

The two approaches, in fact, are manifestations of the differences between the idea of accountability, on the one hand, and responsibility, on the other, as reflected in the seminal debate in the early 1940s between Herman Finer (1941) and Carl Friedrich (1940). The "low road" approach is consistent with Finer's concern for *external* controls over public officials, later apparent in Mosher's (1968) idea of "objective responsibility", which can be understood as official accountability (Gregory 2012). On the other hand, "high road" norms and values are *internalised* by officials, rendering them much more subjectively responsible in their behaviour. The difference is well summed up by Uhr (1993: 4):

> Accountability is about compliance with authority, whereas responsibility is about empowerment and independence. Accountability is the negative end of the same band in which responsibility is the positive end. If accountability is about minimising misgovernment, responsibility is about maximising good government.

A mutually constitutive relationship?

Each approach can be conceptualised as opposing ends of a continuum, reflecting issues of *legality* at the rules-based pole and of *legitimacy* at the integrity-based end (Gregory 2002). The first defines those actions that are *illegal,* according to laws, regulations, rules and codes of conduct (as a form of legalistic hierarchy). While many actions taken by government officials may not be illegal, they may nevertheless be judged as morally and ethically *illegitimate*, constituting forms of official misconduct that may be sanctioned by the courts of public and organizational opinion. For example, the speaker of Australia's Parliament, Bronwyn Bishop, resigned in August 2015 after "abuse of taxpayer funded travel entitlements", described by Prime Minister Tony Abbott as "arguably inside the rules but plainly outside community expectations".[3] Hong Kong's common law offence of "misconduct in public office" covers serious misdemeanours that are not necessarily covered by statutory law. Conversely, some illegal actions may be considered legitimate, say, a whistle-blower who receives strong public support for breaking a law against the disclosure of official information. Laws can codify what is illegitimate behaviour and can also shape societal perceptions of legitimacy. As these views change over time, then laws may also be revised or created in response.

"Low road" approaches on their own will not make honest those officials who for whatever reason are morally and ethically incorrigible but they are necessary in guiding and shaping the behaviour of those, perhaps often the majority, who are neither pure saints nor irredeemable sinners. Obviously, the highest standards of ethical probity in government will be attained when officials are committed to ensuring that their actions are both legal and legitimate. Sometimes, however, the social and political legitimacy of actions, rather than their formal legality, will be decisive, regardless of whether obviously illegitimate actions are also proscribed in law. Public officials' capacity for tentative moral and ethical judgement is at least as important as any instinct they may have for precise legal calculation. Nevertheless, just as "low road" methods will not change the behaviour of obdurate people, nor will attempts to raise officials' ethical awareness succeed in cases where there is little or no receptiveness to them.

Virtually all governmental systems will display some combination of the two approaches, but it is not clear that rules-based and integrity-based modes of securing ethical probity in government are necessarily mutually reinforcing. Much more empirical research is needed. A strong rules-based approach, with concomitant enforcement, reflects the bureaucratic imperative of control but whether or not it is a necessary condition for the development of strong normative commitment remains a moot point. At least in theory, it is possible to conceive of a situation in which rules are either absent or poorly codified and promulgated but where officials nevertheless display high standards of ethical probity. However, a rules-based approach is better understood as a *sine qua non* of ethical probity in government, especially as an integrity-based strategy may take a long time to produce desired, if only marginal, results (Holmes 2015).

It is also plausible that the normative strength of a "high road" approach might be eroded over time by bureaucratic systems that are explicitly based on the belief that officials cannot be trusted. If people are conditioned by the enforcement of rules to see themselves as untrustworthy, to what extent, as a kind of self-fulfilling prophecy, do they tend to become so? And if they do, then by what means can such a tendency be most effectively countered?

While a "low road" approach is fundamental to any modern governmental system, it may become an inadequate means of coping with emergent ethical challenges that flow from broader changes in the administrative environment. Scott and Leung (2012: 50), for example, argue that an "overarching" rules-based approach worked "reasonably well" in Hong Kong after the establishment in 1974 of the Independent Commission Against Corruption (ICAC), when "very specific guidelines" were developed on what constitutes an "advantage". However, this approach is not adequate in dealing with the various types of conflicts of interest that have become more common in recent years. Therefore, the real value of codes of ethics and the like may reside not so much in their content as in the open discussion needed to shape that content.

The impact of New Public Management

During the New Public Management (NPM) "revolution" of the 1980s and 1990s, economic interpretations of political and bureaucratic behaviour emphasised the self-interested motivations of officials rather than their commitment to public service and market-led innovations were introduced to enhance public sector efficiency and accountability (Boston 2011). Although NPM had its origins in and was most assiduously adopted in Western, mainly Anglophone, countries like Britain, New Zealand and Australia, some of its elements have increasingly been adopted in Asian jurisdictions (Cheung 2011).

The career-based personnel systems which preceded NPM had relied overwhelmingly on relational "contracts" which were largely implicit, open-ended, and dependent on agents' willingness to behave according to an ethos of dutiful and ethical public service. NPM, on the other hand, promoted the abolition of public service career systems and their replacement with position-based systems within which "principals" (employers) and "agents" (public employees) entered into specific, usually fixed-term, employment contracts. The NPM approach is consistent with Etzioni's (1975) notion of "remunerative/calculative" compliance, as distinct from his "normative/moral" form, which had previously typified many Western public service systems. The NPM approach is consistent with the principal-agent approaches that are prominent in anti-corruption strategies world-wide (Klitgaard 1988).

In assuming that all governmental officials were, in Le Grand's (2003) metaphorical terminology, essentially "knaves" rather than "knights", NPM promoted contractualised appointments, and rigorous performance management systems, closely linked to incentivised pay for performance. These moves were intended to harness employees' narrow self-interest to the goals of the organization's owners, the better to reduce waste, inefficiency, cynicism, incompetence, and corruption. However, in government organizations "knavish" behaviour can take many forms. Especially in jurisdictions where public administration is strongly "marketised" public officials are more likely to face conflicts of interest of various kinds and "knavishness" is manifest in their failure or unwillingness to recognise these situations as such, despite the existence of rules intended to ensure that such conflicts are properly "managed". "Knavish" behaviour can also be apparent, *inter alia*, in "hitting the target but missing the point", that is, the "gaming" of performance management systems that are intended to ensure purpose-driven (as distinct from rule-driven) compliance; in the surreptitious leaking of information for tactical political and administrative purposes; in the "moral hazard" of shirking, and the "adverse selection" of misleading personal representation; in overly zealous "can-do" attitudes in pursuit of organizational purposes; and in overbearing and officious behaviour towards citizens.

Each approach has its own costs

Public organizations in Western democracies are obliged to display zero tolerance of "hard core" corruption, which is invariably covered by a country's criminal code or is dealt with as common law offences. Most "lesser" forms of unethical or morally dubious behaviour by officials, such as those depicted previously, are proscribed by systemic rules and regulations, which seek to control the ways in which discretionary authority can be exercised. As a rule of thumb, there is likely to be a strongly positive correlation between the size of a public organization's manual of rules and standard operating procedures, on the one hand, and the degree of discretionary authority available to its employees, on the other.

A commitment to a "low road", at the expense of a "high road", approach carries an organizational cost in inverse proportion to the degree of voluntary compliance displayed by organization members. It will enhance the incidence of "goal displacement", wherein the rules and codes increasingly become ends in themselves, as enforcement is used to combat low voluntary compliance, thus inhibiting the organization's capacity to pursue its purposes effectively. Public organizations find it necessary to reduce such costs by also employing integrity-based approaches in securing high standards of ethical probity. The more honest its employees are, the less the need for a rigid and comprehensive panoply of rules and regulations.

In practice, there is no way of objectively calculating the tradeoff, in terms of costs and benefits, over time, between the two approaches. All governmental systems must determine what mix of the two approaches is required to achieve and sustain high levels of ethical probity. As Scott and Leung (2012: 40) argue, a shift from a predominantly rules-based culture to one in which much more emphasis is placed on developing and reinforcing a public service ethos can be problematic. In particular, there are organizational and systemic costs involved in ensuring that public officials are better able to engage in the sort of "moral reasoning" that may be required of them in recognising and dealing appropriately with, for example, conflicts of interest, as their discretionary authority increases. Whereas lower level workers may be trained to recognise conflicts of interest, they cannot normally be expected to take the responsibility for resolving them properly, "theirs not to reason why", so increasingly more decisions are passed up the hierarchy to over-burdened superiors. However, research conducted by Brewer et al. (2015: 407) on the Hong Kong civil service found that there was no evidence of substantial conflict arising out of the increasing use of a value-based approach within a predominantly rules-based system and that the latter approach had been "slightly strengthened" by attempts to introduce elements of the former.

A crucial element in securing high standards of ethical probity in government has always been the understanding that recruitment into government offices, while it may be a pathway to power and authority, and perhaps even fame, does not provide for personal enrichment. It offers a secure and comfortable standard of living, as distinct from the greater financial rewards that people may receive in the business sector, and should not provide opportunities for officials to use their offices for illegitimate and unlawful private gain. It is important, therefore, that this expectation of public office is widely understood within the society that governmental officials are meant to serve. Those seeking public office as a pathway to pecuniary self-enrichment need not apply.

Mixing and matching

While a spirit of ethical probity may pervade a governmental system as a whole, different combinations of rule-based and integrity-based approaches will be needed within individual organizations that compose the system. Different types of task will strongly influence the ways in which an organization will be able to maintain ethical probity amongst its members (Gregory 1995). Some agencies are more liable to corrupt practices than others, as is well recognised in the international literature on corruption. Also, depending on the nature of the organization's central task, some officials will exercise more discretion in their daily work than others. Policing and tax collection carry more risks of corruption than do international diplomacy or scientific research and development, customs collection and immigration more so than town planning or census-taking. Moreover, the people who are employed in public agencies are today much more likely to be members of professional communities than was the case when "technical knowledge", as depicted by Weber, consisted largely of knowledge of the rules. Professionals in public service are governed not only by the rules of the organization in which they work, and by an overarching public service ethos, but also by the norms and standards of the profession to which they belong. There may often be conflict between the two, pulling professionals in different normative directions.

A set of generic values may be adopted as a guiding beacon for public officials across a governmental system such as Hong Kong's "commitment to the rule of law; honesty and integrity above private interests; accountability and openness in decision-making; political neutrality in conducting official duties; impartiality in the execution of public functions and dedication and diligence in serving the community" (Scott and Leung 2012: 48). Such values will not only be core components of an overarching normative model, but will also be reflected in the structures of rules and regulations designed to control individual behaviour.

While "low road" approaches, both across a public service system as a whole, and specifically within particular agencies, are commonly expected to provide a necessary foundation on which high standards of ethical probity can be built and maintained, determinedly corrupt behaviour will find a way around even the most explicit and strongly enforced rules (Gong and Ren 2012). Paradoxically, even when such an approach is largely rhetorical and symbolic, rather than instrumental, it may be more effective because it provides a way of skirting a design contradiction: namely, that in complex governmental systems codes of conduct and of ethics have either to be stated too broadly or too narrowly. If the former, they risk being irrelevant to the particular contextual circumstances facing public officials, and if the latter then they face the same problem of an operating manual that seeks to cover every possible contingency. The pursuit of many governmental purposes depends heavily on inter-agency collaboration, especially in an age of increasing policy complexity. Similarly, the maintenance of high standards of ethical probity depends more on the capacity of agencies, particularly central agencies, to sustain core public service values collectively rather than on individual agencies' codes of conduct.

There can seldom be found an optimal mix of rule-based and integrity-based approaches, in all circumstances over time, and for all agencies, when it comes to securing high ethical standards in public service. Regardless of what mix of rules-based and integrity-based approaches is developed, it is essential that various forms of corruption have first to be recognised as incontrovertibly unacceptable forms of behaviour by government officials (Scott 2013: 91). Until and unless the condemnation of corruption has become established as social and political taboos then no anti-corruption strategy is likely to be effective. In short, what is needed is a viable and sustainable combination of accountability (control) regimes coupled with responsible behaviour by public service employees, a system of "responsible accountability" (Gregory 1999; Gregory and Hicks 1999). Moynihan (2008) argues that the real challenge is how to design compliance systems that appeal simultaneously to both "knights" and "knaves" and that the market model tends over time to reduce the intrinsic public service motivation that is needed to ameliorate its own flaws.

Standards of political ethics

In Western democracies, politicians, like everyone else, are expected to abide by the law. Those among them who constitute the political executive in a national system will also be bound by a body of conventions and protocols, and will be acutely vulnerable to public accusations of unethical, immoral, corrupt or improper behaviour, since these can adversely affect their electoral prospects. They are subject to the judgment of their peers in the legislature and can be strongly sanctioned by them, as well as in the larger court of public opinion. These sanctions can be even stronger in their effects than the panoply of rules, regulations and codes of conduct which constrain the behaviour of bureaucratic (that is, appointed) officials. Nevertheless, the relationship between these two main components of a political system is a key element in the maintenance of high standards of ethical probity in government. In the language of agency theory, officials must be bound to serve their political principals dutifully, competently and honestly. Yet in the "risk and blame games" played out by politicians and officials, both sides can engage in various forms of "cheating" (Hood and Lodge 2006; Hood 2011).

In response to a number of sleaze scandals in British politics during the early 1990s, the Committee on Standards in Public Life (the Nolan Committee) established in 1994 what is still widely seen as an exemplary ethics code, laying out "Seven Principles of Public Life", selflessness, integrity, objectivity, accountability, openness, honesty, and leadership. Notwithstanding this, the perceived deterioration in the ethos of British government led to the passage in 2010 of Britain's Constitutional Reform and Governance Act. This legislation is intended to provide coherence to the patchwork quilt of probity regulation that had emerged as a consequence of the NPM reforms, and embeds a Civil Service Code of core values, namely, integrity, honesty, objectivity and impartiality, that cannot be changed without parliamentary approval. It provides for systematic regulation of the financial interests of members of parliament and also for a separate code for special political advisers who are not civil servants (Heywood 2012).

As Heywood (2012: 485) points out, the Act "reflects the tension between the values-based and compliance-based approaches to integrity management". The ways in which such a tension is resolved over time is likely to have a real impact on levels of public trust in political and governmental institutions. The British House of Commons Public Administration Select Committee in 2007 averred that "A rule based system should never substitute for a culture of high standards, rooted in the traditions of public life and shared by all those who participate in it" (House of Commons 2007: 15). According to the committee, a response to every ventilated allegation would lead to a rule-based system of integrity management that undermined the public trust that it sought to build, with the public asking why the system requires even more safeguards.

Whatever the case, the relationship between political and bureaucratic corruption is unclear, though public administration traditions embody strong assumptions that merit-based and non-corrupt bureaucracies are an essential bulwark against the venal and venial activities of politicians (Painter and Peters 2010). Empirical research by Dahlström et al. (2012) found that professional, merit-based bureaucracies reduce corruption, because the future prospects of these civil servants are independent of the political careers of political executives. In their view, this enhances the opportunities for each group to expose corrupt acts undertaken by the other. However, their argument does not address the degree of "politicisation" of the upper reaches of some professional bureaucracies that has stemmed from aspects of NPM, and issues surrounding the rapid growth in the numbers of political advisers who are not formally civil servants (Peters and Pierre 2004; Eichbaum and Shaw 2010).

High and low roads in some Asian jurisdictions

Notwithstanding these developments in Britain, levels of corruption in Asia are lowest in those two jurisdictions that have a strong British colonial heritage, Singapore and Hong Kong (Quah 2011, 2013). It is clear that in both cases the effective anti-corruption strategies that have been deployed since the early 1960s and the mid-1970s respectively owe much to the institutionalisation of the rule of law and the establishment in both jurisdictions of a single strong, well-resourced and dedicated anti-corruption agency.

In both places, rapid advances made in combating corruption among government officials were founded on a strong regime of rule compliance, buttressed by an entrenched and impartial policy of zero tolerance towards infractions. However, as noted previously, especially in Hong Kong, steps have had to be taken in recent times to institutionalise a more integrity-based system, due to the changing nature of governmental malfeasance, especially the emergence of more conflicts of interest and deferred advantages arising from post-career employment. For their resolution, these demand a greater individual capacity for ethical reasoning, rather than unproblematic compliance with rules. As Scott and Leung (2012) argue, this development has required something of a change in bureaucratic culture, since officials who have become too accustomed to complying with rules find themselves uncertain about what is expected of them, especially when public attitudes are changing in regard to what is seen as corruption and unethical practices, thus creating new pressures on a government which faces new challenges in sustaining public trust and legitimacy. Because no civil service can realistically aspire to be an oasis of ethical purity within a society characterised by high levels of corruption, the ICAC's community relations programme, one of its three core strategies, is instrumental in raising wider public consciousness as to what constitutes corrupt practice in government and in the business sector.

There are also costs to administrative efficiency when officials who have become assiduous rule-followers are almost overnight required to exercise more of their own ethical judgment, but who lack the confidence and experience to exercise such a responsibility and instead prefer to push it back up the bureaucratic hierarchy. As Scott (2013: 98) shows, the greater emphasis being placed on an integrity-based approach to ethical probity in the Hong Kong civil service, especially since the retrocession in 1997, has itself become an integral part of the bureaucratic landscape. In 1998, the Hong Kong government produced a *Civil Servants' Guide to Good Practices*, which laid out the core public service values mentioned previously (Scott and Leung 2012: 48). Eight years later, in 2006, ethics officers, all holding senior line management positions, were appointed in all government agencies to administer programmes run by the ICAC and the Civil Service Bureau, designed to complement the rules-based integrity foundation, and with stronger emphasis on "value-based elements particularly relating to conflicts of interest and professional behaviour".

In larger departments, a generic integrity-based approach can be tailored to the needs of the particular agency. The Hong Kong Police, for example, has "adopted a full-blown approach to value-based integrity management", the aim being to align the personal values of police officers with those of the organization itself (Brewer et al. 2015: 403–404). This "Living the Values" programme periodically highlights one of its core values, such as vision, enhancing honesty and integrity, enhancing police professionalism, building a caring workforce, and fairness in all dealings, through workshops, competitions and videos, encouraging feedback and ideas for implementation.

Similarly, the Singapore Police Force has been able to minimise corruption within its ranks by pursuing policies which since 1999 have included values education for its members (Quah 2014). A *Guide to Ethical Decisions*, promulgated by the Singapore Police Force in 2002, elaborates the "six guiding principles of ethos, the law, honour, conflicts of interest, consequence, and scrutiny", all illustrated by way of questions, scenarios and actual cases (Quah 2014: 201–203).

Across the causeway from Singapore, and ranked third in 2014 among the Association of Southeast Asian countries on Transparency International's Corruption Perceptions Index, Malaysia has recently adopted an approach similar to Hong Kong's. The current Malaysian Anti-Corruption Commission (MACC), set up in 2009, is modelled on Hong Kong's ICAC and thus adopts a three-pronged approach: enforcement, prevention and community education. The following year, Governance and Integrity Committees (*Jitu*) were established in all federal and state government agencies, headed by the respective ministers and state chief executives (*Menteri Besar*). In association with this move, integrity units are being set up in all agencies, staffed by "certified integrity officers", to implement "effective initiatives to institutionalize integrity, manag[e] complaints, prevention, compliance, detection and disciplinary actions in government agencies" (MACC 2013: 4). Unsurprisingly, these initiatives cannot be insulated from the wider politics of Malaysian society, with some commentators questioning the political independence of the *Jitu*. There have also been calls for the MACC to be represented on them (*The Malaysian Insider* 2014). In general, the Malaysian initiatives are a balanced mix of "low road" and "high road" approaches. The emphasis on compliance is apparent in the role of the *Jitu* in government agencies, but their establishment is also framed within a broader drive to raise standards of ethical probity in Malaysian society, as a part of an overarching National Integrity Plan, launched in 2004 by the Malaysian Institute of Integrity, and which includes a Corporate Integrity Pledge, and an annual National Integrity Day. This strategy reflects underlying political, racial and religious tensions in Malaysia, constitutionally a secular state, but one dominated by Muslim politicians and government officials.

Unlike Singapore, South Korea is a "third wave democracy" which has increasingly institutionalised democratic processes since the late 1980s but its development has also been bound up with chronic forms of political corruption. Corruption is defined in the country's criminal code, specifically the Anticorruption Act, which includes a comprehensive Code of Conduct for Public Officials, and restricts the employment opportunities available to corrupt officials who have been found to have engaged in corrupt activities. A Public Servants' Ethics Law has been in force since the 1980s, complementing the Anticorruption Act. It requires all officials to declare their assets, prohibits any use of their offices for private advantage, provides a blind trust system for senior financial authority officials who own substantial stocks, and regulates their opportunities for post-retirement employment. Like Singapore's, South Korea's civil servants constitute a meritocratic elite corps, sustained by means of a highly competitive recruitment examination (the *haengjunggosi*), with most of the successful candidates coming from the country's elite universities. Any form of corruption will result in the termination of the careers of those involved. In 2011, a Protection of Public Interest Whistleblowers Act came into force.

Also in recent years, the rules-based approach to ethical probity in South Korea has been enhanced by measures to support the ethical education of public officials. The country's Anti-Corruption and Civil Rights Commission (ACRC), established in 2008 through an amalgamation of the former Korea Independent Commission Against Corruption, the Ombudsman, and the Administrative Appeals Commission, runs public ethics programmes for civil servants. The ACRC takes into account the hours completed by officials in these courses when it assesses the anti-corruption efforts of individual government agencies (Lee and Jung 2010: 418). South Korea's developmental state is characterised by a relatively corruption-free, highly meritocratic, bureaucracy working in the service of a political elite which has for a long time been entangled with family-dominated business groups, *chaebols*, and which continues to be vulnerable to various forms of corruption.

Like South Korea, Taiwan is an emergent democracy characterised by high levels of corruption, especially in the relationship between politicians and big business interests. Yet, unlike South Korea, its civil service is not a non-corrupt meritocratic elite but is much more susceptible to corruption. Taiwan's President Ma has vowed to combat corruption and a dedicated Agency Against Corruption (AAC) was established in 2011. However, bribery is not defined by the legislation that makes it a criminal offence, and appropriate low-level "facilitation payments" are allowable, though subject to judicial determination as to whether or not they constitute a bribe. The AAC provides ethics guidelines for all employees covered by the Civil Servants Act and *inter alia* these rules set strict limits on the acceptance of gifts and entertainment. Compliance with these rules is monitored by the Government Ethics Office, which, since the early 1990s, has overseen the daily work of about 2,500 ethics officials who are career civil servants located in all government agencies and whose task is to eliminate administrative malpractice in its various forms and to raise levels of integrity awareness. Although these officers do not have statutory powers of criminal investigation, they gather information which is commonly used in the pursuit of prosecutions by the anti-corruption authorities. Morally exhortative rules are also laid down by the country's Central Personnel Administration to enhance levels of self-discipline among public officials. Taiwan promulgated a Public Functionaries' Conflict of Interest Prevention Law, effective from 2002, which is central to its rules-based integrity regime. The law covers conflicts of interest in regard to the financial, property and non-property and career concerns of officials and their relations. Pertinently, this law requires that if an official is aware of a conflict of interest they should immediately file a report.

Unlike in Hong Kong, for example, comparatively little effort is made in Taiwan to enhance officials' capacity for moral and ethical reasoning in ways that would make them more aware of real and potential conflicts of interest. According to Chen and Juang (2010: 573), "That mandatory ethics training [for] every public official has not been offered by ethics staff on a regular basis has been echoed in a cross-cities/counties survey that examined local public servants' perception of administrative ethics…More than one-third of local officials had never been offered any formal ethics training by their organizations…[and]…less than one-quarter of the respondents mentioned receiving training courses regularly provided by government agencies".

Conclusion

In East Asian countries, as in the West, "low road" approaches have been the dominant norm, which is hardly surprising, given that criminal codes and rules and regulations are the very essence of state and bureaucratic control. Even in highly meritocratic and elitist civil services, like those in South Korea and Singapore, where rigorous recruitment and promotion regimes are designed to develop the individual and collective character of public officials above and beyond the norms prevailing in the societies which they serve, a rules-based approach has been deeply entrenched. Nevertheless, Confucian values and norms remain influential in many East Asian governmental systems and are more consistent with a "high road" approach to ensuring the good character of public officials. Frederickson (2002: 610, 625) argues that, "Confucius is to the ethic of bureaucracy as Weber is to the structure and behaviour of bureaucracy", positively asserting that, "A rekindling of Confucian idealism in the modern democratic-capitalist context [in East Asia] would do much to reduce government corruption". However, Confucian ideals can also sit uneasily with the strong Western political and administrative traditions that are found in Hong Kong and Singapore, and which are becoming more influential in South Korea and Taiwan. For example, the 2011 whistle-blower protection legislation in South Korea is partly intended to counteract a Confucian ethic which discourages group "betrayal" by individual members.

Clearly, a country's criminal code will usually define corrupt practices and the penalties that can be applied when they are judged to have been committed, by public officials or anyone else. But because those who exercise public authority on behalf of the citizenry are invariably engaged in decision-making that involves moral and ethical considerations, detailed guidance is provided by bureaucratic rules and regulations and by formal codes of conduct, all designed to achieve and maintain socially and politically acceptable standards of ethical probity in government. Although such standards may shift over time and in response to changing circumstances they are always a reflection of the kind of behaviour that society at large expects of its governmental officials. In countries where the public have high expectations of the moral and ethical behaviour of their officials there will be a much lower tolerance of corrupt behaviour than will be found in jurisdictions where such expectations are less demanding.

Where corruption and administrative malfeasance are much more the rule rather than the exception, as in Vietnam, for example, no matter how formally prohibitive the laws, rules and regulations are, there will be many officials who pay little heed to them. Conversely, in jurisdictions where corruption is uncommon it will be more likely that a "low road" approach to securing high levels of ethical probity is less essential, because government officials will not only be more strongly constrained by social expectations but will also be more likely to be motivated to work in government for reasons which have little to do with the pursuit of narrow and illegitimate self-advantage. In many Asian countries, however, the civil service is the major employer because private sector jobs usually require higher qualifications.

There can be no watertight distinction between rules-based and integrity-based approaches, since rules are undoubtedly a key component of any strategy designed to enhance standards of ethical integrity. After all, laws and rules comprise the formal yardsticks against which ethical behaviour is most easily measured. Nevertheless, over the past ten years or so, it has become apparent that more countries are complementing rules-based approaches with measures explicitly designed to enable public officials to deal appropriately with emergent ethical challenges, especially relating to conflicts of interest and post-retirement employment, that have become more pressing in administrative environments increasingly characterised by market-led, rather than more traditional bureaucratic imperatives. This is the case in both Hong Kong and Singapore, which have inherited a strong rule of law tradition from Britain. It is also true of democratising countries like South Korea and Taiwan, both of which were colonised by Japan for a long time, and in which there continue to be, as in Japan, significant levels of political, rather than administrative, corruption.

Although there is little empirical research on the relationship in governmental systems between predominantly rules-based and integrity-based approaches to maintain ethical probity, it can be surmised that the relationship is a complex one, shaped by changing political and social circumstances prevailing in the wider society, and by governmental reforms carried out for other reasons, for example, in "third wave" democracies, and in the shift from traditional public administration to NPM. The extent to which "high road" methods are invoked to build upon, or even supplant, "low road" compliance will inevitably reflect the political, social and historical circumstances of any particular country or jurisdiction. As in most other aspects of public policymaking and administration, there would seem to be no single and obvious "one best way".

Notes

1 See PUMA (1996: 59–61). The OECD's distinction between "high road" and "low road" approaches is reminiscent of Rohr (1989), though Rohr sees the "high road" as a commitment by officials to social equity. He is critical of both concepts.
2 The UN Convention Against Corruption states that, "once recruited, public servants should be subject to codes of conduct…" https://www.unodc.org/unodc/en/treaties/CAC/convention-highlights.html (accessed 17 August 2015).
3 http://www.stuff.co.nz/world/australia/70759744/australian-speaker-bronwyn-bishop-resigns (accessed 17 Aug 2015).

References

Boston, J. (2011) "Basic NPM ideas and their development", in T. Christensen and P. Laegreid (eds.) *The Ashgate research companion to new public management*, Farnham: Ashgate Publishing, 17–32.
Brewer, B., J.Y.-H. Leung and I. Scott (2015) "Value-based integrity management and bureaucratic organizations: changing the mix", *International Public Management Journal*, 18(3): 390–410.
Cheung, A.B.L. (2011) "NPM in Asian countries", in T. Christensen and P. Laegreid (eds.) *The Ashgate research companion to new public management*, Farnham: Ashgate Publishing, 131–146.
Chen C.-M. and W-J. Juang (2010) "Public service ethics and corruption in Taiwan", in E.M. Berman, M. J. Moon and H. Choi (eds.) *Public administration in East Asia: mainland China, Japan, South Korea, and Taiwan*, London: CRC Press, 563–590.
Cooper, T.L. (2012) *The responsible administrator: an approach to ethics for the administrative role*, 6th edition, San Francisco: Jossey-Bass.

Dahlström, C., V. Lapuente and J. Teorell (2012) "The merit of meritocratization: politics, bureaucracy, and the institutional deterrents of corruption", *Political Research Quarterly*, 65(3): 656–668.

Eichbaum, C. and R. Shaw (eds.) (2010) *Partisan appointees and public servants: an international analysis of the role of the political adviser*, Cheltenham: Edward Elgar.

Etzioni, A. (1975) *A comparative analysis of complex organizations: on power, involvement, and their correlates*, revised and illustrated edition, New York: The Free Press.

Finer, H. (1941) "Administrative responsibility in democratic government", *Public Administration Review*, 1(4): 335–350.

Frederickson, H.G. (2002) "Confucius and the moral basis of bureaucracy", *Administration & Society*, 33(6): 610–628.

Friedrich, C. J. (1940) "Public policy and the nature of administrative responsibility", in C. J. Friedrich and E. S. Mason (eds.) *Public policy*, Cambridge, MA: Harvard University Press, 3–24.

Gilman, S.C. (2005) "Ethics codes and codes of conduct as tools for promoting an ethical and professional public service: comparative successes and lessons", paper prepared for the PREM, World Bank, Washington, DC.

Gong, T. and J. Ren (2013) "Hard rules and soft constraints: regulating conflict of interest in China", *Journal of Contemporary China*, 22(79): 1–17.

Gregory, R. (1995) "Accountability, responsibility, and corruption: managing the 'public production process'", in J. Boston (ed.) *The state under contract*, Wellington: Bridget Williams Books, 56–77.

Gregory, R. (1999) "Social capital theory and administrative reform: maintaining ethical probity in public service", *Public Administration Review*, 59(1): 63–75.

Gregory, R. (2002) "Governmental corruption in New Zealand: a view through Nelson's telescope?" *Asian Journal of Political Science*, 10(1): 17–38.

Gregory, R. (2012) "Accountability in modern government", in B.G. Peters and J. Pierre (eds.) *The Sage handbook of public administration*, 2nd edition, London: Sage Publications, 681–697.

Gregory, R. and C. Hicks (1999) "Promoting public service integrity: a case for responsible accountability", *Australian Journal of Public Administration*, 58(4): 1–15.

Heywood, P. M. (2012) "Integrity management and the public service ethos in the UK: patchwork quilt or threadbare blanket?" *International Review of Administrative Sciences*, 78(3): 474–493.

Holmes, L. (2015) *Corruption: a very short introduction*, Oxford: Oxford University Press.

Hood, C. (2011) *The blame game: spin, bureaucracy, and self-preservation in government*, Princeton: Princeton University Press.

Hood, C. and M. Lodge (2006) *The politics of public service bargains: reward, competency, loyalty – and blame*, Oxford: Oxford University Press.

House of Commons (2007) *Ethics and standards: the regulation of conduct in public life*, Public Administration Select Committee, Volume I, 19 April.

Klitgaard, R. (1988) *Controlling corruption*, Berkeley and Los Angeles: University of California Press.

Le Grand, J. (2003) *Motivation, agency and public policy: of knights and knaves, pawns and queens*, New York: Oxford University Press.

Lee, S.Y. and K.H. Jung (2010) "Public service ethics and anticorruption efforts in South Korea", in E.M. Berman, M. J. Moon and H. Choi (eds.) *Public administration in East Asia: mainland China, Japan, South Korea, and Taiwan*, London: CRC Press, 401–426.

MACC (Malaysian Anti-Corruption Commission) (2013) Presentation at the Australian Public Sector Anti-Corruption Conference, Sydney, 27 November.

The Malaysian Insider (2014) "Have anti-graft officers in new integrity committees, says public accounts committee", 24 July, http://www.themalaysianinsider.com/malaysia/article/have-anti-graft-officers-in-new-integrity-committees-says-public-accounts-c (accessed 21 August 2015).

Mosher, F. C. (1968) *Democracy and the public service*, New York: Oxford University Press.

Moynihan, D.P. (2008) "The normative model in decline? Public service motivation in the age of governance", in J.L. Perry and A. Hondeghem (eds.) *Motivation in public management: the call of public service*, New York: Oxford University Press, 247–267.

Painter, M. and B. G. Peters (eds.) (2010) *Tradition and public administration*, New York: Palgrave Macmillan.

Peters, B. G. and J. Pierre (eds.) (2004) *Politicization of the civil service in comparative perspective: the quest for control*, London: Routledge.

PUMA (Public Management Committee) (1996) "Ethics in the public service: current issues and practice", OECD, *Public Management Occasional Papers*, No. 14.

Quah, J.S.T. (2011) *Curbing corruption in Asian countries: an impossible dream?* Bingley: Emerald Group Publishing.

Quah, J.S.T. (ed.) (2013) *Different paths to curbing corruption: lessons from Denmark, Finland, Hong Kong, New Zealand and Singapore*, Bingley: Emerald Group Publishing.

Quah, J.S.T. (2014) "Curbing police corruption in Singapore: lessons for other Asian countries", *Asian Education and Development Studies*, 3(3): 186–222.

Rohr, J.A. (1989) *Ethics for bureaucrats: an essay on law and values*, 2nd edition, New York: Marcel Dekker.

Scott, I. (2013) "Institutional design and corruption prevention in Hong Kong", *Journal of Contemporary China*, 22(79): 77–92.

Scott, I. and J.Y.-H. Leung (2012) "Integrity management in post-1997 Hong Kong: challenges for a rule-based system", *Crime, Law and Social Change*, 58(1): 39–52.

Uhr, J. (1993) "Redesigning accountability: from muddles to maps", *The Australian Quarterly*, 65(2): 1–16.

Weber, M. (1947) *The theory of social and economic organization*, trans. A. M. Henderson and Talcott Parsons, New York: Oxford University Press.

20

REGIONAL ANTI-CORRUPTION INITIATIVES IN ASIA

Bart W. Édes

Corruption negatively impacts societal cohesion and undermines public faith in government (Seligson 2002; Chang and Chu 2006). Poor and vulnerable people are more dependent on public services than better-off individuals, and, when corruption occurs in the public sector, it has a disproportionate impact on those who can least afford the costs that it imposes (Gupta et al. 2002). On the continent with the largest number of poor people, the case for concerted action by governments to take effective measures to combat corruption is compelling.

In a globalised and increasingly inter-connected world, corruption is often a cross-border phenomenon. One sees this when residents of different countries conspire to transfer funds acquired through the abuse of public power and in situations where illicit commercial transactions involve parties in different jurisdictions. To battle cross-border corruption effectively, governments must collaborate. They can strengthen their collaboration by sharing information and experience, learning from each other's approaches, and working together to build human and institutional capacity.

Over the past two decades, several initiatives have emerged to nurture and support regional cooperation against corruption in Asia and the Pacific. Most of these initiatives have been launched or at least supported by inter-governmental organizations and development aid agencies. Each regional cooperation initiative contributes in some way to raising awareness of the deleterious impacts of corruption, marshalling public and political support for action, and enhancing the knowledge needed by governments to promote integrity and accountability in the public sector effectively.

This chapter briefly examines five anti-corruption cooperation initiatives in Asia, noting their membership, objectives, activities and approaches. While the initiatives described here do not constitute an exhaustive list, they do identify the leading networks and partnerships seeking to enhance co-operation among Asian countries with the aim of reducing corruption. The regional cooperation initiatives are presented in chronological order dating from the year in which they were launched. Table 20.1 summarises key details on each initiative.

Table 20.1 Main features of five regional anti-corruption initiatives in Asia

Anti-Corruption Initiative	Year formed	Secretariat location	Number of members	Objectives
Asia Pacific Group on Money-Laundering (APG)	1997	Bangkok	41	Promotes effective implementation and enforcement of international standards against money laundering and terrorism
OECD Anti-Corruption Network (ACN)	1998	Paris	25	Supports countries in Central and Eastern Europe and the former Soviet Union (including seven Central Asian countries) to prevent and fight corruption
ADB-OECD Anti-Corruption Initiative for Asia and the Pacific	1999	Manila and Paris	31	Supports national and multilateral efforts to fight corruption in Asia and the Pacific
APEC Anti-Corruption and Transparency Experts' Working Group	2004	Singapore	21	Coordinates implementation of the Santiago Commitment to Fight Corruption and Promote Transparency, the APEC Course of Action, and the APEC Transparency Standards
Southeast Asian Parliamentarians Against Corruption (SEAPAC)	2005	Jakarta	10	Strengthens the network of parliamentarians belonging to GOPAC from Southeast Asia to fight corruption and improve governance

Sources: ADB and OECD (2015), APEC (2016), APG (2016), OECD (2016), SEAPAC (2013).

Asia/Pacific Group on Money Laundering

The Asia/Pacific Group on Money Laundering (APG) was launched in Bangkok, Thailand, in 1997. It is a regional body, focused on Asia and the Pacific, and is modeled on the Financial Action Task Force (FATF), itself an inter-governmental body with global membership, established in 1989 (Damais 2007: 69–81; Cox 2014: 21–54). The APG has 41 members including the largest countries in Asia (APG 2012).

The APG does not tackle corruption *per se* but does aim to curb money laundering, preventing acts which make illicit funds appear legitimate. Corruption is one of the main predicate offences for money laundering. More specifically, the APG promotes effective implementation and enforcement of internationally accepted standards against money laundering and the financing of terrorism. The standards are issued by the FATF and set out as forty recommendations.

Initially adopted in 1990, the standards were most recently revised in 2012 to include an obligation on countries to demonstrate the effectiveness of their systems to combat money laundering and terrorist financing (FATF 2015). Other recent revisions include the need for countries to apply an approach based on money laundering and terrorism financing risks to their financial services sector; inclusion of tax evasion as a predicate offence of money laundering; increased focus on beneficial ownership; a broadened scope of politically exposed persons, that is, persons who have been entrusted with prominent public functions, or relatives or known associates of such persons; and implementation of targeted financing sanctions of the United Nations (UN) Security Council with regard to Iran and the People's Democratic Republic of Korea and weapons of mass destruction.

The APG fights money laundering by assessing member compliance with international standards, providing technical assistance and training, researching methods of financing terrorism and money laundering, contributing to the formulation of policy, and informing the private sector of international developments related to money laundering and the financing of terrorism. The APG also helps its members to create national coordination mechanisms to make better use of resources to combat money laundering and the financing of terrorism.

The APG publishes reports on the outcomes of mutual evaluation on countries (APG 2015a). These provide detailed assessments and ratings on compliance with international standards. Other APG publications report on methods, trends and typologies of money laundering and financing for terrorism (APG 2015b) or provide technical guidance to authorities. The research for these publications is carried out to provide decision-makers and operational experts with current information and advice that can help them target policies and strategies effectively.

The attacks of 11 September 2001 in the United States stimulated greater interest in international cooperation to address the issue of cross-border funding for terrorism. The continued disruption caused by extremist acts around the world provides sustained motivation for countries to work together to curb money laundering and the financing of terrorism. The APG maintains its secretariat in Sydney, Australia. Members fund APG activities with contributions based on gross national product. Since its creation, the APG has held an annual general meeting of its members attended by senior officials from member governments together with representatives of observer jurisdictions and organizations.

OECD Anti-Corruption Network

The Anti-Corruption Network for Eastern Europe and Central Asia (ACN) of the Organization for Economic Co-operation and Development (OECD) is an outreach programme of its Working Group on Bribery. The ACN was formed in 1998 to support countries in Central and Eastern Europe and the former Soviet Union in preventing and fighting corruption. It provides a forum for exchanging information, developing best practice, encouraging donor coordination and promoting anti-corruption activities. The ACN carries out its work through general meetings and conferences, sub-regional initiatives, and thematic activities.

Twenty-five countries belong to the ACN, of which seven, the Central Asian countries of Azerbaijan, Kazakhstan, the Kyrgyz Republic, Mongolia, Tajikistan, Turkmenistan and Uzbekistan are from Asia. In addition, OECD member countries and members of the OECD Working Group on Bribery also participate in ACN activities. Each ACN country has a national coordinator. The national coordinators form the Steering Group, which guides the OECD-based Secretariat of the ACN in the preparation, implementation, and assessment of the ACN work programme. The Steering Group typically meets once or twice a year to discuss the work programme, as well as anti-corruption reforms in ACN countries and support for implementation of the United Nations Convention Against Corruption (UNCAC).

The ACN has produced several publications to support its members. Topics covered by these publications include investigation and prosecution of corruption offences, asset declaration for public officials, ethics training for public officials, mutual legal assistance and other forms of co-operation between law enforcement agencies (OECD 2016b). The publications are usually made available in both English and Russian.

In 2003, the ACN established a sub-regional peer review programme known as the Istanbul Anti-corruption Action Plan. The programme supports anti-corruption reforms through country reviews and continuous monitoring of implementation of recommendations, which aim to promote the UNCAC and other international standards and good practices. The first round of monitoring was carried out between 2004 and 2007. The second round took place between 2008 and 2012. The third and most recent round of monitoring began in 2013. The nine countries participating in the Istanbul Anti-corruption Action Plan are Armenia, Azerbaijan, Georgia, Kyrgyz Republic, Kazakhstan, Mongolia, Tajikistan, Ukraine and Uzbekistan.

A 2015 external evaluation of the ACN found its work programme activities highly relevant for members (Trivunovic 2015). The monitoring reports carried out among countries participating in the Istanbul Anti-corruption Action Plan were assessed to provide actionable data to inform national reform programmes and policy dialogue on corruption. Recommendations resulting from these reports are seen to have contributed to greater public sector transparency in Armenia and Georgia and to have assisted countries in meeting their international obligations under the UNCAC and Council of Europe conventions. The evaluation also concluded that the ACN's work positively influenced the political will to implement anti-corruption reforms and provided actionable findings around which national anti-corruption reform efforts can be coordinated and which inform donor activities and policy discussions. Further, it was found that the ACN has built up a critical mass of national officials who have internalised international standards and good practices on anti-corruption policies and law enforcement methods (Trivunovic 2015).

APEC's Anti-Corruption and Transparency Experts' Working Group

Formed in 1989, the Asia-Pacific Economic Cooperation (APEC) is a forum for 21 economies situated along the western and eastern edges of the Pacific Ocean. It promotes commerce across the Asia-Pacific region. At their annual meeting in 2004, APEC leaders established an Anti-Corruption Experts' Task Force, which in 2010 was upgraded to a working group. Its purpose is to implement the Santiago Commitment to Fight Corruption and Ensure Transparency (APEC 2004b), the APEC Course of Action on Fighting Corruption and Ensuring Transparency (APEC 2004a), and the APEC Transparency Standards (APEC 2007). Together, these measures serve to rally APEC support for the UNCAC and other multilateral frameworks promoting transparency and anti-corruption efforts. In their declaration issued in Vladivostok, Russia in 2012, APEC economic leaders encouraged members to implement the UNCAC fully.

The Anti-Corruption and Transparency Experts' Working Group promotes cooperation on extradition, legal assistance and judicial and law enforcement. With regard to this last function, the focus is on asset forfeiture and recovery. The working group meets twice annually on the margins of the first and third annual APEC Senior Officials' Meetings. It is comprised of anti-corruption experts and law enforcement officials from interested APEC member economies, and APEC Observers (for example, ASEAN) as well as representatives from the APEC Secretariat and the APEC Business Advisory Council.

At its 17th meeting, held in Indonesia in 2013, the working group agreed to establish a Network of Anti-Corruption Authorities and Law Enforcement Agencies (ACT-NET) to link law enforcement and anti-corruption officers to improve cooperation among government agencies charged with investigating and prosecuting corruption, bribery, money laundering and illicit trade. The ACT-NET facilitates cooperation among officials to identify and secure return of proceeds of these crimes. Further, it assists in the implementation of working group decisions and other international initiatives against corruption. The ACT-NET reports annually to the working group.

The ACT-NET met for the first time in Beijing in August 2014. Participants (known as "focal points") shared information on topics including asset recovery, criminal investigations, mutual legal assistance, prosecutions, and policy. One year later, the ACT-NET met again, in Cebu, the Philippines. Among other topics, focal points discussed repatriation of fugitives, informal international cooperation, and building of regional capacity for asset recovery and anti-money laundering. As a new body within APEC, the ACT-NET has thus far focused mostly on sharing information and best practice with the aim of developing improved inter-agency coordination and action in the future.

In addition to meetings of the working group and the ACT-NET, APEC has also organized other anti-corruption events, including a workshop on international recovery of the proceeds of corruption held in collaboration with the World Bank in Ningbo, the People's Republic of China (PRC) in February 2014, and a high-level workshop on combatting business bribery. The workshop in Beijing in August 2014 was organized in collaboration with the OECD and the PRC Government's Ministry of Supervision. Special meetings addressing corruption topics are sometimes held alongside meetings of the working group and the ACT-NET.

Between 2013 and 2015, the working group carried out a project on "Designing Best Models on Prosecuting Corruption and Money Laundering". It began as a joint effort of Chile and Thailand to improve investigation and prosecution of corruption. The project has generated the first part of a handbook (APEC 2014), the final version of which is to be published in 2016. APEC has also published other handbooks and guides for its members, including a guide to mutual legal assistance. APEC plans to undertake an independent assessment of the working group in 2016.

Southeast Asian Parliamentarians Against Corruption

The Southeast Asian Parliamentarians Against Corruption (SEAPAC) was formed in March 2005. It constitutes a regional chapter of the Global Organization of Parliamentarians Against Corruption (GOPAC), which was created at a conference of parliamentarians and anti-corruption advocates held in Ottawa, Canada, in October 2002.

GOPAC's vision is to "achieve accountability and transparency through effective anti-corruption mechanisms and inclusive participation and cooperation between parliamentarians, government and civil society" (GOPAC 2015a). To achieve this vision, it pursues the following mission: "assist and support parliamentarians in their advocacy and legislation to make governments accountable and transparent" (GOPAC 2015a).

GOPAC is distinguished by the fact that it is the only global parliamentary network that focuses solely on corruption. It claims a membership of 700 individual members and has four regional chapters in addition to the SEAPAC: Africa, Arab Region, Latin America and the Caribbean, and Oceania. In addition, regional chapters are being formed in South Asia and in the Caribbean.

GOPAC works through Global Task Forces to support the introduction of draft laws and procedures in national parliaments with the aim of promoting good governance and holding the executive accountable to the citizenry. Global Task Forces have been created on Anti-Money Laundering, UNCAC, Parliamentary Oversight, Parliamentary Ethics and Conduct, and Participation of Society.

Among the tools produced by GOPAC are the Guidelines to Strengthen Oversight through Parliamentarian-Donor Collaboration. GOPAC prepared these guidelines in collaboration with the Parliamentary Network on the World Bank and the International Monetary Fund. They were formulated in response to concerns expressed by some parliamentarians that countries have been negatively impacted when donor funds are misused or not allocated for their intended purposes or when projects are perceived to be politically motivated and therefore cancelled with changes in government (GOPAC and The Parliamentary Network 2013). GOPAC has developed other tools for its members, including the Anti-Corruption Assessment tool for Parliamentarians: User Guide, published together with the UNDP (GOPAC and UNDP 2013).

From its founding in 2002 through 2015, GOPAC has held six meetings of its Global Conference of Parliamentarians Against Corruption. The Philippines hosted the fifth Global Conference in 2013 and Indonesia the sixth in 2015. Asian parliamentarians were disproportionately represented at both events because of their venues. Panel sessions at the most recent Global Conference focused on tools and mechanisms to build anti-corruption presentation systems; bringing to justice those committing grand corruption; recovering assets stolen through grand corruption; ethics, conduct and governance for accountable and inclusive institutions; increasing women parliamentarians' leadership on non-traditional issues; and the high cost of institutionalising democracy (GOPAC 2015b).

Much of the focus of GOPAC's attention is on how parliamentarians can hold governments accountable and limit grand corruption, defined by GOPAC as "forms of corruption so grave and whose effect on human life, human rights and human welfare are so catastrophic that they should shock the conscience of the international community and mobilize the will of nations to act across borders" (GOPAC 2015c).

At the conclusion of the Sixth Global Conference, GOPAC members adopted the Yogyakarta Declaration, which lays out GOPAC's three major commitments for the coming years. In particular, members resolved to: express full support and solidarity with the Sustainable Development Goals, especially Goal 16 on Peace, Justice and Strong Institutions (UN 2016); call for appointment of a United Nations special rapporteur on the impact of corruption on human rights, focusing on grand corruption and its impact on socioeconomic and political rights; and endorse the use of legal actions to pursue perpetrators of grand corruption and stress the need to strengthen international cooperation in facilitating the return of stolen assets to the victims of corruption (GOPAC 2015b).

ADB-OECD Anti-Corruption Initiative for Asia and the Pacific

Formed in 1999 by the governments of several Asian and Pacific countries and territories, the ADB-OECD Anti-Corruption Initiative for Asia and the Pacific operates as a regional forum for supporting national and multilateral efforts to reduce corruption in Asia and the Pacific. Its 31 members determine the Initiative's strategies and activities, with the support of a Secretariat jointly hosted by the ADB and the OECD. Most members are represented by the national anti-corruption agency or a similar body. Since 2014, the UN Development Programme (UNDP) has become an active partner in the initiative, jointly sponsoring regional capacity development seminars along with the ADB and the OECD.

Representatives of the member governments sit on the Steering Group, which provides direction for the Initiative. An Advisory Group comprises representatives of selected donor agencies, business groups, and civil society organizations that support the Initiative with technical inputs and resource mobilisation. The Initiative's work was originally based on the Anti-Corruption Action Plan for Asia and the Pacific, which was endorsed by members (ADB and OECD 2001). The Action Plan identifies anti-corruption roles for the public service, the private sector, and citizens. In 2010, the Initiative adopted Strategic Principles to guide future work. Significantly, it made implementation of the UNCAC a priority in order to align with this major global agreement.

The Initiative promotes the UNCAC implementation through capacity building that builds on the exchange of expertise, support to fellow members, and peer learning. The four primary activities of the Initiative are a regional anti-corruption conference held every three years (the most recent one was hosted by Cambodia in 2014); thematic reviews and scoping exercises; capacity building seminars; and annual meetings of the Steering Group. A regional capacity-building seminar is held annually unless a conference is scheduled during the year. This seminar brings together experts and policy makers from within and outside the region to raise awareness and improve understanding of techniques and approaches to curbing corruption. Seminar proceedings are made publicly available. The Initiative's 2015 regional seminar, hosted in Ulaanbaatar, Mongolia, focused on tackling corruption in development projects. Resource speakers shared case studies of how corruption was mitigated and detected in different types of projects.

The 2015 regional seminar also featured a parallel track exclusively for law enforcement practitioners, supported by the Deutsche Gesellschaft für Internationale Zusammenarbeit (GIZ). Participating law enforcement officers shared, in an interactive manner, experiences in investigating and prosecuting corruption, money laundering and tax crimes. The session concluded with the launch of a new Asia-Pacific Law Enforcement Practitioners Network, which will meet again under the rubric of the Initiative at the 2016 regional seminar, to be held in Thimphu, Bhutan. The objective and membership of the new network is very similar to APEC's ACT-NET although the network's geographic reach is far greater because it is not limited to countries and territories bordering the Pacific.

The Initiative periodically conducts thematic reviews concerning some aspect of implementing anti-corruption standards. Reviews typically make recommendations with a country or regional focus. Examples of past reviews include Curbing Corruption in Public Procurement (2006); Mutual Legal Assistance, Extradition and Recovery of Proceeds and Corruption (2007); and Criminalisation of Bribery Offences under the UNCAC (2010). On the request of a member, the Initiative will carry out a country scoping exercise to pinpoint specific challenges to UNCAC implementation. In theory, such a scoping exercise can assist a member in mobilising resources for technical assistance; however, there has been little interest in using this tool.

An independent review found that members believe that the Initiative is helping them to reduce corruption, mainly by peer learning in an informal environment. They appreciate advice on practical, operational matters relevant to anti-corruption agencies. On the other hand, members identified constraints in implementing the Initiative's Action Plan. These include weak international cooperation on mutual legal assistance matters, inadequate financial resources, lack of cooperation from other parts of government, and insufficient professional knowledge and technical assistance. The review also found that members are uneasy about country scoping studies due to a perception that they would alter the Initiative's informal learning environment by introducing compliance pressure (Garnett and Kwok 2009).

Since the independent review was conducted, the Initiative has endeavoured to design regional seminars to respond to members' priority concerns and provide more practical case studies and opportunities for interaction and exchange. Efforts are made to steer members to sources of donor support for their plans. The fledgling Asia-Pacific Law Enforcement Practitioners Network may play some role in promoting improved cooperation on mutual legal assistance matters.

Conclusions

Governments of Asian countries are working more closely than ever before to address various aspects of corruption. Many are doing so through the five regional cooperation initiatives described in this chapter. The initiatives provide useful forums for the exchange of experience, and help to build capacity, generate political support, raise awareness, and mobilise action. While there is overlap in the overall objectives and membership of the five initiatives, they do have distinguishing characteristics that partly explain why they exist separately. For example, the APG focuses only on money laundering and the financing of terrorism. The ACN includes only members from Central and Western Asia with a shared history of communist rule. The SEAPAC's individual members are exclusively current or former parliamentarians. And the national focal points for members of the ADB-OECD Anti-Corruption Initiative for Asia-Pacific are mostly situated in national anti-corruption commissions or similar bodies, rather than in, say, a ministry of justice or law enforcement agency. Thus, each initiative tends to rally authorities with a particular shared geographic focus or specialty within the broader field of anti-corruption. They also differ in terms of the emphasis they put on the peer pressure exerted to encourage compliance with agreed standards and norms.

All of the regional initiatives described in this chapter give strong attention to peer learning and development of practical resources to assist their members. Assessing the impact of these initiatives on reducing corruption in individual countries is very difficult. Attributing particular legal and policy reforms to a certain factor, or factors, is an imperfect science. This is particularly so given the multi-faceted nature of corruption, the many actors and influences involved, and the lack of timely, reliable and comparable data and analysis. One can reasonably surmise, though, that the countries engaged in these initiatives must be receiving at least some value from them, given the time, effort and resources they commit to engagement.

There is some evidence that anti-corruption actions by individual countries have been positively influenced, directly or indirectly, by international cooperation through these regional initiatives. This has been highlighted, for example, by the external evaluation of the ACN and by informal bilateral exchanges held on the sidelines of regional seminars and conferences of the ADB-OECD Anticorruption Initiative for Asia and the Pacific.

A common thread running through the initiatives is support for UNCAC implementation. With the approval of the Sustainable Development Goals, implementation of corruption- and governance-related targets in Goal 16 are likely to command the increasing attention of the regional cooperation initiatives. In light of the overlapping roles and membership of the initiatives, it could be beneficial if they sought cooperation to capitalise on potential synergies more actively in the use of precious resources including political capital, human resources, and grant financing.

This could involve knowledge sharing across initiatives, and participation in, and joint sponsorship of, workshops and meetings. At the 2015 regional seminar of the ADB-OECD

Anticorruption Initiative for Asia and the Pacific, for example, the ACN Secretariat presented a monitoring report on progress in Mongolia's anticorruption reforms. Mongolia is a member of both regional initiatives and hosted the regional seminar. Regional initiatives could also jointly support training events for government officials and other activities geared toward strengthening government capacity to tackle corruption.

Since the regional initiatives described here have now completed several years of activities, a deeper independent analysis of what they have accomplished and their comparative strengths would be very timely. Such an analysis could also propose how the initiatives could more effectively focus their efforts on collaboration with others, including international organizations, national and subnational governments (and different parts of government), civil society, the private sector, academe and the media. With expectations of a major private sector role in supporting achievement of the Sustainable Development Goals, analysis could also extend to how regional initiatives can collaborate with business networks that are working to promote integrity in the public and private sectors, and inclusive, sustainable development.

References

ADB (Asian Development Bank) and OECD (Organization for Economic Co-operation and Development) (2001) Anticorruption plan for Asia and the Pacific, http://www.oecd.org/site/adboecdanti-corruptioninitiative/meetingsandconferences/35021642.pdf (accessed 26 April 2016).

ADB (Asian Development Bank) and OECD (Organization for Economic Co-operation and Development) (2015) General Information, https://www.oecd.org/site/adboecdanti-corruptioninitiative/ADB-OECD-Initiative-Information-Sheet.pdf (accessed 26 April 2016).

APEC (Asia-Pacific Economic Cooperation) (2004a) APEC course of action on fighting corruption and ensuring transparency, http://www.apec.org/~/media/Files/Groups/ACT/04_amm_033rev2.pdf (accessed 26 April 2016).

APEC (Asia-Pacific Economic Cooperation) (2004b) Santiago commitment to fight corruption and ensure transparency, http://www.apec.org/~/media/Files/Groups/ACT/04_amm_032rev1.pdf (accessed 26 April 2016).

APEC (Asia-Pacific Economic Cooperation) (2007) Report on the assessment of APEC economies' implementation of APEC transparency standards, http://www.apec.org/~/media/Files/Groups/Transparency/07_cti_ctirpt_Appdx6.pdf (accessed 26 April 2016).

APEC (Asia-Pacific Economic Cooperation) (2014) Handbook (first part) – Best practices in investigating and prosecuting corruption using financial flow tracking techniques and financial intelligence, http://mddb.apec.org/Documents/2014/ACT/ACT1/14_act1_012.pdf (accessed 26 April 2016).

APEC (Asia-Pacific Economic Cooperation) (2016) Anti-corruption and transparency experts' working group, http://www.apec.org/groups/som-steering-committee-on-economic-and-technical-cooperation/working-groups/anti-corruption-and-transparency.aspx (accessed 26 April 2016).

APG (Asia/Pacific Group on Money Laundering) (2012) Terms of reference, http://www.apgml.org/about-us/page.aspx?p=c735e62b-802b-4895-bda8-b7cf81766943 (accessed 26 April 2016).

APG (Asia/Pacific Group on Money Laundering) (2015a) Mutual evaluations, http://www.apgml.org/mutual-evaluations/page.aspx?p=a901712a-54e4-4b3b-a146-046aefca6534 (accessed 28 March 2016).

APG (Asia/Pacific Group on Money Laundering) (2015b) Typologies – introduction, http://www.apgml.org/methods-and-trends/page.aspx?p=a4a11dca-75f2-4dae-9c25-6215103e56da (accessed 28 March 2016).

APG (Asia/Pacific Group on Money Laundering) (2016) About, http://www.apgml.org/about-us/page.aspx?p=91ce25ec-db8a-424c-9018-8bd1f6869162 (accessed 26 April 2016).

Chang, E.C.C. and Y.H. Chu (2006) "Corruption and trust: exceptionalism in Asian democracies?" *Journal of Politics*, 68(2): 259–271.

Cox, D. (2014) "International money-laundering regulation – the role of Financial Action Task Force 21" in D. Cox (ed.) *Handbook of anti- money laundering*, Chichester: Wiley, 21–59.

Damais, A. (2007) "The Financial Action Task Force", in W.H. Muller, C.H. Kälin and J.G. Goldsworth (eds.) *Anti-money laundering: international law and practice*, Chichester: Wiley, 69–82.

FATF (Financial Action Task Force) (2015) FATF 40 recommendations, http://www.fatf-gafi.org/media/fatf/documents/recommendations/pdfs/FATF_Recommendations.pdf (accessed 26 April 2016).

Garnett H., and T. Kwok (2009) Independent review of the ADB/OECD initiative final report, http://www.oecd.org/site/adboecdanti-corruptioninitiative/meetingsandconferences/44084819.pdf (accessed 28 March 2016).

GOPAC (Global Organization of Parliamentarians Against Corruption) (2015a) Overview, http://gopacnetwork.org/overview/ (accessed 11 May 2016).

GOPAC (Global Organization of Parliamentarians Against Corruption) (2015b) Sixth global conference of parliamentarians against corruption, http://gopacnetwork.org/Docs/6thGlobalConference Report_EN.pdf (accessed 13 May 2016).

GOPAC (Global Organization of Parliamentarians Against Corruption) (2015c) Grand corruption, http://gopacnetwork.org/programs/grand_corruption/ (accessed 11 May 2016).

GOPAC (Global Organization of Parliamentarians Against Corruption) and the Parliamentary Network on The World Bank and the International Monetary Fund (2013) Guidelines to strengthen oversight through parliamentarian-donor collaboration, ttp://gopacnetwork.org/Docs/GOPAC_PN%20Guidelines_FINAL_EN.pdf (accessed on 11 May 2016).

GOPAC (Global Organization of Parliamentarians Against Corruption) and UNDP (the United Nations Development Programme) (2013) Anti-corruption assessment tool for parliamentarians: user guide, http://gopacnetwork.org/Docs/AntiCorruptionAssessmentTool_EN.pdf (accessed 13 May 2016).

Gupta, S., H. Davoodi and R. Alonso-Terme (2002) "Does corruption affect income inequality and poverty?" *Economics of Governance,* 3(1): 23–45.

OECD (Organization for Economic Co-operation and Development Anticorruption Network for Eastern Europe and Central Asia) (2016a) About the network, https://www.oecd.org/corruption/acn/aboutthenetwork/ (accessed 26 April 2016).

OECD (Organization for Economic Co-operation and Development Anticorruption Network for Eastern Europe and Central Asia) (2016b) Documents and publications, https://www.oecd.org/corruption/acn/publicationsdocuments/ (accessed 28 March 2016).

Seligson, M. (2002) "The impact of corruption on regime legitimacy: a comparative study of four Latin American countries", *Journal of Politics*, 64(2): 408–433.

SEAPAC (Southeast Asian Parliamentarians Against Corruption) (2013) Regional action plan of the Southeast Asian Parliamentarians Against Corruption 2013–2016, http://ksap.dpr.go.id/seapac/page/detail/id/111 (accessed 26 April 2016).

Trivunovic, M. (2015) External evaluation ACN Work Programme 2013–2015, http://www.oecd.org/corruption/acn/ACN-External-Evaluation-Report-2015-ENG.pdf (accessed 28 March 2016).

United Nations (2016) Sustainable Development Goals, http://www.un.org/sustainabledevelopment/sustainable-development-goals/ (accessed 28 March 2016).

APPENDIX 1

Selected bibliography on corruption in Asia

Comparative and country studies

This bibliography is designed as an aid for sourcing material on corruption in Asia from both comparative and country perspectives. It includes some, but not all, of the references in the preceding text and many references which are not cited in the text. The criteria for selection is whether the reference provides an overview of corruption, either on a comparative or country basis, or addresses issues which are important to understanding corruption or the success or failure of anti-corruption measures in a particular country. It is intended as a basic reading list which should help to provide some guidance for future research. The bibliography is divided into two parts. The first part deals with comparative studies. The second part consists of country studies listed in alphabetical order and includes citations from the comparative section at the end of each of the country lists.

Comparative studies

Ahmad, N, and O.T. Brookins (2004) "On corruption and countervailing actions in three Southeast Asian nations", *The Journal of Policy Reform,* 7(1): 21–30. [Bangladesh, India, Sri Lanka].

Alatas, V., L. Cameron, A. Chaudhuri, N. Erkal and L. Gangadharan (2009) "Gender, culture, and corruption: insights from an experimental analysis", *Southern Economic Journal,* 75(3): 663–680. [India, Indonesia, Singapore].

Anderson, S. and P.M. Heywood (2009) "Anti-corruption as a risk to democracy: on the unintended consequences of international anti-corruption campaigns", in L.de Sousa, P. Larmour and B. Hindess (eds.) *Governments, NGOs and anti-corruption: the new integrity warriors,* Abingdon: Routledge, 33–49.

Ang, Y. Y. (2014) "Authoritarian restraints on online activism revisited: why 'I paid-a-bribe' worked in India but failed in China", *Comparative Politics,* 47(1): 21–40.

Assegaf, A.R. (2015) "Policy analysis and educational strategy for anti-corruption in Indonesia and Singapore", *International Journal of Asian Social Science,* 5(11): 611–625.

Baker, J. and S. Milne (2015) "Dirty money states: illicit economies and the state in Southeast Asia", *Critical Asian Studies,* 47 (2): 151–176. [Cambodia, the Philippines, Timor-Leste, Vietnam].

Bhargava, V. and E. Bolongaita (2004) *Challenging corruption in Asia: case studies and a framework for action,* Washington, DC: World Bank. [Indonesia, the Philippines, South Korea, Thailand].

Cameron, L., A. Chaudhuri, N. Erkal, and L. Gangadharan (2009) "Propensities to engage in and punish corrupt behavior: experimental evidence from Australia, India, Indonesia and Singapore", *Journal of Public Economics,* 93(7–8): 843–851.

Campbell, N. and S. Saha (2013) "Corruption, democracy and Asia Pacific countries", *Journal of the Asia Pacific Economy*, 18(2): 290–303. [South Asia, South Korea].

Carter, C. and A. Harding (eds.) (2015) *Land grabs in Asia: what role for the law?* London: Routledge.

Chang, E.C.C. and Y.H. Chu (2006) "Corruption and trust: exceptionalism in Asian democracies?" *The Journal of Politics*, 68(2): 259–271. [South Korea, Taiwan].

Cheung, A.B.L. (2008) "Combating corruption as a political strategy to rebuild trust and legitimacy: can China learn from Hong Kong?" in C. Wescott and B. Bowornwathana (eds.) *Comparative governance reform in Asia: democracy, corruption and government trust*, Bingley: Emerald, 55–84.

Choi, J.W. (2009) "Institutional structures and effectiveness of anti-corruption agencies: a comparative analysis of South Korea and Hong Kong", *Asian Journal of Political Science*, 17(2): 195–214.

Clifford Chance (2014) *A guide to anti-corruption legislation in Asia Pacific 2014*, http://www.cliffordchance.com/briefings/2014/10/a_guide_to_anti-corruptionlegislationinasi.html. [China, Hong Kong, India, Indonesia, Japan, Malaysia, the Philippines, Singapore, South Korea, Taiwan, Thailand, Vietnam].

Croissant, A. and B. Martin (eds.) (2006) *Between consolidation and crisis: elections and democracy in five nations in Southeast Asia*, Munster: Lit Verlag. [Cambodia, Indonesia, the Philippines, Malaysia and Thailand].

Davis, J. (2004) "Corruption in public service delivery: experience from South Asia's water and sanitation sector", *World Development*, 32(1): 53–71. [India, Pakistan].

Fritzen, S.A. and S. Basu (2011) "The strategic use of public information in anti-corruption agencies: evidence from the Asia-Pacific region", *International Journal of Public Administration*, 34(14): 893–904. [Hong Kong, India, Singapore, South Korea].

Global Witness (2013) "Rubber barons: how Vietnamese companies and international financiers are driving a land grabbing crisis in Cambodia and Laos", www.globalwitness.org/en/campaigns/land-deals/rubberbarons/.

Göbel, C. (2009) "Warriors in chains: institutional legacies and anti-corruption programmes in Taiwan and South Korea", in L.de Sousa, P. Larmour and B. Hindess (eds.) *Governments, NGOs and anti-corruption: the new integrity warriors*, Abingdon: Routledge, 102–119.

Gong, T. and S.K. Ma (eds.) (2009) *Preventing corruption in Asia: institutional design and policy capacity*, New York: Routledge. [China, India, Japan, Korea, the Philippines, Singapore, Taiwan].

Gong, T., S. Wang and J. Ren (2015) "Corruption in the eye of the beholder: survey evidence from Mainland China and Hong Kong", *International Public Management Journal*, 18(3): 458–482.

Gong, T. and I. Scott (2015) "Conflicts of interest and ethical decision-making: Mainland China and Hong Kong comparisons", in A. Lawton, L. Huberts and Z. Van Der Wal (eds.) *Ethics in public policy and management: a global research companion*, London: Routledge, 257–276.

Hira, A. and K. Shiao (2016) "Understanding the deep roots of success in effective civil services", *Journal of Developing Societies*, 32(1): 17–43. [Hong Kong, Singapore].

Hough, D. (2013) *Corruption, anti-corruption and governance*, London: Palgrave Macmillan, 48–70, 71–92. [Bangladesh, South Korea].

Hutchcroft, P.D. (2014) "Linking capital and countryside: patronage and clientelism in Japan, Thailand, and the Philippines", in A.B. Diego and L. Diamond (eds.) *Clientelism, social policy and the quality of democracy*, Baltimore: Johns Hopkins University Press, 174–203.

James, H. (2010) "Resources, rent-seeking and reform in Thailand and Myanmar (Burma): the economic-politics nexus", *Asian Survey*, 50(2): 426–448.

Jha, S. and P.F. Quisling (2015) "Corruption in Asia and the Pacific: a manifestation of weak governance", in A. B. Deolalikar, S. Jha and P.F. Quisling (eds.) *Governance in developing Asia: public service delivery and empowerment*, Cheltenham: Edward Elgar, 101–136.

Johnson, C. (1998) "Economic crisis in East Asia: clash of capitalisms", *Cambridge Journal of Economics*, 22(6): 653–661.

Johnston, M. (2008) "Japan, Korea, the Philippines, China: four syndromes of corruption", *Crime, Law and Social Change*, 49(3): 205–223.

Kang, D.C. (2002) *Crony capitalism: corruption and development in South Korea and the Philippines*, Cambridge: Cambridge University Press.

Khan, M.H. (1998) "Patron-client networks and the economic effects of corruption in Asia", *The European Journal of Development Research*, 10(1): 15–39. [Bangladesh, India, Malaysia, Pakistan, South Korea, Thailand].

Khan, M.H. (2001) "The new political economy of corruption", in B. Fine, C. Lapavitsas and J. Pincus (eds.) *Development policy in the twenty-first century: beyond the post-Washington consensus*, London and New York: Routledge, 112–135. [Bangladesh, India, Malaysia, Pakistan, South Korea, Thailand].

Khandker, A. (2015) "The effect of economic freedom on corruption: the case of South Asian countries", *International Journal of Economics and Business Research*, 9(4): 403–414. [Bangladesh, Bhutan, India, Maldives, Nepal, Pakistan, Sri Lanka].

Khatri, N., S.E Khilji and B. Mujtaba (2013) "Anatomy of corruption in South Asia", in S. Khilji and C. Rowley (eds.) *Globalization, change and learning in South Asia,* Oxford, Cambridge and New Delhi: Chandos Publishing, 63–81. [Afghanistan, Bangladesh, India, Pakistan].

Kidd, J and F-J Richter (2003) *Fighting corruption in Asia: causes, effects and remedies*, Singapore: World Scientific.

Kumar, C.R. (2011) *Corruption and human rights in India: comparative perspectives on transparency and good governance*, New Delhi: Oxford University Press. [India, Hong Kong, Singapore].

Lee, S.H. and K.K. Oh (2007) "Corruption in Asia: pervasiveness and arbitrariness", *Asia Pacific Journal of Management*, 24(1): 97–114.

Lim, L. Y. C. and A. Stern (2002) "State power and private profit: the political economy of corruption in Southeast Asia", *Asian-Pacific Economic Literature*, 16(2): 18–52. [Indonesia, Malaysia, the Philippines, Singapore and Thailand].

Mathur, A., and K. Singh (2013) "Foreign direct investment, corruption and democracy", *Applied Economics*, 45(8): 991–1002. [China, India, Singapore].

Mohan, M. and V. Sathisan (2013) "Land grabs still plague Myanmar and Cambodia", Asian Business and Rule of Law initiative, http://ink.library.smu.edu.sg/sol_aprl/5.

Myrdal, G. (1972) "Corruption- its cause and effects", in G. Myrdal, *Asian drama: an inquiry into the poverty of nations,* New York: Vintage, 200–210.

Park, C.H. (2008) "A comparative institutional analysis of Korean and Japanese clientelism", *Asian Journal of Political Science*, 16(2): 111–129.

Pye, L. W. (1997) "Money politics and transitions to democracy in East Asia", *Asian Survey,* 37(3): 213–228. [Japan, Korea, Taiwan].

Quah, J.S.T. (2012) "Curbing corruption and enhancing trust in government: some lessons from Singapore and Hong Kong", in J. Liu, S. Jou and B. Hebenton (eds.) *Handbook of Asian criminology,* New York: Springer, 25–47.

Quah, J.S.T. (2013) *Curbing corruption in Asian countries: an impossible dream?* Singapore: Institute of Southeast Asian Studies [Hong Kong, India, Indonesia, Japan, Mongolia, Singapore, South Korea, Thailand].

Quah, J.S.T. (2015) "Evaluating the effectiveness of anti-corruption agencies in five Asian countries: a comparative analysis", *Asian Education and Development Studies*, 4(1): 143–159. [China, Japan, Philippines, Singapore and Taiwan].

Quah, J.S.T. (2016) "Combating corruption in six Asian countries: a comparative analysis", *Asian Education and Development Studies*, 5(2): 244–262. [Brunei Darussalam, Cambodia, Myanmar, Pakistan, Papua New Guinea, Vietnam].

Rodan, G. and C. Hughes (2014) "State-based anticorruption agencies in Indonesia, the Philippines and Thailand", in G. Rodan and C. Hughes, *The politics of accountability in Southeast Asia: the dominance of moral ideologies*, Oxford: Oxford University Press, 143–178.

Sachsenröder, W. (2013) "Political party finances in Southeast Asia: are there any signs of normative development?" Paper presented at the ICIRD 2013 conference, Bangkok, 22–23 August 2013, www.academia.edu/4364178/Party_Funding_and_Party_Finances_in_Southeast_Asia [Cambodia, Indonesia, the Philippines, Laos, Malaysia, Singapore, Timor-Leste, Thailand].

Sun, Y. and M. Johnston (2009) "Does democracy check corruption? Insights from China and India", *Comparative Politics*, 42(1): 1–19.

Toiganbayeva, A., D. Zirker and Z. Kenzhebayeva (2014) "The complex relationship between anti-corruption measures and industrial development levels in Singapore, Hong Kong, Malaysia and Thailand", *World Applied Sciences Journal*, 30(11): 1632–1635.

Tomsa, D and A. Ufen (eds.) (2013) *Party politics in Southeast Asia: clientelism and electoral competition in Indonesia, Thailand and the Philippines*, Abingdon: Routledge.

TI (Transparency International) (2011) *Global corruption report: climate change,* London: Earthscan. [China, India, Sri Lanka].

TI (Transparency International) (2013) *Global corruption report: education,* Abingdon: Routledge. [Afghanistan, Bangladesh, Nepal, Pakistan, Sri Lanka, Vietnam].

TI (Transparency International) (2014) *Fighting corruption in South Asia: building accountability,* www. transparency.org/whatwedo/publication/fighting_corruption_in_south_asia_building_accountability [Bangladesh, India, Maldives, Nepal, Pakistan, Sri Lanka].

TI (Transparency International) (2016) *Corruption Perceptions Index 2015,* https://www.transparency. org/cpi2015.

Tsai, J.H. (2009) "Political structure, legislative process and corruption: comparing Taiwan and South Korea", *Crime, Law and Social Change,* 52(4): 365–383.

Ufen, A. (2015) "Laissez-faire versus strict control of political finance: hegemonic parties and developmental states in Malaysia and Singapore", *Critical Asian Studies,* 47(4): 564–586.

Uslaner, E.M. (2008) *Corruption, inequality and the rule of law: the bulging pocket makes the easy life,* Cambridge: Cambridge University Press, 180–213. [Hong Kong, Singapore].

Wang, C.H. (2015) "Governance performance and political trust in East Asia", *Social Science Quarterly,* doi: 10.1111/ssqu.12223. [Japan, South Korea, Taiwan].

Wong, L. (2013) "Money-laundering in Southeast Asia: liberalism and governmentality at work", *Contemporary Politics,* 19(2): 221–233.

You, J.S. (2015) *Democracy, inequality and corruption: Korea, Taiwan and the Philippines compared,* Cambridge: Cambridge University Press.

Country studies

Afghanistan

Allen, T.S. (2013) "Addressing an ignored imperative: rural corruption in Afghanistan", *Small Wars Journal,* http://smallwarsjournal.com/jrnl/art/addressing-an-ignored-imperative-rural-corruption-in-afghanistan.

Bewley-Taylor, D. (2013) "Drug-trafficking and organised crime in Afghanistan: corruption, insecurity and the challenge of transition", *The RUSI Journal,* 158(6): 6–17.

Beyerle, S.M. (2014) "Community monitoring for postwar transformation: Afghanistan", in S.M. Beyerle (ed.) *Curtailing corruption: people power for accountability and justice,* Boulder: Lynne Rienner, 169–186.

Blunt, P. and S. Khamoosh (2016) "Vexatious voice: the politics of downward accountability and subnational reform in Afghanistan", *Progress in Development Studies,* 16(1): 81–100.

Callen, M. and J. D. Long (2014) "Institutional corruption and election fraud: evidence from a field experiment in Afghanistan", *The American Economic Review,* 105 (1): 354–381.

Carter, J. L. (2013) "Aiding Afghanistan: how corruption and western aid hinder Afghanistan's development", *Foreign Policy Journal,* 18 June, http://www.foreignpolicyjournal.com/wp-content/uploads/2013/06/130610-Carter-Afghanistan.pdf.

Centner, A.J. (2012) "Implementing international anti-corruption standards to improve Afghanistan's education system", *Case Western Reserve Journal of International Law,* 44(3): 847–874.

Chayes, S. (2015) *Thieves of state: why corruption threatens global security,* New York: Norton, 3–66.

De Lauri, A. (2013) "Corruption, legal modernization and judicial practice in Afghanistan", *Asian Studies Review,* 37(4): 527–545.

Geller, A., S. M. M. Rizi and M. M. Latek (2011) "How corruption blunts counternarcotic policies in Afghanistan: a multi-agent investigation", in J. Salerno, S. J. Yang, D. Nau and S.K. Chai (eds.) *Social computing, behavioral-cultural modeling and prediction,* Berlin: Springer, 121–128.

Goodhand, J. (2012) "Corruption or consolidating the peace? The drug economy and post-conflict peacebuilding in Afghanistan", in D. Zaum and C. Cheng (eds.) *Corruption and post-conflict peacebuilding: selling the peace?* Abingdon: Routledge: 144–161.

Government of Afghanistan, *High office of oversight and anti-corruption,* http://anti-corruption.gov. af/en.

Marquette, H. (2011) "Donors, state building and corruption: lessons from Afghanistan and the implications for aid policy", *Third World Quarterly,* 32(10): 1871–1890.

Mullen, R.D. (2010) "Afghanistan in 2009: trying to pull back from the brink", *Asian Survey,* 50(1): 127–138.

Murtazashvili, J. (2015) "Gaming the state: consequences of contracting out state building in Afghanistan", *Central Asian Survey*, 34(1): 78–92.

Singh, D. (2014) "Corruption and clientelism in the lower levels of the Afghan police", *Conflict, Security and Development,* 14(5): 621–650.

Singh, D. (2015) "Explaining varieties of corruption in the Afghan justice sector", *Journal of Intervention and Statebuilding*, 9(2): 231–255.

Singh, D. (2016) "Anti-corruption strategies in Afghanistan: an alternative approach", *Journal of Developing Societies*, 32 (1): 44–72.

TI (Transparency International) and Integrity Watch Afghanistan (2015) *National integrity assessment system Afghanistan 2015*, www.transparency.org/whatwedo/publication/afghanistan_2015_national_ integrity_system_assessment.

Unruh, J. and M. Shalaby (2012) "A volatile interaction between peacebuilding priorities: road infrastructure, (re)construction and land rights in Afghanistan", *Progress in Development Studies,* 12 (1): 47–61.

Wilde, A. and K. Mielke (2013) "Order, stability, and change in Afghanistan: from top-down to bottom-up state-making", *Central Asian Survey*, 32(3): 353–370.

From the comparative studies list, see also: Khatri et al. (2013); TI (2013); TI (2016).

Bangladesh

Ākhatāra, M.I. (2001) *Electoral corruption in Bangladesh*, Farnham: Ashgate.

Anti-Corruption Commission, Bangladesh, http://www.acc.org.bd/.

Bhuiyan, S.H. (2011) "Modernizing Bangladesh public administration through e-governance: benefits and challenges", *Government Information Quarterly*, 28(1): 54–65.

Bhuiyan, S. (2012) "Overcoming electoral corruption: the case of Bangladesh", in J. Mendilow (ed.) *Money, corruption and political competition in established and emerging democracies,* Lanham: Lexington Books, 185–201.

Choe, C., R. Dzhumashev, A. Islam and Z.H. Khan (2013) "The effect of informal networks on corruption in education: evidence from the household survey data in Bangladesh", *Journal of Development Studies*, 49(2): 238–250.

Ehsan, M. (2006) "When implementation fails: the case of anti-corruption commission (ACC) and corruption control in Bangladesh", *Asian Affairs*, 28(3): 40–63.

Feldman, S. and C. Geisler (2012) "Land expropriation and displacement in Bangladesh", *The Journal of Peasant Studies,* 39(3–4): 971–993.

Haque, S.T.M. and S.N. Mohammad (2013) "Administrative culture and incidence of corruption in Bangladesh: a search for the potential linkage", *International Journal of Public Administration*, 36(13): 996–1006.

Hossan, C. and T. Bartram (2009) "The battle against corruption and inefficiency with the help of egovernment in Bangladesh", *Electronic Government, An International Journal*, 7(1): 89–100.

Islam, M.M. (2013) "The toxic politics of Bangladesh: a bipolar competitive neopatrimonial state", *Asian Journal of Political Science*, 21(2): 148–168.

Jamal, I. and P. Pandey (2012) "Inter-organizational coordination and corruption in urban policy implementation in Bangladesh: a case of Rajshahi city corporation", *International Journal of Public Administration*, 35(2): 352–366.

Kashem, M.B. (2005) "The social organization of police corruption: the case of Bangladesh", in R. Sarre, D.K. Das and H.J. Albrecht (eds.) *Policing corruption: international perspectives,* Lanham: Lexington Books, 237–246.

Knox, C. (2009) "Dealing with sectoral corruption in Bangladesh: developing citizen involvement", *Public Administration and Development*, 29(2): 117–132.

Mahmood, S.A.I. (2010) "Public procurement and corruption in Bangladesh: confronting the challenges and opportunities", *Journal of Public Administration and Policy Research*, 2(6): 103–111.

Mahmud, T. and M. Prowse (2012) "Corruption in cyclone preparedness and relief efforts in coastal Bangladesh: lessons for climate adaptation", *Global Environmental Change*, 22(4): 933–943.

Parnini, S.N. (2011) "Governance reforms and anti-corruption commission in Bangladesh", *Romanian Journal of Political Science*, 11(1): 50–70.

Paul, B. P. (2010) "Does corruption foster growth in Bangladesh?" *International Journal of Development Issues*, 9(3): 246–262.

Quddus, M. (2001) "Bureaucratic corruption and business ethics: the case of the garment exports from Bangladesh", *Journal of Bangladesh Studies*, 3(1): 16–24.

Robinson, N. and N. Sattar (2012) "When corruption is an emergency: 'good governance' coups and Bangladesh", *Fordham International Law Journal*, 35(3): 737–779.

Sarkar, A.E (2004) "Administrative reform in Bangladesh: three decades of failure", *International Public Management Journal*, 7(3): 365–384.

Solaiman, S.M. (2014) "Laws whitening black money for boosting national economy: prevention or legalization of corruption in Bangladesh?" *Journal of Money Laundering Control*, 17(2): 141–165.

Transparency International Bangladesh (2014) *National integrity system assessment Bangladesh 2014*, http://www.transparency.org/whatwedo/publication/bangladesh_national_integrity_system_assessment_2014.

Zafurallah, H. and N.A. Siddiquee (2001) "Dissecting public sector corruption in Bangladesh: issues and problems of control", *Public Organization Review*, 1(4): 465–486.

Zafurallah, H and R. Rahman (2008) "The impaired state: assessing state capacity and governance in Bangladesh", *International Journal of Public Sector Management*, 21(7): 739–752.

From the comparative studies list, see also: Ahmad and Brookins (2004); Hough (2013); Khan (1998); Khan (2001); Khandker (2015); Khatri, Khilji and Mujtaba (2013); TI (2013); TI (2014); TI (2016).

Bhutan

Anti-Corruption Commission of Bhutan, http://www.acc.org.bt/.

Transparency International (2015) *Assessment of the Bhutan Anti-Corruption Commission 2015*, Berlin: Transparency International.

From the comparative studies list, see also: Khandker (2015); TI (2016).

Brunei

Anti-Corruption Bureau and Prime Minister's Office, http://www.bmr.gov.bn/Theme/Home.aspx.

Jones, D.S. (2016) "Combatting corruption in Brunei Darussalam", *Asian Education and Development Studies*, 5(2): 141–158.

Norton, Rose, Fulbright (2014) "Business ethics and anti-corruption laws: Brunei Darussalam", www.nortonrosefulbright.com/knowledge/publications/121089/business-ethics-and-anti-corruption-laws-brunei-darussalam.

From the comparative studies list, see also: Khandker (2015); Quah (2016).

Cambodia

Anti-Corruption Unit, www.acu.gov.kh/en_index.php?8e296a067a37563370ded05f5a3bf3ec=163.

Biddulph, R. (2014) "Can elite corruption be a legitimate Machiavellian tool in an unruly world? The case of post-conflict Cambodia", *Third World Quarterly*, 35(5): 872–887.

Brehm, W. C. (2016) "The structures and agents enabling educational corruption in Cambodia: shadow education and the business of examinations", in Y. Kitamura, D.B. Edwards Jr., C. Sitha and J.H. Williams (eds.) *The political economy of schooling in Cambodia: issues of quality and equity*, New York: Palgrave Macmillan, 99–122.

Ear, S. (2013) *Aid dependence in Cambodia: how foreign assistance undermines democracy*, New York: Columbia University Press.

Ear, S. (2016) "Combating corruption in Cambodia", *Asian Education and Development Studies*, 5(2): 159–174.

Feinberg, G. (2009) "The epidemic of petit corruption in contemporary Cambodia: causes, consequences and solutions", *Crime Prevention and Community Safety*, 11(4): 277–296.

Fitzpatrick, D. (2015) "The legal design of land grabs: possession and the state in post-conflict Cambodia", in C. Carter and A. Harding (eds.) *Land grabs in Asia: what role for the law?* London: Routledge, 67–82.

Global Witness (2009) *Country for sale: how Cambodia's elite has captured the country's extractive industries*, Washington, DC: Global Witness Publishing.

Hill, H. and J. Menon (2013) "Cambodia: rapid growth with weak institutions", *Asian Economic Policy Review*, 8(1): 46–65.

Hughes, C. (2006) "The politics of gifts: tradition and regimentation in contemporary Cambodia", *Journal of Southeast Asian Studies*, 37(3): 469–489.

Macinnes, M. (2015) "Land is life: an analysis of the role 'grand corruption' plays in enabling elite grabbing of land in Cambodia", in S. Milne and S. Mahanty (eds.) *Conservation and development in Cambodia: exploring frontiers of change in nature, state and society*, Abingdon: Routledge, 95–119.

Milne, S. (2015) "Cambodia's unofficial regime of extraction: illicit logging in the shadow of transnational governance and investment", *Critical Asian Studies*, 47(2): 200–228.

Samphantharak, K., and E.J. Malesky (2008) "Predictable corruption and firm investment: evidence from a natural experiment and survey of Cambodian entrepreneurs", *Quarterly Journal of Political Science*, 3: 227–267.

Sithirith, M. (2014) "The patron-client system and its effect on resource management in Cambodia: a case in Tonle Sap Lake", *Asian Politics and Policy*, 6(4): 595–609.

Sok, S. (2014) "Limited state and strong social forces: fishing lot management in Cambodia", *Journal of Southeast Asian Studies*, 45(2): 174–193.

Strangio, S. (2014) "Hunsenomics and its discontents", in S. Strangio, *Hun Sen's Cambodia*, New Haven and London: Yale University Press, 131–151.

Transparency International Cambodia (2014) *Corruption and Cambodia's governance system: the need for reform*, www.transparency.org/whatwedo/publication/cambodia_national_integrity_system_assessment_2014.

Un, K. (2005) "Patronage politics and hybrid democracy: political change in Cambodia, 1993–2003", *Asian Perspective*, 29(2): 203–230.

Un, K. and S. So (2009) "Politics of natural resource use in Cambodia", *Asian Affairs: An American Review*, 36(3): 123–138.

Un, K. and S. So (2011) "Land rights in Cambodia: how neopatrimonial politics restricts land policy reform", 84(2): 289–308.

From the comparative studies list, see also: Baker and Milne (2015); Croissant and Martin (2006); Global Witness (2013); Mohan and Sathisan (2013); Quah (2016); Sachsenröder (2013); TI (2016).

Central Asia (Azerbaijan, Kazakhstan, the Kyrgyz Republic, Tajikistan, Turkmenistan, Uzbekistan)

Cokgezen, M. (2004) "Corruption in Kyrgyzstan: the facts, causes and consequences", *Central Asian Survey*, 23(1): 79–94.

Collins, K. (2006) *Clan politics and regime transition in Central Asia*, New York: Cambridge University Press, 38–42, 338–342.

Cooley, A. and J.C. Sharman (2015) "Blurring the line between the licit and the illicit: transnational corruption networks in Central Asia and beyond", *Central Asian Survey*, 34(1): 11–28.

Feoktistova, Y. (2014) "Corruption in higher education and government measures for its prevention", *Procedia- Social and Behavioral Studies*, 112: 167–172.

Frank, A., A. Gawrich and G. Alakbarov (2009) "Kazakhstan and Azerbaijan as post-Soviet rentier states: resource income and autocracy as a double 'curse' in post-Soviet regimes", *Europe-Asia Studies*, 61(1): 109–140.

Isaacs, R. (2014) "Neopatrimonialism and beyond: reassessing the formal and the informal in the study of Central Asian politics", *Contemporary Politics*, 20(2): 229–245.

Knack, S. (2007) "Measuring corruption: a critique of indicators in Eastern Europe and Central Asia", *Journal of Public Policy*, 27(3): 255–291.

Liebert, S. "Challenges of reforming the civil service in the post-Soviet era: the case of Kyrgyzstan", *Review of Public Personnel Administration*, 34(4): 403–420.

McMann, K.M. (2014) *Corruption as a last resort: adapting to the market in Central Asia*, Ithaca: Cornell University Press.

Nicholls, P.M. (2001) "The fit between changes to the international corruption regime and indigenous perceptions of corruption in Kazakhstan", *University of Pennsylvania Journal of International Economic Law*, 22(4): 863–974.

Niyetullayev, N.N. and P. Almond (2014) "Money laundering and the shadow economy in Kazakhstan", *Journal of Money Laundering* Control, 17(2): 128–140.

Nurgaliyev, B., K. Ualiyev and B. Simonovich (2015) "Police corruption in Kazakhstan: the preliminary results of the study", *Review of European Studies*, 7(3): 140–148.

Organization for Economic Co-operation and Development (OECD) (2013) "Azerbaijan", in OECD, *Specialized anti-corruption institutions: review of the models,* 2nd edition, OECD Publishing, 116–120.

Organization for Economic Co-operation and Development (OECD) (2014) "Anti-corruption reforms in Kazakhstan: Round 3 monitoring of the Istanbul anti-corruption action plan", http://www.oecd.org/corruption/acn/Kazakhstan-Round-3-Monitoring-Report-ENG.pdf.

Rasizade, A. (2003) "Azerbaijan in transition to the 'new age of democracy'", *Communist and Post-Communist Studies*, 36(3): 345–372.

Swartz, B., F. Wadsworth and J. Wheat (2008) "Perceptions of corruption in Central Asian countries", *International Business and Economic Research Journal*, 7(3): 71–78.

Transparency Azerbaijan (2014) *Azerbaijan national system integrity assessment* http://www.transparency.org/whatwedo/publication/azerbaijan_national_integrity_system_assessment_2014.

Urinboyev, R. and M. Svensson (2013) "Living law, legal pluralism and corruption in post-Soviet Uzbekistan", *The Journal of Legal Pluralism and Unofficial Law*, 45(3): 372–390.

Yeager, M.G. (2012) "The CIA made me do it: understanding the political economy of corruption in Kazakhstan", *Crime, Law and Social Change*, 57(4): 441–557.

From the comparative studies list, see also: TI (2016).

China

Ang, Y. Y, and N. Jia (2014) "Perverse complementarity: political connections and the use of courts among private firms in China", *The Journal of Politics,* 76(2): 318–332.

Braendle, U. C., T. Gasser and J. Noll (2005) "Corporate governance in China - is economic growth potential hindered by guanxi?" *Business and Society Review*, 110(4): 389–405.

Broadhurst, R. and P. Wang (2014) "After the Bo Xilai trial: does corruption threaten China's future?" *Survival: Global Politics and Strategy*, 56(3): 157–178.

Chen, F. (2000) "Subsistence crises, managerial corruption and labour protests in China", *The China Journal*, 44: 41–63.

Chen, K. (2004) "Fiscal centralization and the form of corruption in China", *European Journal of Political Economy*, 20(4): 1001–1009.

Cole, M. A., R. Elliott and J. Zhang (2009) "Corruption, governance and FDI location in China: a province-level analysis", *The Journal of Development Studies*, 45(9): 1494–1512.

Dai, C. (2013) "Corruption and anti-corruption in China: challenges and countermeasures", in S. Rothlin and P. Haghirian (eds.) *Dimensions of teaching business ethics in Asia*, Berlin: Springer, 61–76.

Dong, B. and B. Torgler (2013) "Causes of corruption: evidence from China", *China Economic Review*, 26: 152–169.

Fu, H. (2015) "Wielding the sword: President's Xi's anti-corruption campaign", in S. Rose-Ackerman and P. Laguenes (eds.) *Greed, corruption and the modern state: essays in political economy,* Cheltenham: Edward Elgar Publishing, 134–160.

Gong, T. (1994) *The politics of corruption in contemporary China: an analysis of policy outcomes*, Westport, CT: Praeger.

Gong, T. (2002) "Dangerous collusion: corruption as a collective venture in contemporary China", *Communist and Post-Communist Studies,* 35(1): 85–103.

Gong, T. (2006) "Corruption and local governance: the double identity of Chinese local governments in market reform", *The Pacific Review*, 19(1): 85–102.

Gong, T. (2011) "An 'institutional turn' in integrity management in China", *International Review of Administrative Sciences*, 77(4): 671–686.

Gong, T. (2015) "Managing government integrity under hierarchy: anti-corruption efforts in local China", *Journal of Contemporary China*, 24(94): 684–700.

Gong, T. and H. Shi (2009) "Management corruption in China's industrial restructuring: how and why state assets get lost", *China Information*, 23(3): 411–445.

Gong, T and A. M. Wu (2012) "Does increased civil service pay deter corruption? Evidence from China", *Review of Public Personnel Administration*, 32(2): 192–204.

Gong, T. and J. Ren (2013) "Hard rules and soft constraints: regulating conflict of interest in China", *Journal of Contemporary China*, 22(79): 1–17.

Gong, T. and N. Zhou (2015) "Corruption and marketization: formal and informal rules in Chinese public procurement", *Regulation and Governance*, 9(1): 63–76.

Guo, Y. (2008) "Corruption in transitional China: an empirical analysis", *The China Quarterly*, 194: 349–364.

Guo, Y. (2011) "Isomorphic effect and organizational bribery in transitional China", *Asian Business and Management*, 10(2): 233–257.

Guo, Y. and S. Li (2015) "Anti-corruption measures in China: suggestions for reforms", *Asian Education and Development Studies*, 4(1): 7–23.

He, Z. (2000) "Corruption and anti-corruption in reform China", *Communist and Post-Communist Studies*, 33(2): 243–270.

Hsu, C. L. (2001) "Political narratives and the production of legitimacy: the case of corruption in post-Mao China", *Qualitative Sociology*, 24(1): 25–54.

Jeffreys, E. (2010) "Exposing police corruption and malfeasance: China's virgin prostitute cases", *The China Journal*, 63: 127–149.

Karkuhnen, P. and R. Kosonen (2016) "Corruption in China: through the lens of Finnish firms", in A.A.C. Texeira, C. Pimenta, A. Maia, and J. A. Moreira (eds.) *Corruption, economic growth and globalization*, London: Routledge, 71–83.

Ko, K. and C. Weng (2011) "Critical review of conceptual definitions of Chinese corruption: a formal-legal perspective", *Journal of Contemporary China*, 20(70): 359–378.

Ko, K. and C. Weng (2012) "Structural changes in Chinese corruption", *The China Quarterly*, 211: 718–740.

Ko, K. and H. Zhi (2013) "Fiscal decentralization: guilty of aggravating corruption in China?" *Journal of Contemporary China*, 22(79): 35–55.

Kwong, J. (1997) *The political economy of corruption in China*, Armonk, NY: M.E. Sharpe.

Leung, J. (2015) "Xi's corruption crackdown: how bribery and graft threaten the Chinese dream", *Foreign Affairs*, 94(3): 32–38.

Li, F. and J. Deng (2015) "The power and misuse of power by China's local procurates in anticorruption", *International Journal of Law, Crime and Justice*, doi: 10.1016/j.ylej.2015.10.002.

Li, F. and J. Deng (2016) "The limits of arbitrariness in anticorruption by China's local party discipline inspection committees", *Journal of Contemporary China*, 25(97): 75–90.

Li, H., H. Xiao and T. Gong (2015) "The impact of economic well-being on perceptions of anti-corruption performance: evidence from China", *Policy and Society*, 34(2): 97–109.

Li, H., T. Gong and H. Xiao (2016) "The perception of anti-corruption efficacy in China: an empirical analysis", *Social Indicators Research*, 125(3): 885–903.

Li, L. (2011) "Performing bribery in China: *guangxi*-practice, corruption with a human face", *Journal of Contemporary China*, 20(68): 1–20.

Li, L. (2012) "The 'production' of corruption in China's courts: judicial politics and decision-making in a one-party state", *Law and Social Inquiry*, 37(4): 848–877.

Li, R. (2013) "Media corruption: a Chinese characteristic", *Journal of Business Ethics*, 116(2): 297–310.

Liu, E. (2016) "A historical review of the control of corruption on economic crime in China", *Journal of Financial Crime*, 23(1): 4–21.

Liu, J. and B. Lin (2012) "Government auditing and corruption control: evidence from China's provincial panel data", *China Journal of Accounting Research*, 5(2): 163–186.

Lu, X. (2000) *Cadres and corruption: the organizational involution of the Chinese communist party*, Stanford: Stanford University Press.

Luo, Y. (2008) "The changing Chinese culture and business behavior: the perspective of intertwinement between *guanxi* and corruption", *International Business Review*, 17(2): 188–193.

Manion, M. (2004) *Corruption by design: building clean government in mainland China and Hong Kong.* Cambridge, MA: Harvard University Press, 84–118.

Manion, M. (2015) "Institutional design and anti-corruption in mainland China", in P. Heywood (ed.) *Routledge handbook of political corruption*, London: Routledge, 242–252.

Manion, M. (2016) "Taking China's anticorruption campaign seriously", *Economic and Political Studies*, 4(1): 3–18.

Mi, Z. and Q. Liu (2014) "Income inequality, fiscal redistribution and governmental corruption: evidence from Chinese provincial data", *Journal of Developing Areas*, 48(4): 119–137.

Millington, A., M. Eberhardt and B. Wilkinson (2005) "Gift giving, *guanxi* and illicit payments in buyer–supplier relations in China: analysing the experience of UK companies", *Journal of Business Ethics*, 57(3): 255–268.

Mo, J.S. (2013) "'Rule by the media'- the role of the media in the present development of rule of law in anti-corruption cases in traditional China", *Asia Pacific Law Review*, 21(2): 223–251.

Ngo, T.W. (2008) "Rent-seeking and economic governance in the structural nexus of corruption in China", *Crime, Law and Social Change*, 49(1): 27–44.

Pei, M (2006) "The dark side of China's rise", *Foreign Policy,* 153: 32–40.

Quah, J.S.T. (2015) *Hunting the corrupt "tigers" and "flies" in China: an evaluation of Xi Jinping's anti-corruption campaign (November 2012 to March 2015),* Baltimore, MD: Carey School of Law, University of Maryland.

Ramirez, C.D. (2014) "Is corruption in China 'out of control'? A comparison with the US in historical perspective", *Journal of Comparative Economics*, 42(1): 76–91.

Rosenbloom D. and T. Gong (2013) "Coproducing "clean" collaborative governance: examples from the United States and China", *Public Performance and Management Review*, 36 (4): 544–571.

Shieh, S. (2005) "The rise of collective corruption in China: the Xiamen smuggling case", *Journal of Contemporary China*, 14(42): 67–91.

Song, X. and W. Cheng (2012) "Perceptions of corruption in 36 major Chinese cities: based on a survey of 1,642 experts", *Social Indicators Research*, 109(2): 211–221.

Sun, Y. (2004) *Corruption and market in contemporary China,* Ithaca, NY: Cornell University Press.

Takeuchi, H. (2013) "Vote buying, village elections and authoritarian rule in rural China: a game-theoretic analysis", *Journal of East Asian Studies*, 13(1): 69–105.

Tam, W. (2011) "Organizational corruption by public hospitals in China", *Crime, Law and Social Change*, 56(3): 265–282.

Wang, P. (2013) "The rise of the red mafia in China: a case study of organised corruption in Chonqing", *Trends in Organized Crime,* 16(1): 49–73.

Wang, Y. (2013) "Court funding and judicial corruption in China", *The China Journal*, 69: 43–63.

Wang, Y. and J. You (2012) "Corruption and firm growth: evidence from China", *China Economic Review*, 23(2): 415–433.

Wedeman, A. (2004) "The intensification of corruption in China", *The China Quarterly*, 180: 895–921.

Wedeman, A. (2005) "Anticorruption campaigns and the intensification of corruption in China", *Journal of Contemporary China*, 14(42): 93–116.

Wedeman, A. (2008) "Win, lose or draw? China's quarter century war on corruption", *Crime, Law and Social Change*, 49(1): 7–26.

Wedeman, A. (2012) *Double paradox: rapid growth and rising corruption in China,* Ithaca: Cornell University Press.

White, J. (2014) "State capitalism and corruption: the case of China", in J. Mendilow and I. Peleg (eds.) *Corruption in the contemporary world: theory, practice and hotspots,* Lanham: Lexington Books, 223–247.

Wu, Y. and J. Zhu (2011) "Corruption, anti-corruption, and inter-county income disparity in China", *The Social Science Journal*, 48(3): 435–448.

Yuen, S. (2014) "Disciplining the party: Xi Jinping's anti-corruption campaign and its limits", *China Perspectives,* 3: 41–47.

Zhang, Q. (2015) "How land grabs are made 'constitutional' in China", in C. Carter and A. Harding (eds.) *Land grabs in Asia: what role for the law?* London: Routledge, 35–47.

Zhu, J. (2008) "Why are offices for sale in China? A case study of the office-selling chain in Heilong-jiang Province", *Asian Survey*, 48(4): 558–579.

Zhu, J. (2012) "The shadow of the skyscrapers: real estate corruption in China", *Journal of Contemporary China*, 21(74): 243–260.

Zhu, J., J. Lu and T. Shi (2013) "When grapevine news meets mass media: different information sources and popular perception of government corruption in mainland China", *Comparative Political Studies*, 46(8): 920–946.

Zhu, L. (2015) "Punishing corrupt officials in China" *The China Quarterly*, 223: 595–617.

From the comparative studies list, see also: Ang (2014); Cheung (2008); Clifford Chance (2014); Gong and Ma (2012); Gong et al. (2015); Gong and Scott (2015); Johnston (2008); Mathur and Singh (2013); Quah (2015); Sun and Johnston (2009); TI (2011); TI (2016).

Hong Kong

Gong, T. and S. Wang (2012) "Indicators and implications of zero tolerance of corruption: the case of Hong Kong", *Social Indicators Research*, 112(3): 569–586.

ICAC (Independent Commission Against Corruption) www.icac.org.hk.

ICAC (Independent Commission Against Corruption) (2015) *40 years in the Operations Department: fighting corruption with the community (1974–2014)*, Hong Kong: Independent Commission Against Corruption.

Lee, F.L.F. (2015) "How citizens react to political scandals surrounding government leaders: a survey study in Hong Kong", *Asian Journal of Political Science*, 23(1): 44–62.

Lethbridge, H.J. (1985) *Hard graft in Hong Kong: scandal, corruption and the ICAC*, Hong Kong: Oxford University Press.

Li, L. (2016) "Measuring the subjective perceptions of the social censure of corruption in post-1997 Hong Kong", *Crime, Law and Social Change*, 65(1): 93–112.

Li, R.B. L. (2014) "Measures to prevent corruption and to encourage cooperation of all sectors of society", Paper presented at the 16th UNAFEI UNCAC training programme, 150–160, www.unafei.or.jp/english/pages/RMS/No92_13VE_Li2.pdf.

Mao, Y., C.S. Wong and K.Z. Peng (2013) "Breaking institutionalized corruption: is the experience of the Hong Kong Independent Commission against Corruption generalizable?" *Asia Pacific Journal of Management*, 30(4): 1115–1124.

Manion, M. (2004) *Corruption by design: building clean government in Mainland China and Hong Kong*, Cambridge, MA: Harvard University Press, 27–83.

McWalters, I. (2015) *Bribery and corruption law in Hong Kong*, 3rd edition, Singapore: LexisNexis.

Michael, B. and I. Carr (2015) "How can the ICAC help foster the widespread adoption of anticorruption programs in Hong Kong?" *North Carolina Journal of International Law and Commercial Regulation*, 40(1): 355–442.

OECD (Organization for Economic Co-operation and Development) (2013) "Hong Kong, China: independent commission against corruption", in OECD, *Specialized anti-corruption institutions: review of the models*, 2nd edition, OECD Publishing, 49–58.

Scott, I. (2011) "The Hong Kong ICAC's approach to corruption control", in A. Graycar and R. G. Smith (eds.) *Handbook of global research and practice in corruption*, Cheltenham: Edward Elgar, 401–415.

Scott, I. (2013) "Engaging the public: the Hong Kong ICAC's community relations strategy", in J.S.T. Quah (ed.) *Different paths to curbing corruption: lessons from Denmark, Finland, Hong Kong, New Zealand and Singapore*, Bingley: Emerald: 79–108.

Scott, I. (2013) "Institutional design and corruption prevention in Hong Kong", *Journal of Contemporary China*, 22, (79):77–92.

Scott, I. (2015) "Governance and corruption prevention in Hong Kong" in L. Van den Dool, F. Hendriks, L. Schaap and A. Gianoli (eds.) *The quest for good urban governance: theoretical reflections and international practices*, Wiesbaden: Springer, 185–204.

Scott, I. and J.Y.H. Leung (2012) "Integrity management in post-1997 Hong Kong: challenges for a rule-based system", *Crime, Law and Social Change*, 58(1): 39–52.

Scott, I. and T. Gong (2015) "Evidence-based policy-making for corruption prevention in Hong Kong: a bottom-up approach", *Asia Pacific Journal of Public Administration*, 37(2): 87–101.

Sutherland, M.R. C (2015) "Anti-money laundering regime in Hong Kong", in B. Rider (ed.) *Research handbook on international financial crime*, Cheltenham: Edward Elgar, 113–124.

Wong, S. H-W (2010) "Political connections and firm performance: the case of Hong Kong", *Journal of East Asian Studies*, 10(2): 275–313.

Yep, R. (2013) "The crusade against corruption in Hong Kong in the 1970s: Governor MacLehose as a zealous reformer or a reluctant hero?" *China Information*, 27(2): 197–221.

From the comparative studies list, see also: Cheung (2008); Choi (2009); Clifford Chance (2014); Fritzen and Basu (2011); Gong et al. (2015); Gong and Scott (2015); Hira and Shiao (2016); Kumar (2011); Quah (2012); Quah (2013); Toiganbayeva et al. (2014); TI (2016); Uslaner (2008).

India

Acharya, A., J. E. Roemer and R. Somanathan (2015) "Caste, corruption and political competition in India", *Research in Economics*, 69(3): 336–352.

Banerjee, A., D. P. Green, J. McManus and R. Pande (2014) "Are poor voters indifferent to whether elected leaders are criminal or corrupt? A vignette experiment in rural India", *Political Communication*, 31(3): 391–407.

Bardhan, P. (2015) "Corruption and development policy (drawing upon the recent Indian debate)", *Journal of Public Economic Theory*, 17(4): 472–479.

Besley, T., R. Pande and V. Rao (2012) "Just rewards? Local politics and public resource allocation in South India", *The World Bank Economic Review*, 26(2): 191–216.

Bussell, J. (2012) "From 'petty' to 'grand' corruption: ownership, management, and the scale of reform", in J. Bussell (ed.) *Corruption and reform in India: public services in the digital age*, Cambridge: Cambridge University Press, 176–204.

Bussell, J. (2014) "Varieties of corruption: the organization of rent-sharing in India", www.princeton. edu/politics/about/file-repository/public/Bussell-Varieties-of-Corruption-Princeton.pdf.

Chakraborty, S. (2013) *Public service reforms in India: a fight against corruption*, Kolkata: Towards Freedom.

Charron, N. (2010) "The correlates of corruption in India: analysis and evidence from the state", *Asian Journal of Political Science*, 18(2): 177–194.

Chatterjee, S. and S.M. Roychoudry (2013) "Institutions, democracy and 'corruption' in India: examining potency and performance", *Japanese Journal of Political Science*, 14(3): 395–419.

Cole, S. (2009) "Fixing market failure or fixing elections? Agricultural credit in India", *American Economic Journal: Applied Economics*, 1(1): 219–250.

Corbridge, S. (2013) "Corruption in India", in A. Kohli and P. Singh (eds.) *Routledge handbook of Indian politics*, London: Routledge, 222–229.

Davis, M.C. (2012) "Human rights and India's struggle against corruption", *Human Rights Quarterly*, 34(2): 624–627.

Dutta, N., S. Kar and S. Roy (2013) "Corruption and persistent informality: an empirical investigation for India", *International Review of Economics and Finance*, 27: 357–373.

Elliott, C. (2012) "Political society, civil society and the state in India", *Asian Survey*, 52(2): 348–372.

Gould, W. (2016) "Corruption and anti-corruption in modern India: history, patronage and the moral patronage of anti-colonialism", in K.A. Jacobsen (ed.) *Routledge handbook of contemporary India*, London, 256–270.

Government of India, *Central Bureau of Investigation*, http://cbi.nic.in/.

Heston, A. and V. Kumar (2008) "Institutional flaws and corruption incentives in India", *The Journal of Development Studies*, 44(9): 1243–1261.

Jeffrey, C. (2002) "Caste, class, and clientelism: a political economy of everyday corruption in rural North India", *Economic Geography*, 78(1): 21–41.

Jenkins, R. (2004) "In varying states of decay? The politics of corruption and anti-corruption in Maharashtra and Rajasthan", in R. Jenkins (ed.) *Regional reflections: comparing politics across Indian states*, New Delhi: Oxford University Press, 219–252.

Jenkins, R. (2006) "Democracy, development and India's struggle against corruption", *Public Policy Research*, 13(3): 147–155.

Kato, A., and T. Sato (2015) "Greasing the wheels? The effect of corruption in regulated manufacturing sectors of India", *Canadian Journal of Development Studies*, 36(4): 459–483.

Kenny, P.D. (2015) "Colonial rule, decolonisation and corruption in India", *Commonwealth and Comparative Politics*, 53(4): 401–427.

Mander, H. (2003) "Corruption and the right to information", in R. Tandon and R. Mohanty (eds.) *Does civil society matter? Governance in contemporary India*, New Delhi: SAGE Publications, 145–166.

Markussen, T. (2011) "Inequality and political clientelism: evidence from South India", *The Journal of Development Studies*, 47(11): 1721–1738.

Nair, M. (2015) "Anti-corruption practices in India", in Y. Zhang and C. Levena (eds.) *Government anti-corruption strategies: a cross cultural perspective*, Boca Raton: CRC Press, 23–42.

Niehaus, P. and S. Sukhtankar (2013) "The marginal rate of corruption in public programs: evidence from India", *Journal of Public Economics*, 104: 52–64.

Pathak, R. D. and R. S. Prasad (2006) "Role of e-governance in tackling corruption: the Indian experience", in R. Ahmad (ed.) *The role of public administration in building a harmonious society,* Manila: Asian Development Bank, 434–463.

Paul, S. (1998) "Corruption in India: who will bell the cat?" *Asian Journal of Political Science,* 6(1): 1–15.

Peisakhin, L. (2012) "Transparency and corruption: evidence from India", *The Journal of Law and Economics,* 55(1): 129–149.

Peisakhin, L. and P. Pinto (2010) "Is transparency an effective anti-corruption strategy? Evidence from a field experiment in India", *Regulation and Governance,* 4(3): 261–280.

Pellissery, S. (2007) "Local processes of national corruption: elite linkages and their effects on poor people in India", *Global Crime,* 8(2): 131–151.

Prasad, A. and S. Shivarajan (2015) "Understanding the role of technology in reducing corruption: a transaction cost approach", *Journal of Public Affairs,* 15(1): 22–39.

Riley, P. and R.K. Roy (2016) "Corruption and anticorruption: the case of India", *Journal of Developing Societies,* 32(1): 73–99.

Roberts, A. (2010) "A great and revolutionary law? The first four years of India's Right to Information Act", *Public Administration Review,* 70(6): 925–933.

Sengupta, M. (2014) "Anna Hazare's anti-corruption movement and the limits of mass mobilization in India", *Social Movement Studies: Journal of Social, Cultural and Political Protest,* 13(3): 406–413.

Shafiq, M. N. (2015) "Aspects of moral change in India, 1990–2006: evidence from public attitudes toward tax evasion and bribery", *World Development,* 68: 136–148.

Sharma, P. (2014) "From India against Corruption to the Aam Aadmi party: social movements, political parties and citizen engagement in India', in R. Cordenillo and S. Van Der Staak (eds.) *Political parties and citizen movements in Asia and Europe,* Stockholm: Asia-Europe Foundation, 39–60.

Singh, G. (1997) "Understanding political corruption in contemporary Indian politics", *Political Studies,* 45(3): 626–638.

Srivastava, M. C. (2016) "Role of media in preventing and combating corruption", *Imperial Journal of Interdisciplinary Research,* 2(2): 170–180.

Sukhtankar, S. (2012) "Sweetening the deal? Political connections and sugar mills in India", *American Economic Journal: Applied Economics,* 4(3): 43–63.

Sukhtankar, S. and M. Vaishnav (2015) "Corruption in India: bridging research evidence and policy options" in S. Shah, A. Panagariya and S. Gokarn (eds.) *India Policy Forum 2014–2015,*11, New Delhi: Sage Publications, 193–275.

Tummala, K.K. (2009) "Combating corruption: lessons out of India", *International Public Management Review,* 10(1): 34–58.

Vadlamannati, K.C. (2015) "Fighting corruption or fighting elections? The politics of anti-corruption policies in India: a sub-national study", *Journal of Comparative Economics,* 43(4): 1035–1052.

Wyatt, A. (2015) "Arvand Kerjiwal's leadership of the Aam Aadmi party", *Contemporary South Asia,* 23(2): 167–180.

From the comparative studies list, see also: Ahmad and Brookins (2004); Alatas et al. (2009) Ang (2014); Cameron et al. (2009); Clifford Chance (2014); Davis (2004); Fritzen and Basu (2011); Gong and Ma (2009); Khan (1998); Khan (2001); Khandker (2015); Khatri et al. (2013); Kumar (2011); Mathur and Singh (2013); Quah (2013); Sun and Johnston (2009); TI (2011);TI (2014); TI (2016).

Indonesia

Allen, W. N. (2014) "From patronage machine to partisan melee: subnational corruption and the evolution of the Indonesian party system", *Pacific Affairs,* 87(2): 221–245.

Bakker, L. and G. Reerink (2015) "Indonesia's land acquisition law: towards effective prevention of land grabbing?" in C. Carter and A. Harding (eds.) *Land grabs in Asia: what role for the law?* London: Routledge, 83–99.

Blunt, P., M. Turner and H. Lindroth (2012) "Patronage's progress in post-Soeharto Indonesia", *Public Administration and Development,* 32(1): 64–81.

Brown, R.A. (2006) "Indonesian corporations, cronyism and, corruption", *Modern Asian Studies,* 40(4): 953–992.

Buehler, M. (2008) "The rise of Shari'a by-laws in Indonesian districts: an indication of changing patterns of power accumulation and political corruption", *South East Asia Research,* 16(2): 225–285.

Buehler, M. (2011) "Indonesia's law on public services: changing state-society relations or continuing politics as usual?" *Bulletin of Indonesian Economic Studies,* 47(1): 65–86.

Blunt, P., M. Turner and H. Lindroth (2012) "Patronage, service delivery, and social justice in Indonesia", *International Journal of Public Administration,* 35(3): 214–220.

Bubandt, N. (2014) *Democracy, corruption and the politics of spirit in contemporary Indonesia,* New York: Routledge.

Budiman, A., A. Roan and V.J. Callan (2013) "Rationalizing ideologies, social identities and corruption among civil servants in Indonesia during the Suharto era", *Journal of Business Ethics,* 116(1): 139–149.

Butt, S. (2011) "Anti-corruption reform in Indonesia: an obituary?" *Bulletin of Indonesian Economic Studies,* 47 (3): 381–394.

Butt, S. (2012) *Corruption and law in Indonesia,* Abingdon: Routledge.

Butt, S. and S.A. Schütte (2014) "Assessing judicial performance in Indonesia: the court for corruption crimes", *Crime, Law and Social Change,* 62(5): 603–619.

Choi, J-W (2011) "Measuring the performance of an anti-corruption agency: the case of the KPK in Indonesia", *International Review of Public Administration,* 16(3): 45–63.

Corruption Eradication Commission, http://www.kpk.go.id/id.

Crouch, H. (1979) "Patrimonialism and military rule in Indonesia", *World Politics,* 31(4): 571–587.

Crouch, H. (2010) "Reforming the constitution and the electoral system", in H. Crouch (ed.) *Political reform in Indonesia after Soeharto,* Singapore: Institute of Southeast Asian Studies, 43–86.

Crouch, H. (2010) "Politics, corruption and the courts", in H. Crouch (ed.) *Political reform in Indonesia after Soeharto,* Singapore: Institute of Southeast Asian Studies, 191–241.

Davidson, J.S. (2007) "Politics-as-usual on trial: regional anti-corruption campaigns in Indonesia", *The Pacific Review,* 20(1): 75–99.

Hadiz, V.R. (2012) "Democracy and money politics: the case of Indonesia", in R. Robison (ed.) *Routledge handbook of Southeast Asian politics,* Abingdon: Routledge, 71–82.

Hamid, A. (2014) "A family matter: political corruption in Banten, Indonesia", *Asian Politics and Policy,* 6(4): 577–593.

Hartwell, E. (2009) *"Wild money": the human rights consequences of illegal logging and corruption in Indonesia's forestry sector,* New York: Human Rights Watch.

Henderson, J.V. and A. Kuncoro (2004) *Corruption in Indonesia,* National Bureau of Economic Research, Working Paper 10674.

Henderson, J.V. and A. Kuncoro (2011) "Corruption and local democratisation in Indonesia: the role of Islamic parties", *Journal of Development Economics,* 94(2): 164–180.

Horowitz, D.L. (2013) *Constitutional change and democracy in Indonesia,* Cambridge: Cambridge University Press, 207–232.

Kramer, E. (2014) "A fall from grace? 'Beef-gate' and the case of Indonesia's Prosperous Justice Party", *Asian Politics and Policy,* 6(4): 555–576.

Kristiansen, S. and M. Ramli (2006) "Buying an income: the market for civil service positions in Indonesia", *Contemporary Southeast Asia: A Journal of International and Strategic Affairs,* 28(2): 207–233.

Kuncoro, A. (2004) "Bribery in Indonesia: some evidence from micro-level data", *Bulletin of Indonesian Economic Studies,* 40(3): 329–354.

Kuncoro, A. (2006) "Corruption and business uncertainty in Indonesia", *ASEAN Economic Bulletin,* 23(1): 11–30.

Mackie, J. (2010) "Patrimonialism: the new order and beyond", in E. Aspinall and G. Fealy (eds.) *Soeharto's new order and its legacy: essays in honour of Harold Crouch,* Canberra: ANU E Press, 81–98.

McLeod, R.H. (2000) "Soeharto's Indonesia: a better class of corruption", *Agenda: A Journal of Policy Analysis and Reform;* 7(2): 99–112.

McLeod, R.H. (2008) "Inadequate budgets and salaries as instruments for institutionalizing public sector corruption in Indonesia", *South East Asia Research,* 16(2): 199–223.

McLeod, R.H. (2011) "Institutionalized public sector corruption: a legacy of the Suharto franchise", in E. Aspinall and G. van Klinken (eds.) *The state and illegality in Indonesia,* Leiden: KITLV Press, 45–64.

Mietzner, M. (2008) "Soldiers, parties and bureaucrats: illicit fund-raising in contemporary Indonesia", *South East Asia Research,* 16(2): 225–254.

Mietzner, M. (2015) "Dysfunction by design: political finance and corruption in Indonesia", *Critical Asian Studies,* 47(4): 611–640.

Olken, B. A. (2006) "Corruption and the costs of redistribution: micro evidence from Indonesia", *Journal of Public Economics,* 90(4–5): 853–870.

OECD (Organization for Economic Co-operation and Development) (2013) "Indonesia: corruption eradication commission", in OECD, *Specialized anti-corruption institutions: review of the models,* 2nd edition, OECD Publishing, 91–94.

Paturnu, A.A. and E.A. Rahman (2014) "Local governance and development outcomes", in H. Hill (ed.) *Regional dynamics in a decentralized Indonesia,* Singapore: Institute of Southeast Asian Studies, 156–185.

Prabowo, H.Y. (2014) "To be corrupt or not to be corrupt: understanding the behavioral side of corruption in Indonesia", *Journal of Money Laundering Control,* 17(3): 306–326.

Robertson-Snape, F. (1999) "Corruption, collusion and nepotism in Indonesia", *Third World Quarterly,* 20(3): 589–602.

Rosser, A. (2012) "Realising free health care for the poor in Indonesia: the politics of illegal fees", *Journal of Contemporary Asia,* 42 (2): 255–275.

Schütte, S.A. (2011) "Appointing top officials in a democratic Indonesia: the Corruption Eradication Commission", *Bulletin of Indonesian Economic Studies,* 47(3): 355–379.

Schütte, S.A. (2012) "Against the odds: anti-corruption reform in Indonesia", *Public Administration and Development,* 32(1): 38–48.

Setiyono, B. and R.H. McLeod (2010) "Civil society organizations' contribution to the anti-corruption movement in Indonesia", *Bulletin of Indonesian Economic Studies,* 46(3): 347–370.

Shin, J.H. (2015) "Voter demands for patronage: evidence from Indonesia", *Journal of East Asian Studies,* 15(1): 127–151.

Silitonga, M. S., G. Anthonio, L. Heyse, and R.Wittek (2015) "Institutional change and corruption of public leaders: a social capital perspective on Indonesia", in R.L. Holzhacker, R. Wittek and J. Woltjer (eds.) *Decentralization and governance in Indonesia,* New York: Springer, 233–258.

Suryadarma, D. (2012) "How corruption diminishes the effectiveness of public spending on education in Indonesia", *Bulletin of Indonesian Economic Studies,* 48(1):85–100.

Varkkey, H. (2013) "Patronage politics, plantation fires and transboundary haze", *Environmental Hazards,* 12(3–4): 200–217.

Vial, V. and J. Hanoteau (2010) "Corruption, manufacturing plant growth, and the Asian paradox: Indonesian evidence", *World Development* 38(5): 693–705.

Von Luebke, C. (2010) "The politics of reform: political scandals, elite resistance, and presidential leadership in Indonesia", *Journal of Current Southeast Asian Affairs,* 29(1): 79–94.

From the comparative studies list, see also: Alatas et al. (2009); Assegaf (2015); Bhargava and Bolongaita (2004); Cameron et al. (2009); Clifford Chance (2014); Lim and Stern (2002); Quah (2013); Rodan and Hughes (2014); Sachsenröder (2013); Tomsa and Ufen (2012); TI (2016).

Japan

Babb, J. (2002) "Politics, business, and the inescapable web of structural corruption in Japan", in E.T. Gomez (ed.) *Political business in East Asia,* London and New York: Routledge, 324–338.

Babb, J. (2005) "Corruption and governance in Japan", in G.D. Hook (ed.) *Contested governance in Japan: sites and issues,* London: Routledge Curzon, 174–191.

Black, W. K. (2004) "The dango tango: why corruption blocks real reform in Japan", *Business Ethics Quarterly,* 14 (4): 603–623.

Bowen, R.W. (2003) *Japan's dysfunctional democracy: the Liberal Democratic Party and structural corruption,* Armonk, NY: M.E. Sharpe.

Carlson, M. (2011) "Money in Japanese politics: regulation and reform", in A. Gaunder (ed.) *Routledge handbook of Japanese politics,* London: Routledge, 70–80.

Carlson, M. and S.R. Reed (2013) "Electoral law violation as campaign effort: turnout in Japan's House of Councillors elections", *Democratization,* 20(7): 1243–1267.

Carpenter, S. (2014) *Japan Inc. on the brink: institutional corruption and agency failure,* Basingstoke: Palgrave Macmillan.

Choi, J.W. (2007) "Government structure and administrative corruption in Japan: an organizational network approach", *Public Administration Review,* 67(5): 930–942.

Christensen, R. (2015) "The rules of the election game in Japan", in R.J. Hrebenar and A. Nakamura (eds.) *Party politics in Japan: political chaos and stalemate in the twenty-first century,* London: Routledge, 22–55.

Cox, G. W. and M.F. Thies (2000) "How much does money matter? 'Buying' votes in Japan 1967–1990", *Comparative Political Studies*, 33(1): 37–57.

Curini, L. (2011) "Negative campaigning in no-cabinet alternation systems: ideological closeness and blames of corruption in Italy and Japan using party manifesto data", *Japanese Journal of Political Science*, 12(3): 399–420.

George Mulgan, A. (2010) "The perils of Japanese politics", *Japan Forum*, 21(2): 183–207.

Johnson, C. (1986) "Tanaka Kakuei, structural corruption, and the advent of machine politics in Japan", *The Journal of Japanese Studies*, 12(1): 1–28.

Johnson, D. (2003) "A tale of two systems: prosecuting corruption in Japan and Italy", in F.J. Schwartz and S.J. Pharr (eds.) *The state of civil society in Japan*, Cambridge: Cambridge University Press, 257–280.

Mitchell, R.H. (1996) *Political bribery in Japan*, Honolulu: University of Hawaii Press.

Nyblade, B. and S. R. Reed (2008) "Who cheats? Who loots? Political competition and corruption in Japan 1947–1993", *American Journal of Political Science*, 52(4): 926–941.

Oyamada, E (2015) "Anti-corruption measures the Japanese way: prevention matters", *Asian Education and Development Studies*, 4(1): 24–50.

Pempel, T. J. (2010) "Between pork and productivity: the collapse of the Liberal Democratic Party", *The Journal of Japanese Studies*, 36(2): 227–254.

Reed, S.R. (1996) "Political corruption in Japan", *International Social Science Journal*, 48(149): 395–405.

Rothacher, A. (2003) "Political corruption in Japan", in M. J. Bull and J.L. Newell (eds.) *Corruption in contemporary politics*, Basingstoke: Palgrave Macmillan, 106–119.

Tanimura, J.K. and M.G. Okamoto (2013) "Reputational penalties in Japan: evidence from corporate scandals", *Asian Economic Journal*, 27(1): 39–57.

TI (Transparency International) (2006) *Country study report, Japan, 2006*, www.transparency.org.

Woodall, B. (2015) "Japanese political finance and its dark side", in R.J. Hrebenar and A. Nakamura (eds.) *Party politics in Japan: political chaos and stalemate in the twenty-first century,* London and New York: Routledge, 56–79.

From the comparative studies list, see also: Clifford Chance (2014); Gong and Ma (2012); Hutchcroft (2014); Johnston (2008); Park (2008); Pye (1997); Quah (2013); Quah (2015); Wang (2015); TI (2016).

Laos

Dwyer, M.B. (2013) "Building the politics machine: tools for 'resolving' the global land grab", *Development and Change,* 44(2): 309–333.

Lao People's Democratic Republic (2005, UNDP draft translation 2006) *Promulgation of the law on anti-corruption,* http://www.ilo.org/dyn/natlex/docs/ELECTRONIC/89795/103234/F-231262531/LAO89795.pdf.

Messerli, P. and O. Schönweger (2015) "Land acquisition, investment and development in the Lao coffee sector: successes and failures", *Critical Asian Studies,* 47(1): 94–122.

Stuart-Fox, M. (2006) "The political culture of corruption in the Lao PDR", *Asian Studies Review,* 30(1): 59–75.

To, P.X., S. Mahanty and W. Dressler (2014) "Social networks of corruption in the Vietnamese and Lao cross-border timber trade", *Anthropological Forum: A Journal of Anthropology and Comparative Sociology,* 24(2): 154–174.

From the comparative studies list, see also: Global Witness (2013); Sachsenröder (2013); TI (2016).

Macao

Godinho, J. (2013) "The prevention of money laundering in Macao casinos", *Gaming Law and Economics,* 17(4): 262–274.

Kwong, B.K.K (2011) "Public ethics and corruption in Macao", in E. Berman (ed.) *Public administration in Southeast Asia: Thailand, Philippines, Malaysia, Hong Kong and Macao,* Boca Raton: CRC Press, 501–518.

Leong, A.V.M. (2004) "Macau casinos and organised crime", *Journal of Money Laundering Control,* 7(4): 298–307.

Lo, S.H. (1993) "Bureaucratic corruption and its control in Macao", *Asian Journal of Public Administration*, 15(1): 32–58.

Lo, S.S.H. (2009) *The politics of cross-border crime in greater China: case studies of mainland China, Hong Kong and Macao*, Armonk, N.Y.: M. E. Sharpe, 131–153.

Macao Special Administration Region (2015) *Commission Against Corruption*, http://www.ccac.org.mo/index.php/en/.

Nelson, I.N. (2013) "A tale of two cities, Macau and Las Vegas", *Gaming Law and Economics*, 17(6): 393–403.

Yu, E.W.Y. (2013) "Anti-corruption approaches in Macao: lawmaking and legal enforcement", *Journal of Contemporary China*, 22(79): 93–108.

From the comparative studies list, see also: TI (2016).

Malaysia

Beh, L. (2011) "Public ethics and corruption in Malaysia", in E. Berman (ed.) *Public administration in Southeast Asia: Thailand, Philippines, Malaysia, Hong Kong and Macao*, Boca Raton: CRC Press, 171–191.

Case, W. (2008) "Malaysia in 2007: high corruption and low opposition", *Asian Survey*, 48(1): 47–54.

Gomez, E.T. (2002) "Political business in Malaysia: party factionalism, corporate development and economic crisis", in E.T. Gomez (ed.) *Political business in East Asia*, London and New York: Routledge, 82–114.

Gomez, E.T. (2012) "Monetizing politics: financing parties and elections in Malaysia", *Modern Asian Studies*, 46(5): 1370–1397.

Hui, W.S., R. Othman, N.H. Omar, R.A. Rahman and N.H. Haron (2011) "Procurement issues in Malaysia", *International Journal of Public Sector Management*, 24(6): 567–593.

Kapeli, N.S and N. Mohamed (2015) "Insights of anti-corruption initiatives in Malaysia", *Procedia Economics and Finance*, 31: 525–534.

Loh, F. K.W. (2014) "Malaysia after Mahathir: late democratization amidst development, the strong developmental state, and developmentalism", in H.H. M. Hsiao (ed.) *Democracy or alternative systems in Asia: after the strongmen*, London: Routledge, 114–136.

MACC (Malaysian Anti-Corruption Commission) http://www.sprm.gov.my/index.php/en/.

Munang, M.N. (2015) "Land grabs in Sabah, Malaysia: customary rights as legal entitlement for indigenous people- real or illusory?" in C. Carter and A. Harding (eds.) *Land grabs in Asia: what role for the law?* London: Routledge, 137–149.

Mutalib, H. M. (2015) "The other side of Malaysia's enviable economic and multiethnic stability: the obstinate resilience of 'money politics'", *Asian Ethnicity*, doi: 10.1080/14631369.2015.1038777.

Sachsenroeder, W. (2014) "Party finances and money politics in Southeast Asia: power broking in the shade", Social Science Research Network paper, http://papers.ssrn.com/sol3/papers.cfm?abstract_id=2450385.

Segon, M., C. Booth and T. O'Shannassy (2010) "Bribery and corruption: a comparative study between Australian and Malaysian managers", in Y.C. So (ed.) *3rd World Business Ethics Forum*, Macau, China, 27–28 October, 1–18.

Siddiquee, N. A. (2010) "Combating corruption and managing integrity in Malaysia: a critical overview of recent strategies and initiatives", *Public Organization Review*, 10(2): 153–171.

Subramaniam, Y. (2015) "Peninsular Malaysia's customary lands: how does legal paternalism facilitate land grabs?" in C. Carter and A. Harding (eds.) *Land grabs in Asia: what role for the law?* London: Routledge, 118–136.

Tan, J. (2015) "Rent-seeking and money politics in Malaysia: ethnicity, cronyism and class", in M.L. Weiss (ed.) *Routledge handbook of contemporary Malaysia*, Abingdon: Routledge, 200–213.

Teh, Y.K. (2002) "Money politics in Malaysia", *Journal of Contemporary Asia*, 32(3): 338–345.

Wain, B. (2009) *Malaysian maverick: Mahathir Mohammad in turbulent times*, London: Palgrave Macmillan, 124–138.

Weiss, M.L. (2015) "The antidemocratic potential of party system institutionalization: Malaysia as morality tale?" in A. Hicken and E.M. Kuhonta (eds.) *Party system institutionalization in Asia: democracies, autocracies, and the shadows of the past*, New York: Cambridge University Press, 25–48.

White, N.J. (2004) "The beginnings of crony capitalism: business, politics and economic development in Malaysia, c. 1955–70", *Modern Asian Studies*, 38(2): 389–417.

From the comparative studies list, see also: Clifford Chance (2014); Croissant and Martin (2006); Khan (1998); Khan (2001); Lim and Stern (2002); Sachsenröder (2013); Toiganbayeva et al. (2014); Ufen (2015).

Maldives

Morrison, S. (2014) "A contractual dispute in the Maldives: some facets in a multi-faceted crisis", *Journal of South Asian Studies*, 2(3): 185–202.
Republic of Maldives, *Anti-Corruption Commission*, http://acc.gov.mv/en/.
Transparency Maldives (2014) *National integrity system assessment, Maldives 2014,* www.transparency.org.
From the comparative studies list, see also: Khandker (2015); TI (2014).

Mongolia

Asia Foundation and Sant-Maral Foundation (2015) *Survey on perceptions and knowledge of corruption: strengthening transparency in Mongolia project,* http//: asiafoundation.org.
Barnes, D.W. (2013) "Mongolia", in World Bank, *Income and asset disclosure: case study illustration,* Washington, DC: The World Bank, 153–172.
Fritz, V. (2007) "Democratisation and corruption in Mongolia", *Public Administration and Development,* 27(3): 191–203.
Landell-Mills, P. (2013) "Mongolia's strong women", in P. Landell-Mills, *Citizens against corruption: report from the front line,* Kibworth Beauchamp: Matador, 50–69.
Png, C.A., M. DeFeo and T. Hicks (2015) "Design and implementation of a capacity development program –experience with combating money laundering and financing of terrorism in Mongolia", *Journal of Money Laundering Control,* 18(4): 488–495.
Reeves, J. (2011) "Resources, sovereignty, and governance: can Mongolia avoid the 'resource curse'?" *Asian Journal of Political Science,* 19(2): 170–185.
Sneath, D. (2002) "Reciprocity and notions of corruption in contemporary Mongolia", *Mongolian Studies,* 25: 85–99.
Sneath, D. (2006) "Transacting and enacting: corruption, obligation and the use of monies in Mongolia", *Ethnos: Journal of Anthropology,* 71(1): 89–112.
Tuya, N. (2006) "Mongolia in 2005: sharing power, dealing with corruption", *Asian Survey,* 46(1): 79–84.
From the comparative studies list, see also: Quah (2013); TI (2016).

Myanmar

Aye, N.N. (2012) "The role of the media in Myanmar: can it be a watchdog for corruption?" in N. Cheesman, M. Skidmore and T. Wilson (eds.) *Myanmar's transition: openings, obstacles and opportunities,* Singapore: Institute of Southeast Asian Studies, 185–203.
Carter, C. (2015) "Winners and losers: land grabbing in the new Myanmar", in C. Carter and A. Harding (eds.) *Land grabs in Asia: what role for the law?* London: Routledge, 100–117.
Cheesman, N. (2012) "Myanmar's courts and the sound money makes", in N. Cheesman, M. Skidmore and T. Wilson (eds.) *Myanmar's transition: openings, obstacles and opportunities,* Singapore: Institute of Southeast Asian Studies, 231–248.
Englehart, N.A. (2012) "Two cheers for Burma's rigged election", *Asian Survey,* 52(4): 666–686.
Ford, M., M. Gillan and H. H. Thein (2016) "From cronyism to oligarchy? Privatisation and business elites in Myanmar", *Journal of Contemporary Asia,* 46(1): 18–41.
Global Witness (2015) *Jade: a Global Witness investigation into Myanmar's 'big state secret',* London: Global Witness.
Meehan, P. (2011) "Drugs, insurgency and state-building in Burma: why the drugs trade is central to Burma's changing political order", *Journal of Southeast Asian Studies,* 42(3): 376–404.
Perry, P. (2005) "Corruption in Burma and the corruption of Burma", in N. Tarling (ed.) *Corruption and good governance in Asia,* Abingdon: Routledge, 186–197.
Quah, J.S.T. (2016) "Minimising corruption in Myanmar: an impossible dream", *Asian Education and Development Studies,* 5(2): 175–194.as yet.

Saha, J. (2013) *Law, disorder and the colonial state: corruption in Burma c.1900,* Basingstoke: Palgrave Macmillan.

Saw, K.S. (2015) "Tackling Myanmar's corruption challenge", *Focus Asia: Perspective and Analysis,* 13: 1–9.

Vlasic, M.V. and P. Atlee (2014) "Myanmar and the Dodd-Frank whistleblower 'bounty': the US Foreign Corrupt Practices Act and curbing grand corruption through innovative action", *American University International Law Review,* 29(2): 441–464.

From the comparative studies list, see also: James (2010); Mohan and Sathisan (2013); Quah (2013); TI (2016).

Nepal

Adhikari, R. (2015) "Public procurement issues and challenges in Nepal", *Journal of Engineering, Economics and Management,* 2(3): 3–27.

Commission for the Investigation of Abuse of Authority, www.ciaa.gov.np.

Kondos, A. (1987) "The question of 'corruption' in Nepal", *The Australian Journal of Anthropology,* 17(1): 15–29.

Manandhar, N. (2009) "The anatomy of a failed anti-corruption project: a case study from Nepal", *U4 Practice Insight,* 3: 1–8.

Manandhar, N. (2015) "Anti-corruption lessons from Nepal", in Y. Zhang and C. Luvena (eds.) *Government anti-corruption strategies: a cross cultural perspective,* Boca Raton: CRC Press: 77–102.

Momen, N. (2013) "Influence of political parties on the judicial process in Nepal", *Asian Studies: Journal of Critical Perspectives on Asia,* 49(1): 150–152.

Neupane, A., J. Soar and K. Vaidya (2012) "Perceived benefits related to anti-corruption from e-tendering system in Nepal", *Asian Journal of Information Technology,* 11(1): 22–29.

NORAD (Norwegian Agency for Development Cooperation) (2011) *Corruption and anti-corruption in Nepal: lessons learned and possible future initiatives,* www.norad.no.

Sharma, K. (2012) "Politics and governance in Nepal", *Asia Pacific Journal of Public Administration,* 34(1), 57–69.

Simkhada, P., E. Van Teijlingen, G. Sharma, B. Simkhada and J. Townend (2012) "User costs and informal payments for care in the largest maternity hospital in Kathmandu, Nepal", *Health Science Journal,* 6 (2): 317–334.

Subedi, M.S. (2005) "Corruption in Nepal: an anthropological inquiry", *Dhaulagiri Journal of Sociology and Anthropology,* 1: 110–128.

Transparency International Nepal (2014) *National system integrity assessment Nepal 2014,* http://www.transparency.org/whatwedo/publication/nepal_nis_2014.

Transparency International Nepal (2015) *Integrity pact in public procurement,* http://issuu.com/tinepal/docs/integrity_pact_in_public.

Truex, R. (2011) "Corruption, attitudes and education: survey evidence from Nepal", *World Development,* 39(7): 1133–1142.

From the comparative studies list, see also: Khandker (2015); TI (2013); TI (2014); TI (2016).

North Korea

Haggard, S., J. Lee and M. Noland (2012) "Integration in the absence of institutions: China–North Korea cross-border exchange", *Journal of Asian Economics,* 23(2): 130–145.

Wang, P. and S. Blancke (2014) "Mafia state: the evolving threat of North Korean narcotics trafficking", *The RUSI Journal,* 159(5): 52–59.

Pakistan

Ahmad, A. (2001) "Historical antecedents of corruption in Pakistan", in A.K. Jain (ed.) *The political economy of corruption,* London: Routledge, 142–154.

Akhtar, A.S. (2011) "Patronage and class in urban Pakistan: modes of labor control in the contractor economy", *Critical Asian Studies,* 43(2): 159–184.

Ali, Z. (2016) "Conflict between social structure and legal framework: political corruption in Pakistan", *Commonwealth and Comparative Politics*, 54(1): 115–137.

Bashir, S., H.R. Khattak, A. Hanif and S.N. Chohan (2011) "Whistle-blowing in public sector organizations: evidence from Pakistan", *The American Review of Public Administration*, 41(3): 285–296.

Farooq, A, M. Shahbaz, M. Arouri and F. Teulon (2013) "Does corruption impede economic growth in Pakistan?" *Economic Modelling*, 35: 622–633.

Government of Pakistan, *National Accountability Bureau*, http://www.nab.gov.pk/.

Haider, A., M.U. Din, and E. Ghani (2011) "Consequences of political instability, governance and bureaucratic corruption on inflation and growth: the case of Pakistan", *The Pakistan Development Review*, 50(4): 773–807.

Hussain, F. and A. Riaz (2012) "Corruption in the public organizations of Pakistan: perceptual views of university students", *The Journal of Commerce*, 4(1): 62–71.

Ismail, A. and K. Rashid (2014) "Time series analysis of the nexus among corruption, political instability and judicial inefficiency in Pakistan", *Quality and Quantity*, 48(5): 2757–2771.

Khan, F. (2007) "Corruption and the decline of the state in Pakistan", *Asian Journal of Political Science*, 15(2): 219–247.

Khan, F. (2016) "Combating corruption in Pakistan", *Asian Education and Development Studies,* 5(2): 195–210.

Khan, M., N.A. Kakakhel and M. Dubnick (2004) "Prosecuting corruption: the case of Pakistan", Institute of Governance, Public Policy and Social Research, Queen's University, Belfast, Working Paper, QU/Gov/11/2004.

Martin, N. (2014) "The dark side of political society: patronage and the reproduction of social inequality", *Journal of Agrarian Change,* 14(3): 419–434.

Rafi, M.M., S.H. Lodi and N.M. Hasan (2012) "Corruption in public infrastructure service and delivery: the Karachi case study", *Public Works Management and Policy*, 17(4): 370–387.

Rinaudo, J.D. (2002) "Corruption and allocation of water: the case of public irrigation in Pakistan", *Water Policy*, 4(5): 405–422.

Smith, L.E.D., A.M. Kushk and M. Stockbridge (2000) "Case studies of corruption in agricultural markets in Sindh province, Pakistan, and implications for market liberalization", *Journal of International Food and Agribusiness Marketing,* 11(1): 19–42.

Transparency International Pakistan (2014) *National integrity system: country report 2014*, http://www.transparency.org/whatwedo/nisarticle/pakistan_2014.

From the comparative studies list, see also: Davis (2004); Khan (1998); Khan (2001); Khandker (2015); Khatri, Khilji and Mujtaba (2013); Quah (2016); TI (2013); TI (2014); TI (2016).

The Philippines

Azfar, O. and G. Tugrul (2008) "Does corruption affect health outcomes in the Philippines?" *Economics of Governance,* 9(3): 197–244.

Batalla, E.V.C. (2015) "Treading the straight and righteous path: curbing corruption in the Philippines", *Asian Education and Development Studies* 4(1): 51–75.

Cariño, L.V. (1985) "The politicization of the Philippine bureaucracy: corruption or commitment?" *International Review of Administrative Sciences*, 51(1): 13–18.

Chaikin, D. and J.C. Sharman (2009) "The Marcos kleptocracy", in D. Chaikin and J.C. Sharman, *Corruption and money-laundering: a symbiotic relationship*, New York: Palgrave Macmillan, 153–186.

Cheung, A.B.L. and D.S. Jones (2013) "Procurement reform in the Philippines: the impact of elite capture and informal bureaucracy", *International Journal of Public Sector Management,* 26(5): 375–400.

Claudio, L.E. (2014) "From scandalous politics to public scandal: corruption, media, and the collapse of the Estrada regime in the Philippines", *Asian Politics and Policy*, 6(4): 539–554.

Co, E.E.A. (2007) "Challenges to the Philippine culture of corruption", in S. Bracking (ed.) *Corruption and development: the anti-corruption campaigns*, Basingstoke: Palgrave Macmillan, 121–137.

Coronel, S. (ed.) (1998) *Pork and other perks: corruption and governance in the Philippines,* Manila: Philippine Centre for Investigative Journalism.

Fajardo, F.J.P. (2014) "A hunger for power and a thirst for wealth: establishing a link between early political corruption and the pork barrel system", *Journal of South Asian Studies*, 2(1): 55–61.

Guth, A.P. (2010) "Human trafficking in the Philippines: the need for an effective anti-corruption program", *Trends in Organized Crime*, 13(2): 147–166.

Hodder, R. (2014) *High-level political appointments in the Philippines: patronage, emotion and democracy*, Singapore: Springer.

Hutchcroft, P.D. and J. Rocamora (2003) "Strong demands and weak institutions: the origins and evolution of the democratic deficit in the Philippines", *Journal of East Asian Studies*, 3(2): 259–292.

Johnston, M. (2010) *Political and social foundations for reform: anti-corruption strategies for the Philippines*, Manila: Asian Institute of Management.

Kushida, K. (2003) "The political economy of the Philippines under Marcos: property rights in the Philippines from 1965–1986", *Stanford Journal of East Asian Affairs*, 3(1): 119–126.

Office of the Ombudsman, http://www.ombudsman.gov.ph/.

Quilala, D.F. (2015) "The Philippines in 2014: unmasking the daang matuwid", *Philippine Political Science Journal*, 36(1): 94–109.

Quimpo, N.G. (2007) "The Philippines: political parties and corruption", *Southeast Asian Affairs*, 277–294.

Quimpo, N.G. (2009) "The Philippines: predatory regime, growing authoritarian features", *The Pacific Review*, 22(3): 335–353.

Quimpo, N.G. (2013) "The limits of post-plunder reform in the Philippines' oligarchic democracy", in E.S.K. Fung and S. Drakeley (eds.) *Democracy in Eastern Asia: issues, problems and challenges in a region of diversity*, New York: Routledge, 119–137.

Reyes, V.C (2009) *Corruption and implementation: case studies in Philippine public administration*, Manila: National College of Public Administration and Governance, University of the Philippines.

Reyes, V. (2012) "Can public funding overcome corruption? A view from the Philippines", in J. Mendilow (ed.) *Money, corruption and political competition in established and emerging democracies*, Lanham: Lexington Books, 145–167.

TI (Transparency International) (2007) *National integrity systems: country study report 2006*, www.transparency.org/files/content/nis/NIS_philippines_2006.pdf.

Transparency International Philippines (2013) *Corruption climate in the Philippines*, www.investphilippines.info.

White III, L. T. (2015) "Corruption", in L.T. White III, *Philippine politics: possibilities and problems in a localist democracy*. Abingdon, Oxon., New York, NY: Routledge, 176–206.

From the comparative studies list, see also: Baker and Milne (2015); Bhargava and Bolongaita (2004); Clifford Chance (2014); Gong and Ma (2009); Hutchcroft (2014) Johnston (2008); Kang (2002); Lim and Stern (2002); Quah (2015); Rodan and Hughes (2014); Sachsenröder (2013); Tomsa and Ufen (2012); TI (2016); You(2015).

Singapore

Corrupt Practices Investigation Bureau, www.cpib.gov.sg.

Koh, T. H. (2012) "National anti-corruption strategy: the Singapore experience", resource material series no.86, 95–103,www.unafei.or.jp/english/pdf/RS_No86/No86_14VE_Hin1.pdf.

Li, S., H.C. Triandis, and Y. Yu (2006) "Cultural orientation and corruption", *Ethics and Behavior*, 16(3): 199–215.

OECD (Organization for Economic Co-operation and Development) (2013) "Singapore: Corrupt Practices Investigation Bureau", in OECD, *Specialized anti-corruption institutions: review of the models*, 2nd edition, OECD Publishing, 59–64.

Oehlers, A. (2005) "Corruption: the peculiarities of Singapore", in N. Tarling (ed.) *Corruption and good governance in Asia*, Abingdon: Routledge, 149–164.

Quah, J.S.T. (2013) "Ensuring good governance in Singapore: is this experience transferrable to other Asian countries?" *International Journal of Public Sector Management*, 26(5): 401–420.

Quah, J.S.T. (2013) "Curbing corruption in Singapore: the importance of political will, expertise, enforcement, and context", in J.S.T. Quah (ed.) *Different paths to curbing corruption: lessons from Denmark, Finland, Hong Kong, New Zealand and Singapore*. United Kingdom: Emerald, 137–166.

Quah, J.S.T. (2014) "Curbing police corruption in Singapore: lessons for other Asian countries", *Asian Education and Development Studies*, 3(3): 186–222.

Quah, J.S.T. (2015) "Singapore's Corrupt Practices Investigation Bureau: four suggestions for enhancing its effectiveness", *Asian Education and Development Studies*, 4(1): 76–100.

Sam, C.Y. (2005) "Singapore's experience in curbing corruption and the growth of the underground economy", *Journal of Social Issues in Southeast Asia*, 20(1): 39–66.

Tan, N. (2013) "Manipulating electoral laws in Singapore", *Electoral Studies*, 32(4): 632–643.

Yu, W. (2015) "Anti-corruption strategies in Singapore: demystifying the Singapore model", in Y. Zhang and C. Lavena (eds.) *Government anti-corruption strategies: a cross-cultural perspective*, Boca Raton: CRC Press, 123–138.

From the comparative studies list, see also: Alatas et al. (2009); Assegaf (2015); Cameron et al. (2009) Clifford Chance (2014); Fritzen and Basu (2011); Gong and Ma (2009); Hira and Shiao (2016); Kumar (2011); Lim and Stern (2002); Mathur and Singh (2013); Quah (2012); Quah (2013); Quah (2015); Sachsenröder (2013); Toiganbayeva et al. (2014); Ufen (2015); Uslaner (2008).

South Korea

Anti-Corruption and Civil Rights Commission of Korea, http://www.acrc.go.kr/eng/index.do.

Apaza, C. R. and Y. Chang (2011) "What makes whistleblowing effective: whistleblowing in Peru and South Korea", *Public Integrity*, 13(2): 113–130.

Beyerle, S. (2014) "Blacklisting corrupt candidates: Korea", in S. Beyerle, *Curtailing corruption, people power for accountability & justice*, Boulder: Lynne Reinner, 37–66.

Ehrlich, C.P. and D.S. Kang (2002) "Independence and corruption in Korea", *Columbia Journal of Asian Law*, 16(1): 1–43.

Chang, C.S., N.J. Chang and B.T. Freese (2001) "Offering gifts or offering bribes? Code of ethics in South Korea", *Journal of Third World Studies*, 18(1): 125–139.

Cho, Y. H. and Choi, B.D. (2004) "e-Government to combat corruption: the case of Seoul metropolitan government", *International Journal of Public Administration*, 27(10): 719–735.

Choi, E. and J. Woo (2012) "Political corruption, economy and citizens' evaluation of democracy in South Korea", *Contemporary Politics*, 18(4): 451–466.

Kalinowski, T. (2016) "Trends and mechanisms of corruption in South Korea", *The Pacific Review*, doi: 10.1080/09512748.2016.1145724.

Kang, D. C. (2002) "Bad loans to good friends: money politics and the developmental state in Korea", *International Organization*, 56(1): 177–207.

Kim, P.S. (2008) "Building national integrity through corruption eradication in South Korea", in B. Bowornwathana and C. Wescott (eds.) *Comparative governance reform in Asia: democracy, corruption, and government trust*, Bingley: Emerald, 155–178.

Kim, S., H.J. Kim and H. Lee (2009) "An institutional analysis of an e-government system for anti-corruption: the case of OPEN", *Government Information Quarterly*, 26(1): 42–50.

Kim, U. and M.D. Whitaker (2013) "Network subversion: the contrasting effects of multiple networks on bribery in South Korea", *International Journal of Law, Crime and Justice*, 41(1): 16–35.

Ko, K. and S.Y. Cho (2015) "Evolution of anti-corruption strategies in South Korea", in Y. Zhang and C. Luvena (eds.) *Government anti-corruption strategies: a cross-cultural perspective*, Boca Raton: CRC Press, 103–122.

Lee, J-H (2006) "Business corruption, public sector corruption, and growth rate: time series analysis using Korean data", *Applied Economics Letters*, 13(13): 881–885.

Lho, K. and J. Cabuay (2005) "Corruption in the Korean public and private sectors", in N. Tarling (ed.) *Corruption and good governance in Asia*, Abingdon: Routledge, 80–97.

Moran, J. (1998) "Corruption and NIC development: a case study of South Korea", *Crime, Law and Social Change*, 29(2): 161–177.

Narayan, R. (2013) "Corruption in government-business relations in Republic of Korea", in H.Y. Cho, L. Surendra and H.J. Cho (eds.) *Contemporary South Korean society: a critical perspective*, Abingdon: Routledge, 143–156.

Park, H. and J. Blenkinsopp (2011) "The roles of transparency and trust in the relationship between corruption and citizen satisfaction", *International Review of Administrative Sciences*, 77(2): 254–274.

Schopf, J.C. (2011) "Following the money to determine the effects of democracy on corruption: the case of Korea", *Journal of East Asian Studies*, 11(1): 1–39.

Schopf, J.C. (2012) "From one-stop graft to costly corruption webs: democratisation and shifting patterns of corruption in Korea", *Asian Journal of Social Science,* 40(5–6): 635–663.

Schopf, J.C. (2015) "Deterring extortive corruption in Korea through democratization and the rule of law", *Journal of Comparative Asian Development*, 14(2): 279–318.

From the comparative studies list, see also: Bhargava and Bolongaita (2004); Campbell and Saha (2013); Chang and Chu (2006); Choi (2009); Clifford Chance (2014); Fritzen and Basu (2011); Göbel (2009); Gong and Ma (2009); Hough (2013); Johnston (2008); Kang (2002); Khan (1998); Khan (2001); Park (2008); Pye (1997); Quah (2013); Tsai (2009); TI (2016); Wang (2015); You (2015).

Sri Lanka

Alam, M.A. (2014) "Women and corruption in public service: the Sri Lankan experience", *Anti-Corruption Research Network,* http://corruptionresearchnetwork.org/acrn-news/blog/women-and-corruption-in-public-service-sri-lankan-experience.

Commission to Investigate Allegations of Bribery or Corruption, www.ciaboc.gov.lk/web/.

de Silva, K.M. (2002) "Corruption in Sri Lanka: the National Legislature 1938–2001", in K. M. de Silva, G.H. Peiris and S.W.R. de A. Samarasinghe (eds.) *Corruption in South Asia: India, Pakistan and Sri Lanka,* Kandy: International Centre for Ethnic Studies, 303–368.

Hettige, S. (2015) "Governance and development in post-independence Sri Lanka", in S. Hettige and E. Gerharz (eds.) *Governance, conflict and development in South Asia: perspectives from India, Nepal and Sri Lanka,* New Delhi: Sage, 69–98.

Höglund, K. and A. Piyarathna (2009) "Paying the price for patronage: electoral violence in Sri Lanka", *Commonwealth and Comparative Politics*, 47(3): 287–307.

Lindberg, J. and C. Orjuela (2011) "Corruption and conflict: connections and consequences in war-torn Sri Lanka", *Conflict, Security and Development*, 11(2): 205–233.

Lindberg, J. and D. Herath (2014) "Land and grievances in post-conflict Sri Lanka: exploring the role of corruption complaints", *Third World Quarterly,* 35(5): 888–904.

Mampilly, Z. (2012) "The nexus of militarization and corruption in post-conflict Sri Lanka" in D. Zaum and C S. Cheng (eds.) *Corruption and post-conflict peacebuilding: selling the peace?* Abingdon: Routledge, 180–198.

Perera-Mubarak, K.N. (2012) "Reading 'stories of corruption' practices and perceptions of everyday corruption in post-tsunami Sri Lanka", *Political Geography*, 31(6): 368–378.

Raymond, J. (2008) "Benchmarking in public procurement", *Benchmarking: An International Journal*, 15(6): 782–793.

Sivakumar, N. (2014) "Conceptualizing corruption: a Sri Lankan perspective", *International Journal of Education and Research*, 2(4): 391–400.

Transparency International Sri Lanka (2014) *National integrity system assessment*, https://issuu.com/tisrilanka/docs/nis2014.

Transparency International Sri Lanka (2015) *Electoral integrity: a review of the abuse of state resources and selected integrity issues during 2015 presidential election in Sri Lanka,* http://www.tisrilanka.org/wp-content/uploads/2015/02/PPPR_2015_ENG_Final.pdf.

From the comparative studies list, see also: Ahmad and Brookins (2004); Khandker (2015); TI (2011); TI (2013); TI (2014); TI (2016).

Taiwan

Agency Against Corruption, http://www.aac.moj.gov.tw/mp290.html.

Batto, N.F. (2005), "Electoral strategy, committee membership, and rent seeking in the Taiwanese legislature, 1992–2001", *Legislative Studies Quarterly,* 30(1): 43–62.

Copper, J.F. (2013) *The KMT returns to power: elections in Taiwan, 2008 to 2012,* Lanham: Lexington Books, 44–50.

Fell, D. (2005) "Political and media liberalization and political corruption in Taiwan", *The China Quarterly*, 184: 875–893.

Fell, D. (2005) "Political change on the political corruption issue", in D. Fell (ed.) *Party politics in Taiwan: party change and the democratic evolution of Taiwan, 1991–2004*, Abingdon: Routledge, 55–84.

Fell, D. (2012) "Is democracy working in Taiwan? Social welfare and political corruption", in D. Fell, *Government and politics in Taiwan,* London: Routledge, 192–210.

Goebel, C. (2016) "The quest for good governance: Taiwan's fight against corruption", *Journal of Democracy*, 27(1): 124–138.

Hsueh, C.Y. (2007) "Power and corruption in Taiwan", *Issues and Studies*, 43(1): 1–39.

Hwang, D.B., P.L. Golemon, Y. Chen, T.S. Wang and W.S. Hung (2009) "*Guanxi* and business ethics in Confucian society today: an empirical case study in Taiwan", *Journal of Business Ethics*, 89(2): 235–250.

Ip, P.K. (2008) "Corporate social responsibility and crony capitalism in Taiwan", *Journal of Business Ethics,* 79(1): 167–177.

Ko, E., Y.C. Su and C. Yu (2015) "Sibling rivalry among anti-corruption agencies in Taiwan: is redundancy doomed to fail?" *Asian Education and Development Studies*, 4(1): 101–124.

Kong, T.Y. (2004) "Corruption and the effect of regime type: the case of Taiwan", *New Political Economy*, 9(3): 341–364.

Lo, S.S.H. (2008) "The politics of controlling *heidao* and corruption in Taiwan", *Asian Affairs: An American Review*, 35(2): 59–82.

Ngo, T.W. (2015) "Social movements under institutional voids: the success and failure of the anti-corruption movement in Taiwan", *Asian Studies,* 1(1): 99–120.

Quah J.S.T. (2015) "Enhancing the effectiveness of Taiwan's anti-corruption agencies in combating corruption", *American Journal of Chinese Studies*, 22(2): 291–307.

Shih, F.L. (2007) "The 'red tide' anti-corruption protest: what does it mean for democracy in Taiwan?" *Taiwan in Comparative Perspective*, 1: 87–98.

Yu, C., C-M Chen, W-J Juang and L-T Hu (2008) "Does democracy breed integrity? Corruption in Taiwan during the democratic transformation period", *Crime, Law and Social Change*, 49(3): 167–184.

Yu, C., C.W. Chen, and M.W. Lin (2013) "Corruption perception in Taiwan: reflections upon a bottom-up citizen perspective", *Journal of Contemporary China*, 22(79): 56–76.

From the comparative studies list, see also: Chang and Chu (2006); Clifford Chance (2014); Göbel (2009); Gong and Ma (2009); Pye (1997); Quah (2013); TI (2016); Tsai (2009); Wang (2015); You (2015).

Thailand

Bowornwathana, B. (2009) "Big businessmen at the helm: the politics of conflict of interest in Thailand", in A. Farazmand (ed.) *Bureaucracy and administration*, Boca Raton: CRC Press, 483–494.

Callahan, W.A. (2005) "Social capital and corruption: vote buying and the politics of reform in Thailand", *Perspectives on Politics*, 3(3): 495–508.

Chachavalpongpun, P. (2014), "'Good coup' gone bad: Thailand's political developments since Thaksin's downfall", in P. Chachavalpongpun (ed.) *"Good coup" gone bad: Thailand's political developments since Thaksin's downfall,* Singapore: Institute of Southeast Asian Studies, 3–16.

Imai, M. (2006) "Mixing family businesses with politics in Thailand", *Asian Economic Journal*, 20(3): 241–256.

Khoman, S. (2015) "Corruption, transaction costs, and network relationships: governance challenges for Thailand", in A.M. Baliscan, U. Chakravorty and M.L.V. Ravago (eds.) *Sustainable economic development: resources, environment and institutions,* Amsterdam: Elsevier, 215–235.

Khoman, S. (2016) "Corruption and network relationships: theory and evidence from Thailand", in A.A.C. Texeira, A. Maia, C. Pimenta and J. A. Moreira (eds.) *Corruption, economic growth and globalization*, London: Routledge, 84–111.

Mutebi, A.M. (2008) "Explaining the failure of Thailand's anti-corruption regime", *Development and Change,* 39(1): 147–171.

Ochoa, R. and A. Graycar (2016) "Tackling conflicts of interest: policy instruments in different settings", *Public Integrity*, 18(1): 83–100.

Office of the National Anti-Corruption Commission, https://www.nacc.go.th/main.php?filename=index_en.

Owen, D.A. (2013) "Conceptualizing vote buying as a process: an empirical study in Thai provinces", *Asian Politics and Policy*, 5(2): 249–273.

Phongpaichit, P. and S. Pinyarangsan (1996) *Corruption and democracy in Thailand*, 2nd edition, Chiang Mai: Silkworm Books.

Punyaratabandhu, S. (2008) "Corruption and government trust: a survey of urban and rural inhabitants in the north and northeast of Thailand", in B. Bowornwathana and C. Wescott (eds.) *Comparative governance reform in Asia: democracy, corruption and government trust*, Bingley: Emerald, 179–200.

Ruengdet, K. and W.Wongsurawat (2015) "The mechanisms of corruption in agricultural price intervention projects: case studies from Thailand", *The Social Science Journal*, 52(1): 22–33.

Sinpeng, A. (2014) "Corruption, morality, and the politics of reform in Thailand", *Asian Politics and Policy*, 6(4): 523–538.

Sopchokchai, O (2016) "Results-based management: an effort to prevent corruption in the Thai public sector", in A.A.C. Texeira, A. Maia, C. Pimenta and J. A. Moreira (eds.) *Corruption, economic growth and globalization*, London and New York: Routledge, 190–210.

Toyama, A. (2013) "The creation of corruption in Thailand: legal provisions and criticism of politicians", *Southeast Asian Studies*, 51(1): 109–138.

United Nations Development Programme (2015) "Advancing anti-corruption efforts in Thailand – a multi-faceted approach", http://www.th.undp.org/content/dam/thailand/docs/publications/UNDP_TH%20AAA%20Prodoc_Signed.pdf.

Vasuvat, S. (2016) "Legal system related to corruption control and corruption causes in Thailand", in A.A.C. Texeira, C. Pimenta, A. Maia and J. A. Moreira (eds.) *Corruption, economic growth and globalization*, London: Routledge, 211–222.

Vichit-Vadakan, J. (2011) "Public ethics and corruption in Thailand", in E.M. Berman (ed.) *Public administration in Southeast Asia: Thailand, Philippines, Malaysia, Hong Kong and Macao*, Boca Raton: CRC Press, 79–94.

Wingfield, T. (2002) "Democratization and economic crisis in Thailand: political business and the changing dynamic of the Thai state", in E.T. Gomez (ed.) *Political business in East Asia*, London: Routledge, 250–300.

From the comparative studies list, see also: Bhargava and Bolongaita (2004); Clifford Chance (2014); Croissant and Martin (2006); Khan (1998); Khan (2001); Hutchcroft (2014); James (2010); Rodan and Hughes (2014); Lim and Stern (2002); Sachsenröder (2013); Toiganbayeva et al. (2014); Tomsa and Ufen (2012); Wescott et al. (2009).

Timor-Leste

Amaral, R. (2013) "Effective measures to prevent and combat corruption and to encourage cooperation between the public and private sectors", Paper presented at the 16th UNAFEI UNCAC training programme, resource material series no.92, 274–277.

Anti-Corruption Commission of Timor-Leste, http//:cac.tl (accessed 17 May 2016).

Blunt, P. (2009) "The political economy of accountability in Timor-Leste: implications for public policy", *Public Administration and Development*, 29(2): 89–100.

Shoesmith, D. (2011) "Timor-Leste: on the road to peace and prosperity?" *Southeast Asian Affairs*, 321–335.

Soares, A. de J. (2013) "Combating corruption: avoiding 'institutional ritualism'", in M. Leach and D. Kingsbury (eds.) *The politics of Timor-Leste: democratic consolidation after intervention*, Ithaca: Cornell University, Southeast Asia Program Publications Press, 85–98.

Soares, A. de J. (2015) "A social movement as an antidote to corruption", in S. Ingram, L. Kent and A. McWilliam (eds.) *A new era? Timor-Leste after the UN*, Canberra: ANU Press, 203–212.

TI (Transparency International) (2015) "Timor-Leste: overview of corruption and anti-corruption", http://www.transparency.org/files/content/corruptionqas/Country_profile_Timor_Leste_2015.pdf.

From the comparative studies list, see also: Baker and Milne (2015); Sachsenröder (2013).

Vietnam

"Anti-corruption as a risk to democracy: on the unintended consequences of international anti-corruption campaigns", in L.de Sousa, P.Larmour and B.Hindess (eds.) *Governments, NGOs and anti-corruption: the new integrity warriors*, Abingdon: Routledge, 33–49.

Arnold, T. and B. Buchanan (2012) "Corruption, foreign direct investment and the cost of doing business in Vietnam" in T. DeSare and D. Caprioglio (eds.) *Foreign Investment: Types, Methods and Impacts*, New York: Nova Scientific Publishing, 163–173.

Bai, J., S. Jayachandran, E.J. Malesky and B.A. Olken (2013) "Does economic growth reduce corruption? Theory and evidence from Vietnam", National Bureau of Research Working Paper, No.19483.

Gainsborough, M. (2003) "Corruption and the politics of economic decentralisation in Vietnam", *Journal of Contemporary Asia*, 33(1): 69–84.

Gainsborough, M (2007) "From patronage to 'outcomes': Vietnam's communist party congresses reconsidered", *Journal of Vietnamese Studies*, 2(1): 3–26.

Gainsborough, M. (2010) "Corruption", in M. Gainsborough, *Vietnam: rethinking the state*, London: Zed Books, 50–70.

Gillespie, J. (2002) "The political-legal culture of anti-corruption reforms in Vietnam", in T. Lindsey and H. Dick (eds.) *Corruption in Asia: rethinking the governance paradigm*, Annandale, NSW: The Federation Press, 167–200.

Gregory, R. (2016) "Combating corruption in Vietnam: a commentary", *Asian Education and Development Studies*, 5(2): 227–243.

Gueorguiev, D. and E. Malesky (2012) "Foreign investment and bribery: a firm-level analysis of corruption in Vietnam", *Journal of Asian Economics*, 23(2): 111–129.

Jandl, T. (2013) "Decentralization, FDI and provincial governance", in T. Jandl, *Vietnam in the global economy: the dynamics of integration, decentralization, and contested politics*, Lanham: Lexington Books, 81–116.

Kerkvliet, B.J.T. (2014) "Protests over land in Vietnam: rightful resistance and more", *Journal of Vietnamese Studies*, 9(3): 19–54.

Le, H. H. (2013) "Navigating the crisis: the VCP's efforts to restructure the economy and fight corruption", *Southeast Asian Affairs*, 348–365.

Le, T. (2015) "Perspectives on land grabs in Vietnam", in C. Carter and A. Harding (eds.) *Land grabs in Asia: what role for the law?* London: Routledge, 150–166.

Maitland, E. (2002) "Corruption and the outsider: multinational enterprises in Vietnam", in T. Lindsey and H. Dick (eds.) *Corruption in Asia: rethinking the governance paradigm*, Annandale, NSW: The Federation Press, 167–200.

Malesky, E.J., D.D. Gueorguiev and N.M. Jensen (2015) "Monopoly money: foreign investment and bribery in Vietnam, a survey experiment", *American Journal of Political Science*, 59(2): 419–439.

Martini, M (2012) "Overview of corruption and anti-corruption in Vietnam", *Anti-corruption Resources Center*, www.u4.no/publications/overview-of-corruption-and-anti-corruption-in-vietnam/.

McCornac, D.C. (2012) "The challenge of corruption in higher education: the case of Vietnam", *Asian Education and Development Studies*, 1(3): 262–275.

Nguyen, N.A, N.M. Nguyen and B Tran-Nam (2016) "Corruption and economic growth, with a focus on Vietnam", *Crime, Law and Social Change*, doi: 10.1007/s10611-016-9603-0.

Nguyen, N.A., Q.H. Doan, N.M. Nguyen and Tran-Nam, B. (2016), "The impact of petty corruption on firm innovation in Vietnam", *Crime, Law and Social Change*, doi: 10.1007/s10611-016-9610-1.

Nguyen, T.T. and M.A van Dijk (2012) "Corruption, growth and governance: private vs. state-owned firms in Vietnam", *Journal of Banking and Finance*, 36(11): 2935–2948.

Nguyen, K.T., Q.A. Do and A. Tran (2012) "One mandarin benefits the whole clan: hometown infrastructure and nepotism in an autocracy", Research Collection School of Economics, Singapore Management University http://ink.library.smu.edu.sg/soe_research/1383.

Nicholson, E. (2002) "The Vietnamese courts and corruption", in T. Lindsey and H. Dick (eds.) *Corruption in Asia: rethinking the governance paradigm*, Annandale, NSW: The Federation Press, 201–218.

Painter, M. (2014) "Myths of political independence, or how not to solve the corruption problem: lessons for Vietnam", *Asian and Pacific Policy Studies*, 1(2): 273–286.

Rand, J. and F. Tarp (2012) "Firm-level corruption in Vietnam", *Economic Development and Cultural Change*, 60(3): 571–595.

Sidel, M. (2013) "Property, state corruption, and the judiciary: the Do Son land case and its implications", H.T. Ho Tai and M. Sidel (eds.) *State, society and the market in contemporary Vietnam: property, power and values*. London, New York: Routledge, 123–139.

Thayer, C.A. (2010) "The trial of Lê Công Định: new challenges to the legitimacy of Vietnam's party-state", *Journal of Vietnamese Studies*, 5(3): 196–207.

Thomsen, L. (2011) "Business–state relations in the differentiated private sector in Vietnam: access to capital and land", *Asian Journal of Social Science*, 39(5): 627–651.

To, P.X., S.Mahanty and W. Dressler (2014) "Social networks of corruption in the Vietnamese and Lao cross-border timber trade", *Anthropological Forum: A Journal of Anthropology and Comparative Studies*, 24(2): 154–174.

Tromme, M. (2016) "What next for anti-corruption research in Vietnam?" *Crime, Law and Social Change,* doi: 10.1007/s10611-016-9607-9.

Vu, H.V., T.Q. Tran, T.V Nguyen and S. Lim (2016) "Corruption, types of corruption and firm financial performance: new evidence from a transitional economy", *Journal of Business Ethics,* doi: 10.1007/s10551-016-3016-y.

Vian, T., D.W. Brinkerhoff, F.G. Feeley, M. Salomon, T.K.V. Nguyen (2012) "Confronting corruption in the health sector in Vietnam: patterns and prospects", *Public Administration and Development*, 32(1): 49–63.

From the comparative studies list, see also: Anderson and Heywood (2009); Baker and Milne (2015); Clifford Chance (2014); Global Witness (2013); Quah (2016); Sachsenröder (2013); TI (2013); TI (2016).

APPENDIX 2

Selected Asian anti-corruption non-governmental organizations (NGOs)

Among many important variables affecting the anti-corruption work of NGOs in Asia, arguably the most significant is the political context within which they are attempting to operate. Three features seem to be particularly critical: the nature of the political regime and the degree of latitude within which NGOs can pursue their objectives; differentiation within anti-corruption civil society organizations; and the level of corruption and strength of the local anti-corruption agency. In respect of the first feature, authoritarian regimes are unlikely to provide NGOs with the political space required for the effective transmission of their views and may see them as potentially counter-productive to government policies. In more democratic systems, the available political space may be populated by other organizations with anti-corruption agendas and even by international NGOs which may advise governments on best anti-corruption practice and also undertake investigative research in particular areas. Where many anti-corruption NGOs have a presence in a country, the task may be to find a differentiated niche which can help to aid anti-corruption efforts. In some countries, civil society is not itself sufficiently developed to provide for this level of differentiation and a lead NGO, for example, a Transparency International chapter, may take on a broad remit to conduct research and make anti-corruption policy recommendations. Finally, we should note that in Singapore and Hong Kong, the Corrupt Practices Investigation Bureau and the Independent Commission Against Corruption have in effect a monopoly on anti-corruption activity; in neither place is there, for example, a chapter of Transparency International or any significant anti-corruption civil society organization.

In the light of this three-fold division, the list of anti-corruption NGOs here reflects particularly the situation in those places where there is sufficient space for an anti-corruption NGO to act as independent commentator on the corruption situation. Our list is not intended to be comprehensive because local anti-corruption NGOs are often ephemeral; rather, it is provided as a potential starting point for an area of research which has received relatively little attention. The listed website addresses are mainly or partially in English. We have not listed some anti-corruption NGOs in Japan and Taiwan because there is no English translation of their aims and activities.

(Continued)

Country	Name	Structure	Aims	Contact address	Commentary
Afghanistan	Integrity Watch Afghanistan (IWA) (founded 2005)		"The mission of Integrity Watch is to put corruption under the spotlight through community monitoring, research, and advocacy. We mobilize and train communities to monitor infrastructure projects, public services, courts, and extractive industries. We develop community monitoring tools, provide policy-oriented research, facilitate policy dialogue, and advocate for integrity, transparency, and accountability in Afghanistan".	Kolola Poshta, Kabul Afghanistan iwaweb.org./ introduction	In 2015, in conjunction with Transparency International and the UNDP, the NGO carried out a national assessment of corruption risks in Afghanistan.
Bangladesh	Transparency International, Bangladesh	Chapter of Transparency International	"To catalyze and strengthen a participatory social movement to promote and develop institutions, laws and practices for combating corruption in Bangladesh and establishing an efficient and transparent system of governance, politics and business".	MIDAS Centre (4th floor), House-5, Road-16 (New) 27 (Old), Dhanmondi, Dhaka - 1209, Bangladesh www.ti-bangladesh.org	TI Bangladesh has campaigned for action against corruption in cricket, for more powers for the official Anti-Corruption Unit and for better fire prevention and regulation of the garment industry.
Cambodia	Pact in Cambodia (founded 1991)	A US-based organization	"Our current and recent work includes improving local governance, fighting against corruption, building savings-led microfinance, providing health education, supporting community forestry and ...community forestry... and providing organizational development assessments and support to Cambodian organizations.	Phnom Penh Centre Building A 3rd floor, Cnr. Sihanouk & Sothearos Blvd or PO Box 149, Phnom Penh, Cambodia www.pactcambodia.org	Pact has programmes concerning governance, economic empowerment and forestry partnerships.

Country	Name	Structure	Aims	Contact address	Commentary
Cambodia	Transparency International, Cambodia (founded 2010)	Chapter of Transparency International	"We strive for all Cambodians to live in a society that is free of corruption. We work together with individuals and institutions at all levels to promote integrity and reduce corruption in Cambodia. Values: Transparency International Cambodia shall respect and adhere to the following values • Integrity • Accountability • Transparency • Solidarity • Justice • Democracy".	Phone (+855) 023 214 430, Email: info@ ticambodia.org www.ticambodia.org	In March 2016, TI Cambodia launched an anti-corruption platform for political parties, which focuses on: the need for appropriate anti-corruption laws; the need for resources for enforcement agencies and the need to understand people's perceptions of corruption.
India	Aam Admi Party (AAD) (founded 2012)	Founded as a political party after differences in the leadership of the India against Corruption movement (q.v. and Ch.14)	The major aim of the party is to create a Jan Lokpal, an independent body to investigate corruption.	www.aamaadmiparty.org	In the 2015 Delhi Legislative Assembly elections, the party won 67 of 70 seats. The party has since suffered from factionalism and eight of its Legislative Assembly members have been arrested.
India	Anti-Corruption Front (ACF) (founded 1997)	Public–Media Coalition against Corruption	"Providing the most powerful platform for common masses to register their complaints against corruption/ bribe, with the help of right minded and honest persons from society and also with the help of some honest officials of various departments and the media".	2151/15, New Patel Nagar, New Delhi - 110 008, India www. anticorruptionfront.org	The NGO has anti-corruption "fronts" with the media and the police and supports "citizen journalists" who report incidents of bribery and corruption.

| India | India Against Corruption (IAC) (founded 2007) | A core committee reports to the Hindustan Republican Association but has also been led by prominent populists and celebrities (see Ch. 14). | "The objectives of the organization are to establish, through revolution, a Republic of the United States of India under a Federal Constitution of the Republic, enforced by organized and armed committees of citizens in a lawful, democratic and Constitutional manner. The basic principle of the organization shall be Universal Suffrage and the abolition of all systems which make any kind of exploitation of man by man possible". | B-59 Defence Colony, New Delhi 110024, India www. indiaagainstcorruption. org.in | The NGO is part of a broader pro-Hindu political movement. On corruption issues, it was particularly prominent in seeking greater transparency, and accountability on the 2010 Commonwealth Games scandals, and pressed for an ombudsman system to investigate corruption. |
| India | India Rejuvenation Initiative (founded 2005) | "A forum of concerned citizens of India (many of whom are former senior public servants) who have committed themselves to the public cause of curbing corruption and restoration of probity and accountability in public life". | "Expose corruption in high places; interact with and support honest civil servants so that they remain honest and work with zeal; provide voice to those at the receiving end of an insensitive and corrupt system; mobilize public opinion for ensuring that 'public representatives' remain 'public servants', and do not become 'political masters'; scrutinize legislations/public policies for flaws which contribute to corruption or protect vested interests; work to ensure that institutions meant to enforce rule of law in our country perform their duties honestly and efficiently". | www.iri.org.in/ about_us.aspx | The NGO focuses principally on corruption in the top echelons of the administration and has expressed concern about the substantial funds of Indian nationals held in Swiss banks. |

(Continued)

Country	Name	Structure	Aims	Contact address	Commentary
India	Mazdoor Kisan Shakti Sangathan (MKSS) (founded 1990)	Mazdoor Kisan Shakti Sangathan is a grassroots organization originally based in rural Rajasthan, India (see Ch. 14).	The goal is to establish the concept of "participatory democracy", to make the people who rule understand that the common man now want his or her share in governance.	Village Devdungri, Post Brar, 313341, District Rajsamand, Rajasthan, India www.mkssindia.org	MKSS was the lead organization in the campaign for the right to information in India. It has exposed corruption through public audits in which official records are read aloud and contrasted with the experience of individual citizens.
India	All India Crime Reforms Organization (founded 1993)	The NGO has branches all over India.	An anti-crime NGO, one of whose aims is "to remove corruption from society".	C-8, Laxman Park, Chander Nagar, New Delhi, 110051, India aicro-ngo.org	The NGO has pressed for stronger legislation on the exploitation of child labour, fraud and property-grabbing from widows.
India	The National Campaign for People's Right to Information (NCPRI) (founded 1996)	A broadly based network of local NGOs which also includes some prominent former government officials among its leaders (see Ch. 14).	"The NCPRI's endeavour is to deepen democracy and achieve constitutional principles through the use of the RTI. Transparency and enforcing accountability facilitates the participation of people in a democracy. This right seeks to empower people to fight corruption and social apathy, to make governments and other public agencies and institutions which impact public welfare, accountable to the people".	B-76, S.F.S. Flats Triveni Apartment, Sheikh Sarai, Phase-I, New Delhi, 110017, India righttoinformation.info	Playing a strong role in the campaign for a Right to Information Act, this NGO has maintained a monitoring role on its implementation and has also strongly supported amendments to the Whistleblowers Act (2014).

Indonesia	Indonesia Corruption Watch (ICW) (founded 1998)	Organized into six divisions concerned with political corruption, public service monitoring, law and justice, budgeting, investigation and publication and fund-raising.	The leading Indonesian NGO whose primary mission is to monitor and report incidents of corruption. ICW is also heavily engaged in prevention and deterrence through education, cultural change, prosecutions and system reform (see Ch.4).	Jalan Kalibata Timur IV/D, No. 6 Jakarta Selatan, 12740, DKI Jakarta. www.antikorupsi.org (Website is not in English)	ICW has campaigned for reforms of the judiciary and for better anti-corruption laws. Some of its members have been arrested by the police but it also received official recognition in 2015 when its former head was appointed as the President's Chief of Staff.
Indonesia	Transparency International, Indonesia (founded 2000)	Started as a chapter of Transparency International but has since acquired Indonesian legal status as an association.	The NGO combines the work of a think-tank and a social movement organization. As a think-tank, TI-I conducts policy reviews and policy or legal drafting, promote policy reforms within government and law enforcement agencies.	Jalan Senayan Bawah No. 17, Blok S, Kelurahan Rawa Barat, Kecamatan Kebayoran Baru, Jakarta Selatan 12180, Indonesia www.ti.or.id/en/	The NGO advises the government on anti-corruption procedures. It has also conducted a Youth Integrity Survey and released a film on the effects of corruption.
Japan	Transparency International, Japan (founded 2004)	Chapter of Transparency International	The chapter aims to organize seminars, publish reports, give lectures and translate basic materials on combating corruption from English to Japanese.	Kita-Shinagawa 1- 9-7-1015, Shinagawa-ku, Tokyo www.ti-j.org/ (Website in Japanese only)	The chapter has reported on Japan's national integrity system and called for urgent action on the "golden parachuting" of former senior officials into highly paid jobs in the private sector and bid-rigging on contracts.

(Continued)

Country	Name	Structure	Aims	Contact address	Commentary
Malaysia	Bersih 2.00 (Coalition for Clean and Fair Elections) (founded 2006)	Coalition of 62 NGOs supported by three major opposition parties.	"Clean the electoral roll; reform postal ballot; use of indelible ink; minimum 21 days campaign period; free and fair access to elections; strengthen public institutions; stop corruption; stop dirty politics".	Unit A-2–8, Block A, Pusat Perniagaan 8 Avenue, Jalan Sungai Jernih 8/1 46050, Petaling Jaya, Selangor, Malaysia www.bersih.org	The coalition has focused on issues of electoral fraud and seeks to bring pressure to bear on the Electoral Commission to ensure that elections are free and fair. It has organized a number of large demonstrations in support of its aims.
Malaysia	Transparency International, Malaysia (founded 1998)	Chapter of Transparency International	"Our Vision: A Nation without Corruption: A Society with Integrity. Our Mission: to eradicate corruption and promote Transparency, Integrity and Accountability throughout Society".	23, Jalan Pantai 9/7, 46000 Petaling Jaya, Selangor, Malaysia www.transparency.org. my	The chapter has raised concerns about corporate governance in relation to the 1 Malaysia Development Berhad scandal.
Maldives	Transparency International, Maldives (founded 2007)	Chapter of Transparency International	"Strives to act as catalyst for reforms that improve transparency and accountability in all sectors; raise public awareness of and initiate public discussion on corruption and its detrimental effects on society and development; and collaborate with individuals and groups from government, businesses, media, and civil society, among others, in the fight against corruption".	Ma. Kurigam 1B, 1st Floor, Ithaa Goalhi, 20222, Male' Maldives transparency.mv/en/	The chapter produced a national integrity report in 2014. It has made efforts to try to ensure the integrity of the electoral process and has been critical of the Anti-Corruption Commission's handling of the scandal involving the government-owned tourism promotion company.
Mongolia	Transparency International, Mongolia	Chapter of Transparency International	"Our vision: A world in which government, politics, business, civil society and the daily lives of people are free of corruption".	Building of Zorig Foundation, 2nd floor, Peace Avenue 17, Sakhbaataar District, Ulaanbaatar, Mongolia www.transparency.mn	In 2015, the chapter opposed the granting of amnesty in corruption cases under a new law. Although the law was passed, a subsequent amendment excludes corruption cases from the amnesty.

Country	Organisation	Type	Mission	Contact	Notes
Myanmar	Myanmar Alliance for Transparency and Accountability (MATA)	More than 400 civil society organizations, civil society networks and individuals are involved in MATA as members.	"A civil society alliance supporting civil society actors to collaboratively advocate for transparency and accountability in all sectors across Myanmar".	No.11(C), 11th floor, Myaynigone Plaza, Sanchaung Tsp., Yangon, Myanmar matacoalition.com/en/ (Website only partially works)	The NGO has promoted Myanmar's admission to the Extractive Industries Transparency Initiative, right-to-information legislation and practical anti-corruption reforms to government.
Nepal	Transparency International Nepal (founded 1996)	Chapter of Transparency International	"To use its lobbying capacity and influence to ensure the best possible outcomes; to encourage corruption complaints; to promote anti-corruption values; to network with affiliated organizations; sectoral focus on the public sector and services offered to citizens".	P.O. Box 11486, Chakhkhu Bakhkhu Marga, New Baneshwor, Kathmandu, Nepal www.tinepal.org	Research studies commissioned in 2016 include work on good governance provisions in the constitution, the hydro-power energy sector and public service delivery. The chapter is also involved in a support programme to foster integrity in the post-earthquake reconstruction.
Pakistan	Pakistan Institute of Legislative Development and Transparency (PILDAT) (founded 2001)	An independent, non-partisan and not-for-profit indigenous think tank focusing on political and public policy research and legislative strengthening.	"PILDAT will work for strengthening democracy and democratic institutions in Pakistan by building the capability of and instituting non-partisan monitoring framework for the elected representatives and legislatures while facilitating greater participation of all segments of the society in the democratic process and development of new political leadership".	No. 7, 9th Avenue, F-8/1, Islamabad 44000, Pakistan www.pildat.org	PILDAT undertakes research on a wide range of governance matters, some of which, such as procurement procedures, relate to corruption issues.

(Continued)

Country	Name	Structure	Aims	Contact address	Commentary
Pakistan	Transparency International, Pakistan (founded 2002)	Chapter of Transparency International	"A civil society organization dedicated to curbing both international and national corruption, its primary objective is to counter corruption in business dealings and to curb corruption on a national level".	Address: 5-C, 2nd Floor, Khayaban-e-It'ehad, Phase VII, D.H.A., Karachi, Pakistan www.transparency.org.pk/	The chapter has an agreement with US Agency for International Development to provide a hotline to report fraud in the utilization of US aid to Pakistan. Its other completed programmes to date have focused mainly on youths.
The Philippines	Transparency International, The Philippines (founded 1995)	Chapter of Transparency International	"Our Mission is to prevent and counter corruption at all levels by promoting transparency, accountability and integrity across all sectors of society. Our Core Values are: transparency, accountability, integrity, solidarity, courage, justice and democracy".	Manila, Philippines www.transparency-ph.org/ (Website does not work)	In 2013, the chapter produced a report on the corruption climate in the Philippines (www.investphilippines.info).
The Philippines	The Council for the Restoration of Filipino Values (CRFV) (founded 1994)		"A non-government organization (NGO) dedicated to the effort in transforming the Filipino public servant and the local government leadership to subscribe to the Code of Ethics and Values that shall provide our nation, the Philippines, with righteous, incorruptible, and sincere service towards a graft free society".	Baguio City, Philippines www.crfv-cpu.org/	The NGO runs programmes which deal in part with integrity, codes of conduct and ethical standards for government officials.
South Korea	People's Solidarity for Participatory Democracy (PSPD) (founded 1994)	The PSPD is financially dependent on membership fees and is "politically impartial". In 2016, it had about 15,000 members.	This NGO has a wide remit focusing on participatory democracy and human rights but also including anti-corruption activities. It seeks to monitor abuse of power by government and private corporations.	16, Jahamunro 9-gil, Jongno-Gu Seoul ROK 110–043 www.peoplepower21.org	The PSPD campaigned to enact the Anti-Corruption Act (1996–2001) and is campaigning to discover the truth about the Sewol ferry tragedy where there was alleged corruption.

Country	Organization	Mission/Aims	Address/Website	Activities
South Korea	Heung Sa Dahn (Young Korean Academy (YKA) (it has had a focus on anti-corruption activities since 2001)	Founded in 1913 to promote national unification, the NGO aims to transmit appropriate moral values to youth and "to eradicate corruption and untruth from our society".	www.yka.or.kr	The NGO runs education programmes which teach youth about corruption through the provision of case studies and discussion of measures to deal with corrupt activities.
South Korea	Transparency International, South Korea (founded 1999)	Chapter of Transparency International	"To raise greater awareness in people, to eliminate the widespread corruption in the society, and to contribute in building a righteous society through anti-corruption activities".	#1006 Pierson Building, 42 Saemunan-ro, Jongno-gu, Seoul 110–761, Korea (South) www.transparency-korea.org	The main activities of the chapter include: anti-corruption movements and activities; research and development of anti-corruption policies and legislation; introduction and implementation of a Citizen's Ombudsman; and international networking.
South Korea	Citizens Coalition for Social Justice (founded 2014)	Has approximately 2000 individuals and organizations as members.	The two major aims are the promotion of the rule of law and combatting corruption and reform of the public education system.	8/fl, KT and G Tower, 416 Yeongdong-daero, Gangnam-gu, Seoul, 06176, Korea www.ccjs.or.kr	The NGO conducts surveys, organizes research activities and hosts international symposia to inform policymakers and the public on the costs of corruption.
Sri Lanka	Transparency International, Sri Lanka (TISL) (founded 2002)	Chapter of Transparency International	"The mission/purpose of TISL's existence is to contribute to increase understanding of corruption, strengthen anti-corruption structures and processes and to appreciate upholding of integrity. Envisioning a nation that upholds integrity, TISLs goal is to support the collective effort to eradicate corruption in order to build a future Sri Lanka which is equitable, peaceful and just".	No 5/1, Elibank Road, Colombo 5, Sri Lanka www.tisrilanka.org/	The chapter produced research reports in 2014 and 2015 on an assessment of national integrity and electoral integrity, respectively.

(Continued)

Country	Name	Structure	Aims	Contact address	Commentary
Thailand	Anti-Corruption Organization of Thailand (ACT)	Coalition of 47 organizations	The Director has said that the "main role of the organization is "to negotiate with government to create laws that can reduce the level of corruption" and "to address public attitudes".	www.anticorruption. in.th (the website is mainly in Thai)	This is the most active anti-corruption NGO in Thailand. It has worked with UNDP and the universities and has had a major success persuading the government to reform the construction and licensing system. It has also created a "Museum of Thai Corruption".
Thailand	Private Sector Collective Action Coalition Against Corruption (CAC) (founded 2010)	Supported by seven leading private sector organizations and led by a Council of ten prominent individuals.	"The aim of the CAC is to create awareness in the private sector of the corruption risk and the need for effective mechanisms to prevent corruption at the company and industry levels".	The Institute of Directors, CMA, Building 2, 2/9 Moo 4 Northpark Project Vibhavadi-Rangsit Road, Bangkok, 102010 thai-cac.com	The NGO certifies private sector companies to CAC anti-corruption standards, runs an ethical leadership programme and has produced a guide to the Bribery Act.
Timor-Leste	Lalenok Ba Ema Hotu (LABEH) (founded 2003)	LABEH is the acronym for "Lalenok Ba Ema Hotu" (The Mirror of the People).	"To promote citizen participation in the fight against corruption and promote transparency, accountability and integrity in Timor-Leste".	No. 30, De Agosto Depan SDN 07 Malinamoc, Comoro Dili, Timor-Leste www.labeh.org	The NGO provides education for youth which includes anti-corruption material. It is supported by a number of international aid agencies and by Transparency International.
Vietnam	Transparency International, Vietnam (founded 2008)	Chapter of Transparency International	"Our Vision: A Vietnam free of corruption where people enjoy social justice, accountability and transparency in all aspects of life. Our Mission: To reduce corruption in Vietnam by increasing demand and promoting measures for transparency, accountability and integrity in government, business and civil society at large".	12B Floor, Machinco Building, 444 Hoang Hoa Tham, Tay Ho, Hanoi, Vietnam www. towardstransparency.vn	The chapter has a broad range of anti-corruption programmes relating to: public service integrity institutional capacity enhancement, civic engagement, business integrity and forest governance.

INDEX